TIMELINES
of
AMERICAN WOMEN'S HISTORY

No study of American history can be complete without a thorough understanding of how women helped shape our nation. Sue Heinemann has compiled the ultimate reference book on the contributions women have made, highlighting remarkable stories and facts that you won't find in your average history book.

In *Timelines of American Women's History*, each area of interest contains a chronological listing of acts of women who dared to challenge and change the world. Spanning 500 years, it shows how American women have overcome obstacles to fight for equality, affirmation, and excellence.

Sue Heinemann received a B.A. from Wellesley College and an M.A. from Hunter College. For more than twelve years she served as an editor, writer, and production manager for *Heresies: A Feminist Publication on Art and Politics*. She has published many articles and reviews on art in *Artforum* and *Arts* magazines, has ghost-written a number of books, and has worked as a freelance editor on a variety of publications.

Timelines of American Women's History was conceived, researched, written, designed, and produced by women.

TIMELINES
of
AMERICAN
WOMEN'S
HISTORY

Sue Heinemann

A Roundtable Press Book/Perigee Book

A Perigee Book
Published by The Berkley Publishing Group
200 Madison Avenue
New York, NY 10016

A Roundtable Press Book

Copyright © 1996 by Sue Heinemann
Book design by Laura Smyth
Cover design by Richard Nebiolo

First edition: March 1996

Published simultaneously in Canada.

The Putnam Berkley World Wide Web site address is
http://www.berkley.com

Library of Congress Cataloging-in-Publication Data

Heinemann, Sue.
    Timelines of American women's history/Sue Heinemann—1st ed.
    p.   cm.
    "A Roundtable press/Perigee book."
    ISBN 0-399-51986-6
    1. Women—United States—History—Chronology. I. Title
HQ1410.H45 1996
305.4'0973—dc20   95-23067
                    CIP

Printed in the United States of America

1 2 3 4 5 6 7 8 9 10

Contents

List of Some Commonly Used Abbreviations

AAU Amateur Athletic Association
ACLU American Civil Liberties Union
AFL American Federation of Labor
AP Associated Press
AWSA American Woman Suffrage Association
CIO Congress of Industrial Organizations
EEOC Equal Employment Opportunity Commisssion
ERA Equal Rights Amendment
GWFC General Federation of Women's Clubs
HEW Department of Health, Education, and Welfare
ILGWU International Ladies' Garment Workers' Union
IWW Industrial Workers of the World
MIT Massachusetts Institute of Technology
MoMA Museum of Modern Art
NAACP National Association for the Advancement of Colored People
NACW National Association of Colored Women
NASA National Aeronautics and Space Administration
NAWSA National American Woman Suffrage Association
NCAA National College Athletic Association
NCNW National Council of Negro Women
NCW National Council of Women
NOW National Organization for Women
NWP National Woman's Party
NWSA National Woman Suffrage Association
PTA Parent-Teachers Association
ROTC Reserve Officer Training Corps
SCLC Southern Christian Leadership Conference
SNCC Student Nonviolent Coordinating Committee
UAW United Auto Workers
UCAPAWA United Cannery, Agricultural, Packing and Allied Workers of America
UFW United Farm Workers
UP United Press
USDA United States Department of Agriculture
USLTA United States Lawn Tennis Association
WAAC Women's Army Auxiliary Corps
WAC Women's Army Corps
WAF Women in the Air Force
WAVES Women Accepted for Voluntary Emergency Service
WCTU Woman's Christian Temperance Union
WEAL Women's Equity Action League
WILPF Women's International League for Peace and Freedom
WTUL Women's Trade Union League
YWCA Young Women's Christian Association

Introduction

Putting this book together has been a joy—to read about and hear the voices of this country's incredible women, past and present, is truly energizing. I only wish I had the space to include them all and tell their stories fully, but that would take volumes, even a whole library. My hope is that the short entries here will arouse your curiosity and lead you on explorations of your own.

For this timeline I have chosen to emphasize the positive, what women have accomplished. Although at every turn there have been (and continue to be) obstacles to women's achievement, it is amazing how many women have persevered and succeeded, enriching all our lives. As you read through the advances in this book, I hope you'll keep in mind that many of these forward steps were made in the face of considerable opposition and are all the more remarkable because of that. But, for me, what is inspiring is what women have *done*—and that is the story presented in this book.

In my own readings I was struck by how long change takes and how recent some victories are. In 1995 we celebrated the 75th anniversary of U.S. women's suffrage, yet it took more than 70 years for women to obtain the vote after the first women's rights convention in 1848, and white men have been voting in this country for more than 200 years. Although today women are totally accepted as jury members, this was not the case until just 20 years ago, when the Supreme Court ruled that women could not be systematically excluded from jury duty because of their sex. Sometimes, in recording the "facts," I wanted to add a marginal note—"it's about time," or "at last!"

Yet, however slow progress may seem sometimes, women have made sure it happens. Listening to women voice their rage, their impatience, their hopes, their desires, is a constant source of inspiration and a prod to further action. The quotations recorded on these pages are just a starting point. Bon voyage.

Amelia Earhart (Library of Congress)

In any effort like this there are many, many people to thank. To the women at Roundtable Press—Susan Meyer, Marsha Melnick, Amy Jonak, Julie Merberg, Alexis Wilson, and Abigail Anderson, I am truly indebted. Not only did Susan and Marsha believe in my idea at first and find a publisher for my book, but in the end everyone pitched in to check the typed information against my thousands of handwritten file cards—a truly daunting task. Everyone at Perigee, especially John Duff and Sheila Curry, was helpful, and I am grateful to them for giving me the chance to do this book. Laura Smyth was wonderful as my designer, readily accommodating my demands. Ginny Croft was much, much more than my copyeditor, providing needed moral support during the final crunch. Marilyn Flaig, aided by Melanie Belkin, worked on an incredibly tight schedule to compile the index and caught many errors for me along the way. Many people also helped in obtaining the photographs. Barbara A. Tenenbaum at the Library of Congress deserves a special thanks for generously spending her time tracking down the photos I wanted; Beverly W. Brannan, Dennis McNew, Susan G. Sharp, Jane Van Nimmen, and Linda Washington all helped in this, for which I am grateful. Still other photos were obtained by Alexis Wilson—again special thanks are due. During the research phase I was constantly surprised by the resources of the Oakland Public Library and the helpfulness of the staff. And Robin James was invaluable in ferreting out information on events in the last two years.

In addition, even though they are not directly involved in the making of this book, I would like to thank all the amazing women I have learned from over the years: from the women at *Heresies: A Feminist Publication on Art and Politics,* to such special friends as Theodora Skipitares, Patricia Jones, Lanie Lee, Jane Grundy, Charlotte Speight, Elaine Summers, Rachel Wiedeman, and Shelley Caldwell. And last, but not least, my thanks to my father, Heinz, my brother, Peter, and my sister-in-law, Dana, for their support.

Malvina Hoffman (New York World-Telegram and Sun Collections, Library of Congress)

Politics and Equal Rights

Suffragist parade, New York City, 1916 (Library of Congress)

1500s

Iroquois women own the land and control the economy by supervising the distribution of food. Each clan mother has considerable political power, for she appoints the new sachem when the old chief dies and can demand his removal from the council if he proves unsatisfactory.

Not only does the Cherokee Women's Council determine the fate of any captives, but the clan mothers can also declare war. They help select the male leaders and have a voice in public policy.

When, around 1540, the Spanish explorer Hernando de Soto marches through what will become Georgia, he is welcomed by the woman ruler, the *cacica* of Cutifachiqui, who gives him her own strand of pearls. De Soto then forces her to guide him through her lands. After two weeks, she tricks him and escapes with a box of valuable pearls.

c. 1600

Near the place later known as Seneca Falls, New York, Iroquois women stage a protest against irresponsible warfare. They refuse to make love or bear children unless they can decide whether to wage war. The men quickly agree to their demand.

1607

Matoaka, nicknamed Pocahontas (c. 1595–1617), allegedly begs her father, chief of the Powhatan Confederacy, to spare the life of Captain John Smith, leader of the new Jamestown settlement in Virginia. Later, in 1613, she is taken hostage by the settlers, and she converts to Christianity. She then marries colonist John Rolfe, with both her father's and the governor's approval. On a trip to London, she is presented at the court, but she dies, probably of smallpox, in England. Seven years after her death, in 1624, John Smith publishes the dramatic account of his rescue that becomes the legend of Pocahontas.

1619

The first Africans, 17 men and 3 women, arrive as indentured servants in Jamestown, Virginia. White women are also imported as indentured servants around this time. Within a few years, however, African slaves begin to be imported in Virginia as well as the other colonies.

1640

When Ann Hibbens of Boston insists that she has the right to complain about the work of male carpenters she hired, the church elders attack her for thinking she can manage these affairs better than her husband, "which is a plain breach of the rule of Christ." She is excommunicated; 16 years later she is hanged for witchcraft.

1643

With her friends, Lady Deborah Moody (c. 1585–c. 1659) leaves the orthodoxy of the Massachusetts colony to set up a community based on religious tolerance in Gravesend, Long Island. After receiving a patent from the Dutch in 1645, she participates in the town council meetings, helping to draw up the plans for the town and select the magistrates.

1648

Margaret Brent (c. 1600–71) demands two votes in the Maryland assembly, as a property owner (she successfully runs her own plantation) and as sole executor of the estate of Lord Calvert, the former governor of Maryland. Although she is denied any vote, the assembly does defend her when Lord Baltimore (Lord Calvert's brother) complains about her use of revenue from his estate to pay off his soldiers, who had recently put down a Protestant rebellion. Her actions, they say, saved the colony from an open revolt (see sidebar).

1655

When Elizabeth Key sues for her freedom in Virginia, her lawyer, William Greensted, argues that her condition is determined by that of her father (a white man), not of her mother (a slave). They win the case, and Key marries Greensted, but in 1662 Virginians enact a law specifically stipulating that the child's condition is determined by that of the mother. The offspring of the master and his slave will remain slaves.

1663

Following the lead of Virginia in 1661, Maryland law makes all blacks in the colony slaves and declares that all newborn African Americans are slaves regardless of the parents' status. In 1664 Maryland outlaws marriage between white women and black men. Other colonies soon enact similar laws.

1671

Awahonks, leader of the Sakonnet in Rhode Island, negotiates a non-aggression treaty with the British settlers to save her people and later supports the British during King Philip's War. Two other women leaders of this time, Weetamoo and Magnus, fight the British (p. 256).

1676

In support of Bacon's Rebellion in Virginia, Sarah Drummond gives lively speeches calling for action and denounces Governor Berkeley. While criticizing Berkeley for not protecting her people from attacks by Bacon's forces, Cocacoeske, leader of the Pamunkey since 1656, sends warriors to help defeat the rebels.

1681

Maria, a slave, is burned at the stake for trying, with two men, to burn down her master's house in Massachusetts. The court condemns her most severely, claiming she lacks "the feare of God before her eyes."

1701

In Albany, New York, six men and six women are selected to serve on a jury, but this is an exception. During much of early American history, women are kept off juries; not until 1975 does the Supreme Court rule that women's automatic exemption from jury duty is unconstitutional.

1704

Sent from France with small trunks (cassettes) carrying their dowries, 25 young "brides" dock at Mobile (Alabama). Appalled at the minimal

"She Rather Deserved Favour"

"As for Mistress Brent's undertaking and meddling with your Lordship's estate here . . . we do Verily Believe and in Conscience report that it was better for the Colony's safety at that time in her hands than in any man's else in the whole Province after your brother's death. . . . We conceive from that time she rather deserved favour and thanks from your Honour for her so much Concurring to the public safety, than to be justly liable to all those bitter invectives you have been pleased to Express against her."
—letter to Lord Baltimore from the Maryland Assembly, *Archives of Maryland*, vol. 1, *Assembly Proceedings, January 1647–March 1648* (Baltimore: Maryland Historical Society, 1883); quoted in *Second to None: A Documentary History of American Women*, vol. 1, edited by Ruth Barnes Moynihan, Cynthia Russett, and Laurie Crumpacker (Lincoln: University of Nebraska Press, 1993)

Coverture: A Marriage Penalty

Following British common law, a single woman or a widow is considered a feme sole; *she has a legal right to own property and enter into contracts and business ventures. When, however, a woman marries, she disappears, becoming a* feme covert *("covered" by her husband). She completely loses any economic independence; everything belongs to her husband. She is not permitted to own property (not even any wages she may earn); she cannot sign contracts; and she is unable to sue for damages or divorce. If she does separate from her husband, she has no right to the custody of her children.*

facilities, they at first refuse to wed any of the colonists but eventually agree to stay.

1706

"Queen Anne" (d. 1725) is the third woman to lead the Pamunkey since 1656. For her people's survival, she attempts to ban the sale of alcohol and land. In 1711 she gets the governor of Virginia to waive the annual tribute required by the British government if she sends her son to the College of William and Mary. Later, in 1715, she addresses the Virginia legislature on the rights of her people.

1708

A black woman is burned alive after seven whites are killed in a slave revolt in Long Island. A Native American man and two black men are hanged.

1712

During William Penn's long illness, his wife, Hannah Callowhill Penn (1671–1726), corresponds from England with the Philadelphia council in order to manage the affairs of Pennsylvania. On her huband's death in 1718, she is his sole executor and plays an important role in helping to hold the province together.

1733

In a letter in the *New York Journal*, a group of women complain: "We are housekeepers, pay our taxes, carry on trade, and most of us are she merchants, and as we in some measure contribute to the support of government, we ought to be entitled to some of the sweets of it."

Mary Musgrove (later Matthews, then Bosomworth, c. 1700–63), the daughter of a white trader and Creek mother, helps James Oglethorpe negotiate with Creek leaders, enabling him to found the colony of Georgia. Later she garners local Native support for him against the Spanish. Before returning to England in 1743, Oglethorpe gives Musgrove his diamond ring and £200, promising much more. Claiming she is "Queen of the Creeks," she eventually gains £2100 from the British.

1755

After taking over when her husband is killed and leading her Cherokee people to victory over the Creek forces, Nanye-hi (later Nancy Ward, c. 1738–1824) is given the title "Beloved Woman." She governs the Women's Council and sits on the Council of Chiefs, where she has a full voice in the decisions. In subsequent years she negotiates several peace treaties with white settlers, at one point expressing surprise that there are no white women negotiators. Later, however, she changes her mind about trusting the whites (see 1817).

1765

In the Massachusetts Superior Court, Jenny Slew (b. c. 1719) wins her case for freedom, after arguing that she was illegally enslaved in 1762 and that because her mother was white, she was born free.

"Let the Daughters of Liberty, nobly arise"
—Anonymous

1767–70

After the British pass the Townshend Acts, charging duties on goods imported by Americans, women organize as Daughters of Liberty and refuse to buy linen, tea, and other British goods. "Stand firmly resolved and bid Grenville to see/That rather than Freedom, we'll part with our Tea," urges one patriotic poet in 1768.

1772

After her husband's death, Queen Esther becomes the leader of the Munsee tribe in northeastern Pennsylvania. For several years she and her people live peacefully with white settlers in the area, but in 1778, after the whites are attacked by another tribe, they kill her son. She then takes revenge, executing some white captives with a stone maul.

1773

Sarah Bradlee Fulton and her sister-in-law help disguise Boston patriots as Indians and have hot water handy to remove the makeup quickly when the men return from dumping British tea into the harbor.

1774

In Edenton, North Carolina, 51 women sign a petition resolving to take political action and boycott British tea and cloth. Other Daughters of Liberty put up broadsides in public places; in a lengthy verse one woman preaches: "Unhappy Boston! wherefore doth thy God/Thus scourge thee with a Tyrant's Iron Rod?/. . . New England, now to meet thy God prepare,/Awake Repentance, Faith and earnest Prayer."

1775

After the first shot is fired, women contribute to the Revolutionary War effort in many ways (see "War and the Military"). Patriotic feelings are intense, and when one man dares to criticize the Revolution, several Daughters of Liberty take off his coat and shirt, cover him with molasses, and then stick on dozens of flower petals.

1776

While her husband, John Adams, works with the Continental Congress in Philadelphia, Abigail Smith Adams (1744–1818) manages the family farm near Boston. In a letter she urges him to give women a voice in the new government (see sidebar). When her husband makes fun of her request, she complains to her friend Mercy Otis Warren (p. 306), a writer of political satire, about his "sauciness" and clearly states her concern about married women's lack of rights. In another letter to her husband, Adams describes how 100 or more Boston women, faced with a coffee shortage, roughed up a stingy merchant, forcing him to hand over the keys to his warehouse, and promptly raided his supply.

New Jersey's new constitution gives the vote to all property owners worth a certain amount, so some unmarried women are eligible. A

"Remember the Ladies"

". . . in the new Code of Laws which I suppose it will be necessary for you to make I desire you would remember the Ladies, and be more generous and favorable to them than your ancestors. Do not put such unlimited power into the hands of the Husbands. Remember all Men would be tyrants if they could. If particular care and attention is not paid to the Ladies we are determined to foment a Rebellion, and will not hold ourselves bound by any laws in which we have no voice, or Representation."
   —Abigail Adams, letter to John Adams, March 31, 1776

"I cannot say that I think you very generous to the Ladies, for whilst you are proclaiming peace and good will to Men . . . you insist upon retaining an absolute power over Wives. But you must remember that Arbitrary power is like most other things which are very hard, very liable to be broken."
   —Abigail Adams, letter to John Adams, May 7, 1776; both in *The Adams Family Correspondence*, edited by Lyman Butterfield (Cambridge, Mass.: Harvard University Press, 1963)

number exercise this right before it is revoked in 1807. In contrast, in 1777 New York specifically denies women voting rights in its constitution, and other states soon repeat this pattern.

According to legend, when a secret committee of the Continental Congress asks Elizabeth ("Betsy") Griscom Ross (1752–1836) to design a flag, she proposes five-pointed stars because they can be cut out much more quickly than six-pointed ones.

1780

Women in Philadelphia and later other cities raise money to clothe the American soldiers. Aligning themselves with great heroines of antiquity, such as Deborah and Esther, the Philadelphia women call for action in a broadside titled "The Sentiments of an American Woman." They describe themselves as "Born for liberty, disdaining to bear the irons of a tyrannic Government."

1781

Elizabeth ("Mum") Bett (later Freeman, c. 1744–1829) claims that her slavery is invalidated by the new Massachusetts constitution, which declares that "all men are born free and equal." She wins her freedom and is even given reparation for a beating by her mistress, but only in 1783 does the Massachusetts Supreme Court declare all slavery illegal.

1783

At the end of the Revolutionary War, women continue active support of the U.S. economy. In 1786, for example, the Ladies Association of Hartford, Connecticut, calls for a boycott of imported silks and ribbons, and urges women to buy American goods as their patriotic duty.

1787

The new U.S. Constitution leaves the determination of who is eligible to vote to each state, but it does not specifically bar women from holding federal office.

"Is the needle and kitchen sufficient . . . ?"
—Judith Sargent Murray

1790

The revised New Jersey election law refers to voters as "he or she."

Two years before British feminist Mary Wollstonecraft's *A Vindication of the Rights of Woman* (1792), Judith Sargent Murray (1751–1820) publishes her essay "On the Equality of the Sexes," which she may have written as early as 1779. Arguing that women's and men's mental abilities are equal, she proposes full education for women (see p. 169).

1791

When Colonel Proctor comes to negotiate with the Seneca chiefs, a delegation of elder women confronts him, insisting that he listen to their words, as they own the land. It is the women who decide to go ahead with peace talks. The same is true in 1795 and 1797.

1797

Lucy Terry Prince (p. 306), a former slave, addresses the U.S. Supreme Court in a property dispute with a neighboring Vermont farmer. She wins the case, and presiding justice Samuel Chase later praises her presentation as one of the best he has heard.

1798

When tax assessors try to collect a new federal tax to support the looming war with France, the women of Quakerstown, Pennsylvania, welcome them with pans of hot water. The militia is quickly called in to control the protestors.

1800

Nancy Prosser helps her husband, Gabriel, plan an uprising of 1,000 slaves near Richmond, Virginia, but the incipient revolt is put down by the militia.

1807

After women vote in relatively large numbers in the 1800 presidential election, New Jersey changes its election law by inserting the words "white" and "male" into the requirements for voters.

1817

To please the U.S. government, the Cherokee adopt a new constitution that eliminates women's power in decision making. Forced to resign, the last Beloved Woman (Nanye-hi, or Nancy Ward) pleads with the Cherokee council not to sell any more land to the white settlers and underlines that to do so "would be like destroying your mothers." Other Cherokee women also petition the council (see sidebar).

1818

In *Observations on the Real Rights of Women, with Their Appropriate Duties, Agreeable to Scripture, Reason and Common Sense*, Hannah Mather Crocker (1752–1829) argues that men and women have equal mental abilities. Women, she states, have been given "the same right of judging and acting for themselves, as . . . the male sex." Yet she disagrees with Mary Wollstonecraft on "the total independence of the sex."

1819

In Hawaii, after her husband's death, Kaahumanu (d. 1832) becomes *kuhina nui*, essentially a coruler, with the new king, Kamehameha II. She uses her power to abolish some of the restrictions on women: for example, persuading the king to abandon the religious taboo against dining with women. Later (1824–32), she is regent for the boy king Kamehameha III (see 1824).

1820

Of 870,860 black women in the United States, 750,010 are enslaved.

1824

Issuing essentially the first code of laws in Hawaii, Kaahumanu prohibits killing and stealing and proclaims that everyone should learn to read and write. Later she establishes a jury system; she also, in 1825, becomes an ardent Protestant convert.

1825

Scottish-born Frances ("Fanny") Wright (1795–1852), whose 1821 book *Views of Society and Manners in America* extolled U.S. women's freedom "as thinking beings," acts on a plan for gradually abolishing slavery. To persuade Congress to let slaves work on public land and buy their freedom with the profits, she sets up a model plantation in Tennessee. The project, however, fails financially and is derailed by charges of "free love." In 1830 she frees all the slaves and pays for their travel to Haiti.

1828

In a 179-page tract, Elizabeth Elkins Sanders (1762–1851) criticizes the expulsion of the Creek and Cherokee people from Georgia by Gen. Andrew Jackson and argues for justice for Native Americans. Later, in 1844, she attacks missionaries for their treatment of Indians.

1829

After first lecturing publicly to mixed audiences in Cincinnati in 1828, Fanny Wright goes on a speaking tour in the East and Midwest. She then buys a church in New York City and turns it into a "Hall of Science," where she lectures on women's rights. "Until women assume the place in society which good sense and good feeling alike assign to them," she declares, "human improvement must advance but feebly. It is in vain that we would circumscribe the power of one half of our race, and that by far the most important and influential."

A crisis occurs in Andrew Jackson's cabinet when he appoints Secretary of War John Henry Eaton, who has just married Margaret ("Peggy") O'Neale Timberlake. The wives of other cabinet members snub her because of gossip about her involvement with Eaton before her first husband's death. These slights anger Jackson and eventually break up his cabinet in 1831. Through this crisis Martin Van Buren emerges as Jackson's successor.

1830

Of 1,162,366 African American women, 996,200 are held in slavery.

"Do you ask what we can do?"
—*Maria W. Stewart*

1832

After publishing her ideas in the *Liberator* (see sidebar), Maria W. Miller Stewart (1803–79) becomes the first American-born female lecturer, speaking on black women's rights and abolition first to the Afric-American Female Intelligence Society, then at Franklin Hall in Boston. Disappointed in the opposition she encounters, she ends her speaking career in 1833. In her farewell address, after pointing to powerful women in the Bible and history, she queries, "What if such women . . . should rise among our sable race?"

African American women organize the Female Anti-Slavery Society of Salem (Massachusetts) with Mary A. Battys as president. In nearby Boston white and black women set up the Boston Female Anti-Slavery Society, which publishes an annual report called *Right and Wrong in Boston*, edited by Maria Weston Chapman (1806–85).

1833

When the newly formed American Anti-Slavery Society refuses to admit women members, about 20 white and black women set up the Philadelphia Female Anti-Slavery Society. In their constitution they underline that slavery and prejudice violate the laws of God and the Declaration of Independence. Charter members include Lucretia Coffin Mott (1793–1880), Esther Moore, Rebecca Buffum, Grace Bustill Douglass, and Charlotte Forten and her three daughters (Margaretta, Sarah Louisa, and Harriet). During the group's 37-year history, its six-member board of managers usually includes two black women.

Boston writer and abolitionist Lydia Maria Francis Child (1802–80) publishes *An Appeal in Favor of That Class of Americans Called Africans*, which denounces slavery and also calls for an end to prejudice and segregation. Her book helps bring Wendell Phillips, Charles Sumner, and other Bostonians into the abolition movement.

1834

One of the first known Chinese women in America, Afong Moy, is exhibited as a curiosity in a New York theater.

1835

A mob threatens a meeting of the Boston Female Anti-Slavery Society at which abolitionist William Lloyd Garrison is scheduled to speak. When the mayor orders the women to leave, Maria Chapman replies, "If this is the last bulwark of freedom, we may as well die here as anywhere." Walking hand in hand, the white and black women then move through the angry mob to Chapman's home.

When white women organize the Ladies' New York City Women's Anti-Slavery Society, they do not let black women join and then propose to "elevate" the city's blacks. In contrast, the Chatham Street Society, a racially mixed women's group, refuses to "join the hypocrisy to persecution by dictating to [African Americans] how they are to improve their character and their prospects." Several black women set up the Manhattan Anti-Slavery Society, which also has one white woman member.

1836

In Boston black women dash into a courtroom and rescue two fugitive slave women before they can be turned over to their "masters." In New York black women stage a similar rescue.

After abolitionist women flood Congress with the signatures they have gathered for antislavery petitions, the legislators pass a "gag rule" to keep these petitions from being read or considered.

"You Are the Wives and Mothers"

". . .why appeal to women *on this subject? We do not make the laws which perpetuate slavery. No legislative power is vested in us; we can do nothing to overthrow the system, even if we wished to do so. To this I reply, I know you do not make the laws, but I also know that you are the wives and mothers, the sisters and daughters of those who do; and if you really suppose you can do nothing to overthrow slavery, you are greatly mistaken. . . .*

"I know this doctrine of obeying God, rather than man, will be considered as dangerous. . . If a law commands me to sin I will break it. . . The doctrine of blind obedience and unqualified submission to any human power, whether civil or ecclesiastical, is the doctrine of despotism, and ought to have no place among Republicans and Christians."

—Angelina Grimké, *An Appeal to the Christian Women of the South* (New York: American Anti-Slavery Society, 1836)

In *Boon* v. *Juliet,* an African American woman defeats her former white master's attempt to keep her children as servants after her period of indentured service ends.

In Philadelphia, Angelina Emily Grimké (later Weld, 1805–79), the daughter of slave owners in the South, publishes her first abolitionist pamphlet, *An Appeal to the Christian Women of the South.* She calls on southern women to free any slaves they own and to speak out against slavery (see sidebar). Warned against ever returning to the South, she starts work in New York as an agent for the American Anti-Slavery Society. Her sister Sarah Moore Grimké (1792–1873) joins her and publishes her *Epistle to the Clergy of the Southern States.*

Gaining five other women signers, newly arrived Jewish immigrant Ernestine Potowski Rose (1810–92) files the first of many petitions to the New York state legislature to let married women own property.

1837

In May the first Anti-Slavery Convention of American Women meets in New York. Of the 200 women attending, at least 20 are black, and Grace Douglass is elected a vice president. The women declare it is time to move out of their "circumscribed limits" and to use their pens, purses, and influence to end slavery.

Angelina Grimké publishes *An Appeal to the Women of the Nominally Free States.* On a lecture tour she and her sister speak to large mixed audiences, converting many to the abolitionist cause but also garnering criticism from clergymen and more traditional women like Catharine Beecher (p. 170). Angelina Grimké asserts: "I believe it is woman's right to have a voice in all the laws and regulations by which she is to be governed, whether in Church or State: and that the present arrangements of society, on these points, are a violation of human rights." She adds that a woman has as much right as a man *"to sit . . . in the Presidential chair of the United States."*

The Mississippi Supreme Court rules that Betsy Allen's property is protected from her white husband's creditors because, under her Chickasaw people's tradition, married women own their property separately. This ruling leads to a change in Mississippi law (see 1839).

1838

Ignoring a Supreme Court ruling, the army forces Cherokee women, men, and children to march 800 miles to Indian Territory, later the state of Oklahoma. Thousands die along the "Trail of Tears."

When the second Anti-Slavery Convention of American Women is held in Philadelphia, an angry mob gathers, throwing stones at the hall. Later that night the crowd burns the hall down and threatens the home of one of the leaders, Lucretia Mott. The next day the women declare "prejudice against color the very spirit of slavery" and urge all abolitionists to sit with African Americans in their places of worship, walk with them on the street, and invite them into their homes.

The first woman to address a legislative body, Angelina Grimké asks Massachusetts legislators to end the slave trade in Washington, D.C. She underlines women's concern with this issue "not only because it is moral and religious, but because it is *political*, inasmuch as we are citizens of this republic."

Sarah Grimké publishes her *Letters on the Equality of the Sexes, and the Condition of Women.* Originally written to Mary S. Parker, president of the Boston Female Anti-Slavery Society, these letters contain her response to the Congregational ministers' Pastoral Letter condemning the Grimké sisters' public speeches (see sidebar).

In Kentucky widowed women are allowed to vote in school board elections under certain conditions.

1839

Mississippi passes the first state law giving a married woman the right to own property in her name, as long as her husband agrees.

The Anti-Slavery Convention of American Women meets for the last time; it dissolves once the American Anti-Slavery Society finally gives women voting rights.

Abigail ("Abby") Kelley (later Foster, 1810–87) lectures against slavery in Connecticut; she later travels for 15 years throughout the Northeast and in the Midwest as an influential abolitionist speaker.

The Grimké sisters compile *American Slavery As It Is: Testimony of a Thousand Witnesses* with Angelina's new husband, Theodore Weld, but they essentially retire from speaking.

1840

Of 1,440,600 African American women, 1,240,938 are held in slavery.

At the American Anti-Slavery Society convention, a dispute arises over women's participation. When conservatives fail to block Abby Foster's nomination to the business committee, they leave. Lucretia Mott and Lydia Maria Child also gain leadership positions in the society.

Several women delegates, including Lucretia Mott, are sent from the United States to the World's Anti-Slavery Convention in London, but the British refuse to accept them. They are allowed to attend only as spectators, seated behind a curtain in the balcony. Elizabeth Cady Stanton (1815–1902), who is there with her husband, a delegate, is outraged at this injustice (earlier in the year, at her wedding, she had the word *obey* deleted from the ceremony). Soon she and Mott, who have become friends, decide "to hold a convention . . . and form a society to advance the rights of women."

Joining forces with Elizabeth Cady Stanton and Paulina Wright (later Davis, 1818–76), Ernestine Rose again petitions and this time speaks before a committee of New York legislators on married women's property rights.

"Whatever Is *Right*"

"I follow [Jesus] through all his precepts, and find him giving the same directions to women as to men, never even referring to the distinction now so strenuously insisted upon between masculine and feminine virtues: this is one of the anti-christian 'traditions of men' which are taught instead of the 'commandments of God.' Men and women are CREATED EQUAL; they are both moral and accountable beings, and whatever is right for a man to do, is right for a woman to do."
　—Sarah Grimké, letter dated July 1837, in *Letters on the Equality of the Sexes, and the Condition of Women* (Boston: Isaac Knapp, 1838)

"Declaration of Sentiments"

"We hold these truths to be self-evident: that all men and women are created equal; that they are endowed by their Creator with certain inalienable rights; that among those rights are life, liberty, and the pursuit of happiness. . . . Whenever any form of government becomes destructive of these ends, it is the right of those who suffer from it to refuse allegiance to it, and to insist upon the institution of a new government. . . .[And] when a long train of abuses and usurpations, pursuing invariably the same object events a design to reduce them under absolute despotism, it is their duty to throw off such government, and to provide new guards for their future security. Such has been the patient sufferance of the women under this government, and such is not the necessity which constrains them to demand the equal station to which they are entitled."

   —"Declaration of Sentiments," Seneca Falls, New York, 1848; in *History of Woman Suffrage*, vol. 1, edited by Elizabeth Cady Stanton, Susan B. Anthony, and Matilda Joslyn Gage (New York: Fowler & Wells, 1881)

1843

Itinerant preacher Isabella Bomefree (c. 1797–1883), who gained her freedom in 1827, changes her name to Sojourner Truth, claiming that God gave her the name *Truth* "because I was to declare the truth to the people." At the end of the year, she joins a utopian community in Massachusetts, meets abolitionists David Ruggles and Frederick Douglass, and is soon one of the most powerful antislavery speakers.

1844

Jessie Ann Benton Frémont (1824–1902) helps her husband, John Charles Frémont, describe his trip to Oregon and California. Published as a Senate document and then commercially, this report greatly influences white settlement of the Far West.

1845

Writer and highly regarded intellectual Margaret Fuller (1810–50) publishes her classic feminist work, *Woman in the Nineteenth Century.* Insisting on woman's need "as a soul to live freely and unimpeded," she calls for an end to "even well-meant restrictions." "We would have every arbitrary barrier thrown down," she declares. "We would have every path laid open to Woman as freely as to Man."

"Resolved, That woman is man's equal"
—Seneca Falls Convention

1848

In February, 44 women send a petition demanding that the New York state legislature repeal its laws affecting women. They argue that the Declaration of Independence states "that governments derive their just powers from the consent of the governed. And as women have never consented to, been represented in, or recognized by this government, it is evident that in justice no allegiance can be claimed from them."

In April, New York passes a law giving married women limited property rights, but it fails to give them control over their wages, for example. Lobbyist Ernestine Rose sees it as "at best . . . for the favored few and not for the suffering many." Meanwhile, in Massachusetts, Mary Upton Ferrin (1810–81) begins her campaign to protect married women's property rights. In the next five years she travels about 600 miles, often on foot, collecting signatures for her petitions.

Elizabeth Cady Stanton, Lucretia Mott, Martha Coffin Wright, Jane Hunt, and Mary Ann McClintock meet and call for a women's rights convention in Seneca Falls, New York, on July 19–20. To their surprise, about 300 people, mostly women, attend. As Charlotte Woodward (later Pierce), a glove sewer, recalls: "As we reached different crossroads, we saw wagons coming from every part of the country, and long before we reached Seneca Falls we were a procession."

   At the convention a "Declaration of Sentiments," drafted by Stanton and modeled on the Declaration of Independence, is read (see sidebar opposite). It condemns women's disfranchisement, their lack of a voice in the laws they must obey, restrictions on their education and employment opportunities, their subordination by the church, the use of a double moral standard, and the theft of married women's full property rights. The group then passes a series of general resolutions calling for women's equal rights. Only one is controversial—a proposal to secure the vote for women—but it narrowly passes after strong arguments by Stanton and Frederick Douglass. This demand takes over 70 years to be fulfilled, and only one woman who signs the resolutions, Charlotte Woodward, lives to cast her ballot.

Two weeks after the Seneca Falls convention, another meeting is held in nearby Rochester, New York. This time a woman runs the meeting (James Mott presided at Seneca Falls at the women's request). The call for women's enfranchisement now heads the list of resolutions; the women also demand a revision of existing property laws and pledge to help raise working women's wages.

The Treaty of Guadalupe Hidalgo, ending the Mexican War, brings Texas, California, and most of the Southwest under U.S. control. As a result, married Mexican women in this area lose their property rights and thus their economic power. They no longer remain in control of their property when they marry, nor can they operate their own businesses, enter into contracts, or sue, as before.

In a daring escape from slavery to freedom, light-skinned Ellen Craft (c. 1826–c. 1891/7) poses as a sickly white master accompanied by "his" slave (her husband, William). Traveling mostly on trains, the two flee from Georgia to Philadelphia. When a federal fugitive slave law is passed in 1850, they are forced to flee again, to England. There they publish their story, *Running a Thousand Miles for Freedom* (1860).

The first three Chinese immigrants to the United States include Maria Seise, a servant of the trader Charles Gillespie.

1849

Harriet Ross Tubman (c. 1820/1–1913) escapes from slavery in Maryland. But when she arrives, she realizes: "I had crossed the line of which I had so long been dreaming. I was free; but there was no one to welcome me to the land of freedom." Determined to rescue her family and others, she soon begins working as a conductor on the Underground Railroad (see sidebar).

Responding to the call for black nationalism by Frederick Douglass, Sarah Mapps Douglass (p. 170), Rachel Lloyd, Hetty Burr, and other black women organize the Woman's Association of Philadelphia.

When the Tennessee legislature declares that married women lack independent souls and thus should not be allowed to own property, feminist and temperance reformer Amelia Jenks Bloomer (1818–94) takes them to task in her journal, *Lily*. If women have no souls, she concludes, then they are free from obeying *any* laws.

"Without Her Equal"

In December 1850 Harriet Tubman makes her first trip back to the South, to lead her sister, Mary Ann Bowley, and her two children to freedom. During the next decade she makes 14 to 18 more forays into the South, bringing out 200 to 300 slaves and guiding them to safety in Canada. (The 1850 fugitive slave law endangers all runaways as well as free blacks in the United States.) In 1857 Tubman is finally able to rescue her parents. Slave owners offer a reward of $40,000 for her capture, but she skillfully disguises herself and at one point even takes her "passengers" south for a while to elude slave hunters. In his 1872 history of the Underground Railroad, William Still describes her as "a woman of no pretensions . . . [but] in point of courage, shrewdness and disinterested exertions to rescue her fellowmen . . . she was without her equal."

"And A'n't I a Woman?"

" . . . from her seat in the corner rose Sojourner Truth. . . .

"'Dat man ober dar say dat womin needs to be helped into carriages, and lifted ober ditches, and to have de best place everywhar. Nobody eber helps me into carriages, or ober mud-puddles, or gibs me any best place!' And raising herself to her full height, and her voice to a pitch like rolling thunder, she asked, 'And a'n't I a woman? Look at me! Look at my arm! (and she bared her right arm to the shoulder, showing her tremendous muscular power). I have ploughed, and planted, and gathered into barns, and no man could head me! And a'n't I a woman? . . . I have borne thirteen chilern, and seen 'em most' all sold off to slavery, and when I cried out with my mother's grief, none but Jesus heard me! And a'n't I a woman?"
—"Reminiscences of Sojourner Truth" by Frances D. Gage; in *History of Woman Suffrage*, vol. 1

1850

Of 1,827,550 black women in America, 1,601,799 are held in slavery.

In April, Emily Robinson, Josephine Griffing, Elizabeth Jones, and other abolitionists organize a women's rights convention in Salem, Ohio. Betsey Mix Cowles presides over the two-day meeting, where men are not allowed to speak or vote. Some men attempt to voice their opinions, but Cowles quickly rules them out of order. Resolving to claim their rights as "human beings," the women send a petition to the Ohio Constitutional Convention demanding suffrage and all other rights extended to men in the new state constitution.

Abolitionist speaker Lucy Stone (1818–93), who had been criticized for discussing women's position in her lectures, joins Paulina Wright Davis and other feminists to call for a national convention on women's rights. Women from nine states attend the two-day meeting in Worcester, Massachusetts, in October. Among the participants are Susan Brownell Anthony (1820–1906), Antoinette Louisa Brown (later Blackwell, 1825–1921), Sojourner Truth, and Lucretia Mott. They agree on a resolution demanding suffrage and equality "without distinction of sex or color."

1851

In Akron, Ohio, Frances Dana Barker Gage (1808–84) presides over a statewide women's rights convention. After Sojourner Truth arrives, many of the women beg Gage not to let her speak, but it is Sojourner Truth who puts the male hecklers in their place, with her much-quoted "A'n't I a Woman?" speech, recorded by Gage (see sidebar).

At the second National Women's Rights Convention in Worcester, Ernestine Rose underlines the degradation of the married property law, where the husband provides for the wife: "Yes! he *keeps* her, and so he does a favorite horse; by law they are both considered his property."

1852

Mary Ann Shadd (later Cary, 1823–93), who emigrated to Canada in 1850 after passage of the fugitive slave law, publishes a 44-page tract, *A Plea for Emigration or, Notes of Canada West, in its Moral, Social and Political Aspect*. This manual presents data on farming conditions in Canada and counters the derogatory propaganda of U.S. slaveholders.

Harriet Beecher Stowe (1811–96) publishes *Uncle Tom's Cabin; or, Life Among the Lowly*, first serialized in the *National Era*. This antislavery novel has a major political impact, gaining supporters for the abolitionist cause and drawing fire from slaveholding men and women in the South. In one year 300,000 copies are sold.

1853

Although she has bought a ticket, Sarah Parker Remond (1826–94) is thrown out of a Boston theater because she is black. She sues the theater and wins. In 1856 she begins lecturing for the American Anti-Slavery Society, first in the United States, then in Europe.

1854

Massachusetts passes the Married Women's Property Act after years of petitioning by Mary Ferrin and others. Married women can now control their own property and make wills. A revision of the divorce law soon gives women equal rights to the guardianship of their children.

In New York, Susan B. Anthony goes door to door, gathering signatures in her campaign for revisions in the married women's property law. At Anthony's urging, Elizabeth Cady Stanton speaks to New York legislators about the legal disadvantages married women face and the need for reform. She is the first woman to address the state senate.

In Massachusetts, Frances Ellen Watkins (later Harper, 1825–1911) gives her first abolitionist lecture, "Education and the Elevation of the Colored Race"; she also publishes her first book of poems.

When Elizabeth Jennings is dragged off a horsecar in New York, she sues the Third Avenue Railroad Company. She wins $225 in damages, as well as a ruling that all "colored persons, if sober, well-behaved, and free from disease" have the right to ride the cars.

1855

On Christmas Eve fugitive slave Ann Wood drives a wagonload of armed youngsters out of Virginia. When stopped, they threaten to keep shooting until they die and are allowed to proceed. Almost all escape to Philadelphia.

When U.S. diplomat John Wheeler arrives in Philadelphia with his slave Jane Johnson, she manages to contact abolitionists, who inform Wheeler that in Pennsylvania she and her children are free. Later, in court, she testifies: "I went away of my own free will; I always wished to be free and meant to be free when I came North." She wins.

1856

In an important test case of the California constitution, Biddy (Bridget) Mason (1818–91) wins her freedom before her Mormon "owners" can take her out of the free state to Texas (see also p. 111).

Expressing the anti-Catholic sentiments of the Know-Nothing Party, Anna Ella Carroll (1815–93) serves as the publicist for its presidential candidate, Millard Fillmore. She produces three campaign pamphlets and a 365-page propaganda tract, *The Great American Battle.*

Susan B. Anthony becomes an American Anti-Slavery Society agent.

1858

After moving to Orange, New Jersey, Lucy Stone protests taxation without representation by refusing to pay her property tax bill without the right to vote. The collector auctions some of her household goods, but a neighbor buys them back.

1859

In the Kansas Territory women are allowed to vote in school elections.

"Fight"

"The one doctrine of my mother's teaching which was branded on my senses was that I should never let anyone abuse me. 'I'll kill you gal, if you don't stand up for yourself,' she would say. 'Fight, and if you can't fight, kick; if you can't kick, then bite.' Ma was generally willing to work, but if she didn't feel like doing something, none could make her do it."

—oral history in "Unwritten History of Slavery; Autobiographical Accounts of Negro Ex-Slaves," Fisk University, Social Science Institute, 1942; quoted in *Black Women in White America,* edited by Gerda Lerner (New York: Vintage Books, 1972)

1860

Of 2,225,086 black women, 1,971,135 are held in slavery. In San Franciso about 85% of Chinese women are essentially enslaved as prostitutes. Kidnapped or lured from their homeland, they are displayed for sale in a huge, closely guarded room.

New York passes a revised Married Women's Property Act, allowing women not only to own property but also to keep their wages, enter into contracts, sue in court, and have equal rights to child custody.

Lydia Maria Child's exchange about slavery with Mrs. Mason, wife of a Virginia senator, is widely distributed as a pamphlet; in response to Mason's remark about the kind treatment of slaves during childbirth, for example, Child says that in the North "after we have helped the mothers, *we do not sell the babies*." Child publishes three other anti-slavery pieces during 1860, including *The Duty of Disobedience to the Fugitive Slave Act*.

At the start of the Civil War, Anna Carroll becomes a publicist for the Union cause and is encouraged by Thomas Scott, assistant secretary of war. She writes two long tracts on the president's power to act against the Confederacy, but she is not an abolitionist.

Sojourner Truth with Abraham Lincoln
(Library of Congress)

1863

When the Emancipation Proclamation frees slaves only in the Confederacy and not in slaveholding Union states, Susan B. Anthony, Elizabeth Cady Stanton, Ernestine Rose, and others organize the National Woman's Loyal League. They send bundles of petitions calling for an end to all slavery to Senator Charles Sumner, who introduces the 13th Amendment. By August 1864 they have collected 400,000 signatures.

A powerful orator, Anna Elizabeth Dickinson (1841–1932) sways the crowd at an election-eve rally in Hartford, Connecticut, and helps the Republicans win by a landslide.

Enraged by high food prices, some 1,000 women go on a rampage in Richmond, Virginia. Led by Mary Jackson, toting her pistol and knife, they barge into shops, taking flour, sugar, and other needed supplies.

San Francisco entrepreneur Mary Ellen Pleasant (1814–1904) lobbies for a law ensuring that African Americans have the right to testify in court. Later, in 1868, she fights against Jim Crow laws by suing a streetcar company when the driver refuses to let her on board.

1864

Invited by a Republican congressman, Anna Dickinson is probably the first woman to speak to the House of Representatives. After inveighing against the South, she calls for the renomination of President Abraham Lincoln, who is seated in the audience.

1865

After President Lincoln's assassination, Mary Eugenia Jenkins Surratt (c. 1820–65), the owner of a boardinghouse where the conspirators met, is arrested. Although she insists on her innocence and the evidence against her is flimsy, she is convicted and executed.

When she is pushed off a streetcar in Washington, D.C., Sojourner Truth gets the conductor arrested for assault and battery.

1866

In May men and women from the American Anti-Slavery Society and women's rights groups join forces to form the American Equal Rights Association in New York. With Lucretia Mott as president and Susan B. Anthony as corresponding secretary, the group campaigns for suffrage for all African Americans and all women.

Thousands of women sign a petition, drafted by Susan B. Anthony and Elizabeth Cady Stanton, demanding that Congress initiate a constitutional amendment to "prohibit the several States from disfranchising any of their citizens on the grounds of sex."

In June, Congress passes the 14th Amendment (ratified in 1868). It states, "All persons born or naturalized in the United States . . . are citizens," and guarantees due process and equal protection under the laws. However, another section refers to voting rights in terms of *male* citizens—the first time this qualification appears in the Constitution. It also specifically excludes Indians "not taxed" from representation.

Even though she cannot vote, Elizabeth Cady Stanton runs for Congress as an Independent. She receives only 24 of the 12,000 votes cast, but she proves that women have the right to seek public office.

In the South white violence against African Americans flares up and "black codes" in state constitutions limit blacks' freedom. In response, Clara Brown, who has built a fortune as a laundress in Colorado, organizes her own wagon train company, staffed by African Americans, to provide southern blacks with transportation to the more liberal West.

1867

At the meeting of the American Equal Rights Association, debate centers on emphasizing voting rights for black men or demanding suffrage for women (black and white) as well. Sojourner Truth speaks out for women's rights (see sidebar), although others, like Frances Watkins Harper in 1869, state that the issue of race, not sex, is more critical.

Josephine White Griffing (1814–72), Belva Bennett Lockwood (1830–1917), and others found the Universal Franchise Association, the first woman's suffrage group in Washington, D.C. Mary Ann Shadd Cary later joins this group.

Susan B. Anthony and Elizabeth Cady Stanton lobby unsuccessfully for woman's suffrage in the new New York state constitution.

Kansas holds a referendum on two separate suffrage amendments, for African Americans and for women. Anthony, Stanton, Lucy Stone and her husband, Henry Blackwell, and others travel throughout Kansas,

"I Have a Right"

" . . . I have a right to have just as much as a man. There is a great stir about colored men getting their rights, but not a word about the colored women; and If colored men get their rights, and not colored women theirs, you see the colored men will be masters over the women, and it will be just as bad as it was before. So I am for keeping the thing going while things are stirring; because if we wait till it is still, it will take a great while to get it going again."
  —Sojourner Truth, at convention of the American Equal Rights Association, 1867; in *History of Woman Suffrage*, vol. 1

but both measures are defeated. During this campaign Stanton and Anthony align themselves with the controversial George Francis Train, a racist, who pledges to finance a women's rights weekly, the *Revolution*.

"Justice, Not Favors!"—*motto of the* Revolution

1868

The first issue of the *Revolution*, edited by Elizabeth Cady Stanton and Parker Pillsbury, appears January 8, with the cry "Men, their rights and nothing more; women their rights and nothing less!" Although the 16-page paper survives only four years, it serves as a major organizing tool. Yet it also reflects anti-immigrant and racist sentiments, posing the educated woman's vote as a counter to that of "Patrick" and "Sambo."

Civil War worker Mary Livermore (p. 258) organizes the first woman suffrage convention in Chicago and becomes president of the resulting Illinois Woman Suffrage Association.

Lucy Stone, Paulina Davis, Julia Ward Howe (p. 310), and others start the New England Woman Suffrage Association, with Howe as president. Davis also helps form a Rhode Island suffrage group, of which she is president. Another founder of the New England group, Isabella Beecher Hooker (1822–1907), anonymously publishes "A Mother's Letters to a Daughter on Woman's Suffrage" in *Putnam's Magazine*.

After learning law from her husband, Myra Colby Bradwell (1831–94) starts an influential weekly, the *Chicago Legal News*, which reviews and advocates legislation. She also heads a legal printing firm. With her husband's help, she gains a special charter from the state to run these businesses as a married woman.

In Vineland, New Jersey, women set up their own election box with a female election judge. Almost 175 women, white and black, cast their "votes" for president. In California, Charley (Charlotte) Parkhurst (1812–79), a stage coach driver assumed to be a man, is reportedly successful in actually voting. Her sex is not discovered until her death.

Anthony and Stanton persuade Senator Samuel Pomeroy of Kansas and Representative George W. Julian of Indiana to introduce the first woman's suffrage amendment into Congress, but it is hardly noticed.

1869

In February, Congress passes the 15th Amendment (ratified 1870), guaranteeing that the right to vote "shall not be denied . . . on account of race, color, or previous condition of servitude." The omission of the word *sex* enrages feminists (see below).

In March, Louisa Rollin speaks to the South Carolina legislature on women's right to vote. Her sisters, Katherine, Charlotte ("Lottie"), and Frances, are also suffragists and active in black political circles during Reconstruction. Lottie chairs the initial 1870 meeting of the South Carolina Woman's Rights Association in Columbia.

Susan B. Anthony (left) and Elizabeth Cady Stanton (UPI/Bettmann)

At the American Equal Rights Association convention in May, the 15th Amendment is hotly debated. Elizabeth Cady Stanton, Susan B. Anthony, and others advocate rejecting any amendment that does not give women the vote, but many abolitionists disagree (see sidebar).

To push for a constitutional amendment guaranteeing women the vote, Stanton and Anthony form the National Woman Suffrage Association (NWSA), with Stanton as president. Later in the year Lucy Stone, Julia Ward Howe, and others establish a counter organization, the American Woman Suffrage Association (AWSA), with Henry Ward Beecher as president. The two groups continue as rivals for over 20 years. Although the NWSA refuses to support the 15th Amendment, it is generally the more radical organization, advocating not just the vote but also reforms in women's wages, working conditions, and property and divorce laws. The AWSA, which supports the 15th Amendment, focuses on women's suffrage, working at the state, rather than federal, level. Its publication is the *Woman's Journal*.

Sorosis (p. 113), a professional women's club in New York, sponsors a Woman's Parliament, but the women do not advocate suffrage. Instead, they propose a parallel government, giving women responsibility for issues, such as education, that naturally fall within their domain.

Active suffragist Myra Bradwell drafts a law to give married women full rights to their earnings, and the Illinois legislature enacts it. She also passes the Illinois bar exam, but the state supreme court refuses to let her practice because she is female, and the U.S. Supreme Court upholds this decision (see 1873).

In Iowa, Arabella Babb Mansfield (1846–1911) also passes the bar exam, and she becomes the first woman admitted to the bar when a judge interprets the word *male* in the state law as including *female*. She does not, however, practice law but continues her college teaching.

In December the territory of Wyoming approves woman's suffrage in its new constitution. The legislature also guarantees married women rights to their own property and approves equal pay for male and female teachers.

1870

In February women in the Utah territory gain the vote and begin to exercise their right in local elections (but see 1887).

In addition to voting, women in Laramie, Wyoming, are the first in the country to sit on a jury. Also in Wyoming, Esther McQuigg Slack Morris (1814–1902), an active suffragist, becomes the first female justice of the peace, in South Pass City.

Sojourner Truth collects signatures in New England and the Midwest for her petition to Congress to reserve lands in the West for settlement by freedpeople. Congress does not respond, but nine years later thousands of blacks flee the South to Kansas and other western states.

Debating the 15th Amendment

Unless women's rights are included now, in the 15th Amendment, Elizabeth Cady Stanton and Susan B. Anthony declare, it will take another generation to secure them (it takes 50 years). As the debate heats up, Stanton states she "does not believe in allowing ignorant negroes and foreigners to make laws for her." On the other side is Frederick Douglass, who stresses the life-and-death issues for blacks in gaining the vote. He argues: "When women, because they are women, are hunted down through the cities of New York and New Orleans; when they are dragged from their houses and hung upon lamp posts; when their children are torn from their arms, and their brains dashed on the pavement . . . then they will have an urgency to obtain the ballot equal to our own." When asked if this isn't true also of a black woman, Douglass agrees that it is, but because she is black.

Led by the Grimké sisters, 40 women in Hyde Park, Massachusetts, brave a severe snowstorm to cast symbolic votes in a separate ballot box. In New Hampshire taxpayer Marilla Young Ricker (1840–1920) asserts her 14th Amendment right to vote as an "elector"; she is turned down but succeeds in voting the next year.

1871

On January 11, before the House Judiciary Committee, Victoria Claflin Woodhull (1838–1927) argues that women have the right to vote under the 14th Amendment. Later she addresses the National Woman Suffrage Association (see sidebar). But Woodhull's views on free love, expressed in her book *Origin, Tendencies and Principles of Government* as well as public speeches, make her a highly controversial figure. Lucy Stone and the AWSA dissociate themselves from her.

Mary Ann Shadd Cary petitions the House Judiciary Committee for her right to vote, under the 14th and 15th Amendments, as a black citizen and registers in Washington, D.C. Other black women attempt to vote in South Carolina.

1872

When Charlotte E. Ray (1850–1911) graduates from law school at Howard University, she becomes the first African American woman admitted to the bar in the United States, but she cannot find many clients because of the double prejudice against her.

Winema (1836–1920) gains media attention when she serves as an interpreter and intermediary in peace negotiations between the Modoc people and whites on the West Coast.

After Susan B. Anthony and the NWSA repudiate her, Victoria Woodhull forms her own Equal Rights Party and announces her candidacy for U.S. president. She names Frederick Douglass as her running mate without his consent. Soon afterward she becomes embroiled in a major scandal by accusing AWSA president and respected minister Henry Ward Beecher of having an affair with Elizabeth Tilton, the wife of a prominent New York newspaper editor. The publicity generated by this scandal hurts the suffrage movement and widens the breach between the NWSA and AWSA. Woodhull herself is jailed for sending "obscenity" through the mails when she publishes her charges in her own paper. She later leaves the country for England.

After Alta M. Hulett (c. 1854–77) is denied admission to the Illinois bar, she drafts a state law opening all professions and employment (except in the military) to women. With the support of Ada H. Kepley (p. 176), Myra Bradwell, and others, she lobbies it through the legislature and then becomes the first woman lawyer in Illinois.

Virginia Louisa Minor (1824–94), president of the Woman Suffrage Association of Missouri, and her husband sue the St. Louis registrar for not letting her register to vote. The case goes to the U.S. Supreme Court as a test of women's 14th Amendment rights (see 1875).

In Rochester, New York, Susan B. Anthony and 16 other women try to vote, claiming their 14th Amendment rights and defying a law against "illegal" voters. After her arrest Anthony defends her stance in public speeches (see sidebar), but at her 1873 trial the judge refuses to let her testify and then directs the jury to find her guilty. At the end he does ask Anthony if she has anything to say, and she promptly lashes out, ". . . you have trampled under foot every vital principle of our government." She refuses to pay her $100 fine, but no action is taken, so she is unable to appeal her case to the Supreme Court.

In Battle Creek, Michigan, Sojourner Truth attempts to vote under the 15th Amendment but is turned away.

"As much as white women need the vote, colored women need it more"—Frances Harper

1873

In the first test of the equal protection of women under the 14th Amendment, the U.S. Supreme Court upholds the rejection of Myra Bradwell by the Illinois bar (see 1870). The court states: "The natural and proper timidity and delicacy which belongs to the female sex evidently unfits it for many of the occupations of civil life." Although Illinois has passed a law opening all professions to women (see 1872), Bradwell never reapplies to the bar. The Illinois Supreme Court finally acts on its own in 1890 and admits her.

After protesting taxation without representation at a town meeting in Glastonbury, Connecticut, Abby Smith (1797–1878) and her sister Julia (1792–1886), both in their eighties, refuse to pay their tax bills. The town promptly confiscates seven of their cows and later sells off land worth $2,000 to pay the $50 still due. The sisters' biting letters to the editor and court battles are reported throughout the country. Other suffragists, like Abby Kelley Foster, then also refuse to pay taxes.

Newspaper publisher Abigail Scott Duniway (p. 292), a leading suffragist in the West, helps found the Oregon Equal Suffrage Association.

1874

Seven years after Kansas, Michigan is the second state to hold a referendum on woman suffrage, but the measure is rejected.

1875

The Supreme Court rules on the suffrage case brought by Virginia Minor (see 1872). Her attorneys point to the 14th Amendment clause: "No State shall make or enforce any law which shall abridge the privileges and immunities of the citizens of the United States." But the court rejects their argument that voting is a right of citizenship. Their decision confirms that a new constitutional amendment is needed.

The U.S. government passes the Page Law to prevent Chinese prostitutes from entering the country. The effect, however, is to keep almost all Chinese women out, as they are put through lengthy questioning before even leaving China.

Michigan and Minnesota are the next two states after Kansas to let women vote in school elections.

1876

At the NWSA convention Harriet ("Hattie") Purvis (1839–post 1903) is elected as the first African American vice president.

When the NWSA asks to read a statement at the July Fourth Centennial celebration in Philadelphia, their request is denied, but they do receive five tickets to the ceremony. Led by Susan B. Anthony, five women march up on the platform, hand the chairman their "Declaration of Rights" (see sidebar), and then pass out copies as they leave the hall. Outside, from a bandstand opposite Independence Hall, Anthony reads the declaration to a large crowd. It highlights six violations of women's rights, including taxation without representation, the lack of a jury of peers, and unequal standards for pay and moral conduct.

1877

The Colorado Suffrage Association mounts a major campaign to pass a referendum giving women the vote. Susan B. Anthony, Lucy Stone, and other leaders tour the state. But the measure is defeated two to one.

1878

Elizabeth Cady Stanton and Susan B. Anthony persuade Senator Aaron A. Sargent of California to present Congress with an amendment giving women the vote. Called the Anthony Amendment, it is reintroduced each year for the next 41 years until it becomes the 19th Amendment to the Constitution. It states simply: "The right of citizens of the United States to vote shall not be denied or abridged by the United States or any State on account of sex."

Matilda Joslyn Gage (1826–98), who has served as president of both the NWSA and New York State Woman Suffrage Association, edits a four-page monthly, *National Citizen and Ballot Box,* for the NWSA.

Mary Jane Garrett organizes 500 black women in New Orleans to protest ongoing violence by whites and to encourage blacks to emigrate to safer states in the West. Some 6,000 blacks travel to Kansas in 1879.

Clara Shortridge Foltz (1849–1934) and Laura de Force Gordon (1838–1907) succeed in amending the California constitution to let women practice law. Later, when they are denied admission to Hastings College of Law, a state school, they both sue and successfully argue the case through the state supreme court.

1879

Massachusetts women win the right to vote in school board elections. The next year Ednah Dow Littlehale Cheney (1824–1904) and Abigail ("Abby") Williams May (1829–88) organize the Massachusetts School Suffrage Association to urge women to go to the polls.

Susette La Flesche (later Tibbles, 1854–1903), using her Omaha name, Inshta Theumba ("Bright Eyes"), joins a speaking tour as interpreter for Standing Bear, the Ponca leader recently arrested when he tried to leave Indian Territory and return with his people to their homeland. Her forceful lectures draw national attention to the government's unjust displacement of the Ponca people and inspire Helen Fiske Hunt Jackson (1830–85) and others to take up the Indian cause.

As a result of lobbying by lawyer Belva Lockwood, Congress passes legislation giving women the right to practice before the Supreme Court. In March, Lockwood is the first female lawyer to argue a case in the Supreme Court.

After helping the U.S. Army in the Bannock Wars (p. 260), Paiute activist Sarah Winnemucca lashes out against the wrongs done to her people and takes their case to Washington, D.C. In January 1880 she extracts a promise from Secretary of the Interior Carl Schurz to let the Paiute return from exile to the Malheur Reservation in Oregon. A government agent, however, thwarts the plan (see 1883).

As president of the National Woman's Christian Temperance Union (WCTU), Frances E. Willard (p. 147) issues guidelines on agitating for the vote in local elections. She emphasizes the connection between fighting against saloons to fighting against those who allow saloons to exist. By 1881 she persuades the group to join the campaign for both state and national suffrage.

1880

In February, Mary Ann Shadd Cary and six other women form the Colored Women's Progressive Franchise Association in Washington, D.C. In addition to demanding equal rights for women, in both voting and employment, they plan a newspaper owned by black women.

New York women win the right to vote in school elections, but when they try to vote they encounter refusal, a variety of threats, and officials who puff cigar smoke in their faces.

Mary Lucinda Bonney (1816–1900), Amelia Stone Quinton (1833–1926), and others gather 13,000 signatures on a petition calling on the government to honor their treaties with Native Americans and to keep white settlers out of Indian Territory. After presenting the 300-foot-long document to President Rutherford B. Hayes and Congress, they establish the Central Indian Committee (later the Women's National Indian Association) and continue petitioning the government.

An amendment to the California Civil Code forbids marriage between any white person and a "Negro, Mulatto, or Mongolian" (or, later, a Filipino). It remains in effect for almost 70 years.

1881

Susan B. Anthony, Elizabeth Cady Stanton, and Matilda Joslyn Gage publish the first volume of *History of Woman Suffrage,* and two more

"The women know as much as the men do, and their advice is often asked. . . . The council-tent is our Congress, and anybody can speak who has anything to say, women and all. They are always interested in what their husbands are doing and thinking about. And they take some part even in the wars. . . . If women could go into your Congress I think justice would soon be done to the Indians."
  —Sarah Winnemucca Hopkins, *Life among the Piutes: Their Wrongs and Claims* (New York: G.P. Putnam's Sons, 1883)

volumes of this major work appear in 1882 and 1886 (see also 1902, 1922). Harriet Jane Hanson Robinson (1825–1911), a former mill-worker and a member of the NWSA, publishes another history, *Massachusetts in the Woman Suffrage Movement*.

The Kentucky Woman Suffrage Association is established with Laura Clay (1849–1941) as president. Like many white southern women, she argues for woman suffrage as a way of maintaining white supremacy.

Helen Hunt Jackson publishes her indictment of the government's Indian policy, *A Century of Dishonor*, in blood-red covers and sends copies to every concerned government official. In 1882, at the government's request, she examines the plight of the Mission Indians in California, but her report is ignored.

1882

Both the Senate and the House appoint committees on woman suffrage, which give favorable reports, but no action is taken.

Led by Rachel Foster Avery (1858–1919), Nebraska women campaign for the vote on a state referendum but do not succeed.

In California lawyer Marion Marsh Todd (1841–post 1913) helps draft the platform of the Greenback Labor Party and runs for state attorney general on its ticket. She gets 1,109 votes.

After living several months on the Omaha reservation, Alice Cunningham Fletcher (1838–1923) drafts and gets Congress to pass a law to give the Omaha individual land allotments (see 1887). She then supervises the division for the government, with the help of Francis La Flesche, Susette La Flesche Tibbles's brother.

There are 48 recorded lynchings of African American women and men. These figures increase in succeeding years.

1883

On an East Coast lecture tour partly sponsored by women reformers, Sarah Winnemucca (Hopkins) gathers signatures on a petition demanding the promised land grants to her people. She also sells her book *Life among the Piutes: Their Wrongs and Claims* (see sidebar).

After a campaign by Abigail Duniway and others, Washington passes a suffrage law, but it is struck down by the territory's supreme court.

"We shall never have equal rights until we take them, nor respect until we command it"—Belva Lockwood

1884

In California a group of women nominate Belva Lockwood to run for president as the National Equal Rights Party candidate. In response to opposition from Susan B. Anthony and Elizabeth Cady Stanton, Lockwood states, "It is quite time that we had our own party." She runs again in 1888.

In contrast to her sister Susette, Rosalie La Flesche Farley (1861–1900) speaks out against citizenship and assimilation; instead, she argues that the Omaha should govern themselves, independent of both the federal and the state governments.

In Tennessee, after refusing to move to a segregated car, Ida Bell Wells (later Barnett, 1862–1931) is thrown off the train. She immediately sues the Chesapeake and Ohio Railroad and wins in the lower court, but the state supreme court overturns the decision in 1887.

1886

Male Wisconsin voters agree to a law allowing women to vote in "any election pertaining to school matters." Olympia Brown, president of the state suffrage association, then tries to vote in a municipal election, claiming it pertains to school matters, but she loses her case.

Lucía ("Lucy") González Parsons (1853–1942), a founder of the radical International Working People's Association in Chicago and labor organizer, mounts a public campaign to protest her husband's and other radicals' arrests for the Haymarket Square riot. Although she takes the case to the Supreme Court, her husband is executed (he is later pardoned). She continues as a labor organizer; much later she helps form the International Labor Defense to assist political prisoners.

1887

The Senate finally debates and votes on the Anthony Amendment (see 1878), with 16 for, 34 against, and 26 absent.

Attacking the continuing practice of polygamy by Mormons, Methodist crusader Angelina Thurston Newman (1837–1910) succeeds in getting Congress to pass the Edmunds-Tucker Act, which disfranchises Utah women. Mormon suffragist Emmeline Woodward Wells (1828–1921) campaigns vigorously against this; after losing the right she has had for 17 years, she helps form a state suffrage group in 1889.

Women win the right to vote in local elections in Kansas, and in April, Susannah Medora Salter (1860–1961) of Argonia (population 500) is elected the first U.S. woman mayor.

The government appoints Alice Fletcher as a special agent to help carry out the new Dawes Severalty Act, which grants Indians individual land allotments along with full U.S. citizenship. When Fletcher works with the Nez Percé, she encounters strong resistance to this law. In the end the act fails to protect the lands of Native peoples.

To mark the centennial of the U.S. Constitution, Lillie Devereux Blake (1833–1913) gives President Grover Cleveland a statement from several NWSA women, pointing out that half the country's citizens are still denied their full constitutional rights.

1888

For the 40th anniversary of the Seneca Falls convention, Elizabeth Cady Stanton and Susan B. Anthony initiate an international meeting of women in Washington, D.C. Representatives from 49 countries and 53 U.S. organizations attend, and two new groups are formed: the International Council of Women and the National Council of Women, with Frances Willard as president and May Wright Sewall (1844–1920) as recording secretary.

1889

Wilhelmina ("Minnie") D. Morgan and an all-woman council are elected to govern Cottonwood Falls, Kansas.

In the five years to 1894, at least eight black women are lynched.

1890

When Congress tries to reject Wyoming's application for statehood because its constitution allows women to vote, Wyoming legislators adamantly refuse to back down. In a close vote Congress then admits Wyoming as the only state where women can vote in federal elections.

After long negotiations—started in 1887 by Lucy Stone; her daughter, Alice Stone Blackwell (1857–1950); and Susan B. Anthony—the two factions of the suffrage movement, NWSA and AWSA, merge into the National American Woman Suffrage Association (NAWSA). Elizabeth Cady Stanton is the first president.

Believing the other organizations are too conservative, Matilda Gage forms the Women's National Liberal Union, which underlines the role of the church in suppressing women.

Mary Elizabeth Clyens Lease (1850–1933) becomes known as a fiery orator for the Farmers' Alliance and the People's (Populist) Party. Traveling throughout Kansas, she gives some 160 speeches, and in 1891 takes her message to Missouri, the Far West, and the South. She allegedly tells farmers to "raise less corn and more hell." Detractors refer to her as the "Kansas Pythoness" or "Mary Yellin."

New Hampshire finally allows women to practice law after Marilla Ricker petitions the state supreme court.

When the Sons of the American Revolution fails to admit women, Ellen Hardin Walworth, Eugenia Washington, Flora Adams Darling, and others form the Daughters of the American Revolution, with First Lady Caroline Scott Harrison as the group's president.

The General Federation of Women's Clubs (GWFC) is organized. (For the reform activities of women's clubs, see "Social Change.")

Although Susan B. Anthony (now 70), Henry Blackwell (65), and others stump the state, South Dakota resoundingly defeats a referendum on woman suffrage.

In 19 states women are now allowed to vote in school elections.

On December 29, at Wounded Knee Creek in South Dakota, U.S. soldiers disarm Big Foot and his Minneconjou (Sioux) people, who are traveling to the Pine Ridge Reservation. Suddenly a shot is fired, and the troops quickly slaughter about 200 people, many of them women and children. "We tried to run," Louise Weasel Bear later recalls, "but they shot us like we were a buffalo."

1891

Liliuokalani (1838–1917) becomes queen of Hawaii after her brother's death. She tries to take power away from American officials and return it to the Crown. However, when she establishes a new constitution in 1893, a group of mostly American residents, backed by U.S. troops, takes over the government (see 1894).

After Harriet Maxwell Converse (1836–1903) derails a New York bill to divide Indian land into individual tracts, she is made a formal member of the Seneca Nation and later an honorary chief.

1892

In Memphis journalist Ida B. Wells launches an antilynching campaign when her friend Thomas Moss and two other black men are murdered by a white mob essentially because their grocery store was taking business away from a white-owned store. After investigating many lynchings, she concludes that the violence is usually sparked by economic competition, not rape. In a fiery editorial in her paper, the *Free Speech*, she asserts: "Nobody in this section of the country believes the old threadbare lie that Negro men rape white women. If Southern white men are not careful . . . a conclusion will then be reached which will be very damaging to the moral reputation of their women." A mob immediately destroys her paper's offices, but fortunately she is in the North at the time. It is not safe for her to return to Memphis.

Elizabeth Cady Stanton retires as NAWSA president, and Susan B. Anthony replaces her. In her famous "Solitude of Self" speech to the NAWSA (and later to House and Senate committees), Stanton underlines women's need for full freedom because of "the individuality of every human soul" (see sidebar).

In *A Voice from the South by a Black Woman of the South*, educator Anna J. Cooper (1858–1964) argues strongly for women's rights, especially with respect to education. "Woman's strongest vindication for speaking [is] that *the world needs to hear her voice*," she contends. "It would be sub-versive of every human interest that the cry of one-half of the human family be stifled."

The Woman's Building opens at the World's Columbian Exposition in Chicago. Organized by the Board of Lady Managers under Bertha Honoré Palmer (1849–1918), it displays women's achievements in 47 nations. Yet, despite repeated requests, African American women are not included in the planning stages and are given only minimal representation. In response, Ida B. Wells prints 20,000 copies of her pamphlet *The Reason Why the Colored American Is Not in the Columbian Exposition* and distributes it during 1893.

"The Arbiter of Her Own Destiny"

". . . consider, first, what belongs to her as an individual, in a world of her own, the arbiter of her own destiny . . . . The strongest reason for giving woman all the opportunities for higher education, for the full development of her faculties, her forces of mind and body; for giving her the most enlarged freedom of thought and action; a complete emancipation from all forms of bondage, of custom, dependence, superstition; from the crippling influences of fear—is the solitude and personal responsibility of her own individual life."

—Elizabeth Cady Stanton, speech to the National American Woman Suffrage Association, "The Solitude of Self," 1892; in *History of Woman Suffrage*, vol. 4, edited by Susan B. Anthony and Ida Husted Harper (Indianapolis: Hollenbeck Press, 1902)

1893

At its convention the NAWSA reveals strong racist and anti-immigrant feelings within its ranks when it passes a resolution pointing out that literate white women outnumber both black and "foreign" voters.

At the World's Congress of Representative Women, held at the Columbian Exposition in Chicago, 330 women present papers and over 150,000 people attend. Speakers range from Lucy Stone (who dies later in the year) to antisuffragist Katherine E. Conway. Anna J. Cooper, Fanny Jackson Coppin (p. 176), and Fannie Barrier Williams (1855–1944) address a special session on "The Intellectual Progress of Colored Women of the United States Since Emancipation."

In a rousing speech in New York, anarchist Emma Goldman (1869–1940) denounces the power of wealthy industrialists and tells striking workers they have a right to take bread to avoid starving. Arrested for inciting a riot, she is sentenced to a year in jail.

Appointed by the Populist Party as president of the Kansas State Board of Charities, Mary Elizabeth Lease then runs for the U.S. Senate but loses. In 1894 disagreements lead to her removal from state office.

To gain positive press coverage for a state suffrage referendum in Colorado, Carrie Lane Chapman Catt (1859–1947) helps organize leading socialites into the exclusive Denver Equal Suffrage League. Even Susan B. Anthony, long a champion of working women, approves this stategy as expedient. And it works: Colorado gives women the vote.

1894

In the next five years (through 1898), 15 or more African American women are lynched.

After a revolt by her supporters fails, Liliuokalani is put under house arrest. Although she formally abdicates in early 1895, she continues to fight against annexation and leads the *Oni pa'a* ("Stand Firm") movement, demanding "Hawaii for the Hawaiians." The U.S. Congress, however, annexes Hawaii in 1898. Almost 100 years later it apologizes for its use of troops to take over the islands.

In a letter to the "Washington Chiefs," Hopi women ask the government not to divide their land into individual tracts owned by men. "Among us," they point out, "the family traces its kin from the mother, hence all the possessions are hers."

When Fannie Barrier Williams tries to join the all-white Chicago Woman's Club, it provokes a heated, lengthy debate, which is covered by the press. In 1895 she becomes the club's first black member.

In Colorado, Clara Clessingham, Carrie Holly, and Frances Klock are the first U.S. women elected to a state house of representatives.

In a drive to convince the New York legislature to give women the vote while revising the state constitution, prominent physician Mary Put-

Liliuokalani (Library of Congress)

nam Jacobi (p. 223) writes the classic pamphlet *Common Sense Applied to Woman Suffrage*. Although women gather 600,000 signatures on a petition, the effort fails.

In New York City, Josephine Shaw Lowell helps organize the Woman's Municipal League to combat political corruption and promote "humanitarian reform." Many other women are active during this period in civic groups (see "Social Change").

"Too long have we been silent"
—Josephine St. Pierre Ruffin

1895

Ida B. Wells-Barnett publishes her pamphlet *A Red Record: Tabulated Statistics and Alleged Causes of Lynching in the United States, 1892–1894*. Attacking white male "chivalry," she writes: "True chivalry respects all womanhood, and no one who reads the record, as it is written in the faces of the million mulattoes in the South, will for a minute conceive that the southern white man had a very chivalrous regard for the honor due women of his race or respect for the womanhood which circumstances placed in his power."

When the male president of the Missouri Press Association writes a letter accusing all black women of being "prostitutes, thieves, and liars," Josephine St. Pierre Ruffin (1842–1924) acts on her outrage and calls for the first national conference of African American women in Boston (see sidebar). The group resolves to fight against lynchings, the erosion of black people's rights in the South, employment discrimination, and segregated transportation. At the end of the meeting, they form the National Federation of Afro-American Women, with Margaret Murray Washington as president and Ruffin as vice president.

Massachusetts holds a nonbinding, "mock" referendum on woman suffrage and lets both women and men vote. A vigorous campaign against the measure is mounted by the Massachusetts Association Opposed to Further Extension of Suffrage to Women (founded in 1882 by Mrs. Henry O. Houghton) and the Man Suffrage Association. Despite prosuffrage efforts by Alice Stone Blackwell, Henry Blackwell, Julia Ward Howe, and others, suffrage loses by 80,000 votes.

1896

On January 4 Utah is admitted to the Union with a state constitution (passed in 1895) reinstating woman suffrage. Utah suffragists Emily Sophia Richards, Emmeline Wells, and Charlotte Ives Cobb Godbe Kirby all contribute to this victory. Later in the year Utah elects the first woman state senator, Martha Hughes Cannon.

Through the efforts of Carrie Chapman Catt, Emma Smith DeVoe, and many others, an Idaho referendum on woman suffrage passes two to one at the polls. The result is disputed by the board of canvassers, but Idaho women take the case to the state supreme court and win.

"We Are Women, American Women"

"Year after year southern women have protested against the admission of colored women . . . on the ground of [their] immorality . . . [and] the charge has never been crushed, as it could and should have been at first. . . . It is to break this silence . . . that we are impelled to take this step, to make of this gathering an object lesson to the world. . . .

"Our woman's movement is woman's movement in that it is led and directed by women for the good of women and men, for the benefit of all humanity. . . . we are women, American women, as intensely interested in all that pertains to us as such as all other American women; . . . willing to join any others in the same work and cordially inviting and welcoming any others to join us."
—Josephine St. Pierre Ruffin, speech to First National Conference of Colored Women, July 1895; quoted in Eleanor Flexner, *Century of Struggle: The Woman's Rights Movement in the United States,* rev. ed. (Cambridge, Mass.: Harvard University Press, 1975)

Four contiguous states—Idaho, Wyoming, Colorado, and Utah—now have full suffrage, but no others will for 14 years.

The National Federation of Afro-American Women and the National League of Colored Women join forces to create the National Association of Colored Women (NACW), with Mary Church Terrell (1863–1954) as president. The group sets up kindergartens and day nurseries as well as demanding woman suffrage and equal rights for all African Americans. Its motto is "Lifting as we climb."

Active in the 1892 formation of the Populist Party, orator and journalist Annie LePorte Diggs (1848–1916) serves on the Populist National Committee. In 1897 she is elected president of the Kansas Woman's Free Silver League.

1897

Helen Kendrick Johnson publishes *Woman and the Republic,* a popular and critically well-received antisuffrage tract. Several other women write similar tracts.

1898

Charlotte Perkins Stetson (later Gilman, 1860–1935) publishes her classic feminist work, *Women and Economics,* stressing the importance of women's financial independence. To free women from constant house-keeping and childcare tasks, she proposes cooperative kitchens and centralized nurseries, all run by hired personnel. She also attacks society's emphasis on woman's sexual role (see sidebar).

Mary Church Terrell, NACW president, speaks to the NAWSA convention on "The Progress of Colored Women." But in 1899, when Lottie Wilson Jackson describes her difficulties in traveling to the convention and proposes a resolution against forcing black women to ride in smoking cars, southerners object and the motion is tabled.

1899

Several women lawyers from New York, Connecticut, and New Jersey establish the Women Lawyers' Club, which in 1908 becomes a national organization (the National Association of Women Lawyers).

There are four recorded lynchings of African American women in the years 1899 through 1903.

1900

Susan B. Anthony chooses Carrie Chapman Catt to succeed her as president of the NAWSA.

Two Radcliffe graduates, Maud Wood Park (1871–1955) and Inez Haynes Gillmore (later Irwin, 1873–1970), set up the first chapter of the College Equal Suffrage League in Massachusetts. Soon Park is recruiting college students and recent graduates in other states. By 1908 the group is a national organization.

In Kansas, where a fusion ticket of Populists, Bryan Democrats, and

Silver Republicans is nominated, Annie Diggs plays such a critical role that regular Democrats dub her "Boss" Diggs.

1902

California activists form the Woman's Socialist Union. Led by Josephine Cole, Mary Garbutt, Anna Ferry Smith, and others, they play an important role in the California suffrage movement.

Speaking in San Francisco's Chinatown, Chinese feminist Xue Jinqin, a student at Berkeley, calls for educational opportunities for women and an end to restrictive customs like foot-binding. Her words and those of other Chinese feminists, such as Zhang Shujun and Du Qingqi, are reported in *Chung Sai Yat Po*, a Chinese-language paper in California.

Just before Elizabeth Cady Stanton dies, she writes President Theodore Roosevelt, asking him to support woman suffrage.

Susan B. Anthony and journalist Ida Husted Harper (1851–1931) publish the fourth volume of the *History of Woman Suffrage*.

1903

The Women's Trade Union League (WTUL) is started (see "Work and Entrepreneurship" for women's labor movement activities).

After a speech by Belle Kearney (1863–1939) stressing that woman suffrage will maintain southern whites' rule, NAWSA president Carrie Chapman Catt reassures southern associations that each state can set its own membership rules and cannot be forced to admit blacks.

1904

When Carrie Chapman Catt resigns, Anna Howard Shaw (1847–1919), a former Methodist minister, becomes the new NAWSA president. She is a strong orator but is not considered a good administrator.

At the International Council of Women in Berlin, Catt and Susan B. Anthony help found the International Woman Suffrage Alliance, with Catt as president. Mary Church Terrell speaks to the ICW in English and German on African American women's advances and obstacles.

Lyda Burton Conley and her sister, Lena (Floating Voice), begin a protest that lasts for years when developers threaten the Wyandotte burial grounds in Kansas. To protect the graves, Lyda Conley studies law and is the first Indian woman admitted to the bar (in 1910). Eventually she argues the case, unsuccessfully, before the Supreme Court.

Six or more black women are lynched in the years 1904 through 1908.

1905

The Equal Rights League, a leftist reform group in New York organized by librarian Maud Malone, opens mock polling places, where women can cast their "votes" on Election Day.

Ella Reeve Cohen (later known as Bloor, 1862–1951) becomes a state organizer for the Socialist Party in Connecticut.

"Failure is impossible!"—Susan B. Anthony

1906

In February, Susan B. Anthony gives her last speech to the NAWSA, concluding with the words above. In March, at age 86, Anthony dies, after fighting more than 50 years for women's rights.

Arguing the case before the Supreme Court, attorney Belva Lockwood gains a record $5 million settlement for the Eastern Cherokee people.

The third referendum on woman suffrage in Oregon is defeated by a narrow margin.

1907

In January, Harriot Stanton Blatch (1856–1940), the daughter of Elizabeth Cady Stanton, forms the Equality League of Self-Supporting Women, which she initially sees as a political extension of the Women's Trade Union League. She serves as president, and labor organizer Leonora O'Reilly (p. 115) is vice president. The 200 women at the first meeting include lawyers, social workers, and factory workers. To encourage working-class participation, there is no membership fee. Later, in 1910, this group becomes the Women's Political Union.

Mary Duffy and Clara Silver, two garment industry unionists, represent the Equality League at the annual hearings on woman suffrage by the New York state legislature (see sidebar). Later in the year the Equality League organizes a speech by Anne Cobden-Sanderson, one of the first British suffragettes to be arrested; it draws a huge crowd.

After lobbying successfully for compulsory education and prohibitions against child labor in the constitution of the new state of Oklahoma, Kate Barnard (1875–1930) is elected commissioner of charities and corrections. The first U.S. woman to win a statewide, as opposed to district, election, she remains in office for two terms and continues her reform agenda. She is not, however, a suffragist.

Although the "Gentleman's Agreement" restricts further immigration of Japanese and Korean workers, it allows those already in America to bring their parents, wives, and children. As a result, more than 20,000 "picture brides" (chosen from photographs) arrive before restrictions are imposed in 1921.

Started by British suffragette Bettina Borrman Wells and led by Maud Malone, the American Suffragettes conduct their first outdoor rally in New York on New Year's Eve. Soon they are holding weekly meetings outdoors. "We . . . believe in standing on streetcorners and fighting our way to recognition, forcing men to think about us," they declare.

1908

With Maud Malone, Harriot Blatch organizes a "trolley car campaign," traveling between Syracuse and Albany and holding outdoor meetings on woman suffrage. Speakers include feminist writer Charlotte Perkins Gilman and larbor organizer Rose Schneiderman (p. 118).

Emma Goldman, an outspoken champion of free speech and radical causes, loses her U.S. citizenship through a government subterfuge.

The National College Women's Equal Suffrage League is established with M. Carey Thomas (p. 179), head of Bryn Mawr College, as president and Maud Park as vice president. In a pamphlet Thomas states: "The right to become citizens of the State is the next and inevitable consequence of education and work outside the home. We have gone so far; we must go farther. We cannot go back."

1909

Upset by the destructive 1908 race riot in Springfield, Illinois, a group of black and white activists meets in New York and starts the National Association for the Advancement of Colored People (NAACP). The founding members include such women as Ida B. Wells-Barnett, Mary Church Terrell, Jane Addams (p. 149), and Mary White Ovington (1865–1951), a social worker and one of the few white associates of the earlier, black-led civil rights group called the Niagara Movement.

Wealthy suffragist Alva Smith Vanderbilt Belmont (1853–1933) rents New York office space for the NAWSA, establishes a national press bureau, and organizes the Political Equality League.

Everywhere women activists speak out on suffrage. Traveling across Massachusetts, four women hold impromptu outdoor rallies in each town they pass through. Illinois suffragists board the "Suffrage Special" from Chicago to Springfield, where 25 women deliver three-minute speeches to the state legislature. Maryland women arrive 600 strong in Annapolis to inform their state legislators that they want the vote.

Lawyer Crystal Eastman (1881–1928), who has studied many industrial accidents, is appointed to the New York State Employers' Liability Commission, where she helps draft a workers' compensation law.

Six or more black women are lynched between 1909 and 1913.

1910

The Equality League of Self-Supporting Women (renamed the Women's Political Union) organizes the first major suffrage parade, down Fifth Avenue in New York. They also operate a suffragist newsstand outside their headquarters, which is open for a couple of hours every day and sells pamphlets, journals, and copies of speeches.

Highly regarded progressive reformer Jane Addams publishes her article "Why Women Should Vote" in the *Ladies' Home Journal*. She argues that in an urban world, women need the vote if they are to protect the home (see sidebar).

Wyoming elects its first female state legislator, Mary G. Bellany.

Kate Richards O'Hare (later Cunningham, 1877–1948), an active lecturer and organizer for the Socialist Party, runs for Congress on its ticket in Kansas.

"No Amount of Private Sweeping"

"In a crowded city quarter . . . if the street is not cleaned by the city authorities no amount of private sweeping will keep the tenement free from grime; if the garbage is not properly collected and destroyed a tenement-house mother may see her children sicken and die of diseases from which she alone is powerless to shield them. . . . In short, if woman would keep on with her old business of caring for her house and rearing her children she will have to have some conscience in regard to public affairs lying quite outside of her immediate household. . . . May we not say that American women need this implement [the ballot] in order to preserve the home?"
—Jane Addams, "Why Women Should Vote," in *Ladies' Home Journal* (January 1910)

Although Oregon fails to pass yet another woman suffrage referendum (its fifth), Washington becomes the first state in 14 years to grant women the vote, approving the measure by almost two to one.

1911

When California announces a referendum on woman's vote, suffragists immediately mount an intensive campaign. The California Equal Suffrage Association joins forces with women's clubs, trade unions, socialist groups, and others to carry the message into every community. Gigantic billboard ads are put up; pageants and plays are staged; student essay contests are held; speakers are whisked from one hall to another in large touring cars—everything is tried. But the liquor interests are also out in full force. Suffragists keep a careful watch at the polls to make sure no finagling occurs. The day after the election, with the city vote in, the papers report that the measure has lost. As the rural vote is tabulated, however, the tables turn. By just 3,587 votes (1.5%), California women win the right to cast their own ballots.

The National Association Opposed to Woman Suffrage is established, with Josephine Marshall Jewell Dodge (1855–1928) as president and headquarters in New York. In the group's journal, *Woman's Protest*, Dodge argues that women can do reform work better without the vote. By 1915 the group has 200,000 members and 25 state associations.

Many Chicanas, including Andrea and Teresa Villareal in Texas and María Talavera and Francisca Mendoza in Los Angeles, actively support the Partido Liberal Mexicano during the Mexican Revolution.

Journalist Jovita Idár (1885–1946) and Soledad Peña organize La Liga Femenil Mexicanista (League of Mexican Feminists) in Laredo, Texas. They pledge support for the struggle *por la raza y para la raza* ("by the race and for the race"). Specifically, they protest lynching, urge equal education for women, and help organize schools for Chicano children.

1912

Julia Clifford Lathrop (1858–1932) becomes the first woman to direct a major federal agency when she is appointed to head the new U.S. Children's Bureau by President William Howard Taft.

At a mass meeting in New York City, members of the Wage Earners' Equal Suffrage League protest the state legislature's failure to support woman suffrage. Unionist Rose Schneiderman ridicules the idea that women might lose their femininity (see sidebar). Mollie Schepps, a shirtwaist maker, cites the terrible Triangle Shirtwaist factory fire (p. 120) and stresses: "The ballot used as we mean to use it will abolish the burning and crushing of our bodies for the profit of a very few."

In New York City suffragist Marie Jenney Howe (1870–1934) and 25 other women start the group Heterodoxy, whose only requirement is that a "member . . . should not be orthodox in her opinions." It resembles consciousness-raising groups of the 1970s. The group sponsors several public forums, such as "Twenty-five Answers to Antis" and

"What Is Feminism?" (in 1914). Members include Elizabeth Gurley Flynn (p. 118), Charlotte Perkins Gilman, Crystal Eastman, and journalists Mary Heaton Vorse and Rheta Childe Dorr.

In New York City a half million people watch as 20,000 marchers demonstrate for woman suffrage.

Jane Addams seconds Theodore Roosevelt's nomination for president at the Progressive Party convention and speaks throughout the country on his behalf. Newspapers at the time call her "one of the ten greatest citizens of the republic."

In Kanab, Utah, Mary Woolley Chamberlain Howard is elected mayor, with an all-female council. The five women run the town for two years.

Six states hold referenda on woman suffrage. The liquor lobby easily defeats the measures in Ohio and Wisconsin, but Arizona, Kansas, and Oregon (on the sixth try) all give women the vote. In Michigan suffrage foes hold back returns in several precincts and then, when the measure is winning, report lopsided results to ensure its defeat. The fraud is obvious, but on a revote suffrage loses.

In honor of her long campaign to win the vote in Oregon, 78-year-old Abigail Duniway, now in a wheelchair, composes the official proclamation, which she then signs with the governor. She is also the first female voter to register in Oregon.

1913

In its first legislative act, the new territory of Alaska gives women the right to vote.

In March, when Woodrow Wilson arrives in Washington, D.C., for his inauguration, almost no one is there to greet him; instead, the crowds are watching 5,000 to 8,000 suffragists, dressed in white, parade down Pennsylvania Avenue. Although the marchers have a permit, the police fail to protect them from angry spectators, who shout insults and even physically assault the women. The public is appalled, and the police chief later loses his job. Yet the two main organizers of the NAWSA-sponsored event—Alice Paul (1885–1977) and Lucy Burns (1879–1966)—are not deterred; they recently studied in England, where they learned confrontational tactics from the British suffragettes.

In March, after forming the Alpha Suffrage Club for black women in Chicago, Ida B. Wells-Barnett travels to Washington, D.C., for the NAWSA parade. When she tries to join the Illinois contingent, she is asked to march in the back of the procession with the other African Americans. "If the Illinois women do not take a stand now in this great democratic parade then the colored women are lost," she argues, but to no avail. Wells-Barnett leaves, but later, during the march, she emerges from the crowd and takes her place beside her only two white supporters in the Illinois group.

In April, Alice Paul, Lucy Burns, Crystal Eastman, and others form

On "True Emancipation"

Emma Goldman champions freedom, but she does not support the woman suffrage movement. In Anarchism and Other Essays (1911), she attacks the snobbishness of the typical middle-class suffragist. "In her exalted conceit," Goldman writes, "she does not see how truly enslaved she is, not so much by man, as by her own silly notions and traditions. Suffrage cannot ameliorate that sad fact; it can only accentuate it." For Goldman, "true emancipation begins neither at the polls nor in the courts. It begins in woman's soul. . . . It is necessary that woman . . . realize that her freedom will reach as far as her power to achieve her freedom reaches. . . . [And] if partial emancipation is to become a complete and true emancipation of woman, it will have to do away with the ridiculous notion that to be loved, to be sweetheart and mother, is synonymous with being slave or subordinate."

In 1914 Heterodoxy (see 1912)
sponsors two mass meetings on
feminism at Cooper Union in New
York. At the first a dozen speakers each present 10-minute state-
ments on "What Feminism Means
to Me." At the second, seven
women discuss different aspects
of "Breaking into the Human
Race." They highlight:
— "The right to work"
— "The right of the mother to
her profession"
— "The right to her
convictions"
— "The right to her name"
— "The right to organize"
— "The right to ignore
fashions"
— "The right to specialize in
home industries"

the Congressional Union for Woman Suffrage and soon begin publishing the weekly *Suffragist*. Although at first an affiliate of the NAWSA,
it is far too radical for that group, and the two split by early 1914.

Women bombard Congress with suffrage petitions. In July a line of
automobiles bears down on the Capitol to deliver 200,000 signatures
for suffrage.

When the Illinois governor refuses to hold a referendum on suffrage,
women focus on gaining limited suffrage by an act of the state legislature. They win with passage of the Presidential and Municipal Suffrage
Bill. Illinois is the first state outside the West to give women at least
some voting power.

Lawyer Hortense Sparks Ward (1872–1944) successfully lobbies the
Texas legislature to pass a law, referred to as the "Hortense Ward Act,"
granting married women property rights. She also helps gain a 54-hour
work week for women and a workers' compensation law.

Objecting to a federal amendment, Kate M. Gordon (1861–1932) sets
up the Southern States Woman Suffrage Conference, which promotes
states' rights as a way to enfranchise white but not black women.

1914

In March, for the first time in 27 years, since 1887, the Woman Suffrage Amendment is brought out of committee and voted on in the
Senate, with 35 for and 34 against.

Despite differences in the governmental systems, the Congressional
Union adopts the British suffragettes' tactic of holding the party in
power accountable for not giving women the vote. Thus, because the
president is a Democrat and Democrats control Congress, they campaign against all Democrats, whether or not they support suffrage. In
addition, CU members begin heckling President Wilson with constant
questions about woman suffrage.

On the ballot in seven states, woman suffrage is defeated in Missouri,
Nebraska, North and South Dakota, and Ohio, but it wins in Montana
and Nevada. As a field secretary for the NAWSA, Jeannette Pickering
Rankin (1880–1973) runs the successful Montana campaign. Anne
Henrietta Martin (1875–1951) of the Nevada Equal Franchise Society
heads the drive in her state.

After a strong voter registration effort by the Alpha Suffrage Club,
many African American women support a black candidate for alderman in the Chicago primaries. Although he loses, the potential power
of the women's votes is clear to both politicians and the press.

When magazine publisher Miriam (Mrs. Frank) Leslie (p. 291) dies,
she leaves Carrie Chapman Catt almost $2 million for suffrage work,
although this is reduced to $1 million by litigation.

After campaigning for Wilson in 1912 as head of the Women's State

Democratic Party, San Francisco lawyer Annette Abbott Adams (1877–1956) is appointed to be the first female federal prosecutor. She serves as assistant U.S. attorney for northern California.

Activist teacher Henrietta Rodman (1878–1923) forms the Feminist Alliance, which "demands the removal of all social, political, and other discriminations which are based upon sex, and the award of all rights and duties in all fields on the basis of individual capacity alone."

Hungarian feminist and pacifist Rosika Schwimmer (1877–1948) tours 22 states, describing the devastation of World War I and urging women especially to pressure Wilson to mediate an end to the war. In 1915 she persuades Henry Ford to sponsor a "peace ship" to Europe, but the press belittles her and the entire venture.

Eleven or more black women are lynched in the five years to 1918.

1915

To protest all war, 3,000 women meet in Washington, D.C., in January and form the Woman's Peace Party, chaired by Jane Addams. Other founding members include Carrie Chapman Catt, Florence Kelley (p. 151), and Emily Greene Balch (1867–1961). Crying "Listen to women for a change," the group soon gains 40,000 members.

Jane Addams presides over the International Congress of Women in The Hague, attended by more than 1,000 women from 12 countries. Calling for mediation to end the war, the group forms a peace committee, which later, in 1919, becomes the Women's International League for Peace and Freedom.

Socialist Jessie Wallace Hughan (1875–1955), Evelyn West Hughan, and Pennsylvania suffragists Tracy Mygatt (1885–1974) and Frances Witherspoon (1887–1974) start the Anti-Enlistment League. In the next two years (before the draft), they get 3,500 people to sign pledges refusing to enlist in the military.

For the first time the Anthony Amendment is voted on in the House, but it loses (204 against, 174 for).

On September 16, in a publicity event organized by the Congressional Union, Sara Bard Field (1882–1974) and two drivers set off from San Francisco in a car to deliver a suffrage petition to Washington, D.C. Mabel Vernon (1883–1975) organizes welcoming parades at a number of stops. After endless trials, from blizzards to breakdowns, Field hands some half-million signatures to President Wilson on December 6.

Black women are the determining factor in electing Chicago's first black alderman, Oscar DePriest.

Despite highly organized door-to-door campaigns, woman suffrage referenda are defeated in four East Coast states: Massachusetts, New Jersey, New York, and Pennsylvania. Led by Carrie Chapman Catt, however, New York suffragists are optimistic; at a rally just two nights

"No Special Privilege"

"I want no special privilege for myself, for my sex, or for my class. I merely demand equal opportunity for all. I want to shoulder my own responsibility and I ask for the ballot to strengthen my arm for its task."
—Kate Richards O'Hare, "Shall Women Vote?" in *Social Revolution* (August 1914)

after the vote, they announce their intention to win in 1917, the next date a referendum can be held.

Impressed with Catt's organizational skills in the New York campaign, NAWSA members urge her to accept the national group's presidency, as Anna Howard Shaw is retiring.

1916

In Chicago, at the Republican Party convention, about 5,000 women march in stormy weather to demand that woman suffrage be included in the party's platform. At the Democratic convention, suffragists present tableaux of women in states with and without suffrage.

Anna Howard Shaw (left) and Carrie Chapman Catt (Library of Congress)

As in 1914, Alice Paul and the Congressional Union campaign against the party in power: the Democrats. As activist Maud Younger (1870–1936) points out, women now have enough votes to swing the election. To organize women voters in suffrage states, they form the National Woman's Party, chaired by Anne Martin. (In 1917 the CU merges into the NWP.) Also, Lucy Burns and some 20 other women board the "Suffrage Special," a railroad car touring the Far West to gain support.

Writer Zitkala-Sa (Gertrude Simmons Bonnin, 1876–1935) helps start the Society of American Indians, the first all-Indian reform group. She lobbies the U.S. government to give all Indians citizenship and to recognize their land claims.

In a speech to the NAWSA convention, President Wilson says they will triumph but "can afford a little while to wait." Anna Howard Shaw responds, "We have waited *so* long, Mr. President! We have dared to hope that . . . yours would be the voice to pronounce the words to bring our freedom." At that point all the women spontaneously stand up and look toward Wilson.

Outlining her "winning plan" to the NAWSA, Carrie Chapman Catt emphasizes passage of a federal amendment but at the same time urges state campaigns to keep up the "suffrage noise." She envisions six years of struggle before the amendment is finally ratified; it takes only four.

Running as a progressive Republican, Jeannette Rankin of Montana is the first woman to be elected to the U.S. House of Representatives.

While addressing Congress soon after his reelection, President Wilson looks up to see a huge yellow banner unfold, asking, "Mr. President, what will you do for woman suffrage?" Immediately, National Woman's Party members begin distributing press releases to the audience.

1917

In January the National Woman's Party starts daily silent vigils in front of the White House with banners asking "How Long Must Women Wait for Liberty?" In May, after U.S. entry into World War I, the banners underline the contradiction between Wilson's fight "to save the world for democracy" and the lack of democracy for U.S. women. When angry bystanders attack the signs and the women, the police arrest the picketers (not their assailants). By August, when signs referring to "Kaiser Wilson" appear, some women are sentenced to 60 days in the Occoquan Workhouse for blocking the sidewalk. Because many of the women are well connected, the press reacts—covering the forced feedings of hunger strikers like Alice Paul and the rough treatment of docile prisoners like 73-year-old Mary Nolan. The women are freed in late November. Throughout the ordeal, however, the NAWSA refuses to support the protestors, and some members quit as a result. In 1918 the federal court of appeals concedes that the demonstrators never committed a crime.

In April, Jeannette Rankin is one of 50-some representatives to vote against U.S. entry into World War I. "I want to stand by my country, but I cannot vote for war," she tells the House. During the remainder of her term, she introduces various bills to help women and children. She is defeated in her bid for the Senate in 1918.

Many women aid the war effort (see "War"), but others oppose it. The DAR expels Jane Addams for her pacifism. Frances Witherspoon and Tracy Mygatt establish the Bureau of Legal Advice in New York to help conscientious objectors. Emma Goldman, who organizes the No-Conscription League with Alexander Berkman, is jailed for advocating war resistance. Similarly, after giving more than 140 antiwar speeches nationwide, socialist activist Kate O'Hare is arrested under the new Espionage Act and jailed in 1919. Socialists mount a strong protest, and she is pardoned in 1920. While imprisoned, she writes two books about her experience and later becomes involved in prison reform.

To protest the murder of African Americans in race riots in Illinois, thousands of black women, dressed in white, join a massive silent march, organized by the NAACP, down Fifth Avenue in New York.

Women gain the right to vote for president after legislative action in six states: Indiana, Michigan, Nebraska, North Dakota, Ohio, and Rhode Island. They also win the right to vote in primaries in Arkansas.

To win a New York suffrage referendum, suffragists gather signatures from over a million women who want the vote. They underline women's contributions to the war effort by including thousands of female war workers in a New York City suffrage parade. The result is a major victory: New York becomes the first East Coast state to give women full suffrage (not just the presidential vote).

1918

In the next 10 years, at least 11 African American women are lynched, including 3 pregnant women.

On January 9 President Woodrow Wilson speaks out in favor of the Anthony Amendment, and the next day it comes up for a vote in the House. Everyone knows the vote will be close. One prosuffrage representative arrives on a stretcher; another refuses to have a broken arm set until after the vote. The final count is 274 for, 136 against—giving just the required two-thirds majority. Yet on October 1, despite a direct plea from Wilson, the Senate fails to pass the measure, falling two votes short of the needed two-thirds majority.

After the Senate vote NAWSA targets four antisuffrage senators for defeat in the upcoming elections. Two lose their seats; the other two see their majority drop.

Two women—Anne Martin of Nevada and Jeannette Rankin of Montana—run for the Senate, but both lose.

State referenda give women complete suffrage in three states: Michigan (which had enacted presidential suffrage in 1917), Oklahoma, and South Dakota. In Texas, where the governor strongly opposes suffrage, women win the right to vote in primaries through legislative action. A literacy test, however, is used to prevent many black and Mexican American women from voting.

Pointing out the need to reach New York women voters, Belle Lindner Moskowitz (1877–1933) helps Alfred E. Smith campaign for governor and becomes a close adviser during his eight years in office.

In Washington, D.C., Kathryn Sellers is the first female judge to head a juvenile court.

Labor expert Mary Van Kleeck (1883–1972) directs the new Women in Industry Service in the Department of Labor. Her assistant is Mary Anderson (1872–1964), a Swedish immigrant who worked in a shoe factory before becoming a labor organizer. They recommend guidelines, such as an eight-hour day, for women workers employed under federal contracts. Their work paves the way for the Women's Bureau (see 1920).

After writing a letter to the *Kansas City Star,* stating, "I am for the people, while the Government is for the profiteers," Socialist Rose Pastor Stokes (1879–1933) is charged under the Espionage Act and given a 10-year sentence. This judgment is overturned in 1920.

1919

The National Woman's Party steps up its demonstrations for suffrage. In the capital women stand over "watchfires," burning copies of Wilson's words. Wealthy New York art collector Louisine Waldron Elder Havemeyer (1855–1929) is arrested for burning Wilson's effigy on the White House lawn. Later, dressed in prison uniforms, she and other NWP women jailed in the suffrage cause board the "Prison Special" for a one-month railroad campaign across the country.

In February the "lame-duck" Senate defeats the Anthony Amendment by one vote, but when the new Congress convenes in May, it is a different story. By a resounding vote of 304 to 89, the House approves the 19th Amendment on May 21. The Senate follows suit on June 3 with a vote of 66 to 30. Within one week three states—Wisconsin, Illinois, and Michigan—ratify the amendment. By the end of the year more than 20 states pass the measure.

When a black group, the Northeastern Federation of Women's Clubs, wants to join the NAWSA, Carrie Chapman Catt discourages them. At her request Susan B. Anthony's friend and biographer, Ida Husted Harper, writes apologetic letters to Mary Church Terrell and NFWC president Elizabeth Carter, asking them to "understand" and wait until suffrage is won (requiring support from the South).

Crystal Eastman and other activists organize the Feminist Congress in New York. They call for not only the vote but also equality in employment, access to birth control, and an end to the double moral standard.

The National Association of Colored Women asks white club women to help protest lynching, protect black voters' rights, improve conditions for domestic workers, and combat racism.

To support the Korean movement for independence from Japan, women start the Korean Women's Patriotic League in California and the Korean Women's Relief Society in Hawaii.

The Women's International League for Peace and Freedom (WILPF) is formally established (see 1915), with Jane Addams as president and Emily Balch as secretary. (Balch's teaching appointment at Wellesley College is not renewed because of her vocal pacifism.) In New York, Frances Garrison Villard (1844–1928), a founding member of the Woman's Peace Party, starts the Woman's Peace Society.

Alice Paul on balcony at National Woman's Party headquarters (Library of Congress)

Mary White Ovington is the first woman to chair the NAACP board of directors. A black woman will not hold this position until 1975.

Ella Bloor and Rosa Stokes help found the U.S. Communist Party.

On her release from prison, "Red Emma" Goldman, who earlier lost her citizenship, is branded a subversive alien and deported to her native Russia. She soon leaves that country and attacks growing Soviet totalitarianism in *My Disillusionment in Russia* (1923).

While President Wilson is incapacitated by a stroke, his wife, Edith Bolling Wilson (1872–1961), serves as his liaison, communicating his instructions. She stresses, however, that she does not make decisions.

The first woman appointed to the New York State Industrial Commission, Frances Perkins (1880–1965) helps mediate strikes and works for labor reforms; in 1928 she becomes state industrial commissioner.

"And the whistles did blow and the bells did ring . . ."
—Carrie Chapman Catt and Nettie Rogers Shuler

1920
In February, anticipating victory for suffrage, the women at the last NAWSA convention formally establish a successor organization, the nonpartisan League of Women Voters (LWV), with Maud Wood Park as president. Its numerous initial concerns include citizenship education, child welfare, and the legal status of women.

Although 38 states approve the 19th Amendment, more than the three-fourths majority needed to pass it, 10 states do not ratify it. They are:
—Alabama
—Delaware
—Florida
—Georgia
—Louisiana
—Maryland
—Mississippi
—North Carolina
—South Carolina
—Virginia

By the end of March, 35 of the 36 required states have ratified the 19th Amendment on woman suffrage. But then state after state shies away from a vote. In August attention focuses on Tennessee, where the governor calls for a special session. Both suffragists and antisuffragists flood the state. The senators quickly approve 25 to 4, but the representatives delay. Finally, when the vote comes to the floor, the deciding "aye" is cast by Harry Burn, the youngest member. His mother, a suffragist, had written him "to be a good boy" and vote for ratification. On August 26 the 19th Amendment is declared official. Two states—Vermont and Connecticut—ratify the amendment later (see sidebar).

The Women's Joint Congressional Committee, headed by Maud Wood Park, is formed as a coalition of 10 large women's groups, including the League of Women Voters, GFWC, National Consumers' League, YWCA, and WTUL. Its aim is to coordinate lobbying efforts on issues of concern to women, including protection of infants, public education, arms reduction, and protective labor legislation. By 1924 it represents 21 groups.

When black women try to register to vote in South Carolina, they face property tax requirements, literacy tests, and other obstacles. Similar difficulties confront African American women in other southern states, despite the efforts of a number of black women voters' leagues.

Invited by the Commission on Interracial Cooperation (CIC), four black women address a conference of southern women, sitting in segregated sections. The day before, Charlotte Hawkins Brown (p. 182) says, she was marched out of her railway car by some white men without a word of protest from the white women in the car. She then gives other examples of racism and urges white women to take a stand, particularly against lynching: "if the white women would take hold of the situation . . . lynching would be stopped." Later, the conference forms the Women's Council of the CIC. When, however, a white woman who attended the 1919 NACW conference reads their statement, she "softens" the wording on suffrage and against lynching.

Jane Addams, Helen Keller, Elizabeth Gurley Flynn, and Crystal Eastman are among those who help found the American Civil Liberties Union (ACLU).

Mary Anderson is named director of the new Women's Bureau in the Department of Labor. She lobbies for improved working conditions for women, including minimum wages and maximum hours. Mary Church Terrell tries unsuccessfully to have a special division for black women included in the bureau.

Suffragist Helen Hamilton Gardener (1853–1925) is appointed to the U.S. Civil Service Commission, where she serves for five years.

Annette Adams becomes the first female U.S. assistant attorney general, serving one year and enforcing Prohibition (even though she personally opposes it).

Henrietta Vinton Davis (1860–1941) chairs an international meeting, held in New York, of the United Negro Improvement Association, Marcus Garvey's popular Pan-Africanist group.

Suffragists start working in the Republican Party. Harriet Taylor Upton (1853–1945) is named vice chair of the Republican National Executive Committee. As vice chair of the New Jersey Republican Party, Lillian Feickert sets up the New Jersey Women's Republican Club, which has 60,000 members by 1922.

Other suffragists run for office. Josephine Bennett campaigns for the U.S. Senate in Connecticut on the National Farmer-Labor Party ticket. In New York, Rose Schneiderman runs for the U.S. Senate on the Labor Party ticket, and Harriot Stanton Blatch and Elinor Byrns are Socialist Party candidates for New York City positions. In Nevada, Anne Martin runs as an Independent for the U.S. Senate.

1921

Under President Warren G. Harding, Mabel Walker Willebrandt (1889–1963) replaces Annette Adams and becomes the second female U.S. assistant attorney general. Dubbed "Prohibition Portia," she, like Adams, enforces Prohibition.

Newly elected Oklahoma representative Alice Mary Robertson (1854–1931), a former missionary educator of Indians and antisuffragist, is the only woman in Congress. Asked to announce the vote on a minor bill, she is, for a few minutes, the first woman to preside over the House.

At the National Woman's Party victory convention, Alice Paul is ready to move on to the next issue: passage of an Equal Rights Amendment (see 1923). She tries to prevent discussion of other issues, such as birth control (see "Health and Medical Care") and voting rights (see below). One NWP member, Mabel Raef Putnam, gets the first state ERA passed, in Wisconsin. This law gives women and men the same rights, but it includes a vague phrase to preserve protective labor legislation.

At the national League of Women Voters convention, black women describe the barriers they face in registering to vote, but the LWV does not take any action. When NAACP field secretary Addie Hunton and other black women ask the National Woman's Party to pressure Congress to investigate these voting rights abuses, Alice Paul and others declare this is a "race" issue not a "woman's" issue. Along similar lines, the NWP decides that Mary Morris Burnett Talbert (1866–1923), former NACW president, represents a group based on race rather than sex and therefore takes back its invitation to have her speak.

Faced with mounting U.S. opposition to picture brides, Japan stops their emigration under the tacit "Ladies' Agreement."

Grace Abbott (1878–1939) succeeds Julia Lathrop as head of the U.S. Children's Bureau and sets up federal prenatal and child health care centers under the new Sheppard-Towner Act (see p. 228).

The new Women's Peace Union of the Western Hemisphere vows they will never, in any way, support war. Another new group, the Women's Committee for World Disarmament, quickly organizes a Disarmament Day (Easter Sunday) and then a Disarmament Week. The efforts of these and other women's peace groups influence President Warren Harding to hold a disarmament conference in Washington, D.C.

After serving as appointees in 1920 (with no vote), women are elected, with full voting power, to the Democratic National Committee. Emily Newell Blair (1877–1951) of Missouri is selected vice chair and starts organizing women's clubs, setting up 2,000 in two years.

When journalist Ruth Hale (1886–1934) asks the State Department to issue a passport under her birth name, she receives one for "Mrs. Heywood Broun." She then helps organize the Lucy Stone League to guarantee a woman the legal right to use her birth name if she wants.

Suffragist Inez Haynes Gillmore Irwin (see 1900) publishes her firsthand *Story of the Woman's Party*.

1922

Under pressure from women delegates, the United Negro Improvement Association choses Henrietta Vinton Davis as fourth assistant president general. Marcus Garvey's second wife, Amy Jacques Garvey (1896–1973), also assumes an important role in the organization, especially after her husband is jailed for supposed mail fraud.

The Women's Joint Congressional Committee successfully lobbies for the Cable Act, repealing earlier statutes that took away a U.S. woman's citizenship if she married *any* foreigner. But the law still states that if an American woman weds "an alien ineligible to citizenship," she forfeits her own citizenship. Thus, any U.S.-born woman who marries an Asian loses her citizenship. Although widowed or divorced white women can regain their citizenship through naturalization, U.S.-born women of Asian descent cannot. This rule remains in effect until 1931.

To get a property deed signed, as the Seminole Nation's own government was destroyed in 1907, President Harding appoints Alice Brown Davis (1852–1935) chief of the Seminole people. When she insists on payment to the Seminole for the land, she is promptly dismissed. Earlier Davis served as an interpreter for her people in negotiations for a homeland and in various court battles.

Ida B. Wells-Barnett publishes her pamphlet *The Arkansas Race Riot*, describing the unjust murder indictment of some black farmers.

Lucille Atcherson is the first woman Foreign Service officer, but only a few more women serve during the 1920s and none in the 1930s.

In Ohio, after winning election to the court of common pleas in 1920, Florence Ellinwood Allen (1884–1966) is elected to the state supreme court—a first for women. "The women were my organization," she says of her successful campaign. "They simply got in touch with women in every county who had been active in the suffrage movement." In 1928 she is reelected by a margin of 350,000 votes.

Suffragist Adelina ("Nina") Otero-Warren (1882–1965), school superintendent for Santa Fe County, runs for Congress on the Republican ticket. Although she loses, she sets a precedent for Latinas.

After her father dies, Winnifred Mason Huck (1882–1936) wins his seat as a U.S. representative from Illinois. In the next 40 years almost half of congresswomen first win seats as relatives of their predecessors.

With much publicity, Rebecca Ann Latimer Felton (1835–1930), a journalist with strong racist and isolationist views, serves one day in the U.S. Senate, filling out the term of a Georgia senator she supported. A new senator has been elected, so she relinquishes her seat the next day.

Working for the NAACP, Mary Talbert organizes the Anti-Lynching Crusaders, urging women to petition the government, to pressure their ministers to speak out, and to give at least $1 each to the campaign. Talbert, also known for saving Frederick Douglass's home, is awarded the NAACP's Spingarn Medal for black achievement. She is the first woman to receive this prestigious award, initiated in 1914.

In December, Ida Harper publishes the fifth and sixth volumes of the detailed *History of Woman Suffrage*.

1923

Delaware admits its first two women, Evangelyn Barskey and Sybil Ward, to the bar. At last, women can practice law in all 48 states.

Jessie Hughan, Tracy Mygatt, Frances Witherspoon, and others start the War Resisters League to support and advise all conscientious objectors, including nonreligious ones.

The National Woman's Party starts a new journal, *Equal Rights,* edited by Edith Houghton Hooker, and introduces its Equal Rights Amendment (nicknamed the Lucretia Mott Amendment) into Congress. This bill states: "Men and women shall have equal rights throughout the United States and every place subject to its jurisdiction." Many women's groups and labor activists oppose the bill because it would eliminate hard-won protective legislation for women workers (see sidebar). Indeed, the Supreme Court invalidates a minimum wage law in the capital essentially because it doesn't give men and women equal rights.

The Women's Joint Congressional Committee pushes for a federal prison for women. Assistant attorney general Mabel Willebrandt drafts the necessary legislation, which is approved in 1924.

Mae Ella Nolan (1886–1973) is the first widow elected to fill her husband's congressional seat (see Huck, 1922). In 1924 she is the first woman to chair a House committee, on Post Office expenditures.

Louise Stanley (1883–1954) is appointed director of the newly formed U.S. Bureau of Home Economics in the Department of Agriculture.

"Some Principle of Equality"

"So we have over-articulate theorists attempting to solve the working women's problems on a purely feministic basis, with the working woman's own voice far less adequately heard. . . .

"The whole question, it seems to me, comes down to this: Shall we let women continue working longer hours than men, for less pay than men, and continue doing two jobs to their husbands' one? And is that sort of thing to continue in the name of the principle of equality? Or shall we agree that the reality of better conditions of employment is more important, both to health and to industrial equality, than is a cherished theory?"
—Mary Anderson, chief of Women's Bureau, "Should There Be Labor Laws for Women?—Yes," *Good Housekeeping* (September 1925)

*"Throughout the suffrage strug-
gle, America's history, her principles, her traditions stood forth to
indicate the inevitability of woman suffrage. . . . Yet the years
went by, decade followed decade,
and twenty-six other countries
gave the vote to their women
while America delayed.*

"Why the delay? . . .

*"We think we have the
answer. It was, not an antagonis-
tic public sentiment, nor yet an
uneducated or indifferent public
sentiment—it was the control of
public sentiment, the deflecting
and the thwarting of public
sentiment, through the trading
and the trickery , the buying and
the selling of American politics.
We think that we can prove it."*

—Carrie Chapman Catt and
Nettie Rogers Shuler, *Woman
Suffrage and Politics* (New
York: Charles Scribner's
Sons, 1923)

Partly to reveal "the devious trail of American politics," Carrie Chapman Catt and Nettie Rogers Shuler (1862–1939) publish *Woman Suffrage and Politics: The Inner Story of the Suffrage Movement* (see sidebar).

1924

The first two women governors are elected on the same day. Nellie Tayloe Ross (1876–1977) wins her late husband's office as Wyoming governor but is not reelected two years later. She is inaugurated two weeks before Miriam Amanda ("Ma") Wallace Ferguson (1875–1961), who wins the Texas governorship after her husband is impeached. A strong opponent of the Ku Klux Klan, Ferguson obtains a law against people wearing masks in public. She also wins amnesty for her husband (later declared unconstitutional). Although not reelected in 1926, she serves another term in 1932.

New Jersey Democrat Mary Teresa Hopkins Norton (1875–1951) is the first East Coast woman elected to Congress. Saying she does "not intend to do any cooking in Congress," she refuses to stand holding a frying pan for a newspaper photographer.

Suffragist and temperance reformer Belle Kearney takes her seat as the first female state senator in the South, in Missouri.

Nannie Helen Burroughs (p. 183) and other club women set up the National League of Republican Women, with Burroughs as president.

Mary Montgomery Booze (1877–c. 1948) from Mississippi is the first black woman elected to the Republican National Committee. She serves for 24 years.

The new Immigration Act singles out Asians, banning all aliens ineligible for citizenship, including the wives of U.S. citizens (although an exception is made for the wives of Chinese merchants). In 1930 wives married to U.S. citizens before 1924 are allowed in.

The Women's Peace Union steps up its campaign for an end to war. At a parade in Washington, D.C., banners declare: "Make War Illegal. Abolish the Army and Navy." It drafts an amendment to this effect.

Members of the DAR, American War Mothers, and similar groups form the National Patriotic Council to support military readiness and to counter women's peace groups such as the WILPF.

During the "Red Scare," the War Department draws a chart linking women's groups and Bolsheviks. They also compose a poem alerting the public to "Miss Bolsheviki's" arrival in town: "In women's clubs she's sure to be found / For she's come to disarm America."

Defying the red-baiting, Anne Martin, Harriot Stanton Blatch, Ruth Hale, and others form the Woman's Committee for Political Action to mobilize women voters to support peace and progressive principles. They back the presidential candidacy of Robert La Follette, whose platform includes women's rights, pacifism, and child labor laws.

1925

Carrie Chapman Catt forms the National Committee on the Cause and the Cure of War, a coalition of women's peace groups representing 5 million women. Although Catt later attacks the DAR and Woman Patriots for red-baiting, she does not invite two of their targets, the WILPF and the Women's Peace Union, into her coalition.

The National Council of Women hosts the meeting of the International Council of Women in Washington, D.C. Beforehand, under pressure from the DAR and the National Patriotic Council, the NCW asks the WILPF to withdraw from the coalition. When peace literature appears in a booth, NCW leaders burn the pamphlets. A different problem arises when the seating is segregated for one event. Mary McLeod Bethune (p. 182), the new president of the NACW, and other black women walk out in protest. The ICW agrees to desegregate all seating.

A special three-woman judicial panel is appointed to rule on a Texas Supreme Court case when all the male justices disqualify themselves because of a conflict of interest. Hortense Ward serves as chief justice and Ruth Brazzil and Hattie L. Henenberg as associate justices for this case, but Texas does not have any permanent female judges until 1934.

Edith Nourse Rogers (1881–1960), a Massachusetts Republican, wins her late husband's seat in Congress. Reelected 17 times, she serves for 35 years. Florence Prag Kahn (1866–1948), a San Francisco Republican, is also elected to her late husband's seat. The first Jewish woman in Congress, she is reelected five times.

The first woman in the U.S. consular service, Pattie Field serves as vice consul in Amsterdam until 1929.

The World Exposition of Women's Progress in Chicago includes a panorama of American women's achievements in the last 25 years.

1926

Zitkala-Sa (Gertrude Bonnin), who has spoken to numerous women's clubs and before Congress on Indian rights, cofounds and serves as president of the National Council of American Indians, a reform group consisting exclusively of Native Americans.

Violette Neatly Anderson (1882–1937) is the first black woman lawyer to practice before the U.S. Supreme Court (see also Prince, 1797).

Emily Balch and two African American women serve on a WILPF commission investigating the U.S. marines' occupation of Haiti. They call for self-government and the removal of U.S. forces.

Publicly smeared as a "Bolshevik spy," pacifist Rosika Schwimmer is denied U.S. citizenship by a Chicago district court because she will not pledge to bear arms to defend the country (see 1929).

After serving as city council president, Bertha Knight Landes (1868–1943) is elected the first female mayor of a major city, Seattle.

10 Women in Congress

1927

Led by lawyer Gail Laughlin (1868–1952), vice chair of the National Woman's Party, 700 women travel in a 200-car caravan across several states to confront President Calvin Coolidge at his summer retreat. They demand his support in passing the Equal Rights Amendment.

Sadie Tanner Mossell Alexander helps found the National Bar Association, a professional group for black lawyers. In 1935 she helps draft a Pennsylvania law against discrimination in public places.

Women are active in protesting the murder convictions of Nicola Sacco and Bartolomeo Vanzetti. Poet Edna St. Vincent Millay gives the profits from her pamphlet *Justice Denied in Massachusetts* to the anarchists' defense. She and 76-year-old socialist Ellen Amanda Hayes (1851–1930) are among those arrested in demonstrations.

In West Virginia, Minnie Buckingham-Harper becomes the first black woman state legislator when she is appointed to her late husband's seat.

1928

After organizing on the state party level, (Anna) Eleanor Roosevelt (1884–1962) leads the women's campaign for the Democratic Party on a national level. She is a strong advocate of social reform, women's concerns, and labor issues, even joining picket lines.

The WILPF gathers 30,000 signatures to urge Congress to sign the Kellogg-Briand Pact condemning war. Ohio Supreme Court judge Florence Allen credits its ratification to women's voting power.

After six years as appraiser of foreign merchandise in the Ohio area, Genevieve Rose Cline (c. 1878–1959) is appointed to the U.S. Customs Court. The first female federal judge, she serves 25 years.

This year marks a high point for women in politics, with 7 women elected to Congress, 12 state senators, and 119 state representatives. After beating seven other candidates in the Republican primaries, Ruth Hanna McCormick (later Simms, 1880–1944) is elected representative-at-large from Illinois by a large majority—a victory hailed as an advance for women—although in 1930, she loses a bid for the Senate. When U.S.-born Ruth Bryan Owen (later Rohde, 1885–1954) of Florida is elected to the House, her opponent complains she has not been a citizen long enough. Owen, who lost her citizenship in 1910 by marrying a foreigner, did not regain it until 1925, due to problems in the 1922 Cable Act. She eloquently pleads her case before the House Elections Committee and later wins needed revisions to the Cable Act.

Vera Micheles (later Dean, 1903–72) starts her 33-year career with the Foreign Policy Association, where she becomes director of research and editor of publications. She argues against isolationism.

1929

The Supreme Court upholds 6 to 3 the 1926 decision to deny citizenship to Rosika Schwimmer, although the dissent written by Oliver

Wendell Holmes decries this violation of "free thought." Schwimmer stays in America but is stateless.

In Texas, María Latigo Hernández (c. 1896–1986) and her husband, Pedro, establish the Orden Caballeros de America, a major Mexican American civil rights and reform group.

1930

Responding to black women's requests that white women take a strong stand against lynching, Jessie Daniel Ames (1883–1972), director of the women's committee of the Council for Interracial Cooperation, forms the Association of Southern Women for the Prevention of Lynching. These white women counter the myth that they need protection and urge their husbands and sons to end racial violence, but they stop short of demanding a federal antilynching law.

Alice Lee Jemison (1901–64), secretary to the president of the Seneca Nation, successfully campaigns for the release of two Seneca women charged in the murder of a white woman in Buffalo, New York. She then serves as a lobbyist for the Seneca people in Washington, D.C.

Daisy Adams Lampkin (c. 1884–1965) is appointed regional field secretary for the NAACP and becomes national field secretary in 1935. She greatly increases its membership.

Women's groups lobby for revisions in the 1922 Cable Act (passed in 1931) to give native-born women who marry foreigners the same citizenship rights as men—for example, the right to reenter the country without being counted in the immigration quota.

During the Depression, many women and men of Mexican descent are deported to Mexico. Some are U.S. citizens.

1931

WILPF president Jane Addams is the first U.S. woman to receive the Nobel Peace Prize, which she shares with Nicholas Murray Butler. She gives $16,000 to the WILPF.

To publicize the 1932 World Disarmament Conference, former suffragist Mabel Vernon (1883–1975) leads a WILPF caravan from California to Washington, D.C., with well-publicized stops in 125 cities.

Gladys Towles Root (d. 1982), a flamboyant lawyer known for her fantastic attire, successfully challenges the constitutionality of a California law that prevented a Filipino man from marrying a white woman.

1932

First appointed in 1931 as a temporary fill-in, Hattie Wyatt Caraway (1878–1950) is the first woman elected to the Senate when she wins a special election in January to finish her late husband's term. In May she gains publicity as the first woman to preside (briefly) over the Senate, and later in the year this Arkansas Democrat wins election to a full Senate term. She serves until 1945.

"Tribute to the Peace Efforts of Women"

"The history of one nation after another shows that it was the mothers who first protested that their children should no longer be slain as living sacrifices upon the altars of tribal gods. Women rebelled against the waste of the life they had nurtured.

"I should like to see the women of civilization rebel against the senseless wholesale human sacrifice of warfare. I am convinced that many thousands of women throughout the world would gladly rise to this challenge.

"The Women's International League for Peace and Freedom was organized at The Hague in 1915. I acted as chairman then and have served as president ever since. It is therefore a tribute to the peace efforts of women that I was chosen to share with Dr. Nicholas Murray Butler in the Nobel peace award."

—Jane Addams, "Disarm and Have Peace," 1932; in *Jane Addams: A Centennial Reader* (New York: Macmillan, 1960)

Mount Holyoke College president Mary Emma Woolley (1863–1947), a peace activist, is one of the U.S. representatives sent to the Geneva Conference on the Reduction and Limitation of Armaments. She is the first female U.S. delegate to a major diplomatic conference.

Mary Norton is the first woman to chair a committee in the House, as head of the District of Columbia Committee (see also 1937).

In New York the Chinese Women's Patriotic Association is established to protest the Japanese invasion of China. The women also speak out on U.S. discrimination against Chinese Americans.

Backed by Eleanor Roosevelt, social reformer Mary ("Molly") Williams Dewson (1874–1962) chairs the Women's Division of the Democratic National Committee, campaigning for Franklin Delano Roosevelt's election as president. She becomes a major force in FDR's appointment of women to federal office. She also increases women's clout within the Democratic Party and trains them to explain New Deal policies.

"The . . . White House wore a startled air [when] its new mistress took over"—Bess Furman, Associated Press

1933

Eleanor Roosevelt is the first First Lady to hold a press conference—for women reporters only—and talks about the Depression and its effect on women. She makes these discussions a regular event and often invites women in the administration to participate. Her press conferences help create a "New Deal for newswomen," claims reporter Ruby Black.

Frances Perkins (1880–1965) becomes the first woman in the cabinet when she is appointed secretary of labor by President Roosevelt. Serving until 1945, she helps draft much of the New Deal legislation, including the Social Security Act, the National Labor Relations Act, the public works section of the National Industrial Recovery Act, and the Fair Labor Standards Act. Molly Dewson, who campaigns vigorously for Perkins's appointment, later comments, "I am convinced that certain women . . . have been more successful in getting labor laws passed and more effective in their administration than any men ever have been or could have been."

Former Wyoming governor Nellie Ross is the first female director of the U.S. Mint.

In North Dakota, Republican state representative Minnie D. Craig is the first woman speaker of a state legislature, but only for three months.

Ruth Owen becomes the first female envoy, serving as the U.S. representative in Denmark and Iceland. She serves until 1936, when she marries Captain Börge Rohde, making her a Danish citizen.

Journalist Lorena A. Hickok quits her job with the Associated Press and travels around the country, reporting on conditions for Harry

Hopkins, head of the Federal Emergency Relief Administration. Her observations are used in the development of New Deal policy. Also under Hopkins, Ellen Sullivan Woodward (1887–1971) supervises emergency relief programs for women, providing aid to 500,000 female heads of household. All of her state directors are women.

1934

Appointed to the Sixth Circuit Court of Appeals in Cincinnati, Florence Allen is the first female judge on a federal court. In her autobiography, *To Do Justly* (1965), she recalls that one male justice reportedly reacted by going "to bed for two days." In 1937, in her most-publicized decision, she upholds the constitutionality of the Tennessee Valley Authority's powers and, by implication, of other New Deal programs. She is not, however, considered for the Supreme Court, despite pressure from women's groups. Moreover, 34 years after her appointment, only one other woman, Shirley Mount Hufstedler, has been named to the court of appeals.

After studying in Germany, Esther Caukin Brunauer (1901–59) testifies before Congress on the Nazi threat and later writes an influential report on the need for national defense (1937).

Prominent reformers, such as Jane Addams and Eleanor Roosevelt, are targeted in Elizabeth Dilling's *The Red Network*, which lists 460-some "suspect" organizations.

1935

Mary McLeod Bethune is awarded the NAACP's Spingarn Medal. She also organizes the National Council of Negro Women (NCNW), a coalition of 14 black women's groups. Bethune is elected president (serving until 1949); other initial officers include Mary Church Terrell, Charlotte Hawkins Brown, and Lucy Diggs Slowe. An early NCNW effort exposes job discrimination by the government; other campaigns fight racism and sexism. These activities are publicized in the group's *Aframerican Woman's Journal*.

Working for the Democratic National Committee, Harriet Wiseman Elliott (1884–1947) sets up study groups, educating over 34,000 women on New Deal policies. Crystal Bird Fauset (1893–1965) directs African American women's activities.

Alice Lee Jemison, the chief Washington lobbyist for the conservative American Indian Federation, opposes the Bureau of Indian Affairs, New Deal policy, and any government involvement in Native affairs.

Lawyer Eunice Hunton Carter (1899–1970) is the only woman and the only African American on Thomas E. Dewey's team investigating racketeering by organized crime. Later in the year she is appointed deputy assistant district attorney for New York City.

Juanita E. Jackson (later Mitchell, 1913–92) directs the NAACP's first national youth program.

"The Husband Owns the Wife's Labor"

In a 1935 article in the Boston University Law Review, *Blanche Crozier underlines the shortcomings of existing married women's property laws. According to the courts' interpretations of the marriage contract, she points out, the wife is essentially an indentured servant. "Everywhere and without exception," she writes, "the husband owns the wife's labor performed at home and of the general nature of housework. It is therefore true that for the great majority of people the husband owns the wife's labor; and any case in which he does not is the result of a considerable departure from the traditional and still typical situation of marriage."*

Women in the FDR Administration

Largely through the prodding of Molly W. Dewson, sometimes called "More Women" Dewson, women's visibility in politics increases during Franklin Delano Roosevelt's administration. Some of these women are:

—Stella Akin, special assistant to the attorney general

—Mary Anderson, director of Women's Bureau

—Marion Banister, assistant treasurer of the United States

—Mary McLeod Bethune, in National Youth Administration

—Molly Dewson and Sue Shelton White, on Social Security Board

—Katherine Lenroot, director of Children's Bureau

—Frances Perkins, secretary of labor

—Josephine Roche, assistant secretary of the treasury

—Nellie Tayloe Ross, director of the U.S. Mint

—Rose Schneiderman, on National Labor Advisory Board

—Hilda Worthington Smith and Ellen Woodward, in the Federal Emergency Relief Administration and Works Progress Administration

1936

Mary McLeod Bethune is asked to oversee job training and placement for black youth in the National Youth Administration (in 1939 her title becomes director of the Division of Negro Affairs). She is the first African American woman to achieve this rank. Later in 1936 she organizes the Federal Council on Negro Affairs, or the "black cabinet," bringing together other black government officials (mostly men) to push for African American concerns.

Jane Margueretta Hoey (1892–1968) is named director of the new Bureau of Public Assistance under the Social Security Board. She administers the welfare provisions of the 1935 Social Security Act.

As the new director of the Women's and Professional Division of the Works Progress Administration, Ellen Woodward supervises the WPA cultural projects.

Through the efforts of Molly Dewson and Eleanor Roosevelt, women for the first time gain equal representation on the Democratic Party platform committee. Over 60,000 women serve as precinct workers during the successful campaign to reelect President Roosevelt.

Concha Ortiz y Pino de Kleven (b. 1912) is the first Chicana elected to a state legislature, in New Mexico. She serves three terms, becoming majority whip and introducing bills to promote bilingual education and to allow women to serve on juries.

In California longtime Communist Party activist Anita Whitney runs for state comptroller and wins 100,000 votes. Other women active in the Communist Party during the 1930s include Anna Damon and Margaret Cowl (who at different times head the party's Women's Commission), Anna Burlak, Ella ("Mother") Reeve Bloor, Elizabeth Gurley Flynn, and Grace Hutchins.

1937

Mary Norton chairs the House Labor Committee and is instrumental in getting the Fair Labor Standards Act through Congress.

Mary McLeod Bethune organizes the government-sponsored National Conference on the Problems of the Negro and Negro Youth, which calls for federal action, including an antilynching law, protection of voting rights, and antisegregation measures.

Alicia Dickerson Montemayor (1902–89) is the first woman elected to a major general leadership position in the League of United Latin American Citizens. Although LULAC introduced Ladies Councils in 1934 (see "Social Change") and women did much behind-the-scenes work for this reform group, they were not initially full members.

1938

In California labor organizer Luisa Moreno helps set up El Congreso del Pueblo de Habla Española (the Spanish-Speaking Con-gress), and Chicana activist Josefina Fierro de Bright (b. 1920) becomes its executive secretary. El Congresso combats anti-alien legislation and police brutality; it also works for better housing and education. Almost a third of the activists are women, and the group emphasizes equality for women, especially in pay. It lasts to 1942.

Black women tell federal officials how the government can best help them and their children at an NCNW-organized conference.

Gladys Pyle (d. 1989) is elected to the U.S. Senate from South Dakota. Later, in 1940, she is the first woman to nominate a presidential candidate at the Republican National Convention.

Crystal Bird Fauset is the first black woman elected to a state legislature, the Pennsylvania Assembly.

1939

Right wingers try to impeach labor secretary Frances Perkins when she will not deport labor leader Harry Bridges for alleged communism. But she defuses this effort in a speech to the House Judiciary Committee.

Mary McLeod Bethune (left) and Eleanor Roosevelt (Bethune Museum and Archives, Washington, D.C.)

Appointed to the Domestic Relations Court in New York City by Mayor Fiorello LaGuardia, Jane Mathilda Bolin (b. 1908) is the first African American woman judge. She focuses attention on racial discrimination in the city's private schools and childcare institutions.

When Eleanor Roosevelt encounters segregated seating at a conference on human welfare in Birmingham, Alabama, she moves her chair to straddle the black and white sections. She also joins the NAACP and addresses its annual meeting.

As minister to Norway when World War II breaks out, Florence ("Daisy") Hurst Harriman (1870–1967) negotiates the return of a U.S. freighter captured at sea by the Germans. In 1940, after Norway is invaded, Harriman helps evacuate Americans and keeps the U.S. government apprised of the situation as she escapes to Sweden.

1940

Viola Pelhame Jimulla, or Sicatuva (1878–1966), becomes chief of the Yavapai tribe in Arizona after her husband's death. Although a five-person tribal council is formed, she remains the leader. Her daughter, Grace Jimulla Mitchell, succeeds her on her death.

The Women's Centennial Congress celebrates 100 women in positions that were closed to women in 1840.

The Republican Party voices support for the ERA at its convention, and the Democratic Party follows suit in 1944.

The first U.S. congresswoman, Jeannette Rankin, is reelected to the House on a pacifist platform (see 1941). Margaret Chase Smith (1897–1995), a Maine Republican, wins her late husband's seat in the House, where she serves four terms. As a member of the Naval Affairs and then the Armed Services Committee, she helps women in the armed forces (see "War").

Why the ERA?

Despite the protection offered by the 1938 Fair Labor Standards Act, the Women's Bureau and trade unionists continue to oppose the Equal Rights Amendment. Yet its supporters argue that many states still have laws that discriminate against women. Some states do not allow married women to enter into contracts, and in a few states a husband can claim his wife's earnings, although the wife cannot claim his. About half the states still keep women off juries, and in some, women cannot even run for elective office. Other inequities surround divorce laws. In one state, for example, a husband is allowed to divorce his wife if he finds out she had sex with someone else before they married, but not vice versa.

1941

Elizabeth Gurley Flynn, kicked off the ACLU executive board for her Communist Party membership in 1940, is elected to the national board of the American Communist Party and in 1942 runs for Congress in New York State, polling 50,000 votes.

In March, Irene McCoy Gaines (c. 1892–1964), president of the Chicago Council of Negro Organizations, helps lead a protest in Washington, D.C., against job discrimination.

Mary McLeod Bethune makes sure that black women, through the NCNW, are represented on the War Department's advisory council on women. Other, nongovernmental groups then include the NCNW in discussions on women's issues.

Eslanda Goode Robeson (1896–1965) helps form the Council on African Affairs to protest colonialism in Africa.

After the attack on Pearl Harbor in December, Jeannette Rankin votes for the second time against entry in a world war. She is the only member of the House to do so, and she is not reelected.

1942

Congresswoman Edith Rogers introduces the bill establishing the Women's Army Auxiliary Corps (see "War").

Mitsuye Endo agrees to serve as a test case for Japanese American citizens who are detained against their will in internment camps after Pearl Harbor. Her petition for freedom leads to the 1944 Supreme Court ruling in *Ex parte Endo,* declaring the detention illegal and granting an "unconditional release."

1943

Senator Hattie Caraway becomes the first woman in Congress to sponsor the Equal Rights Amendment (see sidebar), which is changed to read: "Equality of rights under the law shall not be denied or abridged by the United States or by any State on account of sex." Connecticut women set up an ERA committee, and soon other state groups are established. The General Federation of Women's Clubs comes out in favor of the ERA, as the Federation of Business and Women's Clubs did earlier. To lobby for the ERA, the National Woman's Party backs two new organizations: the Women's Joint Legislative Committee, chaired by Nina Horton Avery, and the St. Joan Society, a group of pro-ERA Catholics, led by Dorothy Shipley Granger. Another pro-ERA group, the Industrial Women's League for Equality, is formed in 1944. Opponents, including many labor activists, also muster their forces and set up the National Committee to Defeat the Un-Equal Rights Amendment in 1944.

After working as a field secretary, Ella Josephine Baker (1903–86) takes over as NAACP national field director.

Frances Payne Bingham Bolton (1885–1977), Republican representative from Ohio, introduces the "Bolton Bill," which helps fund nursing stu-dents and schools and sets up a Cadet Nurse Corps.

1944

Joining the campaign to end racial discrimination in employment, Anna Arnold Hedgeman (1899–1990) becomes executive director of the National Council for a Permanent Fair Employment Practices Committee and lobbies for federal legislation.

The first female officer in either major party, Dorothy Vrendenburgh Bush (1916–91) is secretary of the Democratic National Committee until 1989. She calls the roll and counts the votes at the convention.

Playwright and journalist Clare Boothe Luce (1903–87), a Connecticut Republican elected to the House in 1942, is the keynote speaker at the Republican National Convention.

Former actress Helen Mary Gahagan Douglas (1900–80), a California Democrat, is elected to the House, where she serves three terms. In 1945 she introduces the Pay Equity bill, supported by many women's groups but rejected by the House, and in 1946 she is a delegate to the United Nations (UN) General Assembly.

1945

Virginia Crocheron Gildersleeve (1877–1965), dean of Barnard College, helps draft the UN charter when she serves as the only female U.S. representative to the UN founding meeting in San Francisco. Later in the year President Harry Truman appoints Eleanor Roosevelt as the only female U.S. delegate to the new UN (see sidebar). She then chairs the Human Rights Commission (see 1948).

Ruth Muskrat Bronson (1897–1982), author of *Indians Are People Too* (1944), sets up the Washington, D.C., bureau of the National Congress of American Indians and later serves as executive director, lobbying against threats to tribal sovereignty.

The War Brides Act enables about 200,000 Asian war brides to enter the United States after World War II.

Elizabeth W. Peratrovich (d. 1958), head of the Alaska Native Sisterhood, argues for a civil rights bill before the Alaska legislature. When a senator describes Alaska Natives as "barely out of savagery," she points to the Bill of Rights and asks directly whether she and her family should be forced to live in the slums because of their Tlingit heritage.

"I am not afraid of that challenge"
—Helen Gahagan Douglas

1946

After years of work for the WILPF, Emily Balch is the second U.S. woman (after Jane Addams) to win the Nobel Peace Prize, which she shares with John R. Mott. Recognizing the evil of fascism, she did not

"I Walked on Eggs"

"During the entire London session of the Assembly I walked on eggs. I knew that as the only woman on the [UN] delegation I was not very welcome. Moreover, if I failed to be a useful member, it would not be considered merely that I as an individual had failed but that all women had failed, and there would be little chance for others to serve in the future.

". . . . [A first step was to ask a few women from other countries for an informal discussion over tea, and this idea grew into casual talks over lunch or dinner.] I found that often a few people of different nationalities, meeting on a semisocial basis, could talk together about a common problem with better results than when they were meeting officially as a committee.

"As time went on, there were more and more women serving on various delegations, and ours usually had a woman alternate even while I was still a delegate. Helen Gahagan Douglas, Mrs. Ruth Bryan Rohde, and Edith Sampson all were extremely valuable on the United States delegation."

—Eleanor Roosevelt, "On My Own," in *The Autobiography of Eleanor Roosevelt* (New York: Harper & Brothers, 1958)

oppose U.S. entry into World War II but focused her attention on aiding Jewish refugees and Japanese Americans in internment camps.

Voicing her opposition to the red-baiting in Congress, representative Helen Gahagan Douglas presents her "Democratic Credo" to the House. Underlining her faith in democracy's ability to withstand the challenge of communism, she declares: "The best way to keep communism out of our country is to keep democracy in it."

Esther Brunauer is chosen as U.S. representative to the Preparatory Commission to the United Nations Educational, Scientific, and Cultural Organization (UNESCO) after helping to draw up plans for it.

Lawyer Sadie Alexander is appointed to Truman's Commission to Study the Civil Rights of All Races and Faiths, which recommends desegregation of the armed forces in its 1948 report.

For the first time in more than 20 years, the ERA is voted on in the Senate (see 1943). The count of 38 for and 35 against falls far short of the two-thirds majority needed.

Traveling from Virginia to Maryland, Irene Morgan refuses to sit with other blacks at the back of the bus. Her case goes to the Supreme Court, which rules that segregation on interstate transport is illegal. In 1947, to test this ruling, a biracial group participates in the "Journey of Reconciliation," traveling on interstate buses in the upper South.

1948

Eleanor Roosevelt is given a standing ovation for her work in creating the Universal Declaration of Human Rights, which is passed by the UN General Assembly in December.

Many black women are outraged when Rosa Lee Ingram, a widowed black tenant farmer, and 2 of her 12 children are given the death sentence for killing a white Georgia farmer who, Ingram claims, attacked her. Mary Church Terrell chairs a national committee in their defense, and Charlotta Bass (p. 294), Shirley Graham Du Bois, and others organize Sojourners for Truth and Justice. In 1959 Ingram is finally pardoned.

Lawyer Carol Weiss King (1895–1952), with a long record of contesting the deportation of Communists and aliens, wins Supreme Court recognition of aliens' legal rights and an end to deportation hearings until due process can be provided.

Chinese women immigrants are routinely detained, even though many are the wives of veterans. When Leong Bick Ha hangs herself after being held three months, 100 female detainees stage a protest, refusing to eat for a day.

Representatives Margaret Chase Smith and Edith Nourse Rogers push the Women's Armed Services Integration Act (p. 263) through the House. Smith then runs for the Senate and wins, becoming the only woman in that body (Hattie Caraway lost her seat in 1944). Smith serves 24 years.

When Frieda Barkin Hennock (1904–60) is named the first woman on the Federal Communications Commission, she underlines the need for a female point of view in an area "so peculiarly affecting women." One of her contributions is to save 242 TV channels for educational use.

1949

In Montgomery, Alabama, Mary Fair Burks (d. 1991) organizes black professional women into the Women's Political Council to protest racial discrimination (see 1955).

Isabel Malagran Gonzáles is vice president of the new Asociación Nacional México-Americana, a civil rights organization that protests mass deportations, cultural stereotypes, and police brutality. Other women leaders in this group include Xochitl Ruiz, secretary-general; Florencia Luna, secretary-treasurer; Carmen Contreras, president of the San Francisco chapter; and Dolores Heredia, Chicago chapter president.

Burnita Shelton Matthews (1894–1988) is appointed as the first female judge on a federal district court, in the District of Columbia. Earlier she used her legal skills for the National Woman's Party. Later she presides over the trial of teamster Jimmy Hoffa in 1957.

Perle Skirvin Mesta (1889–1975), an ERA advocate, board member of the Mesta steel firm, and Washington, D.C., political hostess, is named U.S. envoy to Luxembourg, ruled by Grand Duchess Charlotte. She is later the inspiration for Irving Berlin's Broadway hit *Call Me Madam*, starring Ethel Merman.

(Helen) Eugenie Moore Anderson (b. 1909), active in Democratic Party politics, is the first woman named to the post of ambassador, to Denmark. In 1951 she is the first woman to sign a treaty, dealing with commercial and navigational concerns, with a foreign power.

Georgia Neese Clark (b. 1900), an active Kansas Democrat and banker, is the first woman appointed as U.S. treasurer, signing her name on U.S. currency. Other women follow her in this post.

1950

In the Senate, Margaret Chase Smith courageously condemns Joseph McCarthy's witch-hunting of communists in her "Declaration of Conscience" speech. She insists that the Senate not be "debased to the level of a forum of hate and character assassination sheltered by the shield of congressional immunity" (see sidebar).

Representative Helen Gahagan Douglas loses her bid for the Senate after a notorious red-baiting campaign by Richard Nixon.

Anna Marie Lederer Rosenberg (1902–83) is the first woman named assistant secretary of defense and placed in charge of manpower. Previously she served as regional director of the War Manpower Com-

"The Right to Hold Unpopular Beliefs"

"I think that it is high time for the United States Senate and its members to do some soul-searching—for us to weigh our consciences—on the manner in which we are performing our duty to the people of America. . . .

"Those of us who shout the loudest about Americanism in making character assassinations are all too frequently those who, by our own words and acts, ignore some of the basic principles of Americanism:

"The right to criticize;

"The right to hold unpopular beliefs;

"The right to protest;

"The right of independent thought.

"The exercise of these rights should not cost one single American citizen his reputation or his right to a livelihood nor should he be in danger of losing his reputation or livelihood merely because he happens to know someone who holds unpopular beliefs. Who of us doesn't?"

—Margaret Chase Smith, "Declaration of Conscience," speech to Senate, 1950; in *Declaration of Conscience* (New York: Doubleday, 1972)

mission (1942–45) and traveled extensively in Europe, reporting on the soldiers' morale. In 1945 she received the Medal of Freedom.

As an alternate delegate to the UN, Edith Sampson (1901–79), the first African American to hold this post, counters Soviet charges that her appointment is a cover-up for U.S. racism. She emphasizes that she represents *all* Americans and underlines that at least there is the possibility of freedom within a democracy.

After being refused service, Mary Church Terrell and three companions sue a segregated restaurant in Washington, D.C. Terrell, almost 90, also organizes sit-ins and boycotts at other segregated eating places. In 1953 the court rules segregated facilities unconstitutional.

In New York, Jane Grant and 14 other women start a new Lucy Stone League for women's rights.

Juanita E. Jackson becomes the first black woman lawyer in Maryland and later helps win cases desegregating Baltimore secondary schools, public beaches and pools, and restaurants.

1951

Annie Dodge Wauneka (b. 1910) is elected as the first woman on the Navajo Tribal Council and chairs its health committee, after years of work improving communications between Navajo patients and non-Navajo doctors and nurses. She is reelected in 1955 and 1959.

Under the Smith Act, Communist Party activist Elizabeth Gurley Flynn is indicted for conspiring to overthrow the government. She is later sentenced to three years in prison.

Ethel Greenglass Rosenberg (1915–53) is convicted, not of spying, but of "conspiracy to commit espionage," for allegedly typing information for her husband, Julius. Many are outraged when she is given the death penalty, and she refuses to "repent," claiming her innocence. Held in solitary confinement for two years, she is executed, along with her husband, in 1953. In her last letter to her two sons, she says, "Always remember that we were innocent and could not wrong our conscience."

1952

The Democratic Party eliminates its Women's Division and instead names director India Edwards as vice chairperson of the national party in charge of women's activities (with no staff). The Republican Party undergoes a similar reorganization.

Subpoenaed to testify before the witch-hunting House Committee on Un-American Activities (HUAC), playwright Lillian Hellman is willing to answer questions about her own activities but refuses to name possible Communists (see sidebar). She is blacklisted by the film industry, although, unlike others, she is not sent to jail for contempt. Later she describes her ordeal in *Scoundrel Time* (1976).

Newspaper editor Charlotta Bass runs for vice president on the Progressive Party ticket. As the first black woman on a major party ticket, she stresses, "Win or lose, we win by raising the issues."

Leonor Kretzer Sullivan (1902–88), a St. Louis Democrat, defeats the man appointed to her late husband's seat in the House and serves 24 years. She is a sponsor of the food stamp program (enacted in 1964) and the Consumer Credit Protection Act of 1968.

1953

Oveta Culp Hobby (p. 262) becomes the second woman (after Frances Perkins) to serve in the cabinet when President Dwight D. Eisenhower appoints her secretary of health, education, and welfare. She names Jane M. Spaulding of the National Association of Colored Women as her chief assistant in setting up the new department.

Clare Boothe Luce is named U.S. ambassador to Italy, an important diplomatic post, and serves until 1956. Later, in 1959, she is appointed ambassador to Brazil, but her right-wing views spark controversy and she resigns.

1954

As the only woman member of the Seminole delegation to Congress, Laura Mae Osceola (b. 1932) testifies effectively against the proposed termination of government services. Three years later she is appointed secretary-treasurer of her tribe.

Edith Starrett Green (1910–87) of Oregon and Martha Wright Griffiths (b. 1912) of Michigan, both Democrats, are elected to the House, where, in different ways, they support women's rights.

"I wanted to be treated like a human being"
—Rosa Parks

1955

In Montgomery, Alabama, Rosa McCauley Parks (b. 1913), active in the local NAACP, helps ignite the civil rights movement when she is arrested for refusing to give up her bus seat to a white man. Already, for months, the Women's Political Council, headed by Jo Ann Gibson Robinson (b. 1912), has been discussing the possibility of a bus boycott to protest discrimination, and they are ready to swing into action. On December 5, as Parks goes to court, they stage an initial boycott (see sidebar). Backed by the newly formed Montgomery Improvement Association, led by the Rev. Martin Luther King, Jr., and with the support of Montgomery's black women, who often walk miles rather than ride the buses, the boycott continues for 381 more days—until the segregation policy is ruled unconstitutional by the Supreme Court. Parks continues to speak out for basic human rights, although she receives many threats and loses her job. Robinson later describes these events in *The Montgomery Bus Boycott and the Women Who Started It* (1987). (See also the civil rights struggles under "Education.")

"Please Stay Off of All Buses"

"Another Negro woman has been arrested and thrown into jail because she refused to get up out of her seat for a white person to sit down. . . . This has to be stopped. Negroes have rights, too, for if Negroes did not ride the buses, they could not operate. . . . We are, therefore, asking every Negro to stay off the buses Monday in protest of the arrest and trial. . . .Please stay off of all buses Monday."
—leaflet of Women's Political Caucus, December 1955; in Jo Ann Gibson Robinson, *The Montmery Bus Boycott and the Women Who Started It,* edited by David Garrow (Knoxville: University of Tennessee Press, 1987)

"The Killing Had Just Begun"

"After the sit-in, all I could think of was how sick Mississippi whites were. They believed so much in the segregated Southern way of life, they would kill to preserve it. . . . I knew that the killing had just begun. 'Many more will die before it is over with,' I thought. Before the sit-in, I had always hated the whites in Mississippi. Now I knew it was impossible for me to hate sickness. The whites had a disease, an incurable disease in its final stage."
—Anne Moody, in *Coming of Age in Mississippi* (New York: Dial Press, 1968); although the sit-in she describes took place in 1963, it is similar to the early sit-ins in 1960

In San Francisco, Del Martin and Phyllis Lyon initiate the Daughters of Bilitis (DOB), a social club and advocacy group for lesbians' civil rights. The name comes from *Songs of Bilitis* by Sappho, the Greek lesbian poet. Chapters of DOB soon form in other cities.

Longtime Pan-AfricanistP Audley Moore (b. 1898) starts a national campaign to gain reparations for African Americans. "They owe us more than they could ever pay . . . ," she later says. "They stole us from our mothers and fathers and took our names away from us." She also helps found the Universal Association of Ethiopian Women. In 1972 she is given the honorary title "Queen Mother" in Ghana.

1957

As associate press secretary for President Eisenhower, Anne W. Wheaton (c. 1893–1977) is the first presidential spokeswoman.

1958

Ella Baker coordinates the Crusade for Citizenship for the Southern Christian Leadership Conference (SCLC), formed by Martin Luther King, Jr., and others in 1957. To kick off this voter registration drive, she gets 13,000 people to register in 22 states on Lincoln's Birthday.

In Arizona, Mary Velasquez Riley (b. 1908) is the first woman elected to the White Mountain Apache Tribal Council. She lobbies in Congress for her people and helps set up the tribe's Sunrise Ski Resort.

Mildred Loving and her white husband are indicted under Virginia's antimiscegenation laws. At first they agree to leave the state, but they later return to fight the case (see 1967).

Contralto Marian Anderson is a U.S. delegate to the UN.

1959

In Philadelphia, Juanita Kidd Stout (b. 1919) wins a seat on the county court; she is the first black woman to be elected to such a position.

1960

As African American students stage sit-ins to protest segregated lunch counters and other eating facilities in the South (see sidebar), Ella Baker calls for a conference of the leaders of these demonstrations. As a result, the Student Nonviolent Coordinating Committee (SNCC) forms, with Baker as an adviser. Two of the founding members are Ruby Doris Smith (later Robinson, 1942–67), active in the sit-ins in Atlanta, and Diane Nash (b. 1938), a Nashville sit-in organizer.

Appointed as a state magistrate in Alaska, Sadie Brower Neakok (b. 1916) shows the Inupiat how to benefit from the U.S. legal system.

Longtime peace activist Marjorie Swann (b. 1921) and her husband start the New England Committtee for Nonviolent Action, which gives civil disobedience training and protests nuclear weapons and later the Vietnam War. Barbara Deming (1917–85) is also active in this group.

For the first time, in Maine, the Senate race is between two women:

Margaret Chase Smith, the Republican incumbent, and Lucia Marie Cormier, a Democrat. Smith wins more than 60% of the vote. Maurine B. Neuberger, an Oregon Democrat, is also elected to the Senate.

1961

One of the few women in the administration of President John F. Kennedy is Esther Eggersten Peterson, head of the Women's Bureau and assistant secretary of labor. As a strong unionist, she opposes the ERA.

Kennedy establishes a Presidential Commission on the Status of Women, chaired by Eleanor Roosevelt, with Esther Peterson as vice chair. Chosen largely by Peterson, only one of the 26 members (15 women and 11 men) is an avowed ERA supporter: Marguerite Rawalt, a member of the National Woman's Party and the first woman president of the Federal Bar Association. Seven committees are set up to investigate such areas of concern as education, employment, and civil and political rights. Special consideration is also given to black women's problems and media treatment of women. (See 1963 for the report.)

After serving on the New York City Commission on Human Rights, Marietta Peabody Tree (1917–91) is the first female chief U.S. delegate to the UN. In 1964 she is named U.S. ambassador to the UN.

When Washington state authorities violate the treaty rights of several Nisqually fishermen and arrest them, Janet McCloud (b. 1934) and other women mount a vigil in the boats, staging the first "fish-in." With Ramona Bennett, McCloud leads the continuing protest.

Elizabeth Gurley Flynn is the first woman to chair the U.S. Communist Party. In 1962 the government tries to revoke her passport, but she takes the case to the Supreme Court and wins.

After their arrest at a sit-in in South Carolina, the "Rock Hill Four," including Ruby Doris Smith and Diane Nash, refuse to pay bail and spend 30 days in jail instead—initiating SNCC's attention-getting "jail, no bail" tactic. Later in the year Smith and Nash join other civil rights activists on the Freedom Rides, traveling on buses into the Deep South to protest segregation and braving mob violence.

The Supreme Court upholds a Florida law excusing women from jury duty unless they specifically request it. They dismiss Gwendolyn Hoyt's claim of unequal protection when an all-male jury ignored her plea of temporary insanity and convicted her of second-degree murder of her husband. All-male juries are common: Alabama, Mississippi, and South Carolina do not let any women serve on juries; 18 other states automatically excuse any woman who does not wish to serve. (See 1975.)

On November 1, an estimated 50,000 women leave their jobs and their homes in a one-day protest to "End the Arms Race—Not the Human Race." The call to action comes from Women Strike for Peace, a grassroots movement started in Washington, D.C., by Dagmar Wilson, Jeanne Bagby, Folly Fodor, Eleanor Garst, and Margaret Russell.

"Ladies' Day at the Capitol"

The press give front-page coverage to HUAC's downfall at the hands of Women Strike for Peace. "It's Ladies' Day at the Capitol . . . Congressmen Meet Match," proclaims the Chicago Daily News. Chairman Clyde Doyle desperately seeks order as he first bans the women from standing with the witness, then from clapping—only to have them kiss each witness and hand her a bouquet. The first witness, Blanche Posner, calmly insists, "This movement was inspired and motivated by mothers' love for children." When Ruth Meyers is asked whether she is a member of the group, she answers, "No, sir, Women Strike for Peace has no membership." Then, in the coup de grâce, replying to whether she would encourage Communist participation, Dagmar Wilson indicates she has no control over who joins. "In fact," she states, "I would . . . go even further. I would like to say that unless everybody in the world joins us in this fight, then God help us."

Influenced by the Commission on the Status of Women, President Kennedy stipulates that all women and men in the federal government must receive equal consideration for promotion. He also asks Persia Crawford Campbell (1898–1974) to serve on the President's Council of Economic Advisors. In 1964 she becomes the president's representative on international trade negotiations.

Women Strike for Peace steps up pressure for a nuclear test ban treaty. Pushing their children in strollers, they hand out paper doves or fortune cookies bearing messages of peace. In a highly publicized coup, activists in Women Strike for Peace sabotage the House Committee on Un-American Activities in its investigation of "Communist" participation in their group (see sidebar). By 1963 they are denouncing U.S. involvement in Vietnam.

After a voter registration rally in Ruleville, Mississippi, Fannie Lou Townsend Hamer (1917–77) immediately joins a busload to the county courthouse and tries to register. Although she fails her first literacy test, loses her work and home as a sharecropper, and is threatened by gunshots, she is not deterred. By the end of the year she is registered and teaching others how to pass the tests. "The only thing they could do to me was kill me," she later says, "and it seemed like they'd been trying to do that a little bit at a time ever since I could remember."

Sharon Jeffrey helps write the Port Huron statement, outlining the belief in "participatory democracy" that underlines the new Students for a Democratic Society (SDS). In 1963 she and other women work as organizers in the Economic Research and Action Project (ERAP), developing community activism in northern ghettos.

"They must live their own lives again"
—*Betty Friedan*

1963

The Presidential Commission on the Status of Women issues its report, *American Women*, recommending equal pay for comparable work, extension of the Fair Labor Standards Act to include agricultural and other uncovered workers, childcare services for all incomes, paid maternity leave, improved educational opportunities, equal jury service, removal of married women's legal disabilities, and other reforms. Although it does not support the ERA, it urges court action to validate the equality provisions under the 5th and 14th Amendments.

Following the report's direction, President Kennedy sets up an Interdepartmental Committee on the Status of Women within his administration, as well as a Citizens' Advisory Council, with Catherine East as executive secretary of both. He also recommends that states set up their own commissions, and by 1967 all 50 do.

Congress passes the Equal Pay Act, drafted by Edith Green. This law requires that both sexes be paid equally for the same work, but it does not cover administrative, professional, domestic, and agricultural jobs.

In Maryland, Gloria St. Clair Hayes Richardson (later Dandridge, b. 1922) and Inez Grubb, cochairs of the Cambridge Nonviolent Action Committee, demand that the city council desegregate all public facilities. When this is not done, Richardson defiantly leads a series of protests. Tensions grow, and the governor eventually calls in the National Guard. Negotiations begin but later break down, although the 1964 Civil Rights Act brings some resolution.

Ruby Doris Smith joins the SNCC administrative staff, becoming executive secretary in 1966. Bernice Johnson Reagon (p. 365) and other women are also active in SNCC. In Mississippi field secretary Fannie Lou Hamer is arrested and severely beaten; her injuries are permanent.

Just 18 days after the huge civil rights March on Washington, four black youngsters—Addie Mae Collins, Denise McNair, Carole Robertson, and Cynthia Wesley—are murdered when white racists bomb a Baptist church in Birmingham, Alabama.

Betty Goldstein Friedan (b. 1921) publishes her classic exposé, *The Feminine Mystique,* directed to educated middle-class housewives who seem to have everything but suffer from a vague dissatisfaction with their lives, what Friedan calls "the problem that has no name" (see sidebar). An instant bestseller, the book attacks psychologists, educators, advertising, and the media for glorifying the roles of housewife and mother as the epitome of achievement for women. Friedan's work is a turning point, for her and other women. Thrust into a public role, she soon helps form the National Organization for Women (see 1966).

After President Kennedy is assassinated, federal district court judge Sarah Tilghman Hughes (1896–1985) swears in Lyndon B. Johnson as the new president aboard *Air Force One.* Former First Lady Jacqueline Bouvier Kennedy (later Onassis, 1929–94), always the center of much media attention, helps the nation mourn.

The first 31 recipients of the Presidential Medal of Freedom include 3 women: contralto Marian Anderson, educator Genevieve Caulfield, and public health worker Annie Wauneka.

1964

The new Civil Rights Act bans discrimination in public facilities and employment. A key provision for all women is Title VII, which forbids job discrimination on the basis of race, religion, national origin, and sex. The word *sex* is a last-minute addition, pushed by Representative Martha Griffiths, along with Alice Paul and the National Woman's Party. The addition is actually proposed by Representative Howard Smith of Virginia in what many see as a "joke" intended to defeat the whole bill. But Griffiths quickly stands up and checks the laughter of several congressmen, and the bill passes. Margaret Chase Smith makes sure it gets through the Senate.

The act sets up the Equal Employment Opportunity Commission (EEOC) to oversee the law, but it has little enforcement power at first. Within two years, women register some 4,000 complaints, and Title VII becomes a major tool in fighting job discrimination (see "Work").

Virginia Mae Brown (1923–91) is the first woman named to the Interstate Commerce Commission. In 1969 she becomes chair, and she serves until 1979. She is just one of many women President Johnson appoints during his term in office (see sidebar).

Esther Peterson is the first special assistant to the president on consumer affairs, serving under Johnson until 1967 and in 1977 under Jimmy Carter. Later, in honor of her contributions, the Food Marketing Institute starts the Esther Peterson Award for consumer activism.

At the Democratic Party Convention, Ella Baker, Annie Robinson Devine, Victoria Gray, Fannie Lou Hamer, and other members of the new Mississippi Freedom Democratic Party (MFDP) challenge whether the all-white Mississippi delegation represents the state's voters. In a televised speech Hamer vividly describes the beatings she and other African Americans received for trying to vote. Although the Democrats don't seat the MFDP delegation, they agree to reject segregated delegations in 1968.

Senator Margaret Chase Smith runs for president in several Republican primaries and receives 27 votes at the Republican Convention, placing second to Barry Goldwater.

Patsy Takemoto Mink (b. 1927), a Democrat from Hawaii, is the first Japanese American woman elected to Congress. She serves until 1977 and then is reelected in 1990.

Constance Baker Motley (b. 1921), who successfully argued several NAACP cases to integate southern universities, is elected as the first black woman state senator in New York. In 1965 she is elected Manhattan borough president.

1965

After winning on an alternative "Freedom Ballot," Annie Devine, Victoria Gray, and Fannie Lou Hamer challenge the seating of three white congressmen from their Mississippi districts and take their case to the floor of the House, where they are turned down 228 to 143.

On March 25 Viola Gregg Liuzzo (1925–65), a white civil rights supporter from Detroit, is shot to death by the Ku Klux Klan after participating in the five-day march led by Martin Luther King, Jr., from Selma to Montgomery. Three men are convicted of her murder.

In protest against the Vietnam War, 82-year-old Alice Herz, a Nazi refugee, sets herself on fire in downtown Detroit and dies 10 days later. She leaves a note explaining, "I choose the illuminating death of a Buddhist to protest against a great country trying to wipe out a small country for no reason."

Women Strike for Peace keep their congresspeople informed about the Vietnam War's human and financial costs with "Fact a Week" cards.

Claudia Alta Taylor ("Lady Bird") Johnson (b. 1913) is the most politically active First Lady since Eleanor Roosevelt. She tours the country to promote the "Great Society" program and lobbies for the Highway Beautification Act, which is now seen as early environmental legislation.

Lorna E. Lockwood is the first female chief justice of a state supreme court, in Arizona. The next woman to achieve this position is Susie M. Sharp in North Carolina 10 years later.

Howard University law school professor Patricia Roberts Harris (1924–85) is the first African American woman ambassador, to Luxembourg.

Aileen Clark Hernandez (b. 1926) is the one woman appointed to the five-member Equal Employment Opportunity Commission, charged with enforcing the 1964 Civil Rights Act (see also "Work").

Casey Hayden and Mary King, two white women in SNCC, write an anonymous paper protesting the "sexual caste system" and exploitation of women in radical movements. Mailed to women activists in other groups, such as Students for a Democratic Society (SDS), this tract serves as one of the sparks for the women's liberation movement.

1966

In a speech to the House, Representative Martha Griffiths charges that the EEOC has failed to enforce the sex discrimination provisions of the Civil Rights Act. "What is this sickness," she asks, "that causes an official to ridicule the law he swore to uphold and enforce? . . . What kind of mentality is it that can ignore the fact that women's wages are much less than men's, and that Negro women's wages are least of all?" Many women request copies of her speech.

Frustration at EEOC inaction sparks the formation of the National Organization for Women (NOW) at a July meeting of the state status-of-women commissions. Several women propose a resolution to demand EEOC action but are told that the conference is just for information sharing, not action. Outraged, they gather at lunch to set up a new organization for women's rights, called NOW. The purpose, scribbled on a napkin by Betty Friedan, is "to take the *action* to bring women into full participation in the mainstream of American society now . . . in truly equal partnership with men." Telegrams calling for EEOC action are immediately sent out, and on October 29 a formal organization is set up, with Friedan as president and Kathryn ("Kay") Clarenbach, head of the Wisconsin Status of Women Commission, chairing the board. Other officers include Caroline Davis, director of the Women's Department of the United Auto Workers, and Aileen Hernandez, pending her resignation from the EEOC and acceptance (she had not yet been asked, which later caused problems). A statement of purpose (see sidebar), written largely by civil rights activist and lawyer Pauli Murray (1910–85), is adopted, and about 300 charter members sign on.

"The Time Has Come to Confront"

"We believe that the time has come to move beyond the abstract argument, discussion and symposia over the status and special nature of women which has raged in America in recent years; the time has come to confront, with concrete action, the conditions that now prevent women from enjoying the equality of opportunity and freedom . . . which is their right, as individual Americans, and as human beings."
—Statement of Purpose, National Organization for Women, 1966; in Toni Carabillo, Judith Meuli, and June Bundy Csida, *Feminist Chronicles, 1953–1993* (Los Angeles: Women's Graphics, 1993)

Ruby Doris Smith-Robinson becomes executive secretary of SNCC. Other black women, like Muriel Tillinghast and Cynthia Washington, are project directors.

When Constance Baker Motley is appointed to the U.S. district court, she becomes the first black woman federal judge. She is one of only 20 women federal judges.

In New Mexico, Reyes and Patricia Tijerina help form La Alianza Federal de Los Pueblos Libros (Federal Alliance of Free Towns) to reclaim Spanish land grants taken over by the U.S. government. They stage camp-ins on federal lands and other protests.

Barbara Charline Jordan (b. 1936) is elected as the first black senator in the Texas state senate since 1883. In Georgia, Grace Towns Hamilton (1907–92) becomes the first black woman in the state legislature. At the same time Lurleen Burns Wallace (1926–68) is elected to succeed her husband, George Wallace, as governor of Alabama, and vows to continue his battle against integration.

1967

In *Loving* v. *Virginia* (see 1963), the U.S. Supreme Court rules that a Virginia law prohibiting interracial marriage is unconstitutional. This ruling ends antimiscegenation laws in 15 other states as well.

President Johnson issues Executive Order 11375 prohibiting sex discrimination by federal contractors or subcontractors (see "Work").

Betty Mae Jumper (b. 1923) is the first woman to chair the Seminole Tribal Council in Florida. She serves four years and also becomes active nationally, helping to found the United Southeastern Tribes.

At a Women Strike for Peace demonstration, about 2,500 women raid the Pentagon and insist on meeting with "the generals who send our sons to die." Many carry huge posters of napalmed children with the command "Children Are Not for Burning!" Folksinger Joan Baez also generates publicity for the antiwar movement when she is arrested for singing in front of a selective service center in Oakland, California. In Los Angeles, Florence Beaumont (1912–67) protests the Vietnam War by immolating herself in front of the Federal Building.

Another Mother for Peace is organized by Barbara Avedon and other women in Beverly Hills, California, and gains attention through such celebrities as Joanne Woodward, Bess Myerson, and Elaine May. Their logo is "War is not healthy for children and other living things."

Kathleen Neal Cleaver (b. 1945) joins the Black Panther Party and is its national communications secretary. Other women active in the Black Panther Party include Elaine Brown, Ericka Huggins, Assata Shakur (JoAnne Chesimard), and Akua Njere (Deborah Johnson).

The first women's liberation groups appear. Heather Booth, Jo Freeman, Evelyn Goldstein, Amy Kesselman, Sue Munaker, Naomi Weisstein, and others start the Westside group in Chicago after a conference of the radical left fails to take women's issues seriously. Shulamith Firestone and Pam Allen then form New York Radical Women, which publishes *Notes from the First Year* in 1968.

At its annual conference NOW adopts a "Bill of Rights for Women" with eight demands (see sidebar). Two of these demands—for the ERA and the right to choose— prove controversial. (For discussion of reproductive rights, see "Health and Medical Care.")

Georgia Montgomery Davis Powers (b. 1923) is both the first woman and the first African American elected to the Kentucky state senate. In her 20 years in office, she pushes both women's rights and civil rights.

"Sisterhood is powerful"

1968

In January a coalition of about 5,000 women peace activists, called the Jeannette Rankin Brigade (with Jeannette Rankin at the head), march to the Capitol to protest the Vietnam War. At the same time several radical women's groups stage a "Burial of Traditional Womanhood" at the Arlington National Cemetery to raise feminist issues, and they hand out pamphlets claiming, "Sisterhood is powerful."

Just a few days after the assassination of her husband, Martin Luther King, Jr., Coretta Scott King (b. 1927) takes his place at the head of a march of sanitation workers in Memphis. Later she speaks at an antiwar rally in New York. She also helps Ralph Abernathy organize the Poor People's Campaign in Washington, D.C., where she marches with a group of welfare mothers protesting racial discrimination.

In Minneapolis, Mary Jane Wilson joins Dennis Banks, Clyde Bellecourt, George Mitchell, and others to found the American Indian Movement (AIM), with the goal of ending police harassment of Native Americans and improving social services.

In Cleveland the Women's Equity Action League (WEAL) is formed by attorney Elizabeth Boyer and other former NOW members who find the stand on abortion controversial and instead want to focus on discrimination in education and employment. Calling for action that is "incisive but patient, determined but diplomatic" in their statement of purpose, they stress, "WEAL stands for responsible rebellion." Soon WEAL moves its base to Washington, D.C., joining forces with Arvonne Fraser, Bernice Sandler, and others.

Both the federal district court and the Pennsylvania Supreme Court strike down laws that gave longer prison sentences to women than men for the same crime.

Revisions in the Internal Revenue Service Code let widows and single or divorced women over 35 declare head-of-household status with the accompanying deductions.

Eight Demands

The NOW Bill of Rights, adopted in 1967, calls for:
—immediate passage of the Equal Rights Amendment
—enforcement of the 1964 Civil Rights Act forbidding sex discrimination in employment
—paid maternity leave with full job protection
—tax deductions for child-care expenses of working parents
—the establishment of public day-care centers
—legislation to end all discrimination against women in education
—equal rights for poor women, including access to job training, housing, and family allowances
—"the right of women to control their own reproductive lives" by eliminating laws prohibiting abortion and distribution of contraceptives.

"Let's Share Our Feelings"

"We're saying that women have all along been generally in touch with their feelings (rather than underneath them) and that their being in touch with their feelings has been their greatest strength, historically and for the future. . . .

"In our groups, let's share our feelings and pool them. Let's let ourselves go and see where our feelings lead us. Our feelings will lead us to ideas and then to actions.

"Our feelings will lead us to our theory, our theory to our action, our feelings about that action to new theory and then to new action."
—Kathie Sarachild, "A Program for Feminist Consciousness-Raising," 1968; in Redstockings, *Feminist Revolution* (New York: Random House, 1975)

The first female and black assistant secretary of state, Barbara M. Watson heads the department's Bureau of Security and Consular Affairs.

Shirley Mount Hufstedler, Los Angeles County superior court judge, is the second woman (after Florence Allen in 1934) to be named to the U.S. Court of Appeals.

At a White House luncheon given by Lady Bird Johnson, entertainer Eartha Kitt generates public controversy when she attacks the Vietnam War and the nearsightedness of prominent women's approach to racial and social problems.

In Atlantic City, to protest the Miss America Pageant and the image it promotes, 200 women toss bras, girdles, high heels, curlers, false eyelashes, and copies of women's magazines into a huge "Freedom Trash Can." Then they crown a live sheep as the prize "specimen" of the show. No bras are burned, however, as the media claim.

Women's liberation groups proliferate. In Boston, Roxanne Dunbar initiates Cell 16, which publishes the radical journal *No More Fun and Games*. In New York, Valerie Solanis shoots Andy Warhol for allegedly stealing her ideas and publishes her "SCUM (Society for Cutting Up Men) Manifesto." Ti-Grace Atkinson, head of the New York NOW chapter, takes up Solanis's cause. When NOW rejects a proposal to get rid of all leadership positions, Atkinson, writer Kate Millett, and activist civil rights lawyer Flo Kennedy walk out and form the October 17th Movement (later called The Feminists). Also in New York, Robin Morgan and others establish WITCH (originally Witch's International Terrorist Conspiracy from Hell, but later adapted to fit group actions, as in Women Incensed at Telephone Company Harassment). Similar "covens" form in other cities and, dressed as witches, engage in guerrilla theater, hexing companies with discriminatory policies, supermarkets for price hikes, and the like.

In November some 200 women from 30 cities attend the first national women's liberation conference, commemorating the 120th anniversary of the first women's rights meeting at Seneca Falls. The organizers, however, do not to invite radical women of color, leading to tensions later. Kathie Sarachild (born Amatniek, but naming herself as her mother's child) presents a paper on consciousness-raising (CR), a technique developed by the New York Radical Feminists. Soon groups all over the country are using this technique (see sidebar).

Campaigning with the slogan "Unbought and Unbossed" (the title of her later, 1970, autobiography), Shirley St. Hill Chisholm (b. 1924) is the first black woman elected to the U.S. House of Representatives (see sidebar opposite). Representing a Brooklyn, New York, district, she serves for 14 years.

1969

In the new Congress there are only 10 women in the U.S. House of Representatives and 1 in the Senate.

President Richard Nixon appoints Shirley Temple Black (p. 352) as U.S. representative to the UN. He also appoints Nancy Hanks to chair the National Endowment of the Arts, which she does until 1977. During her tenure Hanks persuades Congress to increase the NEA budget about tenfold.

At the urging of Republican congresswomen, Nixon froms the President's Task Force on Women's Responsibility, led by Virginia Allan, former president of the National Federation of Business and Professional Women. Their report, *A Matter of Simple Justice*, is at first repressed by the administration but is finally released after pressure from Elizabeth Duncan Koontz, head of the Women's Bureau. Stronger than the 1963 report, it calls for passage of the ERA and complete legal equality.

Coretta Scott King joins Ralph Abernathy in leading an SCLC protest by hospital workers against racial discrimination in Charleston, South Carolina. She also organizes the Martin Luther King, Jr., Center for Nonviolent Social Change, which formally opens in 1970.

Identifying "the agents of our oppression as men," Shulamith Firestone and Ellen Willis start the New York group Redstockings, claiming to "take the woman's side in everything," be "critical of all past ideology," and use "our feelings as our most important source of understanding," through CR techniques. At a public speakout, 12 women recount their abortion experiences.

Another new group is the New York Radical Feminists, which Firestone cofounds with Anne Koedt. In Boston, Meredith Tax and Linda Gordon start Bread and Roses, taking up the battle cry of the 1912 women strikers in Lawrence, Massachusetts (see "Work"). Heather Booth, Amy Kesselman, Vivian Rothstein, and others form the Chicago Women's Liberation Union.

NOW women institute a number of actions, including picketing men-only restaurants and bars and demonstrating on Mother's Day for "Rights, Not Roses." They also protest abortion laws.

The lesbian rights movement grows out of the confrontation at Stonewall Inn in New York City, after the police harrass the gay patrons.

Grace Thorpe is one of the leaders in the AIM takeover of Alcatraz Island in San Francisco Bay. The protest, which lasts until mid-1971, underlines the penal conditions under which Native Americans live.

The National Women's Hall of Fame is established in Seneca Falls, New York. Among the first inductees are Susan B. Anthony, Marian Anderson, Clara Barton, and Amelia Earhart.

On November 15 thousands of women and men peace activists join in the largest antiwar protest yet, in Washington, D.C.

1970

In the new Congress there are 12 U.S. woman representatives and 1 senator. There are no female governors.

"Women Are Always Organizing"

"Men always underestimate women. . . . If they had thought about it, they would have realized that many of the homes in black neighborhoods are headed by women. . . . The women are always organizing for something, even if it is only a bridge club. They run the PTA, they are the backbone of the social groups and civic clubs, more than the men. So the organization was already there. All I had to do was get its help. . . .

"It was not my original strategy to organize womanpower to elect me; it was forced on me by the time, place, and circumstances. . . . Tremendous amounts of talent are being lost to our society just because that talent wears a skirt. . . . [And] when someone tries to use my sex against me, I delight in being able to turn the tables on him, as I did in my congressional campaign."
—Shirley Chisholm, *Unbought and Unbossed* (Boston: Houghton Mifflin, 1970)

Comanche activist LaDonna Harris (b. 1931), who started Oklahomans for Indian Opportunity in the early 1960s, forms the national Americans for Indian Opportunity. As president, she builds a strong advocacy group for Native political rights and economic development.

Women from 43 nations in 23 states gather to form the North American Indian Women's Association.

Hawaii has three women of Asian descent in public office: Patsy Mink in the U.S. House and Jean Sadako King and Patricia F. Saiki in the state legislature. The only other state with an Asian American woman in office is California, where March Fong Eu is in the state assembly.

In Texas, Maria Hernández and Martha Cotera (b. 1938) help found La Raza Unida Party to fight for Mexican American rights.

In California, Francisca Flores (b. 1913), Graciella Olivárez, Gracia Molina Pick, Yolanda Nava, and other Chicanas establish the Comision Femenil Mexicana Nacional to draw attention to Mexican American women's concerns. They soon open a center for working women and two day-care facilities. Flores also edits the feminist journal *Regeneración (Regeneration)*.

Margarita Bradford Melville (b. 1929), a former nun who was kicked out of Guatemala for her social activism in 1967, is one of the Catonsville Nine, arrested for burning draft records in a Maryland suburb and sentenced to a year in prison. With her husband, she publishes the autobiographical *Whose Heaven, Whose Earth?*

Ada Deer (b. 1935) cofounds the group Determination of the Rights and Unity for Menominee Shareholders (DRUMS). Their goal is to regain federal recognition of the Menominee people and to repeal the 1954 Termination Act, which ended health and education services and threatened loss of tribal lands. Beginning in 1972, Deer serves as the chief lobbyist in Washington, D.C., successfully pushing for the Menominee Restoration Act of 1973.

Representative Martha Griffiths successfully petitions to get the ERA out of the House Judiciary Committee, and it is approved 350 to 15 after only an hour of debate—but the Senate fails to vote on it. The first major union, the United Auto Workers, comes out in favor of the ERA, as does the Department of Labor.

Margaret ("Maggie") Kuhn, forced to retire due to age, forms the Gray Panthers to fight for older citizens' rights. She coins the term *ageism.* and writes *Get Out There and Do Something about Injustice* (1972).

The new League for Women's Rights calls for revisions in the marriage and divorce laws to account for the economic value of housework.

At a meeting of 300 women led by JoAnn Evansgardner and Doris Sassower, the Professional Women's Caucus is formed to promote women's rights, childcare facilities, and women's studies programs.

Conflicts arise over the lesbian presence in the women's movement. After Betty Friedan speaks of a "the lavender menace," lesbian feminists wearing lavender t-shirts stenciled "Lavender Menace" take over a meeting of the Congress to Unite Women. The Radicalesbians present a position paper, "The Woman-Identified Woman," defining lesbianism as a political choice. Later, when NOW holds its annual elections, Friedan tries to keep lesbians from being elected, although in 1971 NOW adopts a resolution accepting lesbian participation.

Aileen Hernandez replaces Friedan as president of NOW, with Wilma Scott Heide chairing the board. Hernandez says, "As a black woman, I particularly think that it is important to be involved in women's liberation. . . . Until women, black as well as others, gain a sense of their own identity and feel they have a real choice in society, nothing is going to happen in civil rights."

On August 26, the 50th anniversary of women gaining the vote, more than 100,000 women across the nation participate in the Women's Strike for Equality, initiated by Betty Friedan and organized by NOW. In New York up to 50,000 women march down Fifth Avenue, and simultaneous demonstrations are held in 90 major cities and many small towns. In rally after rally, speakers underline the inequities women still face. One Boston protestor, for example, chains herself to an oversized typewriter.

Bernice Sandler of WEAL files a sex discrimination complaint against the University of Maryland, where she had firsthand experience, and a number of other colleges (see "Education").

In a case filed by two NOW activists, lawyers Faith Seidenberg and Karen DeCrow, the Supreme Court rules that the men-only policy of McSorley's Olde Ale House, a public restaurant in New York City, is illegal. New York City also passes a law prohibiting sex discrimination in most public facilities—the first such law in a major city.

NOW files a job discrimination complaint against 1,300 corporations.

As the new head of New York City's Commission on Human Rights, Eleanor Holmes Norton (b. 1937) pledges "to see no man is judged by the irrational criteria of race, religion, or national origin. And I assure you that I use the word 'man' in the generic sense, for I mean to see that the principle of nondiscrimination becomes a reality for women as well." In September the commission holds five days of hearings on "Women's Role in Contemporary Society," with testimony from Bella Abzug, Shirley Chisholm, Betty Friedan, Florynce Kennedy, Margaret Mead, Gloria Steinem, and many others.

Four influential works by U.S. feminists are published: *Sexual Politics* by Kate Millett (see sidebar); *The Dialectics of Sex: The Case for Feminist Revolution* by Shulamith Firestone; *The Black Woman,* edited by Toni Cade (later Bambara); and *Sisterhood Is Powerful: An Anthology of Writings from the Women's Movement,* edited by Robin Morgan. Cade's

"Sexual Dominion"

". . . the situation between the sexes now, and throughout history, is . . . a relationship of dominance and subordinance. . . . However muted its present appearance may be, sexual dominion obtains . . . as perhaps the most pervasive ideology of our culture and provides its most fundamental concept of power.

"This is so because our society . . . is a patriarchy. The fact is evident at once if one recalls that the military, industry, technology, universities, science, political office, and finance—in short, every avenue of power . . . is entirely in male hands."

—Kate Millett, *Sexual Politics* (New York: Ballantine, 1970)

*"The Mexican-American move-
ment is not that of just adults
fighting the social system, but it is
a total commitment of a family
unit living what it believes to be a
better way of life in demanding
social change for the benefit of
humankind. When a family is
involved in a human rights
movement, as is the Mexican-
American family, there is little
room for a woman's liberation
movement alone. . . . The
Mexican-American movement
demands are such that, with the
liberation of La Raza [the Race],
we must have a total liberation.
. . . The family must come up
together."*
  —Enriqueta Longauex y
  Vasquez, "The Mexican-
  American Woman," in
  Sisterhood Is Powerful, edited
  by Robin Morgan (New York:
  Vintage Books, 1970)

anthology includes writings by Alice Walker, Nikki Giovanni, Paule Marshall, Pat Robinson, Abbey Lincoln, and others. Morgan's collection includes such essays as "'Kinde, Kuche, Kirche' as Scientific Law: Psychology Constructs the Female" by Naomi Weisstein, "The Politics of Housework" by Pat Mainardi, and "The Mexican-American Woman" by Enriqueta Longauex y Vasquez (see sidebar).

After a courtroom shootout related to the "Soledad Brothers" case, a warrant is issued for the arrest of Angela Yvonne Davis (b. 1944), just because she is the registered owner of the gun involved and has protested the Soledad Brothers' imprisonment. A philosophy professor, Davis first gained attention in 1969 when she was dismissed from UCLA because of her Communist Party membership. Now Davis goes underground, and the FBI puts her on its "10 Most Wanted List." When Davis is apprehended two months later, she is held without bail on murder charges, and a "Free Angela" movement quickly springs up. Singer Aretha Franklin offers to pay her bail "because she's a Black woman who wants freedom for all Black people." In prison Davis co-edits *If They Come in the Morning* (1971), an anthology giving a voice to political prisoners. Later, in 1972, she is finally released on bail, tried, and found not guilty.

An explosion in a Weather Underground bomb factory in a Greenwich Village house kills Diana Oughton and forces Kathy Boudin and Cathy Wilkerson to flee. They and Weather leader Bernardine Dohrn go into hiding. Wilkerson and Dohrn turn themselves in in the late 1970s; Boudin is arrested after an armed robbery in 1981.

Allison Krause and Sandra Scheuer are two of four killed at Kent State University by the Ohio National Guard during antiwar protests. Students are also killed at Jackson State University due to racial tensions.

1971

There are 13 women in the new Congress: 12 in the House and 1 in the Senate. On her first day in the House, New York representative Bella Savitsky Abzug (b. 1920) breaks with tradition and speaks up, demanding that all U.S. troops be immediately withdrawn from Southeast Asia. In 1972 she describes her early experiences in Congress in *Bella! Ms. Abzug Goes to Washington*; she stays for three terms.

After selecting the first seven women for the White House police force in 1970, the Secret Service now approves five women as agents, assigned to protect the president, the vice president, and their families.

Business entrepreneur Romana Acosta Bañuelos (b. 1925) is appointed U.S. treasurer, the first Mexican American woman to hold this post.

Bella Abzug, Shirley Chisholm, Betty Friedan, Gloria Steinem, and others help found the National Women's Political Caucus. A nonpartisan group, the NWPC intends to increase women's political strength by organizing local caucuses, backing women candidates who address women's concerns, and assuring fair representation of women and their issues within the leading parties. They soon pressure the Democratic Party into a guaranteeing nondiscriminatory delegate selection.

Gloria Steinem and Brenda Feigen Fasteau start the Women's Action Alliance, a national center on women's issues.

In Washington, D.C., Rita Mae Brown, Charlotte Bunch, and other activists start a separatist lesbian-feminist collective and begin publishing their ideas in the journal *The Furies* in 1972.

The first national Chicana conference—La Conferencia de Mujeres por la Raza—takes place in Houston, with keynote speeches by lawyer Graciela Olivárez and social work educator Julie Ruiz. There are also a number of regional conferences.

Anne L. Armstrong (b. 1927) is the first woman co-chair of the National Republican Committee, serving until 1973.

The State Department ends its ban on married women in foreign service careers after pressure from women employees. Also, Alison Palmer wins a discrimination suit against the State Department after she was denied the position of political officer by three ambassadors because of her sex. But discrimination continues, and she files a new suit in 1976.

For the first time the Supreme Court declares a law unconstitutional for discriminating against sex. The case, brought by Sally Reed and argued by Ruth Bader Ginsburg (b. 1933), involves an Idaho law that gave preference to a male over a female in administering an estate if all other qualifications were met. (Ginsburg is the initial director of the ACLU's Women's Rights Project.)

Julie Price, Paulette Desell, and Ellen McConnell are approved as the first three female Senate pages.

By a vote of 354 to 23, the House again passes the Equal Rights Amendment (see 1943 for its wording; see also sidebar).

Women's groups demonstrate against AT&T and other companies for sex discrimination. NOW also pressures for childcare tax deductions and stages a "Baby Carriage Brigade" with signs "Are Children as Important as Martinis?"

Despite the lobbying efforts of many women's groups, President Nixon vetoes the Comprehensive Child Care Act, which would have established government-sponsored day-care centers.

1972

After intense lobbying by Wilma Scott Heide of NOW and other women, the Senate follows the House and approves the ERA by a vote of 84 to 8. Hawaii is the first state to ratify the amendment, and by the end of the year 21 other states have followed suit. In addition, 6 states (Colorado, Hawaii, Maryland, New Mexico, Texas, and Washington) add equal rights amendments to their state constitutions; Pennsylvania did so in 1971.

"A Legislative Landmark"

"I consider it [the Equal Rights Amendment] a legislative landmark in the struggle for human equality and recognition of the reality of women's political power. . . . [It] legally establishes, as I see it, that women as a group are physically, mentally and culturally suited for every kind of activity for which men are suited.

"It will have two major effects. First, laws that confer benefits of one kind or another will be extended to both sexes. . . .

"Second, laws that restrict opportunities would be declared unconstitutional. By this I mean 'restrictive' work laws (such as weight and hour limitations), special restrictions on property rights and all other provisions that now penalize women—or men—because of sex."

—Bella Abzug, in *Bella! Ms. Abzug Goes to Washington* (New York: Saturday Review Press, 1972)

Attacking the ERA in her newsletter, Phyllis Schlafly (b. 1924) organizes the National Committee to Stop ERA, which soon has thousands of members. Schlafly claims, "Women's liberation is a total assault on the role of the American woman as a wife and mother, and on the family as the basic unit of society." To emphasize their point of view, her supporters send homemade jams and other delicacies to their legislators, with notes: "Preserve us from a congressional jam;/ Vote against the ERA sham."

Congress passes the Equal Employment Opportunity Act and extends the Equal Pay Act (see "Work"); it also passes the Education Amendments (see "Education").

Chicanas form a caucus within the Raza Unida Party and demand the party take a strong stand on women's rights, including equal pay for equal work, legal abortion, and childcare centers.

Lupe Anguiano (b. 1929), who becomes a program officer in the Department of Health, Education, and Welfare, organizes the Spanish-Speaking Women's National Consultation.

Carmen Maymi (b. 1938), Paquita Vivo, and others form the National Conference of Puerto Rican Women in Washington, D.C.

Carol Burris forms Women's Lobby, Inc., to pressure Congress on women's issues.

Economist Jane Roberts Chapman and attorney Margaret Gates set up the Center for Women Policy Studies and investigate sex discrimination in credit. They reveal that because a married woman's accounts are in her husband's name, even if she is the main earner, she has no credit history if she divorces her husband.

Dixy Lee Ray (b. 1914) is appointed to the Atomic Energy Commission and becomes its chair in 1973. Anne Armstrong becomes President Nixon's counselor and sets up the Office of Women's Programs in the White House. Jean Wilowski (b. 1919) is appointed ambassador to Zambia, the first female ambassador to an African nation.

Wilhelmina Jackson Rolark sets up and heads the new National Association of Black Women Attorneys.

The newly established Clearinghouse on Women's Issues provides information on discrimination.

Teacher Agnes Allen Ross (b. 1910), the new chairperson of the Flandreau Indians in South Dakota, helps oversee the tribe's construction of a motel and establishes health and housing programs.

At the Democratic National Convention, 40% of the delegates are female, compared with 13% four years earlier. Jean Westwood is chosen to chair the party, and Yvonne Braithwaite Burke (b. 1932) is the first African American to vice-chair the convention. The Democratic platform takes a strong stand on women's issues, endorsing the ERA,

Dorothy Height (left), president of the Council of Negro Women, and Shirley Chisholm, 1972 presidential candidate (Bethune Museum and Archives, Washington, D.C.)

educational equality, and equal pay for all workers. At the Republican National Convention, where women are 35% of the delegates, Jill Ruckelshaus of the NWPC also gets women's issues on the platform.

Seeing herself as "a catalyst for change," Shirley Chisholm is the first African American to campaign for the Democratic Party nomination for president. She faces opposition from both women (the NWPC, for example, does not back her candidacy) and black men. Yet she perseveres and receives more than 150 votes on the first ballot. Later she reflects, "I have met far more discrimination as a woman than being black in the field of politics. . . . But, in spite of it all, I went to the Democratic convention . . . and began to open the way for women to think that they can run." At the same Democratic convention, Frances (Sissy) Farenthold, a liberal Texas state legislator and later head of the NWPC, gets 420 votes for vice president.

Among the 15 women elected to the House are Yvonne Braithwaite Burke, the first black woman representative from California; Elizabeth Holtzman (b. 1941), who defeats Emanuel Celler, a strong ERA opponent; Barbara Jordan of Texas, the first black woman from the South; and Patricia Schroeder (b. 1940), a Colorado Democrat. However, Margaret Chase Smith loses her bid for reelection, so when the new session starts in 1973, there are no women in the Senate.

Ramona Bennett is elected Puyallup tribal chairperson after spending years traveling to Washington, D.C., and lobbying for tribal recognition (see sidebar). At the National Tribal Chairman's Association meeting, where she first has to overcome male resistance to her presence, she raises the issue of Native children who lose their culture through adoption, a concern that leads to the 1978 Indian Child Welfare Act.

1973

The new National Black Feminist Organization insists that "there can't be liberation for half the race" and urges a fight against both racism and sexism. In the San Francisco Bay Area, Black Women Organized for Action also points to the dual struggle and stresses the need for organizing and taking action rather than just talking.

The West Coast Lesbian Feminist Conference is held in Los Angeles.

At its annual meeting NOW adopts a resolution supporting its lesbian members and pledging to fight for legislation prohibiting discrimination based on sexual orientation.

In Taft, Oklahoma, Leila K. Smith Foley is elected the first African American woman mayor in the 48 contiguous states.

Carmen Maymi is the first Puerto Rican–born director of the Women's Bureau in the Department of Labor; she also serves as deputy assistant secretary for employment standards.

Vilma Martinez (b. 1943) becomes president of the Mexican American Legal Defense and Education Fund and serves until 1982. In this posi-

"A Matter of Life and Death"

"If I couldn't get an appointment with a congressman, I'd wait outside his door for the bell to ring calling him into chambers to vote. I'd have my papers ready, and when he came out, I'd run with him. . . .

"Our tribe lacked recognition, we had a very high rate of infant mortality and suicide, we were losing our children through adoption. Families were living in condemned housing, and there were fires. We needed protection, law enforcement, education, job programs. It was a matter of life and death."

—Ramona Bennett, interviewed by Jane Katz, in *Messengers of the Wind: Native American Women Tell Their Life Stories* (New York: Ballantine Books, 1995)

"Our Women Played a Major Part"

"At one time [during the siege at Wounded Knee] a white volunteer nurse berated us for doing slave work while the men got all the glory. We were betraying the case of womankind, was the way she put it. We told her that her kind of women's lib was a white, middle-class thing, and that at this critical stage we had other priorities. Once our men had gotten their rights and their balls back, we might start arguing with them about who should do the dishes. But not before.

"Actually, our women played a major part at Wounded Knee. We had two or three pistol-packing mamas . . . taking their turns on the firing line, swapping lead with the feds. The Indian nurses bringing in the wounded under a hail of fire were braver than many warriors."

—Mary Crow Dog, in *Lakota Woman*, with Richard Erdoes (New York: HarperPerennial, 1991)

tion she lobbies successfully to extend the Voting Rights Act of 1965 to protect Mexican American citizens and fights a court battle to obtain public education for the children of illegal aliens.

In South Dakota women are active in AIM's 71-day takeover of Wounded Knee in response to federal agents' armed harassment of the Pine Ridge Reservation. Gladys Bissonette (with her husband, Pedro) and Ellen Moves Camp start the Oglala Sioux Civil Rights Organization, which is willing to use arms in self-defense if necessary, and they urge, "Go ahead and make your stand at Wounded Knee. If you men won't do it, you can stay here and talk for all eternity and we women will do it" (see sidebar). Later, as a result of government reprisals against AIM, 21 women are among the 69 people killed at Pine Ridge. AIM activists Lorelei Means and Madonna Gilbert Thunderhawk help set up the "We Will Remember Survival School."

As a fugitive from the FBI, Jane Alpert publishes the influential "Mother Right: A New Feminist Theory" in *Ms.*, attacking the left's sexism and turning to women's biologically based maternal qualities as a foundation for a different society. Alpert surrenders in 1974 and serves time for her part in several 1969 bombings of government buildings.

Two funds are set up as a result of the NWPC conference in Houston: the National Women's Education Fund to train women for political participation and the Women's Campaign Fund to help finance women candidates. At the conference Chicanas present a number of resolutions, although only one—allowing ethnic caucuses—is passed.

The AFL-CIO endorses the ERA, and eight more states ratify it (a total of 30). In a NOW action women literally give blood for the ERA.

Supreme Court rulings on abortion (see "Health") and benefits for married women in the military (see "War") back women's rights.

Lindy Boggs (born Marie Corinne Morrison Claibone) is elected to complete her husband's term in Congress and is reelected for 17 years.

Although Gene Cox, the daughter of a congressman, served as a page for one day in 1939, Felda Looper is the first regular House page.

1974

The Mexican American Women's National Association (MANA) is set up. This pro-choice, feminist group lobbies Congress for regulations to end sterilization abuse. It also works to increase educational opportunities and starts a Hermanitas ("Little Sisters") program.

As the House Judiciary Committee investigates the possible impeachment of President Nixon, representatives Elizabeth Holtzman and Barbara Jordan gain respect for their astute comments. In her televised statement in favor of impeachment, Jordan asserts, "My faith in the Constitution is whole. It is complete. It is total. I am not going to sit here and be an idle spectator in the diminution, the subversion, and the destruction of the Constitution."

Lorelei DeCora Means, Madonna Thunderhawk, Phyllis Young, and others start Women of All Red Nations (WARN), an activist group. "What we are about," says Young, "is drawing on our traditions, regaining our strength as women in the ways handed down to us by our grandmothers, and their grandmothers before them."

Elaine Brown is the only woman to chair the Black Panther Party, an experience she details in her 1992 autobiography, *A Taste of Power*.

When Esther Lau charges white Los Angeles policemen with sexual harassment and physical assault, the case focuses attention on similar abuses of the basic civil rights of other women of color.

In part through the efforts of the Center for Women Policy Studies (see 1972), Congress passes the Equal Credit Opportunity Act, forbidding the denial of credit on the basis of sex or marital status.

The state of Pennsylvania prohibits sex bias in insurance policies.

The Fair Housing Act of 1968 is extended to forbid discrimination in rentals, sales, or financing on the basis of sex. Congress also passes the Educational Equity Act (see "Education").

After regaining federal recognition for her people, Ada Deer chairs the Menominee Restoration Committee and helps structure the new tribal government.

Patricia ("Patty") Hearst, daughter of the publishing magnate, is kidnapped by the Symbionese Liberation Army, undergoes a "conversion," and joins them in robbing banks, purportedly to free the oppressed. After her arrest in 1976, she serves two years in prison for armed robbery.

Karen DeCrow, NOW president, and 16 other leaders of women's groups meet with President Gerald Ford to discuss women's needs. It is the first invitation to the White House since NOW began.

After serving as Connecticut's secretary of state and then as a U.S. representative, Ella Tambussi Grasso (1919–81) wins the governorship in Connecticut by a huge majority. For the first time a woman governor is elected entirely on her own, without succeeding a husband. She serves as governor until 1980.

Federally, 18 women are elected to the House but 0 to the Senate. In state elections March Fong Eu wins as secretary of state in California, the first woman of Asian descent in such a position. Elaine Noble is the first "out" lesbian elected to state office, as a Massachusetts state legislator. Overall, women in state legislatures increase to 587, although this is still less than 10% of the total. Locally, Janet Gray Hayes (b. 1926) is elected mayor of San Jose, California, the first female to run a city with a population of over half a million. Inspired by her success, Lila Cockrell wins the mayoral election in San Antonio, Texas, the following year.

Only 3 new states ratify the ERA, for a total of 33 of the 38 needed.

In *Taylor* v. *Louisiana* the Supreme Court rules that women cannot be systematically excluded from jury duty. At the time Louisiana is the only state that will not call a woman for jury duty unless she specifically asks in writing to serve. The court states that this practice violates the Sixth Amendment rights of the defendant (in this case a man) to a jury "drawn from a fair cross section of the community."

In *Thelma Stanton* v. *James Stanton*, the Supreme Court invalidates a Utah law that requires that child support be paid until age 21 for a son but only to age 18 for a daughter. Citing a violation of the daughter's 14th Amendment rights, the court points out: "No longer is the female destined solely for the home and the rearing of the family, and only the male for the marketplace and the world of ideas."

After serving as assistant attorney general, Carla Anderson Hills (b. 1934) is named secretary of the Department of Housing and Urban Development. She is only the third woman in a cabinet-level position.

Attorney Margaret Bush Wilson (b. 1919) is the first black woman to chair the board of the NAACP. "I was literally born and raised in the NAACP," she comments, "and the issues that it faces have been a part of my earliest experiences."

Representative Cardiss Robertson Collins (b. 1931) of Illinois is both the first woman and the first African American to serve as Democratic whip-at-large in the House.

Economist Alice Mitchell Rivlin (b. 1931) initiates the Congressional Budget Office and serves as its director until 1983.

The first American Indian Women's Leadership Conference is held.

When anti-American sentiments emerge at the UN Conference on International Women's Year in Mexico City, several U.S. women are determined to improve relations. Michaela Walsh, for example, starts Women's World Banking, and Fran Hosken publishes *WIN News*.

In a much-publicized trial, Joan (Joanne) Little is acquitted of murder charges in the 1974 killing of a white prison guard in self-defense when he raped her in her jail cell in Beaufort, North Carolina. Civil rights activists and women's groups use her case to underline the all-too-common sexual abuse of black women within the prison system.

In Halifax, Virginia, Cora Tucker starts Citizens for a Better America to fight for black residents' rights. The group boycotts stores that don't employ African Americans, registers voters, protests a proposed nuclear waste dump, and fights against welfare program abuses.

Only one new state (North Dakota) ratifies the ERA. On the other side, Phyllis Schlafly organizes her Eagle Forum as an "alternative to women's liberation." The group opposes the ERA, school busing, government-sponsored childcare, and abortion while advocating voluntary school prayer and taking a law-and-order stance.

1976

AIM organizer Anna Mae Pictou Aquash (1945–76) is murdered, execution style, on Pine Ridge Reservation in South Dakota. At the time the FBI wants to question her about the killers of two agents during a 1975 shootout at Pine Ridge. No one is arrested for her murder, but Native women gather to give her a proper burial. "The executioners of Anna Mae did not snuff out a meddlesome woman," says Shirley Hill Witt. "They exalted a Brave Hearted Woman for all time."

The Organization of Pan Asian American Women is formed to coordinate the efforts various groups for women of Asian and Pacific Islander descent. Also, Asian Women United of California is started to foster Asian American women's social and economic welfare.

The National Alliance of Black Feminists is organized in Chicago.

Irma Vidal Santaella, New York state's first Puerto Rican woman lawyer, helps start the National Association for Puerto Rican Civil Rights.

Ambassador to Ghana since 1974, Shirley Temple Black becomes the first female chief of protocol under President Ford. (Later, from 1989 to 1992, she serves as ambassador to Czechoslovakia.) Anne Armstrong is appointed ambassador to Great Britain.

ERAmerica is formed to channel money to states where it will be most effective. Drawing on suffragists' tactics, NOW members mount a daily pro-ERA vigil outside the White House during summer. No new states ratify the federal ERA, but Massachusetts approves a state ERA.

Barbara Jordan is the first African American and the first woman to give the keynote speech at the Democratic National Convention in its 144-year existence. That this is possible, she says, "is one additional bit of evidence that the American Dream need not forever be deferred."

Dixy Lee Ray wins election as governor of Washington. New congresswomen include Barbara Mikulski of Maryland and Mary Rose Oakar of Ohio (both the first Democratic women from their states). In California, Maxine Waters (b. 1938) wins election to the state assembly from South Central Los Angeles and by 1984 chairs the Democratic caucus there. In Mississippi, where she was once refused the right to vote and was jailed over 70 times in her fight for civil rights, Unita Blackwell (b. 1933) is elected mayor of Mayersville; she is the first African American woman mayor in the state's history.

1977

President Jimmy Carter's administration has two women at cabinet level. Patricia Roberts Harris, the first black woman in the cabinet, serves initially as secretary of housing and urban development (HUD) and in 1979 as secretary of health, education, and welfare (HEW). She gains media attention at her senate confirmation hearings, where she is questioned about her sensitivity to the needs of the poor (see sidebar). Juanita Morris Kreps (b. 1921) becomes the first woman secretary of

"If You Think That I Have Forgotten"

"You do not understand who I am. . . . I am a black woman, the daughter of a Pullman car waiter. I am a black woman who even eight years ago could not buy a house in parts of the District of Columbia. I didn't start out as a member of a prestigious law firm, but as a woman who needed a scholarship to go to school. If you think that I have forgotten that, you are wrong."
—Patricia Roberts Harris, Senate Confirmation Hearings, 1977; quoted in *Epic Lives: One Hundred Black Women Who Made a Difference*, edited by Jessie Carney Smith (Detroit: Visible Ink Press, 1993)

"Our Liberation Is a Necessity"

"Above all else, our politics initially sprang from the shared belief that Black women are inherently valuable, that our liberation is a necessity not as an adjunct to somebody else's but because of our need as human persons for autonomy. . . . We realize that the only people who care enough about us to work consistently for our liberation is us. Our politics evolve from a healthy love for ourselves, our sisters, and our community which allows us to continue our struggle and work."
—The Combahee River Collective, "A Black Feminist Statement," 1977; quoted in *All the Women Are White, All the Blacks Are Men, But Some of Us Are Brave*, edited by Gloria T. Hull, Patricia Bell Scott, and Barbara Smith (Old Westbury, N.Y.: Feminist Press, 1982)

commerce. An economics professor at Duke University, she is the author of *Sex in the Marketplace: Women at Work* (1971) and *Women and the American Economy: A Look to the 1980s* (1976), among other works.

Eleanor Holmes Norton becomes the first woman to chair the Equal Employment Opportunity Commission, and within two years she helps cut the huge number of pending cases in half. Educator Mary Frances Berry serves as assistant secretary for education, the first African American woman in this post. Graciela Olivárez is the highest-ranking Latina in the government, as director of the Community Services Administration.

Educator Mari-Luci Jaramillo (b. 1928) serves as U.S. ambassador to Honduras, where she helps oversee the first free elections.

Law professor Rose Elizabeth Bird is appointed the first woman chief justice of the California Supreme Court.

In San Francisco, Judy Heumann, who in the early 1970s organized Disabled in Action, leads 100 demonstrators in a 25-day takeover of the Department of HEW to insist on enforcement of the 1973 Rehabilitation Act, prohibiting discrimination on the basis of a "handicap."

In Arizona, Dene women begin protesting the fencing off of joint-use lands in the Big Mountain area by the Bureau of Indian Affairs. Pauline Whitesinger physically confronts one of the work crews; later protests are led by Roberta Blackgoat, Ruth Benally, and others.

The Combahee River Collective, formed in 1974, issues "A Black Feminist Statement" (see sidebar) to help other groups organize. The Boston-based lesbian feminist collective, named after the river where Harriet Tubman led U.S. troops to free 750 slaves, actively protests against sterilization abuse, violence against women, and homophobia.

Eleanor Cutri Smeal (b. 1939) becomes the first salaried president of NOW and vows to wage an all-out national fight for the ERA, using a special ERA Strike Force.

On Equality Day (the anniversary of ratification of the 19th Amendment), 4,000 women pay tribute to suffragist Alice Paul (who died earlier in the year) and march to the White House to urge passage of the ERA, which Paul initiated.

As part of the UN International Women's Year, more than 2,000 delegates and 18,000 observers attend the government-sponsored National Women's Conference, chaired by Bella Abzug, in Houston. For the opening a lighted torch is passed 2,600 miles from Seneca Falls to Houston. First Lady Rosalyn Carter, Betty Ford, Ladybird Johnson, and Coretta Scott King are among the participants at the meeting. About 35% of the delegates are women of color, and 20% are low income. Although right-wing activists pack 11 state delegations with antifeminists, the conference still approves a 25-point action plan that includes commitments to the ERA, reproductive choice, and lesbian and minority rights. Black delegates voice their own action plan for African American women.

At a simultaneous counterconvention in Houston, Phyllis Schlafly organizes the Pro-Family Movement, which opposes much of what the National Women's Conference supports. Schlafly contends that the ERA is not only unnecessary but a step down for women.

The power of right-wing women is evident in Dade County, Florida, where evangelist singer Anita Bryant, leader of Save Our Children, successfully campaigns to overturn a local ordinance prohibiting discrimination against homosexuals.

Only one state (Indiana) approves the ERA during the year. ERA supporters must constantly fight not only campaigns to pass the ERA but also ones to rescind it. To gain more time, representative Elizabeth Holtzman introduces a bill to extend the deadline for ratification.

To investigate women's needs and devise appropriate legislation, the women in Congress form the bipartisan Congresswomen's Caucus (later Congressional Caucus on Women's Issues).

1978

About 100,000 people crowd in front of the Capitol in Washington, D.C., to affirm their support for the ERA and to urge Congress to extend the deadline beyond March 1979. Seven more years are requested, but Congress only extends the deadline to June 30, 1982. So far 35 states have ratified the amendment, but 3 more are needed. No new states ratify the amendment this year, despite effective economic boycotts of states that have not approved the ERA.

Economist Nancy Hays Teeters (b. 1930) becomes the first woman on the Federal Reserve Bank's board of governors. She serves until 1984.

In San Francisco, Dianne Goldman Feinstein (b. 1933), president of the board of supervisors, takes over as mayor after her predecessor, George Muscone, is murdered for his support of gay rights. She is the elected in her own right and serves until 1988.

Bella Abzug and Carmen Votaw, president of the National Conference of Puerto Rican Women, head the new 40-member National Advisory Committee for Women. However, in 1979, President Carter fires Abzug, and Votaw and 27 members resign in protest.

In the elections women win only 17 seats in the House (a loss of 2), but gain a Senate seat and increase their representation on the state level from 7% to 11%. Nancy Landon Kassebaum (b. 1932), a pro-ERA and pro-choice Republican, wins the Kansas race for U.S. senator, to become the only woman in that body. Geraldine A. Ferraro (b. 1935) of Queens, New York, is elected to her first term in the House. On the state level, Polly Baca (b. 1943) is the first Latina elected to a state senate, in Colorado. Jean King becomes the highest-ranking Asian woman, as lieutenant governor of Hawaii.

1979

Federal judge Shirley Hufstedler, seen by many as a Supreme Court candidate, is appointed as the first secretary of education. Patricia Roberts Harris becomes secretary of health and human services.

In an upset election, Jane Margaret Byrne (b. 1934) beats Mayor Richard Daley's annointed successor in the Democratic primary and goes on to win the race for Chicago mayor with 82% of the vote.

Yvonne Braithwaite Burke, Patsy Mink, Bella Abzug, and others set up WOMEN, USA to fight for equality, especially economically.

There are enough women to form the National Association of Women Judges as a networking group. Amalya Lyle Kearse (b. 1937) is the first woman and the second African American appointed to the Second Circuit Court of Appeals, in Manhattan. Margarita Esquiroz (b. 1945) is the first Cuban American woman state judge in Florida.

Althea T. L. Simmons (1924–90) serves as the chief lobbyist for the NAACP in Washington, D.C., and directs its bureau there.

Cardiss Robertson Collins is the first woman to chair the Congressional Black Caucus.

NOW and other groups head off attempts to revoke ERA ratification in 13 states. They do not, however, gain any new states.

Owanah Anderson (b. 1926) starts the Ohoyo Resource Center, which publishes *Ohoyo One Thousand: A Resource Guide of American Indian/ Alaska Native Women* in 1982.

The first National March for Lesbian and Gay Rights brings about 100,000 demonstrators to the capital.

Both lesbians and black women are upset when Arlie Scott, an "out" lesbian, and Sharon Parker, an African American, lose the elections for NOW vice president and secretary, respectively. At the newly formed Black American Political Association of California, Aileen Hernandez, former NOW president, criticizes the group for not electing even one woman of color to national office.

1980

Mary Frances Berry and Blandina Cárdenas Ramírez (b. 1944) are appointed to the U.S. Commission on Civil Rights. Ramírez is the first Hispanic American on the commission.

Initiated by NOW, the National Judicial Education Program to Promote Equality for Women and Men in the Courts aims to inform judges about gender bias, which affects divorce, child support, and other legal issues. Norma Wikler is the first director, followed by Lynn Hecht Schafran in 1981.

Ruth Bader Ginsburg becomes a judge on the U.S. Court of Appeals in the District of Columbia and serves until 1993.

At the instigation of Australian physician and activist Helen Caldicott, Women's Action for Nuclear Disarmament (WAND) forms to lobby the U.S. government for a nuclear-free world.

During the Women's Pentagon Action, 2,000 women encircle the Pentagon to protest U.S. militarism, and 140 are arrested for blocking the three main entrances. Women also erect gravestones for the women killed by government actions.

Geraldine Ferraro chairs the Democratic Party Platform Committee. At the convention, women are almost 50% of the voting delegates and ensure a strong ERA and pro-choice platform. Thousands of women demonstrate outside the Republican National Convention when the party refuses to include the ERA in its platform. In related protest one black woman carries as sign reading: "Will the party that freed the slaves becomes the party that enslaves women?"

Women's Rights National History Park is established in Seneca Falls, New York, and includes both the site of the 1848 convention and Elizabeth Cady Stanton's home.

As the official U.S. representative, Sarah Weddington signs the UN Convention on the Elimination of All Forms of Discrimination Against Women at the mid-decade UN International Women's Conference.

Congress passes a law requiring the State Department to expand opportunities for women and minorities.

About 1,000 women attend the First National Hispanic Feminist Conference, initiated by Sylvia Gonzales of NOW.

Many Native women participate in the Long Walk from California to the UN in New York to protest the treatment of Indians (see sidebar).

In one of the largest demonstrations ever in Chicago, some 90,000 ERA supporters press for passage of the amendment. The vote in the Illinois legislature, however, is two short of the needed three-fifths majority. No states pass the ERA during the year.

Republican Paula Hawkins is the first woman senator from Florida. Carol Kawanami is the first Japanese American woman to be elected mayor, in Villa Park, Orange County, California.

1981

Sandra Day O'Connor (b. 1930) is the first woman appointed to the U.S. Supreme Court. Her experience includes service in Arizona as an assistant attorney general, a state senator and majority leader (the first woman), an elected city superior court judge, and a justice on the state court of appeals. At the time of her appointment, women represent only 5.4% of all federal judges and less than 5% of state court judges.

Jeane Jordan Kirkpatrick, a Georgetown University political science professor, is appointed as the first woman to serve as permanent U.S. ambassador to the UN. Later she comments: "I suppose the first time I

"This Doesn't Reach the News"

"When we walk, it's a spiritual walk, it's a prayer, it's a sacrifice and a suffering. We walk to establish, even for five minutes, a dialogue. . . . We want a world court so we can have our say. There's no justice for Native people in this country. All of us who are walking, we face repression—phones being tapped, murder; 300 people missing around South Dakota. This doesn't reach the news. When women are being sterilized, this doesn't reach the news. . . . We are America's best-kept secret, the skeleton in America's closet, the Indian people."
    —Rocky Olguin, interviewed by Merle Temkin, in *Heresies: A Feminist Magazine on Art and Politics,* issue 13: *Feminism and Ecology* (1981)

Against Equal Rights

Although 35 states ratify the Equal Rights Amendment, *15 do not. The states that oppose the ERA are:*

- —*Alabama*
- —*Arizona*
- —*Arkansas*
- —*Florida*
- —*Georgia*
- —*Illinois*
- —*Louisiana*
- —*Mississippi*
- —*Missouri*
- —*Nevada*
- —*North Carolina*
- —*Oklahoma*
- —*South Carolina*
- —*Utah*
- —*Virginia*

*There are 4 states that vote to rescind their earlier passage of the ERA, but this is not thought to be constitutional.

thought about the diplomatic corps, as an exclusive male preserve, was when I was at the UN and realized that not only was I the first woman ever to represent the United States . . . I was the first woman to represent any major power."

Julia Chang Bloch is appointed assistant administrator in the Agency for International Development in Washington, D.C., the highest position at the time for an Asian American woman.

Kathy Niederhofer Whitmire becomes mayor of Houston, the fourth largest U.S. city. She serves for 10 years, and during this time other women rise to such positions of power within the city as chief of police, superintendent of schools, and district chief of the city hospitals.

When Harriet Elizabeth ("Liz") Byrd enters the Wyoming House of Representatives, she is the first African American legislator in the state.

The National Bar Association, a group of African American lawyers, chooses Arnetta R. Hubbard as its first woman president.

Sharon Parker and Veronica Collazo start the National Institute for Women of Color to build connections between different groups.

Janet McCloud establishes the Northwest Indian Women's Circle.

Women's groups increase their efforts to secure the ERA before the deadline expires in 1982. NOW mounts a major ERA Countdown campaign with former First Lady Betty Ford as honorary chair and Alan Alda as co-chair. Polls show that 63% of Americans support the ERA, with only 32% opposed. Yet no new states ratify the ERA.

In *Kirchberg v. Feenstra* the U.S. Supreme Court unanimously strikes down a Louisiana law that let a husband dispose of joint marital property without his wife's consent.

1982

Aiko Yoshinaga Herzig, while working for the government Commission on Wartime Relocation and Internment of Civilians, uncovers key documents showing that the army knew there was no "military necessity" for interning Japanese Americans during World War II but went ahead anyhow. Her research backs up the words of numerous Japanese American women, who break a silence of 40 years to speak of their internment experiences at congressional hearings (see 1988).

On June 30, the deadline for ratification, the ERA is still 3 states short of the 38 needed for ratification (see sidebar). Among the main arguments used to defeat the amendment are the specter of women being drafted and forced to serve in combat, the potential loss of alimony and child custody preference in divorce cases, and the possibility that tax money would have to be used for abortions. Antifeminists also stress absurd but highly symbolic scenarios, such as unisex public toilets.

To counter a speech by Phyllis Schlafly in Cleveland, Ohio, a group of activists called "Ladies Against Women" show up adorned with neat hats and white gloves and carrying signs with messages like "Suffering Not Suffrage."

Mildred Imach Cleghorn (b. 1910), who was born in captivity in Fort Sill, Oklahoma, becomes the leader of the Fort Sill Chiricahua/Warm Springs Apache Tribe.

In the elections women double their seats in the state senates of two anti-ERA states: Florida (from four to nine) and Illinois (from four to eight). In California, Barbara Levy Boxer (b. 1940), a Democrat, wins election to the U.S. House, where she serves for 10 years; Gloria Molina (b. 1948) is the first Chicana elected to the state assembly; and Loretta Glickman is the first black woman elected as mayor of a city with more than 100,000 people, in Pasadena.

Betty Bumpers starts Peace Links to boost the number of women in the peace movement; she also forms Grandmothers for Peace.

At the urging of Judge Marilyn Loftus, New Jersey appoints the first Task Force on Women in the Courts, to investigate gender bias in the judicial system. During the next decade many other states appoint similar study groups; all discover widespread gender bias.

Maine schoolgirl Samantha Smith writes a letter to Soviet prime minister Yuri Andropov, asking for peace. She is invited on a much-publicized trip to the USSR and continues her efforts for peace on her return. She is killed in a plane crash with her father in 1985.

1983

Elizabeth Hanford Dole (b. 1936) is named secretary of transportation, serving until 1987, and Margaret Heckler becomes secretary of health and human services, serving to 1985. Katherine D. Ortega (b. 1934) is named U.S. treasurer and serves six years. Linda Chavez (b. 1947) becomes staff director for the U.S. Commission on Civil Rights; she later issues a controversial memo opposing quotas and affirmative action.

President Ronald Reagan fires three women on the U.S. Commission on Civil Rights—Mary Frances Berry, Blandina Ramírez, and Jill Ruckelshaus—when they criticize his record on civil rights. Berry and Ramírez sue to be reinstated and win their case in court.

In the last 12 years the number of women in state legislatures has risen from 362 to 992, and the number of women in Congress from 11 to 24, although this is still less than 5%.

Inspired by British women's camping out at Greenham Common to protest the deployment of nuclear missiles, U.S. activists set up the Women's Peace Encampment outside the Seneca Army Depot in New York. On July 30 about 135 women begin a peaceful 15-mile walk from Seneca Falls to the site of the encampment in honor of the earlier women activists of Seneca Falls and "to bring their courageous spirit to the Encampment." In the town of Waterloo, they are confronted by a shouting, flag-waving mob; when they sit down to avoid violence, 54

"Not a Very Threatening Walk"

"There were about 135 of us. Walking to honor our women's history, written, unwritten. To honor in particular the history of women from this country. Not a very threatening walk, you might have thought."
—Barbara Deming, "A New Spirit Moves Among Us," 1984

"Our intent was to walk, not to do civil disobedience. We sat to diffuse the violence, to decide our course, and to make the denial of our constitutional rights clear. One of the things we love most about our country is the Bill of RIghts. These rights were denied when the police . . . arrested us instead of the people threatening us."
—Statement of the Waterloo 54, Waterloo, New York, 1983; both quotes in Barbara Deming, *Prisons That Could Not Hold* (San Francisco: Spinsters Ink, 1985)

are arrested (see sidebar). Later, when supporters begin a vigil around the school used as a jail, the governor calls in the state police.

Coretta Scott King leads half a million protestors in a 20th-anniversary renewal of the seminal 1963 civil rights march.

Irma Vidal Santaella is the first Puerto Rican justice on New York's state supreme court. Earlier she helped draft provisions to eliminate English literacy tests and thus protect Latinos' voting rights.

As a result of a discrimination suit filed by Ellen Starer, a national insurance company agrees to make disability rates the same for men and women in Pennsylvania. To draw attention to continuing inequities in the insurance industry that cost women at least $1 billion a year, NOW activists stage protests across the country in June.

In Kentucky, Martha Layne Collins (b. 1936), who has served as lieutenant governor since 1978, is the first woman elected to be governor. She quickly acts to improve educational standards, restrict strip mining, and institute other reforms.

In Monterey, California, Lily Chen is elected as the first Chinese American woman mayor in the country.

"All issues . . . are women's issues"—Geraldine Ferraro

1984

Congress passes the Retirement Equity Act, cosponsored by Geraldine Ferraro—a law making it easier for women, especially widows and divorcees, to collect benefits under pension plans. Congress also enacts the Child Support Amendments, introduced by Representative Barbara Kennelly of Connecticut, which require withholding of wages and interstate enforcement of child-support orders. These provisions are later strengthened by the 1988 Family Support Act.

Shirley Chisholm and C. DeLores Tucker (b. 1927) start the National Political Congress of Black Women to encourage African American women to run for office and assume leadership positions. In four years it has 8,500 members.

Peggy Noonan leaves CBS News to serve as speechwriter for President Reagan and quickly shows his staff the value of sound bites.

When Geraldine Ferraro becomes Walter Mondale's running mate on the Democratic Party ticket, it is the first time a woman is nominated for vice president in one of the two major parties. Although she is a Roman Catholic, Ferraro refuses to impose her church's views on others and insists on a woman's right to choose an abortion—a position that is attacked by the church. Later, after losing the election, she describes the difficulties of her campaign in *Ferraro: My Story* (1985; see sidebar opposite).

Several other women are also candidates in this election: Sonia Johnson (p. 216) runs for president on the Citizens Party ticket; Nancy

Ross is the Alliance Party's vice-presidential candidate; and Angela Davis is nominated for vice president by the Communist Party.

U.S. treasurer Katherine D. Ortega (b. 1934) gives the keynote speech at the Republican Convention.

Aulana L. Peters (b. 1941) is the first African American woman on the Securities and Exchange Commission.

Winona LaDuke and Ingrid Washinawatok set up the Indigenous Women's Network, and about 200 women attend the first meeting in 1985. The group soon begins publishing *Indigenous Women.*

Mary Frances Berry, a leader of the Free South Africa movement, is one of a number of prominent African Americans arrested in demonstrations against apartheid and U.S. policies toward South Africa.

In Vermont, Madeline May Kunin (b. 1933), a former lieutenant governor, wins a close race for governor. She is the first woman and the first Jew elected to this office in the state. In her first term she eliminates the state's deficit, increases educational spending, and introduces strong environmental protections. She is reelected in 1986 and 1988.

1985

In the last 15 years the number of Asian American women in elected office has increased from 4 to 40, all in the West, mostly in California and Hawaii—but Patricia Saiki of Hawaii is the only one in Congress.

Ellen Malcolm starts EMILY's List to give financial backing to pro-choice Democratic women candidates for state and federal office. The name "EMILY" stands for "Early Money Is Like Yeast."

Bella Abzug helps start the Women's Foreign Policy Council, which aims to increase the participation of women in foreign policy decisions. Other groups promoting women's visibility in foreign policy include Women for Meaningful Summits and the Jane Addams Conference.

Rozanne L. Ridgway, former ambassador to East Germany, is named assistant secretary for European and Canadian affairs.

When the present chief resigns in December, Wilma P. Mankiller (b. 1945), elected deputy chief in 1983, becomes the first woman principal chief of the Cherokee Nation in Oklahoma, with more than 67,000 members. Elected in her own right in 1987, she is reelected by a landslide in 1991. "For Cherokee women," she later says, "serving in leadership roles in government and other professions represents a return to the matrilineal traditions that were prevalent prior to European contact, a tradition I have relied on in serving all Cherokee people."

Montana is the first state to forbid sex discrimination in all insurance.

California state senator Diane Watson starts the National Organization of Black Elected Legislative Women to increase the numbers in both elected and appointed state positions.

"I Ran As a Woman"

". . . I wanted people to vote for me not because I was a woman, but because they thought I would make the best Vice President.

"There is no doubt, however, that I ran as a woman, and brought a different perspective. . . .

"The discrimination toward women in my lifetime alone had been outrageous. And I had felt it every step of the way. . . .

"Even after three years in Congress, I could not get a VISA card from Citibank the first time around. . . . And I was a woman with clout. What about women who were not members of Congress?"

—Geraldine A. Ferraro, in *Ferraro: My Story,* with Linda Bird Franke (New York: Bantam Books, 1985)

"Elect More . . . Women"

"The best way to assure recognition of women's political concerns is to elect more officeholders who not only are pro-women's issues but are women themselves. Women should think seriously about running for office and encourage other women to do so. The quickest way for us to elect more women to public office is for more women to run as candidates. Running for office requires enormous drive, determination, and an understanding of the realities of getting elected. But it is also easier than you might think."

—Eleanor Smeal, "Women on the Ballot—And in Office," in *Why and How Women Will Elect the Next President* (New York: Harper & Row, 1984)

Maureen Reagan leads the American delegation to the UN Conference on Women in Nairobi, marking the end of the Decade for Women. Sissy Farenthold and 40 other women from 15 countries organize Peace Tents to encourage dialogue between U.S. and Soviet and Israeli and Palestinian women. About 2,000 U.S. women are among the 15,000 at the meeting, which seeds many international connections.

Attorney Antonia Hernández (b. 1948) takes over as president and general counsel for the Mexican American Legal Defense and Education Fund (MADLEF) and fights to protect immigrants' rights.

Marie Prezioso of West Virginia is the first female president of Young Democrats of America.

1986

Congress approves 6 of the 22 provisions of the Economic Equity Act, backed by the Congressional Caucus for Women's Issues. Included are pensions reforms, a greater tax deduction for a single head of household, and continuation of health insurance coverage for widows, divorcees, and their children.

Some 125,000 women join the March for Women's Lives to protect abortion and birth control rights (see "Health").

Barbara Mikulski, congresswoman from Maryland, defeats Republican candidate Linda Chavez to become the first Democratic woman elected to the Senate without succeeding her husband. Her election doubles the number of women in the Senate—from one to two.

Two women also oppose each other in the Nebraska gubernatorial race: Republican Kay Stark Orr and Democrat Helen Boosalis. Orr wins, becoming the first woman elected governor of Nebraska. She serves until 1991.

1987

The National Women's Conference Committee issues *Decade of Achievement, 1977–1987,* edited by Susanna Downie. The report underlines the growth of grass-roots women's groups, including rape crisis centers, battered women's shelters, and women's centers, as well as the networking around such issues as childcare, pay equity, health care, and family leave (for discussions of these developments, see "Work," "Social Change," and "Health").

To push for a range of women's concerns, former NOW president Eleanor Smeal, Peg Yorkin, Toni Carabillo, Judith Meuli, and Kathy Spillar start the Fund for the Feminist Majority. One of their first actions is a campaign to urge feminists to run for office (see sidebar).

After her son is lynched, Beulah Mae Donald sues the United Klans of America and secures a $7 million judgment, effectively eliminating that branch of the Ku Klux Klan.

In Michigan, Dorothy Comstock Riley (b. 1924) becomes chief justice of the state supreme court after serving as an associate justice since 1982. She is the first Latina in this position.

Alison Palmer and the Women's Action Organization win their class action suit against the State Department for sex discrimination in the foreign service. At the time only 4.8% of senior foreign service officers are women.

The Supreme Court rules that male-only clubs like the Rotary Clubs violate laws against discrimination in public accommodations. Earlier, in 1984, the court ruled that the Jaycees must admit woman members.

Women gain important mayoral victories. After serving seven years as a state legislator, Carrie Saxon Perry (b. 1931) is the first black woman elected as mayor of a major city, in Hartford, Connecticut. When Annette Strauss is elected mayor of Dallas and Betty Turner wins in Corpus Christi, the state of Texas has female mayors in four large cities; the other two are Kathy Whitmire in Houston (who is reelected) and Janice Coggeshall in Galveston. In North Carolina, Sue Myrick is elected mayor of Charlotte.

In San Francisco women's rights advocate Nancy Pelosi (b. 1940) wins the congressional seat of the late Sala Burton.

1988

Congress passes the Civil Rights Restoration Act to strengthen anti-discrimination provisions that had been weakened by Supreme Court decisions. For example, it restores the full thrust of the prohibition of sex discrimination in education, which had been limited by the Supreme Court in *Grove City College* v. *Bell* (see "Education"). The law also includes the Danforth Amendment, which does allow federally funded institutions to refuse to perform abortions. Although President Reagan vetoes the act, Congress overrides him.

Partly through the intense lobbying efforts of Grayce Uyehara of the Japanese American Citizens League, Congress apologizes for the internment of Japanese Americans during World War II and agrees to pay reparations.

The Supreme Court upholds a New York City ordinance prohibiting discrimination in clubs that have more than 400 members, offer regular meals, and accept nonmember payments (such as a business paying an employee's dues). Essentially, this law bans certain men-only clubs where business deals were worked out over lunch.

At the urging of the National Women's Political Caucus, 45 groups join in the bipartisan Coalition for Women's Appointments to push for more women appointees in top-level government jobs.

To increase their visibility and underline issues of concern to African American women, 13 women mayors form the Black Women Mayors' Caucus. In four years their number has increased to 66.

After almost 30 years as a judge in Philadelphia, Juanita Kidd Stout becomes the first African American woman on a state supreme court, in Philadelphia. She has to retire in 1989, when she turns 70.

Susan Estrich (b. 1952), a law professor at Harvard University and the first woman president of the *Harvard Law Review* (in 1976), manages the campaign of Democrat Michael Dukakis for president (she began in 1987). She is the first woman to do this for a major party.

Texas state treasurer (Dorothy) Ann Willis Richards (b. 1933) gains attention for her feisty keynote speech at the Democratic National Convention. Peggy Noonan is credited with writing much of George Bush's acceptance speech at the Republican nomination.

Running for president on the New Alliance Party ticket, Lenora Fulani is the first woman and the first African American to be listed as a candidate on the ballots of all 50 states.

1989

Elizabeth Dole, former secretary of transportation, becomes secretary of labor in the Bush administration, serving until 1990. Carla Hills, former secretary of housing and urban development, serves in the cabinet as U.S. trade representative, negotiating trade agreements and trying to expand markets abroad. (For other appointments, see sidebar.)

Late in the year, pediatrician Antonia C. Novello (b. 1944), director of the National Institute of Child Health and Human Development, is the first woman and first Latina appointed U.S. surgeon general. Attention focuses on her opposition to abortion, but she stresses her "message of empowerment for women, children, and minorities."

The new Congress has the most women to date: 25 representatives and 2 senators. In a special election later in the year, Indiana Democrat Jill Long wins a seat in the U.S. House, bringing the total to 26 there.

Judith Chang Bloch is the first Asian American to become a U.S. ambassador, to Nepal.

Madeleine Korbel Albright (b. 1937) becomes president of the Center of National Policy.

After receiving the Reebok Human Rights Award, activist Winona LaDuke starts the White Earth Land Recovery Project, to return some of the land originally promised to the Chippewa in Minnesota.

The Leadership Conference for Female Chiefs meets for the first time.

Women mayors make new gains. Civil rights activist Unita Blackwell chairs the National Conference of Black Mayors. In Texas the four biggest cities have women mayors: El Paso (Suzie Azar), Dallas (Annette Strauss), Houston (Kathy Whitmire), and San Antonio (Lila Cockrell)—with the last three among the ten largest U.S. cities. In Hialeah Gardens, Florida, Gilda Oliveros becomes the first Cuban American woman mayor in the country.

After serving for seven years in the Florida state legislature, Ileana Ros-Lehtinen (b. 1952) is elected to the U.S. House. A conservative Republican who strongly opposes abortion and Fidel Castro, she is the the first Cuban American in the House.

1990

To draw attention to the Wintu people's appeal for tribal recognition by the government, Caleen A. Sisk-Franco (b. 1952), chair of the Toyon Wintu Center in California, goes on a 21-day hunger strike.

In its revised Code of Judicial Conduct, the American Bar Association specifically lists sexual harassment as misconduct and prohibits judges from belonging to discriminatory groups.

Three women, all Democrats, win governorships: Joan Finney in Kansas, Ann Richards in Texas, and Barbara Roberts in Oregon. In California, Democrat Dianne Feinstein loses to Pete Wilson by only three percentage points. Altogether 6 women are elected lieutenant governor, 10 secretary of state, 3 attorney general, and 12 state treasurer. In the U.S. House, women win 28 of 435 seats (less than 6%). Among the new members are Maxine Waters of Los Angeles and Eleanor Holmes Norton, a nonvoting delegate from Washington, D.C.

Washington, D.C., elects its first woman mayor: Sharon Pratt Dixon (later Kelly, b. 1944). She is the first black woman to head one of the top 20 cities in the country.

Representative Lynn Martin of Illinois is named the new secretary of labor after Elizabeth Dole resigns to head the American Red Cross.

1991

Minnesota becomes the first state with a majority of women on its supreme court.

Gloria Molina becomes the first woman on the influential Los Angeles County Board of Supervisors. She is also the first Hispanic supervisor in more than 100 years.

Nadine Strossen (b. 1950) becomes the first woman president of the American Civil Liberties Union.

As the new director of the Peace Corps, Elaine L. Chao is the top-ranking Asian American in the Bush administration.

Debbie Doxtator is chairperson of the Oneida in Wisconsin, and six of the nine council members are women. Doxtator helps build a successful gambling business. "I think [money] is important," she says, "because tribal governments have been stymied from operating their governments for a number of years due to their dependent relationship with the U.S. government."

In October, National Public Radio exposes a report made by law professor Anita Hill (b. 1956) to the Senate Judiciary Committee that Supreme Court nominee Clarence Thomas sexually harassed her when

"The response to my Senate Judiciary Committee testimony has been at once heartwarming and heart-wrenching. In learning that I am not alone in experiencing harassment, I am also learning that there are far too many women who have experienced a range of inexcusable and illegal activities—from sexist jokes to sexual assault—on the job. . . .

"How do we capture our rage and turn it into positive energy? Through the power of women working together, whether it be in the political arena, or in the context of a lawsuit, or in community service. . . . Making the workplace a safer, more productive place for ourselves and our daughters should be on the agenda for each of us."
—Anita Hill, "The Nature of the Beast," *Ms.* (January–February 1992)

she worked for him a decade earlier. The all-male committee doesn't even consider the charges—at least not until outraged women politicians and activists demand that the Senate postpone confirmation until Hill's charges are given a full hearing. Millions of Americans watch the drama unfold on television, as Hill and Thomas present their totally different accounts. Although the Senate confirms Thomas 52 to 48, the issue of sexual harassment has been highlighted (see sidebar and section on "Work"). Moreover, appalled at the attacks on Hill's character during the hearings, feminists throughout the country vow to change the overwhelmingly male composition of Congress in the next elections. In the last few months of the year, NOW is flooded with 13,000 new members.

Journalist Susan Faludi publishes *Backlash: The Undeclared War Against American Women,* documenting the attacks on women's progress during the last decade. She points out that "the antifeminist backlash has been set off not by women's achievement of full equality but by the increased possibility that they might win it. It is a preemptive strike that stops women long before they reach the finish line."

After much compromising, the Civil Rights Act of 1991 is signed into law with provisions to protect against job discrimination, although these are weaker than originally intended.

1992

In this election year, women's groups launch an all-out effort to put more women in office. Fund for the Feminist Majority mounts its "Feminization of Power" drive, coordinated by Katherine Spillar. EMILY's List, the Women's Campaign Fund, and other groups raise money for a record number of candidates. NOW, led by Patricia Ireland, sponsors an "Elect Women for a Change" campaign. NOW also helps organize the 21st Century Party, a national party committed to both diversity and an equal representation of women in political office.

In New York, enraged by the treatment of Anita Hill, the Women's Action Coalition (WAC) forms as a nonhierarchical "alliance of women committed to *direct action* on issues affecting the rights of all women." Hundreds of women, energized by a corps of drummers, join with other groups to protest court treatment of rape victims, nonpayment of child support, threats to abortion laws, and other concerns. Soon 35 cities have their own WACs.

To protest the government's refusal to admit Haitian refuges, 83-year-old choreographer Katherine Dunham stages a hunger strike.

Affirming "We Won't Go Back! We Will Fight Back!" a record 750,000 protestors join a NOW-sponsored March for Women's Lives in the capital to protect the right of choice.

Barbara Franklin is appointed secretary of commerce, joining Lynn Martin and Carla Hills in the cabinet. Shirley D. Peterson becomes the first woman to head the Internal Revenue Service.

In Indiana, Pamela Fanning Carter becomes the first black woman appointed as state attorney general.

Three Latinas are appointed as federal judges: Irma Gonzalez and Lourdes G. Baird in California and Sonia Sotomayor in New York, where she is the first Latina on the Southern District Court.

At the Democratic National Convention, Barbara Jordan, former Texas representative in the House, gives the keynote speech. Governor Ann Richards of Texas chairs the convention, and Senator Barbara Mikulski nominates Albert Gore for vice president. Gloria Molina cochairs William ("Bill") Jefferson Clinton's campaign

At the Republican National Convention, Secretary of Labor Lynn Martin nominates George Bush for president, and Barbara Bush and Marilyn Quayle, as the wives of the candidates, are featured speakers on the campaign theme of "family values." The most moving speech, however, is a plea for AIDS understanding given by Mary Fisher, an HIV-positive mother.

A record number of women run for office, leading to a record number of women in office. The election adds four new women (all Democrats) to the Senate, tripling the number from two to six. California, the country's most populous state, elects two women senators: representative Barbara Boxer (for a full term) and former San Francisco mayor Dianne Feinstein (for a partial term; see 1994). Illinois elects the first black woman senator, Carol Moseley-Braun (b. 1947), who served as an Illinois state representative for 10 years and in 1987 became the first African American in an executive position in Cook County, as recorder of deeds. She is the only African American in the Senate at the time and only the second since Reconstruction. Washington state elects its first woman senator: Patty Murray (b. 1950), who served in the state senate.

In the U.S. House 48 women are elected, including a number of firsts. Leslie Byrne (b. 1946), a Democrat, is the first woman elected to Congress from Virginia; Eva Clayton (b. 1934), a Democrat, is the first congresswoman from North Carolina and one of the first two African Americans from that state since Reconstruction; Cynthia McKinney (b. 1955), a Democrat, is the first African American congresswoman from Georgia; Carrie Meek (b. 1926), Democrat, is the first black congresswoman from Florida; Lucille Roybal-Allard (b. 1941), a California Democrat, is the first Mexican American congresswoman; and Nydia Margarita Velázquez (b. 1953), a New York City Democrat, is the first Puerto Rican congresswoman.

1993

Women hold a record number of positions in state as well as federal government (see also 1992 election results above). They now represent 20.4% of the state legislators—and almost 40% in the state of Washington. Three women are governors (see 1990), 11 lieutenant governors, 8 attorneys general, 13 secretaries of state, and 19 state treasurers.

Women are mayors in 19 of the top 100 U.S. cities, including the second and third largest cities in California: San Diego (Susan Goldring) and San Jose (Susan Hammer).

The all-male Senate Judiciary Committee, which angered many feminists for its interrogation of Anita Hill, gains two female members: Senators Dianne Feinstein and Carol Moseley-Braun. Pat Schroeder and Marilyn Lloyd chair two subcommittees of the House Armed Services Committee, but there are still no woman chairs of any of the standing full committees.

President William ("Bill") Jefferson Clinton's administration includes a record number of women at top levels: Madeleine Albright, former director of the Center for National Policy, is the second woman ambassador to the UN (after Jeane Kirkpatrick under Reagan). Carol M. Browner (b. 1955), former secretary of environmental regulation in Florida, heads the Environmental Protection Agency, a post given cabinet status. Jocelyn Elders (b. 1933), a pediatrician and former head of the Arkansas Public Health Department, becomes the first female African American surgeon general. Hazel R. O'Leary (b. 1938), former power company executive and a Department of Energy regulator under Presidents Ford and Carter, is secretary of energy, the first woman and the first African American to hold this post. Janet Reno (b. 1938), former state prosecutor in Dade County, Florida, is the first woman attorney general. (Clinton's first choice, Zoë E. Baird, is forced to withdraw because she hired an illegal immigrant to care for her children. Clinton's second choice, Kimba M. Wood, withdraws because of media attention to the "Nannygate" issue—even though she did nothing illegal and always paid Social Security taxes for her help.) Donna E. Shalala, former chancellor of the University of Wisconsin at Madison, is secretary of health and human services. Laura D'Andrea Tyson, an economics professor, is the first woman to chair the Council of Economic Advisors.

Among the other important appointments are gay rights activist Roberta Achtenberg as assistant secretary for fair housing and equal opportunity, actress Jane Alexander as chair of the National Endowment for the Arts, Harriet C. Babbitt as permanent representative to the Organization of the American States, Carol Bellamy as director of the Peace Corps, Bonnie Cohen as chief financial officer and aassistant secretary of the interior for policy management and budget, Lynn E. Davis as undersecretary for international security affairs, Menominee activist Ada Deer as the first woman assistant secretary for Indian affairs, Mary Lowe Good as undersecretary for technology in the Department of Commerce, Jo Ann Harris as head of the Justice Department's criminal division, Judith Heumann as assistant secretary for special education and rehabilitative services, Madeleine Kunin as deputy secretary of education, Dee Dee Myers as press secretary, Karen Nussbaum (former executive director of 9 to 5, the National Association of Working Women) as head of the Women's Bureau in the

Department of Labor, Alice M. Rivlin as deputy director of the Office of Management and Budget, Joan Spero as undersecretary of state for economic and agricultural affairs, and Sheila Widnall as secretary of the Air Force in the Defense Department.

However, when Lani Guinier, a law professor and former NAACP attorney, is proposed for assistant attorney general, she is attacked by the right for her strong affirmative action stance and forced to withdraw.

Pamela Digby Churchill Harriman, a major Democratic Party fundraiser, is the first woman ambassador to France.

Republican Kay Bailey Hutchinson, former Texas state treasurer, wins the U.S. Senate seat left vacant by Secretary of the Treasury Lloyd Benson. The total number of women in the Senate is now seven.

First Lady Hillary Rodham Clinton (b. 1947) is named as chair of the administration's task force on health care reform. Later she consults with the Congressional Caucus for Women's Issues.

Ruth Bader Ginsburg, who is at the time serving on the U.S. Court of Appeals in the District of Columbia and has successfully argued several important women's rights cases before the Supreme Court, is appointed as the second woman on the U.S. Supreme Court (see sidebar). She is the first Jewish justice on the court in 24 years.

Judith Kaye becomes the first woman chief judge of the New York Court of Appeals, and Carmen Beauchamp Ciparick, a former state supreme court justice, is the first Puerto Rican woman on the federal court of appeals in New York.

Elaine Jones is the first woman director of the NAACP Legal Defense and Education Fund.

Protesting the continued imprisonment of Indian rights activist Leonard Peltier and highlighting other issues of concern to Native Americans, Mary Jane Wilson is a one of the leaders of the "Walk for Justice" from Alcatraz in San Francisco to Washington, D.C.

Carrie and Mary Dann win the Right Livelihood Award, known as "the alternative Nobel Peace Prize," for their battle on behalf of the Western Shoshone to protect their land.

Defying Ku Klux Klan threats, Ruth Woods, mayor of Vidor, Texas, carries out the integration of public housing ordered by the courts.

Former radical Katherine Ann Power, a fugitive from the FBI since 1970, gains media attention when she turns herself in and is sentenced for her part in a bank robbery during which a policeman was killed.

Secretary of Energy Hazel O'Leary goes public with information that the government conducted radiation experiments on unsuspecting citizens during the 1940s and 1950s; she acknowledges the government's responsibility for this injustice and seeks restitution for the victims.

"At Least Half the Talent Pool"

"The announcement the president just made . . . . contributes to the end of the days when women, at least half the talent pool of our society, appear in high places only as one-at-a-time performers. Recall that when President Carter took office in 1976, no woman had ever served on the Supreme Court, and only one woman, Shirley Hofstedler of California, then served at the next federal court level, the United States Court of Appeals.

"Today Justice Sandra Day O'Connor graces the Supreme Court bench, and close to 25 women serve at the federal Court of Appeals level, two as chief judges. I am confident that more will soon join them."
—Ruth Bader Ginsburg, speech after nomination to Supreme Court by President Clinton, June 1993; quoted in *The 1995 Information Please Women's Sourcebook*, edited by Lisa DiMona and Constance Herndon (Boston: Houghton Mifflin, 1994)

Only 12 Women Governors

Only 11 states have ever had women governors, and only one (Texas) has ever had a second woman governor:
—Alabama (Lurleen Wallace)
—Connecticut (Ella Grasso)
—Kansas (Joan Finney)
—Kentucky (Martha Layne Collins)
—Nebraska (Kay Orr)
—New Jersey (Christine Todd Whitman)
—Oregon (Barbara Roberts)
—Texas (Miriam Ferguson and Ann Richards)
—Vermont (Madeleine Kunin)
—Washington (Dixy Lee Ray)
—Wyoming (Nellie Tayloe Ross)

Republican Christine Todd Whitman is the first woman elected governor of New Jersey (see sidebar). In Minneapolis, Sharon Sayles Belton is the first woman and first African American elected mayor.

1994

For the first time the U.S. Department of Justice has a majority of 9 women in the 15 top-level positions: Attorney General Janet Reno, Deputy Attorney General Jamie Gorelick, six assistant attorneys general, and the head of the Environment and Natural Resources Division.

Roberta Cooper Ramo is the first woman elected president of the American Bar Association since its founding in 1878. Martha Barnett is in the second most powerful position, as chair of the House of Delegates. Ramo says, "I may be the first woman president of the ABA, but I'm not going to be the last."

Adelante Con Nuestra Visión is the first national leadership conference for Latina lesbians.

Lois De Berry, Tennessee speaker pro-tempore, is the first female president of the National Caucus of Black State Legislators.

Patricia Fleming replaces Kristine Gebbie as the country's AIDS czar.

Congress passes the Violence Against Women Act (see "Social Change"). This is just one of the 66 bills of importance to women enacted during the two-year tenure of the 103d Congress.

In the midterm elections women lose five seats overall in the House. Of the eight new Republican congresswomen, all but one oppose abortion.

1995

The 10 states with the most women in their legislatures are, in order: Washington, Nevada, Colorado, Arizona, Utah, New Hampshire, Oregon, Maryland, Idaho, and Kansas. The state with the fewest women legislators is Alabama.

Myrlie Evers-Williams, who fought 31 years to put the racist killer of her first husband, Medgar Evers, in jail, is elected chair of the NAACP.

Three years after 10 women first alleged improper sexual advances, Senator Robert Packwood resigns.

As executive director, Nora Slatkin is the first woman to hold a senior post at the Central Intelligence Agency.

In August women across the country celebrate the 75th anniversary of women's suffrage.

At the UN's Fourth World Conference on Women in Beijing, First Lady Hillary Rodham Clinton speaks out against abuses against women. "It is a violation of human rights when women are denied the right to plan their own families, and that includes being forced to have abortions or being sterilized against their will."

Work and Entrepreneurship

"Rosita the Riveter": Southern Pacific workers during World War II
(Arizona Historical Society/Tucson #63527)

Early Native Women at Work

Native American women perform a variety of tasks. They are primarily responsible for raising crops: plowing the land and otherwise preparing the soil, sowing the seed, weeding and tending to the plants, and finally harvesting the food. Cotton, corn, beans, and squash are some of the crops they grow, as well as medicinal herbs. Women then prepare the food, drying vegetables and curing meat brought back by male hunters. In the Northeast they also tap maple sugar. Clothing is made by the women, who tan animal hides. Some weave blankets and baskets. Some even construct the homes, putting up the tipis, for example. In addition, women care for and teach the children. Most of this work is done communally.

1600s

European women settlers produce much of what their families eat and use. Although the men usually plow the land, the women tend to the crops, help with the harvest, and cook or preserve the food. Learning much from Indian women, the settler women collect and dry wild herbs for medicinal and other uses. They spin and dye their own yarn, weave their own fabrics, and sew their family's clothes by hand. Candles and soap are also made at home, and sometimes women construct furniture. Whatever is needed to keep the family business going, women do. Some shoe horses, run the mill, keep the books, grind eyeglasses, mind the store, or stitch uppers to the soles of shoes.

Women also work as indentured servants for five to seven years to pay off the cost of their trip to the colonies. If they are lucky, they may receive a reward of land or money at the end of their term. Under their contracts, they are not allowed to marry, and usually if they become pregnant, they have to work extra time. Their work is similar to that of other women settlers, but they usually do the heavy labor and least desirable tasks, from hauling buckets of water to herding and milking the cows. Later a few women serve as indentured apprentices, learning how to be a midwife or seamstress, but this is not common.

In 1638 Margaret Brent (c. 1600–71) arrives in Maryland, where she and her sister, Mary, receive the first known land grant to women and set up their own estate. Margaret Brent's name later appears in many court records, indicating that she handles her own business affairs. In 1647 she is the sole executor of Governor Calvert's estate (see p. 11).

One of the first American women known to run a printing press is Mrs. Jose Glover in Cambridge, Massachusetts, in 1638.

In the 1640s New Amsterdam women manage the farms and small businesses while their husbands are away trading furs. In New England women help the colonies increase their production of cloth—spinning, weaving, and sewing at home.

Slavery begins to be institutionalized at this time. African women are forced to work in the fields, sowing and harvesting crops. They also are required to cook, wash, sew, and wait on their masters' families. This forced labor continues more than 200 years (see "Politics").

In his 1643 writings about the Narragansett, Roger Williams, the founder of the Rhode Island settlement, describes the Native women's work, taking down, carrying, and setting up the "mats," or house coverings, when their people move from summer to winter homes. They also "plant, weede, and hill, and gather and barne all the corne."

After her first husband's death in 1660, Margaret Hardenbrook de Vries (later Philipse, n.d.–1690) takes over his business as a merchant, buying and shipping furs to Holland in return for Dutch products, which she sells in New Amsterdam. She probably also owns her ships. Although she remarries, she continues to run her own business.

Near Albany, New York, Maria Van Cortlandt Van Rennselaer (1645–1688/9) successfully manages a 24-square-mile estate after her husband's death in 1674 and clears the title to the property when the English reconquer the area.

Dinah Nuthead inherits her husband's printing press in 1695 and moves it to Annapolis, where she runs the business.

1700s

Although the rules of coverture restrict married women (see p. 12), women do run a number of businesses throughout the century (see sidebar). An early entrepreneur is Martha Turnstall Smith, who already operates a whaling business in Long Island in 1707. About a fifth of all colonial newspapers are edited by women (see "Journalism"). On the frontier, women do the household work (including making their own cloth and other supplies) and share the farming tasks with men; they also learn to use muskets and handle canoes.

Objecting to the rules that make it difficult for women to own property, Magdalena Zeh and a troop of women, waving brooms and rakes, force a law-enforcing sheriff off "their land" in 1715 and insist on their right to squat along a river in New York.

In 1718 Pennsylvania expands the definition of feme sole (p. 12) trading to let sailors' wives and deserted wives run their own businesses.

Mary Spratt Provoost Alexander (1693–1760) continues her first husband's trading ventures after her second marriage in 1721. She imports a variety of goods to sell in her New York store and possibly equips a military expedition during the French and Indian War.

In 1734 New York maids organize to protest abusive treatment by their mistress's husbands.

After several years of experimentation while running her father's plantation, Elizabeth ("Eliza") Lucas Pinckney (c. 1722–93) harvests the first successful indigo crop in South Carolina in 1744. She distributes seeds to other planters, and soon indigo replaces rice as the colony's main export. In 1747, for example, 100,000 pounds are shipped to England. Later Pinckney experiments with silkworms on her husband's estate.

In Boston women operate the 400 spinning wheels at a new "manufacturing house" in 1769. Similar businesses soon start in other cities; by the mid-1770s, for example, a Philadelphia company has 400 women manufacturing cotton thread.

Abigail Stoneman (d. 1777) adds a ballroom to her teahouse near Newport, Rhode Island, in 1769. She later runs a coffeehouse in Boston, a tavern in Newport, and another coffeehouse in New York.

On the Pennsylvania frontier, Susanna Wright (1697–1784) wins a £10 reward in 1771 for raising the largest number of silkworms, and her

Women Workers in the 1700s

This list shows just some of the occupations of women during the 1700s:

—barber (Elizabeth Butler)
—blacksmith (Jane Burgess)
—bookstore owner (Ann Smith)
—butcher (Margaret Oliver and her mother)
—candle and soap maker (Elizabeth Franklin)
—glazier and painter (Mary Stevenson)
—gunsmith (Jane Massey)
—pewterer (Mary Willet)
—net-maker (Hannah Beales)
—rope-maker (Sarah Jewell)
—shoemaker (Mary Wilson)
—shipwright (Elizabeth Russell)
—silversmith (Jane Inch)
—tanner and leather dresser (Mary Robinson)
—turner (Ann Page)
—upholsterer (Rebecca Weyman)

silk is later used for a dress presented by Benjamin Franklin to Queen Charlotte of England. A "Renaissance" woman, Wright owns a huge library and is known as an intellectual and a poet. Often she acts as a judge, settling disputes between neighbors, and she also makes her own medicinal remedies with herbs.

During the Revolutionary War, as in later wars, women take over much of the men's work, running farms and businesses. Some even manufacture guns and cannons.

Baltimore newspaper publisher Mary Katherine Goddard (p. 290) becomes the first postmistress, in 1775. But by 1789 the job is considered desirable and she is replaced by a man, ostensibly because he can travel and oversee other departments in the region. Although 200 businessmen support her petition to keep her job, her request is denied.

Sally Ainse (or Montour), an Oneida fur trader, buys property in the Detroit region in 1778 and continues her successful business. Later, in 1787, she moves to Ontario. She loses her property there, however, when the British purchase the area from the Chippewa, even though her land was not supposed to be included.

In Boston in the 1790s, hundreds of women work for a manufacturer of sailcloth. Others do piecework at home, making "cards" for combing wool and cotton. During this time the first cotton-spinning mill opens in Pawtucket, Rhode Island.

1800–19

In the South black women held in slavery are forced to work not only on plantations but also in cotton mills, food-processing plants, foundries, and other types of manufacturing. Some are required to dig canals, build levees, and pull carts in mines.

Jane Aitken (1764–1832) runs the family book printing and binding business after her father's death in 1802. She is best known for printing the four-volume Thomson Bible in 1808.

In 1814 in Waltham, Massachusetts, Deborah Skinner operates what is believed to be the first power-driven loom. By 1817 three more looms in Fall River, Massachusetts, are run by women: Hannah Borden, Mary Healy, and Sallie Winters.

In the area that becomes Texas, Doña María del Carmen Calvillo (1765–1865) is one of several Mexican women in the early 1800s who own and manage large estates. She adds an irrigation system, a granary, and a sugar mill to her prosperous ranch.

In New York in 1819, the Bank for Savings is the first place where women can open their own accounts.

1820–29

Eulalia Arrila de Pérez (c. 1773–1878) is one of several Mexican women who serve as *llaveras* (keepers of the keys) at the Spanish missions. At the San Gabriel Mission in California, where she works from 1821 to 1835, she is in charge of all the supplies, distributing them as needed. She also oversees the laundry, the processing of olive oil and wine, the sewing and fitting of clothing, and much more.

In an 1824 account of her life as a captive with the Seneca, Mary Jemison (1743–1833) describes the women's work (see sidebar). Earlier she preferred to stay among the Seneca when given a choice. When, however, settlers force the Seneca to move, she remains on lands she owns, but she does not adopt the settlers' lifestyle.

In Pawtucket, Rhode Island, in 1824 women weavers join men in a strike to protest a cut in wages and increased hours. Although it is a joint action, the women hold separate meetings.

Lavinia Waight and Louise Mitchell form the United Tailoresses Society of New York and later hold a strike in 1825. They are the first group of women to strike on their own (see also below).

Maria Gertrudes Barcelo (1800–52), called "La Tules," starts her gambling business in 1825. In a few years she has her own casino, complete with huge mirrors and elegant carpets, in Santa Fe. A flamboyant beauty and skilled monte dealer, she dominates Santa Fe society for years.

In Pennsylvania, Rebecca Pennock Lukens (1794–1854) oversees the business operation of the Brandywine Iron Works after her husband's death in 1825, and her brother-in-law supervises the workers. She soon supplies customers from Boston to New Orleans and builds the business from debt to a $100,000 enterprise. It is later renamed Lukens Steel.

In Dover, New Hampshire, in 1828 the first group of female mill workers goes on strike to protest new work regulations, including a latecomers' fine that is a third of a day's wages, a ban on talking at work, and mandatory church attendance. The women march down the street with banners and even shoot off gunpowder, but they soon return to work. The next year Salome Lincoln (p. 201) leads women mill workers in Taunton, Massachusetts, on strike after a pay cut is announced. Despite her urging, her colleagues go back to work before full pay is restored.

1830–39

Women in the United Tailoresses Society of New York, led by Lavinia Waight, strike for higher pay for their piecework in 1831. "Why should not women engage in the duties of trade and legislation?" Waight asks. At the time even working a 16-hour day may not provide a living wage. The women hold out for about five weeks but then go back to work.

In Lynn, Massachusetts, women shoemakers form a society in 1833 and affirm their "inalienable" right to assemble. They win higher pay from their strike, but the benefit is soon lost through decreased work.

After a wage cut in 1834 in Lowell, Massachusetts, several women organize, handing in their notice and demanding their savings at the same time. The mill owners promptly fire the leader, and soon some

"Our Labor Was Not Severe"

"Our labor was not severe . . . Notwithstanding the Indian women have all the fuel and bread to procure, and the cooking to perform, their task is probably not harder than that of white women, who have those articles provided for them; and their cares certainly are not half as numerous, nor as great. In the summer season, we planted, tended and harvested our corn, and generally had all our children with us; but had no master to oversee or drive us, so that we could work as leisurely as we pleased."

—Mary Jemison, as told to James Seaver, *A Narrative of the Life of Mrs. Mary Jemison* (Canandaigna, N.Y.: J.D. Bemis, 1823)

800 women walk off their jobs in rage. "Union Is Power," they pro-claim, but they are threatened with strikebreakers and hounded by the clergy and press until they return to work. Two years later, organized into the Factory Girls' Association, some 1,500 women walk out after another wage cut. One 11-year-old, Harriet Hanson (later Robinson, 1825–1911) helps lead her cohorts out. "As I looked back at the long line that followed me, I was more proud than I have ever been since," she later recalls in her book *Loom and Spindle* (1898). As they parade down the street, the women sing "Oh! isn't a pity, such a pretty girl as I/Should be sent to the factory to pine away and die?" The group, however, soon runs out of money; some women are kicked out of their boardinghouses; and the leaders are fired and blacklisted.

Similar strikes occur in New York and Pennsylvania mills around this time. More than 40,000 women work in cotton mills, as the economy shifts from self-sufficient home production to mass manufac-turing. Most are single young women, often recruited from rural areas. They work 12- to 16-hour days for $1 to $3 a week, at least half of which goes to pay their board in company-owned housing.

"Try Again!"—Lowell mill workers' slogan

1840–49

Led by Sarah Bagley, mill workers organize the Lowell Female Labor Reform Association in 1844 and take demands for better work conditions to the state legislature (see sidebar). At the same time a former mill worker, Harriet Farley (later Donlevy, c. 1813–1907), who edits the *Lowell Offering,* a monthly written by mill workers, refuses to air the demands for better working conditions. She insists on publish-ing moralistic literary material. When Bagley and others turn instead to the *Voice of Industry,* the *Offering* is forced to close down for a while.

Irish women, fleeing the potato famine, arrive in the United States around this time. Many work as domestics, but others begin to replace the New England farm women in the mills.

Led by Elizabeth Gray, New York City seamstresses in the mid-1840s organize the Female Industry Association, which also includes straw workers, lace and fringe makers, and similar workers. Their efforts to raise the pay for their piecework, however, meet with little success.

1850–59

Women make up 13% of paid workers in 1850. Most are employed in agriculture or as domestic workers, but more than 225,000 work in factories, and this number steadily increases over the ensuing years.

In 1851 in New York, 6,000 female stitchers join forces in the Shirt Sewers Cooperative Union and pledge to share their profits. A similar cooperative organization is formed in Philadelphia. Both succeed in getting orders.

Ohio passes the first 10-hour-day law for women workers in 1852.

After leaving her teaching job, Clara Barton takes a job as a clerk in the Patent Office in 1854 and is probably the first woman regularly employed in a government office.

In New York City the first day-care nursery opens in 1854 at Nursery and Child's Hospital, allowing working mothers who are ex-patients to leave their children there. Similar centers are soon started in Troy, New York; Philadelphia; and other cities.

After winning her freedom from slavery in 1856 (p. 23), Biddy Mason begins working as a midwife and saves her money to buy a homestead in Los Angeles. One of the first African Americans to own property in California, she amasses a fortune through her real estate transactions.

Successful dairy owner Margaret Gaffney Haughery (1813–82) receives a bakery as payment for a debt in 1858. She converts it to a steam bakery, introduces packaged crackers, and soon has the largest export operation in New Orleans. Later she gives much of her money to charity.

1860–69

Many women are among the 88 workers killed and 116 badly injured when a poorly constructed mill collapses in Massachusetts in 1860.

In Lynn, Massachusetts, female shoe workers join male workers in an 1860 strike for increased wages. About 800 women, carrying signs proclaiming "American Ladies Will Not Be Slaves," march through the streets during a winter blizzard. Other towns soon join the protest.

In addition to launching a fashion magazine, complete with tissue-paper patterns, Ellen Curtis Demorest (1824–98) and her husband open Mme. Demorest's Emporium of Fashions in New York. She is soon the undisputed leader of American fashion. In addition to employing many women in her patternmaking operation, Demorest links up with Susan A. King, a real estate entrepreneur, to start the Woman's Tea Company in 1872, with women agents selling the tea.

Around 1860 Margaret Getchell (later LaForge, 1841–80) begins working in R. H. Macy's dry goods store in New York. She quickly rises from cashier to bookkeeper to superintendent, and by 1869 is in charge of some 200 employees, mostly women.

During the Civil War women fill in for men in factories and stores. Many assume various government jobs, becoming known as "government girls." Others serve as nurses (see "War").

Led by Kate Mullaney, the Troy Collar Laundry Union goes on strike in 1863 and wins a pay increase. Yet the women still spend 12 to 14 hours a day in 100-degree rooms washing, starching, and ironing men's detachable collars.

In New York in 1864 about 100 sewers organize the Working Women's Union "to improve our social condition." At the time they may earn as little as 17 cents for a 15-hour day. Similar groups start in Boston and

The Lighthouse Heroine

In Newport Harbor, Rhode Island, Ida Lewis (1842–1911) becomes the unofficial lighthouse keeper after her father has a stroke. She makes the first of many dramatic rescues in 1858—saving four young men after their boat capsizes. A few years later she hauls in not only some herders but also their runaway sheep. She receives national attention in 1869, when a New York reporter details her intrepid rescue of two soldiers whose sailboat overturned in a storm. Without taking time to put on shoes or a coat, she rushed out onto the cold seas and pulled the two nearly dead men into her rowboat. Susan B. Anthony picks up the story and publicizes it in the Revolution. *Yet it takes another 10 years and several more rescues before the government finally appoints Lewis as the official lighthouse keeper in 1879. Her last known rescue is in 1906, at age 64, when she saves a female tourist.*

Philadelphia. In Detroit the Sewing Women's Protective Association has sewing machines for women to use in its office and gets customers to buy from the women directly, without going through a contractor.

In 1865 Cincinnati women sewers petition the president to end the army's subcontracting system for uniforms, as "we are unable to sustain life for the price offered by contractors, who fatten on their contracts by grinding immense profits out of the labor of their operators."

The number of women store clerks increases in the mid-1860s, but their wages are low and they must stand for hours (there is no place to sit). They can be fined just for being a second late back from a break.

In Jackson, Mississippi, black washerwomen resolve in 1866 to all charge the same rate for their services and publish a letter to the mayor in the local paper to inform the public of their need for a living wage.

Most freedwomen earn a living as sharecroppers, wage laborers, or tenant farmers, and many file complaints with the Freedman's Bureau about abusive treatment. One woman describes how, while she was putting on her shoes, her employer dragged her from her room and threatened to kill her if she did not milk the cows immediately.

In 1867 the cigarmakers are the first national union to accept women and African Americans, although they do not admit nonskilled factory workers and homeworkers until 1875.

In 1868 Susan B. Anthony helps form the Working Women's Association in New York City to improve workers' conditions and encourage women to join unions. Backed by this group, typesetter Augusta Lewis (later Troup, c. 1848–1920) organizes the Women's Typographical Union No. 1, which within a few months has 30 members. Lewis and Anthony, however, clash in 1869, when Lewis and other women unionists insist on supporting a strike by male typographers but Anthony urges women to take advantage of the strike to gain employment. In 1869, in a major reversal of policy, the International Typographical Union admits women, in large part because the women refused to work as scabs during the men's strike.

Aroused by an earlier public forum on women sewers' plight, middle- and upper-class women establish the Working Women's Protective Union in New York in 1868; similar groups form in other cities. These "unions" give free legal aid to workers to help them collect what they are due in court. The groups also lobby successfully for laws to penalize employers who fail to pay workers, and act as employment agencies.

At its 1868 convention the National Labor Union, which urges women to unionize and supports equal pay for equal work, admits four female delegates: Susan B. Anthony, Mary Kellogg, Mary MacDonald (all from Working Women's Protective Unions), and Elizabeth Cady Stanton of the National Woman's Suffrage Association. Kate Mullaney of the Troy Collar Laundresses Union is singled out for praise, after winning another pay increase for her members, and she is elected to office. (Her union, however, loses an 1869 strike and then dissolves.)

Incensed when she is denied entrance to a New York Press Club affair in 1868, journalist Jane Cunningham Croly (p. 291) joins with other professional women to form the first career women's club, Sorosis, in New York. Writer Alice Cary (1820–71) is elected president, and the members meet biweekly at Delmonico's as a kind of support group.

Six women are among the first contract laborers brought from Japan to Hawaii in 1868.

In Lynn, Massachusetts, in 1869 women shoe stitchers from 12 lodges in six states (including California) form the first national women's labor organization, the Daughters of St. Crispin. Under Carrie Wilson as president and Abbie Jacques as secretary, the member lodges soon double to 24. By 1870 the women gain recognition from the men's union, the Knights of St. Crispin, along with support for their demand of equal pay. The group lasts until 1876.

Mary Ann Cary (p. 22) speaks before the Colored National Labor Union in 1869 and is elected to the union's executive committee.

1870–79

In 1870 Augusta Lewis is elected corresponding secretary of the International Typographical Union—the first woman in this position in a national union. At the end of her one-year term, however, she reports: "It is the general opinion of female compositors that they are more justly treated by what is termed 'rat' foremen, printers and employers than they are by union men."

Backed by Cornelius Vanderbilt, Victoria Claflin Woodhull (1838–1927) and her sister Tennessee Celeste Claflin (1846–1923) open a brokerage firm in New York in 1870. The sisters, who have a reputation as spiritualists, surprise Wall Street with their success. Having conquered one male domain, Woodhull turns to politics (p. 28).

Through the efforts of lawyer Belva Lockwood (p. 25), Congress passes an 1872 law giving women federal employees equal pay for equal work.

Massachusetts limits women and children to a 60-hour work week in 1874. Similar laws are soon passed in Illinois and Minnesota.

In 1877 in Chicago, typesetter Alzina Parsons Stevens (1849–1900) sets up the Working Woman's Union to press for women workers' concerns. She later moves to Toledo, Ohio, where she continues as labor organizer and advances from proofreader to editor of the *Toledo Bee*.

Labor organizer Mary Harris ("Mother") Jones (1830–1930) joins striking railroad workers in Pittsburgh in 1877. Soon she is traveling to wherever the need for organizing is greatest. As she later explains, "My address is like my shoes. It travels with me. I abide where there is a fight against wrong."

Two Different Fortunes

In 1874 heiress Hetty Robinson Green (1834–1916) begins augmenting her fortune by purchasing real estate and mortgages in fast-growing cities like Chicago, where she eventually amasses property valued at $5–6 million. She also is a major money lender. Later the media jump on her eccentric frugality, such as living in run-down housing and using free medical clinics, to dub her "the witch of Wall Street." But her estate is worth some $120 million at her death.

In 1875 Lydia Estes Pinkham (1819–83) starts marketing a homemade remedy for "women's weakness," called "Mrs. Lydia E. Pinkham's Vegetable Compound." Her patent medicine, packaged with almost 20% alcohol as a preservative, is a huge success, and the picture of her on the product label (initiated in 1879) becomes known throughout America. She writes all the advertising copy and personally answers all the letters sent to her "Department of Advice." The business continues to thrive for years after her death.

In 1878, a year after the first switchboard is introduced, Emma M. Nutt (c. 1849–1926) is hired in Boston as the first female telephone operator. Soon many women telegraph operators are retrained to work the switchboards. By 1900 some 35,000 women are phone operators. Another invention that affects women's employment is the Remington typewriter (introduced in 1873). Already the company claims, "No invention has opened for women so broad and easy an avenue to profitable and suitable employment."

Determined to expand job opportunities for women, Mary Foot Seymour (1846–93) starts the first secretarial school for women, the Union School of Stenography, in 1879 in New York. Soon she is running four schools and an employment bureau. In 1889 she launches the bimonthly *Business Woman's Journal* and sets up the Mary F. Seymour Publishing Company, with all-female officers.

Lucy Parsons (p. 33), a seamstress as well as a labor activist, is a vocal member of the Working Women's Union in Chicago, speaking out for the rights of homemakers and other wageless workers in 1879.

1880–89

One of the first women to join the Knights of Labor in Chicago is Elizabeth Flynn Rodgers (1847–1939), a homemaker who heads the newly formed Local Assembly No. 1789 (all women) in 1881 and who in 1886 becomes the first woman head of a district assembly. The Knights of Labor actively supports women workers and by 1886 has 192 women's assemblies with 50,000 female members. Other early women leaders in the union include Mary Hanafin and Mary Stirling, two shoe workers from Philadelphia.

In Atlanta in 1881 washerwomen demand higher pay and organize a strike force of 3,000—the largest known labor action by black women at the time. Called the "Washing Amazons" by the *Atlanta Constitution*, the women defy police attacks and other threats, declaring, "We mean business . . . or no washing." But they do not win.

In New York wealthy social worker Grace Hoadley Dodge (1856–1914) begins an informal discussion group for young female factory workers in 1881. In a few years the Working Girls Club rents a building, providing lodging, a library, health care, and a variety of classes. By 1885 several similar clubs in New York join together in an association, and by 1890 there is a national group, which puts out the magazine *Far and Near*, edited by Maria Bowen Chapin.

Mary F. Hoyt (1858–1958), who has the top score on the 1883 Civil Service exam, is the first woman appointed under the new system, which assigns government jobs based on merit and exam scores. She starts out as a clerk in a Treasury Department agency.

At its 1883 convention the two-year-old Federation of Organized Trade and Labor Unions—in 1886 the American Federation of Labor (AFL)—voices its support of women's unions and equal pay for equal work. One of the few women attending the meeting is Mrs. Charlotte Smith, president of the Woman's National Industrial League, although she is not seated as a delegate until 1884. However, despite this early show of support, many AFL men do not support women's unions.

In 1885 carpet weavers strike in Yonkers, New York, after the company fires some women for joining the Knights of Labor. About 2,500 women walk out in support, but they do not win union recognition.

In 1885 Elizabeth Bailey takes over her husband's circus, producing "Mollie Bailey's Show"—the first circus run by a woman.

"Women . . . should have all the benefits that can be given to men"—*Leonora Barry*

Following recommendations of the 16 women delegates, the 1886 Knights of Labor convention sets up a women's department with a paid investigator: Leonora M. Kearney Barry (later Lake, 1849–1930), a hosiery worker. During the next year she travels to many factories, helping women organize and detailing their horrible working conditions. In 1887 she reports on her findings (see sidebar), and her observations foster the passage of a factory inspection law in Pennsylvania. She continues her reports and organizing work until 1890, when she marries and becomes active in suffrage and temperance work.

In 1886 New York collar factory worker Leonora O'Reilly (1870–1927) joins the Knights of Labor and starts the Working Women's Society, which gains the support of Josephine Shaw Lowell (p. 147). In addition to backing women strikers, this group informs the public about women's working conditions.

With extensive newspaper advertising, Harriet Hubbard Ayer (1849–1903) is, in 1886, the first U.S. woman to launch a successful cosmetics business, marketing a facial cream she claims was used by Madame Récamier, the famous beauty of Napoleon's time. Later, after losing her business in a family dispute, she becomes a journalist.

In 1887 Harriet Russell Strong (1844–1929) first plants walnuts on the semiarid land she owns in California. She also develops and patents a series of storage dams to improve irrigation. Her enterprise is so successful that she is soon known as the "walnut queen."

Elizabeth Morgan, who began working in British mills at age 11, helps organize the Ladies Federal Union No. 2703 under the AFL in 1888. The union is made up of a variety of workers, including bookbinders, music teachers, candymakers, and laundresses. As soon as 10 workers from one trade join, a new local is created for that industry. By 1892 there are 23 new unions. Morgan also helps start the Illinois Women's Alliance, a lobbying group for better labor legislation (see p. 148).

Women take an active leadership role in the National Farmers' Alliances that form as local cooperatives in rural areas in the late 1880s.

"Give Us Your Assistance"

"Men! ye whose earnings count from nine to fifteen dollars a week and upward, cease, in the name of God and humanity, cease your demands and grievances and give us your assistance for a time to bring some relief to the poor unfortunate, whose week's work of eighty-four hours brings her but $2.50 or $3 per week.

". . . The abuse, injustice and suffering which the women [in a linen thread plant] endure from the tyranny, cruelty and slave-driving propensities of the employers is something terrible to be allowed existence in free America. In one branch . . . women are compelled to stand on a stone floor in water the year round, most of the time barefoot, with a spray of cold water flying constantly against the breast. . . ."
    —Leonora M. Barry, report to general assembly of Knights of Labor, 1887; quoted in Gerda Lerner, *The Female Experience: An American Documentary* (Indianapolis: Bobbs-Merrill, 1977)

Two Women Join the Food Business

Amanda Theodosia Jones (1835–1914) sets up the Woman's Canning and Preserving Company in 1890 to put her newly invented vacuum process to work. Calling her business "women's work for women," she insists on having women run the company. "This is a woman's industry," she declares. "No man will vote our stock, transact our business, pronounce on women's wages, supervise our factories. Give men whatever work is suitable, but keep the governing power. This is a business training school for working women." Although Jones resigns after a dispute in 1893, the company flourishes.

Rose Markward Knox (1857–1950) and her husband start their gelatin business in Johnstown, New York, in 1890. To interest women in her product, Knox comes out with a booklet of "Dainty Desserts" in 1896. After her husband's death in 1908, she runs the business on her own and gears her advertising toward women, with helpful hints titled "Mrs. Knox Says." She also sponsors research on new uses for gelatin. By 1925 the company is worth $1 million.

More than 4 million U.S. women are wage earners in 1890, making up 17.2% of the workforce. Nonwhite women represent a fourth of this number. They are forced to work primarily in domestic service or agricultural jobs; only about 3% do factory work.

In 1890 Mary Burke, head of the Retail Clerks International Protective Association, is the first woman delegate to an AFL convention. She pushes through a resolution to have women organizers; the first, however, is not appointed until 1892.

Kate Gleason (1865–1933) takes over as secretary and treasurer of her father's machine-tool company in 1890 and greatly increases its sales. Her promotional efforts are so effective that she is at times credited with inventing the beveled-gear planer (her father's design). She builds the firm into the top U.S. producer of gear-cutting machines.

In 1890 stenographer Alice B. Sanger is the first woman to work in the White House executive office, under President Benjamin Harrison.

About 500 women workers, led by Mary Evaline, strike against pay cuts at shirt and collar manufacturers in Troy, New York, in 1891. They get the backing of the AFL and win their demands, although a few years later the union collapses after another wage battle.

After organizing women bookbinders in Chicago, Mary Kenney (later O'Sullivan, 1864–1943) serves as the first woman general organizer of the AFL in 1892 and quickly organizes New York garment workers, Troy shirtwaist workers, and a number of groups in Boston. She also joins Boston social reformer Mary Kimball Kehew (1859–1918) to start the Union for Industrial Progress, which promotes trade unionism among women. Kenney's appointment, however, only lasts for five months, and the AFL does not appoint another full-time woman organizer until 1908, when it hires Annie Fitzgerald.

Illinois passes an 1893 law banning child workers under age 14, setting an eight-hour work day for women, regulating sweatshops, and providing for state factory inspectors. This law is largely the result of the findings of Hull House reformer Florence Kelley (1859–1932), who was hired in 1892 by the Illinois Bureau of Labor Statistics to look into sweatshop conditions in the garment industry. Kelley is named the initial chief factory inspector and given a staff of 12.

Helen Campbell publishes *Women Wage-Earners* (1893), describing the appalling conditions uncovered by the Massachusetts Bureau of Labor.

In 1895 in New York, 50 women bookbinders organize one of the most successful early unions, winning a six-day, 48-hour work week and other benefits.

In 1896 Maryland passes a law requiring seats for female sales clerks, but later (in 1904) they have to amend this to stipulate that the women be allowed to sit on the seats.

Harriet Smith Pullen takes her four children to search for gold in Alaska in 1897. She quickly makes a profit selling baked apples to all the gold hunters and soon has her own restaurant. Within a year she also operates a freight serivce and later starts a hotel.

Agnes Nestor (1880–1948) becomes the spokesperson for the striking workers at a Chicago glovemaking factory in 1898. Another leader is Elisabeth Christman (1881–1975). After 10 days of picketing, the strikers win their demands and go on to start a union.

In 1899 in Richmond, Virginia, Maggie Lena Mitchell Walker (c. 1867–1934) takes charge of the Independent Order of Saint Luke, a mutual-aid society that was established in 1867 by Mary Ann Prout. Walker immediately launches a major membership drive. She urges the development of black-owned businesses and stresses economic independence for African Americans. To this end she starts several new ventures, including a newspaper, the *St. Luke Herald*, in 1902 and a bank in 1903 (see also below).

1900–9

In 1900 more than 5 million women are wage earners, about a fifth of all U.S. women. The greatest increase in the last 30 years is in female office workers, who now represent nearly 77% of all office workers. These jobs are almost entirely held by native-born white women. Two other areas of dramatic increase are in the number of telephone and telegraph operators and of sales clerks. Yet these jobs represent only a small percentage of the total. Nearly 30% of all working women are domestics or in related "service" industries. Others work on farms, as teachers, or in factories (mostly garment or textile manufacturing).

When the International Ladies' Garment Workers' Union (ILGWU) is formed in 1900, the membership is primarily the male cutters and pressers of women's clothing. Only later in the decade do large numbers of women join, although the top leadership remains male.

Working for the United Mine Workers, Mother Jones helps organize the mining strikes in Pittsburgh, both in 1900 and 1902. She forms an army of strikers' wives, outfitted with dishpans and brooms, to prevent scabs from entering the mines (see sidebar). When women are later arrested, Jones urges them to take their babies with them to jail and "to sing to them all night long." The women are quickly released.

In 1902 Agnes Nestor helps organize the International Glove Workers Union, a coalition of 27 locals. Elected vice president in 1903, she serves as an officer until 1938 (see also 1913).

In Chicago in 1902, sausage packers Mollie Daly and Hannah O'Day ask Mary McDowell of the University of Chicago Settlement House to help them start a union with the members of their Maud Gonne Club (named for the Irish patriot). They become a local of the Amalgamated Meat Cutters and Butchers Workmen of North America, but in 1904 a strike undoes all the stockyard workers unions.

"They Were Heroic Women"

"Up the mountain side, yelling and hollering, she [an Irish-born striker's wife] led the women, and when the mules came up with the scabs and the coal, she began beating on the dishpan and hollering and all the army joined in with her. [The scabs fled.]. . . .

"From that day on the women kept continual watch of the mines to see that the company did not bring in scabs. . . . They were heroic women. In the long years to come the nation will pay them high tribute for they were fighting for the advancement of the country."
—Mary Harris Jones, recollection in *Autobiography of Mother Jones* (Chicago: Charles H. Kerr, 1925)

Middle-class reformers and women labor organizers join forces to form the national Women's Trade Union League (WTUL) in 1903. The group aims both to unionize women workers and to bring public attention to working women's concerns. Its motto is "The eight-hour day; a living wage; to guard the home." The initial officers are Mary Kehew, president; Jane Addams, vice president; Mary Kenney O'Sullivan, secretary; and Mary Donovan (a shoe worker), treasurer. Board members include Leonora O'Reilly from the ILGWU, Ellen Lindstrom from the United Garment Workers, and Mary Freitas of the Textile Workers. Both union and nonunion women workers, as well as nonworking supporters, are invited to become members.

To publicize ongoing abuses of child labor in 1903, Mother Jones first leads striking textile workers' children (who also work in the mills) on a march in Philadelphia. "Philadelphia's mansions were built on the broken bones, the quivering hearts and drooping heads of these children," she admonishes. She then takes them on a 125-mile trek to President Theodore Roosevelt's summer home, but he refuses to meet with them.

After working "undercover" in several factories, writers Marie Louise Van Vorst and her sister-in-law, Bessie McGinnis Van Vorst, expose the abuses they found in *The Woman Who Toils* (1903). Marie reports on her work in a Massachusetts shoe factory and a South Carolina cotton mill; Bessie, on a Pittsburgh cannery and a Buffalo knitting mill.

A 1903 Oregon law limits women factory and laundry workers to a 10-hour day; it leads to a major Supreme Court case in 1908 (see below).

In 1903 in Richmond, Virginia, Maggie Lena Walker is the first African American and first woman to establish and head a U.S. bank, the St. Luke Penny Savings Bank. Two years later, in 1905, she starts a department store, the Emporium, although this venture is not as successful. She is a strong advocate of economic independence for women.

In New York in 1904, Lane Bryant (Lena Himmelstein) opens a store that specializes in clothes for pregnant and heavy-set women. She later expands with a chain of Lane Bryant stores.

After organizing the first women's local of the Jewish Socialist United Cloth Hat and Cap Makers' Union in 1902, Rose Schneiderman (1882–1972) leads her co-workers on a successful 13-week strike in 1905. "So we must stand together to resist," she reflects, "for we will get what we can take—just that and no more." She also joins the New York WTUL, is elected vice president in 1906, and in 1910 beomes a full-time organizer for the WTUL.

Lucy Parsons is one of the main speakers at the 1905 founding convention of the Industrial Workers of the World, or Wobblies. Elizabeth Gurley Flynn (1890–1964) joins the IWW a year later and quickly becomes one of its main speakers and organizers.

In 1906 Margaret Dreier Robins (1868–1945) becomes president of the national WTUL, serving until 1922, often donating money, and helping to build an effective alliance of working and nonworking women. The WTUL and its branches back most of the women's strikes of this period. Many of the WTUL board members are labor organizers, such as Mary Anderson and Emma Steghagen (shoe workers), Josephine Casey (railroad ticket takers), Elisabeth Christman and Agnes Nestor (glove makers), Stella Franklin (department store clerks), Elizabeth Maloney (waitresses), Rose Schneiderman (cap makers), Melinda Scott (hat trimmers), and Maud O'Farrell Swartz (typographers).

In *Muller* v. *State of Oregon* (1908), the Supreme Court upholds Oregon's 10-hour work day for women. The winning argument, presented by Louis Brandeis, is built from facts compiled by Helen Marot, Florence Kelley, and Josephine and Pauline Goldmark. It is an important victory for advocates of protective laws; the ruling, however, also stresses the notion of women's physical weakness.

"We strike for justice"—shirtwaist worker's sign

In 1909 in New York, when women shirtwaist workers at two companies try to organize, they are fired and immediately form a picket line, persevering despite arrests and beatings from police. When New York WTUL president Mary Dreier (1875–1963), the sister of Margaret Dreier Robins, is arrested, it generates press attention. On November 22, 1909, a mass meeting is called at Cooper Union to discuss a general strike. After lengthy speeches by AFL head Samuel Gompers and others, 16-year-old Clara Lemlich, a striking worker who was beaten while picketing, gets up. "I am tired of listening to speakers who talk in general terms," she asserts. "What we are here for is to decide whether or not we shall strike. I offer a resolution that a general strike be declared—now!" The women in the audience then rise to take a traditional Jewish pledge, affirming their resolve.

Called the "Uprising of the 20,000," it is the largest strike of women workers to date (there are some male strikers, too). During the 13-week strike, women picketers brave clubbings and arrests. The WTUL supports them, registering union members, raising bail, and generating press attention. Although the women do not win all their demands (most shops settle individually), they prove that women can organize.

1910–19

In Chicago, Bessie Abramowitz (later Hillman, c. 1895–1970), Anne Shapiro, and 12 other women walk off their jobs at a large clothing manufacturer when their piece rate for sewing buttons is suddenly cut. The male-led trade unions at first refuse to support them, but the women call a meeting at Hull House and in a month have 18,000 other city garment workers (many of them men) behind them. The workers hold out for and win union recognition. Abramowitz goes on to help found the Amalgamated Clothing Workers of America in 1914 and serves as a vice president.

Women Writing on Labor Reform

As part of the six-volume Pittsburgh Survey *examining social conditions in that city, Elizabeth Beardsley Butler writes* Women and the Trades *(1906), which underlines the low wages and unsafe conditions. It is used to help push for protective legislation. Another book in this series is Crystal Eastman's* Work Accidents and the Law *(1910), which is used as an argument for workers' compensation laws.*

Josephine Clara Goldmark (1877–1950) publishes one of several detailed studies revealing the need for labor reform: Child Labor Legislation Handbook *(1906). Later reports include* Fatigue and Efficiency *(1912), showing how long hours reduce productivity;* The Case for the Shorter Working Day *(1916); and* The Case Against Nightwork for Women *(1918).*

"Too Much Blood Has Been Spilled"

"This is not the first time girls have been burned alive in the city. Every week I must learn of the untimely death of one of my sister workers. . . .

"I can't talk fellowship to you who are gathered here. Too much blood has been spilled. I know from my experience it is up to the working people to save themselves. The only way they can save themselves is by a strong working-class movement."
—Rose Schneiderman, memorial speech for shirt-waist workers, 1911; in *All for One*, with Lucy Goldthwaite (New York: Paul S. Eriksen, 1967)

Young Jewish garment workers on strike with signs "Abolish our slavery!" (Library of Congress)

In Los Angeles, Alice Stebbins Wells becomes the first female police officer in the country. She encourages other women to join the force and helps form the International Association of Policewomen in 1915.

On March 25, 1911, in New York City, fire breaks out at the Triangle Shirtwaist Factory, where the 1909 uprising began. The exits are locked (against the law) and the fire ladders cannot reach the top floors, so 146 workers (mostly young immigrant women) jump or burn to death. The WTUL holds a memorial meeting at which Rose Schneiderman gives an impassioned speech (see sidebar), and 100,000 some mourners march down Fifth Avenue. Later a New York Factory Investigation Commission is formed, but the factory owners are completely acquitted.

In 1911 Emma R.H. Jentzer (1883–1972) is the first woman to serve as a special agent in the Bureau of Investigations (later the FBI).

A pay cut triggers a strike of male and female mill workers in Lawrence, Massachusetts, in 1912. One of the IWW organizers is Elizabeth Gurley Flynn, and the women strikers play a prominent role, carrying banners proclaiming, "We Want Bread and Roses, Too!" Police fire into the picketers, killing Anna Lo Pizzo; they also beat women strikers, causing two pregnant women to lose their babies. When the strikers try to send their children out of town to safety, police club the children and their mothers, causing a public outcry. "A reign of terror prevailed in Lawrence which literally shook America," Flynn later recalls. Congress begins an investigation, and the owners agree to settle.

In 1912 Massachusetts passes the first minimum-wage law for women and children after a report compiled largely by Molly Dewson. Mabel Edna Gillespie serves on a committee to administer the new law, but it lacks enforcement power. Other states soon pass similar laws, but the Supreme Court strikes them down in 1923.

Josephine Carey leads a 1912 strike of corset factory workers in Kalamazoo, Michigan, to complain about the foreman's demand for sexual favors in return for providing thread.

In 1912 Christine McGaffey Frederick (1883–1970), a household management expert, sets up the League of Advertising Women (later Advertising Women of New York) when existing groups refuse to admit women.

In 1913 Agnes Nestor is elected president of the International Glove Workers Union, and Elisabeth Christman is secretary-treasurer.

After removing loopholes in California's maximum-hour laws, reformer Katherine Philips Edson (1870–1933) helps draft a 1913 minimum-wage law for women and serves on the commission to enforce it.

In 1914 the WTUL starts a school in Chicago to train women labor leaders. Its first three students, Fannia Cohn, Myrtle Whitehad, and Louisa Mittlestadt, all become effective organizers. By the time the school closes in 1926, it has trained 40 women organizers.

In 1914 Mary Phelps ("Polly") Jacob (later Caresse Crosby) secures a patent for her "backless brassiere," which she created with the help of her maid to replace her corset and better show off her evening gown. Warner Brothers Corset Company soon buys her patent for just $1,500.

Dorothy Jacobs (later Bellanca, 1894–1946), who in 1909 organized buttonhole sewers in Baltimore, is elected to the executive board of the two-year-old Amalgamated Clothing Workers of America in 1916. The following year she becomes its first full-time woman organizer.

After leading a successful strike of Chicago's dress and white goods workers in 1915, Fannia Cohn is elected as the first woman vice president of the ILGWU in 1916.

In 1917 in Norfolk, Virginia, 600 black women waitresses, domestics, nurses, and tobacco stemmers organize to demand higher pay and improved working conditions, but when the stemmers try to strike, they are quickly arrested. In New Orleans, Ella Pete organizes 1,000 African American women in the Domestic Servants Union.

During World War I women take over many of the men's jobs, working in blast furnaces, smelting brass and copper, producing chemicals, and manufacturing automobiles and railway parts. They run streetcars and elevators and deliver the mail. Their wartime work leads to the 1918 formation of the Women in Industry Service in the Department of Labor, later the Women's Bureau (1920).

Mabel Gillespie organizes the first stenographers union in 1918 and serves as its president.

After the war most women lose their new jobs and higher pay. In 1919 in Cleveland, for example, male unions protest the use of female streetcar conductors. Detroit streetcar operators manage to hold onto their jobs, but no new women are hired.

In 1919 Julia Sarsfield O'Connor (later Parker, 1890–1972) leads the New England Telephone Operators on a six-day strike that disrupts service in five states. The women win their wage demands.

In Clarksville, Tennessee, in 1919 the Woman's Bank opens under Brenda Runyon with an all-female staff. It continues until 1926, when it merges with another bank.

To address white-collar women workers' needs, Lena Madesin Phillips (1881–1955) starts the National Federation of Business and Professional Women's Clubs (BPW) in 1919. Lawyer Gail Laughlin is the first president, and Phillips is executive secretary. In a year the group has 26,000 members, about half clerical workers, organized in 287 clubs in 47 states. Their slogan is "At least a high school education for every business girl." Phillips also starts the BPW journal, *Independent Woman*.

In Los Angeles in 1919, Georgia Hill Robinson becomes the first African American policewoman.

Two Cosmetics Empires

In New York, Florence Nightingale Graham (c. 1878/84–1966) opens a beauty salon on Fifth Avenue with Elizabeth Hubbard in 1910, but she soon takes over the business and repaints the sign "Elizabeth Arden" (partly inspired by a Tennyson poem). Four years later she starts offering her own line of cosmetics, including a facial cream called Amoretta. By skillful advertising and marketing, she expands her operation to more than 100 salons and 300 products and a name that is known worldwide.

After attracting a wealthy clientele in London and Paris, Helena Rubinstein (1871–1965) opens a beauty salon in New York in 1914, then in other U.S. cities. From a business that allegedly began with 12 pots of face cream made for her mother, Rubinstein builds a vast cosmetics empire, becoming the arch rival of Elizabeth Arden. She helps create the celebrated vamp look of film star Theda Bara and becomes a celebrity in her own right.

"Guess I Have a Right To"

When two female leaders of the picketers are tried for disobeying an injunction, they turn the tables on their prosecutors. Trixie Perry appears in a red, white, and blue dress and a cap sewn from a U.S. flag. The attorney questions her: "You are dressed in a United States flag and the colors?" She replies, "I guess so, I was born under it, guess I have a right to." Later when the attorney asks her about blocking the road, she rejoins, "A little thing like me block a big road?" The other young woman on trial, called "Texas Bill," behaves in a very ladylike manner on the stand and makes the soldiers look ridiculous for accusing her of "assaulting" them.

1920–29

Almost 20% of all Japanese American women are wage earners in 1920; about 34% work in agriculture and nearly 27% as domestics.

To develop policies for women workers, the Women's Bureau, directed by Mary Anderson, is set up in the Labor Department (see "Politics").

In St. Louis and Cleveland in 1920, black women refuse to buy goods in clothing and department stores where they can't work.

Of the female business and professional workers in 1921, about 50% are teachers and 37% are secretaries. One college graduate writes, "Can it be in the divine order of things that one Ph.D. should wash dishes a whole lifetime for another Ph.D. just because one is a woman and the other a man?"

A number of women sell bonds for top Wall Street firms. Betty Cook of Hemphill Noyes, Mary Riis of Shearson, and Louise Watson of J. P. Morgan Guaranty start the Women's Bond Club of New York in 1921.

In 1921 women printers successfully lobby to repeal provisions of a New York law that prohibits night work and limits their hours so that they are unable to work on morning editions.

Bryn Mawr College holds its first summer school program to train women in union leadership skills in 1921 (see also "Education").

In *Adkins* v. *Children's Hospital* (1923), the Supreme Court strikes down a minimum-wage law for women in the District of Columbia enacted by Congress in 1918. The justices contend that, with the vote, women are now essentially equal to men, so they no longer need special protection. The decision knocks out all existing state minimum-wage laws and leads to one cartoonist's caption: "This decision affirms your constitutional right to starve."

Ida Kaganovich Rosenthal (1886–1973) and her husband set up the Maiden Form Brassiere Company in 1923 to market their new cup-shaped bra. Rosenthal at first gave it away with dresses sold in her shop, but women kept asking for the bra alone.

Ethel Puffer Howes starts the Institute for the Coordination of Women's Interests at Smith College in 1925 to see how women can best combine a careeer, marriage, and motherhood. She sets up a day-care program, a cooked-meal service, and training for "home assistants." She also investigates the possibilities of home-based freelance work.

After they are repeatedly denied a wage increase, women at a rayon plant in Elizabethton, Tennessee, walk out in 1929. After an initial agreement breaks down, a second strike starts and armed troops are called in. The women defiantly block a road and refuse to walk 12 miles to jail (see sidebar). They also parade down the street "draped in the American flag and carrying the colors," so the soldiers have to salute them again and again. The government finally sends in Anna

Weinstock, its first female negotiator, to reach a settlement. She receives headlines for resolving the dispute, but the workers lose.

"But understand, all workers, / Our union they do fear"—Ella May Wiggins

During a 1929 textile mill workers' strike in Gastonia, North Carolina, labor organizer Ella May Wiggins, a mother of nine, is shot and killed by vigilantes. She is known for writing songs to organize workers.

In 1929 Marjorie Merriweather Post (1887–1973)—who inherited the Postum Cereal Company in 1914 and participated in major decisions (although as a woman she could not sit on the board)—insists on the value of Clarence Birdseye's food-freezing patents and persuades the board to buy them. This decision helps make the company, renamed General Foods, the largest of its kind in the country.

In 1929 Marjorie Child Husted directs the Betty Crocker Homemaking Service Service at General Mills; she turns the fictional "Betty Crocker" into an endearing "real" person for consumers, in this way boosting sales.

1930–39

About 11 million women are wage earners in 1930, nearly 30% still in domestic and personal services. Among professional workers, 75% are teachers or nurses. Relatively few workers (1 in 34) belong to unions.

During the Depression many women lose their jobs, especially women of color. During the decade black women's employment rate drops from 43.3% to 33.5%, while white women's goes from 22.9% to 21.8%. Moreover, much of the New Deal legislation doesn't cover agricultural or domestic work, the two main employment areas for women of color.

In 1931 Dorothy Shaver (1897–1959) is named vice president overseeing advertising, publicity, and the bureau of fashion at Lord and Taylor in New York. She promotes many female American designers and introduces such ideas as a fashion department just for teenagers.

The 1932 National Economy Act forbids more than one family member from holding a government job, and it is the wife who loses her job. A 1933 rule actually requires a female civil servant to take her husband's name, just to make sure no one cheats. Yet, despite public opposition to married women in the workforce, the percentage of married women workers actually increases during the Depression.

Dorothy Jacobs Bellanca organizes hundreds of shirt workers for the Amalgamated Clothing Workers of America between 1932 and 1934. In Allentown, Pennsylvania, she gets attention when she and the governor's wife, Cornelia Bryce Pinchot, lead strikers age 13 to 18.

In 1933 Congress establishes the National Recovery Administration, which determines maximum hours and minimum wages for both male

Women in the Skies

In 1930 Ellen Church, a registered nurse, is the first airline stewardess on a flight by Boeing Air Transport (later United Airlines) from Cheyenne, Wyoming, to Oakland, California. She picks seven other stewardesses, who are also required to be nurses. In addition to serving a box lunch and coffee on board, they put the luggage on board, help fuel the planes, and join the pilots in pushing the planes into the hangars at the end of the day.

In 1932 Ruth Nichols, already famous for setting several air records, is the first woman hired as a pilot for commercial passenger flights, on New York and New England Airways.

Olive Beech (1903–93) helps found Beech Aircraft Corporation in 1932. Later, during World War II, she turns it into the main supplier of training planes for the U.S. armed forces.

and female workers in manufacturing. Although this does not establish equal pay for equal work, most women factory workers do benefit. Not included, however, are the many women who work as domestics, professionals (teachers and nurses), clerical workers, and farm laborers.

In 1933 Latinas join a cotton pickers' strike in California. To deter scabs, they tear open the cotton sacks and dump the contents on the ground. In St. Louis, Connie Smith leads a strike of 900 black women pecan workers who want better pay and working conditions and an end to different treatment of black and white workers. White workers support the strikers; they refuse an offer of more money and instead march downtown with the black women, 1,500 strong. The strike is a success.

In 1933 Massachusetts innkeeper Ruth Graves Wakefield accidentally invents the chocolate chip cookie, named the Toll House cookie after her inn. It is so popular that by 1939 Nestlé is packaging chocolate bits for use with Wakefield's recipe and buys rights to the Toll House name.

In New York in 1934, Dora Jones starts the Domestic Workers' Union, gaining 350 members in five years, three-fourths African American.

"To us no strike is ever lost. Whatever the immediate outcome, we eventually win."—Rose Pesotta

After successfully organizing Los Angeles dressmakers for the ILGWU in 1933, Rose Pesotta (1896–1965) is elected in 1934 as ILGWU vice president, the only woman on the board. Ten years later, when she retires in 1944, she stresses that one woman on the board is not enough for a union that is 85% women. Also working for the ILGWU in 1934 is Angela Bambace (1898–1975), who organizes women cloakmakers in Baltimore and encourages Italian American women to unionize.

Like Pesotta, Dorothy Bellanca becomes the only woman vice president on the executive board of the Amalgamated Clothing Workers of America in 1934; she serves until 1946.

Tillie Lewis (Myrtle Ehrlich) starts growing Italian tomatoes in California in 1934 and eventually builds her canning operation into a multimillion-dollar enterprise, Tillie Lewis Foods. She is the first to can unskinned tomatoes and to artificially sweeten canned fruit.

Lillie Mae Jackson of the NAACP starts a national "Buy Where You Can Work" campaign in 1935 to make stores hire African Americans.

With her husband and others, Manuela Solis Sager helps start the South Texas Agricultural Workers Union in 1935.

A 1935 *Fortune* magazine article on 16 women executives singles out Josephine Roche, head of a Colorado coal-mining company and assistant secretary of the treasury, as the businesswoman of the decade. Other women cited include Elizabeth Arden, Helena Rubinstein, and Mrs. Taube Coller Davis, who advises department stores.

In 1935 Gretchen Schoenleber, president of Ambrosia Chocolate Company in Milwaukee, is the first woman member of a commodity exchange, the New York Cocoa Exchange.

When the United Electrical and Radio Workers forms in 1936, it welcomes women workers. By 1937 they are 40% of its membership.

In a suit brought by Elsie Parrish against her employer, the West Coast Hotel Company, the Supreme Court in 1937 reverses its 1923 *Adkins* decision and upholds a Washington state minimum-wage law for women. In its decision the court deplores the "exploitation of a class of workers who are in an unequal position with respect to bargaining power" and contends, "What these workers lose in wages the taxpayers are called upon to pay. The bare cost of living must be met."

During the 44-day sit-down strike of auto workers at General Motors in Flint, Michigan, in 1937, women provide the men, seated at their machines, with food and other necessities (see sidebar).

To protest poor pay, women salesclerks at several dime stores in New York hold a sit-down strike in 1937. Locking themselves in, they bed down behind the counters at night. They win their raises.

Margaret Fogarty Rudkin (1897–1967) sells bread baked at her home (Pepperidge Farm) to a local Connecticut grocer in 1937. Her market quickly expands, and by 1939 *Reader's Digest* features her in an article, "Bread de Luxe." It is the start of a multimillion-dollar baking industry.

In San Francisco, Chinese American women organize an ILGWU affiliate in 1938 and strike for 13 weeks against a chain store's garment factory. They win their immediate demands, but the plant later closes.

The 1938 Fair Labor Standards Act establishes minimum wages and maximum hours for both sexes and forbids employment of children under 16. It does not, however, include agricultural and domestic workers, thereby failing to protect many women of color.

Labor organizer Emma Tenayuca (b. 1916) initially leads pecan shellers in San Antonio on a successful 1938 strike, but the United Cannery, Agricultural, Packing and Allied Workers of America (UCAPAWA) fears her Communist Party affiliation and replaces her with Luisa Moreno (c. 1906/7–92). During the next decade Moreno also organizes cotton workers, beet workers, and cannery workers. She serves as international UCAPAWA vice president and state vice president for the Congress of Industrial Organizations (CIO). Politically active, she is deported during the McCarthy witchhunts of the 1950s.

Some 1,000 Japanese American women join cannery unions in 1938.

In Richmond, Virginia, Louise ("Mama") Harris leads a spontaneous strike of tobacco stemmers in 1938. White ILGWU women shock the town by backing the black workers' demonstration. The strikers' demands are met within 18 days.

"We Organized on Our Own"

During the 1937 auto workers strike, Genora Johnson initiates the Women's Emergency Brigade. The women, sporting red berets and armbands, help run the picket lines, stave off police attacks, and even break the factory windows when tear gas is used on the men inside. "We organized on our own without the benefit of professional leadership," Johnson later says, "and yet, we played a role, second to none, in the birth of a union [the United Auto Workers] and in changing working families' lives forever."

After aiding the sleeping car porters' union since 1925, local auxiliaries coalesce in 1939 in the International Ladies' Auxiliary Order to the Brotherhood of Sleeping Car Porters, headed by Halena Wilson. Their anthem is "Marching Together," written by Rosina Corrothers-Tucker.

In 1938 Beatrice Fox Auerbach (1887–1968) starts managing the family department store, G. Fox and Company, in Hartford, Connecticut, and increases business tenfold by 1965. She is one of the first to give employees a five-day week, retirement plans, and other benefits.

In 1939 at the California Sanitary Canning Company in Los Angeles, Chicana and Russian Jewish women walk out for higher pay, improved working conditions, and union recognition. UCAPAWA organizer Dorothy Ray Healey helps lead the workers, who run constant pickets, set up a boycott, and finally take their children to protest at the owners' homes. After two-and-a-half months, they win most of their demands.

Two women welders during World War II (Library of Congress)

1940–49

Roughly a fifth of white women and a third of black women are wage earners in 1940. Although a third of white workers have clerical jobs, only 1.4% of black women do. About 60% of black compared with 10% of white women workers are domestics. Among Japanese American women earners, almost 38% are in agriculture and 24% in personal services, such as laundries. Married women workers often have difficulty finding jobs, especially in banks, insurance companies, public utilities, and teaching.

In 1940 Georgette Klinger opens her New York salon, introducing the skin-care products she developed in Europe. Her business grows into a multimillion-dollar concern; in 1972 she adds Klinger for Men.

After the U.S. entry into World War II in late 1941, the government urges industry to tap into "womanpower," and Congress passes the 1942 Lanham Act, establishing public nurseries (until the end of the war only) for the children of women working for the war effort. The defense industry alone hires 2 million women during the war. They quickly learn how to construct airplanes and ships, put together machine guns, and wire electrical equipment. Altogether 6 million new women enter the labor force, including a large number of married women. "Rosie the Riveter" is a popular war propaganda symbol. "Almost overnight," remarks Mary Anderson, head of the Women's Bureau, "women were reclassified from a marginal to a basic labor supply." Not all women, however: about 50,000 Japanese American women spend the war in internment camps.

In 1942, when Hope Skillman Schary (1908–81) starts Skillmill, a textile company, she hires only women; later she becomes a women's rights activist.

In Winston-Salem, North Carolina, in 1943 African American women stage a spontaneous strike at a tobacco plant after an elderly man dies from overwork; they succeed in forming a union. One of the leaders,

Moranda Smith (1915–50), becomes the first black woman to serve as a regional director in the South (p. 128). Despite threats from the Ku Klux Klan, she travels all through the South, organizing workers.

By 1944 the number of women in unions has increased almost four-fold since 1940, from 800,000 to 3 million. Because so many women join, the United Auto Workers creates a women's division, led by Mildred M. Jeffrey and Lillian Hatcher. The United Federal Workers elect Eleanor Nelson as the first woman to head a national union in more than 40 years, since Agnes Nestor in 1913. Nelson is also the only woman on the CIO national executive board. At the United Electrical, Radio and Machine Workers of America, Ruth Young is elected to the exectuve board.

In 1944 Soia Mentschikoff becomes probably the first woman partner in a major Wall Street firm, but there are hardly any others until the late 1970s or 1980s.

As the war ends in 1945, many women lose their jobs, especially in heavy industry. The Latinas who worked the copper mines in Arkansas, for example, all give their jobs to returning soldiers. In the Detroit auto industry the women employees drop from 25% to 7.5% of the workforce, despite protests from UAW women leaders. At war's end 36% of women work, but by 1947 this falls to 28%.

In 1945 Dorothy Shaver becomes president of Lord and Taylor, with an annual salary of $110,000, the highest of any woman in the country but about a quarter of what men in a similar position receive.

Using an old family recipe, Bertha West Nealey and Ruth Bigelow set up their own company, Constant Comment Tea, in 1945. The name is from a friend's remark to Nealey: "My dear, your tea was the hit of the party. There was nothing but constant comment."

Bell Telephone hires its first black female phone operator in 1945.

Estée Mentzer Lauder and her husband start their cosmetics empire in 1946 by selling a face cream made by her uncle.

"The Voice With a Smile Will Be Gone for a While"
—telephone strikers' cry

The largest walkout of U.S. women occurs in 1947, when 350,000 telephone workers, two-thirds women, go on strike against American Telephone and Telegraph. The protests are settled locally, but the strike leads to the formation of the Communications Workers of America.

In 1948 the Supreme Court upholds a Michigan law banning women bartenders except for the "wife or daughter of the male owner."

In 1949 in Los Angeles, Romana Acosta Bañuelos (b. 1925) starts a tortilla factory, which expands into the highly successful Ramona's Mexican Food Products.

On a Billboard

"If you've used an electric mixer in your kitchen, you can learn to run a drill press. "If you've followed recipes exactly, you can learn to load shell."
—from 1943 billboard ad; cited in *America's Working Women: A Documentary History*, edited by Rosalyn Baxandall, Linda Gordon, and Susan Reverby (New York: Vintage Books, 1976)

In 1949 Moranda Smith becomes the southern regional director for the Food, Tobacco, Agricultural and Allied Workers and a member of its national executive board—the highest position to date for any African American woman in the labor movement.

1950–59

Almost 30% of all women work in 1950, and they represent about a quarter of the total workforce. More than half of single women work, and nearly a quarter of married women, a big increase from 1940.

Chemist Hazel Gladys Bishop starts her own cosmetics firm in 1950 to market her "lasting lipstick," which doesn't smear. She soon quits the firm but continues to develop new cosmetics.

In June 1951, after Chicano miners in New Mexico have been on strike eight months, the company gets an injunction against their picketing and hires scabs. But the women take over the picket lines and refuse to let the scabs through, chanting, *"No les dejen pasar"* ("Don't let them pass"). Neither tear gas nor arrests stop the women from going back to the picket line (see sidebar). A year later the strike is won. The women's story is later told in the film *Salt of the Earth*.

Lillian Vernon starts her company in 1951 with an ad in *Seventeen* magazine for belts and purses. She soon is sending out her own catalog and expands into a multimillion-dollar mail-order business selling housewares and novelty items.

In 1952 Mary McCusker is the first woman elected to the American Institute of Banking.

In 1953 Ernestine G. Foster Bowman (later Procope) starts E. G. Bowman Company, providing insurance for black families' homes. In the 1970s she gains corporate clients, and by the 1990s she heads the largest black-owned insurance brokerage agency.

Women helicopter pilots start their Whirly Girls association in 1955.

In 1955 women earn an average of 63 cents for every dollar men earn; this figure will actually drop in the next decade.

As the new president and chairperson of the board of A. M. Kidder, a brokerage house, in 1956, Josephine Holt Perfect Bay (1900–62) is the first woman to head a member firm of the New York Stock Exchange.

The National Manpower Commission publishes *Womanpower in Today's World* (1957), highlighting the large number of women, including married women, in the workforce. It also reveals that women are mostly confined to what is seen as "women's work" and points out that 95% of doctors, lawyers, and scientists are men. A second report, *Work in the Lives of Married Women* (1958), indicates the need for day care.

In 1957, as president of Laguna Beach, California, Federal Savings and Loan, Lorna Mills is the first woman to head a federally chartered savings and loan company.

Mary Roebling, president of a Trenton, New Jersey, bank since 1937, is the first woman elected to the board of governors of the American Stock Exchange, in 1958.

When Mildred Custin is named president of Bonwit Teller in Philadelphia in 1958, she is one of only six women department store presidents at a time when women are 90% of the shoppers and 80% of the workers in clothing factories.

In 1959 Ruth Bowen starts Queen Artists (later Queen Booking Corporation) in a tiny office, and in five years it is the biggest black-owned entertainment agency.

Gregoria Montalbe and Sophia Gonzales lead an ILGWU-organized strike against Tex-Son, a garment plant in San Antonio, in 1959.

Led by Local 1199, workers (mostly women) at six New York hospitals go on strike for higher wages in 1959. Defying police attacks and arrests, they stay out for 46 days to win a raise. Their action paves the way for union recognition in 1962 and a 1963 state law acknowledging collective bargaining rights of city hospital workers.

1960–69

About 35% of all women work in 1960, including more than 30% of all married women. The rate of pay, however, has dropped since 1955. Women now average 60 cents for every dollar men earn, and women of color average even less, about 42 cents per dollar. About 30% of women work in clerical jobs; for black women, this figure is close to 11%.

In 1962 Dolores Fernández Huerta (b. 1930) helps César Chávez start the Farm Workers Association (later the United Farm Workers, or UFW) and becomes its main contract negotiator. She helps coordinate the grape boycott on the East Coast in 1968–69, as well as the lettuce, grape, and Gallo wine boycotts of the 1970s. Arrested more than 20 times, she almost dies after a clubbing by police in 1988.

Another important UFW organizer is Jessie Lopez de la Cruz, the union's first woman organizing in the fields. "When I became involved with the union," she recalls, "I felt I had to get other women involved."

Felice Nierenberg Schwartz establishes Catalyst, a nonprofit organization, in 1962 to assist women with their career choices and problems.

Harvard Business School first admits women in 1962. At the University of Michigan a conference for women on management attracts 36 female executives from 19 states.

The 1963 Equal Pay Act establishes equal pay for equal work, but it does not cover domestics, agricultural workers, executives, administrators, and professionals.

Dusty Roads and Nancy Collins of the Airline Stewards and Stewardesses Association denounce the mandatory retirement age of 32 at a 1963 press conference. It takes five years to change this rule (see below).

Enterprising Inventors

In 1951 Marion Donovan invents a disposable diaper, called the Boater, and manufactures it herself when no one will take it on. She later sells her company for $1 million.

In 1956 executive secretary Bette McMurray Nesmith (later Graham, 1924–80) develops a white paint to correct typing mistakes and begins selling her Mistake Out to other secretaries. She soon changes the name to Liquid Paper, applies for a patent and trademark, and by 1968 is producing 10,000 bottles a day.

In 1959 Ruth Handler invents Barbie, the first teenage doll, which quadruples the sales of Mattel, the toy company she cofounded with her husband in 1945. Later she creates Ken. In the 1970s, after undergoing a mastectomy, she creates her Nearly Me breast prostheses and swimsuits for cancer victims.

Entrepreneurs for the 1960s

In 1963 Jean Slutsky Nidetch uses her own experience as a compulsive eater to establish Weight Watchers, which provides group reinforcement and dieting instructions for millions of overweight women.

In Texas in 1963, Mary Kay Ash starts Mary Kay Cosmetics, using women to sell her products through home demonstrations. She encourages the women as entrepreneurs, and by 1993 more women earn over $100,000 working for Mary Kay than for any other U.S. company.

In 1966 Mary G. Berg Wells (later Lawrence) cofounds Wells, Rich, Greene, soon one of the hottest ad agencies on Madison Avenue. She becomes chief executive officer and chairs the board. One of the firm's early, attention-getting successes is a new look for Braniff International Airlines, with the planes brightly painted and stewardesses attired in uniforms by well-known designers.

Muriel ("Mickey") Siebert establishes her own discount brokerage firm in 1967 and is the first woman to buy a seat on the New York Stock Exchange, after overcoming a "new" financing rule set by the NYSE and finding a sponsor (nine men initially turned her down despite her proven record in a top Wall Street firm).

Title VII of the 1964 Civil Rights Act bans sex discrimination in employment; the Equal Employment Opportunity Commission (EEOC) is the enforcing agency (see pp. 71–72).

In 1964 Bennetta Washington (1918–91) sets up the new Job Corps program for women, with training centers across the country.

At the 1964 United Auto Workers convention, 200 women and a few men start a group called Help Equalize Representation (HER), headed by Joanne Wilson and Elizabeth Jackson. By 1966 they succeed in getting Olga Madar elected to the UAW International executive board.

Mary Draper Janney and Jane Phillips Fleming start Washington (later Wider) Opportunities for Women (WOW) in 1964 to develop women's job skills, provide employment counseling, help women enter nontraditional fields, and assist with locating day care.

In 1965 Romana Bañuelos helps start the Pan-American National Bank in East Los Angeles, the only Chicano-owned bank at the time. In 1969 she chairs the board of directors.

Julia Walsh and Phyllis Peterson are the first women members of the American Stock Exchange, in 1965.

"Breaking Free at Last"—button by Vivian Jones

At the Lincoln Nursing Home in Baltimore in 1966, about 20 black women workers go on strike and start the Maryland Freedom Union with the support of the Congress of Racial Equality (CORE). Women from two other nursing homes join them, and Vivian Jones is elected president. Her button design of two black hands breaking out of chains (see above) becomes well known. The union also organizes retail workers and negotiates contracts for them at three big chain stores.

In 1968, after a five-year fight, Dusty Roads and Nancy Collins win their complaint against the airlines when EEOC guidelines prohibit airlines from dismissing "overage" stewardesses. The EEOC also rules against the airlines' restriction on employing married women.

Following two years of protests by NOW, the EEOC in 1968 bans sex-segregated advertising in newspaper "Help Wanted" columns unless employers can show that sex is a "bona fide occupational qualification."

Turned down for a job as an agent-telegrapher because of her sex, Leah Rosenfeld wins a discrimination case against Southern Pacific Railroad in 1968. The Ninth Circuit Court rules that Title VII of the Civil Rights Act supersedes California's protective legislation, which effectively prevents women from holding jobs that require overtime.

Federally Employed Women is formed by Daisy Fields and others in 1968 to fight employment discrimination by the U.S. government.

In Atlanta in 1968, Dorothy Lee Bolden helps organize the National Domestic Workers Union to teach women how to win better conditions from their employers. The group succeeds in raising wages from a low of $3.50 a day to a minimum of $13.50 plus carfare.

In New York labor organizer Lillian Davis Roberts (b. 1928) defies a state law against strikes by public employees to lead a walkout by state hospital workers in 1968. There is a public outcry when she is jailed for two weeks. Later, in 1981, as the first black woman to serve as state industrial (or labor) commissioner, she fights against sweatshops.

Venita Walker VanCaspel sets up her own brokerage firm in 1968 and is the first female member of the Pacific Stock Exchange.

In 1969 in the Fifth Circuit Court, NOW lawyers Marguerite Rawalt and Sylvia Roberts win Lorena Weeks's case against Southern Bell, which had denied her a job as a switchman because of a Georgia law restricting the weights women could lift. The attorneys point out that as a secretary, Weeks already has to lift a typewriter weighing more than the limit. When Weeks finally starts her new job in 1971, she faces both racial and sexual putdowns, and women activists protest.

In Charleston, South Carolina, Mary Ann Moultrie leads black women hospital workers on a 113-day strike in 1969 to gain wage increases and union recognition (see sidebar). Huge rallies, supported by civil rights leaders like Coretta Scott King, ensue, along with beatings and mass arrests. The workers persevere and win many of their demands through their union, Local 1199B. Later in the year the National Union of Hospital and Health Care Employees (District 1199) is established. Two women serve on the 17-member executive board: Doris Turner as secretary and Mary Ann Moultrie as vice president.

1970–79

Close to 44% of all women work in 1970, including about 41% of married women. Women are moving into skilled trades, gaining employment as carpenters, electricians, plumbers, and machinists. However, most women are still concentrated in poorly paid jobs. The average amount women earn has dropped to about 59 cents for every dollar men earn. It is even less for women of color, although the gap between white and nonwhite women has narrowed.

In 1970 women file job discrimination complaints against a number of institutions, including *Newsweek* and other magazines (see "Journalism") and universities (see "Education"). NOW files complaints against 1,300 corporations.

In *Phillips* v. *Martin-Marietta Corporation* (1971), the Supreme Court rules that the company cannot refuse to hire Ida Phillips or any other woman because she has preschool children unless it also denies employment to fathers with young children.

After Harriet Rabb and women law students file sex discrimination charges at 10 of New York's top law firms, New York City Human Rights Commissioner Eleanor Holmes Norton rules in their favor in

"We Can and We Will Overcome"

"We 400 hospital workers—almost all of us women, and all of us black—were compelled to go on strike so that we could win the right to be treated as human beings. . . .

"We had to fight the entire power structure of the state of South Carolina. . . . All because 400 black women dared to stand up and say we were not going to let anybody turn us around. . . .

"A year ago, nobody ever heard of us. We were forgotten women, second-class citizens. . . .

"We have demonstrated to the city of Charleston, to the state of South Carolina, and to the people all over America that we can and we will overcome. And nobody, just nobody, is going to turn us around."
—Mary Ann Moultrie, Local 1199B organizer; quoted in Philip S. Foner *Women and the American Labor Movement: From World War I to the Present* (New York: Free Press, 1980)

the test case in 1971. After further legal action, all the firms agree to nondiscriminatory hiring practices.

In 1972 Congress extends the Equal Pay Act of 1963 to include executive, administrative, and professional personnel. It also passes the Equal Employment Opportunity Act, which enables the EEOC to take legal action to enforce its decisions.

In 1972 in Washington, D.C., 13 women start the Association of Women Business Owners (changed to National AWBO in 1974). Other new organizations include the Federation for Professional Women and the National Association for Female Executives. Also, the Institute for Women and Work, sponsored by Cornell University, begins its research into women's roles in the workplace.

Juanita Morris Kreps serves as the first woman director of the New York Stock Exchange in 1972. In the same year she publishes *Sex in the Marketplace: American Women at Work* and is given the James B. Duke professorship at Duke University.

In 1972 Joanne E. Pierce and Susan Lynn Roley are the first women FBI agents since J. Edgar Hoover took over the bureau in 1924.

In Texas in 1972, about 4,000 Chicanas formally strike against Farah Manufacturing Company after a drive for unionization beginning in 1969. In 1970 a poster featuring Rosa Flores, fists raised, shouting "*Viva la Huelga!*" ("Long Live the Strike!") helped spur a national boycott of the company's pants for men and boys. The strike lasts almost two years, until 1974, when the women win union recognition.

In a suit brought by NOW against the *Pittsburgh Press,* the Supreme Court rules in 1973 against sex-segregated employment ads.

American Telephone and Telegraph (AT&T)—described by the EEOC as "without doubt the largest oppressor of women workers in the U.S." —signs a $38 million settlement in 1973 giving back pay to 13,000 women, as well as 2,000 men of color. It also sets affirmative action goals, including hiring women for traditional men's jobs and vice versa.

Under pressure from women's groups, the Office of Federal Contract Compliance in 1973 finally issues its revised guidelines, which not only prohibit sex discrimination in employment by any federal contractor but also require affirmative action to correct existing imbalances.

In 1973 the Civil Service Commission eliminates height and weight requirements that discriminated against the hiring of women to police parks, prevent fires, or help control drugs.

The Federal Home Loan Bank forbids sex discrimination by savings and loan institutions in 1973. In the same year the first Feminist Credit Union is established in Detroit, Michigan.

The new Stewardesses for Women's Rights speaks out in 1973 on job discrimination, public image, and health concerns for women flight attendants. Office workers also begin to organize, forming Women Employed in Chicago, Women Office Workers in New York, and 9 to 5 in Boston.

In 1973 Kate Zollar Miller and her husband begin publishing *Career Woman,* a recruitment magazine for women entering the job market.

As second officer for Frontier Airlines, Emily Howell flies Boeing 737 jets in 1973, the first woman to do so for a regularly scheduled commercial airline. Bonnie Tiburzi is the first female jet pilot hired by a major airline, American Airlines, in 1973.

More than 3,000 women from 58 unions attend a 1974 Chicago meeting where the Coalition of Labor Union Women (CLUW) is formed. Olga Madar, who became the first female vice president of the United Auto Workers in 1970, is the first president. Addie Wyatt (Amalgamated Meat Cutters), Myra Wolfgang (international vice president of the Hotel, Motel and Restaurant Employees' Union), Edith Van Horne (UAW), and Dorothy Haener (UAW) are among those who help set up CLUW. Unlike the earlier WTUL, the group is made up entirely of union members; their goals are to combat sexism within unions, push for legislation addressing women workers' needs, and organize the 30 million women workers who are not in unions.

In 1974, for the first time, the nation's 1.5 million domestic workers are covered by the minimum-wage law.

Annabelle Valle, Amalia Mendoza, and Martha Cotera form the Mexican American Business and Professional Women of Austin in 1974. A similar group forms in El Paso the following year.

"I told one of the guys that I had to feed my . . . kids just like he did"—*Ann Warren, steelworker*

A number of women begin working in coal mines in 1974, and by 1979 they are ready to hold the first National Conference of Women Coal Miners. Women also enter the steel industry in 1974, after steel companies settle a $56 million suit for sex and race discrimination.

In North Carolina, Crystal Lee Jordan Sutton's struggle to organize textile workers at J. P. Stevens mills pays off in 1974, when workers choose the Textile Workers Union of America to represent them. But J. P. Stevens continues to resist unionization, and in 1977 the Coalition of Labor Union Women calls for a boycott of its products. Sutton's story is later the basis for the movie *Norma Rae,* starring Sally Field.

Simmons College Graduate School of Management opens in 1974 to teach women how to move up in the corporate world.

Working Women United Institute is set up in 1975 to combat sexual harassment at work. In its initial survey 70% of the women report at least one instance of sexual harrassment.

Entrepreneurs in Fashion

Among the women who launch fashion design businesses in the late 1960s and 1970s are:

Susie Tompkins, who starts Esprit de Corps in 1968, featuring a youth-oriented casual look.

—Jessica McClintock, who sets up her own company in 1969 and gains attention for her Gunne Sax line of prairie-style dresses.

—Nancy Heller, who launches her business in 1971 by selling rhinestone-studded size 16 men's undershirts.

—Diane Von Furstenberg, who starts her business in 1971 with her design for a simple jersey wrap dress.

—Carole Little, who cofounds her company in 1975 and emphasizes colorful prints in her designs.

—Elisabeth Claiborne Ortenberg, who starts her own Liz Claiborne line of clothes for professional women in 1976.

—Josie Cruz Natori, who transforms the lingerie industry in 1977 with her nightshirts featuring Philippine embroidery.

—Adrienne Vittadini, who develops her line of women's sportswear from her knitted sweaters of 1979.

The First Women's Bank and Trust Company opens in New York City in 1975, with Madeline H. McWhinney as its first president, followed by Lynn Salvage in 1976.

After a year-long strike at a San Francisco garment factory, 125 Chinese American women in an ILGWU local win their demands in 1976.

Working Women: National Association for Office Workers, headed by Karen Nussbaum, is formed in 1976 from five local groups. In four years it has 12 chapters with a membership of 10,000.

The first issue of *Working Woman* (1976) features such successes as day-care director Elaine Bloom, restaurateur Cindy Ayers, database manager Maureen Grove, and TV journalist Betty Rollin.

In Pennsylvania in 1976, Roberta A. Kankus is the first woman to be licensed as an operator at a commercial nuclear power plant.

To raise money for the Oneida community center in 1976, Alma Webster and Sandra Ninham run a Sunday afternoon bingo game, which is the start of the reservation's multimillion-dollar gambling operation.

When Iris Rivera's boss asks her to make him coffee in 1977, she refuses because "(1) I don't drink coffee, (2) it's not listed as one of my job duties, and (3) ordering the secretary to fix the coffee is carrying the role of homemaker too far." She is promptly fired, sparking a lunch-hour protest of 50-some other secretaries in Chicago's Loop. Women Employed takes up Rivera's cause, gaining publicity and getting Rivera's job back.

American Woman's Economic Development Corporation is set up in 1977, with Beatrice Fitzpatrick as director, to provide training and advice for women entrepreneurs.

In Denver in 1977, Juana Maria Bordes starts the Mi Casa Resource Center to provide job training, language skills, and counseling for low-income women of color, especially Chicanas. By 1988 they have placed almost 300 women in full-time jobs.

The 1978 Pregnancy Discrimination Act amends Title VII of the 1964 Civil Rights Act to ban employment discrimination against pregnant women. This law counters several recent Supreme Court decisions that let employers deny pregnant women disability benefits, although in 1977, in *Satty* v. *Nashville Gas Company,* the court did uphold Nora Satty's right to retain her seniority during maternity leave.

New 1978 regulations from the Labor Department are designed to increase the number of women construction workers.

Appalachian women start the Coal Employment Project in 1978 to get the mines to hire more women and minority workers.

For the first time, in 1978 New York City allows women to apply for firefighters' jobs, but they must pass tests of physical ability. When all

79 applicants fail, Brenda Berkman sues for a less biased test and wins. In 1982 the first 11 women Fire Academy graduates enter the force.

A 1979 Supreme Court ruling upholds the use of affirmative action programs in private industry. However, in another case the court upholds a Massachusetts law that gives veterans (98% of whom are male) automatic preference in civil service jobs as long as they pass the exam.

Companies can no longer require women, but not men, to wear uniforms if the jobs are comparable, according to a 1979 court decision.

By 1979 there are close to 300 women on the boards of major U.S. corporations, almost double the number four years earlier.

The National Association of Black Women Entrepreneurs is formed by Marilyn French-Hubbard and others in 1979 to offer advice and training, as well as networking, for black businesswomen.

In 1979 Long Island Railroad conductor Deirdre Hickey is the first woman to operate all freight and passenger trains on a commuter line.

1980–89

In 1980 more than half of all women are in the workforce, including just over 50% of married women. They still, however, earn only an average of 59 cents to the male worker's dollar. At the top level, 427 of the top 1,300 companies have at least one women on the board of directors. Also, the number of women entrepreneurs has increased 56% in the last decade, five times the rate for men.

In 1980 Joyce Miller, vice president of Amalgamated Clothing and Textile Workers and past president of the Coalition of Labor Union Women, is the first woman on the 35-member AFL-CIO executive council. A second woman, Barbara Hutchinson, is elected in 1982, and a third, Lenore Miller, in 1987.

New EEOC guidelines in 1980 list sexual harassment as a form of prohibited sexual discrimination. In Minnesota the supreme court rules the employer is responsible for sexual harassment by employees.

The Iowa Civil Rights Commission in 1980 upholds firefighter Linda Eaton's right to breastfeed her son at work during her personal time. Faced with continuing harassment on the job, however, Eaton resigns.

After seven years, design engineer Helen Kim wins a sex discrimination suit against the Los Angeles transportation department in 1980.

Gertrude Stutz, president of Henri Bendel since 1957, buys the store in 1980 and transforms it into one of the trendiest shops in New York.

In 1981 in San Jose, California, about 1,5000 mostly female municipal employees attack wage discrimination in a system-wide strike of city workers; they are the first women to win salaries based on comparable worth. In Chicago 60 female custodians win their suit against the city for wage discrimination.

Executives of the 1970s

Some of the women reaching the top levels of management during the 1970s are:

—Ellen R. Gordon, first woman president, Tootsie Roll Industries.

—Mercedes A. Bates, first female vice president, General Mills.

—Beverly C. Lannquist, vice president, Morgan Stanley and Company (investment house).

—Jeannette Lee, first female vice president, Hallmark Cards, in charge of corporate design.

—Diana K. Mayer, first woman vice president, Citicorp.

—Rose Totino, first female vice president, Pillsbury, after buyout of her frozen-pizza business.

—Jane Cahill Pfeiffer, former IBM vice president; first woman chair, NBC's board of directors.

—Virginia Dwyer, first female vice president and treasurer, AT&T.

—Betsy Ancker-Johnson, former assistant secretary of commerce for science and technology; first woman vice president in auto industry, in charge of environmental activities at General Motors.

Entrepreneurs of the Early 1980s

These are a few of the many women who set up successful new businesses in the early 1980s:

—Gae Veit starts Shingobee Construction in 1980 in Minnesota, hiring mostly other Native American workers.

—In 1980 Lin W. Lan sets up the Pacific Pioneer Insurance Company to serve the Asian American business community in California.

—In 1982 Jan Davidson founds her own California-based educational software publishing company, whose products include Math Blaster.

—Jenny Craig and her husband start the Jenny Craig weight loss program in 1982.

—In 1983 Judy Sims and her husband set up Software Spectrum, marketing microcomputer business software.

—June Morris establishes Morris Air in 1984, at first offering vacation trips to Hawaii and then discount airfares between cities in the West.

—Donna Karan starts her own fashion design firm in 1984 after a decade as Anne Klein's successor.

—In 1985 Kavelle Bajaj sets up I-Net, a computer networking and systems integration firm.

Women's professional and labor groups form the National Committee on Pay Equity as an advocacy group and source of information for women with wage discrimination complaints.

In New York more than 10,000 Asian American seamstresses walk off their jobs in 1982 and march en masse through Chinatown. They win their demands in a new ILGWU contract.

There are 62 women partners at the top eight accounting firms in 1983, but this represents only 1% of the total.

Asian Immigrant Women Advocates forms in Oakland, California, in 1983 as a community-based organizing group. It helps garment workers, for example, organize to collect back pay from contractors.

In a suit brought by Elizabeth Ann Hishon against the law firm King and Spalding, the Supreme Court rules in 1984 that any discimination on the basis of sex in promotion to the position of partner violates the 1964 Civil Rights Act.

According to *Savvy* magazine, the top 12 women business owners in 1984 are, in order: Estée Lauder (cosmetics), Katharine Graham (*Washington Post*), Mary Wells Lawrence (Wells, Rich, Green: advertising), Mary C. Crowley (Home Interiors and Gifts: a Dallas firm), Mary Hudson (Hudson Oil Works: petroleum), Mary Kay Ash (cosmetics), Donna Wolf Steigerwaldt (Jockey International: clothing), Colombe Nicholas (Christian Dior: fashion), Helen K. Copley (Copley Press: newspaper publishing), Diane Von Furstenberg (fashion), Lana Jane Lewis-Brent and Leona Lewis (Sunshine-J Stores: retail chain), and Elisabeth Claiborne Ortenberg (fashion).

The number of women in managerial positions has more than doubled between 1965 and 1985, going from 14% to 33%. Yet a third of women are still in low-paying clerical jobs. Even in new fields women are overrepresented at the bottom and underrepresented at the top: for example, only a third of computer programmers are women, compared with two-thirds of word processors and computer operators.

In California in 1985, Asian American seamstresses win a three-year battle, supported by the U.S. Department of Labor, against T&W Fashions for better pay and working conditions. In Boston, after organizing to win job retraining when they are laid off, Chinese women garment workers help set up the Chinese Progressive Alliance Workers Center as a support group and resource facility.

In 1985 Betty Tianti becomes the only female to head a state AFL-CIO, in Connecticut. In the American Federation of State, County, and Municipal Employees, a third of all locals are headed by women. The largest U.S. postal workers' local, in the New York metropolitan area, is led by Josie McMillian. In a much-publicized 1985 strike at Yale University, women clerical workers win a contract correcting wage disparities.

"A claim of 'hostile environment' sex discrimination is actionable"—U.S. Supreme Court

In *Meritor Savings Bank* v. *Mechelle Vinson* (1986), the Supreme Court rules that sexual harassment is a form of sex discrimination prohibited by federal law. In several other cases the court reaffirms the constitutionality of affirmative action programs, and it clarifies that there is no need to prove each applicant was actually discriminated against in the past. In another ruling, in a case brought against Dayton Christian Day Schools, the court holds that religious organizations must comply with laws forbidding sex discrimination in employment.

Women own more than a quarter of American businesses in 1987, and the revenues of women-owned businesses have more than tripled in the last decade.

In *California Federal Savings and Loan* v. *Guerra* (1987), the Supreme Court upholds a state law requiring companies to give women up to four months of leave for childbirth without loss of their jobs. Yet in another case the court upholds a Missouri law denying unemployment benefits to a woman who voluntarily leaves her job for childbirth, since the same law applies to other disabilities.

In a case brought by a male job applicant, the Supreme Court rules in 1987 that employers can consider sex in hiring a qualified applicant for a job from which women have been traditionally excluded. As a result, Diane Joyce keeps her new job as a dispatcher for road crews in Santa Clara County, California.

Women in Franchising forms in 1987 to provide training in this area.

Elaine Garzarelli of Shearson Lehman Brothers gains attention as a top Wall Street market analyst after predicting the 1987 October crash. Other women who achieve firsts in 1987 in investment banking include Marilyn LaMarche, as an active partner at Lazard Frères; Karen Bechtel, Catherine James, and Marie-Elaine LaRoche, as managing directors at Morgan Stanley; Barabara Alexander, as managing director at Salomon Brothers; and Jeanette Loeb, as partner at Goldman, Sachs.

Congress passes the 1988 Women's Business Ownership Act, which gives women the same rights and protections in applying for commercial credit as they gained for individual credit under the Equal Credit Opportunity Act. It also sets up the National Women's Business Council to help women in their dealings with federal agencies.

Carmen Ortiz starts the Hispanic Women's Chamber of Commerce in 1988, which offers seminars to help Latinas get started in business.

In 1989 Ann Hopkins wins her suit against the accounting firm Price Waterhouse, which did not promote her to partner even though she generated more business for the firm than any other candidate. In a victory for women's rights, the Supreme Court rules that as long as an

Firsts for the 1980s

Breakthroughs for women continue during the 1980s. A few of these follow.

—Caroline Leonette Ahmanson in San Francisco and Jean A Crockett in Philadelphia are the first two women to chair regional federal reserve banks, in 1981.

—Vicki Saporta is the first woman director of organizing for the International Brotherhood of Teamsters, in 1983.

—Betsy Carroll of People Express is the first woman to fly a jumbo jet across the Atlantic for a commercial airline, in 1984.

—Geri B. Larson is the U.S. Forest Service's first woman supervisor in 1985, in charge of Tahoe National Forest in California.

—Penny Harrington is the first woman police chief of a major city, in Portland, Oregon, in 1985—after filing more than 40 sex discrimination complaints during her career. She is forced to resign in 1986, however, after clashes with the mayor and male union leaders.

—Dorothy Brunson is the first black woman to own a TV station, WGTW in Philadelphia (her license is approved in 1986, and she wins various legal challenges in 1991).

—María Elena Durazo is the first Latina to head a major union in Los Angeles, as president of the Hotel and Restaurant Employees local, in 1989.

employee can give clear evidence that sex bias exists, it is up to the employer to prove that this was not the reason for denying promotion.

A 1989 article by Felice N. Schwartz, president of Catalyst, stirs up controversy over the "Mommy Track." Schwartz's call for flexible schedules to meet the needs of mothers in the corporate world is seen as encouraging a two-tier system.

1990–95

About three-fourths of women age 25 to 54 are wage earners in 1990. About 24% of lawyers are now women, compared with only 3% two decades ago. Almost half of all accountants are women, double the number 20 years ago. Similar gains can be seen in many other professions. Yet white men still hold 95% of the top management jobs in the biggest corporations. And although the gap between men's and women's average earnings has narrowed, women still make only 67 cents for every dollar men make.

A 1991 Labor Department report shows that only 6.6% of executive employees are women, and a similar study by the Feminist Majority Foundation reveals that fewer than 3% of Fortune 500 companies' top executives are female. Faced with these statistics, the new Civil Rights Act sets up a Glass Ceiling Commission, chaired by the secretary of labor, to investigate obstacles to promotion of women and minorities to the top positions.

In 1991 a Minneapolis federal district judge approves the first class-action suit charging sexual harassment, filed by 100 women ironworkers. The complaints of Anita Hill (see "Politics") and Paula Coughlin (see "Military") bring media attention to sexual harassment.

The Supreme Court rules in 1991 that a company, in this case Johnson Controls, cannot cite "fetal protection" as a reason for barring women of childbearing age from jobs that involve exposure to substances that may lead to birth defects. Earlier, some women underwent sterilization in order to get these dangerous but high-paying jobs.

In 1991 AT&T pays a record $66 million to settle a 1978 discrimination complaint filed with the EEOC by employees who were forced to go on unpaid leave when they were six or seven months pregnant.

In 1991 American Airlines ends its rigid weight rules after losing in court. At Continental Airlines, Terri Fischette is fired when she doesn't wear makeup, but press ridicule and the courts force her reinstatement.

Debora de Hoyos is, in 1991, the first Latina managing partner at one of the 12 largest U.S. law firms: Mayer, Brown and Platt in Chicago.

Several women assume top jobs in advertising in 1991: Rochelle Lazarus is president of the New York office of Ogilvy and Mather Worldwide, Susan Gilette heads the Chicago office of DDB Needham, and Helayne Spivak is executive vice president and executive creative director at Young and Rubicam. In 1992 Charlotte Beers is named chairperson and CEO of Ogilvy and Mather Worldwide, the fifth largest ad agency in the world. She oversees more than 7,000 employees. Beers is also the first woman president of the American Association of Advertising Agencies.

Women's average earnings in 1992 are 71 cents to the male dollar. Some women professionals with doctorate degrees earn 77 cents to the dollar, but women at the low end earn only 65 cents to the dollar.

Congress passes the 1992 Women in Apprenticeship and Nontraditional Occupations Act, giving community-based groups money to train women for jobs in traditionally male fields.

In 1992 State Farm Insurance pays a record $157 million settlement in a sex discrimination suit, more than a dozen years after Muriel Kraszewski initiated the complaint. Kraszewski had been told she needed a college degree to be a sales agent (although men didn't need one); more than 800 women joined her in the suit.

Donna Redel is the first woman to head an American futures exchange, as chair of the Commodity Exchange of New York in 1992.

In 1992 women-owned businesses employ more workers in the United States than the Fortune 500 companies do worldwide. A 1993 survey shows 41 of the 50 corporations with the largest profits have at least one woman director. However, women represent only 6.2% of the corporate directors in the Fortune 500 and 500 service companies.

In *Harris* v. *Forklift Systems* (1993), the Supreme Court sides with Teresa Harris and rules that a complainant does not have to prove "severe psychological injury" or an inability to work well to sustain the charge of sexual harassment. The main criterion is if any "reasonable person" would find the situation abusive.

In 1993 the Ms. Foundation for Women sponsors its first Take Our Daughters to Work Day, designed to build girls' self-esteem and open their eyes to a variety of career possibilities for women.

Barbara Spyridon Pope starts the Foundation for the Prevention of Sexual Harrassment and Workplace Discrimination in 1993. As former assistant secretary of the Navy for manpower and reserve administration, she was involved in the Tailhook investigation (see "War").

The 1993 Family Medical Leave Act finally goes into effect (vetoed earlier by Geoge Bush, it is passed again and signed by Bill Clinton). It guarantees up to 12 weeks of unpaid time off for family reasons, such as childbirth or a family member's illness.

After 170 years the Texas Rangers, an elite corps of state troopers, gain two women in 1993: Cheryl Campbell Steadman and Marie Reynolds Garcia. Steadman quits after a year, citing sexual harassment.

The International Association of Women Chefs and Restaurateurs forms in 1994 in San Francisco to encourage women in the field.

Top 10 Women Business Owners

These women are listed by the National Association of Women Business Owners as the top 10 for 1994:

—*Marian Ilitch, Little Caesar Enterprises (pizza chain)*

—*Joyce Raley Teel, Raley's (grocery store chain)*

—*Lynda Resnick, Roll Industries (varied)*

—*Antonia Axson Johnson, Axel Johnson (communications)*

—*Liz Minyard and Gretchen Minyard Williams, Minyard Food Stores*

—*Linda Wachner, Warnaco Group (clothing)*

—*Jenny Craig, Jenny Craig (weight-loss program)*

—*Donna Wolf Steigerwaldt, Jockey International (clothing)*

—*Donna Karan, Donna Karan (clothing)*

—*Helen Copley, Copley Press (newspaper publisher)*

In 1994 Rena Weeks, who had worked as a secretary at a large and prestigious law firm in San Francisco, is awarded a record $7.1 million (later reduced) for sexual harassment by her boss.

Beverly Harvard is the first African American woman to head a major police department, in Atlanta in 1994.

In 1995 the Glass Ceiling Commission reports that 95% of the senior management positions are held by white men.

Social Change

Reformer Jane Addams (center) with two of her early
Hull House associates, Julia Lathrop (left) and Mary
McDowell (Library of Congress)

A Story of Survival

Many Native American women hold positions of power within their communities, both economically and politically. Some nations are matrilineal, with women owning the property and controlling the children. But during the next couple of centuries, their lives radically change. Native women's story is one of survival and of preservation of traditions in the face of continual attack. Many actively resist the European invasion, as evidenced by the women warriors (see "War").

For most African women, too, the first 250 years are a story of survival. Brought against their will, first as indentured servants, then as slaves, they are not only forced to do hard labor but often raped and beaten by their white masters. As one woman describes much later, "Slavery was the worst days that was ever seed in the world. They was things way past tellin.'" Women held in slavery resist in many ways, from outright rebellion and escape (see "Politics") to subtle sabotage and use of herbal medicines to avoid the pain of bringing children into a world of slavery.

1600s–1700s

In the British colonies married women settlers are usually treated as their husband's property in the legal codes, following the principle of coverture (see p. 12). In Massachusetts the women's lives are further circumscribed by Puritanism, and attempts at change are often met with the accusation of witchcraft (see "Religion"). Although premarital sex by an engaged couple is tolerated, pregnancy outside marriage or engagement is not. Adultery is one of the most heinous crimes. One early Massachusetts law (1631) makes adultery by either a man or a woman punishable by death, but a decade later the penalty is revised to a whipping and public humiliation through the wearing of the letter *A*.

The first Catholic nuns, who arrive in the 1720s, set up schools and perform other charitable work (see "Religion").

Women first organize in groups during the Revolutionary War (see "Politics" and "War"). In the late 1700s they start forming charitable groups to help other women (see below).

Free black women in Philadelphia start one of the first mutual-benefit organizations, the Female Benevolent Society of St. Thomas, in 1793. Many other African American women start mutual-aid societies, paying dues and using the money to help members who become sick or widowed or who are otherwise in need. Philadelphia alone gains 60 mutual-aid societies by 1838.

Quaker Ann Parrish (1760–1800) and 23 other women start meeting in 1795 as the Friendly Circle, later changing their name to the Female Society of Philadelphia for the Relief and Employment of the Poor. They set up a House of Industry, giving poor women employment as spinners and hiring older women in an early day-care center. Parrish also starts the Aimwell School for poor children.

In New York City, Isabella Marshall Graham (1742–1814), her daughter Joanna Graham Bethune (1770-1860), and 14 other women organize the Society for the Relief of Poor Widows with Small Children in 1797. In the first winter alone they assist 98 widows and 223 children. Highly organized, they keep careful records and establish strict rules of "worthiness" for aid. By 1804 they have raised money to buy a house and set up a spinning and tailoring operation, as well as a school.

In New York City in 1798, Catherine Brown Murray and other Quaker women start the Female Association for the Relief of the Sick Poor, and for the Education of Such Female Children as Do Not Belong to, or Are Not Provided for by Any Religious Society. Their school becomes part of the public school system in 1845.

1800–19

In Boston in 1800, Elizabeth Peck Perkins (c. 1735–1807), who earlier ran her own business, joins other women to start the Boston Female Asylum, with Perkins as director. In another group, the Boston Society for Missionary Purposes, the women sell their knitting and sewing to raise money for missionaries to the West, but they also take clothing and food (along with spiritual "advice") to the neighborhood poor. Many other similar groups form throughout the country, in both cities and more rural areas.

Rebecca Gratz (1781–1869) helps start the Female Association for the Relief of Women and Children in Reduced Circumstances in Philadelphia in 1801. In 1815 she helps found a nonsectarian orphan asylum; she also establishes the Female Hebrew Benevolent Society (1819) and the Jewish Foster Home and Orphan Asylum (1855). By some accounts, she is the model for Sir Walter Scott's Rebecca in *Ivanhoe*.

In 1806 in New York City, Joanna Bethune sets up the Orphan Asylum Society, which soon constructs its own building. She teaches in its school; later she leads in the Sunday school movement and establishes the first "infant schools" (see "Education").

The African Female Benevolent Society of Newport, Rhode Island, works in 1809 with a male-led society to raise money for a school, as there are no public schools for black children in Newport until 1842.

Writer Margaret Bayard Smith (1778–1844) joins with other women to set up the Washington Female Orphan Asylum in 1815 to keep orphans from being housed with criminals.

1820–29

As a form of insurance against hard times, women continue to form mutual-aid societies with constitutions spelling out the requirements of membership. In Philadelphia, for example, 200 working-class women form the Daughters of Africa Society in 1821.

Female charitable associations proliferate during the 1820s. One example is the Society for Employing the Poor, formed in 1820 in Boston; another is the New York Asylum for Lying-In Women, started to help low-income pregnant women in 1823.

In Philadelphia in 1823, Mary Waln Wistar organizes the Female Prison Association of Friends, which visits women prisoners. The group begins by getting the prisoners needed clothing; giving sewing and writing lessons, as well as spiritual advice; and finding places for released prisoners. Soon they are campaigning for a separate home for young offenders and later for a matron for the women prisoners.

New York black women start the African Dorcas Society in 1827 and meet weekly to sew clothes for children in the African free schools.

1830–39

Ladies' Magazine editor Sarah Hale starts the Boston Seaman's Aid Society in 1833 to give work to widowed women, and it soon grows to include vocational training, a nonprofit business, a school, and residential facilities. The group takes an activist stand in petitioning for better wages for women workers; they declare that it is "a shame and disgrace for any one, who writes himself *man*, to make a fortune out of the handy-work of poor females!" A similar group is the Providence Employment Society, set up for seamstresses in Rhode Island.

"I Tell What I Have Seen"

> "I tell what I have seen—*painful and shocking as the details often are*. . . .
>
> "*I come as the advocate of helpless, forgotten, insane and idiotic men and women; of beings, sunk to a condition from which the most unconcerned would start with real horror; of beings wretched in our Prisons, and more wretched in our alms-houses*. . . . *Chained, naked, beaten with rods and lashed into obedience*. . . .
>
> "*The use of cages all but universal*. . . . "
>
> —Dorothea Dix, "Memorial to the Legislature of Massachusetts," 1843; quoted in Gerda Lerner, *The Woman in American History* (Reading, Mass.: Addison-Wesley, 1971)

"*This is the appropriate work for* women"
—*member of Female Moral Reform Society*

A small group of middle-class New York women form the Female Moral Reform Society in 1834 to fight against prostitution not only by converting prostitutes to Christianity and shutting down the brothels but also by exposing the double standard and condemning male licentiousness. The women state that "the licentious man is no less guilty than his victim, and ought, therefore, to be excluded from all virtuous female society." Missionaries (at first male but later female) visit the brothels to pray and sing hymns to the prostitutes and their customers. The group publishes a weekly bulletin, the *Advocate of Moral Reform*, and sets up a home for prostitutes as well as an employment service for its converts. In 1839 a national organization is set up, with 445 local chapters. By 1846 the group succeeds in getting a Massachusetts law prohibiting seduction, followed by one in New York in 1848.

Two white Quakers, Anna M. Shotwell and Mary Murray, start the first Colored Orphan Asylum in New York in the mid-1830s, with matron Rachel Johnson and other black women running most of the daily operations. After a mob destroys the orphanage in 1863, it moves to Riverdale as the Riverdale Children's Association.

1840–49

Shocked by the conditions she finds when she begins teaching a Sunday school class for prisoners in 1841, Dorothea Lynde Dix (1802–87) reports in 1843 to the Massachusetts legislature on the inhumane treatment of some 950 jailed women and men whose only crime is mental illness (see sidebar). Her plea leads to immediate provision of more hospital beds for the insane. In 1845 she publishes *Remarks on Prisons and Prison Discipline in the United States,* proposing many changes that are later adopted. Traveling thousands of miles in the next 40 years, she compels 15 states and Canada to set up 32 mental hospitals.

When Eliza Farnham takes over as matron of women in Sing Sing prison in 1844, she does away with the unpopular rule of silence, brings in a piano to encourage singing, and adds homelike touches, such as curtains and flowers. She is fired, however, in 1848.

Led by Elizabeth King, Baltimore Quakers set up the Women Friends Association for Visiting the Penitentiary in 1846. They start by teaching women prisoners to read and write, then establish a school and library; they also help place released prisoners.

In New York in 1846, Abby Hopper Gibbons and other women open possibly the world's first halfway house for released female prisoners. Philadelphia women open a similar house in 1853.

1850–59

Women in church missionary societies organize charitable activities both at home and abroad (see also "Religion"). One example is the Ladies' Home Missionary Society of the Methodist Episcopal Church, which in 1850 is the first to send missionaries into the notorious Five Points area of lower Manhattan. At first they rent a room, but in 1853 they buy an old brewery and convert it into 20 apartments, baths, a school, and a chapel.

In 1852 Susan B. Anthony is outraged when, as women, she and other members of the Daughers of Temperance (an auxiliary started in 1842) are not allowed to speak at a rally. She sets up the Woman's New York State Temperance Society, with Elizabeth Cady Stanton as president. The following year Anthony helps organize the Whole World's Temperance Convention in New York after Antoinette Brown (later Blackwell, p. 203) and other female delegates are shouted down at the World's Temperance Convention.

Quaker minister Amanda M. Way (1828–1914), a leader in the Indiana Woman's Rights Society, sets up the Woman's Temperance Army to shut down local saloons in 1854.

When in 1855 Lucy Stone marries Henry B. Blackwell, the brother of medical pioneers Elizabeth and Emily Blackwell, she insists on keeping her birth name; other women who follow her lead in this are known as Lucy Stoners. The wedding ceremony includes a statement against the inequities in the marriage laws, and this is later publicized.

A forerunner of the Young Women's Christian Association, the Ladies' Christian Union is started in 1858 in New York by Mrs. Marshall O. Roberts. It stresses its concern with the "welfare of women, particularly the young and unprotected employed in stores and manufactories."

1860–69

The Woman's Union Missionary Society and similar groups begin working in schools and hospitals in 1860, as well as proselytizing among the "heathen" immigrants in inner cities (see "Religion").

In 1862 Elizabeth Keckley (1818–1907), a former slave who is a dressmaker for Mary Todd Lincoln, helps start the Contrabond Relief Association to assist freed African Americans in the capital.

In a sensational 1864 trial in Illinois, Elizabeth Ware Packard (1816–97) proves her sanity to avoid being committed for a second time to a state mental hospital. She then lobbies successfully to have the commitment laws changed in several states. Although she writes several books on the need for married women's rights, she gains the most attention for her exposés of insane asylums, such as *The Prisoner's Hidden Life* (1868).

As general agent for the National Freedmen's Relief Association of the District of Columbia in 1865, Josephine White Griffing (1814–72)

Dress Reform

Although not the first to create an alternative to women's unwieldy long skirts, Elizabeth Smith Miller (1822–1911) popularizes her "short dress" and "Turkish trousers" when, in 1851, she introduces the outfit to Elizabeth Cady Stanton (her cousin) and Amelia Bloomer. After Bloomer features the style in her reform journal, Lily, *it becomes a hit and is soon called the "Bloomer costume." But the outfit becomes a subject of ridicule in the male press, and Stanton and others eventually give up its comfort to focus attention on more basic reforms in women's rights.*

Members of the Dress Reform Association, formed in the mid-1850s, continue to press for less confining, more comfortable clothes for women One of the most outspoken advocates of this reform is Lydia Sayer Hasbrouck (1827–1910), who ridicules "the vasty depths and breadths" of hoop skirts in her magazine, Sibyl, *started in 1856.*

raises assistance money and operates a kind of settlement house, offering temporary shelter, vocational training, and counseling.

The first group to call itself the Young Women's Christian Association (YWCA) is established in Boston in 1866. Soon similar groups form to address their concern for the moral life of young women workers living away from home in the cities. Many set up dormitories and other services.

Women are active participants in the new Grange, or Patrons of Husbandry, organized to help farmers after the Civil War. Although not in the top leadership positions, women vote equally with men and hold office; they also put together many of the group's social and cultural activities. By 1885 the Grange openly supports suffrage and other women's rights.

In 1867 Baltimore educator Mary Ann Prout (c. 1800–84) starts an African American group, later called the Independent Order of Saint Luke (see p. 117), to insure the sick and pay burial fees.

The New England Woman's Club, with Caroline Seymour Severance (1820–1914) as president, forms in 1868 as one of the first women's clubs, along with Sorosis in New York (p. 113). A reform-oriented group, it helps start Girls' Latin School in Boston and the Cooperative Building Association; it also lobbies for women on the school board.

In 1869 the Sisters of Charity start the first Foundling Asylum (later the New York Foundling Hospital), headed by Sister Irene (Catherine Fitzgibbon, 1823–96). Sister Irene encourages unwed mothers to keep their babies and actively places infants in foster homes so that they are not sent to prisons or almshouses for care.

1870–79

The Philadelphia Colored Women's Christian Association, probably the first black YWCA, is started in 1870. White and black YWCAs remain segregated until the mid-1940s.

Frances Wisebart Jacobs (1843-92) begins her charity work by establishing an orphanage and the Hebrew Benevolent Ladies Aid Society in Denver in 1872. She later helps set up Denver's Charity Organization Society, a coalition of several groups. In 1900 she is the only woman among the 16 outstanding Colorado pioneers honored with a stained-glass portrait in the state capitol building.

Appalled by the treatment of Indiana women prisoners, who have to bathe outside in front of male guards and then endure nighttime visits, Sarah Smith and other Quaker women get the state to open a women's prison run entirely by women in 1873.

In Philadelphia, Fanny Baker Ames (1840–1931) and her husband help set up the Relief Society of Germantown in 1873 and use the first social workers, female volunteers who visit the poor and report back on the families most in need.

The "Woman's Crusade" for temperance takes hold in Ohio in the winter of 1873–74. In Hillsboro a temperance lecture inspires about 50 women, led by Eliza Jane Trimble Thompson (1816–1905), to invade saloons, praying and singing, to convince the owners to close down. All through the state, women repeat this action (see sidebar). Eliza Daniel Stewart (1816–1908), known as "Mother" Stewart for assisting Union soldiers during the Civil War, starts several temperance unions and leads a band of zealous, praying women into the bars of Springfield.

Following the Ohio Woman's Crusade, the Woman's Christian Temperance Union (WCTU) is founded in 1874 in Cleveland, with Annie Turner Wittenmyer (1827–1900) as the first president. Frances Willard (1839–98) is elected corresponding secretary. Within 20 years the national organization has 200,000 members. Operating under the slogan "For God and Home and Native Land," many of these women express anti-Catholic and anti-immigrant sentiments.

In San Francisco in 1874, the Women's Occidental Board sets up the Presbyterian Mission Home, a woman's shelter in Chinatown. Director Margaret Culbertson and later Donaldina MacKenzie Cameron lead police-backed raids to rescue Chinese women held and abused as prostitutes or *mujai* (indentured servants). By 1908 about 1,000 have been housed and educated in the refuge.

Josephine Shaw Lowell (1843–1905) is the first woman on the New York State Board of Charities, in 1876. Her reports on institutional conditions lead to many reforms, including the first home for mentally retarded women (1885) and police matrons in all stations (1888).

While teaching at a New York industrial school for immigrant girls in 1876, Emily Huntington (1841–1909) initiates the "kitchen garden" (inspired by the "kinder-garten"). Using little brooms and pots, she teaches youngsters "how to make their homes more comfortable" and prepares them for domestic service. The idea catches on; by 1880 there is a Kitchen Garden Association in New York, and the concept spreads not only to other U.S. cities but also to Europe and Asia.

After lobbying by Ellen Cheney Johnson (1829–99) and her friends, the Massachusetts Reformatory Prison for Women opens near Framingham in 1877 and is soon well known for its innovations. When Johnson becomes superintendent in 1884, she rewards well-behaved inmates with increasing privileges and encourages literacy, actually requiring prisoners to carry a library book with them at all times.

"Do Everything!"—Frances Willard

Frances Willard becomes president of the WCTU in 1879 and is the prime mover of the group until her death in 1898. Rallying to her cry (above), the highly moralistic, mostly Protestant WCTU women not only battle the abuses of alcohol but also tackle prostitution and take up the cry of women's suffrage (see p. 31). Willard turns the annual

"Women Singing and Praying to God"

"That day . . . is one long to be remembered in Washington [Ohio], as the day upon which occurred the first surrender ever made by a liquor-dealer, of his stock of liquors of every kind and variety, to the women, in answer to their prayers and entreaties, and by them poured into the street. Nearly a thousand men, women, and children witnessed the mingling of beer, ale, wine, and whiskey, as they filled the gutters and were drunk up by the earth, while the bells were ringing, men and boys shouting, and women singing and praying to God who had given the victory."
—Annie Wittenmyer, in *History of the Woman's Temperance Crusade* (Boston: James H. Earle, 1882)

conventions into energizing events, complete with banners, flowers, and music. Her speaking tours make headlines across the country, and her words are eagerly read (see sidebar).

As registrar for the Boston Associated Charities in 1879, Zilpha Drew Smith (c. 1852–1926) sets up a model training system for charity workers and establishes the need for supervision of social workers.

1880–89

Following the example of British reformer Octavia Hill, Ellen Collins buys and renovates three New York tenement houses in 1880. Through careful management, she offers tenants a well-maintained residence at low rent—as long as they follow certain rules of good behavior. A similar effort is undertaken in 1884 by Edith Wright (later Gifford), who sets up "Wrightsville," offering well-maintained properties in a Philadelphia slum at low rents and establishing services such as a library and bank. Cornelia Hancock serves as the resident manager.

In 1881 Clara Barton (1821–1912) sets up the U.S. branch of the International Red Cross and in 1882 persuades the Senate to approve the Geneva Treaty, letting Red Cross workers rescue wounded soldiers during war. Rushing to the site of any disaster, Barton personally manages the Red Cross relief work during the Michigan forest fire of 1881, the midwestern floods of 1884, and other calamities during her 23-year presidency.

Pressured by Mary Hanchett Hunt (1820–1906) of the WCTU, Vermont is the first state to require temperance instruction in the public schools, in 1882. All states have similar laws by 1901. Beginning in 1883, Frances Harper (p. 23) works as a WCTU superintendent, organizing temperance drives in the black community. Later she writes an article criticizing the racism of women in the WCTU.

The national YWCA is founded in 1886, with Mrs. Henry Fowl Durant as president. Around the same time, largely in reaction to Christian women's insensitivity to Jewish immigrants' culture, New York women set up the Young Women's Hebrew Association (YWHA) as an auxiliary to the men's YMHA. Julia Richman is the first president.

In 1888 working women join middle-class reformers in the Illinois Women's Alliance, a coalition of 30 women's groups. They lobby for female factory inspectors, sweatshop regulation, abolition of child labor, compulsory education, and protective legislation for working women. The group dissolves soon after the new state law of 1893 (see "Work").

Led by Lillie Devereux Blake, New York suffragists win passage of an 1888 law requiring women doctors for women patients in mental institutions. In 1892 they secure matrons in all police stations.

Inspired by Toynbee Hall in a London slum, a group of Smith College graduates, led by Jean Fine and Helen Rand, open College Settlement in 1889 on New York's Lower East Side. This community center, offering educational and recreational facilities, is the second U.S. settlement house and the first started solely by women. Living at the center, women workers take part in the neighborhood they serve. Other settlement houses linked to women's colleges are soon established in Boston and Philadelphia.

"An effort to add the social function to democracy"
—Jane Addams

After visiting Toynbee Hall, Jane Addams (1860–1935) and her friend Ellen Gates Starr (1860–1940) set up residence in 1889 in Hull House, the third and most famous U.S. settlement house, in Chicago. Offering a meeting place, classes, youth clubs, a day nursery, and other services, the center is soon a hit, attracting thousands of neighborhood people. As it grows, it encompasses a gymnasium, a dispensary, an art gallery, a residence for young working women, and more (see sidebar). By 1910 the complex takes up a city block. Beyond its role in the neighborhood, Hull House becomes a hub for progressive women reformers, such as Julia Lathrop, Florence Kelley, and sisters Edith and Grace Abbott. Its residents push for protective labor laws, industrial safety, compulsory schooling, juvenile courts, and the like.

Local WCTU chapters provide various charitable services by 1889. For example, Chicago WCTU women run two day nurseries, a free medical clinic for 1,600 patients a year, a shelter serving 4,000 homeless women a year, an inexpensive restaurant, an industrial school, and more.

1890–99

After compiling statistics on the terrible working conditions of sales clerks, Alice Woodbridge and others in the Working Women's Society contact Josephine Shaw Lowell, Maud Nathan, and other influential women. Deciding that the best way to bring about change is to involve the buying public, Lowell and Nathan found the National Consumers League of New York in 1890. They put together a "white list" of stores meeting certain work standards and encourage customers to use only these stores. They also publicize abuses, such as women forced to stand continuously for 12 hours without any seats available.

In 1890 in Hampton, Virginia, educator Janie Porter Barrett (1865–1948) starts Locust Street Social Settlement, one of the first settlement houses for African Americans.

The General Federation of Women's Clubs (GFWC) forms in 1890 as a coalition of about 200 local clubs. African American women's clubs, however, are not admitted. Although most clubs started as literary or educational groups, many now support a range of reform activities. The Chicago Woman's Club, for example, lobbies for women doctors at the county mental institution and kindergartens in the public schools. The GFWC soon makes a point of stating that its members are "guardians of the civic housekeeping of their respective communities."

"Arousing the Social Energies"

". . . The one thing to be dreaded in the Settlement is that it lose its flexibility, its power of quick adaptation, its readiness to change its methods as its environment may demand. It must be open to conviction and must have a deep and abiding sense of tolerance. It must be hospitable and ready for experiment. . . . Its residents must be emptied of all conceit of opinion and all self-assertion, and ready to arouse and interpret the public opinion of their neighborhood. They must be content to live quietly side by side with their neighbors until they grow into a sense of relationship and mutual interests. . . . In short, residents are pledged to devote themselves to the duties of good citizenship and to the arousing of the social energies which too largely lie dormant in every neighborhood given over to industrialism."

— Jane Addams, *Philanthropy and Social Progress* (1893)

The Black Women's Club Movement

In response to racism and social welfare needs of the black community, African American women form their own clubs in the 1890s. In 1892 Anna J. Cooper, Mary Church Terrell, and others start the Colored Woman's League of Washington, D.C., and in New York, Victoria Earle Matthews and Maritcha Lyons start the Woman's Loyal Union. In 1893 in Boston, Josephine St. Pierre Ruffin, her daughter Florida, and Maria Baldwin start the Woman's Era Club. In 1894 they launch the monthly Woman's Era, *an important guide to black women's activities nationwide.*

Told they need a national organization to participate first in the planning of the 1893 Columbian Exposition and then in the National Council of Women, D.C. women form the National League of Colored Women. But the first national conference is called by Josephine Ruffin after a racist incident (p. 37); this leads to the formation of the National Federation of Afro-American Women in 1895. In 1896 the two groups merge in the National Association of Colored Women (p. 38), which actively supports temperance and social welfare reforms. Its member clubs establish homes for the elderly, orphanages, kindergartens, educational programs, and more.

Frances Willard is elected president of the new World's Woman's Christian Temperance Union, founded in Boston in 1891. The group presents anti-alcohol and -drug petitions signed by 7 million to governments throughout the world. During the same year Frances Harper advises black temperance workers that if any WCTU women "draw the line at color, draw your line at self-respect and fight without them."

In 1893 the College Settlements Association opens Denison House in Boston, headed by Helena Dudley (1858–1932). Dudley immediately organizes a sewing room to help out 300 women during the year's depression. She also opens the center to the labor movement and helps organize women garment workers.

At an 1893 conference in Chicago, the National Council of Jewish Women is formed with Hannah Greenbaum Solomon as its first president. In addition to fostering religious understanding, the council fights anti-Semitism and runs many social service programs.

In Philadelphia in 1893, Drs. Rebecca J. Cole (p. 222) and Charlotte Abbey set up the Woman's Directory to give medical and legal assistance to poor women, prevent infanticide, and fight baby farming.

In 1893 Lillian D. Wald (1867–1940) and her friend Mary Brewster move into New York's Lower East Side community, determined "to live in the neighborhood as nurses, identify ourselves with it socially, and . . . contribute to it our citizenship." In 1895 Wald starts the "Nurses Settlement" on Henry Street. Her program of visiting nurses establishes the field of public health nursing (see "Health"). In addition, the Henry Street Settlement becomes a leading New York community center, providing neighborhood services and pushing for reforms. By 1913 it has seven buildings on Henry Street as well as two uptown branches.

In 1894 in Jersey City, Cornelia Foster Bradford (1847–1935) sets up New Jersey's first settlement house, Whittier House, and helps fight for state and local reforms in housing, health care, and child welfare. In Chicago in 1894, Mary Eliza McDowell (1854–1936) directs the new University of Chicago Settlement in "Packingtown," near the stockyards and meat-packing plants. She leads the drive for a community park, a branch library, public bathhouses, and the closing of an open garbage dump and the sewage-infested Bubbly Creek.

In the mid-1890s Mexican American women are active in *mutualistas* (mutual-aid societies), such as Tucson's Alianza Hispano-Americana.

After running the U.S. branch of the Salvation Army, Maud Ballington Booth (1865–1948) and her husband start Volunteers of America in 1896. She heads the Volunteer Prison League, which converts and rehabilitates ex-convicts, helps them find employment, and provides housing in "Hope Halls."

In 1896 Harriet Lawrence Hemenway calls a meeting to stop the slaughter of birds used to provide feathers for ladies' hats, and the

Massachusetts Audubon Society is formed. With the help of Minna Hall, she recruits both women and men to protest the fashions of the day. Although hers is not the first Audubon Society, it spurs the formation of many more.

In New York in 1897, Victoria Earle Matthews (1861–1907) starts the White Rose Home and Industrial Association for Working Girls to provide shelter for young African American women arriving from the South in search of jobs. The home soon becomes a community center, offering classes on black history as well as vocational training. In 1898 Matthews and her assistants begin meeting boats at the piers to protect women from unscrupulous employment agents. By 1905 she officially establishes the White Rose Travelers' Aid Society, which helps more than 50,000 newly arrived black women in the next 10 years.

Carry Nation (Library of Congress)

Marion F. Curney starts St. Rose's, the first Catholic settlement house, on New York's West Side in 1898.

Lillian Ames Stevens (1844–1944) assumes leadership of the WCTU after Frances Willard's death in 1898 and focuses its efforts on the growing campaign for state and federal prohibition laws.

In 1899 the National Consumers' League forms, with Florence Kelley as its general secretary. She travels throughout the country, setting up 60-some local leagues, urging consumers to boycott stores and products of companies with unfair labor practices, and fighting for the passage of protective labor legislation and regulation of sweatshops. The NCL's "white labels," started in 1907, alert customers to products by companies offering decent working conditions.

As the new head of the Independent Order of Saint Luke in 1899 (see "Work"), Maggie Lena Walker not only establishes new businesses but also sets up scholarships and starts a school for delinquent girls.

Tearfully singing temperance hymns, Carry Moore Nation (1846–1911) succeeds in closing all the saloons in her Kansas hometown in 1899. By the next year she is physically attacking bars throughout the state. Alone or with supporters, singing hymns and cursing sinners, she marches into the saloons, swings her hatchet or tosses bricks, and smashes everything in sight. Jailed again and again, she gains national attention for her "hatchetations." She carries her crusade onto the vaudeville circuit and into the U.S. Senate, where she is thrown out for shouting her views from the gallery.

Baltimore social worker Mary Ellen Richmond (1861–1928) publishes *Friendly Visiting among the Poor* (1899), a guide to her new casework method, involving systematic study of each client's social conditions.

1900–9

As president of the Woman's Era Club, Josephine St. Pierre Ruffin attends the 1900 convention of the General Federation of Women's Clubs but is denied a seat because her club has only black members.

Although eligible to attend as a member of another, mostly white club, she refuses, calling attention to the racism within the GWFC.

At Milwaukee's first settlement house, founded by two Jewish women's groups in 1900, Lizzie Black Kander (1858–1940) teaches a popular cooking class. To save students time in copying recipes, she raises money to print 1,000 copies of *The Settlement Cook Book: The Way to a Man's Heart* (1901). Its huge sales help support the settlement house.

After drafting and lobbying for a 1901 Pennsylvania law setting up special juvenile courts, detention homes, and a probation system, Hannah Kent Schoff (1853–1940) successfully campaigns for similar reforms in other states and later conducts a broad survey of juvenile delinquency, published as *The Wayward Child* (1915).

In New York in 1902, Mary Kingsbury Simkhovitch (1867–1951) starts Greenwich House, a settlement house that eventually supports a theater and art workshops as well as vocational training and a variety of community services. It also sponsors influential studies on housing, unemployment, racism, and other problems.

Sponsored by the WCTU, Katherine Pettit (1868–1936) and May Stone in 1902 set up one of the first rural settlements, Hindman Settlement School in Kentucky. By 1911 they have 200 some students studying academic subjects as well as a variety of crafts.

Evangeline Cory Booth (1865–1950) takes over as commander of the U.S. Salvation Army in 1904. She sets up hospitals for unwed mothers, "Evangeline Residencies" for working women, homes for the elderly, and disaster relief services (after the 1907 San Francisco earthquake).

Lillian Wald and Florence Kelley help found the National Child Labor Committee in 1904 to fight for a ban on all child labor.

In 1905 Winifred Holt (1870–1945) and her sister Edith start the New York Association for the Blind, which emphasizes vocational training rather than charity. The group's motto is "Light through Work." In 1913 they open a permanent center, called the Lighthouse, with educational, recreational, and employment facilities. Soon there are Lighthouses in other cities and abroad.

The National League for the Protection of Colored Women is set up in 1906 by Frances A. Kellor and others. It sends agents to meet black women migrants at the docks and train terminals of major cities and help them find decent housing and employment.

Women help gain passage of the 1906 Pure Food and Drug Act. Journalist Ella Bloor (a pseudonym for Ella Reeve Cohen, 1862–1951) probes conditions in Chicago's meat-packing industry to back up Upton Sinclair's fictional exposé, *The Jungle,* and her reports are widely read. Clubwoman Alice Lakey (1857–1935) gets thousands of women to flood the Senate with petitions for the law's approval.

With an unprecedented gift of $10 million, Margaret Slocum Sage (1828–1918) sets up the Russell Sage Foundation in 1907 to find ways to ameliorate social conditions.

To raise money to fight tuberculosis, Emily Bissell (1861–1948) prints Christmas seals in 1907 and sells them in Wilmington, Delaware. By the next year the stamps are sold nationally, bringing in $135,000.

"Thy Neighbor as Thyself"—Neighborhood Union motto

Led by Lugenia Burns Hope (1871–1947), Atlanta women organize the Neighborhood Union in 1908 to help black communities They hold cleanup campaigns, build playgrounds, set up children's clubs, establish community centers, provide day care, and much more. In 1924 their efforts lead to Atlanta's first black high school; they also establish the first public housing for African Americans.

In 1908 Grace Abbott, Sophinisba Breckinridge (1866–1948), and other Hull House social workers establish the Immigrant Protective League, headed by Abbott. The group starts by meeting young immigrant women at the station and helping them find employment, but it soon is helping immigrant families with the schools and in court.

In 1908 in Brooklyn, New York, physician Verina Morton-Jones (1865–1943) heads the Lincoln Settlement House, the first to focus on the needs of the African American community there.

In San Francisco in 1908, Korean women form Hankuk Puin Hoe to ensure Korean language education and foster Korean women's unity.

After a campaign by Anna M. Jarvis, the first Mother's Day is observed in 1908 in Philadelphia and Grafton, West Virginia (where Jarvis's recently deceased mother had lived). Jarvis's constant petitioning leads to the establishment of the national holiday in 1914.

Hannah Bachman Einstein (1862–1929) starts the Widowed Mothers' Fund Association in 1909 in New York to give mothers regular aid so that they don't need to go out to work. She calls for a "government pension" for widowed mothers and later works with Sophie Simon Loeb (1876–1929) for passage of New York's pioneering child welfare law of 1915.

In 1909 Jane Addams is the first female president of the National Conference of Charities and Correction (later the National Conference of Social Work). She also publishes *The Spirit of Youth and the City Streets*, followed by her autobiography *Twenty Years at Hull House* (1910).

1910–19

Hoping to stem the traffic in prostitution, a number of women lobby for the 1910 Mann Act, which forbids transporting women across state or national borders for "immoral purposes." In effect, however, this law limits all women's movements.

Women Prison Reformers

At the Massachusetts Reformatory for Women in 1910, Jessie Donaldson Hodder (1867–1931) institutes a number of reforms, including a strong educational and recreational program. Many of her changes are based on the work of Katharine Bement Davis (1860–1935) at the Bedford Hills women's prison in New York.

In Pennsylvania, Martha Platt Falconer (1862–1941) sets up a cottage system in 1910 at Sleighton Farm, a girls' reformatory, with young college graduates as matrons. She also starts a student government.

As New York's new commissioner of corrections in 1914, Katharine Davis sets up a farm school for delinquent boys, plans a detention home for girls, and instigates legal reforms in sentencing and parole.

As chief probation officer in Philadelphia in 1917, Jane Deeter Rippin (1882–1953) sets up the nation's first multifunctional detention center for women. It includes a dormlike prison, court, employment agency, day nurseries, and diagnosis and treatment facilities.

Under the auspices of the YWCA, Edith Terry Bremer (1885–1964) starts the International Institute in New York in 1910. It offers classes and helps with jobs, housing, and other problems for young female immigrants. The helpers are mostly former immigrants trained as social workers. The emphasis is on cultural diversity rather than assimilation.

In 1911 Kansas City, Missouri, enacts the first mother's pension law, providing widowed or abandoned mothers with money to raise their children. Later in the year Illinois passes the first statewide law, and by 1913 a dozen more states have similar laws (see also 1909).

In 1911 the new Liga Femenil Mexicanista affirms, "Educate a woman and you educate a family" (see "Politics").

As head of the new Children's Bureau in 1911, Julia Lathrop pushes for laws against child labor and spurs investigation into infant and maternal mortality, juvenile delinquency, mother's pensions, child development, and the like. She enforces a 1916 federal child labor law before it is struck down by the Supreme Court. She also lays the groundwork for the 1921 Sheppard-Towner Act (see "Health").

In Virginia in 1912, Ora Brown Stokes (1881–1957) starts the Richmond Neighborhood Association to help black working women, and it soon expands to support a day nursery, a residence for young girls, and other community services.

A Cleveland woman's club headed by Jane Edna Hunter (1882–1971) opens the Phillis Wheatley Home in 1913, providing housing, training, and an employment service for young black women. By 1927, in its new 11-story building, it is the largest black women's residence.

In 1913 in Harlan County, Kentucky, Katherine Pettit and Ethel de Long (1878–1928) start the Pine Mountain Settlement School, offering basic education, encouraging traditional crafts, and setting up health clinics, especially for the treatment of trachoma and hookworm.

Chairing the GFWC's conservation department, Mary King Sherman (1862–1935) begins her campaign in 1914 for a national park service (established in 1916) and for national parks in the Rockies (1915) and the Grand Canyon (1919). She is called the "National Park Lady."

Largely through the efforts of Daisy Florence Simms (1873–1923), the YWCA sponsors 375 "industrial clubs" for women working in factories, laundries, and stores by 1915. In addition to offering classes and spiritual guidance, these clubs support the drive for labor reform.

Black women's clubs open the Virginia Industrial School for Colored Girls in 1915 as a rehabilitation center. Another joint efforct by black women's clubs is the 1916 Negro Women's Club Home in Denver, which provides housing for "deserving" women and day care.

With ratification of the 18th Amendment establishing Prohibition in 1919, the WCTU shifts direction, concentrating on enforcement, as well as child welfare and Americanization of immigrants. Its membership grows, helped by the attention-getting gestures of its president, Anna Adams Gordon (1853–1931), who in 1923 dumps 300 bottles of illegal whiskey into a city sewer.

1920–29

One of the goals of the National Council of Catholic Women, formed in 1920, is improving the welfare of women factory workers. This group quickly expands, with 1,700 local chapters by 1930.

With increasing acceptance of her standards for psychiatric social work, Mary Cromwell Jarrett (1877–1961) in 1920 starts a club that becomes the American Association of Psychiatric Social Workers. Also, in 1921, about 750 social workers, mostly women, form the American Association of Social Workers.

As the new head of the Children's Bureau, Grace Abbott is in charge of putting the 1921 Sheppard-Towner Act into effect, setting up more than 3,000 centers offering prenatal and child health care. She fends off constant attacks on the program, which Congress ends in 1929.

Zitkala-Sa, or Gertrude Bonnin, gets the GWFC to set up the Indian Welfare Committee in 1921. With its backing, she investigates abuses in the government treatment of Native Americans. The GWFC also works with the Indian Rights Association for voting rights, better education, health care facilities, and other reforms.

"Round in knowledge and square in dealings"
—Square and Circle Club

Seven Chinese American women start the Square and Circle Club in 1924 to provide community services. The name alludes to a saying from a Chinese poem (above).

In 1926 YWCA members no longer have to be Protestant Christians. Through its industrial clubs it continues to help organize and educate women workers. By 1930 the YWCA has 600,000 members.

The first federal prison for women begins operation in Alderson, West Virginia, in 1927. Planned largely by superintendent Mary Belle Harris (1874–1957), it is a model for prison reform, styled after a boarding school, with no intimidating walls or armed guards. The program offers education, vocational training, physical exercise, and self-government.

Edith Abbott and Sophinisba Breckinridge, the authors of several pioneering social work studies, launch the *Social Service Review* in 1927.

In Jacksonville, Florida, Eartha Mary Magdalene White (1876–1974), a successful businesswoman and the city's first black social worker, opens the Clara White Mission in 1928 in memory of her adoptive mother. Living at the mission, she offers food, shelter, and clothing for those in need. During the Depression, the mission provides relief for thousands.

African Americans in the YWCA

In 1917 the YWCA sets up a division to help in the war effort. Eva del Vakia Bowles (1875–1943), who became the Y's first black employee in 1905, runs the section for African American women. In two years she starts new centers in about 30 cities and increases black membership to 12,000, but then her division is shut down.

In Atlanta, when Lugenia Hope tries to set up a Phillis Wheatley YWCA in a black community in 1919, a white Y field supervisor objects. Hope and others protest the racial inequities within the Y, and by 1924 Elizabeth Ross Haynes is the first African American woman on the national board. However, the Ys are not integrated until 1946.

The American Woman's Association, founded in 1910 as the Working Girls' Vacation Association, opens a New York clubhouse in 1928 with housing and recreational facitilities for 1,200 professional women.

In 1929, after WCTU president Ella Alexander Boole tells Congress, "I represent the women of America," Pauline Morton Sabin (1887–1955) founds the Women's Organization for National Prohibition Reform to fight for repeal of the 18th Amendment. In a year the group gains 100,000 members; in four it is three times the size of the WCTU.

Helen Merrell Lynd (1896–1982) and her husband, Robert, publish an anthropological-sociological study of everyday life in Muncie, Indiana— *Middletown: A Study in Contemporary American Culture* (1929). They do a follow-up study: *Middletown in Transition* (1935).

At the Council of Women for Home Missions, a nondenominational Protestant missionary group, Edith Lowry (1897–1970) begins her 32 years as director of the program for migrant workers in 1929.

Dorothy Harrison Wood Eustis (1886–1946) sets up her guide-dog training school, the Seeing Eye, in Tennessee in 1929, moving it to Morristown, New Jersey, the following year. The idea began with a request from a blind salesman, who had read her 1927 article on Germany's use of guide-dogs for blind veterans. Already training German shepherds for policework, Eustis decided to start the first U.S. guide-dog program.

1930–39

Fannie B. Peck and 50 other women form the Housewives' League of Detroit in 1930 and in four years gain 10,000 members, pledged to buy from black businesses and support the black community economically. Similar groups organize in Chicago, New York, and other cities.

"We cannot live alone"—Dorothy Day

In 1933 Dorothy Day (1897–1980) and Peter Maurin start the Catholic Worker movement, combining religious, social, and political concerns. The *Catholic Worker*, a paper edited by Day (p. 295), expresses their belief in pacifism and direct social action (see sidebar). She also helps establish houses of hospitality, offering food, clothing, and shelter for those in need, as well as farming communes. A leading proponent of nonviolent resistance, she actively participates in labor struggles and civil rights and peace demonstrations.

In 1934 in El Paso, Texas, Mrs. J. C. Machuca and others start the first ladies' auxiliaries of the five-year-old League of United Latin American Citizens. The women help run health clinics and orphanages, organize youth activities, teach English, and register voters, but they are not initially considered full members (see p. 60).

Catherine Krouse Bauer (1905–64) helps set up the American Federation of Labor Housing Conference (LHC) in 1934 to push for a federal housing program. As LHC executive secretary, she successfully lobbies for America's first public housing legislation in 1937.

In 1935 Mary McLeod Bethune forms the National Council of Negro Women (p. 59), which works for civil rights and social reforms.

Many women are active in the social welfare programs set up under Franklin Roosevelt. One example is Jane Hoey (1892–1968), who serves as the first director of the Bureau of Public Assistance of the Social Security Board from 1936 to 1953 (see also "Politics").

In 1937 Catherine de Hueck opens Friendship House in Harlem, employing young Catholic women to help the neighborhood poor.

As director of California's prison system in 1939, Kate O'Hare Cunningham immediately institutes reforms to make this the most progressive penal system in the country.

1940–49

Mollie Moon (1912–90) founds the National Urban League Guild in 1942 to raise money for the Urban League, formed in 1911 to fight for better conditions for African Americans in the cities.

During the war many women work on relief efforts, joining the Red Cross and other groups. Jewish women from Hadassah, the National Council of Jewish Women, and other groups are active in helping refugees from Nazi Germany.

The Service Bureau for Women's Organizations is started in 1945 in Connecticut to help train women in community organizing. It also conducts its own studies and serves as an informational source.

In 1946 the YWCA finally adopts an interracial charter to integrate black women into its programs rather than maintaining separate black and white branches.

In 1946 in Philadelphia, Margaret Roselle Hawkins and Sarah Strickland Scott start the Links to sponsor educational, cultural, and civic programs for the African American community. Within three years there are 14 chapters in eight states.

In 1947 Katharine Lenroot, chief of the U.S. Children's Bureau, helps initiate what becomes the U.S. Committee for UNICEF. Early members include Mary McLeod Bethune and Mrs. Oswald B. Lord.

Marjory Stoneman Douglas publishes *The Everglades: River of Grass* (1947) and lobbies vigorously to protect this area.

In 1949 Dorothy Rogers Tilly (1883–1970) starts the Fellowship of the Concerned, an interracial and interfaith women's group that works for justice for African Americans in the courts and other areas.

1950–59

Throughout the 1950s women continue to be active in a variety of volunteer organizations. Many do church work or participate in the activities of local YWCAs, PTAs, Junior Leagues, Red Cross branches, and the like. A 1955 report estimates there are 115 all-women volunteer associations and 20 million women volunteers. At minimum wage, their work is worth more than $2.5 billion annually.

There is also the ongoing activity of social workers and settlement house leaders, such as Helen Hall, who in 1959 is honored after serving 25 years as director of the Henry Street Settlement House. Dorothy Day, who publishes her autobiography, *The Long Loneliness,* in 1952, continues her social activism at her hospitality houses. For many black women, social reforms are linked to civil rights actions (see "Politics").

In 1957 Sadie Ginsberg and Elinor Guggenheim start what becomes the Day Care and Child Development Council of America to push for government-backed day care, as existed during World War II (p. 126).

Alice Herrington starts Friends of Animals in 1957, and Helen Jones organizes the Society for Animal Rights in 1959.

In 1958 Ethel Percy Andrus, who set up the National Retired Teachers Association in 1947, establishes and serves as the first president of the American Association of Retired Persons (AARP), which becomes a strong advocate for older people's needs and rights.

1960–69

With *Silent Spring* (1962), an exposé of the overuse of pesticides and their damage to the environment, biologist Rachel Carson (1907–64) helps start the environmental movement. Both she and her work are vilified by the agricultural chemical industry and others, but Congress and the president quickly set up committees to investigate her charges.

The 1964 New York murder of Christine ("Kitty") Genovese, witnessed by almost 40 neighbors, who ignore her cries for help, provokes national discussion of urban isolation and indifference.

Led by Dorothy Irene Height (b. 1957), the National Council of Negro Women begins promoting many new programs addressing social issues in 1965. During the next 15 years, they help set up such projects as Youth Career Development, Operations Sisters United, and Ujamma to deal with the special problems of black youth. Other programs, such as Operation Cope or Women's Rights and Housing, are aimed at the needs of low-income women.

In the mid-1960s, 30 women form the Indianapolis Women's Crusade against Crime, which has 50,000 members by the end of the decade.

In 1965 Chicago nuns start The Place as a center for inner-city teenage girls. New York nuns also are active in the inner cities, helping to organize a rent strike and running activities for youngsters.

In Atlanta in 1965, neighborhood residents organize the Vine City Foundation, directed by Helen Howard, to help other local residents. They set up an emergency service to assist in whatever way is needed, from applying for welfare to raising bail. In the next three years they add a nursery, a medical clinic, a family-counseling service, youth programs, a monthly newspaper, and more.

Women on welfare organize in 1967. In California, for example, Alicia Escalante starts the East Los Angeles Welfare Rights Organization and later founds the Chicano National Welfare Rights Organization. Many local groups join forces in the National Welfare Rights Organization, led by such black activist welfare recipients as Johnnie Tillmon (chair) and Etta Horn and Beulah Sanders (vice chairs). They help educate women about applying for benefits and lobby for respect within the system and for job-training and day-care programs (see sidebar). By 1969 there are 22,000 members, but the NWRO lacks funds to continue beyond 1975.

In 1967 Mary Sinclair begins a 17-year campaign to stop construction of a nuclear power plant in Midland, Michigan. From initial questions about safety to court battles, despite defeats and criticism, she persists, until opinion turns and the plant is abandoned.

Helen Natalie Jackson Claytor becomes the first African American president of the national YWCA in 1967.

Marie Cirillo, a former nun, starts work as a community organizer in a Tennessee coal-mining community in 1967. With Jean Luce, another former nun, and Louise Adams, the town's postmistress, she helps the community set up a health clinic in 1968 and later an economic development organization. She also campaigns against strip mining.

In Jacksonville, Florida, Eartha M. M. White expands her community service (1920s) by opening a nursing home for welfare patients in 1967.

Sister Kathleen Clark starts Casa de los Niños, a shelter and school for abused children, in Tucson in late 1960s. Later 38 similar centers open.

"I'm going to keep doing"—Clara McBride Hale

After raising many foster children, Clara McBride ("Mother") Hale (c. 1905–92) takes in the baby of a crack-addicted mother in 1969 and four years later opens Hale House in Harlem to care for the infants of drug-addicted mothers. Age does not stop her. "My people need me," she explains. "They need somebody that's not taking from them and is giving them something."

To lobby for air-pollution control, chemist Ruth Weiner forms Colorado Citizens for Clear Air in 1969.

Mifaunwy Shunatona Hines starts the American Indian Community House in New York City in 1969 to provide educational, cultural, social, health, and information services to local Native Americans.

In Mississippi in 1969, Fannie Lou Hamer (p. 70) starts the Freedom Farm Cooperative, a nonprofit group that provides land for families to raise food and livestock. Within a year 1,500 people get their food

---

"It Can Happen to Anybody"

"Welfare's like a traffic accident. It can happen to anybody, but especially it happens to women. . . .

"If I were president, I would solve this so-called welfare crisis in a minute and go a long way toward liberating every woman. I'd just issue a proclamation that 'women's' work is real work.

"In other words, I'd start paying women a living wage for doing the work we are already doing—child-raising and housekeeping. . . .

"For me, Women's Liberation is simple. No woman in this country can feel dignified, no woman can be liberated, until all women get off their knees. That's what NWRO is all about—women standing together, on their feet."

—Johnnie Tillmon, "Welfare Is a Women's Issue," in *America's Working Women*, edited by Rosalyn Baxandall, Linda Gordon, and Susan Reverby

These are just a few of the many local programs begun by women in the early 1970s:

—In 1970 Lucy Poulin starts Homeworkers Organized for More Employment (HOME) in Hancock City, Maine. It begins as a crafts cooperative and grows to include a food co-op, day-care facilities, a learning center, a land trust, and more. "I think we need to create systems where it's easier for people to be good," says Poulin.

—In 1971 in San Francisco, Mimi Silbert starts Delancey Street, a rehabilitation center for criminals, with strict rules and a two-year training program designed to give them several marketable skills. In the next 20 years it grows to support 500 residents in San Francisco, who earn their keep by running a restaurant and other enterprises. The program also expands to other cities.

—In 1973 in San Antonio, Texas, Gloria Rodriguez founds Avance to give low-income mothers information about parenting. Also in San Antonio, Lupe Anguiano organizes a "Let's Get Off Welfare" campaign and in six months helps place more than 500 women in jobs.

from the initial 40-acre site. "Hunger has no color line," says Hamer. "What I'm really trying to do . . . is to wipe out hunger."

1970–79

In 1970 California is the first state to pass a no-fault divorce law, letting couples divorce for "irreconcilable differences." By 1981 every state except Illinois and South Dakota has a similar law.

One of the first feminist self-help groups, Women in Transition forms in 1971 in Philadelphia to offer support services for divorced or separated women, battered wives, and single mothers. In 1975 they publish the *Women's Survival Manual: A Feminist Handbook on Separation and Divorce.*

"Rape is violence not sex"—protester's sign

New York Radical Feminists holds a speakout and conference on rape in 1971. They point out the unreasonable corroborative evidence required to prove a rape in court and the 1% conviction rate for complaints the New York police deems "founded." In California the Bay Area Women Against Rape is formed to support rape victims and combat their "criminal" treatment by the justice system. A year later the first emergency rape crisis line is set up in Washington, D.C. By 1976 there are 400 independent rape crisis centers for women that offer self-defense courses, support groups, and counseling.

The Ms. Foundation for Women is set up in 1972 to support projects initiated by women.

In Chicago in 1972, Gale Cincotta organizes a national conference for neighborhood housing groups, attended by 2,000 activists from 38 states, who then form National People's Action, with Cincotta as chair. The group works for improved housing, bank loans for people in low-income communities, energy money, and health care. For Cincotta, victory is the point "where people really have a say in their lives, where *they* call the shots."

In 1973 Heather Booth founds the Midwest Academy, an organizing school for community, union, peace, and other activists. It leads to the formation of Citizen Action in 1979.

In San Francisco in 1973, Margo St. James helps establish a group for prostitutes' rights called COYOTE (Cut Out Your Old Tired Ethics). They fight for the legalization of prostitution, as well as decent legal representation for prostitutes who are arrested.

The first U.S. battered women's shelters open in 1973: Rainbow Retreat in Tucson, Arizona, and Women's Advocates in St. Paul, Minnesota. Another early center is Boston's Transition House, started by Betsy Warrior in 1975. By 1979 there are more than 250 U.S. shelters.

Lawyer Marian Wright Edelman (b. 1939) sets up the Children's Defense Fund in 1973 to fight for public recognition of children's rights and needs (see sidebar). In 1987 she helps put together the Act for Better Child Care, and in 1992 her book, *The Measure of Our Success: A Letter to My Children and Yours*, is a bestseller.

In Oklahoma in 1974, lab technician and union organizer Karen Silkwood believes her employer, Kerr-McGee Nuclear Corporation, is falsifying their quality-control records, and she has been gathering evidence to prove that charge as well as safety abuses. On her way to show her findings to a *New York Times* reporter and union official, she is killed in a mysterious car crash. Her story is the basis for the movie *Silkwood*, starring Meryl Streep and Cher.

After a three-year campaign by women's groups, in 1974 New York no longer requires a rape victim to give independent corroboration of the crime. The issue of legal and institutional changes to help rape victims is taken up by the Feminist Alliance Against Rape's new newsletter.

In 1974 Tish Sommers and Laurie Shields form the Alliance for Displaced Homemakers to address the problems divorced and widowed homemakers face in trying to find outside employment. They successfully lobby for the first Displaced Homemakers Act (1975) in California. This law sets up a pilot center to offer job training and counseling, which opens at Mills College in Oakland in 1976.

Describing the work of Boston Widowed to Widowed, the book *Helping Each Other in Widowhood* (1974), compiled by Phyllis Silverman and others, leads to the formation of similar self-help groups in other cities.

Women lawyers set up Equal Rights Advocates in 1974 to provide free legal help to low-income women.

In 1975 the National Congress of Neighborhood Women is set up in Brooklyn, New York, as an outgrowth of a 1974 conference. To empower working-class women through education, several community-based programs are developed, including high school equivalency, skills training, and college studies at a nearby community college. Also in Brooklyn around this time, the Sisterhood of Black Single Mothers brings 200 women together to run clothing and baby-sitting cooperatives and to share information.

Carnela Gloria Lacayo sets up the National Association for the Hispanic Elderly in 1975 to secure housing and social services as well as employment for older Latino citizens.

Susan Brownmiller's book *Against Our Will: Men, Women, and Rape* (1975) exposes the prevalence of violence against women and stresses that it is "nothing more or less than a conscious process of intimidation by which *all men* keep *all women* in a state of fear." Another new book is Diana E. Russell's *The Politics of Rape: The Victim's Perspective* (1975).

In 1976 Nebraska makes marital rape a crime (only in 1993 do all states have such laws). Across the United States there are now more than 400 programs for battered women and rape victims. In Boston,

"I Could Help Change the World"

"I have always believed that I could help change the world because I have been lucky to have adults around me who did—in small and large ways. . . .

"The Children's Defense Fund was conceived in the cauldron of Mississippi's summer project of 1964 and in the Head Start battles of 1965. . . . [I] learned that critical civil and political rights would not mean much to a hungry, homeless, illiterate child and family if they lacked the social and economic means to exercise them. And so children—my own and other people's—became the passion of my personal and professional life. For it is they who are God's presence, promise, and hope for mankind."

—Marian Wright Edelman, in *The Measure of Our Success: A Letter to My Children and Ours* (New York: HarperPerennial, 1992)

Local Initiatives in the Later 1970s

Casa Myrna Vazquez opens as the first battered women's shelter set up by women of color. A new national newsletter, *Aegis,* is the first devoted to domestic violence. Two new books on the issue are Del Martin's *Battered Wives* and Betsy Warrior's *Battered Women's Directory.*

In San Francisco in 1976, Women Against Violence in Pornography and the Media Against Women is formed by Diana Russell and others. In Los Angeles, another group, Women Against Violence Against Women (WAVAW), demonstrates against the porn film *Snuff,* which features the killing and dismemberment of a woman as entertainment. The first national feminist conference on pornography is held in 1978 in San Francisco, with a large "Take Back the Night" march to draw attention to women's right to walk the streets at night without fear. Soon thousands of women across the country stage similar marches.

In New York in 1976, the Single Parent Family Project opens a storefront center and helps establish neighborhood support groups.

In 1976, as president of the Cochran Tenant Management Corporation in St. Louis, Bertha Knox Gilkey (b. 1949) organizes residents to run the public housing complex and obtains federal funding to renovate it. The group sets up a day-care center and fights off drug sellers.

In California in 1977, after being imprisoned for almost two years, Inez Garcia is acquitted of all charges in the killing of one of the men who brutally raped her. Originally she was found guilty of second-degree murder, even though the man threw a knife at her when she confronted him, but her claim of self-defense finally holds on appeal. In another case Francine Hughes is acquitted, on the grounds of "temporary insanity," of murdering her husband by setting fire to his bed. Since 1963 he had assaulted her, but she received no help from police or social workers, and even when she divorced him, he stayed. Her story is told by Faith McNulty in *The Burning Bed: The True Story of an Abused Wife* (1980).

In 1977 women's groups join with church and health care organizations in the Infant Formula Action Coalition (INFACT), which stages a huge international boycott against Nestlé products. They eventually get the company to stop its aggressive advertising of infant formula at the expense of breast-feeding in developing countries.

Ellen Thurston forms American Funds for Alternatives to Animal Research in New York in 1977.

The National Association of Cuban-American Women forms in 1977 to help immigrants find their way in American society. The Organization of Chinese American Women starts with a similar intent.

The National Coalition Against Domestic Violence forms in 1978, bringing shelters and other groups together to publicize the issue.

In Berkeley, California, Laura X sets up the National Clearinghouse on Marital and Date Rape in 1978 to lobby for state laws against marital rape. In Oregon, which has such a law, John Rideout is the first man indicted for marital rape, but he is acquitted (he is later jailed for harassing his wife after they break up).

In 1978 Tish Sommers and Laurie Shields start the Older Women's League Educational Fund, which in 1980 becomes the Older Women's League (OWL). They focus on the problems older women face with Social Security and pension benefits, health insurance, and the like. Largely through Sommers and Shields's earlier efforts, the government allocates money for centers for displaced homemakers; also, Massachusetts passes a Displaced Homemakers Act to protect these women. In 1979 the Displaced Homemakers Network (later Women Work!) is formed as a lobbying group.

In Niagara Falls, New York, Lois Gibbs organizes the Love Canal Homeowners Association in 1978 to prod government agencies to clean up the toxic waste dump that is causing health problems in her neighborhood. Her protests draw national attention to the issue (see sidebar), and in 1981 she sets up the Citizen's Clearinghouse for Hazardous Wastes to advise other communities on how to organize and deal with the problem.

"Challenging people to create a new world . . ."
—Lupe Anguiano

Lupe Anguiano founds the National Women's Employment and Education Project in 1979 to find jobs for welfare mothers and train them for these jobs. Model programs are started in eight states. "The welfare program needs to be changed so that it supports [a] working woman," insists Anguiano, "so that when the woman goes and applies for a job, she is offered child care, transportation, or whatever she needs."

In *Califano* v. *Webster* (1979), the Supreme Court rules that welfare benefits must be paid equally to families whether the need arises because of the mother's or the father's unemployment.

Rape crisis centers in 20 states join forces in the National Coalition Against Sexual Assault in 1979.

In 1979 Joyce Tischler cofounds and serves as executive director of Attorneys For Animal Rights (AFAR, later Animal Legal Defense Fund). They initiate legal fights to protect animals.

After seeing the TV documentary *The Killing Ground*, describing Lois Gibbs's efforts at Love Canal, Cathy Hinds and Cheryl Washburn start a group in 1979 to fight for cleanup of the toxic waste dump in their Maine town and, in 1982, obtain federal funding for the work.

The National Center for Women and Family Law is organized in 1979 to offer legal resources to low-income women. Its National Battered Women's Law Project, for example, gives information on dealing with domestic violence.

"To Try to Save Their Families"

". . . Women are no longer at home, because it is unsafe. . . . Now women who would never have volunteered for anything have given up two years of their lives to try to save their families, working in our office, conducting phone surveys, going door to door. . . .

"The first thing we learned when we started organizing was how valuable the media can be. We learned what would get us national attention, like our survey on women who became pregnant during the construction of the containment system on the canal proper. . . . There were 15 pregnancies during this time. Of the 15, only one normal baby was born. . . . We found that numbers, long chemical names and statistics confused people, so we arranged a series—a horror story of the day. . . . Readers became furious with the government for allowing this to happen."
—Lois Gibbs, speech at "Women and Life on Earth Conference," 1980; in *Heresies*, issue 13 (1981)

After her daughter is killed by a drunk driver, Candy Lightner organizes Mothers Against Drunk Driving (MADD) in 1980 and starts lobbying for tougher drunk driving laws in California. But, as she explains, "MADD is far more than legislation. It is victims assistance, it is group support, it is public education, it is court monitoring, trying to change the system, and it's trying to change attitudes and behavior."

In 1980 Ingrid Newkirk helps found People for the Ethical Treatment of Animals (PETA), which organizes boycotts of cosmetics companies that use animal testing. Other women protest fur trapping and ranching practices; repeated demonstrations against women wearing furs during the 1980s succeed in getting designers to feature fake fur by the end of the decade.

Ynestra King, Celeste Wesson, Grace Paley, and others organize the 1980 conference "Women and Life on Earth: Ecofeminism in the 1980s" in Massachusetts (see also p. 216). Susan Adler and others hold a West Coast ecofeminist conference in 1981. Later, in 1985, King and Starhawk cofound the WomanEarth Feminist Peace Institute.

Expanding a New York group started in 1970, Jewell Jackson McCabe in 1981 launches the National Coalition of 100 Black Women, which gains 7,000 members in the next 10 years. In addition to facilitating networking among black women professionals, the group sponsors programs to develop leadership skills among teenagers.

Sarah Kemp Brady becomes a leader in the gun-control movement after her husband is permanently injured in an attempted assassination of President Reagan in 1981. Her persistent efforts result in the passage of the Brady Handgun Control Law in 1993.

Based in Alaska, Dolores ("Polly") Whaley starts Missing Children of America in 1981 to help track down children who have disappeared.

In 1982, as the new head of the National Urban Coalition, Ramona Hoage Edelin works to better conditions for low-income city residents.

The 1983 gang rape of a woman in a bar in Bedford, Massachusetts, focuses national attention on male violence. Four of the men are later given prison sentences for aggravated assault. The attack on the woman's own character, as if she were responsible for the attack, is the subject of the film *The Accused*, starring Jodie Foster.

Attorney Catharine MacKinnon and Andrea Dworkin, author of *Pornography: Men Possessing Women* (1981) and other works, draft an antipornography law, which is passed by the Minneapolis council in 1983 but vetoed by the mayor. A similar law is enacted in 1984 in Indianapolis but struck down by the courts as interfering with free speech. Some women's groups, such as the Feminist Anti-Censorship Task Force (FACT), oppose MacKinnon and Dworkin's proposal.

In 1984 several new federal laws result from pressure from women's

Local Initiatives in the Early 1980s

These are just a few of the many local programs begun by women in the early 1980s:

—In a Milwaukee housing project in 1981, June Martin-Perry starts Each One Reach One, a mentoring program for African American teenagers.

—In Las Vegas, Celeste Tate and a male friend start a supermarket in 1982 to provide inexpensive food for those in need. For a few dollars people can buy a cart of groceries, much of it donated by local casinos. Tate helps lead workshops to teach others to set up similar stores.

—In Baltimore in 1982, Kathy Levin starts Magic Me, a confidence-building program in which inner city children help people in old-age homes. The program later spreads to other cities.

—In New York in 1983, Rita Zimmer opens a homeless women's shelter, which grows into the group Women in Need, running several shelters, day-care services, a food canteen, and workshops on AIDS prevention and treatment of alcoholism.

—In San Diego, California, Theresa Do initiates the Refugee Women's Association in 1983 as a way for newly arrived Chinese women to help each other and fight for their rights.

groups. Congress approves the Family Violence Prevention and Services Act, which helps fund battered women's shelters. It also passes the Retirement Equity Act, providing pension protection for homemakers. With the Child Support Amendments, Congress calls for paycheck withholding if fathers are delinquent with child support, but this is not fully enforced.

Mothers of East Los Angeles is first organized in 1984 to oppose a state prison in their neighborhood; the group also battles against a proposed toxic waste incinerator in 1986. Their ongoing efforts finally bear fruit in the 1990s, with the defeat of both projects.

In 1985 Tracey Thurman wins her suit against a Connecticut police department for negligence and violation of her civil rights. In 1983 a police officer stood by and just watched as her husband attacked her, stabbing her repeatedly and kicking her in the head. (Her husband received a 15-year sentence for this abuse.)

The New York Asian Women's Center, formed in the mid-1980s, sponsors programs to combat violence against Asian women.

The first support group for battered lesbians starts in Seattle in 1985.

Formed in 1985, the National Assault Prevention Center, with Sally Cooper as executive director, holds workshops to help children deal with different forms of abuse.

Gloria Bonilla-Santiago organizes the New Jersey Hispanic Women's Task Force in 1985 to set up resource centers for low-income Latinas in the state. She also publishes *Breaking Grounds: Hispanic Women Developing Effective Leadership*.

In 1986 the National Council of Negro Women starts its Black Family Reunion celebrations, offering workshops, exhibits, and entertainment.

Elizabeth Morgan goes to jail in 1987 rather than reveal the whereabouts of her daughter to her ex-husband, who she believes has sexually abused the child. Her case becomes a cause célèbre, and she is finally released two years later by an act of Congress. Later she wins custody of her daughter in New Zealand.

In 1987 in Detroit, Clementine Barfield starts So Sad to help families who have lost a child, as she has, to city violence. In 1988 Cynthia Harris reacts to her son's murder by setting up the Stop! The Madness Foundation in Washington, D.C., to combat drug-related crime.

In 1987 in Philadelphia, Sue Osthoff and Barbara Hart establish the National Clearinghouse for the Defense of Battered Women.

1990–95

After her son is killed for his expensive jacket, Brenda Muhammad organizes Mothers of Murdered Sons (MOMS) in 1990 in Atlanta. Chapters soon open in other major cities. "We need to bring attention to the problem of young blacks killing young blacks," she says.

Protecting the Land

A number of Native American women help lead protests to protect their peoples' lands from environmentally destructive development during the 1980s. Two examples are:

—JoAnn Tall, who leads 150 people to camp out in 1987 at a proposed weapons test site in a Black Hills canyon that is an ancient burial site. "How dare you descecrate our church?" she asks. She later helps found the Native Resource Coalition to fight against the use of Native lands for toxic waste dumps.

—Sarah James, who helps organize a conference at which the Gwich'in people protest oil and gas development on the Alaska coastal plain, home to the Porcupine caribou. As chair of the Gwich'in Steering Committee, she testifies at state and federal hearings. "Why don't we accept responsibility to save the earth for the next generation?" she asks.

In 1990 Judy Bari, an EarthFirst! activist in California, helps organize Redwood Summer to stop clear-cutting in old-growth forests. She gains workers, support by pledging that protesters will no longer spike the trees. Before the summer starts, however, she is badly injured when a pipe bomb mysteriously explodes in her car.

In 1991 women students at Brown University begin a graffiti campaign to publicize the names of male students who commit date rape. At a university-sponsored forum to discuss the issue, a woman stands up every three minutes to indicate the frequency of attacks on women throughout the country. The school sets up procedures for handling complaints and a mandatory date rape seminar. Other colleges, such as Swarthmore in 1992, also start date rape prevention programs.

In *Sexual Violence: Our War Against Rape* (1993), Linda A. Fairstein, director of New York's Sex Crimes Prosecution Unit, describes both the progress and difficulties in prosecuting rape crimes. She notes, for example, how the "ugly and offensive attacks" on the victim's character during the trial of "preppie" murderer Robert Chambers led, in 1990, to an extension of New York's rape shield law to murder victims.

Congress passes the 1994 Violence Against Women Act, which funds services for victims of rape and domestic violence, allows women to seek civil rights remedies for gender-related crimes, and provides training to increase police and court officials' sensitivity. Several states also pass laws to protect women against violence. New York becomes the second state (after Florida) to say that rapists cannot claim that the victim's dress provoked their crime. New Jersey and Pennsylvania add stalking to their definitions of abuse. California distributes information on domestic violence to any couple applying for a marriage license.

Education

Teacher in a one-room school in the West during the 19th century
(Denver Public Library, Western History Department)

Coeducation in the Late 1700s

In Connecticut, an early coeducational academy opened by Timothy Dwight in 1783, lets girls attend classes, but not at the same time as boys. Rhode Island Quakers start a coeducational boarding school in 1784; similar Quaker schools open in 1796 near Poughkeepsie, New York, and near Philadelphia in 1799. At these schools boys and girls receive separate but roughly equal educations—although the girls do not study Latin and Greek, and the boys abstain from needlework. The two sexes are carefully kept apart; even brothers and sisters may visit only once every two weeks. One difference between the sexes at these schools is in the pay scale: male teachers receive more than female teachers.

1600s

In New England parents are required to teach their boys to read and write, but girls are usually taught only reading. By the end of the century, only 50% of the women in New England, compared with 80% of the men, can sign their names. In the South the figure is much lower, with only 25% of the women able to read and write. To learn their letters, New England girls often attend dame schools, taught by older women in their homes. Reading is the main "course," but writing, spelling, and sewing are also sometimes taught. In 1647 Massachusetts allows girls to attend summer sessions at its public schools, but they cannot advance beyond the grammar school level.

1700–49

Although most girls who receive any education continue to be taught at home or in dame schools, there are a few alternatives. When they arrive in New Orleans in 1727, Catholic nuns set up a school, teaching French settlers, blacks, and Native Americans (see "Religion"). In 1742 Benigna von Zinzendorf (later de Watteville, 1725–89) opens a Moravian boarding school for girls in Pennsylvania. There girls receive lessons in reading and writing, as well as religion and domestic skills. (The school later becomes the Moravian College and Seminary for Women.) A second Moravian boarding school for girls is started in 1746.

1750–99

In 1754 Philadelphia Quakers establish a public school for girls, where the daughters of both wealthy and poor families learn not only reading and writing but also French, Latin, and the classics. Several students are known for their later contributions: historian Deborah Norris (later Logan), minister and teacher Rebecca Jones, and journalist Sally Wister.

An early school for African American children is set up in 1761 in Williamsburg, Virginia, by Dr. Bray's Associates, an English group. Its teacher, Anne Wager, gives reading lessons as well as religious instruction, but slave owners often refuse to let her pupils stay for long.

In 1764 a Dedham, Massachusetts, teacher, Susannah Brittano, leaves all her savings to found a school taught by women. In Rhode Island at this time, Sarah Osborn (p. 200) holds separate classes for African Americans while running a dame school. The instruction is mostly religious, but she teaches reading and writing to any who want to learn.

In 1776 Abigail Adams writes of the need for education for women. "If we mean to have Heroes, Statesmen and Philosophers," she contends, "we should have learned women." As she points out, it is women who are the first educators of men. Another early plea for female education is by Judith Sargent Stevens (later Murray) in her 1779 essay, "Desultory Thoughts upon the Utility of Encouraging a Degree of Self-Complacency, Especially in Female Bosoms," published in 1784.

In 1787 the Young Ladies Academy of Philadelphia opens, offering rigorous instruction, with exams every few months, in reading, writing, composition, grammar, rhetoric, geography, arithmetic, and the like. In his address to the first year's graduating class, Benjamin Rush emphasizes the importance of educating women because of their influence on the young—a philosophy that guides female education for many years.

In "On the Equality of the Sexes" (1790), Judith Sargent Murray contends that much of the alleged inferiority of the female sex is due to the lack of equal educational opportunities (see sidebar).

In Litchfield, Connecticut, in 1792 Sarah Pierce (1767–1852) starts teaching in her home and by 1798 the demand is so great that townspeople give her a building. (In 1827 the school is incorporated as the Litchfield Female Academy.) She insists that both girls and boys need "the discipline of the mind," and she believes in regular exercise, requiring a walk each evening. Pierce also writes some of the texts, including a four-volume history using a question-and-answer format to make the subject interesting to students.

Graduating students at the Young Ladies Academy of Philadelphia defend their right to speak in public. In 1792 Molly Wallace asks, "And if [we are taught] to read, why not to speak?" In 1793 Priscilla Mason decries the lack of places for women to speak: "The Church, the Bar, the Senate are closed against us. Who shut them? *Man;* despotic man."

In New York, Catherine ("Katy") Williams Ferguson (c. 1774–1854), a former slave, starts a Sunday school in her home for poor black and white children living in her neighborhood or a nearby almshouse. She gives them religious lessons; soon a local minister offers her space in his church's basement, as well as assistants to teach secular subjects.

In 1797 Susanna Haswell Rowson (c. 1762–1824) opens her Young Ladies Academy in Boston to offer girls education beyond the elementary level. She prepares texts in geography, history, spelling, and Bible studies; brings in European-trained music teachers; and encourages public speaking. As Judith Murray writes in 1798: "Female academies are everywhere establishing."

1800–19

A few women's literary clubs offer a kind of self-directed continuing education for women with some leisure time. An early example, from 1800, is the Woman's Literary Society in Chelsea, Connecticut.

Catholic nuns continue to educate girls, as at the boarding school established by Elizabeth Seton near Baltimore in 1809 (see "Religion").

In Vermont in 1814, Emma Hart Willard (1787–1870) studies the books of her husband's nephew, a student at Middlebury College, and uses this knowledge to teach classical and scientific subjects to pupils at a female seminary she runs in her home.

On the Missouri frontier in 1818, Rose Philippine Duchesne, a French nun, and her colleagues set up boarding schools for girls and also offer day classses for Indian and African American girls (see "Religion").

"What Partiality!"

"... Are we deficient in reason? We can only reason from what hath been denied us, the inferiority of our sex cannot fairly be deduced from thence.

"... Will it be said that the judgment of a male of two years old, is more sage than that of a female's of the same age? I believe the reverse is generally observed to be true. But from that period, what partiality! how is the one exalted and the other depressed, by the contrary modes of education which are adopted! ... Grant that their minds are by nature equal, yet who shall wonder at the apparent superiority."
—"Constantia" (Judith Sargent Murray),
"On the Equality of the Sexes," *Massachusetts Magazine* (1790)

"A reform with respect to female education is necessary"—Emma Willard

In 1819 Emma Willard lobbies the New York state legislature with her pamphlet *An Address to the Public . . . Proposing a Plan for Improving Female Education* (see sidebar). When her request for state funding for a secondary school for girls is denied, the town council of Troy, New York, raises $4,000, enabling Willard to purchase a building and open the Troy Female Seminary in 1821. Willard's curriculum includes mathematics and sciences as well as traditional moral and religious instruction. Students draw maps to learn geography and sketch the heart, arteries, and veins to understand physiology—although Willard covers textbook pictures of human anatomy with thick paper, as most parents consider these too shocking for young women. Within 10 years there are 100 boarders and 200 day students at the Troy Female Seminary, and it serves as a model for other secondary and teacher-training schools. In 1895 it is renamed the Emma Willard School.

An early seminary for southern white women is the Elizabeth Female Academy (also called "college") in Washington, Mississippi, in 1819.

One of the first known female black teachers in the South is Julian Froumountaine, who runs a free school for African Americans in Savannah, Georgia, in 1819. When, in the 1830s, it becomes illegal to teach blacks in the South, she conducts her lessons secretly, as do a number of other black women.

1820–29

In 1820 Ann Marie Becroft sets up the first seminary for African American girls in Washington, D.C. Throughout the 1820s, similar schools are begun by other black women educators, including one in Philadelphia by Sarah Mapps (later Douglass, 1806–82), later an outspoken member of the Philadelphia Female Anti-Slavery Society.

In 1823 Catharine Beecher (1800–78) and her sister Mary open a girls' school in Hartford, Connecticut, which is formally established as the Hartford Female Seminary in 1827. There Catharine Beecher helps develop standards for teacher training and introduces calisthenics to the school curriculum. She continues to promote educational institutions and teaching roles for women, establishing the Western Female Institute in Cincinnati in 1832. She is not, however, an advocate of female suffrage or an abolitionist like her sister Harriet Beecher Stowe.

The first public high school for girls opens in Worcester, Massachusetts, in 1824. It is followed two years later by one in New York City. But other large cities, such as Philadelphia, do not open secondary schools to females until after the Civil War.

In 1824, as head of the new Adams Female Seminary in East Derry, New Hampshire, Zilpah Grant (1794–1874) sets up a demanding three-year course of study. When her Calvinist beliefs cause conflict with the Unitarian trustees in 1828, she leaves and sets up the Ipswich Female Seminary, with the help of Mary Lyon (1797–1849; see p. 172).

To offer childcare for working-class parents, Joanna Graham Bethune (1770–1860) starts the first free school for "infants," age one-and-a-half to five years, in 1827. She later establishes the Infant School Society.

In 1828–29 lectures from New York to St. Louis, Fanny Wright (p. 16), calls for equal education for women and underlines the importance of free inquiry into all beliefs. She argues, "Until women assume the place in society which good sense and good feeling alike assign to them, human improvement must advance but feebly. . . . Are [women] cultivated?—so is society polished and enlightened. Are they ignorant?—so is it gross and stupid. Are they wise?—so is the human character elevated. Are they enslaved?—so is the whole human race degraded."

In Baltimore the Oblate Sisters of Providence, the first U.S. order of black nuns, open a female boarding school in 1829. They teach not only religion but also grammar, composition, geography, history, art, and domestic skills. On alternate days classes are conducted in French.

1830–39

Prudence Crandall (later Philleo, 1803–90) opens a girls' school in Canterbury, Connecticut, in 1831. The next year Sarah Harris (later Fayerweather, 1802–68), the daughter of a local African American farmer, asks to be admitted as a day student so that she can learn enough to teach black children. Crandall agrees, and when white parents threaten to withdraw their daughters from classes, she refuses to back down. Instead, she closes the school and, with the help of abolitionists, reopens it in 1833 as a boarding school for young black women, offering teacher training. The white community responds with violence (see sidebar). Similar attacks on schools for African American girls occur in New Hampshire in 1835 and Ohio in 1836.

Two black literary clubs form in 1831: the Female Literary Association of Philadelphia and the Afric-American Female Intelligence Society of Boston. Similar clubs start in Providence (1832) and New York (1834).

In 1833 Oberlin College is established in Ohio as the first college offering equal education to both sexes and all races. It promises to bring "within the reach of the misjudged and neglected sex all the instructional privileges which hitherto have unreasonably distinguished the leading sex from theirs." Women, however, are generally consigned to a literary "ladies' course." In 1837 the first four women enter Oberlin, and three—Mary Hosford, Elizabeth Smith Prall, and Caroline Mary Rudd—receive degrees in 1841. Another early graduate (1847) is Lucy Stone (p. 22), who turns down the "honor" of writing a speech for graduation because only men are allowed to read the speeches.

In 1833 in Missouri, local families start the Columbia Female Academy (later Stephens College), under Lucy Wales, to give their daughters a similar education to that of their sons, minus Greek and Latin.

"Where Is Justice?"

To protest Prudence Crandall's school for African American girls, the Connecticut townspeople break windows, stuff manure down the well, and throw stones at students. Shopkeepers refuse to sell the school any food, and the state passes a "black law," forbidding the teaching of African Americans from out of state (many of Crandall's pupils come from Boston, Providence, and New York). One student describes the Canterburians as "savage." In her words: "The place is delightful; all that is wanting to complete the scene is civilized men. Last evening the news reached us that the new ['black'] law had passed. The bell rang, and a cannon was fired for half an hour. Where is justice? . . . When we walk out, horns are blown and pistols fired."

Crandall is arrested under the new law and spends a night in jail, giving rise to a nationwide outcry by abolitionists. Although her conviction is eventually overturned, repeated mob violence forces her to close the school in the fall of 1834. With her husband, she moves west, where she continues to teach and advocate women's rights.

In Boston in the mid-1830s, Susan Paul (1809–41) runs a school for African American children and organizes student concerts to benefit the abolition movement. In contrast, in the South, another black teacher, Milla Granson, has to conduct her classes late at night in secret in order to teach other Mississippi slaves how to read and write.

In Macon, Georgia Female College (later Wesleyan College) receives a charter in 1836 but does not open until 1838, granting its first degree in 1840. Although called a "college," it is closer to a female seminary. Its curriculum, however, does include mathematics, science, and Latin.

After helping her husband develop a system to translate the Seneca language into written form, missionary Lavinia Wright (1809–86) compiles a bilingual text in 1836 to teach reading and writing, as well as Christianity, to the Seneca.

After raising money from many women (see sidebar), Mary Lyon in 1837 opens the Mount Holyoke Female Seminary in South Hadley, Massachusetts, with 80 students age 17 or older. Students must pass an exam to be admitted and are required to help with domestic chores to keep the school's costs down. The rigorous three-year course, emphasizing grammar, algebra, geography, history, science, and philosophy, comes close to college standards. So great is the demand for this advanced education that in 1838 Mount Holyoke must turn away 400 applicants.

At the Perkins Institution, a Boston school for the blind, Laura Bridgman (1829–89) is the first blind deaf-mute to be educated, learning to read by touching raised letters on different objects in 1837.

In 1839, as grammar schools proliferate, Massachusetts opens the first public teacher-training school. Women teachers, paid less than men, are increasingly in demand, especially on the expanding frontier.

Transcendentalist Margaret Fuller (p. 20) begins her "conversations," attracting Boston women to discuss topics from art to health to women's rights. Later men attend these evenings as well, held at the bookshop of Elizabeth Peabody (1804–94), also a highly regarded Transcendentalist.

1840–49

In Maryland in 1841, Almira Hart Phelps (1793–1884), the sister of Emma Willard, heads the Patapsco Female Institute, training future teachers and homemakers. For science classes she uses mostly her own texts, such as the highly popular *Familiar Lectures on Botany* (1829).

In 1843 in Farmington, Connecticut, Sarah Porter (1813–1900) opens Miss Porter's School for Girls, an elite boarding school, which emphasizes gracious manners as well as academic excellence. For many years Porter teaches all the subjects herself, including basic skills as well as Latin, German, chemistry, music, mathematics, history, and the like.

In *The Duty of American Women to Their Country* (1845), Catharine Beecher urges women to take up teaching and extend their moral influence over the two million or so unschooled children. She lectures on this topic in the East, portraying teaching as a natural outgrowth of women's duties in the home and underlining that women teachers are less expensive. In 1847 she helps found the National Popular Education Board, which sends many Protestant women teachers to instruct children in the West. She later, in 1852, sets up the American Women's Educational Association to establish teacher-training schools in the West. Partly through her efforts, teaching—especially at the elementary level—becomes a female occupation.

At the 1848 women's rights convention at Seneca Falls (p. 20), Elizabeth Cady Stanton stresses woman's need for education (see sidebar).

In Boston in 1848, when Sarah Roberts is denied admission to a white school near her home and forced to travel to a black school, her father files suit. But the Massachusetts Supreme Court upholds segregation in the first known opinion giving the "separate but equal" argument.

In Illinois in 1849, Anna Peck Sill (1816–89) opens a girls' school, later called the Rockford Female Seminary (and in 1892 Rockford College), which is modeled on Mount Holyoke and becomes the leading girls' school in the Midwest.

1850–59

The Cherokee Female Seminary, modeled on Mount Holyoke, is set up in Oklahoma in 1850. Although originally supported by the Cherokee Council as a way of fostering traditional Cherokee education, it is soon dominated by its missionary sponsors and works to undermine Native culture. Most classes are taught by non-Indian women, and mixed-blood and full-blood Indians are segregated.

Graduating from Oberlin College in 1850, Lucy Sessions is the first African American woman to receive a degree in its literary course.

In Tennessee in 1851, Mary Sharp College, considered by many as the first true woman's college, is established, offering higher mathematics, Latin, and Greek as well as other courses.

In Washington, D.C., white educator Myrtilla Miner (1815–64) opens the Colored Girls School in 1851 with six students. She trains teachers, who go on to run their own schools. Although Miner bravely defends her school from mob violence, even taking out her pistol at times, she also shows a condescending attitude toward her pupils. The school closes in 1860 but is later revived as the Miner Normal School, eventually becoming part of the District of Columbia Teachers College.

"How little I . . . knew of what awaited me"
—Caroline Wilkinson, schoolteacher on frontier

Throughout the 1850s Protestant women teachers travel alone to set up schools on the western frontier. Bound for Michigan in 1852, for example, Flora Davis Winslow writes, "I teach school because I wish to be independent. . . . I go West to do the Will of my Heavenly Father."

"To Find Out Our Own Sphere"

"Man's intellectual superiority cannot be a question until woman has had a fair trial. When we shall have had our freedom to find out our own sphere, when we shall have had our colleges, our professions, our trades, for a century, a comparison then may be justly instituted. When woman, instead of being taxed to endow colleges where she is forbidden to enter—instead of forming sewing societies to educate 'poor, but pious,' young men, shall first educate herself, when she shall be just to herself before she is generous to others; improving the talents God has given her, and leaving her neighbor to do the same for himself, we shall not hear so much about this boasted superiority."
—Elizabeth Cady Stanton, "Address Delivered at Seneca Falls," 1848; quoted in *Elizabeth Cady Stanton/Susan B. Anthony: Correspondence, Writings, Speeches*, edited by Ellen Carol DuBois (New York: Schocken Books, 1981)

"Exalt Those Who Labor with You"

"Do you not see that so long as society says a woman is incompetent to be a lawyer, minister or doctor, but has ample ability to be a teacher, that every man of you who chooses this profession tacitly acknowledges that he has no more brains than a woman? And this, too, is the reason that teaching is a less lucrative profession, as here men must compete with the cheap labor of woman. Would you exalt your profession, exalt those who labor with you. Would you make it more lucrative, increase the salaries of the women engaged in the noble work of educating your future Presidents, Senators and Congressmen."

—Susan B. Anthony, address to New York state teachers' convention, 1853; in *History of Women Suffrage,* vol. 1

In Yellow Springs, Ohio, Antioch College is established in 1852 as the first college to treat women and men equally in its educational program. It hires Rebecca Mann Pennell as the first woman teacher at a coeducational college. She teaches a range of subjects, from didactics to physical geography. Although she attends faculty meetings with the men and shares other privileges, she soon discovers that her salary is lower.

Philadelphia Quakers set up the Institute for Colored Youth in 1852 to offer a classical high school education to black students of both sexes.

Clara Barton starts a free public school in Bordentown, New Jersey, in 1852. It is soon so successful that the local government decides it must have a male principal to run it—and Barton leaves.

The Woman's Medical College of Pennsylvania in 1852 admits a few nonmedical science students (for medical education, see "Health").

At an 1853 convention of New York schoolteachers, Susan B. Anthony ignores the rule barring women from speaking and tells the men what they need to do to gain more respect for the profession (see sidebar).

In 1855 in New York, the new Elmira Female College has a curriculum similar to that of Amherst. It graduates only about 10 students a year.

In 1855 the University of Iowa is the first state school to admit women. In 1858 the board of managers tries, but fails, to exclude women.

In California in 1855, Mary Atkins (1819–82) takes over the Benicia Seminary, turning it into a success that evolves into Mills College.

In the mid-1850s Susie King Taylor (p. 259) is learning to read from her grandmother's friend, a free black woman who conducts secret classes in Georgia. As Taylor later describes, "We went every day about nine o'clock, with our books wrapped in paper to prevent the police or white persons from seeing them."

In her Wisconsin home in 1857, Margrethe Meyer Schurz (1833–76), who learned about the kindergarten movement in her native Germany, opens the first American kindergarten. She later influences Elizabeth Peabody in Boston to start the U.S. movement (see 1860).

After teaching 10 years in public schools, Betsey Mix Cowles (1810–76) becomes superintendent of schools in Painesville, Ohio, in 1858.

In 1859 in New Harmony, Indiana, Constance Owen Fauntleroy starts the Minerva Society, an early women's study club. Their motto is: "Wisdom is the crown of Glory."

Sarah Jane Woodson (later Early, 1825–1907), who received a degree from Oberlin College, is the first black woman to teach at a college, at Wilberforce University in Ohio in 1859.

1860–69

In Boston in 1860, Elizabeth Peabody starts the first English-speaking kindergarten and does much to publicize the idea. In 1863 she writes a text on kindergartens with her sister Mary Peabody Mann, and in 1873 she starts the *Kindergarten Messenger*, a journal devoted to the subject.

After secretly teaching slaves and free blacks in her home, Mary Smith Kelsey Peake (1823–62) gains the support of the American Missionary Association and opens a day school in Hampton, Virginia, in 1861. She soon has 50 children during the day and 20 adults in the evening. Other schools for African Americans soon open in the South (see sidebar).

The 1862 Morrill Act, granting public lands for the establishment of state colleges with programs in agriculture and industrial arts, increases the educational institutions open to women. For example, although Cornell University opens in 1868 with only male students, when Jenny Spencer later demands admittance, she has to be accepted because it is a land-grant school.

Mary Jane Patterson (1840–94) is the first African American woman to receive a full B.A. degree from Oberlin College, in 1862. She goes on to teach, becoming in 1871 the first principal of Preparatory High School (later the M Street School) in Washington, D.C., the city's only high school for black students.

The University of Wisconsin admits 30 women to its teacher-training department in 1863, and during the Civil War women are also allowed to take other classes, as long as there is space. After the war, however, this practice stops and a separate female college is set up. Only in 1873 is coeducation reestablished.

Sarah J. Smith Thompson Garnet (1831–1911) is the first black woman school principal in New York City.

Near Philadelphia, Quakers start the coed Swarthmore College in 1864. On its board of managers are an equal number of men and women.

Vassar College, chartered in 1861, opens in Poughkeepsie, New York, in 1865, with the goal of providing women with top-quality higher education. To gain qualified students, a preparatory program is set up, and it dominates the program for the next 20 years. The faculty, mostly women, includes the well-known astronomer Maria Mitchell (p. 240), who encourages her students to open their minds to new ideas. "We cannot accept anything as granted, beyond the first mathematical formulae," she insists. "Question everything else."

The National Teachers' Association (later the National Education Association), which was founded in 1857, first admits women in 1866.

Scotia Seminary (later, in 1932, Barber-Scotia College) is started in 1867 as a Presbyterian boarding school for black girls in Concord, North Carolina. Most of the teachers are white, and the emphasis is on domestic skills, although teacher training is offered.

In 1867 Congress establishes Howard University, which not only admits women students but also has women on its faculty.

Freedmen's Schools

In 1862 in the Sea Islands of South Carolina, Laura Matilda Towne (1825–1901) and Ellen Murray, two white teachers from Philadelphia, set up Penn School, one of the earliest freedmen's schools. Northern abolitionist Charlotte Forten (later Grimké, 1837–1914) is the first black teacher hired for the project; she later describes her experiences in "Life on the Sea Islands," published in the 1864 Atlantic Monthly.

Working for the newly established Freedmen's Bureau or the American Missionary Association in 1865, black and white women teachers contend with mob violence to establish schools for African Americans in the South. By 1869 there are more than 9,000 teachers, mostly women, educating African American children in the South.

In 1867, at the new Clarke Institution for Deaf Mutes in Massachusetts, director Harriet Burbank Rogers (1834–1919) is the first to teach U.S. deaf children to lip-read and speak. In 1869 Sarah Fuller (1836–1927) takes charge of the new Boston School for Deaf-Mutes, where she also emphasizes speaking rather than signing.

The women's study club movement starts with Sorosis in New York (p. 113) and the New England Women's Club in Boston in 1868. Many relatively affluent women join clubs to broaden their education. The movement quickly spreads, with some clubs becoming specialized, such as San Francisco's Portia Club, which focuses on law and government.

In New York in 1868, Maria Kraus-Boelte and her husband start the first kindergarten-training school.

In 1869 Phoebe Couzins and Lemma Barkaloo are the first two women admitted to a law school, St. Louis Law School (later Washington University School of Law) in Missouri. The first woman to graduate from a law school, however, is Ada H. Kepley, at Union College in Chicago. Couzins graduates soon afterward, and Barkaloo (who doesn't finish) is the first woman admitted to the Missouri bar (in 1870).

Fanny Jackson (later Coppin, 1837–1913), an Oberlin graduate, is the first black woman to head the Institute for Colored Youth in Philadelphia in 1869. She introduces a teacher-training course in 1871 and vocational training in 1889.

In 1869 Indiana, Kansas, and Minnesota all admit women to their universities; only Indiana accepts women from out of state.

1870–79

After women raise $100,000 to back up their demands, the University of Michigan agrees to accept women in 1870. Other schools accepting women include the University of California (from the home state only), the University of Illinois, and Ohio State. Although the University of Missouri admits women, it does not let them in all classes until 1871 and even then they do not have full access to the library. In contrast, at the University of Cincinnati, where tuition is free, women make up half the student body from the start. In New York, when City College refuses to accept women, Hunter College (initially called Female Normal and High School) is created, offering teacher training and free tuition.

In 1870 Ellen Swallow (later Richards, 1842–1911) is the first woman allowed to attend the Massachusetts Institute of Technology. As she later learns, she is given free tuition so that the president can tell the trustees she isn't really a student. Although she receives a B.S. in 1873, she is refused a doctorate in chemistry. Richards later initiates home economics, a field providing work for women chemists.

Pioneer women, such as Emily Biggs in 1871 in Kansas (see sidebar), often start their own informal schools during this time.

In 1871 Frances Willard, later the leader of the WCTU (p. 147), is the first president of the Evanston College for Ladies. When it merges with Northwestern University in 1873, she becomes dean of women.

After taking over the Benecia Ladies Seminary in 1865, Susan Tolman Mills (1825–1912) and her husband, Cyrus, move the school in 1871 to Oakland, California, where it eventually becomes Mills College.

At an 1873 meeting called by Jane Croly of the club Sorosis, 400 women form the Association for the Advancement of Women to promote both higher education and professional possibilities for women. Speakers at this meeting include Julia Ward Howe, Maria Mitchell, Catharine Beecher, Elizabeth Peabody, and Antoinette Blackwell. Mary Rice Livermore is selected as the first president.

In 1873 Boston University is the first coeducational college in Massachusetts. In Greensboro, North Carolina, Methodist Episcopalians start Bennett Seminary (later Bennett College for Women) for male and female African American students.

Through the efforts of the New England Women's Club, four women are elected to the Boston School Committee in 1873, but the men refuse to seat them. The next year, after passage of a new state law affirming women's place on the board, six women—including Lucretia Crocker, Abby W. May, and Lucretia Peabody Hale—are elected.

In 1873 Susan Elizabeth Blow (1843–1916) opens the first public U.S. kindergarten, in St. Louis, and in 1874 starts the first public training school for kindergarten teachers.

Julia Ward Howe edits *Sex and Education: A Reply to Dr. E. H. Clarke's "Sex in Education"* (1874), denouncing the Harvard psychology professor's claim that too much study destroyed women's sex organs and caused mental disorders. Clarke's 1873 book, however, remains highly influential. "We were haunted in those days, by the clanging chains of that gloomy little specter, Dr. Edward H. Clarke's *Sex in Education*," educator M. Carey Thomas (p. 179) later recalls.

The Chautauqua movement has its origins in a Methodist Episcopal summer program in upstate New York in 1874. The adult education soon expands to include a correspondence course and traveling lecturers. Many educated women earn a living as Chautauqua speakers.

Two new women's colleges open in Massachusetts in 1875: Smith and Wellesley, both originally founded in 1870 (see sidebar).

In 1875 in Mississippi, Mount Holyoke graduate Sarah Ann Dickey opens Mount Hermon Female Seminary, which trains many black elementary school teachers. An equal number of blacks and whites sit on its board.

After teaching cooking to working women at the Women's Educational and Industrial Society's school, Juliet Corson (1841–97) starts her own cooking school in New York in 1876. She gains attention with an 1877

The Opening of Wellesley and Smith

From its opening in 1875 (and all through its history), Wellesley has a woman president, although Ada Lydia Howard (1829–1907) carefully follows founder Henry F. Durant's policies. The teachers are all women, but men are added the next year. Most of the initial 300 students are enrolled in the preparatory department to build up their skills; by 1881 Wellesley has encouraged separate prep schools, such as Dana Hall, so it drops this department.

At Smith, which opens a day later, there are only 14 students, as the strict admissions standards follow men's colleges in requiring Greek and math, for example. The president is a man, and there are no female presidents for 100 years, until Jill Ker Conway in 1975. The college's founder, however, is a woman: Sophia Smith (1796–1870), who left money for a woman's college in her will. "It is my opinion," she wrote in her will, "that by the higher and more thoroughly Christian education of women, what are called their 'wrongs' will be redressed, their wages will be adjusted, their weight of influence in reforming the evils of society will be greatly increased; as teachers, as writers, as mothers, as members of society, their power for good will be incalculably increased."

"No, I Will Not Submit"

". . . [My friend Judéwin] had overheard the paleface woman talk about cutting our long, heavy hair. . . . Among our people, short hair was worn by mourners, and shingled hair by cowards!

". . . when Judéwin said, 'We have to submit, because they are strong,' I rebelled.

"'No, I will not submit! I will struggle first!' I answered.

". . . I remember being dragged out, though I resisted by kicking and scratching wildly. In spite of myself, I was carried downstairs and tied fast in a chair.

"I cried aloud all the while until I felt the cold blades of the scissors against my neck, and heard them gnaw off one of my thick braids. Then I lost my spirit."

—Zitkala-Sa, "Impressions of an Indian Childhood," Atlantic Monthly (January 1900)

pamphlet, *Fifteen Cent Dinners for Families of Six,* and the idea of cooking schools spreads. In 1879 Mary Bailey Lincoln (1844–1921) starts a school in Boston, and Sarah Heston Rorer (1849–1937) does the same in Philadelphia in 1883; both also publish cookbooks.

The Massachusetts Society for the University Education of Women, started in 1877, is an early scholarship organization.

When Helen Magill (later White, 1853–1944) obtains a doctorate in Greek at Boston University in 1877, she is the first woman to receive a Ph.D. at a U.S. school.

In 1878 Girls' Latin School in Boston is the first public college preparatory school in Massachusetts.

Mary Seymour opens a secretarial school in New York in 1879 (p. 114).

The "Harvard Annex," with classes taught by Harvard faculty, opens in 1879 with 27 women students. In 1882 it is formally incorporated as the Society for the Collegiate Instruction of Women, with Elizabeth Cary Agassiz (p. 240) as president. Although the teachers are from Harvard, there is no official connection until 1894, when the school is renamed Radcliffe College.

In 1879 the new Carlisle School in Pennsylvania uses military-style discipline to train young Indian women in domestic skills as a way of "civilizing" Native peoples. Many similar industrial schools for Indians are started by whites in the next 30 years. Later, Zitkala-Sa describes her 1884 experience in one of these schools (see sidebar).

1880–89

By 1880 there are about 40,000 women in colleges, representing 32% of all students, almost a fourfold increase since 1870.

Susette LaFlesche Tibbles (p. 31) presents a paper on "The Position, Occupation and Culture of Indian Women" to the Association for Advancement of Women in 1881.

White missionaries Sophia B. Packard and Harriet Giles start the Atlanta Baptist Seminary for black women and girls in a church basement in 1881. Within a year enrollment has jumped from 11 to 150. In 1884, having moved to a permanent site, the school is renamed Spelman Seminary (later College). Its emphasis is on teacher training and homemaking skills at first; in 1886 it adds the first nurse training school for African Americans.

In 1881 in Philadelphia, Eliza Sproat Turner (1826–1903) and other club women start evening classes for working women and later form the New Century Guild of Working Women. Classes emphasize vocational skills, while study groups investigate history, philosophy, and the like.

The Association of Collegiate Alumnae is formed in 1882 by 65 women graduates as a networking organization and to counter arguments like that of Edward Clarke against higher education for women. They also establish the first women's fellowships for graduate study abroad. Later, after merging with similar western and southern associations, the ACA becomes the American Association of University Women (1921).

As Wellesley's second president in 1882, Alice Freeman (later Palmer, 1855–1902) is in full charge of the school. After establishing allied prep schools, she raises admission standards to the college level. Later, in 1892, she is the first dean of women at the University of Chicago.

"There is not any right or justice"—Mary Tape

When Mary and Joseph Tape are not allowed to enroll their daughter, Mamie, in a local San Francisco school in 1884, they take their case to court in the first test of Chinese American children's right to attend public schools. Although in 1885 the California Supreme Court rules Mamie must be admitted, the school board still refuses. "It seems no matter how a Chinese may live and dress," Mary Tape writes the board, "so long as you know they [are] Chinese then they are hated as one." The board eventually sets up a segregated Chinese Primary School.

New schools in 1884 include the Methodist-sponsored Women's College of Baltimore (later Goucher) near Johns Hopkins University and the South's first state college for women: the Mississippi Industrial Institute and College for the Education of White Girls of the State of Mississippi, which only becomes coeducational in 1982. In Richmond, Virginia, the new Hartshorn Memorial College for Women features teacher training, college prep, and college courses. In 1888 it receives a charter as the first liberal arts college for black women, and the first three women graduate in 1892.

At her death Bernice Pauahi Bishop (1831–1884), a Hawaiian social leader, leaves her estate to the founding of a girls and a boys school, later called the Kamehameha Schools.

Founded by Quakers, Bryn Mawr College opens near Philadelphia in 1885; it is the first women's college to offer graduate study. M. (Martha) Carey Thomas (1857–1935), its first dean and professor of English, is a major force in establishing its curriculum. In 1894 she becomes president of the college, serving until 1922. Insistent on top-notch academic education, without any traces of a finishing school, she is also a white elitist, expressing the racist and anti-immigrant sentiments of the day.

Alice Rufie Jordan defiantly registers at Yale University's law school in 1885, pointing out that the catalog does not exclude women. She manages to receive her degree in 1886, but Yale quickly adds a paragraph to its catalog to clarify that, unless specified, its classes are open only to men. No other women attend its law school until 1918.

Believing in the importance of black women teachers, Lucy Craft Laney (1854–1933), one of Atlanta University's first graduates, opens a school for black children in Augusta, Georgia, in 1886. In two years it expands from 5 to 234 students. As Haines Normal and Industrial Institute, it

Kindergartens

The kindergarten movement is strongly influenced by women. In the early 1880s the West Coast leader is Kate Douglas Wiggin, who started the first free kindergarten in the Far West, the Silver Street school in San Francisco, in 1878. She later becomes known for her children's books.

In the late 1880s Elizabeth Harrison in Chicago establishes a model training school; Anna E. Bryan in Louisville, Kentucky, leads the move away from an authoritarian stance to an emphasis on the child's own learning ability; and Lucy Wheelock in Boston sets up her own training course and in 1896 starts a kindergarten training school (later Wheelock College).

In the 1890s Anna Bryan's student Patty Smith Hill gains attention as an innovator; she later heads the department at Teacher's College, Columbia (1910). Sarah Stewart initiates the founding of the International Kindergarten Union (1892) to promote kindergartens and teacher training.

The first black kindergarten is set up in 1890 in Washington, D.C., by Emma Grayson Merritt, principal of Garnet School (and later supervising principal of all black schools in the city). Anna Murray sets up the first African American kindergarten-training school in the capital in 1896.

becomes one of the best secondary schools in the South, at a time when no public high schools in the state are open to African Americans.

In 1887 Anne Sullivan (later Macy, 1866–1936) of Boston's Perkins Institution for the Blind travels to Alabama to try to teach Helen Keller (1880–1968), who is blind, deaf, and mute. In the first month Keller makes the pivotal connection between water pumped over her hand and the word *w-a-t-e-r* spelled on her palm. By 1900 Keller is admitted to Radcliffe, and in 1902 she describes her experience in *The Story of My Life* (1902). Sullivan spends her life with Keller.

In memory of her daughter, Josephine Louise Le Monnier Newcomb (1816–1901) founds H. Sophie Newcomb Memorial College in New Orleans in 1887. Although connected to the all-male Tulane University, this women's college has its own teachers, buildings, and policies.

In 1889 in New York, Barnard College opens as Columbia's annex for women, after a vigorous campaign by Annie Nathan Meyer (1867–1951). Although it uses Columbia College's faculty at first, Barnard remains separate and eventually recruits its own faculty.

At the Agassiz Grammar School in Cambridge in 1889, Maria Louise Baldwin (1856–1922) is the first African American female principal in Massachusetts. When the school is expanded in 1916, she is in charge of 12 white teachers and 500 students, almost all white.

In Baltimore in 1889, Henrietta Szold (1860–1945) organizes one of the first adult schools to teach immigrants English as well as U.S. customs. The settlement houses that start at this time also have an educational component (see "Social Change").

Helen Keller (left) with Anne Sullivan
(Library of Congress)

1890–99

The number of female teachers jumps from 90,000 to 250,000 between 1870 and 1890. More than 60% of all U.S. schoolteachers are women.

The Association of Collegiate Alumnae offers its first graduate fellowship for study abroad in 1890. It helps support the first U.S. women at several German universities, including Margaret Maltby (1895 physics Ph.D., Göttingen) and Ira Hyde (1896 physiology Ph.D., Heidelberg).

As the first female student at Brown University, Mary Emma Woolley (1863–1947), future Mount Holyoke president, sits as a "guest" in men's classes in 1891 and joins the new, separate women's course in 1892.

In 1892 the University of Chicago opens, admitting women to both its undergraduate and graduate programs and including women on its faculty (see 1902). Alice Freeman Palmer is dean of women, assisted by Marion Talbot (1858–1948), who later takes over the job.

In 1892 in Mayesville, South Carolina, Emma J. Wilson starts her African American school with almost no money. Even after the school is accredited in 1896, she has hardly any state funding. She and her students grow their own food and construct all the buildings.

In 1892 the University of Kansas offers a sociology course called "Status of Women in the United States," an early example of "women's studies."

Under president Elizabeth Billings Mead (1832–1917), Mount Holyoke drops its seminary course by 1893 and is solely a college.

Radcliffe College is chartered to grant its own degrees in 1894, but it uses the Harvard faculty and the diplomas are countersigned by Harvard's president. Elizabeth Agassiz is president of Radcliffe, and Agnes Irwin (1841–1914) is the first dean. Only in 1965 do Radcliffe students receive Harvard degrees.

Both Colorado and Wyoming elect women to the post of state superintendent of public instruction in the mid-1890s.

Mary Church Terrell (p. 38) is the first black woman appointed to a board of education, in Washington, D.C., in 1895. She serves 16 years.

Trinity College, the first national liberal arts college for Catholic women, is founded by Sisters Julia McGroarty and Mary Euphrasia near the all-male Catholic University of America in Washington, D.C., in 1897 and admits its first students in 1900.

At the urging of Alice McLellan Birney (1858–1907), backed by Phoebe Apperson Hearst (1842–1919), some 2,000 women gather in Washington, D.C., in 1897 to form the National Congress of Mothers to encourage mothers' active participation in their children's education. Birney is elected president, and within two years the group has 50,000 members. In 1924 this group becomes the National Congress of Parents and Teachers (later the Parent-Teachers Association, or PTA).

In South Carolina in 1897, Tuskegee Institute graduate Elizabeth Evelyn Wright establishes the Denmark Industrial School (later Vorhees College) for African American students..

Catharine Goggin, an elementary schoolteacher, forms the Chicago Teachers Federation in 1897 to promote female teachers' interests. When the board of education says there is no money for higher wages, Goggin and Margaret Haley investigate, discover corporations that are not paying full taxes, and successfully fight in court for better pay. Haley later fights for other reforms, including a state pension plan for teachers (1907) and a state tenure law (1917).

In 1897 Anna Julia Cooper is the only female member of the new American Negro Academy, which fosters scholarly research.

Frustrated by existing law schools' refusal to admit women, lawyers Ellen Spencer Mussey and Emma M. Gillett open the coeducational Washington Law School in 1898 in the capital.

By 1899 northeastern women's colleges have graduated only six black women: one each at Mount Holyoke and Vassar, two each at Wellesley and Radcliffe. These figures do not increase much in the next 10 years.

Graduate Education for Women

The University of Chicago, Yale, and Princeton open their graduate programs to women in the early 1890s, but several other top schools do not admit women.

In 1893 Florence Bascom (p. 243) is the first woman to receive a Ph.D. from Johns Hopkins University, in geology. However, she is an exception; other women are not admitted to the graduate school until 1907.

Mary Whiton Calkins (1863–1930), who in 1891 established the first experimental psychology laboratory at a woman's college (Wellesley), passes her Harvard doctorate exam in 1895 but, as a woman, is denied a degree, despite William James's praise for her work. Ten years later she rejects the offer of a Radcliffe degree instead.

Librarians

One of women at the forefront of librarianship is Mary Cutler Fairchild, who serves as vice director of the New York State Library School from 1889 to 1905 and helps formulate library training standards that become the model for the rest of the country. In Brooklyn, New York, in 1895, Mary Wright Plummer helps design one of the first children's rooms in a public library.

Throughout the early 1900s women are instrumental in setting up public library systems. For example, Katharine Sharp founds the Illinois State Library School; Lutie E. Stearns travels throughout Wisconsin to establish public libraries; and Alice Tyler triples the number of libraries in Iowa as secretary of the state library commission. Beginning in 1905, Sarah Byrd Askew is instrumental in establishing New Jersey's public libraries (she introduces the first bookmobile in 1920).

In 1901 in an Iowa school, Jessie Field (later Shambaugh, 1881–1971) starts the Boys Corn Club and Girls Home Club, laying the foundation for 4-H clubs. In 1906, as county superintendent of schools, she sets up more clubs and creates a three-leaf clover pin, each leaf bearing a letter *H* (for Head, Heart, and Hands). In 1913 a fourth *H* is added (for Home, later Health). The national 4-H organization forms in 1914.

In Chicago, when she marries and, as a result, is fired for "misconduct," schoolteacher Mary Murphy takes the case to court in 1901 and wins.

In 1902 in Sedalia, North Carolina, Charlotte Hawkins (later Brown, c. 1883–1961) opens her own school, the Alice Freeman Palmer Memorial Institute, when the American Missionary Association stops funding her rural grammar school for African American children.

In Georgia in 1902, Martha McChesney Berry (1866–1942) starts her Boys' Industrial School, with its innovative work-study program, in a log cabin on her father's plantation. In 1909 she adds a girls school and in 1926 a junior college.

In 1902 at the new Simmons College for Women in Boston, many students already work at office or teaching jobs. The program offers academic and secretarial courses, as well as a course in domestic skills. In 1904 the college open s one of the first schools for social workers.

At the University of Chicago women are 52% of the undergraduates but have received 56% of the Phi Beta Kappa awards in the school's first 10 years. In 1902 in reaction, the school segregates male and female freshmen and sophomores, but this ends in five years. At Stanford, where women also earn more honors than men, the school initiates a quota system limiting female admissions from 1904 to 1933.

New York's 1903 compulsory education law is in large part due to a report by Helen Marot, Florence Kelley, and Josephine Goldmark.

In Florida, Mary McLeod Bethune (1875–1955) opens the Daytona Educational and Industrial Institute, with just $1.50. "We burned logs and used the charred splinters as pencils, and mashed elderberries for ink," she later recalls. The girls' school quickly grows, adding a trades school, nurses training, a high school, and teacher training. In 1923 it merges with Cookman Institute, becoming coed (later called Bethune-Cookman College).

The first public vocational high school for girls opens in 1904 in Boston, with Florence M. Marshall as principal.

As superintendent of the Emahaka Mission school for girls in Oklahoma in 1906, Alice Brown Davis fights a losing battle to keep the school under the control of the Seminole people rather than the federal government.

In 1907 Ada Louise Comstock (1876–1973) is the first dean of women at the University of Minnesota, where she teaches rhetoric and oratory. Later, from 1923 to 1943, she is president of Radcliffe College.

Alpha Kappa Alpha, the first Greek-letter sorority for African American women, is started at Howard University by Ethel Hedgeman and eight other students in 1908.

Portia Law School begins in 1908 in Boston as a bar-review course in the evenings; in 1919 it grants degrees and in 1969 becomes the New England School of Law.

In Tarrytown, New York, Mother Marie Joseph Butler (1860–1940) starts the Marymount School, with just one student. Her goal—to establish a first-rate college for Catholic women—is achieved in 1918, and she soon opens branches both in other states and abroad.

"We specialize in the wholly impossible"
—motto of National Training School for Women and Girls

In 1909 Nannie Helen Burroughs (1879–1961), an activist in the black Baptist church (p. 183), heads the new National Training School for Women and Girls, a church-supported boarding school in Washington, D.C. Although the program emphasizes domestic science and "the three B's" (Bible, bath, and broom), it also offers instruction in printing, shoe repair, barbering, and other trades, as well as a required course in black history. More than 2,000 women attend the school in its first 25 years.

In 1909 Ella Flagg Young (1845–1918) becomes the first female superintendent of a major public school system, in Chicago, and a year later is elected the first woman president of the National Education Association. She fights to raise teachers' professional status, adds vocational and physical education to the curriculum, and tries (unsuccessfully) to add sex education. When she is not reappointed superintendent in 1913, Chicago women—now voters—protest and she is reinstated.

1910–19

More than one-and-a-half times as many women attend college in 1910 as in 1900. Yet, as Marion Talbot, University of Chicago dean of women, asserts in *The Education of Women* (1910): "It is time . . . some of the needless barriers [are] removed from the path of women scholars."

In 1910 Charlotte Vetter Gulick and her husband help start the Camp Fire Girls, the first nonsectarian, interracial national group for U.S. girls.

Denied membership in the all-white Association of Collegiate Alumnae, Sarah Winifred Brown, Mary Church Terrell, and other African American women start the College Alumnae Club in 1910.

Mary Branch Munford (1865–1938) forms the Co-ordinate College League in 1910 to establish a women's program at the state-supported University of Virginia. Although the legislature repeatedly defeats the proposal, it does admit women to the College of William and Mary in

The New Discipline of Home Economics

The new field of domestic science, or home economics, originates in a series of summer conferences, initiated by Ellen Richards, beginning in 1899 in Lake Placid, New York. It is seen as a way of saving the home and the family group in the wake of growing industrialization. "The study of household arts, if taught in the right spirit," claims Richards, "must make the home a more interesting place."

The Lake Placid meetings set standards, course outlines, and reading lists for the new discipline, professionalizing housework. In 1908 the American Home Economics Association is formed. Ellen Richards is the first president and editor of the new Journal of Home Economics.

The women who establish home economics as an academic discipline include Isabel Bevier (who sets up a house as a laboratory for her students at the University of Illinois), Abby Marlatt (University of Wisconsin), Agnes Fay Morgan (University of California), Mary Swartz Rose (Teachers College, Columbia), and Flora Rose and Martha Van Rensselaer (both at Cornell). Only in this field can women scientists become professors and department chairs.

Experiments in Education

Women start several experimental schools during this period:

—In 1911 in Kentucky, Cora Stewart begins the "Moonlight School" program, using volunteer teachers to instruct adult workers on moonlit nights, when it is easier to find the path to the school. On the first night more than a thousand eager students show up. The movement spreads to other states and abroad.

—In New York in 1916, Helen Parkhurst (1887–1973) starts a school (later the Dalton School), where she uses her "laboratory plan," allowing children to progress at their own pace.

—In Denver in 1916, Emily Griffith (c. 1880–1947) opens her Public Opportunity School, offering free day and evening classes to children and adults. The idea is to give people the chance to learn whatever they need to know. In the first week 1,400 students sign up.

—In 1921 in New York, Elisabeth Irwin (1880–1942) starts the "Little Red School House," an experimental public elementary school, where the curriculum is modified to meet the needs of different ability groups.

1918. Graduate programs at the University of Virginia admit women in 1920, but undergraduate women are not accepted until 1970.

One of La Liga Feminíl Mexicanista's first activities in 1911 is to set up classes for Chicano children (see also "Politics").

In 1911 Katherine Gibbs (1865–1934) decides to open a secretarial school that stresses both business skills and a firm liberal arts education. Her first school, in Providence, Rhode Island, becomes so popular during World War I that she soon founds other schools.

Cornell University appoints its first women professors in 1911, in home economics. There are no female assistant professors in the College of Arts and Sciences until 1947, and no full professors until 1960.

In Savannah, Georgia, in 1912, Juliette Gordon Low (1860–1927) organizes the first American Girl Guides, following the British program. To reach "tenderfoot" rank, the girls learn to tie knots and light a campfire, among other things. In 1915 she establishes a national organization, the Girls Scouts of America.

The 1914 Smith-Lever Act gives impetus to the growing home economics movement by funding domestic science courses along with other vocational programs at land-grant colleges.

In 1914 the National Women's Trade Union League starts a training school for women labor organizers (see "Work"). Also around this time, under Julia Stuart Poyntz and later Fannia Cohn, the ILGWU establishes educational programs for garment industry workers.

In New York in 1914, Henrietta Rodman leads a successful fight to allow married women to continue teaching. In 1915 the Teacher's League also wins teachers the right to maternity leave after Bridget Pexitto and others contest their dismissal.

A 1915 California law lets districts hire teachers to make home visits, and this is soon used to acculturate Mexican American children.

The 14 Catholic women's colleges in 1915 include Trinity College (Washington, D.C.), Manhattanville of the Sacred Heart (New York), and St. Catherine, St. Theresa, and St. Scholastica (all in Minnesota). In 1919 Emmanuel College in Boston is the first Catholic college for women in New England. It emphasizes a liberal arts education.

In 1916 Ethel Percy Andrus (1884–1967) is the first woman high school principal in California, at the Abraham Lincoln High School in Los Angeles, where she tries to emphasize the value of diversity.

Russell Sage College of Practical Arts opens in Troy, New York, in 1916 with Eliza Kellas (1864–1943) as president. At first it is tied to the Emma Willard School, but in 1927 it becomes a separate institution.

With the 1917 Smith-Hughes Act the government increases its support for home economics, as well as other vocational courses, by promoting secondary school programs and such student groups as Future Homemakers of America.

In 1917 Nina Otero-Warren (p. 53) becomes superintendent of schools in Santa Fe County, New Mexico, the first Latina in this post.

Mabel Smith Douglass (1877–1933) is the first dean of the New Jersey College for Women (later Douglass College), set up in 1918 to avoid coeducation at Rutgers University. She heads the school for 14 years.

Effie Chew is, in 1918, the first Chinese American woman to teach in the public schools.

After running the first training program for psychiatric social work-ers during the summer of 1918, Mary Jarrett (1877–1961) helps set up the Smith College Training School for Social Work in 1919.

1920–29

In 1920 Susan Miller Dorsey (1857–1946) is the second woman super-intendent of a large school system, in Los Angeles. During her nine years on the job, school enrollment jumps from 90,000 to 220,000.

The number of female undergraduates in 1920 has doubled since 1910.

In 1921 the first three African American women receive their Ph.D.s: Eva Dykes in English philology from Radcliffe, Sadie Tanner Mossell (later Alexander) in economics from the University of Pennsylvania, and Georgiana Simpson in German from the University of Chicago.

In 1921 Bryn Mawr holds its first Summer School for Women in In-dustry, a program for working women initiated by union women, M. Carey Thomas (the college president) and Hilda Smith (a social wel-fare professor). The 60-some students give up their paycheck for two months to learn history, economics, labor law, and the like and develop leadership skills. In the same year Fannia Cohn at the ILGWU helps set up the Workers' Education Bureau, with information on different programs, and the Brookwood Labor College, a residential school.

The American Association of University Women forms in 1921 out of the Association of Collegiate Alumnae and the Southern Association of College Women. Ada Comstock, then dean at Smith College, is the first president, followed by Aurelia Reinhardt, head of Mills College, in 1923. A parallel group, the National Association of College Women, is soon set up by black women in 1924, with Lucy Diggs Slowe, Howard University dean of women, as president.

In 1924 in Mississippi, Lum Gong sues to have his daughters attend a white rather than a black school. The case goes to the U.S. Supreme Court, which agrees with the lower courts' decision to classify Chinese Americans as "colored" and to thereby "preserve the purity and integri-ty of the white race."

In the mid-1920s Polingaysi Qoyawayma (Elizabeth Q. White, c. 1892–1990) begins her 30-year teaching career in the Indian Service

Pioneers in Early Chidhood Education

In 1916 Lucy Sprague Mitchell cofounds the Bureau of Educa-tional Experiments (later the Bank Street College of Education) in New York. Three years later, in 1919, Harriet Johnson opens the City and County School as part of the bureau. It is probably the first U.S. nursery school.

The British nursery school movement is introduced into this country in 1922 by Abigail Eliot, with her Ruggles Street Nursery in Boston. Also in 1922, Edna Noble White sets up a nursery school in Detroit at the Merrill-Palmer Insti-tute, where she serves as director and helps pioneer child develop-ment research.

At the instigation of Patty Smith Hill, the National Commit-tee on Nursery Schools (later the National Association for Nursery Education, or NANE) is started in New York in 1925, with Lois Hay-den Meek (later Stolz) as the first permanent chair.

The first African American nursery school is started by Dorothy Howard in Washington, D.C., in 1927. Early laboratory schools are set up at Hampton Institute under Phyllis Jones Tuly in 1929 and Spelman College under Pearlie Reed in 1930.

New Women's Colleges

A few new four-year women's colleges are established during the 1920s and 1930s, including:

—Mary Baldwin College in Staunton, Virginia, which becomes a full four-year college in 1923 after serving as a junior college since 1916. Originally started as Augusta Female Seminary in 1842, it is one of the oldest Presbyterian schools for women in the country.

—Spelman College in Atlanta, which converts from a seminary to a four-year college in 1924. Although at first many of the teachers are white women, by 1937 there are twice as many black teachers as white.

—Bennett College in Greensboro, North Carolina, which becomes a black women's college in 1926 after existing as a coeducational school since 1873.

—Scripps College in Claremont, California, which opens in 1927. Funded largely by publisher Ellen Browning Scripps, it emphasizes courses in the humanities.

—Sarah Lawrence College for Women in Bronxville, New York, which opens in 1928. It offers small tutorials but has high tuition fees.

—Bennington College in Vermont, which opens in 1932 as a small experimental women's college with a focus on the arts.

system. Much later she describes her experience in *No Turning Back: A Hopi Indian Woman's Struggle to Survive in Two Worlds* (1964).

In 1924 Florence Rood is the first woman president of the American Federation of Teachers.

As a counterpart to the all-white National Congress of Parents and Teachers, Selena Sloan Butler and others start the National Congress of Colored Parents and Teachers in 1926, with Butler as president.

Lucy Diggs Slowe of Howard University invites deans and other counselors of female black students to a 1929 conference to develop a support network and articulate black women's educational concerns. The group continues to meet, formally organizing as the Association of Deans of Women and Advisers to Girls in Negro Schools in 1935.

1930–39

In 1930 women are about 44% of college students. At black colleges women are two-fifths of the graduates, double the number of 1920.

At Howard University, librarian Dorothy Burnett Porter (later Wesley) in 1930 begins converting stored-away boxes of books and information on African Americans into the Moorland-Spingarn Research Center.

In 1930 Anna J. Cooper, who received a Ph.D. from the Sorbonne in 1925 at age 66, becomes president of Freylinghuysen University, for black wage earners. She tries in vain to help it survive the Depression.

In San Antonio, Texas, María Latigo Hernández forms La Liga de Defensa Escolar in 1934 to fight against segregation and call for improved school buildings and adequate textbooks and teachers.

As president of St. Mary's College in Notre Dame, Indiana, from 1934, Sister Madeleva (Mary Evaline) Wolff (1887–1964) makes many improvements, such as establishing the country's first graduate program in theology for Catholic women (1943).

In Philadelphia in 1938, Miriam Stubbs Thomas and other black women start a club with cultural activities for children, later called Jack and Jill. The idea spreads and in 1946 a national group, Jack and Jill of America, is formed with Dorothy B. Wright as president.

1940–49

By 1940 more girls graduate from high school than boys. At the college level more black women than men now receive undergraduate degrees, although the overall figure for women is only 40% of the total. The number of women college teachers reaches a high of almost 28%, but this figure drops to 22% by 1960.

In 1940 May Hill Arbuthnot, who founded the first nursery schools in Ohio, coauthors the "Dick and Jane" readers that teach millions of U.S. children how to read in the next few decades.

In 1943 Radcliffe students can attend all classes at Harvard, although they do not receive Harvard degrees until 1963. Also at Radcliffe, the Schlesinger Library on the History of Women in America, a major resource collection, is established. Later in the decade the Sophia Smith Collection is set up at Smith College.

Former Mount Holyoke professor Nellie Neilson (1873–1947) is the first woman president of the American Historical Association in 1943.

When, in 1946, Ada Lois Sipuel (later Fisher, b. 1924) is denied admission to the University of Oklahoma law school as an African American, she goes to the NAACP, which takes on the case and wins in a landmark 1948 Supreme Court ruling that the state must provide equal educational opportunities for blacks and whites and cannot require students to wait for a segregated facility. Sipuel finally starts classes in 1949, but she is relegated to a chair labeled "colored" and cordoned off from her classmates. She perseveres, graduates in 1951, and in 1992 is appointed to the University of Oklahoma board of regents.

1950–59

In 1950 Harvard law school admits its first 12 women, but it indicates that, as it is already turning down good men, only the very best female candidates need apply.

In 1952 Frances Rappaport Horwich creates the first educational TV program for preschoolers, "Ding Dong School."

In its historic *Brown* v. *Board of Education of Topeka* decision (1954), the Supreme Court argues that segregated schools are "inherently unequal" and thus unconstitutional. The case originated when Linda Brown was denied admission to an all-white school in her neighborhood. In 1979 Linda Brown Smith (later Buckner) files a new suit against the city for continuing to maintain segregated schools.

In 1954 the Sister Formation Movement protests the inadequate training of many nuns teaching in parochial schools and asks that all teaching nuns earn a college degree and appropriate credentials.

At Bennett College in 1955, Willa B. Player becomes the first African American woman president of a four-year college. She later supports the student sit-ins to desegregate the town's lunch counters.

At the New York public library in 1955, Jean Blackwell Hutson becomes curator of the Schomburg Collection, building it into the Schomburg Center for Research in Black Culture.

In 1956, after fighting in court to attend graduate school at the University of Alabama, Autherine Juanita Lucy (later Foster, b. 1929) starts classes as the school's first black student. On the third day a white mob throws eggs at her while shouting "Let's kill her!" The school immediately suspends her for her "safety" and, when she is reinstated, promptly expels her for "libelous" comments about racism at the university. In 1992 she finally receives her maaster's degree from the school, the same year that her daughter, Grazia, gets a bachelor's degree.

Autherine Lucy (center) with NAACP attorney Thurgood Marshall (right) and NAACP executive secretary Roy Wilkins (Library of Congress)

In 1956 Rose Hum Lee (1904–64) is the first Chinese American woman to chair a university department, as head of the sociology department at Roosevelt University in Chicago. She later writes *The Chinese in the United States of America* (1960).

In 1956 in South Carolina, Septima Poinsette Clark (1898–1987) loses her teaching job and retirement benefits when she refuses to drop out of the NAACP and accept a new state law barring teachers and other city employees from joining civil rights groups. She then works for the Highlander Folk School in Tennessee, and in 1961, as director of education and teaching for the Southern Christian Leadership Conference, she defies threats by the Ku Klux Klan and others to set up "citizenship schools" (see sidebar). In 1976 she finally gets her state benefits restored.

In 1957 Daisy Lee Gatson Bates (b. 1920), president of the Arkansas NAACP, leads the nine African American teenagers who try to integrate a Little Rock high school in the face of mob violence. In her later book, *The Long Shadow of Little Rock* (1962), she describes the courage of Minnijean Brown, Elizabeth Eckford, Thelma Mothershed, Melba Pattillo, Gloria Ray, Carlotta Walls, and the three boys who have to endure constant taunts and assaults from their classmates.

In Ganado, Texas, in 1957, Isabel Verver starts a preschool to prepare Chicano children for the first grade. Her program is picked up by the state three years later and expanded to reach 15,500 preschoolers.

In the *Education of Women: Signs for the Future* (1957), a special commission on women, set up by the American Council on Education in 1953, recommends establishing flexible higher education programs to meet the needs of women with children. Their suggestion comes at a time when there are almost no continuing education programs.

"We started fighting for our rights"—María Sánchez

Not allowed to be a regular New York City schoolteacher because of her accent, María E. Sánchez is, in 1958, one of the first "substitute auxiliary teachers" mediating between the Puerto Rican community and the school system. She soon organizes the Society of Puerto Rican Auxiliary Teachers and later helps start bilingual education programs.

In 1959, as a visiting teacher of political science, Hannah Arendt is the first woman given full professorial status at Princeton University. The first woman allowed to teach at Princeton—Ludmilla Buketoff Turkevich, starting in 1944—is still relegated to the position of "lecturer" on Russian and Spanish literature.

In *A Century of Higher Education for American Women*, Mabel Newcomer reports on a decline since 1920. Although women were 47% of all college students in 1920, they are now, as of 1958, only 35.2%. Three of five women at coeducational schools are in secretarial, home economics, nursing, or teaching fields. Fewer than 10% of doctorates are awarded to women, compared with almost 17% in 1920.

To encourage college attendance by older women, the University of Minnesota starts an innovative continuing education program, designed by Virginia Senders, around 1960. It includes such support services as babysitting, remedial training, and job counseling. Similar programs soon appear at other colleges, and the growth of junior and community colleges also increases the number of older women students. There are 20 continuing education programs by 1963 and 500 by 1975.

In 1960 new Radcliffe president Mary Ingraham Bunting sets up the Radcliffe Institute for Independent Study (later the Bunting Institute), directed by Constance E. Smith. It provides fellowships for women, in their mid-thirties or so, to pursue scholarly or artistic studies on a part-time basis. Some 200 women apply for the first 20 spots (see sidebar).

After a two-year legal fight, Charlayne Hunter (later Gault) is one of the first two black students at the University of Georgia in Athens in 1961. "There was conflict and there was pain. . . . But I emerged as a whole person and the university came out the better for it," she later reflects. She goes on to become a prominent journalist.

In New York in 1961, Antonia Pantoja helps start the Aspira Clubs, which encourage Puerto Rican teenagers to pursue higher education.

In Chicago in 1962, four black mothers stage a sit-in to protest de facto segregation and poor conditions at their children's elementary school.

Katherine Dexter McCormick builds a women's dorm at MIT in 1962, along with a second one in 1968, to put an end to the school's excuse that there is not enough housing for more women students.

In 1962 Jeannette Henry cofounds the American Indian Historical Society and later publishes *Textbooks and the American Indian* (1970).

In 1963 Vivian Malone is one of two black students who defy segregationist Governor George Wallace and enter the University of Alabama. In 1965 Malone is the school's first African American graduate.

The 1964 government-sponsored Head Start program develops in part from the work on preschool enrichment programs by such women as Susan Gray, Cynthia Deutsch, and Annamarie Roeper.

The University of Michigan establishes its Center for Continuing Education of Women in 1964.

In 1964 in California, Bettina Aptheker helps lead the Berkeley Free Speech Movement, one of the early student protests.

In 1965 in Miami, Florida, a community-wide continuing education program involving four local colleges is set up. It reaches women age 21 to 79, with previous educational backgrounds ranging from elementary school to postdoctorates.

After a three-day sit-in at a New York board of education meeting in

"These Women . . . Now Had a Chance"

"The institute's first program for independent studies offered fellowships . . . to women who wished to use their talents in a productive way. The idea was to allow women who were living at home to be able to afford such mundance services as baby-sitters or part-time help so they could continue to work on the subjects in which they were interested. We supplied each of them with a studio or appropriate place to study without interruption, and access to the Harvard libraries and to any courses that they chose to audit. The exciting thing was that these women who had been stuck at home, and not recognized by society as having important contributions to make outside the home, now had a chance."

—Mary Ingraham Bunting, interviewed by William P. Rayner, in *Wise Women* (New York: St. Martin's Press, 1983)

The Start of Women's Studies

The first women's studies courses appear in 1969. San Diego State College offers five courses in women's studies; this becomes a 10-course program in 1970. At Cornell University, Sheila Tobias organizes a conference on women, leading to a six-course interdisciplinary program in 1970. Additional women's studies programs soon take shape at Portland State University in Oregon, New York's City College, Sacramento State University, and the University of Washington.

In 1970 Sheila Tobias puts together 17 syllabi from women's studies courses in Female Studies I, *and this is immediately followed by* Female Studies II, *edited by Florence Howe, with 64 course outlines. Howe also cofounds the Feminist Press, a publishing house, during this year.*

In 1971 courses on women are added at the elementary school level in Berkeley, California, and the high school level in Stoughton, Wisconsin.

1966, Dolores Torres and others take charge of their neighborhood schools in the Ocean Hill–Brownsville area of Brooklyn. The United Federation of Teachers objects and goes on strike, winning in 1968.

In 1967 Mary Gambrell is the first woman to head a major coeducational school, as president of New York City's Hunter College, which began admitting men in 1964.

In a Harlem school in 1967, Lillian Weber introduces the "open corridor" program, which lets students of different ages interact and fosters learning by individuals or in small groups rather than a large class.

From 1966 to 1968 there are 18 all-male and 35 all-female colleges that become coeducational.

In 1968 Elizabeth Duncan Koontz (1919–89) becomes the first African American president of the National Education Association and helps initiate its Center for Human Relations.

The Women's Research Center opens in Berkeley, California, in 1968.

At New York's Lehman College in 1969, Maria Teresa Babín (1910–89), author of *Introducción a la Cultura Hispanica* (1949), starts the first department of Puerto Rican studies in the United States.

The Children's Television Workshop, headed by Joan Ganz Cooney, first airs the innovative children's educational TV program *Sesame Street* in 1969. When feminists critique the program for showing women in stereotyped roles, Cooney institutes changes.

Alice de Rivera wins admission as the first female student at New York's Stuyvesant High School in 1969. Before, only one of the city's three public schools that specialized in science accepted girls. Other female high school students sue to take shop rather than home economics.

In 1969 Yale University admits its first female undergraduates, and Vassar College admits men. Princeton goes coeducational in 1970.

In 1969 the Modern Language Association sets up a Commission on the Status of Women in the Profession, chaired by Florence Howe, and in 1970 women form a caucus within the MLA. Similarly, the Committee on Women in the Historical Profession starts and in 1970 issues a report, compiled by Willie Lee Rose, on women's status in the field.

1970–79

Only one of 411 tenured professors at the Harvard Graduate School of Arts and Sciences is a woman in 1970. At the University of Connecticut 33% of the instructors are women, but only 4.8% of the full professors are; similar inequities exist at most other colleges.

In 1970 in the Department of Health, Education, and Welfare, Lupe Anguiano helps develop the Bilingual Education Act. Working for the U.S. Civil Rights Commission, Cecilia Cosca and Cecilia Preciado de Burciaga prepare reports on the education of Mexican Americans.

"If discriminations based on sex were eliminated ..."
—Bernice Sandler

Using Executive Order 11246 (prohibiting discrimination by federal contractors), Bernice ("Bunny") Sandler puts together a class-action sex discrimination complaint, which the Women's Equity Action League initially files in 1970 against more than 100 colleges. Citing statistics like those above, Sandler prepares more than 80 pages of documentation. The charges cover the entire state systems of California, Florida, and New Jersey, as well as many prominent universities, including the University of Maryland, which had denied Sandler a full-time position. Later in the year WEAL files charges against all U.S. medical schools. Also, Representative Edith Green, who is on WEAL's advisory board, initiates congressional hearings on sex discrimination in education.

As the result of a class-action suit, the University of Michigan is, in 1971, the first school to establish a clear-cut affirmative action plan for hiring and promoting women.

In 1971 NOW files a sex discrimination complaint against all public schools with the U.S. Department of Labor. It points out that 78% of all elementary school principals are men, although about 85% of all the teachers are women; at the secondary level 96% of the principals are men, but almost 50% of the teachers are women.

Title IX of the 1972 Education Amendments passed by Congress bans sex discrimination in any educational institution, from preschool to the graduate and postdoctorate levels, that receives federal funds. The only exemptions are for U.S. military training schools and certain religious groups. The new act also includes a provision that extends the Equal Pay Act to administrative, executive, and professional employees (i.e., teachers). The Nixon administration, however, is slow to establish guidelines, and WEAL has to file suit to prod it into action.

In 1972 the Ford Foundation is the first major foundation to support research in women's studies. Two new journals—*Women's Studies* and *Feminist Studies*—also give a boost to scholarship in this area. In addition, the Berkshire Conference on the History of Women (originally held in 1928) is revived, meeting first at Douglass College and then every three years at another women's school.

In 1972 Women on Words and Images (a group in Princeton, New Jersey) publishes *Dick and Jane as Victims: Sex Stereotyping in Children's Readers*. Meanwhile, Scott Foresman, a major textbook publisher, issues *Guidelines for Improving the Image of Women in Textbooks*.

When Gail and Thomas Parker are appointed president and vice president of Bennington College in 1972, they are the first wife-husband team to head a four-year college.

A 1972 National Education Association report reveals that thousands of black teachers have lost their jobs since the 1954 desegregation ruling.

A number of research centers and other women's educational organizations are established in the 1970s, including:

—Higher Education Resource Services (HERS), started in 1972, first at Brown, then at Wellesley, with additional offices opening later at the University of Denver and the University of Utah.

—The Wellesley College Center for Research on Women, set up in 1974, with Carolyn Elliott as its initial director. Other research centers open at Stanford University and the University of California, Davis.

—The Lesbian Herstory Archives, founded in New York in 1974 by Deborah Edel and Joan Nestle.

—The National Coalition for Women and Girls in Education, set up in the mid-1970s by Holly Knox from NOW's Project on Equal Education Rights, Bernice Sandler, and others. The group's goal is to make sure Title IX is enforced and to help communities identify problems.

In 1972, as superintendent of the 300-some parochial schools in the New York archdiocese, Sister Elinor Rita Ford is the first woman to head the Catholic schools in a major city.

In 1973 a curriculum workshop at the University of California at Los Angeles leads to the publication of *New Directions in Education: Estudios Femeniles de la Chicana,* edited by Anna Nieto-Gomez.

In 1973 the EEOC files its first sex discrimination suit against a university, Tufts, where Christiane L. Joost and Barbara E. White, two assistant professors in fine arts, were not rehired. At the University of Minnesota, Shymala Rajender wins her sex discrimination suit.

In 1973 Antonia Pantoja establishes and serves as the first president of the Universidad Boricua and Puerto Rican Research and Resource Center in Washington, D.C., a bilingual institution.

By 1974 hundreds of colleges offer women's studies courses, and there are more than 80 full programs in the field. In addition, 230 women's centers at college campuses provide support services such as counseling; information on health, childcare, and the like; and lectures.

Congress passes the 1974 Women's Educational Equity Act, introduced by representative Patsy Mink. It provides funding for the development of nonsexist teaching materials and model programs that encourage full educational opportunities for women, without stereotypes.

Ruling on cases brought by two schoolteachers, Jo Carol LaFleur of Cleveland and Ann Elizabeth Nelson of Chesterfield City, Virginia, the Supreme Court says in 1974 that it is unconstitutional to force a teacher to leave her job when she is five months pregnant.

A 1974 statewide conference for Chicanas on education is organized in Texas by Olga de Leona and Imelda Ramos. In Austin, Martha P. Cotera founds and directs the Chicana Research and Learning Center.

In 1974 Faith Smith helps start the Native American Educational Services, an Indian-oriented college system, "to make higher education meaningful to Native people."

In Chicago in 1975, Marva Nettle Collins starts the Westside Preparatory School, emphasizing self-esteem and the three R's to improve learning by black children from the inner city.

In 1975 Gloria Randle Scott is the first African American president of the Girl Scouts, USA. In 1987 she becomes the second woman president of Bennett College.

Signs: A Journal of Women in Culture and Society, edited by Catharine Stimpson, starts publication in 1975 and is a major force in the development of women's studies.

Congress agrees to the admission of women to the U.S. military service academies in 1976 (see "War").

The National Women's Studies Association is formed in 1977 to promote the field's development. By 1978 there are already 15,000-some courses and more than 275 programs; by 1992 there are 670 programs.

The experimental Hampshire College, opened in 1977, has a woman president, Adele Simmons.

In 1977 Susan Vorchheimer loses her bid for a place at Philadelphia's all-male Central High School when the Supreme Court decides that the all-female Girls' High is equal (but see 1983).

After a new British law opens the Rhodes scholar program to women, 13 U.S. women are among the first 24 females to win scholarships to study at Oxford University in 1977.

In 1977 the Women's Research and Education Institute (WREI) is established in Washington, D.C., in association with the Congressional Caucus on Women's Issues. In 1987 it begins publishing a yearly report on the status of women.

In a historic first, more U.S. women than men enter college in 1978.

A 1978 report shows that the number of female principals at secondary schools has dropped from 10% in 1965 to 7%.

The number of women receiving law degrees has greatly increased during the decade, from 5.4% of the total in 1970 to 28.5%. The number of female M.D.s has similarly jumped from 8.4% to 23%. The percentage of Ph.D.s has doubled, from 13% to 26%.

The Association of Black Women Historians is formed in 1979 and starts a newsletter called *Truth*. Also, in Washington, D.C., the National Archives for Black Women's History and the Mary McLeod Bethune Memorial Museum open.

1980–89

The first national Asian Pacific American women's conference on equal educational opportunities is held in Washington, D.C., in 1980.

In California, the National Women's History Research Project is established in 1980 with Molly Murphy MacGregor as executive director. Its goal is "to promote the multicultural study of women's history in the K-12 classroom." It also lobbies successfully for the first National Women's History Week in 1981.

Mujeres Activas en Letras y Cambio Social (MALCS) is started in 1981 by Adaljiza Sosa-Riddell and other educators to foster Latina scholarship and inclusion of the Latina perspective in academic studies.

In 1981 Jewel Plummer Cobb, medical scientist and former dean of Douglass College, is named president of Cal State University at Fullerton, the first black woman president in the California system.

The American Historical Association publishes influential historian Gerda Lerner's *Teaching Women's History* (1981).

Some Administrative Firsts for the 1970s

A number of firsts for women in college administration occur during the 1970s:

—In 1974 Lorene Rogers is the first woman president of a major university, in charge of the University of Texas at Austin.

—In 1975 Smith College gains its first female president in its 100-year existence: Jill Kerr Conway. Wheaton College also gains its first woman president: Alice Frey Emerson.

—In 1976, when history and law professor Mary Frances Berry becomes chancellor of the University of Colorado at Boulder, she is the first African American woman to head a major research university. In 1977 she takes a leave to serve as the top U.S. educational officer (p. 88).

—In 1978, after serving as provost and then acting president at Yale University, Hanna Holborn Gray is the first female appointed as president of the University of Chicago.

—In 1978, for the first time, all Seven Sister colleges have female presidents: Jill Ker Conway at Smith, Matina Horner at Radcliffe, Jacqueline Mattfeld at Barnard, Mary McPherson at Bryn Mawr, Elizabeth Kennan at Mount Holyoke, Barbara Newell at Wellesley, and Virginia Smith at Vassar.

In *North Haven Board of Education* v. *Bell* (1982), the Supreme Court rules that the Title IX, prohibiting sex discrimination in schools receiving federal funds, applies to employees as well as students.

In Montana in 1982, Jeanine Pease-Windy Boy starts Little Big Horn College with a rundown house and two trailers. It soon becomes an accredited two-year college and by the early 1990s is used by 300 Crow Reservation residents a year. Many courses are taught in Crow.

In a 1982 report for the Association of American Colleges, *The Classroom Climate: A Chilly One for Women?*, Roberta Hall and Bernice Sandler point to the different treatment of men and women by faculty.

In 1983 women earn more than half the undergraduate degrees, about half the master's degrees, and a third of Ph.D.s. However, women are only 27% of full-time faculty and 11% of full professors. The number of female senior administrators at institutions of higher education has increased, but it is still only 1% of the total.

With the enrollment of women at Columbia College in 1983, all of the Ivy League schools are coeducational.

In 1983 in Philadelphia, a judge orders Central High School, the top academic public school, to admit girls to its classes.

The National Council for Research on Women is organized in 1983 as an alliance of about 30 (and later more) existing research centers.

In *Grove City* v. *Bell* (1984), the Supreme Court limits the application of Title IX to the specific school programs that receive federal funds, but Congress later restores the law's full reach (see 1988).

SAGE: A Scholarly Journal on Black Women, edited by Patricia Bell-Scott and Beverly Guy-Sheftall, starts publishing in 1984.

In 1985 the number of women heading institutions of higher learning has doubled since 1975, although it is still only 10% of the total.

After being denied educational benefits because she is less that one-fourth Indian, although she is an enrolled member of the Sherwood Valley Pomo, Deanne Zarr wins her case on appeal in 1985.

"To make women's studies truly the study of all women"—*Johnnetta B. Cole*

Johnnetta B. Cole publishes the anthology *All American Women: Lines That Divide, Ties That Bind* (1986) to give voice to the differences and the commonalities among U.S. women. In 1987 she becomes the first African American woman to head the 106-year-old Spelman College—an appointment that, in her words, "belonged to all Black women."

In 1986 in New York, Isaura Santiago becomes president of Hostos Community College in the South Bronx, where 80% of the students are women who work.

The 1986 Higher Education Amendments provide financial aid to part-time students, thereby assisting many women.

In 1987 Congress makes March Women's History Month (see sidebar).

After a nine-year court battle, English professor Julia Prewitt Brown is the first woman given tenure at Boston University, in 1987.

Over President Reagan's veto, Congress passes the 1988 Civil Rights Restoration Act, reaffirming that the ban on sex discrimination in Title IX applies to all programs in a school that receives federal funding.

In 1988 Lambda Delta Lambda at the University of California, Los Angeles, is the first lesbian sorority.

In 1989 Rita Esquivel is the first Mexican American to direct the Office of Bilingual Education and Minority Language Affairs in the Department of Education. Later she becomes the first woman director of the Adult Education Center in California.

1990–95

In 1990 women are over half the instructors and lecturers at U.S. colleges but just 26.4% of associate professors and 12.8% of full professors.

Wearing T-shirts claiming "Better dead than co-ed," Mills College students go on strike for two weeks in 1990, until the administration reverses its decision to admit men and keeps Mills a women's college. The number of women's colleges has been halved in the last 20 years.

Mujeres Activas en Letras y Cambio Social starts the Chicana/Latina Research Project at the University of California in 1990, with the goal of setting up a permanent institute at the Davis campus.

In a 1990 case brought by Rosalee Tung and the EEOC against the University of Pennsylvania, the court rules that no tenure review material can be kept secret.

In 1990 Marguerite Ross Barnett is the first woman and first African American president of the University of Houston.

At Harvard law school, only 3 of 61 tenured professors are African American and only 5 are women; none are African American women in 1990. In protest, Derrick Bell—the school's first black professor—takes a leave of absence until a black woman is given tenure. He later gives up his job rather than support the ongoing injustice.

Neurosurgeon Frances K. Conley resigns from Stanford University Medical School to protest sexual harassment at the school in 1991. She returns when the school adopts procedures to deal with the problem.

In 1991 mathematician Delores Richard Spikes, the first black graduate (in 1971) of Southern University in Louisiana, is chosen as the first woman to head a university system, the Southern University system.

In Minnesota in 1991, Katy Lyle wins a complaint against her high

A Debate about Women's Studies

In the late 1980s and 1990s a debate grows over women's studies programs and who defines feminism. Among the writings on the role of women's perspective in the curriculum are the following:

—Marilyn R. Schuster and Susan R. Van Dyne, editors, Women's Place in the Academy: Transforming the Liberal Arts Curriculum *(1985)*

—Carol Pearson et al., editors, Educating the Majority: Women Challenge Tradition in Higher Education *(1989)*

—Caryn McTighe Musil, editor, The Courage to Question: Women's Studies and Student Learning *(1992)*

—The AAUW Report: How Schools Shortchange Girls (1992; see text)

—Myra and David Sadker, Failing at Fairness: How America's Schools Cheat Girls *(1994)*

—Christina Hoff Sommers, Who Stole Feminism? How Women Have Betrayed Women *(1994)*

—Daphne Patai and Noretta Koertge, Professing Feminism: Cautionary Tales from the Strange World of Women's Studies *(1995)*

school, which did nothing to protect her from sexual harassment and had to be asked more than a dozen times to remove offensive graffiti.

The American Association of University Women issues two influential reports: *Shortchanging Girls, Shortchanging America* (1991) and *How Schools Shortchange Girls* (1992). Their studies reveal that from elementary school, teachers encourage boys more than girls, and that by high school this leads to a marked decline in girls' self-esteem. Evidence of this drop in self-esteem in adolescent girls (especially white and Latina girls) is also presented by Carol Gilligan and her colleagues in *Making Connections* (1990) and Peggy Orenstein in *SchoolGirls* (1994).

The Supreme Court rules in 1992 that students can claim damages for sexual harassment as a form of sex discrimination banned by Title IX.

At Boalt Hall, the law school at the University of California, Berkeley, Herma Hill Kay is the first woman dean, in 1992.

In 1993 Nannerl Overholser Keohane, former president of Wellesley College, is the first female president of Duke University. Judith Rodin, former provost of Yale University, is named the first permanent female president of an Ivy League school—the University of Pennsylvania—replacing acting president Claire Fagin.

The University of Virginia is, in 1993, the first school to explicitly prohibit sexual relationships between teachers and undergraduates.

In Cambridge, Massachusetts, some 2,000 women attend the first Black Women in the Academy conference in 1994. The keynote speakers are Lani Guinier, Angela Davis, and Johnetta Cole.

In 1994 Ruth J. Simmons is named the first African American president of a Seven Sister college, Smith College.

Congress adopts many provisions of the Gender Equity in Education Act, to train teachers, promote math and science learning by girls, counsel pregnant teenagers, and prevent sexual harassment.

In 1995, at age 87, Oseola McCarty gives the $150,000 she saved as a washerwoman to support scholarships for African Americans at the University of Southern Mississippi. "I wanted to share my wealth with the children," she explains.

Religion and
Spirituality

Arapaho women performing the Ghost Dance in the 1890s (Smithsonian Institution, National Anthropological Archives, photo #55-297)

1500s

Women figure prominently in many Native creation stories, suggesting their importance for the community's spiritual life. The Iroquois speak of Sky Woman, who lands on the back of Grandmother Turtle, and they thank the Three Sisters for providing food. Selu, or Corn Mother, is at the center of Cherokee beliefs, and the Tewa Pueblo tell of Blue Corn Woman and White Corn Maiden. Hard Beings Woman, or Huruing Wuhti, is key to Hopi origins, while Thought Woman, or Tse che nako, precedes all material creation in Keres beliefs. Spider Woman, Earth Woman, Changing Woman, Serpent Woman—all attest to woman's power in Native belief systems.

As part of the community's spiritual life, women take on the roles of healer, dreamer, shaman. These functions continue throughout recorded history, in some cases into the 1990s (see sidebar).

1600s

In 1635 Anne Hutchinson (1591–1643) begins holding religious discussion meetings at her Massachusetts home. At first just women attend, but she soon attracts a following of influential men as well. Her belief in a "covenant of grace," with salvation directly from God rather than through moral righteousness, runs counter to the prevailing Puritan doctrine. Moreover, she suggests the social equality of men and women by highlighting their spiritual equality, and she directly criticizes the clergy. As a result, she is tried in 1637 as "one of those that have troubled the peace of the commonwealth and the churches," and especially for holding meetings, which is not "fitting for [her] sex." Throughout her questioning by Governor John Winthrop, she is defiant. "Do you think it not lawful for me to teach women and why do you call me to teach the court?" she asks. Later she insists: "Now if you do condemn me for speaking what in my conscience I know to be truth I must commit myself unto the Lord." A threat to Puritan orthodoxy, she is banished and later excommunicated. She and her family move to Rhode Island, then to New Netherland, where she is killed by Indians.

Anne Hutchinson is not alone in defying the Puritan authorities. Mary Oliver is tried in 1638 for arguing against the power of the clergy. Other early rebels against the Puritan male clergy's authority include Katherine Finch, Philp(a) Hammond, and Ann Hibbens (p. 10).

In 1641 a black woman is accepted into the Puritan congregation after displaying her religious belief for many years.

In 1646 in New Haven, Anne Eaton, the governor's wife, attacks the baptism of infants, and three of her female supporters are put on trial. One, Mrs. Leech, is not afraid to point to the "untruths" she finds in the church's doctrine.

Most early Quaker women settle in Pennsylvania, where they are free to practice their religion (but see sidebar opposite). Women play a strong role in religious life, serving equally with men as ministers and conducting their own business meetings, beginning in the 1670s. They are entrusted with overseeing moral behavior, caring for those in need, and determining if a couple is ready for marriage. Their accepted public role later helps give rise to such early feminists as Lucretia Mott and Susan B. Anthony.

In 1676 Kateri Tekakwitha (1656–80) converts to Christianity and defies stones thrown by her Mohawk people to observe the Sabbath. She later flees to the Jesuit mission near Montreal, where she is the first Indian to take sacred vows. Known for her devotion, she inflicts severe penances on herself, fasting and sleeping on thorns. After her death miracles are reported; 300 years later, in 1980, she is beatified by the Roman Catholic church.

A 1676 account by a French missionary describes a Micmac medicine woman's "conversion" of rosary beads for her own religious purposes.

In 1692 in Salem, Massachusetts, several young girls engage in playacting after listening to stories about Barbados and magic spells told by Tituba, a slave. Their play develops into the mass hysteria of the Salem witchhunts and the execution of 14 women and 6 men. The highly respected Rebecca Nurse is among those who refuse to confess to witchcraft and are therefore hanged. Tituba also refuses to confess and is imprisoned for 13 months before being sold by her owner.

1700–49

On Nantucket, Mary Coffyn Starbuck becomes an important Quaker minister in the early 1700s. Many other Quaker women travel to England and within America as ministers.

In 1711 Cotton Mather publishes some writings of his sister Jerusha in *Memorials of Early Piety*. Other Puritan women leave written testimonies of their faith in the form of instructions to surviving family members.

A 1715 Maryland law stipulates that children can be taken away from a Catholic mother to be educated if her Protestant husband dies.

Ursuline nuns from France arrive in 1727 in New Orleans, where they set up a hospital, school for girls, and orphanage. They teach African and Native American children as well as whites.

The Ephrata Cloister, a Dunker community, is established in Lancaster, Pennsylvania, in 1732. The women spin, prepare medications, make sulfur matches, weave baskets, and the like to maintain their cloister, and they establish the rules for their sisterhood. Known for their singing, the sisters often compose their own hymns.

During the first Great Awakening, a religious revival beginning with the teachings of Jonathan Edwards in 1734, many women are converted. Edwards's own mother, Esther Stoddard Edwards, is known locally for her religious influence and holds Bible discussions in her home.

In 1741 the Moravians establish a community in Bethlehem, Pennsylvania. Women play an important role in both the economy and the

The Ordeals of Early Quaker Women

During the 1650s Quaker women, who often travel in pairs as ministers of their faith, begin to arrive in America. Mary Fisher and Ann Austin, for example, are the first two Quakers to arrive in Boston. They are immediately arrested, strip-searched, imprisoned for five weeks, and then sent away on a ship. Such treatment, however, does not deter the women missionaries. In 1657 Mary Dyer, who earlier was forced to leave Massachusetts as a supporter of Anne Hutchinson and who then converted to Quakerism, makes the first of three trips to Boston. Banished, she returns in 1659 to support two imprisoned Quakers; sentenced to hang, she is reprieved just as the noose is being tightened around her neck. Dyer opposes the ban on Quakers and restrictions on religious freedom, so she returns in 1660, when she is hanged. In 1959 a statue in her memory is built in Boston.

In 1661 two more Quaker missionaries, Elisabeth Hooten and Joan Brocksopp, arrive in Boston; they are taken out into the wilderness and simply left there. After they walk to Rhode Island, Hooten refuses to give up. When she returns the next year with her daughter, the two are tied to a cart, stripped to the waist, and publicly whipped through several towns.

Two Different Prophets

In 1774 Shaker preacher Ann Lee (1736–84) arrives in New York from England and in 1776 establishes a community in Niskeyuna (later Watervliet) near Albany. Her doctrine, which encourages celibacy, stresses a communal life built on simplicity and charity, as well as the equality of the sexes and the races. Mother Ann's visions guide her community, which quickly grows to several thousand. A pacifist, she is jailed for several months during the Revolutionary War. In 1783 she is severely beaten during a preaching tour and dies soon afterward. In 1787 Lucy Wright (1760–1821) is named as Ann Lee's female successor in the "female line," and she sends out missionaries to spread the Shaker doctrine.

In 1776, during a severe illness, Jemima Wilkinson (1752–1819) believes she dies and then is revived by Christ in order to preach. Calling herself the "Publick Universal Friend," she travels for 14 years throughout the Northeast preaching repentance, salvation for all, each individual's direct relation to God, pacifism, and opposition to slavery. In 1790 she settles in western New York with her followers.

religious life of the community; within the female groups, for example, they conduct their own Bible studies and write religious autobiographies. Early Moravian leaders include Anna Nitschmann, Mary Spangenberg, Anna Mack, Elisabeth Böhler, and Anna Maria Lawatsch.

During the 1740s Sarah Haggar Wheaten Osborn (1714–96) begins holding her weekly prayer meetings for women. In a 1755 publication, she writes about the "Nature, Certainty and Evidence of True Christianity," expressing her revivalist beliefs. By the mid-1760s hundreds attend the meetings in her Rhode Island home.

1750–99

In 1766 Barbara Ruckle Heck (1734–1804) cofounds the first Methodist church in America, in New York City. Reportedly, on seeing some men playing cards, she throws the cards into the fire and begs her cousin to preach. She then oversees the building of the first church, the John Street Methodist Church, in 1768.

Sophia Hume is one of the many traveling Quaker ministers of the time. In her preaching she speaks of a woman's right to pursue the dictates of her own conscience. One of her sermons, *An Exhortation to the Inhabitants of the Province of South Carolina*, is published in 1774.

Two charismatic women preachers, whom some see as Messiahs, attract followers in the 1770s: Ann Lee and Jemima Wilkinson (see sidebar).

Although New England Puritan women are not allowed to preach from the pulpit, a number use broadsides to preach their beliefs, as Daughters of Liberty, during the Revolutionary War.

In the early 1780s Abigail Franks in Pennsylvania and Cynthia Miers in New Jersey stir up controversy over their "mixed blood" when they apply for membership in their Quaker meetings. It takes a few years for them to be admitted.

In 1790, after the restrictions against Catholics have been lifted in Maryland, Ann Teresa Mathews (Mother Bernardina, 1732–1800) and Frances Dickinson (Sister Clare Joseph, 1755–1830) establish the first convent in the new United States (which does not yet include New Orleans). In 10 years they have 14 nuns in their Carmelite order.

In New York, Katy Ferguson starts an early Sunday school for black and white children in 1793 (see "Education").

When Jemima Wilkinson preaches repentance to the Iroquois in 1794, three Indian women, addressing the Council of Six Nations, call in turn for "the white people to repent" and to "wrong the Indians no more."

During the Second Awakening, from about 1795 into the 1830s, a number of women conduct their own prayer meetings for women.

In 1796 Elizabeth, a former slave, begins preaching in Maryland. Asked if she is ordained, she indicates that "if the Lord has ordained me, I need nothing better."

1800–9

In 1802 U.S. Quaker Hannah Jenkins Barnard (c. 1754–1825) is charged in London with heresy when she defies the male leaders there and insists on a selective reading of the Bible, which allows individuals to decide whether to believe in miracles like the virgin birth.

In 1809 Elizabeth Ann Bayley Seton (1774–1821), a wealthy widow who converted to Catholism, starts a religious order (later called the Sisters of Charity of St. Joseph) in Baltimore, soon moving to Emmitsburg, Maryland. She opens a boarding school and gives free lessons to local girls. Her order spreads to Philadelphia and New York. Considered a saint by many during her lifetime, Seton is canonized in 1975, the first U.S.-born saint.

1810–19

After opening a Catholic school in Kentucky, Mary Rhodes (1783–1853) and two friends establish the Sisters of Loretto in 1812. They soon start other schools in Kentucky; in the next 100 years the order sets up 100 schools, two full colleges, and one junior college.

In 1812 Ann Hasseltine Judson and Harriet Atwood Newell are the first two women to accompany their husbands abroad as Congregational missionaries, to Burma and the Isle of France (Mauritius).

In 1813 in Kentucky, Catherine Spalding (1793–1858) becomes the superior of the new Sisters of Charity (later of Nazareth). Modeled on Elizabeth Seton's community, the order sets up the Nazareth Academy (1814), a convent (1818), other schools, an orphanage, and a hospital.

An early Protestant preacher is Abigail Roberts, who is converted by Nancy Cram in 1814 and then establishes a number of churches.

Given permission to hold prayer meetings and "exhort" by Richard Allen, bishop of the African Methodist Episcopal (AME) Church, Jarena Lee begins her preaching career around this time (see 1836).

In 1818 Rose Philippine Duchesne (1769–1852) and four other French nuns from the Society of the Sacred Heart set up their first free school for girls on the Missouri frontier. Although they are forced to close this, they eventually establish a convent, schools, and an orphanage in St. Louis, as well as other schools, including one for Potawatomi girls. Duchesne is canonized in 1988.

1820–29

In 1824 Kapiolani (c. 1781–1841), a Hawaiian chicftess and convert to Christianity, defies the fire goddess Pele. She treks 100 miles to the Kilauea crater, descends 500 feet to a ledge above the molten lava, and declares that Pele cannot harm her for she is protected by the Christian God. Her act does much to convert other Hawaiians to Christianity.

Isabella Bomefree, who later changes her name to Sojourner Truth (p. 20), begins her preaching career in 1827. Another new preacher is Salome Lincoln (later Mowry; see sidebar). After leading a mill

"I Then Arose and Began to Speak"

When the preacher does not arrive at a meeting in Rochester, Massachusetts, Salome Lincoln realizes she must speak: "I sat a few moments trembling under the cross: and then fell upon my knees and commenced praying. While in prayer, the power of God was manifested—and the fear of man taken away. I then arose and began to speak."
—quoted in Gerda Lerner,
*The Female Experience:
An American Documentary*
(Indianapolis: Bobbs-Merrill, 1977)

workers' strike, Lincoln concentrates on her preaching in the 1830s, traveling to Boston and other towns to hold revival meetings.

Cynthia Farrar (1795–1862) is the first single woman missionary sent out by the American Board of Commissioners for Foreign Missions. She spends more than 30 years setting up Christian schools in India.

In 1828 Zilpah Elaw, a traveling evangelist preacher, speaks out against slavery in her sermons. She addresses other African Americans as well as whites not only in the Northeast, but also in Washington, D.C., and the slaveholding states of Maryland and Virginia.

In 1829 Elizabeth Clovis Lange (Mother Mary Elizabeth, 1784–1882) and three other women start the first black Catholic community, the Oblate Sisters of Providence, in Baltimore. They teach black children and travel outside the convent to care for the sick.

1830–39

A 1832 pastoral letter from the Presbyterian General Assembly approves of women's prayer meetings but forbids speeches to "promiscuous" (mixed-sex) gatherings.

Mary Frances Clarke (1803–87) and four other women start the Sisters of Charity of the Blessed Virgin Mary in Philadelphia in 1833; in 1843 they travel to the frontier town of Dubuque in Iowa territory, where they open St. Mary's Female Academy (later Clarke College).

A dismissed novice, Rebecca Reed, augments anti-Catholic sentiment with false rumors about the Ursuline nuns in Charlestown, Massachusetts. A mob burns down the convent in 1834. Reed then writes one of the first anticonvent tracts, *Six Months in a Convent* (1835). Another polemic used by Protestant ministers to stir up prejudices against Catholics is Maria Monk's *Awful Disclosures of the Hotel Dieu Nunnery of Montreal* (1836), which sells 300,000 copies in 25 years.

In 1835 Phoebe Worrall Palmer (1807–74) holds her first prayer meetings for women and soon becomes an important figure in the "holiness" movement. By 1839 her Tuesday meetings for the "promotion of holiness" include men. In 1845 she publishes *The Way of Holiness.*

"I must preach the gospel"—*Jarena Lee*

In 1836 Jarena Lee publishes *The Life and Religious Experience of Jarena Lee, a Coloured Lady, Giving an Account of Her Call to Preach the Gospel* In this work she takes issue with the church's refusal to accept women preachers (see sidebar).

Sarah Grimké attacks the Congregational clergy for their 1838 pastoral letter condemning public speaking by women (see "Politics").

In Philadelphia philanthropist Rebecca Gratz (1781–1869) starts the first Hebrew Sunday School, which is free for both boys and girls. She continues to direct the school for 32 years.

1840–49

During the 1840s several new Catholic sisterhoods are established in different parts of the country (see sidebar).

In 1842 Emma Hale Smith (1804–79) is named president of the Female Relief Society, a charitable organ of the Mormon Church.

In 1848 Margaret, Catherine, and Leah Fox claim to be spiritualist mediums, privy to the messages of the strange rappings in their house. They start holding seances, and soon "spirit circles" are the rage. Margaret later calls their powers a hoax but then changes her story again.

Women share fairly equally with men in running the Oneida Association, a Perfectionist community established near Syracuse, New York, in 1848. Almost from the start, they adopt the bloomer costume and short hair; they later take on "manly" work and invade the machine shop. Women also play an important role in the utopian community Brook Farm, started as a Transcendentalist venture in 1841.

When Barbara Heinemann (1795–1883) shows her prophetic ability in 1849, the Inspirationists honor her as a religious leader and *Werkzeug* (God's instrument). With Christian Metz, the sect's original leader, she directs a new settlement, the Amana Society, in Iowa. In 1867 she becomes its sole spiritual head, although male elders handle the political and economic affairs of the community and women are not generally highly regarded.

1850–59

In 1852 María Dominica (born Concepción Argüello, c. 1791–1857) becomes the first nun in California. She is called "La Beata" ("the Blessed One") for her work with the poor and the sick.

In 1852 Anne Ayres (1816–96) establishes the first Episcopal sisterhood in the United States, the Sisterhood of the Holy Communion in New York. They do mostly nursing work.

The work of Catholic nuns as nurses during various yellow fever epidemics in the 1850s helps to lessen anti-Catholic feelings.

Sister Benedicta (Maria Sybilla) Riepp (1825–62) starts America's first Benedictine convent in Pennsylvania in 1852, along with a school.

In 1853 Antoinette Brown (later Blackwell, 1825–1921) is the first U.S. woman ordained as a minister in a Protestant denomination, serving the First Congregational Church of Butler and Savannah, New York. Earlier, after finishing her studies for a theological degree at Oberlin in 1850, she was not allowed to receive either her degree or a license to preach. Now, at her ordination ceremony, the ordaining minister admits, "If she has not that right [to preach the gospel] already, we have no power to communicate it."

Mother Mary Baptist Russell (1829–98) establishes the Sisters of Mercy in San Francisco in 1854, quickly opening a convent and a

New Catholic Orders of the 1840s

In 1840 Mother Theodore Guérin (1798–1856) and five other nuns from the Sisters of Providence arrive in Indiana from France and start their convent of St. Mary-of-the-Woods near Terre Haute. In 1841 they open the first girls' academy in Indiana. "In truth how much good there is to do here," Mother Guérin writes, "and how great and sublime the mission confided to us! But one must be a saint to fulfill it."

Sister Louise (Josephine) Van der Schrieck (1813–86) arrives in Cincinnati in 1840 with seven other sisters to establish the order of Notre Dame de Namur of Belgium. She becomes superior-provincial and helps start almost 50 parochial elementary schools in the East.

In 1841 Mother Mary Aloysia Hardey (1809–86) establishes the first convent of the Society of the Sacred Heart in the East, in New York City. She sets up 16 other houses and moves her headquarters to Manhatttanville, where the convent school becomes College of the Sacred Heart and later Manhattanville College.

Sisters of the Holy Family, the second black Catholic order, is set up in 1842 by Henriette Delille (1813–62) and Cuban-born Juliette Gaudin (1808–88) in New Orleans.

school. During the 1855 cholera epidemic the sisters help with the nursing, and in 1857 they open the first Catholic hospital, St. Mary's, on the Pacific Coast.

In Michigan in 1854, Mother Angela Gillespie (1824–87) takes charge of the Sisters of the Holy Cross and soon makes this a major teaching order in the Midwest. Under her almost 40 institutions, from schools to hospitals and orphanages, are established.

In *Promise of the Father: or, A Neglected Specialty of the Last Days* (1859), holiness movement preacher Phoebe Palmer calls on women to take up preaching: "Answer, ye thousands of Heaven-touched lips, whose testimonies have so long been repressed in the assemblies of the pious."

Rebecca Cox Jackson (1795–1871) starts a black Shaker community in Philadelphia in 1859. Her vision underlines the "Mother in the Deity," the loving, comforting aspect of God.

1860–69

With her husband, Ellen Gould Harmon White (1827–1915) formally organizes the Seventh Day Adventists in Battle Creek, Michigan, in 1860. Her visions, which began in 1844, guide the group's interpretation of the Bible, and she helps set the dietary and similar regulations. Her 500 books and thousands of articles and pamphlets include the autobiographical *Sketch of the Christian Experience and Views of Ellen G. White* (1851) and the nine-volume *Testimonies for the Church* (1855).

In 1861 the interdenominational Woman's Union Missionary Society of America forms to send single women as missionaries to the women in India, Japan, China, and other lands. Its magazine, *Missionary Link,* connects the women sponsors with the women in the field. In 1868, however, individual denominations begin setting up their own groups.

Catholic nuns represent about a fifth of the nurses during the Civil War. They willingly treat victims of smallpox and other contagious diseases. They also baptize dying soldiers who request this.

In her 44-page 1862 pamphlet, *Rights of Women in the Church,* Barbara Kellison declares: "You might as well try to convince me that I have no soul as to persuade me that God never called me to preach his Gospel."

In 1863 Olympia Brown (1835–1926), later an active suffragist, is the first woman ordained as a minister by the Northern Universalist Association. Six months later Augusta Chapin (1836–1905) is also ordained as a Universalist minister; in 1870 she is the first woman to serve on the council of the Universalist church.

At different times several Quaker women, including Eliza Kirkbride Gurney and Elizabeth Rous Comstock, hold prayer meetings with President Lincoln to encourage emancipation of all slaves.

In 1864 Fanny Cosby (1820–1915) begins writing her thousands of hymns, such as "Safe in the Arms of Jesus," for the Methodist Church.

In 1865 Harriet Starr Cannon (1823–96) and four others set up the Community of St. Mary, an Episcopal sisterhood, in New York City. It is the first to be officially sanctioned by the church since the 1500s. The sisters set up a free hospital for poor children, convent schools, homeless shelters, and orphanages.

In 1866 Margaret McDonald Bottome (1827–1906) and nine other women form a Bible study group, calling themselves King's Daughters. Each woman organizes another group of 10, and the organization quickly proliferates. In 1887 men are admitted, and in 20 years there are more than a half-million members in the Order of the King's Daughters and Sons.

Beginning in 1868, separate women's missionary societies are set up in the different denominations (see sidebar). Except for the initial Congregational group, most of the societies are initiated by women, and they give thousands of women organizational leadership skills. The belief is that women are the best missionaries to other women. One Presbyterian publication calls this "woman's work for woman." However, the underlying prejudices of these women can be seen in the title of a typical publication, *Heathen Woman's Friend*.

The African Methodist Episcopal Church establishes women's first official position: "stewardess," or assistant to the clergy.

In 1869 Margaret ("Maggie") Newton Van Cott (1830–1914), an evangelical preacher, receives a local preacher's license, the first given to a woman in the Methodist Episcopal Church. In the next 33 years she travels thousands of miles, holding special meetings for mothers as well as "Praise Meetings" and "Love Fests." She reportedly converts 75,000.

1870–79

About 1870 Amanda Berry Smith (1837–1915) starts holding revival meetings within African Methodist Episcopal churches, and she soon extends her preaching to white Methodists. In 1878 she sets out on a 12-year mission, preaching holiness and temperance in England, India, and Liberia. She later publishes *An Autobiography: The Story of the Lord's Dealing with Mrs. Amanda Smith* (1893).

The Woman's Centenary Association, the first national organization of church women, forms in 1871 with Caroline White Soule (1814–1903) as its first president. They propose to help needy preachers, conduct missionary work at home and abroad, and promote the education of women ministers.

The first female Unitarian minister to be ordained is Cecilia C. Burleigh (c. 1827–75) in 1871 in Brooklyn, Connecticut.

When Ann Eliza Webb Young sues for a divorce from Mormon leader Brigham Young in 1873, it generates headlines in the press. She lectures against polygamy throughout the country and in 1876 publishes *Wife No. 19, or The Story of a Life in Bondage*.

Women's Missionary Societies

1868: *Woman's Board of Missions (Congregational)*

1869: *Woman's Foreign Missionary Society (Methodist Episcopal)*

1870: *Woman's Foreign Missionary Societies of the Presbyterian Church, USA*

1871: *Woman's Auxiliary (Protestant Episcopal)*

1873: *Woman's Baptist Foreign Mission Society*

1874: *Woman's Parent Mite Missionary Society of the African Methodist Episcopal Church; Christian Woman's Board of Missions (Disciples)*

1875: *Woman's Board of Foreign Missions of the Reformed Church of America*

1877: *Woman's American Baptist Home Missionary Society*

1878: *Woman's Executive Committee for Home Missions (Presbyterian); Woman's Board of Foreign Missions (Methodist Episcopal Church South)*

1879: *Woman's Missionary Society of the Evangelical Lutheran Church*

1880: *Congregational Women's Home Missionary Association*

1884: *Woman's Home Missionary Society (Methodist Episcopal)*

1888: *Woman's Missionary Union (auxiliary to Southern Baptist Convention)*

1912: *Woman's Auxiliary, Presbyterian Church in the United States*

The Christian's Secret of a Happy Life (1875), by evangelist preacher Hannah Whitall Smith (1832–1911), is a highly popular fundamentalist text, selling more than 2 million copies worldwide.

In *Science and Health* (1875), Mary Baker (later Eddy, 1821–1910) puts forth the basic tenets of her Christian Science doctrine. Based on her personal experience, she believes that the body can be cured by faith. "Spirit is the real and eternal; matter is the unreal and temporal," she proclaims. She spreads her ideas primarily by teaching and in 1879 charters her Church of Christ, Scientist in Boston. Two years later she starts a teaching college and in 1883 begins publishing a monthly journal. By 1890 there are 20 Christian Science churches and more than 250 practitioners.

Russian-born Helena Petrovna Hahn Blavatsky (1831–91), a mystic, cofounds the Theosophical Society in 1875 and in 1877 publishes *Isis Unveiled: A Master-Key to the Mysteries of Ancient and Modern Science and Technology*, claiming Tibetan origins for the movement.

"God made man and woman equal"
—Martha McWhirter

Already organized as a prayer group, the Sanctificationists of Belton, Texas, begin pooling their resources for communal support in 1879. Led by Martha White McWhirter, the "sisters" start a laundry business in 1882; they also sell milk and butter and later cut and haul wood. When one of their members is attacked by her husband, they build her a house; soon they have constructed three more houses. "It was no longer a woman's duty to remain with a husband who bossed and controlled her," according to McWhirter. In 1886 the sisters convert an existing house into a hotel. The self-sufficient Woman's Commonwealth is guided by McWhirter's decisions and group religious discussions in which they intepret their dreams and spiritual visions. Later, in 1898, the group moves to Mt. Pleasant, near Washington, D.C.

1880–89

In 1880, after failing to win ordination in the Methodist Episcopal Church, Anna Howard Shaw (1847–1919) is the first woman ordained as a Methodist Protestant minister. She later pursues a medical degree and becomes a major leader in the suffrage movement (see "Politics").

In 1881 the Woman's Baptist Missionary Training School, the first such school for women, is established in Chicago. During the next 50 years many similar schools are started, offering instruction in religion as well as practical work in city missions.

In 1885 Lucy Rider Meyer (1849–1922) and her husband set up the Chicago Training School for City, Home, and Foreign Missions, which soon becomes a center of religious social work activity. In 1887 Meyer starts the first deaconess home in the Methodist Episcopal Church, which serves as a model for many others. Athough they do not take

Mary Baker Eddy (Library of Congress)

vows, the women live together and can be identified by their uniform: a long black dress, white collar, and black hat. They set up and run many charitable Protestant institutions, such as hospitals and schools. Countering the picture of a deaconess "as a goody-goody kind of woman," Meyer writes that "there is nothing a woman *can* do in the line of Christian work that a deaconess may not do." Specifically, she cites physicians and hospital superintendents as well as nurses.

When Lenore Simonds Piper (1859–1950), a famous medium, is investigated by a renowned expert in psychic frauds in 1887, she convinces him that her powers are genuine.

After the Methodist Episcopal Church General Conference refuses to seat Frances Willard (p. 147) and four other women as delegates in 1887, Willard condemns the church in an address to the WCTU. In *Woman in the Pulpit* (1889), she indicates that there are 500 female evangelist preachers, 350 Quaker women ministers, and a number of female pastors. She includes testimonies from several of these.

Reacting to Bishop Henry McNeal Turner's 1885 ordination of Sarah Ann Hughes, an evangelist preacher, the African Methodist Episcopal General Conference specifically forbids women's ordination in 1888.

Within the populist Cumberland Presbyterian Church, which already allows women elders, Louisa Woosley is ordained as a minister in 1889 in Nollin, Kentucky. The main body of Presbyterians, however, does not allow women to serve as ministers until 1955.

In 1889 Mother Frances Xavier Cabrini (1850–1917) arrives in the United States to help immigrants from Italy. She opens the first U.S. house of the Missionary Sisters of the Sacred Heart in New York City and eventually sets up many schools, hospitals, orphanages, and convents throughout the United States. In 1946 she is canonized as the first American saint.

1890–99

Myrtle Page Fillmore (1845–1931) and her husband found the Society of Silent Unity (later the Unity School of Christianity) in 1890.

Amelia E. Johnson's *Clarence and Corinne, or God's Way* (1890) is the first Sunday school book by an African American.

In 1891 Sacred White Buffalo (Josephine Crowfeather, or Ptesanwan-yakapi, 1867–93), a Benedictine nun, starts the first Native American order, the Congregation of American Sisters, in North Dakota. As Mother Mary Catherine, she initiates the short-lived order's work in teaching English and nursing the sick.

In Pennsylvania, Sister (later Mother) Mary Katharine Drexel (1858–1955) establishes the Sisters of the Blessed Sacrament for Indians and Colored People in 1891. Under her the order expands to some 500 sisters and starts close to 70 schools. In 1915 it founds the first Catholic college for African Americans, Xavier University, in New Orleans.

Two Offshoots of Mary Baker Eddy

After breaking with Mary Baker Eddy, Emma Curtis Hopkins (1853–1925) sets up the Christian Science Theological Seminary in her Chicago home in 1887 and publishes the magazine Christian Metaphysician. Calling her doctrine "Spiritual Science," Hopkins influences the later New Thought movement. In the 1920s she publishes the 12-volume High Mysticism.

Augusta Simmons Stetson (1842–1928), a student of Mary Baker Eddy, is ordained as the pastor of the First Church of Christ, Scientist in New York in 1890, and the following year she sets up a training institute. Later Eddy tries to curtail her growing power, and in 1909 her license as a Christian Science teacher is revoked. Stetson, however, remains dominant in the New York church, especially after Eddy's death in 1910. In later writings Stetson advocates Nordic supremacy.

*"The world has seemingly awaited
the advent of heroic souls who
once again should dare all things
for the truth. The woman who
possesses love for her sex, for the
world, for truth, justice and right,
will not hesitate to place herself
upon record as opposed to false-
hood, no matter under what
guise of age or holiness it appears. A generation has passed
since the great struggle began,
but not until within ten years has
woman dared attack upon the
veriest stronghold of her oppression, the Church.*

*". . . During the ages, no
rebellion has been of like importance with that of Woman against
the tyranny of Church and State. .
. . We note its beginning; its progress will overthrow every existing
form of these institutions; its end
will be a regenerated world."*
—Matilda Joslyn Gage,
Woman, Church and State
(1893; reprint, Watertown,
Mass.: Persephone Press, 1980)

In 1892 Belle Harris Bennett (1852–1922) starts the Scarritt Bible and Training School in Kansas City, Missouri, for Methodist women.

In the early 1890s Ray Frank (later Litman, 1864–1948) temporarily serves as a rabbi for several West Coast towns, as no rabbi is available. After speaking at the Congress of Jewish Women (below), she starts a congregation in Chicago, although she doesn't call herself a rabbi.

For the World's Parliament of Religions, held at the World's Columbian Exposition in Chicago in 1893, Hannah Greenebaum Solomon (1858–1942) organizes the Jewish Women's Congress. Papers are presented by Henrietta Szold, Josephine Lazarus, and Ray Frank. The meeting leads to the formation of the National Council of Jewish Women, with Solomon as the first president. This organization promotes religious study and engages in social service work. Also, after the meeting, Rosa Sonneschein starts the *American Jewess* magazine.

Women's rights leader Matilda Joslyn Gage (1826–98) publishes *Woman, Church and State* (1893), in which she condemns the church as a major source of women's oppression (see sidebar).

In 1894 the African Methodist Episcopal Zion Church ordains Julia A. J. Foote (1823–1900), an evangelist preacher and missionary since 1879, as its first female deacon. Soon afterward, in 1895, Mary J. Small is ordained as a deacon, and she becomes the church's first female elder in 1898. Foote also becomes an elder, in 1900.

By 1894 about 1,000 Protestant female missionaries have gone abroad.

Unitarian minister Caroline Bartlett (later Crane, 1858–1935) forms the People's Church in Kalamazoo, Michigan, in 1894. She emphasizes community service, establishing a free kindergarten, gym, various clubs and educational courses, an orchestra, and the like.

In 1895, at the age of 80, Elizabeth Cady Stanton stirs up controversy with the first volume of *The Woman's Bible*, in which she revises biblical passages that degrade women. Clergymen vehemently denounce her interpretations, and suffragists at the 1896 NAWSA convention pass a resolution dissociating themselves from this work by one of their original leaders. Undeterred, Stanton publishes a second volume in 1898.

The new leader of the Theosophical Society of America, Katherine Westcott Tingley (1847–1929), establishes a utopian community in Point Loma in southern California in 1897. There she constructs an exotic edifice, made of wood but designed to look like marble. Her emphasis, however, is on social reform. Her International Brotherhood League, started in 1897, promotes interracial understanding and aids workers, prisoners, and others. In *The Voice of the Soul* (1928), Tingley describes her belief in the divinity within each person.

In 1897 a New York temple listens to social reformer Maud Nathan's lecture "The Heart of Judaism" instead of a sermon—one of the first instances of a woman speaking during a Jewish service.

Harriette Emilie Cady's *Lesson in Truth* (1897) is influential in the New Thought movement. Also important is Ella Wheeler Wilcox's later *The Heart of New Thought* (1902).

1900–9

At the National Baptist Convention of 1900, Nannie Helen Burroughs (1879–1961) speaks on "How the Sisters Are Hindered from Helping." As a result, an auxiliary, the Women's Convention, is formed, with S. Willie Layten as president and Burroughs as corresponding secretary. The group sets up settlement houses, works for basic rights, and is a voice for reform.

In 1900 Sister (later Mother) Mary Alphonsa Lathrop (born Rose Hawthorne, 1851–1926) takes her initial vows and founds a Dominican order, which is devoted to the care of terminally ill cancer patients in New York.

After the Methodist Church forbids her from preaching, Alma Bridwell White (1862–1946) starts her own revivalist group, the Methodist Pentecostal Union Church (later the Pillar of Fire Church) in 1901 in Denver. In 1907 she moves her headquarters to New Jersey (see 1918).

Through the efforts of Nannie Helen Burroughs, Woman's Day is instituted by the National Baptist Convention in 1907. For Burroughs the idea of a day on which women raise money for missionary work is to give women leadership and public speaking experience (see sidebar).

Many women are active in the Pentecostal movement. For example, after she is healed in Los Angeles, Florence Crawford establishes the Pentecostal Apostolic Faith movement in Portland, Oregon, in 1907. Lizzie Woods Roberson establishes a women's department in the Church of God in Christ and travels widely setting up new churches.

1910–19

In *Western Women in Eastern Lands: Fifty Years of Woman's Work in Foreign Missions* (1910), Helen Barrett Montgomery describes the increase in women missionaries from 1 to more than 4,600. She also notes that because of women's successful fund-raising, men in the church now want control over women's organizations. In fact, the Methodist Episcopal council reorganizes in a way that cuts women's representation. This action spurs Belle Harris Bennett to push for lay voting rights for women. "God made man and woman coordinate," she asserts, and she stresses that this relationship must prevail in the church. Finally the Methodist Episcopal Church, South, grants these rights in 1918.

Led by Henrietta Szold, Jewish women in New York City form the Hadassah Chapter of the Daughters of Zion in 1912. Its main goal initially is to provide health services for Palestine. It also promotes Jewish religious and cultural life in opposition to assimilation efforts.

In 1914 the National Federation of Temple Sisterhoods is organized, with 5,000 members from 52 local groups. It promotes work by

"A Million Women Singing!"

"A million women praying! A million women singing! A million women desiring! A million women laboring for the coming of the kingdom in the hearts of all men, would be a power that would move God on his throne to immediately answer the petitions. It would mean spiritual dynamite that would blast Satan's greatest stronghold and drive sin to its native heath. Can we have such a day?"
    —Nannie Helen Burroughs, 1908 report to Woman's Convention; in *Women and Religion in America*, vol. 3, edited by Rosemary Redford Ruether and Rosemary Skinner Keller (New York: Harper & Row, 1986)

women within the synagogue and the community. In the same year *Methods of Teaching Jewish Ethics,* coauthored by Julia Richman, is published posthumously.

In 1916 the Handmaids of the Most Pure Heart of Mary, later a Franciscan order, becomes the third black Catholic order.

After her father dies in 1916, Martha Bad Warrior, or Red Eagle Woman (1854–1936), becomes the keeper of the Sacred Calf Pipe Bundle for her Lakota people.

In *The Voice of Isis* (1917), Harriette Augusta Curtiss, cofounder of the Order of Christian Mystics, celebrates the sacred female principle, an idea she develops further in *The Divine Mother* (1921).

In 1918 Alma White becomes bishop of the Pillar of Fire Church, the first woman bishop in a Christian church. Each year she travels thousands of miles conducting her jumping and shouting revival meetings. Everywhere she sets up congregations and gains new members. She also becomes a strong supporter of the Ku Klux Klan and writes several anti-Catholic and anti-Semitic tracts.

Henrietta Szold (see sidebar) directs the department of education of the new Zionist Organization of America in 1918 and helps organize the American Zionist Medical Unit, sent to Palestine.

Conservative Jewish women form the Women's League of the United Synagogues of America in 1918 to carry out charity work, religious education, and fund-raising.

In 1919 Madeline Southard, a Methodist preacher in Kansas, forms the American Association of Women Preachers, which publishes the journal *Woman's Pulpit* starting in 1921.

1920–29

The Methodist Epicsopal Church agrees to license local women preachers in 1920 and begins ordaining them in 1924. They are not, however, allowed to be members of the annual conference until 1956.

The National Catholic Women's Council (later National Council of Catholic Women) is organized at the bishops' request. Agnes Gertrude Regan (1869–1943) is the first executive secretary. One aspect of the council is the training of social workers, and in 1921 it sponsors the National Catholic Service School for Women.

Mother Mary Joseph Rogers (1882–1955) leads the Foreign Mission Sisters of St. Dominic (later the Maryknoll Sisters of St. Dominic), established in 1920, as an outgrowth of a group begun in 1914. In 1921 six sisters are sent to China. By 1955 the order has grown to 1,160 sisters in 84 missions worldwide.

When Helen Montgomery is elected president of the Northern Baptist Convention in 1921, she is the first woman in charge of a Protestant denomination's governing body.

Judith Kaplan (later Eisenstein) is the first girl to celebrate her bat mitzvah, an initiation ceremony introduced in 1922 by her father, Rabbi Mordecai Kaplan, the founder of Reconstructionist Judaism. The following year Martha Neumark, a student at Hebrew Union College, is turned down when she seeks ordination as a rabbi.

Evangelist preacher Aimee Semple McPherson (1890–1944) dedicates the Angelus Temple of her International Church of the Foursquare Gospel in Los Angeles in 1923. A faith healer and dramatic speaker, she attracts crowds of 5,000 or more to her sermons, which are staged with colorful pageantry and offer a doctrine of hope. At the temple she maintains food and clothing for those in need, an employment bureau, and other services. During the next 20 years her church membership grows to 22,000 in America and abroad. In 1926 she attracts media attention when she disappears for several days, claims she was kidnapped, and then is charged by the district attorney, who believes she made up the story. The case is later dropped, and her sermons continue to draw a huge audience.

Aimee Semple McPherson
(Library of Congress)

"Her glory was in giving life, not taking it"
—Charlotte Perkins Gilman

Charlotte Perkins Gilman publishes *His Religion and Hers* (1923), differentiating between death-based, authoritarian male beliefs and birth-based, altruistic female ones.

Belle Carter Harman is the first woman ordained as a deacon (1924) and then as an elder (1926) in the Methodist Episcopal Church.

About 33% of the pastors in the Church of God, based in Anderson, Indiana, are women in 1925; by 1975 this declines to 3%. This trend is also found in other holiness and pentecostal groups.

The Women's Labor Zionist Organization of America (Pioneer Women) is started in 1924 to help women in Palestine become self-supporting workers. It works closely with the Women's American ORT (Organization for Rehabilitation through Training), founded by Jewish women in 1927.

In 1926 Edna Baxter (1890–1985), a Methodist Episcopal deaconess, begins teaching at the Hartford Theological Seminary, where she eventually becomes the first woman professor.

In 1927, at the request of the Presbyterian General Council, Katharine Bennett and Margaret Hodge report on "Causes of Unrest Among Women of the Church." They underline the women's resentment at the male takeover of the missionary organizations women started and the desire for a greater role in the church (see 1930).

1930–39

In 1930 the Presbyterian Church in the USA (northern) approves women elders but refuses to let women be ordained as ministers. Sarah

E. Dickson becomes the first woman elder. Later, in 1938, the Presbyterians create a new category of "commissioned church worker," but they specifically state that this does not include ministerial rights.

Henrietta Szold is the first woman to receive an honorary Doctor of Hebrew Letters from the Jewish Institute of Religion in 1930. In 1933 she becomes a leader in Youth Aliyah, which helps 30,000-some children leave Nazi Germany for Palestine.

In 1933 Dorothy Day helps start the Catholic Worker movement (see "Social Change").

In 1934 the United Lutherans allow women to serve as delegates and as members of the church council and of boards and commissions.

Helen Haddassah Levinthal is the first woman to graduate from the Jewish Institute for Religion in 1939, but the president refuses to ordain her.

As professor of applied theology at Garrett Biblical Institute, Georgia Harkness (1891–1974) becomes, in 1939, the first woman to teach in a field other than Christian education at a major theological seminary. A strong advocate of full rights for women in the church, she also calls for the church to take a stand on contemporary social and moral issues.

When the northern and southern Methodist Episcopal Church and the Methodist Protestant Church come together in 1939, they arrive at a compromise on women preachers. Women can now become preachers in the southern branch, but no new women preachers in any branch are allowed conference membership. This situation holds until 1956.

1940–49

In 1940 two Dutch women, Lydwine van Kersbergen and Joan Overboss, bring the Grail, a Catholic women's movement, to the United States. Seeing women as social transformers, the group at first takes a back-to-the-land approach and later turns its attention to urban issues.

In 1940 Mills College president Aurelia Henry Reinhardt (1877–1948) is the first woman moderator of the American Unitarian Association.

In 1943 St. Mary's College in Indiana offers the first graduate program in theology for Catholic women. It continues until 1969, when Marquette University and the University of Notre Dame first allow women into graduate courses in theology.

Essie Parrish (1902–79) succeeds Annie Jarvis in 1943 as the official dreamer of the Kashaya Pomo in southern California. She later helps make a number of films on Kashaya culture, including *Chishkle, or Beautiful Tree*. She is also well known as a basketweaver.

The American Lutheran Church seats its first female delegate in 1944.

In 1945 Conservative Jews change men's traditional morning prayer so that the man no longer thanks God for not making him a woman.

In 1946 in Pennsylvania, Kathryn Kuhlman (c. 1907–76) begins conducting her healing services and revivals, which draw thousands.

Saint Frances Xavier Cabrini, who founded the Missionary Sisters of the Heart in 1889, is the first American citizen to be cannonized by the Catholic Church, in 1946.

In 1948 the African Episcopal Church ordains its first woman minister, Martha J. Keys.

In Wrentham, Massachusetts, Trappist nuns establish their first U.S. convent, in 1949.

Theologian Georgia Harkness publishes *The Gospel and Our World*, arguing for a Christianity with meaning for the people. Her other, later works include *Christian Ethics* (1957), *The Bible Speaks to Daily Needs* (1959), and *Women in Church and Society* (1971).

The Society for the Advancement of Judaism, New York's Reconstructionist synagogue, is the first to count women in the *minyan*, the quorum of 10 required for public worship.

1950–59

In Mississippi, Paula Ackerman serves briefly as the rabbi of her congregation, after her husband dies in 1951, until a new rabbi is found.

Kathleen Bliss publishes *The Service and Status of Women in the Church* (1952), based on reports to the World Council of Churches, in 1948.

Josie Head Swift Limpy (Stands Near the Fire) serves as keeper of the Sacred Hat Bundle, which represents women's fertility, for the Northern Cheyenne between 1952 and 1957.

Yeshiva University opens Stern College for Women in 1954 to offer higher education to Orthodox Jewish women.

In 1954 the Christian Methodist Episcopal Church first allows women to be ordained.

The first female cantor is Mrs. Sheldon Robbins, at a Reform synagogue in Long Island, in 1955.

In 1956 the Presbyterian Church in the USA finally approves ordination for women, and Margaret E. Towner is the first to be ordained. At the same time the Methodist Church gives all women ministers full status, including conference membership. The Harvard Divinity School also now accepts women.

In Chicago, Johnnie Coleman begins preaching to 35 African Americans in 1956. Her congregation eventually grows to 10,000 and occupies the 32-acre Christ Universal Complex.

In Detroit, Charleszetta Campbell ("Mother") Waddles founds her Perpetual Mission for Saving Souls of All Nations in 1957. An ordained pentecostal minister, she emphasizes hope in her sermons and

Thousands of nuns leave their Catholic orders between 1965 and 1970, and by 1970 the number of women entering the orders is less than a tenth of what it was a decade earlier. At the same time several new organizations of Catholic nuns emerge:

—In 1968 the Leadership Conference of Women Religious forms out of the earlier Conference of Major Superiors of Women Religious (1956).

—In 1968 some 155 nuns organize the National Black Sisters' Conference, pledging to work for the liberation of black people.

—In 1969 the National Coalition of American Nuns is established to support the civil rights and antiwar movements and to call for equal rights for women within the Catholic Church. Several former nuns are also active in social and antiwar protests in the late 1960s. One example is Margarita Melville of the Catonville Nine (p. 78).

—In 1970 Latina nuns organize Las Hermanas in part to protest the prejudices they face in the Irish-dominated Catholic Church, where they are often assigned to housekeeping chores.

offers immediate help, including health care, food, job training, and other services, to the community.

One of the first women ministers in the Puerto Rican barrio in New York, Leonicia Rosado Rosseau serves as pastor of Damascus Christian Church beginning in 1957. With the Christian Youth Crusade, she sets up a program to fight drug abuse. As she tells it: "The kids would say, 'Mama, we came for the bird and you gave us the Word!'"

1960–69

In 1960 Madalyn Murray (later O'Hair), an atheist, begins her fight against school prayer in the Baltimore public schools, where her son is enrolled. After much harassment, she wins her case in a landmark 1963 Supreme Court ruling that prayer and other forms of religious observance in public schools violate the constitutional separation of church and state. Murray publishes the monthly *American Atheist* and sets up the Freethought Society of America.

In 1961 the Catholic Church allows nuns and schoolgirls to read at a mass performed for women in a convent or a school.

The southern Presbyterian church finally allows women to serve as deacons, elders, or ministers in 1964, and in 1965 Rachel Henderlite is the first woman to be ordained, as minister of All Souls Presbyterian Church in Richmond, Virginia.

In 1964 Patty Crowley, a leader in the Christian Family Movement, presents "A Woman's Viewpoint" to the Papal Birth Control Commission and speaks against the rhythm method of birth control. "No amount of theory by men can convince women that this way of making and expressing love is natural," she contends.

In 1964 Aimee García Cortese (b. 1929), ordained by the Wesleyan Methodist Church in Puerto Rico, returns to her native South Bronx to preach at the Thessalonica Christian Church. She also serves as the first woman chaplain for the state department of corrections.

Episcopal bishop James Pike ordains Phyliss Edwards to the diaconate in 1965, sparking controversy about women's status (see 1970).

Theologian Rosemary Radford Ruether begins her teaching career in 1965 and in 1967 publishes *The Church Against Itself.*

When the Reconstructionist Rabbinical College opens in Philadelphia in 1968, it admits women.

In the new United Methodist Church of 1968, which includes the old United Brethren and Evangelical Church, women are allowed to be ordained as ministers.

Mary Daly publishes her first book, *The Church and the Second Sex,* in 1968. The following year her contract is not renewed at the Jesuit-run Boston College, students and others protest until she is reinstated. By 1971, however, she has gone beyond a call for reform within the church and symbolically leads women out of Harvard Memorial Church after delivering the Sunday sermon there (a first for a woman).

1970–79

The Lutheran Church in America and the American Lutheran Church both agree to ordain women in 1970, although the Lutheran Church: Missouri Synod does not. Barbara Andrews (c. 1934–78) is the first woman ordained in the American Lutheran Church, in 1970 in Minneapolis. Judith Hird is the first pastor in the Lutheran Church in America, in 1972 in Toms River, New Jersey.

The Episcopal Church approves women deacons in 1970 but does not yet let them be ordained as priests. Suzanne Hiatt, a leader in the movement for ordination, is the first woman ordained under this rule.

In Berkeley, California, the Center for Women and Religion is set up in 1970 for women involved in theological education. It publishes the journal *Women and Religion*.

Paula Hyman and other Jewish women form Ezrat Nashim ("the help of women") in 1971 and the following year ask the convention of Conservative rabbis to allow women's full participation in religious observances. They win the right for women to be counted in the *minyan* and to be called to the Torah.

Lois Stair is the first woman moderator of the General Assembly of the United Presbyterian Church in the USA in 1971.

In 1972 Sally Priesand is the first U.S. woman to be officially ordained as a rabbi in Reform Judaism. She later writes *Judaism and the New Woman* (1975).

Catholics for a Free Choice is formed in 1973 (see also "Health").

As the first female moderator of the United Church of Christ in 1973, Margaret A. Haywood is the first black woman to head a major Protestant denomination in the United States.

In Philadelphia in 1974, in a nonsanctioned ceremony, four Episcopal bishops ordain 11 women deacons to the priesthood. This challenge provokes two years of debate within the church, leading to official approval of women's ordination in 1976 (see below).

In 1974 Claire Randall becomes the first female secretary of the National Council of the Churches of Christ, a coalition of 30 Protestant and Eastern Orthodox denomiantions.

Sandy Eisenberg Sasso is the first woman ordained as a Reconstructionist rabbi, in 1974.

Womanshare, started in 1974 in Oregon, is one of the first woman-only communities. Others form in Wisconsin, Minnesota, and New Mexico.

In 1975 Barbara Herman becomes the first American woman cantor in Reform Judaism, at a New Jersey temple.

A Different Kind of Religion

From the early 1970s, women begin to define a feminist approach to religion. A few important works are:

—The First Sex *(1971), in which Elizabeth Gould Davis portrays women's original power and argues for "a return to the values of the matriarchates."*

—Beyond God the Father: Toward a Philosophy of Women's Liberation *(1973), in which Mary Daly rejects the male God of Christianity and proposes a new feminist theology.*

—The Gods and Goddesses of Old Europe, 7000 B.C. to 3500 B.C.: Myths, Legends, and Cult Images *(1974), in which archaeologist Marija Gimbutas describes the Goddess worship of prehistoric Europe.*

—Religion and Sexism *(1974), in which Rosemary Radford Ruether presents a variety of sources showing the history of sexism in religion.*

The second half of the 1970s brings a flood of writings on women's spirituality, including:

—Merlin Stone's When God Was a Woman *(1976).*

—Mary Daly's Gyn/Ecology: The Metaethics of Radical Feminism *(1978).*

—Susan Griffin's Woman and Nature: The Roaring Inside Her *(1978).*

—Naomi Goldenberg's The Changing of the Gods: Feminism and the End of Traditional Religions *(1979).*

—Elaine Pagels's The Gnostic Gospels *(1979).*

—Starhawk's The Spiral Dance: A Rebirth of the Ancient Religion of the Great Goddess *(1979).*

—Carol P. Christ and Judith Plaskow's anthology Womanspirit Rising: A Feminist Reader in Religion *(1979), with writings by Mary Daly, Rita Gross, Elaine Pagels, Rosemary Radford Ruether, Merlin Stone, and others.*

There are also several magazines on women's spirituality, including WomanSpirit *and* Lady-Unique-Inclination-of-the-Night, *as well as articles and special issues on the subject in* Quest, Sinister Wisdom, Heresies, Parabola, Chrysalis, *and other publications.*

In Detroit 1,200 Catholic women form the Women's Ordination Conference in 1975 to push for women Roman Catholic priests.

Elizabeth Ann Seton, who founded the Sisters of Charity of St. Joseph in 1809, is canonized as the first American-born saint in 1975.

In the mid-1970s Pilulaw Khus, a Chumash elder, and others occupy Point Conception, a sacred site of the Chumash people, when public utilities ignore old treaties and draw up plans for a new plant there. "We won that one," Khus later says, "and it's still clean out there. Our spirits can still travel back and forth out there."

In the mid-1970s Sister Thea (Bertha) Bowman (1937–90), the first black member of the Franciscan Sisters of Perpetual Adoration, creates intercultural awareness programs and establishes the Hallelujah Singers.

From the mid-1970s the women's spirituality movement and Goddess worship take hold. Starhawk (Miriam Simos) is one of many women who develop feminist rituals and a new "thealogy." Some, like Z Budapest, draw on witchcraft; others borrow from Native American culture.

In 1976 the General Convention of the Episcopal Church approves the ordination of women as priests and bishops, and it accepts the 15 who were unofficially ordained earlier (including the 11 in 1974), as long as they undergo new, "regular" ceremonies. Jacqueline Means, one of the Philadelphia 11, is the first to be officially ordained, in 1977. Also, in 1977 Pauli Murray (p. 73) is the first African American woman Episcopal priest; Beverly Messenger-Harris is the first woman rector in charge of an Episcopal parish (Sherrill, New York); and Mary Michael Simpson is the first Episcopal nun ordained as a priest, as well as the first female canon. In 1978 Simpson becomes the first ordained woman to preach at Westminster Abbey in London.

In Sherman, Texas, in 1978, Sara Berenice Mosely is the first woman chosen to head the governing body of a Presbyterian church.

Lakota women form *Sina Wakan Win Oklakiciye'* (Sacred Shawl Woman's Society) in 1979 to help improve conditions for women, particularly to help heal the family and curtail domestic violence.

Sister Mary Theresa Kane, president of the Leadership Conference of Women Religious, implores Pope John Paul II during his U.S. visit in 1979 to consider the ordination of women. Her demand is backed up by 53 nuns, with blue armbands, who stand up during her speech.

The Mormon Church puts Sonia Johnson on trial in 1979 for her open sup-port of the ERA in opposition to the church leaders. She is excommunicated and later writes *From Housewife to Heretic* (1981).

1980–89

Influenced by Susan Griffin's *Woman and Nature* (1978) and Carolyn Merchant's *The Death of Nature* (1980), as well as the ideas of Ynestra King, Charlene Spretnak, and others, the ecofeminist movement gains momentum in the 1980s. It bridges the environmental, feminist, and women's spirituality movements (see also p. 164).

In 1980 Marjorie Matthews is the first female U.S. Methodist bishop.

At Reform Judaism's School of Sacred Music in New York, only one applicant for training as a cantor is not a woman in 1982.

In 1983 the Jewish Theological Seminary (for Conservative Jews) agrees to allow women to pursue rabbinical studies, and in 1985 Amy Eilberg becomes the first woman Conservative rabbi.

The first Women-Church conference, an outgrowth of the Catholic Women's Ordination Conference, is held in 1983 for women who are forming their own female-dominated places of worship in homes and on college campuses. Ten years later, in 1993, Diann L. Neu and Mary E. Hunt edit the *Women-Church Sourcebook* as an organizing tool.

In 1984 Leontyne T. C. Kelly is the first African American and the second woman ordained as a bishop in the United Methodist Church. She is in charge of the northern California area.

In a *New York Times* ad in October 1984, 26 nuns are among the 97 Catholics stating that a "diversity of opinions" on abortion exists within the church. The church authorities insist that all the nuns must take back or at least "clarify" their statement. After four years of harassment, two of the nuns—Barbara Ferraro and Patricia Hussey—finally leave their order. As they explain, "For us to stand with women, we need to renounce the differences, privileges, and even limitations that are part of membership in a religious community in a patriarchal church."

"We have asked for bread and you have given us stone"—Las Hermanas

At a 1985 bishops' meeting, four women from Las Hermanas—Beatriz Diaz-Taveras, Maria Teresa Garza, Ada Maria Isasi-Diaz, and Carmen Villegas—give each bishop a stone. "Put these stones on your altars when you celebrate Eucharist," they say, "and remember us Hispanic women, struggling for our liberation and the liberation of our people!"

In Massachusetts in 1985, Sandra Boston de Sylvia starts Pilgrim Warrior Training, a retreat that lets women find sacred power in nature.

The Religious Coalition for Abortion Rights, formed by 31 groups in 1985, insists that abortion is a personal decision of conscience and that restrictive laws violate religious as well as reproductive freedom.

Rivka Hunt and Judy Bernstein form the Women's Tefillah Network in 1985 to support Orthodox Jewish women who want to lead their own prayer groups.

The Methodists revise their hymnal to be gender-neutral in 1988.

In 1989 Barbara C. Harris (b. 1930) is ordained as the first female

More Writings

During the 1980s many more books addressing women's spirituality appear, including:

—*Charlene Spretnak's* anthology The Politics of Women's Spirituality: Essays on the Rise of Spiritual Power within the Feminist Movement *(1982).*

—*Rosemary Radford Ruether's* Sexism and God Talk *(1983) and* Women-Church *(1986).*

—*Susannah Heschel's* On Being a Jewish Feminist *(1983).*

—*Elisabeth Schüssler Fiorenza's* In Memory of Her: A Feminist Theological Reconstruction of Christian Origins *(1984)*

—*Luisah Teish's* Jambalaya: The Natural Woman's Book of Personal Charms and Practical Rituals *(1985).*

—*Paula Gunn Allen's* The Sacred Hoop: Recovering the Feminine in American Indian Traditions *(1986).*

—*Riane Eisler's* The Chalice and the Blade: Our History, Our Future *(1987).*

—*Carol Christ's* The Laughter of Aphrodite: Reflections on a Journey to the Goddess *(1987).*

—*Kate G. Cannon's* Black Womanist Ethics *(1988).*

—*Renita J. Weems's* Just a Sister Away: A Womanist Vision of Women's Relationships in the Bible *(1988).*

—*Judith Plaskow and Carol Christ's anthology* Weaving the Visions: New Patterns in Feminist Spirituality *(1989).*

suffragan bishop in the Episcopal Church, in the diocese of Massachusetts. An early member of the Union of Black Episcopalians, she is a strong advocate of the rights of African Americans and women.

Elected moderator of the Presbyterian Church, USA, in 1989, Joan Salmon Campbell is the first black woman to lead the church.

1990–95

In 1990 Joan Brown Campbell is chosen as the second woman to head the largest U.S. ecumenical group, the National Council of Churches.

A new 1990 translation of the Bible for Protestant churches avoids sexist, racist, and homophobic language.

Christian Lesbians Out Together forms in 1991 to protest discriminatroy church policy.

Monica Sjöö and Barbara Mor publish *The Great Cosmic Mother: Rediscovering the Religion of the Earth* (1991).

A 1992 report on women in the United Methodist Chuch reveals that 60% of church members are women but only 34% of the delegates to the General Conference and 11% of the clergy are women.

In 1992 April Ulring Larson is the first American woman elected as a bishop in the Evangelical Lutheran Church, the largest Lutheran denomination in the United States.

In 1993 Mary Adelea McLeod is elected diocesan bishop, in charge of the Anglican church in Vermont.

Among the 1993 feminist theological publications are Sandy Boucher's *Turning the Wheel: American Women Creating the New Buddhism*, Rita Gross's *Buddhism After Patriarchy*, Ada María Isasi-Díaz's *En la Lucha: A Hispanic Women's Liberation Theology*, and Delores S. Williams's *Sisters in the Wilderness: The Challenge of Womanist God-Talk*.

In Beverly Hills, California, Laura Geller becomes the first senior rabbi of a congregation in a large metropolitan area, in 1994.

Walking in the Sacred Manner (1995) by Mark St. Pierre and Tilda Long Soldier presents the wisdom of holy women of the Northern Plains peoples (see sidebar).

In 1995 the Canon Law Society of America cautiously voices support for letting Catholic women serve as deacons but not priests.

Health and Medical Care

Operating room, St. Luke's Hospital, New York, 1899 (Library of Congress)

The Early Healers

Throughout history there are older Native American women who are healers, using their knowledge of herbs to cure illnesses and serving as midwives at births. Some of these women assist medicine men; some become medicine women in their own right. Later accounts reveal that among the Yurok in northern California, for example, the doctors are all women. The art of healing is closely tied to spiritual life, and many women healers are dreamers with spiritual powers (see "Religion").

Among the early European settlers, women usually serve as midwives. One of the first is Bridget Lee Fuller, who arrives on the Mayflower in 1620 and practices for more than 40 years, until her death in 1664. In fact, women so dominate midwifery that a man is tried for trying his hand at it in 1646. Yet women "doctoresses" pose a threat to authorities. Jane Hawkins, a follower of Anne Hutchinson, is banished from Massachusetts in 1640 in part because of her medical practice, in which she uses fertility potions and insists that patients' faith can help effect a cure. In 1648 Margaret Jones is the first to be hanged as a witch for her use of herbal medicines and healing practice.

The Dutch seem more accepting of women's healing role. New Amsterdam's first hospital, built in 1658, is run by a woman.

1700s

Women deliver most babies in the 1700s. A few have formal training as midwives. For example, Elizabeth Phillips, who arrives in Boston in 1719, studied in London and earned a license to practice midwifery; she delivers some 3,000 babies before her death in 1761. The best account of midwifery during this period comes from Martha Moore Ballard, who begins her practice in Maine in 1777 and keeps a detailed diary of her work. By 1812 she has delivered close to 1,000 babies, at times traveling miles through the woods in stormy conditions to do so.

During the Revolutionary War, some women nurse battlefield victims.

In Philadelphia, African American women earn praise for nursing both black and white victims of the yellow fever epidemic during 1793.

1800–29

In the early 1800s women on the *llano* (bordering today's Texas and New Mexico) are *curanderas* or *medicas,* treating ailments with herbal remedies and serving as midwives. Throughout the 1800s Catholic nuns set up hospitals and provide nursing (see "Religion").

In the 1820s, after gaining much of his knowledge from Mrs. Benton, a female herbalist who learned much from Native American women, Samuel Thomson initiates his "family botanic medicine," which encourages everyone, including women, to be a doctor. Almost a quarter of U.S. citizens participate in this popular health movement.

Abortion before the quickening, the point during pregnancy when movement by the fetus is first felt, is acceptable in early America. In 1821, however, Connecticut specifically bans abortions after the quickening; in the next 40 years 20 other states enact abortion laws.

1830–39

After studying anatomy and physiology with a British couple, Harriot Kezia Hunt (1805–75) and her sister, Sarah, open their medical practice in Boston in 1835. They emphasize hygiene, rest, diet, and exercise and provide what is essentially psychotherapy. Most of their patients are women and children. To broaden her knowledge, Harriot applies to Harvard Medical School and is accepted in 1850. However, when she tries to attend the lectures, the male students protest so vigorously, she is forced to withdraw.

When the American Physiological Society is established in Boston in 1837, almost a third of its members are women. A number of these women, including Harriot Hunt, become known as lecturers.

In 1838 Mary Neal Gove (later Nichols, 1810–84) begins lecturing to women on anatomy, physiology, and hygiene. She sees health reform as a way of increasing women's freedom and promotes a vegetarian diet, fresh air, cold baths, and the like. In the mid-1840s she begins to advocate water-cure treatments (hydropathy) and free love. Later she becomes involved in spiritualism and converts to Catholicism.

In the late 1830s Ann Trow Lohman (1812–78), known as "Madame Restell," advertises as a midwife and "female physician" in New York. In 1841 she is arrested for performing an abortion, after her patient dies, and acquires notoriety as an abortionist. In 1847 she is jailed for defying a new law banning abortions after the quickening (see 1878).

1840–49

In 1843 Harriot Hunt starts the Charlestown Ladies' Physiological Society in Massachusetts. In Philadelphia, Ann Preston (1813–72) and other Quaker women hold discussions on physiology around this time.

In 1849 Elizabeth Blackwell is the first female M.D., followed by Lydia Folger Fowler in 1850 (see sidebar).

In 1848 the Boston (later New England) Female Medical College opens to give women training as midwives (but not as physicians).

1850–59

To give women a chance to learn medicine, Quaker physicians establish the Female (later Woman's) Medical College of Pennsylvania in Philadelphia in 1850. Ann Preston and Hannah Longshore (1819–1901) are among the first seven to graduate in 1851, at a ceremony guarded by police due to threats of violence. Longshore serves as a demonstrator at the Boston Female Medical College in 1852 and then sets up her practice as the first woman doctor in Philadelphia. Preston begins teaching at her alma mater in 1853 and later is its first woman dean (1866).

After Harriot Hunt's failed attempt to study at Harvard in 1851, the trustees vote to exclude women, a rule that prevails until 1946.

In 1851 Sarah Adamson (later Dolley, 1829–1909), a graduate of Central Medical College, is the first woman to intern in a U.S. hospital, at Blockley Hospital in Philadelphia (see also 1886). Earlier, Elizabeth Blackwell went to England for her internship.

In 1853 Elizabeth Blackwell opens a part-time dispensary in New York to treat low-income women when she cannot get a job in any hospital. Her sister, Emily (1826–1910), studying medicine at Western Reserve University in Cleveland, graduates with honors in 1854 and goes to Europe for further study.

An early female dentist is Eveline Roberts James, who studies with her husband and assumes his Connectictut practice when he dies in 1855.

During the 1850s dress reformers (see "Social Change") call attention to the way tight corsets interfere with women's health. Another reformer is Catharine Beecher (p. 170), who writes *Letters to the Public on Health and Happiness* (1855) and *Physiology and Calisthenics* (1856).

Starting in 1857, women doctors open their own hospitals (see p. 222).

1860–69

Beginning with Connecticut in 1860, states enact laws prohibiting all abortions, both before and after quickening.

The First Two Female M.D.s

In 1847 Elizabeth Blackwell (1821–1910) is the first woman to attend a medical college, after the male students at Geneva Medical College in Geneva, New York, vote for her admission, seeing it as a joke. For Blackwell, however, "the idea of winning a doctor's degree gradually assumed the aspect of a great moral struggle, and the moral fight possesses immense attraction for me." Despite the hostility of both the townspeople and students, she graduates in 1849, the first U.S. woman to earn a medical degree.

In 1847 Lydia Folger Fowler (1822–79), who travels to lecture women on anatomy and physiology, publishes Familiar Lessons on Physiology *and* Familiar Lessons on Phrenology. *In 1849 she enters Central Medical College in upstate New York, and in 1850 is the second U.S. woman to receive a medical degree. When she starts teaching midwifery and the diseases of women and children at her alma mater in 1851, she is the first woman professor of medicine. The school, however, closes in 1852.*

The First Hospitals

Unable to practice in male-run hospitals, women start their own:

In 1857 Elizabeth and Emily Blackwell, with Marie Zakrzewska (1829–1902), open the New York Infirmary for Women and Children, the first U.S. hospital run by women doctors. Zakrzewska, a German-born midwife who got her medical degree at Western Reserve College, is the resident physician, and Emily is in charge of surgery. By 1859 they have so many patients, they move to a larger building.

When women are banned from Philadelphia hospital teaching clinics in 1858, Ann Preston leads in founding the Woman's Hospital of Philadelphia in 1861. The hospital allows students at the Woman's Medical College to gain practical experience. After completing postgraduate work in obstetrics in Paris, Emeline Horton Cleveland (1829–78) serves as the hospital's chief resident, beginning in 1862. The college adds a nursing school in 1863.

In 1862 Marie Zakrzewska opens the New England Hospital for Women and Children in Boston to provide clinical training for women doctors and to allow women patients to be treated by women physicians. The hospital also provides training for nurses.

From the start of the Civil War in 1861, women organize nursing services and set up hospitals (see "War"). It is through these efforts that nursing begins to develop as a profession.

In 1863, after much lobbying for a charter, Clemence Harned Lozier (1813–88), a graduate of Syracuse Medical College, opens the New York Medical College and Hospital for Women, a homeopathic school. By 1888 it has graduated some 200 women physicians.

Women midwives continue to play an important role on the frontier. In 1862, for example, Mary Heathman Smith begins her practice in Utah, where she delivers about 1,500 babies in the next 30 years.

Rebecca Lee (later Crumpler, 1833–post 1883) is the first black woman to receive a medical degree, from the New England Female Medical College in 1864. Two other early African American women doctors are Rebecca J. Cole, an 1867 Woman's Medical College of Pennsylvania graduate, and Susan Smith (later McKinney, then Steward), an 1870 New York Medical College for Women graduate.

In 1865 Mary Harris Thompson (1829–95) leads in founding the Chicago Hospital for Women and Children, where she heads the medical and surgical staff. She pursues advanced training at the Chicago Medical College, but when that school closes its doors to women in 1870, she sets up the Woman's Hospital Medical College, the first women's medical college in the Midwest. In 1874 she adds a nursing school. The first female surgeon in Chicago, Thompson specializes in abdominal and pelvic surgery and develops the widely used abdominal needle.

Lucy Hobbs Taylor (1833–1910) is the first U.S. woman to receive a dental degree, as an 1866 graduate of the Ohio College of Dental Surgery. She actually began practicing in Cincinnati in 1861 after studying privately but was not allowed to attend the college then. She also practiced in Iowa, where she was elected to the state dental society.

Seventh Day Adventist cofounder Ellen White helps set up the Western Health Reform Institute (later the Battle Creek Sanitarium) in 1866 in Michigan.

In 1868 the Blackwell sisters open the Woman's Medical College of the New York Infirmary. It is the first school in the country to create a chair in preventive medicine. During its 31 years, before it merges with Cornell University Medical School, it graduates 364 women physicians. The Blackwells' New York Infirmary is also one of the first hospitals to send doctors into tenements to teach health care to mothers, in 1868.

Ann Preston, dean of the Woman's Medical College of Pennsylvania, persuades Philadelphia hospitals to let her students attend teaching lectures in 1869. When they are jeered and spat at, she responds in the Philadelphia press: "Wherever it is proper to introduce women as patients, there also it is but just and in accordance with the instincts of the truest womanhood for women to appear as physicians and students."

In 1869 Mary Stinson is the first woman doctor to serve in a psychiatric department, as assistant physician in the woman's department in the asylum in Worcester, Massachusetts.

Howard University Medical School begins admitting women in 1869; by 1900 it graduates 23 black and 25 white women.

1870–79

When the University of Michigan accepts female medical students in 1870, it is the first state school to do so. Amanda Sanford is its first graduate, in 1871. Also, in 1870, Mary Harris Thompson opens the Woman's Hospital College in Chicago (see p. 222).

After receiving the first degree awarded to a woman from the Ecole de Médecine in Paris in 1871, Mary Putnam (later Jacobi, 1841–1906) teaches at the Woman's Medical College in New York and organizes the Association for the Advancement of the Medical Education of Women in 1872. In addition, she helps set up the children's dispensary at Mount Sinai Hospital in 1873. She is one of the top physicians in the country and publishes more than 100 papers during her career.

The first nursing schools are established in 1872–73 (see sidebar).

The 1873 Comstock Act forbids interstate commerce in contraceptive or abortion devices. Even sending information by mail is prohibited.

In 1875 Drs. Charlotte Blake Brown and Martha E. Bucknell help set up the Pacific Dispensary for Women and Children (later San Francisco Hospital for Children). In 1880 they add a nurses' training school.

Emeline Cleveland is probably the first U.S. woman to perform major surgery when she successfully removes an ovarian tumor in 1875.

Lydia E. Pinkham (p. 113) first markets her famous compound in 1875.

As an Illinois State Medical Society delegate, Sarah Hackett Stevenson (1841–1909) is the first woman seated at an American Medical Association convention, in 1876. She later publishes *The Physiology of Woman* (1880) and is the first woman on the Illinois board of health (1893).

Mary Putnam Jacobi wins Harvard University's Boylston Prize for her paper "The Question of Rest for Women during Menstruation" in 1876. This recognition leads to her election as the first woman member of the New York Academy of Medicine (1880).

In 1878 Ann Lohman ("Madame Restell") is tricked into selling contraceptives to ardent anti-obscenity crusader Anthony Comstock (in disguise). Rather than face trial, she commits suicide.

Denied membership in the Massachusetts medical society, Boston women in 1878 form their own group, the New England Hospital Medical Society, with Marie Zakrzewska as president.

In 1879 Mary Eliza Mahoney (1845–1926) is the first African American to graduate from a nursing school, at the New England Hospital

The First Nursing Schools

In 1872 Drs. Marie Zakrzewska and Susan Dimock (1847–75) start a school of nursing, the first in the United States, at the New England Hospital for Women and Children. Linda Richards (1841–1930) is the first nurse to graduate, in 1873; she later develops the nursing program at the Massachusetts General Hospital School of Nursing and at Boston City Hospital before serving as a missionary in Japan.

Three nursing schools open in 1873: at Bellevue Hospital in New York City, Massachusetts General Hospital in Boston, and Connecticut Hospital in New Haven. Bellevue is the first to use Florence Nightingale's teaching methods. Hospitals dominate early nurse training and often exploit nurses as unpaid workers.

More Pioneering Nursing Schools

The first African American nursing school is set up at Atlanta Baptist Seminary (later Spelman) in 1886. The first hospital training school for black nurses is not established until 1891, when Provident Hospital opens in Chicago.

Isabel Hampton (later Robb, 1860–1910) sets up the new nursing school at Johns Hopkins in 1889, establishing high standards and paving the way for an eight-hour work day for students. Many of her ideas are put into effect by her successor, Adelaide Nutting (1858–1948), who takes charge of the school in 1894.

for Women and Children. The school admits only one black and one Jewish student per class.

1880–89

About 13,000 U.S. women work as nurses in 1880, but only about 560 are graduates of hospital training schools. Important new nursing schools are established during the 1880s (see sidebar).

In 1880 Dr. Alice Bennett is the first woman to direct the female division of a mental hospital, at Pennyslvania's state hospital. She opposes physical restraints and introduces occupational therapy.

Drs. Emily Pope and Emma Call publish *The Practice of Medicine by Women in the United States* (1881), based on a survey of 430 doctors.

Clara Barton starts the American Red Cross in 1881 (see p. 148).

Women continue to found charity hospitals. In Rochester, New York, Dr. Sarah Dolley and others set up the Provident Dispensary Association in 1886 to give medical care to low-income women and their children. In Minneapolis in 1886, Dr. Martha Rogers Ripley starts Maternity Hospital, providing care for both married and unmarried mothers.

1890–99

Dr. Susan La Flesche (later Picotte, 1865–1915), the first Native American graduate of the Woman's Medical College of Pennsylvania, starts work on the Omaha reservation in Nebraska in 1890, eventually serving 1,300 Indians there. She later, in 1913, helps set up a hospital nearby.

In 1890 Ida Gray is the first African American woman to receive a doctor of dental surgery degree, from the University of Michigan.

In 1891 Dr. Halle Tanner Dillon (later Johnson, 1864–1901) endures a 10-day exam to become Alabama's first licensed woman doctor and the first black woman to practice in the state (a white woman is practicing without a license). She is the resident physician at Tuskegee Institute.

Dr. Isabelle Cobb (1858–1947) is the second Native American graduate of the Women's Medical College of Pennyslvania, in 1892; she later practices in Indian Territory (Oklahoma), where she conducts surgery in people's homes because there are no local hospitals.

Johns Hopkins Medical School admits women in 1893, but only after Mary Garrett, M. Carey Thomas, and others raise $500,000 (most of it given by Garrett). A similar attempt to use a financial bribe to open Harvard Medical School to women was tried in 1881 but failed.

Exiled from Mexico for her healing powers as a *curandera* and anticlerical preachings, which help incite the Yaqui, Teresa Urrea (1873–1905) arrives in El Paso in 1893. Later, after being exploited by a medical firm for a "curing crusade," she builds a hospital in Clifton, Arizona, in 1904.

In 1893 Anna D. Gregg and Georgianna Patton are the first two female graduates of the all-black Meharry Medical College in Nashville.

In 1895 Lillian Wald starts her Nurses' Settlement on Henry Street in New York (p. 150). She initiates a program of visiting nurses to provide health care to low-income neighborhoods throughout the city. By 1913 there are 92 nurses making 200,000 visits a year.

In 1896 Dr. Kong Tai Heong (1875–1951), a graduate of Canton Medical College, arrives in Hawaii. With her physician husband, she sets up the first Chinese hospital in Honolulu. She works primarily as an obstetrician, delivering more than 6,000 babies in the next 50 years.

In 1897 two widowed sisters, Drs. Alice Berry Graham and Katharine Berry Richardson, start Children's Mercy Hospital in Kansas City, Missouri. They set up a fund to treat crippled children unable to pay.

In 1897 Isabel Hampton Robb helps found and is the first president of the Nurses' Associated Alumnae of the United States and Canada (later American Nurses' Association), which lobbies for nursing standards.

In 1898 Elizabeth Hurdon (1868–1941), a gynecologist and pathologist, is the first woman on the Johns Hopkins Hospital staff; she is also the first woman on the medical school faculty.

After Cornell University admits women to its medical school in 1898, Woman's Medical College of the New York Infirmary closes in 1899. Emily Blackwell comments that she has "always regarded co-education as the final stage in the medical education of women." Other women's colleges also close. By 1903 only 3 of the 17 schools in 1893 remain. A major consequence is the loss of teaching jobs for women doctors.

1900–9

In 1900 Sophia French Palmer (1853–1920) is the first editor of the *American Journal of Nursing*, the official organ of the group that becomes the American Nurses' Association.

Serving as an army nurse in Cuba, Clara Maass (1876–1901) volunteers for a yellow fever experiment in 1901 and lets an infected mosquito bite her to see if that is how the disease spreads. She becomes ill and dies, but she proves that the mosquito is the carrier of the disease.

In 1901 Dr. Matilda Arabella Evans (1872–1935) establishes the first black hospital and nurses' training school in Columbia, South Carolina. She also sets up a free public health clinic.

In 1902 Lillian Wald sends a visiting nurse, Lina L. Rogers, to work in a local school; the experiment expands to cover the entire New York City school system—the world's first public school nursing program.

In 1903, despite the protests of male medical interns, Dr. Emily Dunning (later Barringer) becomes the first female ambulance surgeon, driving a horse-drawn vehicle to emergency cases in New York City.

In 1905 Dr. Elizabeth Bass and other women start a free dispensary in New Orleans, as they are not allowed to work in existing hospitals. By 1908 their facility is a full hospital (later the Sara Mayo Hospital).

Medical Discoverers

In 1894 Anna Wessel Williams (1863–1954) isolates a diphtheria strain (later called Park-Williams #8) and helps develop an effective antitoxin. She then works on rabies vaccine production and discovers distinctive cells that identify the disease (called Negri bodies, after the Italian man who published his simultaneous findings first). In 1905 Williams comes up with a new staining method that is the standard for rabies diagnosis for the next 34 years.

Dorothy Reed (later Mendenhall, 1874–1964) shows in 1901 that Hodgkin's disease is not a form of tuberculosis, as is thought at the time. She discovers a distinctive blood cell, later called the Reed cell (also Sternberg-Reed or Reed-Sternberg cell), which can be used to diagnose the disease.

Appointed to the Johns Hopkins medical faculty in 1902, Dr. Florence Sabin (1871–1953) begins her research into lymphatics and changes prevailing ideas about how these tiny vessels originate (see 1917; also "Science").

Letting Babies Live

Working for the New York City health department, Dr. Sara Josephine Baker (1873–1945) initiates an experimental preventive health plan for children in 1908. In one tenement district her team of 30 nurses instructs mothers on basic hygiene and encourages breast feeding—as a result, the infant mortality rate drops significantly. The city then sets up the nation's first division of child hygiene, with Baker as director. She introduces "baby health stations," offers a free training school for midwives, designs a special container making it is easy to give silver nitrate drops to prevent blindness in newborns, and establishes "Little Mothers' Leagues" to teach young girls how to care for their siblings while their mothers are at work. In 10 years, by 1918, the infant mortality drops from 144 per 1,000 live births to 88.

Promoting health care for blacks, the Women's Improvement Club of Indianapolis opens possibly the first U.S. tuberculosis camp in 1905.

Around 1905 Lillie Rosa Minoka-Hill (1876–1952), a Woman's Medical College graduate, sets up practice in Oneida, Wisconsin, although she is not officially licensed until 1934. She runs a clinic out of her kitchen and travels miles to treat patients, as the area has no other doctors.

Lavinia Dock (1858–1956), who worked at the Henry Street Settlement, writes the two-volume *History of Nursing* (1907) with Adelaide Nutting. Dock adds two more volumes in 1912.

In 1907 Dr. Esther Clayson Pohl (later Lovejoy, 1869–1967) is the first woman to head the board of health in a large city, in Portland, Oregon. She greatly improves sanitation standards and sets up school nurses.

Barred from membership in southern state associations and thus from the Nurses' Associated Alumnae, black nurses form the National Association of Colored Graduate Nurses in 1908, with Martha Minerva Franklin (1870–1968) as president.

In 1909 Jane Armina Delano (1862–1919) chairs the new National Committee on Red Cross Nursing; in addition, she is president of the Nurses' Associated Alumnae and superintendent of the Army Nurse Corps—helping to coordinate all these efforts. In 1912 she focuses exclusively on the Red Cross nurses, building up a body of professionally trained nurses with volunteer nurses' aides. Due to her efforts, nurses are able to react immediately when World War I later breaks out.

1910–19

In 1910 women are 6% of all U.S. physicians, but this figure declines in later years. There are about 1,000 hospital nursing schools, a number that more than doubles by 1927. Medical education, however, is curtailed by Abraham Flexner's 1910 report, which condemns 85% of medical schools and sets very high standards.

Dr. Alice Hamilton (1869–1970) supervises an Illinois survey of industrial poisons in 1910. Focusing on lead, she pinpoints 578 victims of lead poisoning and 77 harmful processes. Her meticulous work helps the state set safety regulations. In 1911 she undertakes similar work for the federal government. She becomes one of the world's leading experts in the new field of industrial toxicology.

In 1911 Clara Dutton Noyes (1869–1936) starts the first U.S. school for midwives, at Bellevue Hospital in New York. In her book *The Midwife in England* (1913), another trained nurse, Carolyn Van Blarcom (1879–1960), reveals that the United States is the only major power that does not offer adequate training or require licensing of midwives. On the other hand, a 1912 Johns Hopkins study shows that most U.S. physicians are not as competent as midwives, yet by 1930 doctors have replaced most midwives and dominate childbirth.

The National Organization for Public Health Nursing is formed in

1912 with Lillian Wald as president and Ella Crandall (1871–1938) as executive secretary. Crandall travels as much as 82,000 miles in a year to establish links with farflung public health nurses.

Mary Cromwell Jarrett (1877–1961) uses the social casework method for psychiatric patients in 1913 and pioneers psychiatric social work.

"Every child a wanted child"—*Margaret Sanger*

Margaret Higgins Sanger (1883–1966), convinced of the need for birth control from her work as a nurse and midwife, calls for legalization of contraceptives in her new, feminist publication, the *Woman Rebel* (1914), which the post office bans from the mails. Indicted under the Comstock Act, she flees to Europe. Before leaving, however, she arranges for distribution of her pamphlet *Family Limitation,* detailing contraceptive techniques. Her husband is then arrested when he inadvertently gives a copy to an anti-vice agent. With the death of her daughter in 1915, Sanger returns, and charges against her are dropped.

Among the 1,000-some new members admitted to the American College of Surgeons in 1914 are the first two women: Dr. Alice Gertrude Bryant (1862–1942) and Dr. Florence West Duckering (1869–1951).

In a 1914 *McClure's* article, Marguerite Tracy and Constance Leupp describe "twilight sleep," which uses scopolamine-morphine anesthesia to make childbirth painless. Surgeon Bertha Van Hoosen (1863–1952), who has used the method since 1904, joins other women in a public crusade for its use, helps form the National Twilight Sleep Association, and publishes a 1915 book on the method. Yet problems arise, as the anesthesia is often not properly administered, so its popularity declines.

The American Medical Women's Association, a lobbying and support group, is founded in 1915. Dr. Bertha Van Hoosen is its first president.

Suffragist Mary Ware Dennett (1872–1947) organizes other middle-class women into the National Birth Control League in 1915 to lobby for legalization of birth control information.

Margaret Sanger, her sister Ethel Byrne, and Fania Mindell open the first U.S. birth control clinic in the Brownsville section of Brooklyn, New York, in 1916 (see sidebar). In 1917 Sanger cofounds the New York Birth Control League, which campaigns for doctors' right to prescribe contraceptives and publishes the *Birth Control Review.* In contrast, Dennett's rival group argues for an end to all restrictions on birth control as a free speech issue.

In 1917 Dr. Florence Sabin (1871–1953) is the first female full professor at Johns Hopkins Medical School, but one of her male students is appointed over her to head the histology department.

During World War I many women serve as nurses in the Army Nurse Corps and Red Cross (see "War"). The American Medical Women's Association sets up an emergency-relief committee and in 1918 begins

"Women . . . Flocked to the Clinic"

Margaret Sanger, Ethel Byrne, and Fania Mindell hand out leaflets in Yiddish, Italian, and English to announce their birth control clinic. As Sanger describes, "Women . . . flocked to the clinic with the determination not to have any more children than their health could stand or their husbands support." For 10 days the clinic flouts the law to offer birth control information and sell contraceptive devices and copies of "What Every Girl Should Know." It is no surprise that the women running the clinic are arrested. The trial and Esther Bryne's hunger strike in jail gain publicity for Sanger's cause, and New York soon lets doctors prescribe contraceptives for "the cure and prevention of disease."

Margaret Sanger (to left of baby) at birth control trial (Library of Congress)

Medical Researchers

In 1917 Alice Evans (1881–1975) links the human disease brucellosis (undulant fever) to supposedly separate diseases in cows and goats. Pasteurizing milk, she finds, kills the brucellosis microbes and thus prevents the disease in humans. Her discovery, however, is rejected by scientists and the dairy industry for many years. In 1928 she is elected president of the Society of American Bacteriologists, but not until the 1930s is pasteurization of milk required.

In 1918 Martha Wollstein (1868–1939), with Harold Amoss, finds a way to speed the production of antimeningitis serum and develops standardization criteria.

In 1919 Louise Pearce (1885–1959), with Wade Hampton Brown, develops a drug (tryparsamide) that cures sleeping sickness. She goes to the Belgian Congo in 1919 to test the drug's effectiveness on humans suffering from the disease. For her successful work, she receives the Order of the Crown of Bel-gium and later, in 1953, the King Leopold II Prize.

In 1923 Gladys Henry Dick (1881–1963) and her husband determine the streptococcus that causes scarlet fever and in 1924 develop a skin test for susceptibility to scarlet fever.

establishing hospitals in France, where women doctors (not allowed in the army) help the war-ravaged communities. Later, as the American Women's Hospitals Service (chaired by Esther Pohl Lovejoy), this group helps with other disasters or medical problems, such as the Tokyo earthquake of 1923 or the prevalence of pellagra in South Carolina.

In 1918 Frances Elliott (later Davis, c. 1882–1965) is the first black nurse enrolled in the Red Cross but is specially classified as "colored."

Mary Ware Dennett merges her group with the new Voluntary Parenthood League in 1919 to lobby for free access to contraceptive information. Her sex education article, "The Sex Side of Life" (1918), originally written for her teenage sons, is increasingly in demand (see 1928).

The Circle of Negro Relief forms in 1919 as an outgrowth of wartime work. In 1921 it institutes a public health nursing program for blacks.

In 1919 Dr. Alice Hamilton becomes the first woman assistant professor, in industrial medicine, at Harvard Medical School, although she is not allowed to participate in commencement exercises.

1920–29

Backed by a coalition of women's groups, the 1921 Sheppard-Towner Act—the first federal health care program—aims at lowering the infant mortality rate. It provides funds for public health clinics that offer prenatal care, checkups for infants, and advice to mothers on good health care. Under the direction of Grace Abbott of the Children's Bureau, 3,000 clinics, largely staffed by women, are established. Yet many male physicians oppose the program, and funding is not renewed in 1929.

Margaret Sanger sets up the American Birth Control League in 1921, which evolves into the Federation of Planned Parenthood in 1942. She also opens the Birth Control Research Bureau, headed by Dr. Hannah Stone, in 1923 to prove the effectiveness of contraceptive techniques. It serves as the model for other birth control clinics—such as the second U.S. clinic, established by Dr. Rachelle Yarros in Chicago in 1923. Sanger herself develops new arguments for birth control, praising it for letting women enjoy sex but also advocating it as a means of eugenics.

In 1922 Dr. Edith Maas Lincoln starts a chest clinic for children at New York's Bellevue Hospital. During the next 30 years she paves the way in drug treatment of TB, using streptomycin as early as 1949.

Mary Breckinridge (1881–1965) starts the Kentucky Committee for Mothers and Babies (later the Frontier Nursing Service) in 1925 in the Appalachians. Her British-trained nurse midwives gradually replace the lay midwives in the area; each covers a 75-square-mile area, providing not only midwifery but also prenatal and other health care services.

In *Buck* v. *Bell* (1927), the Supreme Court rules against Carrie Buck, who protested against a Virginia law that orders sterilization for any inmate of a state institution for the "feeble-minded." Buck was committed to the institution after she was raped and became pregnant.

In 1928 Mary Dennett is tried for violating the Comstock Act by sending out her article on sex education after the post office banned it as obscene. She wins on appeal and writes *Who's Obscene?* (1930).

In her 1929 report on sexual behavior in 2,200 middle-class women, Katharine Bement Davis concludes that sex is "physically necessary to the woman as well as the man."

In 1929 the American Association of Nurse Midwives forms, mostly with members of Mary Breckinridge's Frontier Nursing Service.

1930–39

Martha Wollstein is elected in 1930 as the first female member of the American Pediatric Society.

George Hoyt Whipple, a 1934 Nobel Prize winner for work on pernicious anemia and related diseases, publicly credits Frieda Robschert-Robbins, his research associate, as equally deserving of the award.

In 1935 Alpha Kappa Alpha, the first black women's sorority (1908), sets up the Mississippi Health Project, directed by Dorothy Ferebee. It uses mobile health units to provide care in the Mississippi Delta.

In *United States* v. *One Package* (1936), the Supreme Court overturns the Comstock Act and rules it is not obscene for doctors to send contraceptive material through the mails. The decision is a victory for Margaret Sanger and her associates, who initiated the case. In 1937 the American Medical Association approves study of birth control in medical schools.

In 1937 Dr. Elise Strang L'Esperance (c. 1878–1959) starts the Kate Deprew Strang Cancer Prevention Clinic in New York City, the first organized effort to detect cancer in women at an early stage. Staffed by women doctors, the successful clinic serves as a model for others.

In 1939 the Birth Control Federation of America (Margaret Sanger's renamed organization) initiates the "Negro Project," a thinly veiled racist effort to control the growing black population in the South.

Challenging Freudian ideas about penis envy, Karen Danielsen Horney (1885–1952) publishes *New Ways in Psychoanalysis* (1939). She develops her own school of therapy stressing sociocultural influences on neurosis.

1940–49

In the 1940s Sanapia (1895–1984) begins her practice as an eagle doctor. To treat "ghost sickness," she combines prayers, songs, herbs, peyote, and psychological counseling. Later anthropologist David E. Jones records her story in *Sanapia, Comanche Medicine Woman* (1972).

For the role of nurses and doctors during World War II, see "War."

Dr. Sara Jordan (1884–1959) is elected the first woman president of the American Gastroenterological Association in 1942.

Margaret Sanger's organization changes its name to Planned Parenthood Federation of America in 1942.

Researchers in 1930s

In 1930 Dr. Cora Downs publishes her first report on tularemia and helps define this disease.

In 1932 Dr. Matilda Moldenhauer Brooks shows that methylene blue works as an antidote to both cyanide and carbon monoxide poisoning in humans.

Around 1932 Florence Seibert, a biochemist, isolates a pure form of tuberculin. In 1941 she uses it to develop an effective skin test for tuberculosis, but this is not widely used for another 10 years.

In 1938 Dorothy Hansine Andersen (1901–63), a pathologist, presents her research on cystic fibrosis, which she is the first to recognize as a distinct disease. She later develops diagnostic criteria.

In 1938 Ruth Darrow (1895–1956) postulates the existence of what is later identified as the Rh factor.

In 1939 Hattie Alexander (1901–68), a pediatrician and microbiologist, reports the first successful treatment of influenzal meningitis in infants using a rabbit serum she has developed.

In 1939 Pearl Kendrick helps develop a vaccine against whooping cough and later improves on this to include protection against diphtheria and tetanus as well.

Researchers in 1940s

Physician Grace Goldsmith coauthors a 1940 paper on vitamin C deficiency in pellagra, the first of her many nutritional discoveries.

Microbiologist Gladys Hobby is on a team that purifies penicillin in 1940 and treats patients with injections. She later helps develop Terramycin, another antibiotic.

Anatomist Berta Vogel Scharrer and her husband, Ernst, develop the theory of neurohormones and neurosecretion in the early 1940s.

In 1942 Dorothy I. Fennel is part of a team that develops a new pencillin species, which is named for her: Penicillium fennelliae. Another important penicillin researcher is Elizabeth McCoy.

Helen Brooke Taussig, a pediatric cardiologist, believes that "blue" babies have a malformed pulmonary artery, and she works with heart surgeon Alfred Blalock to develop an operation to correct this. The first successful Blalock-Taussig operation is performed at Johns Hopkins in 1944.

In the mid-1940s Icie Macy Hoobler's research into the composition of human milk helps define women's nutritional needs.

Gerty Cori shares the 1947 Nobel Prize for Physiology and Medicine (see "Science").

Dr. Myra Logan (1908–77), one of the first African American women in the American College of Physicians and Surgeons, is the first U.S. woman to perform heart surgery, in 1943.

"Women still have real grounds for envying men" — *Clara M. Thompson*

In her 1943 paper "'Penis Envy' in Women," psychotherapist Clara M. Thompson attributes any penis envy to cultural, not biological, factors. In contrast, Freudian analyst Helene Deutsch stresses female passivity and masochism in her two-volume *The Psychology of Women* (1944–45).

The first 12 women enter Harvard Medical School in 1945.

Dr. Martha May Eliot is the first woman president of the American Public Health Association, in 1947. Her contributions to maternal and child health are commemorated later in an award in her name (1964).

Adelle Davis writes *Let's Cook It Right* (1947) and other books that help inspire the health food movement. Her books are criticized for giving false nutritional information but remain highly popular.

Mary Elizabeth Lancaster Carnegie, who helped set up the nursing program at Florida A&M College, is the first black woman elected to the board of the Florida State Nurses Association, in 1949. Nine states and Washington, D.C., still refuse to admit black nurses into their state chapters, but the American Nurses' Association finally—largely through the efforts of Mabel Keaton Staupers (1890–1989)—lets black nurses join directly. As a result, the National Association of Colored Graduate Nurses votes to dissolove in 1949 and merge with the American Nurses' Association. Staupers later describes the battle of black nurses to win acceptance in both civilian and military roles in *No Time for Prejudice: A Story of the Integration of Negroes in Nursing in the United States* (1961).

1950–59

In *Principles of Intensive Psychotherapy* (1950), analyst Frieda Fromm-Reichmann details her work, also cited by her patient Joanne Greenberg ("Hannah Green") in *I Never Promised You a Rose Garden* (1964).

At New York Medical College in 1950, Dr. Margaret Giannini sets up the Mental Retardation Institute, one of the first such treatment clinics.

In 1952 Dr. Virginia Apgar (1909–74) develops her Apgar Score, a quick way of gauging a newborn's health and determining if any medical emergency exists. This system—which assesses color, heart rate, reflexes, muscle tone, and breathing—is soon adopted for all births.

Based on interviews with 8,000 women, *Sexual Behavior in the Human Female* (1953) by Alfred C. Kinsey and his colleagues counters prevailing ideas on female sexuality. It indicates that most women have clitoral orgasms and that almost half of women have sex before marriage.

Trials of the new oral contraceptive developed by Gregory Pincus, with funding from Katherine Dexter McCormick, begin in the mid-1950s. The main study of "the Pill" is carried out on low-income Puerto Rican women, who are not given physical examinations. When five women die in this study, no autopsies are performed.

The American College of Nurse-Midwives is founded in 1955.

Dr. Emma Sandler Moss becomes the first woman president of the American Society of Clinical Pathologists in 1955.

La Leche League is started in 1956 by Marian Tompson and Mary White in suburban Chicago to encourage mothers to breast-feed their infants. About the same time the Lamaze method, promoting natural childbirth without drugs, is imported from France. Marjorie Karmel's book *Thank You, Dr. Lamaze* (1959) helps popularize the movment.

When Planned Parenthoold publishes *Abortion in the United States* (1958), some medical journals are afraid to review it. At the time most states treat abortion as a criminal act. Only two states allow "therapeutic" abortions, to save a mother's life, and none permit abortions for victims of rape or incest.

Dr. Marion E. Kenworthy (1891–1980), Columbia University's first female professor of psychiatry in 1930, is the first woman president of the American Psychoanalytic Association in 1958.

Dr. Helen Taussig becomes the first female full professor at Johns Hopkins Medical School in 1959, almost 15 years after developing her pioneering "blue" baby operation.

In 1959 Dr. Lena Frances Edwards (1900–86), one of the first African American obstetrician gynecologists in 1948, establishes Our Lady of Guadelupe Maternity Clinic in Hereford, Texas, to serve migrant workers. In 1964 she receives the Presidential Medal of Freedom.

1960–69

The Food and Drug Administration (FDA) approves the first birth control pill (Enovid) in 1960 (see above).

In 1960 Dr. Frances Oldham Kelsey becomes director of new drugs at the FDA when Dr. Barbara Moulton resigns in frustration at the commercialism of the drug approval process. Kelsey resists pressure from a drug firm and blocks the licensing of thalidomide, a tranquilizer and sleeping pill, because of reports by Dr. Helen Taussig and others of its role in causing severe birth defects, such as legless and armless infants. In 1962 Sherri Chessen Finkbine, a star on the TV show *Romper Room*, goes public with her story to warn women against the drug—as a result she can't get an abortion in the United States and has to go to Sweden. Kelsey earns a presidential award for protecting women from the drug.

In 1960 Dr. Nina Starr Braunwald is the first U.S. woman to do open-heart surgery, installing an artifical mitral valve.

For her key role in setting up U.S. vocational rehabilitation services,

Researchers in 1950s

In 1950, with Solomon Berson, physicist Rosalyn Sussman Yalow develops radioimmunoassay (RIA), which uses radioactive particles to detect enzymes, hormones, and other biologically active substances in the body. The technique is used to diagnose diabetes, thyroid diseases, hypertension, and other conditions as well as to test for hepatitis in blood bank supplies. For this work Yalow shares the 1977 Nobel Prize (see "Science").

At the Sloan-Kettering Institute, Gladys Anderson Emerson, the first to isolate vitamin E, begins pioneering work on the relation of nutrition and cancer in 1950.

In 1952 Dr. Dorothy Horstmann boosts the effort to develop a polio vaccine by identifying the virus in victims' blood at a very early stage in the disease.

Dr. Rita Levi-Montalcini coauthors a 1954 paper revealing a substance that stimulates nerve cell growth, later called nerve growth factor. Her work, with Stanley Cohen, on this substance leads to a 1986 Nobel Prize.

At the New York University–Bellevue Medical Center Infertility Clinic, where she becomes director in 1958, Dr. Sophia Josephine Kleegman improves the Pap smear test. She later coauthors Infertility in Women (1966).

In 1962 Dr. Gertrude Elion develops a drug that helps avoid rejection in kidney transplant operations. She helps discover many more effective drug treatments before sharing the Nobel Prize in 1988.

In 1963 Elizabeth Stern publishes the first report connecting the herpes simplex virus to cervical cancer. A decade later, in 1973, she reports on a study of 11,000 women showing a connection between the Pill and a precursor of cervical cancer.

In 1963 physiological chemist Mary L. Petermann is the first woman member of the Sloan-Kettering Institute for Cancer Research. She is known for her earlier pioneering work on ribosomes (initially called Petermann's particles) and her studies of protein synthesis.

In 1964 biophysiologist Judith Graham Pool describes a method (now standard) of isolating the antihemophiliac factor in blood.

In the later 1960s Nancy Sabin Wexler launches a crusade for research on Huntington's disease (which she has a 50% of getting) that leads to major new findings. In 1993 she receives the Albert Lasker Award for these efforts.

Dr. Mary Switzer is the first woman to receive one of medicine's top honors, the Albert Lasker Award, in 1960.

Dr. Rebecca Craighill Lancefield, who clarified the connection between streptococcal infection and rheumatic fever, is the first woman president of the American Association of Immunologists, in 1961.

Dr. Janet Graeme Travell, in 1961, is the first woman to serve as White House physician, as President John F. Kennedy's personal doctor. Later she describes her experiences in *Office Hours: Day and Night* (1968).

In 1961 Patricia Maginnis and Lana Phelan start the Society for Humane Abortion in California to demand access to abortion as a woman's right. In 1966 Maginnis sets up the Association to Repeal Abortion Laws in California, which provides lists of abortion doctors and offers free classes in self-abortion.

The 1964 Nurses Training Act and the 1968 Health Manpower Act provide federal funding for nursing schools.

Dr. Hattie Alexander, a pioneer in curing influenzal meningitis, is the first woman president of the American Pediatric Society, in 1964.

In 1964 Dr. Mary Steichen Calderone founds and serves as executive director of the Sex Information and Education Council of the United States (SIECUS).

Virginia Satir's book *Cojoint Family Therapy* (1964) describes her pioneering work in this field.

In *Griswold* v. *Connecticut* (1965), the Supreme Court overturns a law making it a crime for anyone to even use contraceptives. It cites a marital couple's right to privacy as implicit in the Bill of Rights.

Charlotte Bertha Bühler is the first president of the Association for Humanistic Psychology, formed in 1965. She later coauthors *An Introduction to Humanistic Psychology* (1972) with Melanie Allen.

Helen Brooke Taussig becomes the first woman president of the American Heart Association in 1965. In the same year Grace Goldsmith is elected president of the American Institute of Nutrition.

Virginia Eshelman Johnson coauthors *Human Sexual Response* (1966) with William H. Masters. They argue for a woman's right to sexual pleasure and give legitimacy to the clitoral orgasm. In their later *Human Sexual Inadequacy* (1970), they dispel myths about women's frigidity and point instead to the effects of the double standard.

As dean of the Tulane School of Public Health and Tropical Medicine in 1967, Grace Goldsmith is the first woman to head a U.S. school of public health. In the same year cancer researcher Dr. Jane C. Wright is the first African American woman to serve as an associate dean, at New York Medical College, where she is also professor of surgery.

Two early women's medical institutions disappear in the late 1960s: the

New England Hospital for Women closes and becomes a community health center in 1968, and the Woman's Medical College of Pennsylvania admits men in 1969 and thus deletes *Woman's* from its name.

Feminist Anne Koedt's "The Myth of the Vaginal Orgasm" (1969) is a widely read essay calling for recognition of women's sexual needs.

In *The Doctor's Case Against the Pill* (1969), Barbara Seaman points to studies revealing adverse side effects, such as blood clots or cancer, from the Pill. After 1970 Senate hearings on the pill (which feminist activists disrupt in protest), the FDA adds an insert on potential side effects. European countries take the high-dose original Pill off the market in the early 1970s, but it is available in the United States until 1988.

In *On Death and Dying* (1969), Dr. Elisabeth Kübler-Ross defines the emotional issues faced by the terminally ill and calls for attention to the dying person's needs by both doctors and relatives.

1970–79

The Boston Women's Health Book Collective puts out its initial newsprint book, later named *Our Bodies, Ourselves,* in 1970. An outgrowth of the collective's discussion of health issues, the book integrates medical information with personal experience. In two years 2,000 copies are sold by word of mouth and in women's centers. Mass-market distribution begins in 1973, with a revised edition published by Simon and Schuster.

When Effie O'Neal Ellis is named special assistant for health services to the American Medical Association in 1970, she is the first black woman doctor given an administrative position in the AMA.

In 1970 Dr. Helen Rodriguez takes over as head of pediatrics at Lincoln Hospital in the South Bronx in the midst of protests against the lack of Latino doctors. She speaks out against the sterilization of Latinas without their permission and against child sexual abuse.

In 1971 Dr. Roberta Fenlon becomes the first woman president of a state medical society, in California.

The National Black Nurses' Association forms in 1971, with Lauranne B. Sams as president. It points out that the American Nurses' Association has not had a black president or vice president since opening its membership in 1951.

The first Feminist Women's Health Center is started in Los Angeles in 1971 by Carol Downer and Lorraine Rothman. A self-help clinic, it offers gynecological and pregnancy testing, instruction on conducting self-examinations and menstrual extractions (early abortions using a suction device invented by Rothman), and other information. Many other women's health clinics start around this time. Somerville Women's Health Project (near Boston) and Fremont's Women's Clinic (Seattle) are two that offer services in low-income areas.

Although the number of women doctors is increasing, in 1971 Alaska,

Abortion Reform

In 1967 Colorado is the first state to revise its abortion law, allowing hospital abortions (after approval by a panel of three doctors) in cases where pregnancy is the result of rape or incest, poses a threat to the woman's physical or mental health, or is likely to give rise to a severely deformed child. Both California and North Carolina pass similar reforms in 1969.

In 1969 the new National Association for the Repeal of Abortion Laws (NARAL) sponsors the first national conference on abortion rights. (Later the group is renamed the National Abortion Rights Action League.) Women's groups campaign to repeal abortion laws. Redstockings members, for example, hold speakouts and disrupt New York State hearings to testify as "the real experts." In Chicago, where abortion is illegal, women form an underground abortion referral collective called "Jane," as that is the name each woman uses when supplying information or counseling. The women also learn how to perform safe early abortions.

Four states legalize abortion in 1970: Alaska, Hawaii, New York, and Washington. In other states, such as California, Georgia, Texas, and Wisconsin, lower courts declare abortion laws invalid on privacy grounds—leading to the Supreme Court case in 1973.

Protests Against the Medical Norm

In Women and Madness *(1972), psychologist Phyllis Chesler challenges psychiatry's definition of madness and documents how independent or "deviant" behavior by women is curtailed.*

In The Cultural Warping of Childhood *(1972), Doris Haire, a leader of the International Childbirth Association, condemns the medicalization of childbirth in the United States and documents the lower rate of infant mortality in countries where midwives handle most births.*

In Why Would a Girl Go into Medicine? *(1973), Dr. Margaret Campbell (actually Mary Howell, former associate dean of Harvard Medical School) details the discrimination women medical students face, from lack of housing facilities to "entertaining" slides of nude women during lectures.*

In Why Me? What Every Woman Should Know about Breast Cancer to Save Her Life *(1975), Rose Kushner presents a strong case for fewer radical mastectomies. Her efforts lead the National Institutes of Health in 1979 to back a biopsy procedure that gives women a choice in breast surgery.*

Nevada, New Hampshire, and Wyoming only have one woman gynecologist each, and 11 other states each have five or fewer.

The first findings appear in 1971 linking diethylstilbestrol (DES) to vaginal cancer in the daughters of women who took the drug to avoid miscarriages. When existing agencies fail to mount a warning campaign for those at risk, women form two groups, Coalition for the Medical Rights of Women and DES Action, in the mid-1970s.

In *Eisenstadt* v. *Baird* (1972), the Supreme Court rules that states cannot restrict an unmarried person's access to contraceptives. The majority opinion states: "If the right of privacy means anything, it is the right of the individual . . . to be free from unwarranted government intrusion into matters so fundamentally affecting a person as the decision wheth-er to bear or beget a child."

The Feminist Counseling Collective forms in 1972 in Washington, D.C., to offer an alternative to traditional psychotherapy.

In its 1973 rulings on two cases, *Roe* v. *Wade* and *Doe* v. *Bolton*, the Supreme Court strikes down the abortion laws of Texas and Georgia. Essentially it removes all restrictions on abortion during the first three months of pregnancy, leaving the decision to the woman and her doctor, on the grounds of an individual's right to privacy. The court then says states can regulate abortion in the second trimester to protect the woman's health and they can prohibit abortion entirely in the third trimester, once the fetus is "viable." This landmark ruling effectively cancels the abortion laws in 46 states (only Alaska, Hawaii, New York, and Washington have laws in line with the court's standards). The winning arguments in both cases were presented by women: Sarah Weddington in *Roe* and Margie Pitts Hames in *Doe*.

In 1973 Lois Fister Steele begins directing the Indians Into Medicine program at the University of North Dakota, designed to increase Native American medical professionals. She then gets her M.D. degree and writes *Medicine Woman* (1985) on challenges to traditional practices.

As the first female medical director of the Cook County Hospital in 1973, Dr. Rowine Hayes Brown helps lobby for a law requiring doctors to report suspected cases of child abuse.

In *Eating Disorders: Obesity, Anorexia, and the Person Within* (1973), Dr. Hilde Bruch expounds on her pioneering work on this subject.

By 1974 several freestanding birth centers, providing an alternative to hospital births, have opened. In 10 years there are more than 100.

An expert on newborns' diseases, Dr. Mary Ellen Avery is, in 1974, the first woman to chair Harvard Medical School's pediatrics department.

Both First Lady Betty Ford and Happy Rockefeller, wife of New York's governor, speak in public about their mastectomies in 1974 and urge women to get checkups for breast cancer.

Thousands of women attend the first national women's health conference, held in 1975 in Boston. By this time there are about 50 feminist health centers in the country.

In 1976 the National Women's Health Network is set up in Washington, D.C., as a consumers' group focused on women's health care. It serves as a clearinghouse, supplying information on health issues and legislation affecting women and working to increase women's voice in health care. Another, strongly activist group formed at this time is the Women's Health Action Movement (WHAM) in New York. It demonstrates, for example, at the Democratic National Convention to draw attention to women's health issues.

In *Planned Parenthood* v. *Danforth* (1976), the Supreme Court strikes down several provisions in a Missouri antiabortion law. It says the woman does not need her husband's written consent, although she can be required to give her own written consent. Although it invalidates a provision requiring minors to obtain parental consent, it indicates it might consider such a provision if it gave the minor an appeal route.

The Hyde Amendment (originally 1976, then renewed) cuts off Medicaid funding for abortion; in 1977 Rosie Jiminez, a 27-year-old single mother earning her teaching degree, dies after an illegal, low-cost abortion in Texas. In several 1977 cases the Supreme Court rules states have no obligation to pay for "unnecessary" abortions with Medicaid funds.

In *The Hite Report* (1977), Shere Hite presents the results of 3,000 questionnaires on women's sexuality.

The Committee for Abortion Rights and Against Sterilization Abuse (CARASA) is formed in New York in 1977.

"There can be no compromise position"—Faye Wattleton

In 1978 Faye Wattleton is the first woman and first African American to serve as president of the Planned Parenthood Federation of America. "All women . . . must be free to take charge of their lives and make their own personal decisions," she insists.

Dr. Jennifer Niebyl at Johns Hopkins directs an important 1979 study of cleft-lip syndrome, the second most common birth defect.

In 1979 the Supreme Court rules against a Massachusetts law requiring unmarried minors to obtain consent for an abortion from both parents or a judge if they refuse.

1980–89

Toxic shock syndrome, a potentially fatal bacterial infection, appears to be linked to tampon use, so the FDA requires warning labels for tampons in 1980. Some super-absorbent brands are taken off the market.

In 1981 Byllye V. Avery starts the National Black Women's Health Project to promote self-help health care groups and educate African

Abuses in the 1970s

An Alabama family-planning clinic sterilizes two black teenagers, 12 and 14, in 1973 without clearly explaining the procedure to them or their mother. The Southern Poverty Law Center files a class-action suit, but only ineffectual government guidelines against such abuses result.

In 1973 reporter Barbara Katz reveals that the Dalkon Shield, a widely used intrauterine device, has a 10% pregnancy rate and can cause fatal infections. Her exposé helps spur the FDA to have it taken off the market in 1974, but the manufacturer does not institute a removal program until 1984—and then only after a long campaign by the National Women's Health Network.

A 1974 study by Women of All Red Nations reveals that the Indian Health Services has sterilized 42% of Native American women of childbearing age without their informed consent. In 1975 in California, 10 Chicanas, backed by the Comisión Feminil Mexicana Nacional, sue a county medical center for sterilizing them without their consent.

In 1975 Julie Roy wins a highly publicized case against Renatus Hartogs, a prominent New York psychiatrist, for sexual abuse during her psychotherapy.

1980: *In* Harris *v.* McRae *it upholds the* Hyde Amendment, *denying Medicaid funds even for medically necessary abortions.*

1981: *In* H.L. *v.* Matheson *it upholds a law calling for parental notification "if possible" when a minor seeks an abortion.*

1983: *In* Akron *v.* Akron Center for Reproductive Health, *it strikes down a law requiring abortions after the first trimester to be in a hospital, for doctors to say that life begins at conception and list all negative effects of abortion, and for women to wait 24 hours after giving consent. In* Planned Parenthood *v.* Ashcroft *it upholds a law requiring a minor to obtain either parental or judicial consent.*

1986: *In* Thornburgh *v.* American College of Obstetricians and Gynecologists, *it invalidates a law that has a detailed list of anti-abortion information the doctor must present. In its decision the court reaffirms its decision in* Roe: *"A woman's right to make that choice [to end her pregnancy] freely is fundamental."*

1989: *In* Webster *v.* Reproductive Health Services, *it upholds a law that starts off with a statement that life begins at conception, bans publicly funded facilities from performing abortions except to save the mother's life, and requires all physicians to test for fetal viability at 20 weeks.*

American women on health issues. By 1989 there are almost 100 local groups and 2,000 members. Under Avery's direction, the organization produces films on teenage pregnancy and runs educational programs on cancer and infant mortality.

In 1982 the Supreme Court rules that the Mississippi University for Women cannot exclude men from its nursing school. In the majority opinion, written by Sandra Day O'Connor, it states that the school's policy "tends to perpetuate the stereotyped view of nursing as an exclusively woman's job."

Nora W. Coffey helps found the HERS (Hysterectomy Educational Resources and Services) Foundation in 1982 after her own operation, in order to help women make informed decisions. Two other new groups are the Cesarean Prevention Movement, to protest unnecessary C-sections, and the Midwives' Alliance of North America, to promote the use of midwives as an alternative.

In 1983 medical researcher Mathilde Krim helps establish the AIDS Medical Foundation (later American Foundation for AIDS Research). In 1984 molecular biologist Flossie Wong-Staal is the first person to clone the HIV virus, a major research advance.

In 1984 Dr. Alexa Canady is the first black female neurosurgeon. Also, Dr. Luella Klein is the first woman president of the American College of Obstetricians and Gynecologists, and Dr. Carol C. Nadelson is the first female president of the American Psychiatric Association.

The 1984 TV documentary *Four Corners of Earth* features Susie Billie, a medicine woman of the Seminole people, who combines herbal remedies, songs, and rituals in her healing practice.

The 1984 death of singer Karen Carpenter focuses attention on anorexia nervosa among young women. Later, in *Fasting Girls* (1988), Joan Jacobs Brumberg claims thousands of U.S. women die of it every year.

The 1985 report by the Public Health Service Task Force on Women's Issues underlines the need to increase research on women's health.

The Organización Nacional de la Salud de la Mujer Latina, or National Latina Health Organization, is formed in 1986 in Oakland, California, with Luz Alvarez Martinez as its director.

As medical director of Cook County Hospital in Chicago in 1986, Dr. Agnes D. Lattimer is the only African American woman to be the chief medical officer at a large city hospital.

For the 1986 NOW-backed "March for Women's Lives," 125,000 people converge on the capital to demand the continued legality of birth control and abortion. In 1989 half a million demonstrate.

The "Baby M" case draws attention to the issue of surrogate mothers. Mary Beth Whitehead agreed to be artificially inseminated and bear a child for William Stern, as his wife, Elizabeth, was physically unable to have children. After the birth, Whitehead wants to keep the child, so a court battle ensues. In 1987 the lower court rules against Whitehead, describing her as "impulsive." Although a higher court judge states that a mother should be able to change her mind after birth, he still awards the child to the Sterns, whom he considers a more stable family.

In 1987 Jane Rideout and her colleagues patent AZT (azidothymidine) for treatment of patients with HIV after Rideout sends it to Martha St. Clair for testing in mice and it inhibits the growth of the virus.

Charon Asetoyer starts the Native American Women's Health and Education Resource Center in South Dakota in 1988. It provides information on health concerns from family planning to AIDS.

The FDA approves the cervical cap as a contraceptive in 1988.

The Reagan administration institutes what is called the "gag" rule in 1988: family planning clinics that receive federal funds are not allowed to tell pregnant women that abortion is an option or provide referrals to abortion clinics, even when asked.

The 1988 death of teenage Rebecca ("Becky") Bell from an illegal abortion becomes a rallying cry for opponents of parental consent laws.

Antonia Novello is the first female surgeon general, in 1989 (see p. 98).

1990–95

In 1990 the FDA approves Norplant, a contraceptive device that is implanted under the skin and gradually releases progestin on a timed basis.

Dr. Roselyn Payne Epps becomes the first African American woman president of the American Medical Association in 1990.

Congress approves the 1990 Breast and Cervical Cancer Mortality Prevention Act, intended to increase the availability of mammograms and Pap smears to low-income women. It is the first part of the 20-bill Women's Health Equity Act, prepared by the Congressional Caucus for Women's Issues to improve research, services, and preventive care for women. Also, pressured by women's groups, the National Institutes of Health set up the Office of Research on Women's Health, headed by Dr. Vivian P. Pinn, in 1990.

Midwives attend more than seven times as many births in 1990 as in 1975; about a third of these are at freestanding birth centers.

In 1991 Dr. Bernadine Healy, a cardiologist, is the first woman to direct the National Institutes of Health. She soon proposes the "Women's Health Initiative," a 14-year study of 150,000 some women to investigate the development of breast cancer, heart disease, and osteoporosis in older women.

A 1991 report by the Feminist Majority and American Medical Women's Association indicates that there are no women in charge of any U.S. medical schools and that 98% of the department chairmen

---

Supreme Court on Abortion: 1990s

1990: *In* Hodgson v. Minnesota *the court rules that a state may require a pregnant teenager to notify both of her biological parents, provided a judicial bypass is available. The court also upholds a similar Ohio law requiring notification of only one parent.*

1991: *In* Rust v. Sullivan, *the court upholds the "gag rule," banning abortion information in federally funded family planning clinics.*

1992: *In* Planned Parenthood of Southeastern Pennsylvania v. Casey, *the court reaffirms a woman's basic right to choose an abortion during the first trimester but allows restrictions if they do not impose an "undue burden." In this case it allows an anti-abortion lecture, a 24-hour waiting period, and a parental consent requirement for minors with the provision of judicial bypass. It does not, however, agree that a married woman needs her husband's consent.*

1993: *In* Bray v. Alexandria Women's Health Clinic, *the court does not forbid blockades of abortion clinics on the grounds of sex-based discrimination.*

1994: *In* NOW v. Scheidler, *the court allows the use of the anti-racketeering law (RICO) to sue demonstrators blocking access to abortion clinics or otherwise conspiring to keep women from obtaining legal abortions.*

New Congressional Initiatives

In 1992 Congress passes the Mammogram Quality Assurance Act, which sets standards for mammogram facilities; it also passes the Infertility Prevention Act to fund screening and treatment of chlamydia and other sexually transmitted diseases.

In 1993 Congress passes the National Institutes of Health Revitalization Act, which requires women to be adequately repre-sented in federal research studies (a recent long-term study on the effectiveness of aspirin in curtail-ing heart attacks, for example, was conducted only on men and then simply generalized to women). This law also expands research in areas of particular concern to women, such as osteoporosis, contraception, breast and ovarian cancer, and menopause.

and 79% of the faculty are men. The problem of harassment in medical schools is underscored by Dr. Frances Conley, one of the first female neurosurgeons, who resigns from her tenured position at Stanford Medical School in protest.

Dr. Susan M. Love, author of *Dr. Susan Love's Breast Book* (1990), co-founds the National Breast Cancer Coalition in 1991. With 600,000 signatures, it pressures Congress to raise breast cancer research fund-ings and helps win a threefold budget increase in 1992.

In 1992, deliberately defying an FDA ban, Leona Benten brings in RU-486, an abortion-inducing drug that is legal in Europe. When the drug is seized, she takes the case to the Supreme Court, but it refuses to require that the drug be returned to her.

About 750,000 attend the 1992 pro-choice rally in Washington, D.C.

There are more than four times as many women physicians in 1992 as in 1970, and women represent 18% of the total number instead of 7%. The greatest number are in internal medicine, with the next largest concentration in pediatrics.

In 1993 President Clinton lifts the "gag rule" imposed on federally funded family planning clinics as well as the ban on fetal tissue research. He also supports studies toward FDA approval of RU-486.

In 1993 Dr. Jocelyn Elders is the first black surgeon general. She stresses the need for prevention and education in controlling the rising AIDS rate, increased violence against women, teenage pregnancy, infant mortality, and breast cancer. Her outspokenness on sex educa-tion, however, leads to a political uproar, forcing her to resign in 1995.

Right-wing violence against abortion clinics escalates: a Florida doctor is murdered by an antiabortion demonstrator in 1993; another Florida doctor and his escort are murdered in 1994, as well as two receptionists at two different Boston clinics.

In 1994 researchers locate a breast cancer gene, after geneticist Mary-Claire King spurred the search in 1990 with her finding of a chromo-some 17 abnormality that was linked to breast cancer susceptibility.

Dr. Susan J. Blumenthal becomes the first deputy assistant for women's health in 1994.

Science and Invention

Bureau of Plant Industry in U.S. Department of Agriculture in 1905 (courtesy of National Archives and Records Administration)

Early Inventors

The first known American woman inventor is Sybilla Righton Masters. A 1715 patent issued in London to her husband names her as the creator of a device for processing Indian corn using a stamping instead of grinding method. A 1716 patent is for a way of preparing palmetto leaves to make hats.

Catherine Littlefield Greene persuades Eli Whitney to invent a device to separate the seeds from cotton and possibly offers design ideas for his 1793 cotton gin.

In 1793 Mrs. Samuel Slater is the first woman to receive a U.S. patent, for her improved cotton sewing thread, probably used in her husband's early cotton mills.

Many women's patents in the early 1800s involve hats or other items of clothing. Nancy Johnson creates a hand-cranked machine for making ice cream (1843), and Sarah O. Mather an underwater lamp and telescope (1845).

In the late 1850s Martha Hunt Coston finishes her husband's design for a signal flare and patents it. Widely used in the Civil War, it let distant ships quickly communicate information. It is later known as the Very signal, after a man adds minor improvements.

In 1864 Mary Jane Montgomery devises planking to keep barnacles away from the hulls of warships. She also patents some improved locomotive wheels.

1750–1849

By 1757 botanist Jane Colden (later Farquhar, 1724–66) has catalogued more than 300 plants in the lower Hudson Valley. Among the new plants that she discovers is the gardenia.

In 1829 Almira Hart Lincoln (later Phelps, p. 172) publishes the first of her popular science textbooks, *Familiar Lectures on Botany*.

During the 1840s women begin creating their own scientific societies, such as the Female Botanical Society of Wilmington, Delaware.

In 1841 Orra White Hitchcock does the technical drawings for her husband's report on Massachusetts geology. Another early geology illustrator is Sarah Hall, who also works with her husband.

Lucy Way Say, who assisted her husband with his entomological studies, is the first woman elected to a male scientific society, as associate member of Philadelphia's Academy of Natural Sciences in 1841.

Maragretta Hare Morris (1797–1867) publishes her article distinguishing two species of Hessian fly in 1841. She becomes the first woman member of the Philadelphia Academy of Science.

In 1847, using her two-inch telescope, Maria Mitchell (1818–89) discovers a new comet and is awarded a gold medal by Denmark's king. "Nature made woman an observer," she later says. In 1848 she is the first woman in the American Academy of Arts and Sciences in Boston.

1850–69

In 1850 Maria Mitchell and Margaretta Morris are the first women admitted to the American Association for the Advancement of Science, followed by Almira Phelps in 1859.

In 1859 Hepsa Ely Sillman publishes her theory of meteorites' origins.

As professor of astronomy at the new Vassar College in 1865, Maria Mitchell sets up the observatory there and develops a strong program for women. She at first thinks, "How much women need exact science," but later revises this to "How much science needs women."

Elizabeth Cary Agassiz (1822–1907) coauthors *A Journey to Brazil* (1867) with her husband, Louis, a well-known naturalist. Earlier she published *A First Lesson in Natural History* (1859) and another text.

In 1868 Mary Evard devises her "Reliance Cook Stove," which allows dry baking on one side and moist on the other.

1870–79

In 1870 Kate Furbish (1834–1931) starts collecting and sketching botanical specimens in Maine. The Furbish lousewort is one discovery.

In 1870 Margaret ("Mattie") Knight (1838–1914) obtains a patent for an attachment that allows paper to be folded into square-bottomed bags. Her detailed diary entries recording her experiments help prove her patent case when a man who saw her model being built tries to take the credit. "I'm not surprised at what I've done," she says. "I'm only sorry I couldn't have had as good a chance as a boy, and have been put to my trade regularly." She gains 27 patents in all (see also 1890s).

Ellen Swallow (later Richards) begins her chemistry studies in 1870 as the first woman at the Massachusetts Institute of Technology (see p. 176). To encourage other women scientists, she opens the Woman's Laboratory at MIT in 1876, which lasts until the school admits women students in 1883. She publishes articles on mineral chemistry and is the first woman elected to the American Institute of Mining Engineers in 1879. Her interest in food chemistry leads to an 1879 report on impurities that is a key factor in the Massachusetts food and drug act. Eventually Richards's interest in sanitary chemistry and what she calls "oekology," combining nutritional and environmental concerns, propels her into founding the discipline of home economics.

In 1872 Emily Warren Roebling oversees Brooklyn Bridge's construction when her husband, the designer, is incapacitated. Becoming an expert in civil engineering, she supervises until the bridge is done in 1883.

Many women attend Elizabeth and Louis Agassiz's summer workshops for seaside naturalists in 1873-74 . The Women's Education Association of Boston sponsors similar classes, leading to the 1888 founding of the Marine Biological Laboratory in Woods Hole, Massachusetts.

At an 1874 meeting suggested by Rachel Bodley, professor of chemistry and dean at the Women's Medical College of Pennsylvania, the American Chemical Society is formed. The women at the conference are excluded from the group photo, and no new women are admitted until the 1890s. The American Association for the Advancement of Science also restricts its female membership in the 1870s, so only two women are elected: Sophie Herrick and Ellen Swallow Richards.

In 1876 Elizabeth Bragg is the first U.S. woman with a degree in civil engineering, from the University of California, Berkeley; other women gain engineering degrees in the 1870s from the University of Illinois.

Sarah Frances Whiting (1847–1927), after studying the facilities at MIT, opens the second undergraduate physics lab in the country, at Wellesley College in 1878. The next year she starts astronomy classes.

In 1879 Katherine Jeannette Bush starts work in Yale's Peabody Museum of Natural History and becomes an expert on marine invertebrates. In 1901 she is the first woman to get a Ph.D. in zoology at Yale.

1880–89

After inventing a device to reduce pollution from smokestacks, Mary Walton in 1881 devises a way to reduce the sound from the elevated railways; she sells her idea to the Metropolitan Railroad.

In 1881, fed up with the sloppy work of his male assistant, Harvard College Observatory director Edward Pickering hires Williamina Paton Stevens Fleming (1857–1911). The following year Mary Palmer Draper

Women's Ingenuity on Display

At the Woman's Pavilion at the 1876 Centennial Exhibition in Philadelphia, 85 women display their inventions. Elizabeth Stiles receives the top prize for her multifunctional desk, which folds to just 18 inches thick but then opens to 7 feet.

In addition to Mattie Knight (see text), interesting female inventors of the 1870s include:

—Mary Carpenter (later Hooper), who in 1870 patents a sewing machine with an easy-to-thread needle. Her 1876 machine for braiding and sewing straw allows hat makers to sew their products in one motion.

—Jane Wells, who in 1872 devises a baby jumper, allowing an infant "to dance, swing, and turn itself in any direction."

—Amanda Theodosia Jones (p. 116), a poet and spiritualist, who in 1873 co-patents a vacuum process for canning food without cooking it first. She later patents several improvements as well as an oil burner.

—Helen Augusta Blanchard, who in 1873 creates the first of her improvements on the sewing machine, a forerunner of the zigzag machine.

—Mary Nolan, who in 1877 patents her interlocking bricks made of pulverized glass and clay, a mixture she calls Nolanum.

backs a large star classification project at Harvard in memory of her husband, Henry Draper. Fleming soon helps develop a system of classifying stellar spectra; she also hires other women assistants for the project, which gives women astronomers work for several decades. During her 30 years at Harvard, Fleming identifies about 10 new novas, 300 variable stars, and 59 nebulas.

After entering Johns Hopkins University in 1878 as a "special" student, Christine Ladd (later Franklin, 1847–1930) submits her Ph.D. dissertation, "On the Algebra of Logic," in 1882, but as a woman, she is refused a degree. Only 44 years later, in 1926, does she receive it.

In 1882 botanist Sarah Plummer Lemmon identifies a new plant genus, later named after her: *Plummera floribunda.*

Elizabeth Knight (later Britton, 1858–1934) writes the first of almost 350 papers on mosses in 1884. Later she is instrumental in setting up the New York Botanical Garden in 1891 and tends its moss collection. The moss genus *Bryobrittonia* and 15 moss species are named for her.

British-born Charlotte Angas Scott (1858–1931) heads the math department at Bryn Mawr College in 1885; she writes many papers on plane analytical geometry and an 1894 text, in print for about 70 years.

In 1886 Mary Jane Rathbun (1860–1943) starts her 53 years of work in the department of marine invertebrates at the National Museum; although not even given the position of assistant curator until 1907, she effectively runs the department. She becomes an expert on crabs.

Rachel Lloyd (1839–1900) is probably the first U.S. woman to receive a Ph.D. in chemistry, in 1886 at the University of Zurich.

In 1886 Emily Gregory, a botany professor at Bryn Mawr with a Ph.D. from Zurich, is the first woman in the American Society of Naturalists. Ida Keller, also a botanist at Bryn Mawr, is the second, in 1892.

Winifred Haring Edgerton (later Merrill, 1862–1951) is the first woman to receive a Ph.D. in mathematics at a U.S. university and the first woman to obtain any degree at Columbia University, in 1886.

In 1887 Effie Southworth (later Spalding) is the first female science assistant in the Bureau of Plant Industry in the Department of Agriculture. During the next 30 years some 20 women are hired to study crown galls, corn blight, and other plant diseases. Because women are not eligible for the post of junior botanist or pathologist, they are less expensive than men.

In 1888 Rosa Smith Eigenmann (1858–1947) coauthors the first of 15 papers on fish published with her husband in the next five years. The first major woman ichthyologist, she also writes 20 papers on her own.

Mary Whitney (1847–1921) succeeds Maria Mitchell in 1888 as the director of the Vassar College Observatory. She and her staff publish more than 100 papers, many in the *Astronomical Journal.*

1890–99

Williamina Fleming publishes the *Draper Catalogue of Stellar Spectra* (1890), which classifies 10,351 stars by their spectras. In 1899 she is named curator of astronomical photographs, the first woman in such a position at Harvard.

For the 1890 Patent Office centennial, Charlotte Smith publishes the newsheet *Woman Inventor*. No women are asked to the celebrations, but Smith gets women admitted to the new Association of Inventors.

Mary Whiton Calkins (1863–1930) sets up the first psychology lab at a women's college (Wellesley) in 1891. In her own work she stresses that ideas cannot be separated from the conscious "self" thinking them.

In 1892 Kate Olivia Sessions (1857–1940) starts what becomes Balboa Park in San Diego as a part of her nursery. She introduces many plants to the area, such as queen palms and various acacias and bougainvilleas.

At the 1892 International Congress of Psychology, Christine Ladd-Franklin introduces her theory of color vision, which is highly regarded at the time, although no longer considered valid.

Florence Bascom (1862–1945) is the first woman to receive a Ph.D. from Johns Hopkins University, in geology in 1893. She becomes the first woman fellow of the Geological Society of America in 1894, and in 1896 she is the first female assistant geologist for the U.S. Geological Survey, for which she investigates the Mid-Atlantic Piedmont area.

The only woman admitted to the Botanical Society of America when it forms in 1893 is Elizabeth Knight Britton.

In 1893 Bertha Lamme (1869–1954) is the first U.S. woman to receive a mechanical engineering degree, from Ohio State University. Later she possibly helps her brother develop the power system for Niagara Falls.

Alice Eastwood (1859–1953) succeeds Katharine Brandegee as botanical curator of the California Academy of Sciences in 1894. After the 1906 San Francisco earthquake she saves key specimens from the fire. She subsequently adds some 340,000 specimens to the herbarium.

The two women charter members of the American Mathematical Society, formed in 1894, are Charlotte Scott and Ruth Gentry. In the same year Margaret Washburn and Christine Ladd-Franklin are the first female members of the American Psychological Association. Also, Mary Blair Moody and her son are elected to the Association of American Anatomists, which does not admit any more women for eight years.

In 1895 Anna Botsford Comstock (1854–1930), known for her drawings of insects, helps set up nature-study courses in New York public schools and is a leader in the nature-study movement, writing such popular texts as *The Handbook of Nature* (1911). In 1899 she is the first female assistant professor at Cornell University, but the trustees object. She becomes a lecturer until 1913, when her professorship is reinstated.

More Inventions

The first known black woman inventor is Sarah E. Goode, who patents her folding bed in 1885; Miriam E. Benjamin patents her "gong and signal chair," used to call congressional pages, in 1888.

Julia Brainerd Hall helps her brother develop an electrolytic reduction process for aluminum production in 1886, although her brother receives all the credit.

In 1886 Carrie J. Everson patents her version of the oil flotation system used to extract ores in mining, although her process doesn't catch on until later, after the patent expires.

Another 1886 invention is Josephine G. Cochran's dishwasher, which she sells to hotels and restaurants in Chicago.

During the 1890s Margaret Knight patents a number of new devices, including a shoe-cutting machine (1890) and a numbering machine (1894). She later develops several rotary engines (1904).

Harriet R. Tracy patents her "lock and chain stitch" sewing machine in 1892, as well as a safety device to slow the descent of elevators if the power fails. She constructs one of her elevators for the Woman's Building at the 1893 World's Columbian Exposition.

Cynthia Westover (later Alden) devises a street-cleaning cart in 1892, and it is soon used in many cities.

In 1898 Elizabeth Knight Britton and Annie Smith Morrill start what later becomes the American Bryological Society. Marcia Keith and Isabelle Stone help found the American Physical Society in 1899.

In 1902 the American Physiological Society accepts its first female member: Ida Hyde, who does pioneering work in experimental physiology at the University of Kansas. The next woman is not accepted until 1913.

In 1903 the Association of American Geographers has two women charter members: Martha Krug Genthe and Ellen Churchill Semple (1863–1932), who publishes her first book, American History and Its Geographic Conditions (1903). Semple later becomes the association's first woman president, in 1921.

In 1905 Mary Whiton Calkins is the first woman president of the American Psychological Association. In 1918 she is the first woman president of the American Philosophical Association.

In 1906 Charlotte Scott is the first woman to hold office, as vice president, in the American Mathematical Society. The next female vice president will not be until Mary W. Gray in 1976.

In 1895 Margaret Maltby (1860–1944) is the first U.S. woman (and second woman) to earn a Ph.D. (physics) from the University of Göttingen; in 1896 Mary Winston (later Newson, 1869–1959) gains her Ph.D. (mathematics) there. Ida Hyde (1857–1945) is the first woman to earn a Ph.D. (physiology) at the University of Heidelberg, in 1896.

Antonia Maury (1866–1952), working at the Harvard Observatory since 1888, publishes her 1897 study on the spectra of bright stars, using her own classification system. Her boss rejects her system, but it is later hailed as a stepping stone for modern theories of astrophysics.

1900–9

Harriet Ann Boyd (later Hawes, 1871–1945) discovers and begins excavating a Minoan site at Gournia in Crete in 1901. She is the first woman to direct an important archaeological dig.

Florence Merriam Bailey (1863–1948) publishes her much-used *Handbook of the Birds of the Western United States* (1902). In 1908 the California mountain chickadee *(Parus gambeli baileyae)* is named for her.

Ethnomusicologist Alice Cunningham Fletcher (1838–1923) helps found the American Anthropological Association in 1902. She writes *The Hako: A Pawnee Ceremony* (1904) and *The Omaha Tribe* (1911).

Zelia Nutall, who found two codices by Mexican artists, publishes *Codex Nutall* (1902) and *The Book of the Life of the Ancient Mexicans* (1903).

Based on studies of male beetles, Nettie Maria Stevens (1861–1912) reports in 1905 that the X and Y chromosomes determine an individual's sex. Credit for this important discovery, however, is often given to a man who published a slightly later paper.

Mary Agnes Meara Chase (1869–1963), a top botanical illustrator, begins studying grasses in 1905, eventually becoming the principal scientist for systematic agrostology in the Department of Agriculture. She collects 12,200 sets of plants and authors some 70 publications.

In 1907 Mary Engle Pennington (1872–1952) becomes a bacteriological chemist in the USDA's Bureau of Chemistry. In 1908 she is named head of the new Food Research Laboratory, where she establishes standards for refrigeration in railroad cars.

In 1907 Williamina Fleming reports her discovery of 222 variable stars.

Mary Emily Sinclair (1878–1955) publishes three papers on the calculus of variations in 1907 to 1909 and in 1908 is the first woman to receive a mathematics doctorate from the University of Chicago.

In 1908 Vassar psychology professor Margaret Washburn (1871–1939) publishes her major work, *The Animal Mind* (see also 1931).

1910–19

Eloise Gerry is the first woman scientist in the U.S. Forest Service in 1910 and becomes an expert on gum products. Alice Evans, later known for her work on brucellosis, is the first woman scientist in the USDA's Bureau of Animal Industry, in 1910.

With Alice Walker, Hetty Goldman (1881–1972) directs an archaeological excavation of a Neolithic village in Greece in 1911. She later carries out a number of other digs in Asia Minor.

Gertrude Rand (1866–1970) begins her collaboration with Clarence Ferree (later her husband) in 1911. They study the effects of illumination on color perception and develop the Ferree-Rand perimeter used in diagnosing visual difficulties.

In 1913 Maude Menten (1879–1960) helps develop the Michaelis-Menten equation used to measure the rate of enzyme reactions.

Pathologist Maud Slye (1869–1954) in 1913 first presents findings, from studies of mice, that susceptibility to cancer is hereditary. In her continuing work on heredity in cancer, she uses some 150,000 mice.

In 1913 chemist Emma Perry Carr (1880–1972) sets up a research program at Mount Holyoke, where she, her colleague Dorothy Hahn, and students help pioneer the field of absorption spectroscopy.

Mildred Lenora Sanderson (1889–1914) makes an important contribution to the theory of modular invariants in her 1913 Ph.D. dissertation.

In *The Psychology of Management* (1914), Lillian Moller Gilbreth (1878–1972) underlines psychological as well as physiological factors in scientific industrial management. She and her husband are recognized authorities on industrial engineering, and in 1921 she is the first female member of the Society of Industrial Engineers. In the 1920s she becomes a household efficiency expert; 2 of her 12 children later describe life in the Gilbreth family in the book *Cheaper by the Dozen*.

In 1918 Anna Johnson Pell (later Wheeler, 1883–1966) begins teaching mathematics at Bryn Mawr. She contributes to the new field of functional analysis, and in 1927 is the first woman to give the highly regarded Colloquium Lectures to the American Mathematical Society.

Emmeline Moore joins the New York State Conservation Department in 1919, where she adds to knowledge of fish diseases and pollution.

1920–29

In 1920 Olive Clio Hazlett (1890–1974) publishes the first of several important papers on modular invariants and covariants, expanding the work of Mildred Sanderson.

Paleontologist Julia Anna Gardner joins the U.S. Geological Survey in 1920 and contributes to knowledge of Gulf and Coastal Plains fossils.

Ida Bengston, the first woman scientist in the U.S. Public Health Service Hygienic Laboratory (later the National Institutes of Health) in 1916, identifies a new strain of the botulism bacillus in 1922.

Fanny Carter Edson (1887–1952) begins work as a geologist for

Astronomical Observations

After working at the Harvard Observatory since 1896, Annie Jump Cannon (1863–1941) takes over as curator of astronomical photographs on Williamina Fleming's death in 1911. In The Henry Draper Catalogue *(1918–24) and* The Henry Draper Extension *(1925–49), she classifies the spectra of some 350,000 stars. She is so adept at this that she can classify three stars a minute.*

In 1912 Henrietta Swan Leavitt (1868–1921), working at the Harvard Observatory since 1902, points out the regular relationship between period and luminosity in Cepheid variable stars, a finding that is later used to measure the stars' distance from earth. In the course of her work, she discovers about 2,400 variable stars—about half of the total identified at the time.

Firsts for Scientists in the 1920s

Among significant firsts are:

—In 1924, after her 1923 publication on monocytes, Florence Sabin (p. 227) becomes the first woman president of the American Association of Anatomists. In 1925 she is the first woman elected to the National Academy of Sciences and the first asked to join the prestigious Rockefeller Institute.

—The first female Ph.D. candidate at the Harvard Observatory is Cecilia Payne (later Gaposchkin, 1900–79), whose highly acclaimed 1925 thesis relates spectral classes to the stars' actual temperatures.

—In 1927 cost engineer Elsie Eaves (1890–1983) is the first female member of the American Society of Civil Engineers.

—In 1928 Alice Evans is the first female president of the Society of American Bacteriologists.

—In 1929 Florence Merriam Bailey is the first woman fellow of the American Ornithologists' Union (after being its first female associate member in 1885). In 1931 she receives its Brewster Medal for her Birds of New Mexico (1928).

—In 1929 Margaret Ferguson is the first woman president of the Botanical Society of America.

—In 1929 the Society of Experimental Psychologists admits its first two women: Margaret Washburn and June Downey.

Roxana Oil (later Shell) in 1924. When the first well is drilled in Oklahoma's productive Marshall pool, she analyzes the cores and persuades the crew to keep drilling when they want to stop.

In 1925 Ynes Mexia (1870–1938) takes her first botanical collecting trip to Mexico, gathering 500 specimens, including the *Mimosa mexiae* (named after her). On her 1926–27 trip she gathers 1,600 specimens, including a new genus *(Mexianthus mexicanus)*. Later explorations take her to Brazil and Peru, where she collects about 300 types of ferns.

In the mid-1920s electrical engineer Edith Clarke (1883–1959) develops a calculating device that allows engineers to predict how electrical power systems will behave.

In 1925 paleontologists Esther Richards Applin and Alva Christine Ellisor with Hedwig Kniker publish a paper on the use of microfossils from exploratory oil drillings to date the beds and help predict where petroleum is likely to be found. During the 1920s women micropaleontologists are often employed to read drilling samples.

In 1926 psychologist Florence Goodenough reports on the "Draw-a-Man" test she devised to study children's concept formation. She later develops the Minnesota Preschool Scale (1932) to evaluate children's mental status and writes *Developmental Psychology* (1934).

Augusta Fox Bronner (1881–1966) coauthors *A Manual of Individual Mental Tests and Testing* (1927). She later, in 1932, serves as president of the American Orthopsychiatric Association.

In 1928 Emma Perry Carr and her researchers begin using ultraviolet absorption spectra to illuminate the structure of hydrocarbons. Aided by Mary Lura Sherrill and Lucy W. Pickett, she contributes to an understanding of the carbon-carbon double bond.

Anthropologist Margaret Mead (1901–78) publishes her seminal *Coming of Age in Samoa* (1928), followed by *Growing Up in New Guinea* (1930) and *Sex and Temperament in Three Primitive Societies* (1935).

1930–39

In 1931 the National Academy of Sciences elects Margaret Washburn as its second woman member (after Florence Sabin). It gives Annie Jump Cannon its Draper Medal but does not invite her to be a member.

Mayme Irwin Logsdon (1881–1967) writes her two-volume *Elementary Mathematical Analyses* (1932–33) and *A Mathematician Explains* (1935).

Anthropologist Ella Cara Deloria (1888–1971) publishes *Dakota Texts* (1932), a bilingual collection of myths; she also coauthors *Dakota Grammar* with Franz Boas and later writes a popular text, *Speaking of Indians* (1944), focusing on her own Sioux culture.

Anthropologist Ruth Benedict (1887–1948) publishes the seminal *Patterns of Culture* (1934), suggesting different cultures are defined in terms of different personality types.

Anthropologist Frederica de Laguna's *The Archaeology of Cook Inlet, Alaska* (1934) is one of the first studies of ancient peoples in this area.

In 1935 Ethel Browne Harvey (1885–1965) publishes her pioneering work on cell division and differentiation in sea urchin eggs. Her discovery that cell division can be stimulated without fertilization adds to the understanding of the role of cytoplasm in life processes.

The American Chemical Society's Francis P. Garvan Award for a distinguished woman chemist is established in 1935. It is first awarded to Emma Perry Carr in 1937.

In 1937 Margaret Morse Nice (1883–1974), who advances the idea of territoriality to explain birds' nesting behavior, is named a fellow of the American Ornithologists' Union.

Geologist Eleanora Bliss Knopf (1883–1974) writes *Structural Petrography* (1938); she also studies formations near the New York and Connecticut border for the U.S. Geological Survey (c. 1925–55).

In 1938 General Electric announces physicist Katherine Burr Blodgett's creation of a nonreflecting, or "invisible," glass by applying a gelatinous film to its surface. She also uses the film for a gauge that can measure extremely thin transparent and semitransparent materials. Her work has important uses in optics, chemistry, metallurgy, and other disciplines. Blodgett later develops methods to de-ice airplane wings.

After 25 years of work Cecilia Payne-Gaposchkin is finally appointed as an astronomer at Harvard College Observatory. She analyzes the spectra of all 2,000 known variable stars.

Biochemist Jane Anne Russell publishes an important 1938 article on the role of pituitary hormones in carbohydrate metabolism.

In 1939 Winifred Goldring (1888–1971), known for her studies of Devonian plant fossils, is the first woman state paleontologist, in New York. In 1949 she is the Paleontology Society's first woman president.

Studying carbohydrate metabolism, Gerty Radnitz Cori (1896–1957) and her husband, Carl, synthesize the first test-tube glycogen in 1939.

Anthropologist Elsie Clews Parsons (1875–1941), known for her earlier collections of folklore, publishes her two-volume *Pueblo Indian Religion* (1939), the culmination of 20-some years of research. In 1940 she is elected president of the American Anthropological Association.

1940–49

Libbie Henrietta Hyman (1888–1969) publishes the first volume in her six-volume *The Invertebrates* (1940–67). This encyclopedic work, for which she does most of the illustrations as well, covers about a million invertebates, although she never completes the section on higher mollusks and arthropods. In 1954 she is elected to the National Academy of Sciences for her efforts and in 1960 awarded the gold medal of the Linnaean Society.

1930s Archaeologists

Hetty Goldman writes her classic work on Eutresis (1931) and in 1932 begins excavations at Gözlü Kule in Tarsus, Turkey. In 1936 she is the first woman professor at the Institute for Advanced Studies in Princeton, New Jersey.

Ann Axtell Morris describes her work with her husband at Chichen Itza in Digging in the Yucatan (1931) and her study of pictographs in Digging in the Southwest (1933).

Florence Hawley (later Ellis) uses tree-ring dating, ceramic analyses, and statistics in her 1934 study of the peoples of Chaco Canyon. In 1936 she publishes the standard manual on prehistoric pottery in New Mexico.

Elizabeth W. Campbell and her husband publish a paper on the Pinto Basin site in the California desert in 1935.

Marjorie Ferguson (later Lambert) begins excavating prehistoric Rio Grande pueblos in 1937 and becomes one of the first women curators of archaeology, at the Museum of New Mexico.

Bertha Dutton's 1938 report on Chaco culture is based on her excavations in New Mexico.

Marie Wormington, an early curator of archaeology at the Denver Museum, writes Ancient Man in North America (1939) and Prehistoric Indians of the Southwest (1947), a standard text for many years.

Gerty Cori (Archives, Washington
University School of Medicine)

Fleeing Nazi Germany, Tilly Edinger (1897–1967) begins work at
Harvard's Museum of Comparative Zoology in 1940. Her early mono-
graph on fossil invertebrates' brains and *The Evolution of the Horse
Brain* (1948) lay the groundwork for paleoneurology.

After 20 years of ongoing research on radiation effects and 50 technical
articles, Edith Hinkley Quimby (1891–1982) receives a medal from the
American Radiation Society in 1940.

Judith Graham (later Pool, 1919–75) coauthors a 1942 paper on the
use of a new microelectrode to study the resting and action potentials
in a frog muscle. She later does key work in blood physiology (p. 232).

While working as an electrical engineer at General Electric, Edith
Clarke publishes her important text *Circuit Analysis of AC Power
Systems, Symmetrical and Related Components* (1943).

At least 85 women participate in the development of the first atomic
bomb through the Manhattan Project. Physicist Leona Woods Marshall (later Libby), for example, helps design the first nuclear reactor
and later works on plutonium production reactors. Physicist Maria
Goeppert Mayer (1906–72) joins the isotope separation team and helps
find a way to extract the uranium-235 used for the bomb. At Los Ala-
mos physicist Elda Anderson (1899–1961) tracks the fission process.
Other women working on various aspects of the project include Mary
Argo, Margaret D. Foster, Elizabeth Riddle Graves, Jane Hamilton
Hall, Joan Hinton, Katherine Way, and Chien-Shiung Wu.

In 1944 Barbara McClintock (1902–92), known for her work in the
early 1930s on genetic crossing-over in Indian corn, is the third woman
elected to the National Academy of Sciences.

In 1944 chemist Ivy Parker is the first editor of *Corrosion*, published by
the National Association of Corrosion Engineers. She serves as editor
for 21 years. Her specialty is preventing corrosion of oil pipelines.

While serving in the Navy in the mid-1940s, Grace Brewster Murray
Hopper (1906–92) develops the operating program for the first automatic, digital computer.

Ruth Benedict publishes *The Chrysanthemum and the Sword: Patterns of
Japanese Culture* (1946). Only after the book's huge success and a grant
from the Office of Naval Research for a research project under her
direction does Columbia University make her a full professor in 1948.

In 1947 sculptor Alice King Chatham designs the helmet used by Air
Force pilot Chuck Yeager when he breaks the sound barrier. She develops other high-tech head gear for the Air Force and later NASA.

In 1947 Madeline Dorothy Kneberg publishes her work with Thomas
Lewis on the Archaic period in Tennessee.

In 1948 Edith Clarke is the first woman elected as a fellow of the
American Institute of Electrical Engineers.

In her seminal paper "On Closed Shells in Nuclei" (1948) and a sequel in 1949, Maria Goeppert Mayer outlines her shell theory of nuclear structure and postulates a "spin-orbit force." She later clarifies the idea in *Elementary Theory of Nuclear Shell Structure* (1955), written with J.H.D. Jensen. In 1948 she also coauthors the classic text *Statistical Mechanics* with her husband, Joseph Mayer.

Chemist and engineer Maria Telkes and architect Eleanor Raymond create the first solar-heated house, in 1948 in Dover, Massachusetts.

In 1948 Gertrude Rogallo and her husband, Francis, invent what they call a "flexible wing," first used in kites and then later developed into the Rogallo wing used in hang-gliding.

Margaret Mead publishes *Male and Female: A Study of the Sexes in a Changing World* (1949).

Agnes Fay Morgan receives the 1949 Garvan Medal for her pioneering work on the chemistry of vitamins. She was one of the first to report adrenal damage from acid deficiency and protein damage from heat.

1950–59
Botanist and plant ecologist Emma Lucy Braun (1889–1971) publishes *Deciduous Forests of Eastern North America* (1950), drawing on her 25 years of research, covering 65,000 miles. She is also elected as the first woman member of the Ecological Society of America, in 1950.

Barbara McClintock presents her seminal paper "Chromosome Organization and Genic Expression" (1951), explaining her idea of "jumping genes," for which she wins the Nobel Prize in 1983. Her belief that some genes randomly shift their positions on the chromosome in sequential generations is loudly denounced; not until the mid-1960s do scientists begin to recognize the validity of her ideas.

"All the life of the planet is interrelated"—Rachel Carson

Biologist Rachel Carson (1907–64) publishes her best-selling *The Sea Around Us* (1951), which wins a National Book Award. She follows it with *The Edge of the Sea* (1955) and the *Sense of Wonder* (1956).

In 1952 Beatrice Hicks founds and serves as the first president of the Society of Women Engineers. Also in 1952 the SWE gives its first annual achievement award to Maria Telkes for work on solar energy.

In 1952 Grace Brewster Murray Hopper invents the first computer compiler, ending the need to write new machine instructions for each software package. She also works on the computer language COBOL.

In 1952 Gertrude Rand, who helped develop the lighting system in New York's Holland Tunnel, is the first woman in the Illuminating Engineering Society.

In *Discontinuous Automatic Control* (1953), Irmgard Flügge-Lotz advances ideas that spur development of automatic airplane controls. La-

Medical Science

Maude Menten coauthors a 1944 paper outlining a new azo-dye method, which is used to diagnose different forms of leukemia and other diseases. She also pioneers in the molecular study of hemoglobin.

In the mid-1940s biochemist Sarah Ratner, later a Garvan Medal winner (1961), does important work on the role of enzymes in amino acid metabolism.

In 1948 microbiologist Elizabeth Lee Hazen and chemist Rachel Brown discover an antifungal antibiotic they later name nystatin (manufactured as Mycostatin). It has many uses, from treating athlete's foot and yeast infections to saving paintings and books from severe damage. They set up a nonprofit corporation to channel the profits from their patent into further research.

In 1949 Elda Anderson helps pioneer health physics, to protect humans and the environment from radiation effects.

In 1950 Jewell Plummer (later Cobb) begins her cancer research, focusing on melanin and melanoma, at the National Cancer Institute.

In 1950, with Solomon Berson, nuclear physicist Rosalyn Sussman Yalow develops radioimmunoassay (see p. 231).

In 1954 Rita Levi-Montalcini describes the nerve growth factor (see p. 231).

Honors for women scientists in the 1950s include:

—The National Academy of Sciences elects three women members: physicist Maria Goeppert Mayer (1956), plant structure expert Katherine Esau (1957), and physicist Chien-Shiung Wu (1958).

—Garvan Medal recipients include Katherine Blodgett (1951, "invisible" glass), Gladys Emerson (1952, vitamin E chemistry), Betty Sullivan (1954, cereal chemistry), Allene R. Jeanes (1956, initial dextran research and development of blood-volume expander), Lucy W. Pickett (1957, molecular structure studies with ultraviolet spectroscopy), and Arda A. Green (1958, isolation of luciferases, which make fireflies glow).

—Society of Women Engineers award recipients include Elsie Gregory MacGill (1953, designer of her own plane), Edith Clarke (1954, electrical engineering theorist), and Margaret H. Hutchinson (1955, chemical engineer).

—In 1958 Marie Wormington is the first woman president of the Society of American Archaeologists, and Marion E. Kenworthy is the first woman president of the American Psychoanalytic Association.

ter, in 1970, she is the second woman fellow of the American Institute of Aeronautics and Astronautics.

In 1955 Angelina Rose Messina (1910–68), who helped prepare a definitive catalog of microfossils, cofounds the journal *Micropaleontology*.

Lois M. Haibt helps develop FORTRAN, a computer language, in 1955, and Grace Elizabeth ("Libby") Mitchell designs a major early IBM computer operating system.

In 1955 Eugenie Clark is appointed executive director of the new Cape Hazard Marine Biological Lab in Florida, where she becomes an expert on sharks and pioneers in revealing their learning behavior.

Astronomer Cecilia Payne-Gaposchkin is finally made a full professor at Harvard in 1956, after more than 30 years of work in which she has analyzed about 2,000 bright variable stars. She is the first woman to hold a professorship not restricted to women.

Archaeologist Marija Gimbutas's *Bronze Age Cultures in Central and Eastern Europe* (1956) is a pioneering work in this area.

In 1956 physicist Chien-Shiung Wu heads a team that disproves the theory of the conservation of parity and shows that atomic particles do not always behave in a symmetrical fashion, but instead display right- and left-handedness. Her experimental work backs up the theoretical analysis of her colleagues Tsung-Dao Lee and Chen-Ning Yang, who win the 1957 Nobel Prize. She is elected to the National Academy of Sciences in 1958.

Betty Jane Meggars coauthors a 1957 paper on archaeological studies at the mouth of the Amazon, one of the first investigations of this area.

Working with mouse cells, Katherine K. Sanford is in 1958 the first person to successfully clone a mammalian cell, isolating it and getting it to produce identical offspring.

1960–69

About 27% of biologists are women, 26% of mathematicians, 9% of chemists, 4% of physicists, and 1% of engineers in 1960.

In 1960 Mary Beth Stearns, a solid-state physicist, becomes principal scientist at the Ford Motor Company, where she contributes to the understanding of why some solids are magnetic and others are not.

Women scientists working in NASA's space program in the early 1960s include Jocelyn R. Gill, Mildred Mitchell, and Nancy G. Roman.

Marian Emily ("Happy") White, the first woman Ph.D. in anthropology at the University of Michigan, in 1956, publishes a 1960 paper on the Iroquois. A strong advocate of archaeological conservation, she even lies on the ground to prevent bulldozers from destroying a site.

Theodora Kroeber publishes *Ishi in Two Worlds: A Biography of the Last Wild Indian in North America* (1961) and *Ishi, Last of His Tribe* (1964).

Rachel Carson publishes *Silent Spring* (1962), attacking the abuse of chemical pesticides, especially DDT (see also p. 158).

Helen Wendler Deane (1917–66) publishes *The Adrenocortical Hormones—Their Origin, Chemistry, Physiology, and Pharmacology* (1962).

In 1963 geneticist Ruth Sager reveals clear evidence of DNA outside the nucleus in the cytoplasm and later publishes *Cytoplasmic Genes and Organelles* (1972).

Elizabeth Armstrong Wood, past president of the American Crystallographic Association, publishes the *Crystal Orientation Manual* (1963) followed by a popular science book, *Crystals and Light* (1964).

Joanne Simpson, the first female Ph.D. in meteorology, directs the U.S. Weather Bureau's experimental laboratory in Florida (1965–73).

In 1965 biologist Elizabeth Gantt begins studies of red algae leading to the discovery of phycobilisomes, key factors in photosynthesis.

For her sightings of comets and minor planets, astronomer Elizabeth Roemera has a minor planet named after her in 1965.

In 1965 Stephanie L. Kwolek creates a synthetic fiber, Kevlar, that is stronger than steel and used in a variety of products, from bulletproof vests to space vehicles.

Rita Guttman, known for her work on nerve membranes, is the first woman on the Council of Biophysical Study.

In 1967 Dian Fossey, sponsored by Louis Leakey, goes to Rwanda to study mountain gorillas. In three years she gets these large primates to accept her presence, something no one has ever done before. Her observations in her 1976 doctoral thesis establish the baseline for gorilla research. Fossey becomes increasingly concerned with protecting the gorillas from poachers and is asked to leave the country because of these activities. In 1983 she writes *Gorillas in the Mist*, the basis for the later movie. In 1985 she is mysteriously murdered in Rwanda.

Mildred Spiewak Dresselhaus is named MIT professor of electrical engineering in 1968 and in 1977 directs its Center for Materials Science and Engineering. She works on the electronic structure of semimetals.

The Association for Women in Psychology results from a 1969 symposium organized by Jo-Ann Evans Gardner.

Marguerite Shue-Wen Chang invents a device to help trigger underground nuclear explosions in 1969.

1970–79

Cynthia Irwin-Williams directs the excavation of the Salmon Ruins in New Mexico, beginning in 1970. In 1977 she is the second woman president of the Society of American Archaeologists.

In 1970 marine biologist Sylvia Earle Mead and her all-woman team

Honors in the 1960s

Honors for women scientists in the 1960s include:

—Marie Goeppert Mayer shares the 1963 Nobel Prize for Physics with J.H.D. Jensen and Eugene P. Wigner for her work on nuclear shell theory. She is the first U.S. woman to win in physics.

—Garvan Medal recipients include Mary L. Caldwell (1960, isolation of enzymes), Sarah Ratner (1961, protein metabolism), Mildred Cohn (1963, oxygen 18 enzymes), Birgit Vennesland (carbohydrate metabolism), Gertrude E. Perlmann (1965, protein synthesis), Mary L. Petermann (1966, ribosomes and cellular chemistry), and Gertrude Elion (1968, drugs for chemotherapy).

—Society of Women Engineers award winners include Esther Marley Conwell (1960, solid state studies), Grace Murray Hooper (1964, computer programming), and Isabella Lugoski Karle (1968, molecular structure studies with electron and X-ray diffraction).

—New National Academy of Sciences members are zoologist Libbie Hyman (1961), anatomist Berta Vogel Scharrer (1967), and neurobiologist Rita Levi-Montalcini (1968).

In the 1970s the National Academy of Sciences for the first time adds more than one woman in a year. New members are:
—1970: Rebecca Craighill Lancefield and Ruth Patrick
—1971: Mildred Cohn and Eleanor Jack Gibson
—1972: Gertrude Scharff Goldhaber and Elizabeth Shull Russell
—1973: Beatrice Mintz, Helen M. Ranney, and Helen B. Taussig
—1974: Estella Bergere Leopold and Sarah Ratner
—1975: Gertrude Mary Cox, Frederica Annis de Laguna, Dorothy M. Horstmann, Dorothea Jameson, Margaret Mead, and Rosalyn Yalow
—1976: Charlotte Friend and Julia Bowman Robinson
—1977: Elizabeth Florence Colson, Elizabeth Fondal Neufeld, Ruth Sager, and Evelyn Maisel Witkin
—1978: E. Margaret Burbidge, Mary R. Haas, Isabella L. Karle, Elizabeth Cavert Miller, and Mary Osborn
—1979: Gertrude Henle, Maxine F. Singer, and Salome G. Waelsch.

spend two weeks in an underwater capsule off the Virgin Islands; they swim 6 to 10 hours daily to study plant and animal life.

Ruth Benerito receives the 1970 Garvan Medal for her work on cellulose. Other recipients include Mary L. Good in 1973 for her work in spectroscopy (in 1988 she is American Chemical Society president), Joyce Kaufman in 1974 for calculations of drugs' affect on neurons, and Marjorie Horning in 1977 for developing safe medications for infants.

The Association for Women in Science forms in 1971 to increase educational and job opportunities for women scientists and engineers.

Mathematician Mina Spiegel Rees becomes the first woman president of the American Association for the Advancement of Science in 1971.

In 1973 the reference work *American Men of Science* is renamed *American Men and Women of Science.*

For her work on the first lunar landing, Barbard Crawford Johnson receives the 1974 Society of Women Engineers achievement award; in 1975 SWE honors Sheila E. Widnall for her aerodynamics research.

In the mid-1970s Mary Beth Stearns invents the High Resolution Electron Spectrometer (HRES).

Ruth Patrick receives the prestigious John and Alice Tyler Ecology Award in 1975. The diatometer she invented helps identify pollution in freshwater rivers and lakes.

Bodel Schmidt-Nielsen is the first woman president of the American Physiological Society, in 1975. In 1976 Anna J. Harrison is the first woman president of the American Chemical Society and Margaret Burbidge the first female president of the American Astronomical Society. In addition, Margaret Mead is president of the American Association for the Advancement of Science, Elizabeth Dexter Hay is president of the American Society for Cell Biology, and Isabella Karle is president of the American Crystallographic Association.

"The world cannot afford the loss of the talents of half its people"—Rosalyn Yalow

In 1977, for her work with radioimmunoassay, Rosalyn Yalow shares the Nobel Prize for Physiology or Medicine with two male scientists. In accepting, she says that "we must feel a personal responsibility to ease the path for those [women] who come after us" (see also above).

Astronomer Christine Jones Forman is part of the team that discovers superclusters of galaxies in 1977.

In her 1978 Ph.D. thesis Birute Galdikas sets the baseline for orangutan behavior, after 12 years spent getting them to accept her presence.

In 1979 mathematician Ruth M. Davis becomes assistant secretary of energy for resource applications.

1980–89

In 1980 Betsy Ancker-Johnson is honored by the Institute of Electrical and Electronics Engineers for her work on plasmas in solids. She is one of the few female members of the National Academy of Engineering.

Helen Murray Free receives the 1980 Garvan Medal for developing the dip and read self-test for diabetics.

In 1980 Julia Bowman Robinson is the second woman, since Anna Pell Wheeler in 1927, to give the prestigious Colloquium Lectures to the American Mathematical Society, and in 1983 she is elected as its first woman president. She uses number theory to solve logic problems.

Astronomer Vera Cooper Rubin, who in the 1970s pioneered in revealing the invisible "dark matter" in the universe, is elected to the National Academy of Sciences in 1981 (see sidebar).

Doris Malkin Curtis is the first woman president of the American Geological Institute, in 1981. In 1990 she is the first woman president of the Geological Society of America.

Biologist Ruth Hubbard focuses on sociological issues, editing *Biological Woman—The Convenient Myth* (1982) and *Women's Nature: Rationalizations of Inequality* (1983).

In 1982 Martina Kempf invents a computer program that reacts to spoken commands, called Katalavox (from the Greek *katal* and the Latin *vox*, signifying "understand voice"). It is later used for microsurgery as well as to allow people to maneuver their wheelchairs.

Sherry Turkle publishes *The Second Self: Computers and the Human Spirit* (1984), on how computers are changing the way people think.

In 1984 Cathleen Synge Morawetz is the first woman to head New York University's Courant Institute of Mathematical Sciences.

Evelyn Fox Keller publishes *Reflections on Gender and Science* in 1985.

In 1986 Susan Solomon, an atmospheric chemist for the National Oceanic and Atmospheric Administration, hypothesizes on how chlorofluorocarbons could cause a hole in the ozone layer and in 1987 leads an 18-man team to the Antarctic to test her idea.

By 1986 about 25% of scientists are women, but they are still less likely than men to be full professors or on a tenure track. Only 3.5% of the National Academy of Sciences members are women (51 members); since the academy's 1863 founding, only 60 women have been elected.

In 1987 Sheila Widnall is elected president of the Association for the Advancement of Science.

In 1987 Philippa Marrack and her husband, John Kaplan, publish a paper on their innovative work on the immune system. They have discovered a way to track T cells and study their responses to different antigens; they are also investigating superantigens.

Honors in the 1980s

Three U.S. women scientists earn the Nobel Prize in Physiology or Medicine in the 1980s:

—Barbara McClintock, in 1983 for work on "jumping genes"

—Rita Levi-Montalcini, with Stanley Cohen, in 1986 for work on the nerve growth factor

—Gertrude B. Elion, with two men, in 1988 for developing various drugs, such as the immunosuppressant used in the first heart transplant

New women in the National Academy of Sciences are:

—1980: Eloise R. Giblett

—1981: Marian E. Koshland, Vera C. Rubin, and Thressa C. Stadtman

—1982: Margaret Bryan Davis

—1983: Lynn Margulis, Mary-Lou Pardue, and Joan A. Steitz

—1984: Marilyn Gist Farquhar, Elizabeth D. Hay, Mary Ellen Jones, and Janet D. Rowley

—1985: Mary-Dell Chilton, Mildred S. Dresselhaus, Sandra M. Faber, and Martha Vaughan

—1986: Susan W. Kieffer, Liane B. Russell, and Karen K. Uhlenbeck

—1987: Jane E. Buikstra

—1988: Frances K. Graham, Ann M. Graybiel, Patty Jo Watson, and May Jane West-Eberhard

—1989: Philippa Marrack, Jane A. Menken, Barbara H. Partee, and Ora M. Rosen

NAS Members: 1990s

New women members of the National Academy of Sciences in the first half of the 1990s are:

—1990: Esther M. Conwell, Gertrude B. Elion (1988 Nobelist), Nina Fedoroff, P. S. Goldman-Rakic, Sarah Blaffer Hrdy, and Cathleen S. Morawetz

—1991: Mary Edmonds, Mary K. Gaillard, Susan E. Leeman, and Jane S. Richardson

—1992: Margaret J. Geller, Carol A. Gross, Olga F. Linares, Susan Solomon, and JoAnne Stubbe

—1993: Christine Guthrie, Nancy Kleckner, Sydney Kustu, Sharon R. Long, Eleanor E. Maccoby, Alexandra Navrotsky, and Marina Ratner

—1994: Mary Ellen Avery, May R. Berenbaum, Marye Anne Fox, Judith P. Klinman, Pamela A. Matson, Matilda White Riley, Myriam F. Sarachik, Lucy Shapiro, and Ellen S. Vitetta

—1995: Clara Franzini-Armstrong, Judith Kimble, Anne O. Krueger, Carla J. Shatz, and Mary Lou Zoback

Helen Donnis-Keller heads a team that by 1987 has mapped all 46 chromosomes.

In 1988 Sallie Baliunas is honored by the American Astronomical Society for her observations of a cycle of highs and lows in sunspot activity in distant stars.

1990–95

The U.S. Patent Office celebrates its 200th anniversary in 1990 with a special exhibit on women inventors. In 1991 the National Inventors Hall of Fame, established in 1973, inducts its first woman: Gertrude B. Elion. Elizabeth Lee Hazen and Rachel Fuller Brown enter in 1994.

Mimi Koehl receives a 1991 MacArthur grant for her study of comparative biomechanics. As part of her research she builds models of flying frogs and other animals, using materials from carpet scraps to dental plastic to Jell-O. Another 1991 grantee is chemist Jacqueline Barton, who wins the Garvan Medal in 1992.

By 1992 astronomer Carolyn Shoemaker has discovered 26 comets, more than anyone else.

In 1993 Martha Sloan is the first woman president of the Institute of Electrical and Electronic Engineers in its 108-year history.

In 1995 theoretical physicist Shirley Ann Jackson is both the first woman and the first African American to chair the U.S. Nuclear Regulatory Commission.

War and the Military

Yeomanettes, women in U.S. Navy, during World War I (Library of Congress)

"The British Are Coming!"

Several women carry messages of the British troops' approach:

Sybil Ludington (1761–1839) rides 40 miles during the night to alert the countryside and call soldiers to arms after a British attack on a supply depot in Danbury, Connecticut, in 1777.

In a similar feat, 22-year-old Deborah Champion gallops for two days through enemy lines to carry intelligence information to Gen. George Washington.

Listening through a keyhole, Lydia Barrington Darragh (1729–89) learns of Gen. William Howe's 1777 plans to surprise Washington. She inveigles a pass to travel outside Philadelphia and warns a soldier friend she encounters on the road.

In 1781 Emily Geiger rides 100 miles through enemy territory in South Carolina to deliver key information from Gen. Nathaniel Greene to Gen. Thomas Sumter. Stopped by Tories en route, she quickly reads and swallows the message before being searched and is allowed to continue on her way.

After she hears the British brag of their plans for an attack, teenage Susanna Bolling crosses the Appomattox River at night to warn General Lafayette, in 1781.

Following a 1671 nonaggression pact with colonial leaders, Awashonks, squaw sachem of the Saconnet in Rhode Island, sends some of her warriors to help the settlers during King Philip's War in 1675. In contrast, two other women leaders in the area, Weetamoo and Magnus, side with King Philip. Weetamoo drowns during the war, while Awashonks resettles her people in Sandwich, Massachusetts. Mary White Rowlandson, an English settler captured by the Indians, describes Weetamoo in her 1682 account of her three-month captivity.

After Hannah Duston (1657–c. 1736) is captured by the Abnaki in 1697, she is marched 100 miles north of her Massachusetts home. With the help of an English boy (also a captive), she steals the Indians' hatchets, kills and scalps 10 of them, takes a canoe, and escapes.

After her husband is killed in a battle in 1755, Nanye-hi (p. 12) leads the Cherokee warriors to rout the Creek forces. Her courage earns her the title of Beloved Woman and a place on the council of chiefs.

Becoming the mistress and possibly wife of William Johnson, the British head of Indian affairs in the North, in 1759, Molly Brant (Gonwatsijayenni, c. 1736–96) allies her Mohawk people with the British. When the Revolutionary War breaks out, she helps persuade the Iroquois to back the British and warns the British of an impending attack.

In 1775, soon after the first shots of the Revolutionary War are fired at Lexington, Prudence Wright commands a troop of women, dressed in men's clothes and armed with pitchforks and muskets, who prepare to defend the town of Pepperell, Massachusetts, from the British. They ambush a British spy and send his information on to colonial leaders.

During the Revolutionary War, thousands of women follow the troops, cooking their meals and nursing the wounded as well as supplying water and bullets to soldiers under fire. A few even fill in at the front when needed. For example, in 1776, after her husband is killed defending Fort Washington, New York, Margaret Cochran Corbin (1751–c. 1800) takes his place at the cannon until she, too, is wounded (she later receives half a soldier's regular disability pay for her heroism). Similarly, at the 1778 Battle of Monmouth in New Jersey, Mary Ludwig Hays (later McCauley, c. 1754–1832)—who had been lugging "pitchers" of water to thirsty soldiers—takes over the cannon when her husband collapses. In the legend that grows around "Molly Pitcher," she remains unperturbed as a cannonball rips through her lower skirts, and is made a sergeant on the battlefield. Whatever the truth, she does eventually get a pension from the Pennsylvania assembly.

Catherine Van Rennsselaer Schuyler (1734–1803) ignores warnings about warring Indians and travels to the family's summer estate near Albany in 1777 to burn the wheat fields so the British cannot harvest them. Impressed by her resolve, other patriots also burn their fields.

In 1779 Nancy Morgan Hart (c. 1735–1830) allegedly overcomes five to six armed Tories when they invade her Georgia cabin. At their insistence she prepares a meal, but she sneaks her daughter out to alert the neighbors. After lulling the men with her homemade whiskey, she takes up a rifle, kills one as he tries to attack her, fatally wounds another, and keeps the rest under guard until she is rescued.

Esther De Berdt Reed (1746–80), Sara Franklin Bache (1743–1808), and 37 other Philadelphia women organize in 1780 to raise funds for Washington's army. They use the money to buy linen for some 2,000 shirts, which they then sew.

In 1782, disguised in men's clothing, Deborah Sampson (later Gannett, 1760–1827) enlists in a Massachusetts regiment as Robert Shurtleff (see sidebar). Wounded twice in battle, she treats herself to avoid discovery. She serves 18 months before a fever forces her into a hospital, where her sex is discovered. Later she earns money by speaking about her experience. According to some sources, she is of African descent.

When gunpowder runs low during an Indian attack on Fort Henry in West Virginia in 1782, Elizabeth ("Betty") Zane (c. 1766–c. 1831) dashes out to the supply house some 50 yards away, braving Indian fire, to return with the needed ammunition.

In 1791 Ann Bailey (1742–1825), a frontier scout, helps save Fort Lee in West Virginia from an Indian onslaught. When ammunition runs low, she defies the attackers' fire, tears out of the fort, gallops 100 miles to Fort Union, and returns three days later with the needed gunpowder.

1800–49

Disguised as a man, Lucy Brewer enlists as George Baker and serves aboard the USS *Constitution* during the War of 1812. She joins in the victorious battle against the British ship *Guerriere*.

Thinking quickly, First Lady Dolley Payne Todd Madison (1768–1849) escapes from the presidential house with a Gilbert Stuart portrait of George Washington and vital government papers before the British burn the capital in 1814.

In the Milwaukee area Josette Juneau (1803–55) advocates peace between her Native people and the white settlers. In 1835 she remains on guard all night to protect a white settlement from a Potawatomi attack.

In the 1840s Woman Chief (c. 1806–58) gains a reputation among the Crow as a woman warrior. After she thwarts a Blackfoot raid and then leads several successful guerrilla attacks against them, she is invited onto the council of chiefs. She later acts as a peacemaker in the upper Missouri area but is eventually killed in an ambush.

During the Mexican War, Sarah Borginis serves as a brevet colonel under Gen. Zachary Taylor and helps defend Fort Brown in 1846. Another woman who, disguised as a man, fights in this war is Eliza Allen, who recounts her adventures in *The Female Volunteer* (1851).

"I Burst the Tyrant Bonds"

"Wrought upon at length by an enthusiasm and frenzy that could brook no control, I burst the tyrant bonds which held my sex in awe, and clandestinely, or by stealth, grasped an opportunity, which custom and the world seemed to deny, as a natural privilege. And whilst poverty, hunger, nakedness, cold and disease had dwindled the American armies to a handful . . . I threw off the soft habiliment of my sex, and assumed those of the warrior, already prepared for battle."

—Deborah Sampson Gannett, speech in Boston, 1802; quoted in Elizabeth Evans, *Weathering the Storm* (New York: Paragon House, 1975)

Civil War Veterans

The best-known female Union soldier is Canadian-born Sarah Emma Edmonds (1841–98), who enlists in a Michigan regiment as Frank Thompson and participates in such battles as Fredericksburg in 1862. At times she adopts a double disguise, dressing up as a "woman" to carry intelligence information behind enemy lines. In 1863 she turns to nursing rather than soldiering, and in 1865 she publishes a fictionalized account of her adventures, Nurse and Spy in the Union Army.

Loreta Velazquez, as Lt. Harry T. Buford, fights at the first Battle of Bull Run as well as others and later describes her exploits in The Woman in Battle *(1876). Jennie Hodgers serves as Albert D.J. Cashier and continues in disguise until her sex is discovered when she moves into an old soldiers home. Mary Scaberry (Charles Freeman), Sarah Rosetta Wakeman (Lyons Wakeman), and Frances Hook are just some of the known female soldiers; many others are probably buried in graves labeled "unknown."*

1850–99

During the Civil War (1861–65) a number of women, disguised as men, fight on the battlefield (see sidebar)

Several women spy for the Confederacy. One of the most flamboyant is Belle Boyd (1844–1900), who serves as a courier for Generals Beauregard and Jackson. At Front Royal, Virginia, in 1862 she races across a field, exposed to Union fire, to deliver information to Jackson. Later she is arrested, imprisoned, and then sent South, where she is treated as a heroine. In 1864, when she attempts to carry messages to England aboard a blockade runner, she is caught and banished to Canada. Her exploits are recorded in *Belle Boyd, in Camp and Prison* (1865).

Rose O'Neal Greenhow (c. 1815–64) sends key information hidden in her courier's hairdo to alert the Confederates of the plans for the first Battle of Bull. Placed under house arrest, she continues to run a Confederate spy ring from her Washington, D.C., home. Even when she is imprisoned, she manages to get her messages out and she defiantly flies a Confederate flag from her window. Like Boyd, she is exiled to the South, where she is a heroine. She then travels to London for the Confederacy but drowns on her way home.

On the Union side women also serve as spies. In Richmond, Virginia, Elizabeth Van Lew (1818–1900) reportedly helps prisoners escape. She then sets up her own spy ring, but to divert suspicion, she dresses and acts strangely, becoming known as "Crazy Bet." Using a secret code, she keeps the Union army informed of conditions as they approach her city. A major source of information is one of Van Lew's servants, Mary Elizabeth Bowser, who takes a job in Jefferson Davis's house, where she reads dispatches, listens in on discussions, and then reports to Van Lew.

Actress Pauline Cushman (1833–93) gains valuable information for the Union forces as she travels to several Confederate camps in Tennessee, supposedly looking for her brother. Caught with some stolen maps, she escapes, but then is recaptured and sentenced to die. Just in time the Union troops arrive.

Women are best known for their role as nurses during the Civil War. Soon after the war breaks out, Drs. Elizabeth and Emily Blackwell (p. 221) help form the Woman's Central Relief Association in New York and begin training nurses for war work. Their effort spurs the formation of the U.S. Sanitary Commission, which is nominally run by men but whose work of caring for wounded Union soldiers is mostly carried out by women.

Dorothea Lynde Dix (p. 144) is appointed superintendent of Union army nurses in 1861. She accepts only those who are over 30, plain, and Protestant, but her rigidity causes friction and she later has to take anyone who will work.

Jane Blaikie Hoge (1811–90) and Mary Ashton Rice Livermore (1820–1905) take charge of the Northwestern Sanitary Commission, eventually coordinating the efforts of 3,000 local aid societies and delivering tons of vegetables and fresh fruit, along with clothing and hospital supplies, to the front. In all they are credited with furnishing about two-thirds of the Union army's needs. Livermore later describes her experience in *My Story of the War* (1887).

Mary Ann Ball Bickerdyke (1817–1901), gratefully called Mother Bickerdyke by many soldiers, works directly in the field, "carrying system, order, and relief wherever she" goes, according to Mary Livermore. No matter how primitive the facilities, she manages to wash the linen, heat some nourishing soup, clean wounds, and offer calming words. She even combs the battlefield to make sure all the living have been rescued. When one doctor asks whom she works for, she replies, "I have received my authority from the Lord God Almighty; have you anything that ranks higher than that?"

Clara Barton (1821–1912) sets up her own supply system and leads mule trains with food and medical supplies to the front. On the battlefields she administers first aid and warms up soup and coffee. Many refer to her as the "Angel of the Battlefield."

Susie Baker Taylor (later King, 1848–1912) serves as a laundress and nurse for the African American troops in South Carolina. She later publishes *A Black Woman's Civil War Memoirs* (1902).

On the Confederate side several women establish hospitals. Sally Louisa Tompkins (1833–1916) runs a hospital in her house in Richmond, Virginia, and is made a captain in the Confederate cavalry so that she can continue her venture when all private hospitals are shut down. Stressing sanitation, she saves all but 73 of the 1,333 patients she treats over four years. Sallie Gordon Law (1805–94) organizes a hospital in Memphis; when the city is captured, she buys morphine, quinine, and other drugs and personally takes them South. Ella King Newsom (later Trader, 1838–1919) sets up hospitals at several battle sites and earns a reputation as "the Florence Nightingale of the South."

In 1863 Dr. Mary Edwards Walker (1832–1919) becomes an assistant surgeon in the Union army in Tennessee. Dressed in a slightly modified officer's union, she is captured on one of her trips behind enemy lines to treat civilians. After the war she is the first woman to receive the Congressional Medal of Honor, but it is revoked in 1917 and only restored in 1976. An advocate of dress reform, she adopts trousers, a jacket, a bow tie, and a top hat in civilian life.

Harriet Tubman (Library of Congress)

"We weakened the rebels"—*Harriet Tubman*

In addition to working as a spy and nurse, Harriet Tubman (p. 21) in 1863 leads Col. James Montgomery and several hundred black soldiers on a raid up the Combahee River in South Carolina, where they destroy valuable property and free 800 slaves.

Mary Ann Shadd Cary (p. 22) becomes the only official female recruiter during the war, when the governor of Indiana commissions her to sign up African American volunteers in 1864.

In 1865, after the war, Clara Barton sets up an office to trace missing soldiers for their families. She also marks the graves of the 13,000 men killed in the Confederate prison in Andersonville, Georgia.

In the 1860s–80s a number of Native American women stand out as warriors. For example, Ehyophsta (Yellow Haired Woman) helps defend her Cheyenne people from a Shoshoni attack in 1869. Brown Weasel Woman helps Blackfoot warriors recapture some stolen horses and then protects the herd from two Crow attackers, killing one of them. Given the name Running Eagle, she leads a number of raids, including an attack on Flathead warriors in which she is killed in 1878. Two Crow women, The-Other-Magpie and Finds-Them-and-Kills-Them, fight at the Battle of the Rosebud in 1876 (see sidebar). A noted Cheyenne woman warrior, both at the Battle of the Rosebud and the Cheyenne Breakout (1878) is Buffalo Calf Road. In 1878 Sarah Winnemucca (Thocmetony, p. 31) serves as a scout for the army in the Bannock Wars and rescues her father and other Paiute warriors from the Bannock camps. Major Apache warriors include Dahteste, Gouyen, Ishton, Lozen, and Siki Toklanni. Dahteste and Lozen are the two messengers sent by Geronimo to negotiate his final surrender in 1886.

During the 1898 Spanish-American War, Dr. Anita Newcomb McGee (1864–1940) is acting assistant surgeon general and recruits 1,200 female nurses to help in the camps. She then drafts legislation to set up a permanent Army Nurse Corps, passed in 1901. Although recruited for the war effort, black nurses are not allowed to join the ANC.

As head of the American Red Cross, Clara Barton is active in the relief effort and personally rides the mule trains to bring in supplies.

1900–19

Dita H. Kinney is the first commander of the Army Nurse Corps, created in 1901 (see above). The Navy Nurse Corps is organized in 1908, under Esther Vorhees Hanson, but Navy nurses are allowed only on hospital, not combat, ships. Only single women are accepted as navy nurses until 1944; black nurses are not admitted until 1945.

In 1913 Jovita Idár and Lenor Villegas de Magnón form La Cruz Blanca (the White Cross) to aid the wounded on the Texas border during the Mexican Revolution.

Led by Jane Delano, the Red Cross Nursing Service is immediately ready with 8,000 trained nurses upon the U.S. entry into World War I in 1917, and supplies 20,000 altogether. Also, in a month 400 army nurses ship out for Europe, with a total of 10,000 serving overseas. More than 50 receive medals for their service. Julia Stimson (1881–1948) directs the nurses for the American Expeditionary Forces, as described in *Finding Themselves* (1918). Through the efforts of Adah Samuels Thoms (c. 1863–1943), president of the National Association of Colored Graduate Nurses, black women are at last admitted into the Red Cross Nursing Service and thus the Army Nurse Corps in 1918.

Beginning in 1917 with Loretta Walsh, the navy enrolls women "yeomanettes" in its reserve, mostly for clerical work but also as electricians, camouflage designers, and other jobs. The marines follow, swearing in Opha Mae Johnson as the first "marinette" in 1918. The army, however, refuses to sign up women. In all, about 12,500 yeomanettes and 300 marinettes serve before being demobilized at the war's end in 1918.

When Marguerite Baker Harrison (1879–1967) goes to Germany as a reporter in 1918, she is really gathering military intelligence for use at the Versailles peace conference. Later she goes to Russia but is caught, forced to act as a counterspy, and then imprisoned for 10 months—as recounted in *Marooned in Moscow* (1921).

1920–39

Appointed superintendent of the Army Nurse Corps in 1919, Julia Stimson helps persuade Congress to give army nurses "relative" rank in 1920, making them second in command to the medical officers in military hospitals, although they do not gain full commissioned status, with its accompanying privileges, until 1947. Stimson herself is promoted to major in 1920, the first woman given that rank.

During the 1920s Anita Phipps is director of women's programs for the army. She proposes a women's service corps to the War Department, but her idea is rejected. Her position is eliminated in 1931.

When the Naval Reserve Act is revised in 1925, only male citizens are allowed to enroll.

Olive Hoskins is, in 1926, the first female warrant officer in the army.

1940–59

In 1940 Alice Throckmorton McLean (1886–1968) starts the American Women's Voluntary Services, training 18,000 women to drive ambulances, administer first aid, set up mobile kitchens, and the like before Pearl Harbor. After the U.S. entry into World War II in December 1941, training in cryptography, mechanics, and other areas is added. About 325,000 AWVS volunteers do relief work at armed forces posts during the war; many others help by selling war bonds. Women also serve in the Red Cross and other relief groups, such as the United Service Organizations, set up by Mary Shotwell Ingraham (1887–1981) to offer social services to the armed forces. Various local patriotic groups are also formed, including the Women's Ambulance and Defense Corps in Chicago, the Green Guards in Washington, D.C., and the Spanish-American Mothers and Wives Association of Tucson (which volunteers in hospitals, sells war bonds, and the like). Still other women take jobs in the defense industry (see "Work").

In 1941 Representative Edith Nourse Rogers introduces a bill to establish the Women's Army Auxiliary Corps, which is passed a year later, in May 1942. The idea is to use women in noncombat positions to free men to fight. At first WAAC members are governed by the army but have no military status and receive no benefits. Only in 1943 is the "auxiliary" status dropped, giving Women's Army Corps members

Civilian Efforts for World War I

Many women help the war effort on the home front. Suffragist Anna Howard Shaw coordinates these efforts as chair of the Woman's Committee under the Council of National Defense. Among the expatriate women active in relief work in Europe, Gertrude Stein and Alice B. Toklas drive an ambulance for the American Fund for the French Wounded, and Edith Wharton cares for more than 600 war orphans (the Belgian and French governments later honor her for her war work). Other women help the Red Cross or YWCA relief efforts overseas. Vera Scott Cushman, for example, sets up 140 hostess houses for nurses and other women workers. Women physicians (not allowed in the army) organize hospitals in France through the American Women's Medical Association.

African American women form the Circle for Negro War Relief in 1917 as an interracial counterpart to the Red Cross (which does not yet admit black nurses), and the YWCA Colored Women's War Council provides social services for black soldiers. YWCA workers Addie Waites Hunton and Kathryn M. Johnson later describe their experience and the racism in the armed forces in Two Colored Women with the American Expeditionary Forces *(1920).*

"This Unhappy War"

On February 19, 1942, President Franklin D. Roosevelt signs Executive Order 9066, allowing some 112,000 people of Japanese descent, many of them U.S. citizens, to be placed in internment camps. In Nisei Daughter *(1953), Monica Sone recalls her feeling of foreboding with the bombing of Pearl Harbor: "I knew instinctively that the fact that I was an American in birthright was not going to help me escape the consequences of this unhappy war." Soon she is part of Family #10710, with a tag on her coat lapel. Yet a number of Japanese American women leave the camps to serve as WACs or army nurses.*

Private Margaret Fukuoka, WAC
(photo by Ansel Adams,
Library of Congress)

full military status. Oveta Culp Hobby is appointed director in 1942 and supervises some 100,000 women at the height of the war. The first WAAC force overseas arrives in Algiers in January 1943. By July 1943 Capt. Mary Agnes Hallaren leads a battalion in Europe. As in the rest of the army, however, black WAC members are segregated. The first African American officer in WAAC is Charity Adams (later Earley), who commands the only black WAC battalion to serve in Europe. She later describes her experience in *One Woman's Army: A Black Officer Remembers the WAC* (1986).

In July 1942 the navy creates the WAVES (Women Accepted for Volunteer Emergency Service, or colloquially, Women Are Very Essential Sometimes) as part of its reserve, with full military status from the start. Wellesley College president Mildred McAfee Horton is its first director, overseeing 86,000 women at its peak.

In September 1942 two civilian women's pilot groups form to aid the war effort. Nancy Harkness Love commands 40 highly experienced women pilots in the Women's Auxiliary Ferrying Squadron, which flies planes from the factories to the bases. Jacqueline Cochran (p. 272) organizes the Women's Air Service Pilots, under contract to the Army Air Corps. The two groups merge as WASPs in August 1943. During the war WASP pilots not only deliver new planes but also help in training male pilots, try out planes with reported mechanical trouble, and tow targets for gunnery practice. "We flew 60 million miles in various aircraft, from small primary trainers up to the B-29 Super Fortress," WASP pilot Ann Darr recalls. One licensed pilot who is turned down by the WASPs, however, is Janet Harmon Waterford (later Bragg), because she is African American.

In late 1942 women join the U.S. Coast Guard for the first time, in the reserve corps SPARS (from the motto *Semper paratus*, "always ready"), directed by Dorothy Constance Stratton. The group grows to 10,000 by the end of the war, but there are no black women until 1944.

In 1943 the marines finally accept women reservists, under the direction of Ruth Cheney Streeter, a Civil Air Patrol pilot. Although most women who serve do clerical work, they are taught how to parachute and to operate antiaircraft guns.

U.S.–born Mildred Harnack-Fish, a German Resistance fighter, is captured and executed in Berlin's Plotzensee Prison in 1943.

During the war 57,000 women serve as army nurses and 11,000 as navy nurses. As superintendent of the Navy Nurse Corps, Sue Dauser in 1942 secures the same "relative" rank for her nurses that army nurses have (see 1920). Of the military women, the nurses suffer the greatest casualties; also several hundred are held as prisoners of war in the South Pacific. Some 1,600 Army Nurse Corps women are decorated for their service. Leah Fox, head nurse at Hickam Field, Hawaii, is the first woman to receive the Purple Heart, after she is wounded in the bombing of Pearl Harbor. Racism, however, is a problem in the nursing corps: the army uses a quota system to limit black nurses, and the navy does not accept any. When a proposal is made in 1945 to draft nurses to remedy a shortage, Mabel Keaton Staupers, executive secretary of the National Association of Colored Graduate Nurses, publicly asks why black nurses aren't used and helps to end the exclusionary practices.

A total of about 350,000 women serve in the military in World War II, plus about 2,000 WASPs, who are denied military status and thus any benefits in 1944 (they belatedly receive military recognition in 1977).

Representative Frances Payne Bolton and army nurse Florence Blanchfield help get the Army-Navy Nurse Act passed in 1947, giving nurses full military rank—although a ceiling is put on the top rank. Col. Blanchfield is the first woman to receive a regular army commission.

In 1948 Congress passes the Women's Armed Services Integration Act, giving women regular military status, although limits are set on the top rank as well as the number of top offiers. Also, WAC is designated as a separate body in the army, although the other corps are not separated. The new top-ranked officers are Col. Mary A. Hallaren, WAC director; Capt. Joy Bright Hancock, WAVES director; Col. Katherine Towle, director of the Regular Women Marines; and Col. Geraldine Pratt May, director of Women in the Air Force (WAF).

In 1949 the Air Force Nurse Corps is set up, as well as the Army and Air Force Medical Specialists Corps. Also, in 1949 the first 19 women enter the Air Force Officer and Candidate School in San Antonio.

In 1950, when the Korean War breaks out, army nurses begin setting up hospitals in Pusan just four days after the first troops land. Some 500 to 600 nurses serve in the war zone (all other women are kept out of the combat area). Despite the value of WASPs' work in World War II, the air force does not use women pilots even in noncombat jobs.

In 1953 Lt. Fae Margaret Adams (WAC) is the first woman physician to receive a regular army commission.

By the end of the 1950s military women can no longer serve in such fields as intelligence, weather, and control tower operation. Most are assigned to purely secretarial jobs.

1960–79

Military nurses assist Iranian earthquake victims in 1962 and help in other, similar disasters.

In 1965 army nurses set up a field hospital in Vietnam; air force nurses help airlift injured soldiers out; and navy nurses work aboard the hospital ship USS *Repose*. By early 1966 there are 300 military nurses in Vietnam and Thailand. Some of these nurses also help provide medical care for Vietnamese civilians in rural areas.

Maj. Kathleen Wilkes and M. Sgt. Betty Adams help set up the Vietnamese Women's Armed Forces Corps, modeled on WAC in 1965. The first contingent of WACs, under Capt. Peggy E. Ready,

Two Different Treason Trials

In 1948, Iva Ikuko Toguri d'Aquino is arrested as "Tokyo Rose" (in fact 14 different voices). A U.S. native, she was stranded in Japan during the war. With no means of support, she took a typing job at Radio Tokyo. Eventually she was forced to broadcast on "Zero Hour," although she tried to caricature the messages. One navy officer even joked that Tokyo Rose should be given a reward for providing the men with entertainment, as the propaganda was so obvious. Yet, using trumped-up evidence, the government brings in a conviction on one of eight counts, and she serves more than six years in jail. In 1977 she finally receives a full pardon from President Ford.

Also in 1948 Mildred E. Gillars, known as Axis Sally, is tried for treason for her well-paid radio broadcasts of Nazi propaganda to U.S. troops during the war. Convicted in 1949, she serves 12 years of a 30-year sentence.

arrive in Vietnam in 1966. In 1967 Sgt. Barbara J. Dulinsky is the first woman marine in a combat theater, and Lt. Col. June H. Hilton leads the first WAFs in Vietnam.

In 1967 Public Law 90-130 removes the ceiling on rank as well as the 2% limit on the number of women in the services.

In 1968 Clothhilde Dent Brown is the first African American woman colonel in the army.

The air force opens its Reserve Officer Training Corps (ROTC) to women in 1969; by 1970 about 500 women have enrolled. Also, the first women enter the Joint Armed Forces Staff College in 1969 and the Air War College in 1970.

The first WAF to brief officers on air strikes is Maj. Norma A. Archer, as operations officer of a photographic squadron in Vietnam in 1969.

In 1970 several women fight military policies calling for the automatic discharge of pregnant women, and the air force and marines institute a policy of waivers, allowing women to return after giving birth.

When the Vietnam peace treaty is signed in 1973, about 10,000 women, mostly nurses (see sidebar), have served. Eight female nurses have died in the war, as well as a number of civilian foreign service and Red Cross workers, a journalist, and a social worker.

Lt. Pamela Chelgren is the first woman in the National Oceanic and Administrative Corps, in 1972.

In a suit brought by Air Force Lt. Sharron Frontiero and argued by Ruth Bader Ginsburg, the Supreme Court rules in 1973 that married women officers are entitled to the same family benefits as married male officers and do not have to prove their spouse is dependent on them.

The first six navy women win flight wings in 1973, but their duties are limited, as they can't be assigned to combat ships, even to deliver mail.

The U.S. Merchant Marine Academy is the first service academy to admit women, in 1974, and it graduates its first eight women in 1978.

In 1974 Jill Brown is the first black woman pilot in the U.S. military. Also in 1974, Sally Murphy is the army's first female helicopter pilot, and in 1975 Joellen Drag is the navy's first woman helicopter pilot, and Sp4c. Debra Houghton is the first female army tank driver. Dr. Donna P. Davis is the first black woman physician in the military, in the Naval Medical Corps in 1975.

In the face of several lawsuits, Congress passes a 1975 law requiring all the service academies to admit women. By fall of 1976 women are 6% of the new class at the U.S. Naval Academy in Annapolis, 8% at the U.S. Military Academy in West Point, and 10% at the Air Force Academy in Colorado Springs. The first women also enter the U.S. Coast Guard Academy (not covered by the law).

In 1975 the Department of Defense ends the policy banning women with children from serving, and in 1976 the Second Circuit Court rules that a female marine cannot automatically be discharged when she becomes pregnant.

Juanita Ashcraft is the first woman assistant secretary in the U.S. Air Force, as assistant secretary for manpower and reserve affairs in 1976.

The first 10 air force women graduate as pilots in 1977. "When you step out of the airplane and take off your helmet, the transient maintenance guys almost fall over backwards. That sort of keeps us going," Capt. Kathy LaSauce later remarks.

In 1977 two U.S. Coast Guard cutters are assigned mixed crews on a permanent basis, with 10 enlisted women and 2 officers on each. By 1978 the U.S. Coast Guard is the first service to remove all restrictions on assignments for women. By 1979 two women are in command of 95-foot cutters, including Beverly Gwinn Kelley, who shares a citation with her crew for their rescue work during a 1980 Hawaiian storm.

A court case brought by navy electrician Yona Owens, charging sex discrimination when she is not given a job on a noncombat ship, results in a 1978 ruling in her favor. Under a new law, then, the navy lets women to go to sea on noncombat ships, and on November 1, 1978, the first eight female ensigns report for ship duty.

The first five women, one from each military branch, join the White House Honor Guard in 1978. One is Air Force Sgt. Elizabeth Foreman, who wrote First Lady Rosalynn Carter to push for the change.

1980–95

The first 217 women graduate from the army, navy, air force, and Coast Guard service academies in 1980. At this time women are 8.5% of military personnel; about 54% are in traditional female jobs, but others are flight mechanics, truck drivers, military police officers, and the like.

In *Rostker* v. *Goldberg* (1981), the Supreme Court upholds the restriction of the new draft registration requirement to men only. In the 1980 congressional debate, representative Patricia Schroeder had argued: "If the country needs . . . the draft, then of course women will have to go."

The air force opens an additional 1,645 jobs to women in 1986, letting them serve in 95% of all positions. In 1987 the navy opens about 10,000 new noncombat positions to women, and in 1988 the army lets women serve in 3,000 new noncombat positions, as well as 6,000 National Guard and 1,700 reserve jobs.

In 1988 Congress approves a memorial to the 10,000 women who served in the armed forces in Vietnam.

During the 1989 military action in Panama, Capt. Linda L. Bray makes headlines when she leads 30 military police to take over a supposedly lightly guarded kennel for attack dogs. Only after a three-hour firefight

The First to Receive Stars

In 1970 Anna Mae Hays, the head of the Army Nurse Corps, is the first woman brigadier general; in the same ceremony Elizabeth P. Hoisington, WAC director, is made a brigadier general.

In 1971 Jeanne Holm, WAF director, is promoted to brigadier general, as is Ethel Ann Hoefly, Air Force Nurse Corps head, a few months later.

In 1972 Alene B. Duerk, head of the Navy Nurse Corps, becomes the first woman rear admiral (lower half).

In 1973 Jeanne Holm of the air force is the first woman major general.

In 1976 Fran McKee is the first female line officer, rather than nurse, in the navy to achieve the rank of rear admiral.

When WAC is dissolved as a separate division in the army in 1978, its last commander, Mary Clarke, becomes the first female major general in the army. In the same year Margaret A. Brewer, who directed the Women Marines before its dissolution in 1977, becomes the first woman brigadier general in the marines.

The first black women brigadier generals are Hazel Winifred Johnson, head of the Army Nurse Corps, in 1979; Sherian Grace Cadora in the regular army in 1985; and Marcelite Jordon Harris in the air force in 1990.

Some Firsts in the 1980s and 1990s

Here are a few of many firsts:

—In 1983 Colleen Nevius is the first female navy test pilot; in 1988, Jacqueline Parker is the first in the air force.

—In 1984 Kristine Holdereid is the first woman to gradaute at the top of her class at a military academy, the U.S. Naval Academy.

—In 1985 Comdr. Roberta L. Hazard is the first woman to head the navy's largest training facility, in Great Lakes, Illinois.

—In 1986 Terrie A. McLaughlin is the first female outstanding cadet at the Air Force Academy.

—In 1989 Kristin Baker is the first woman named captain of the West Point cadet corps.

—In 1990 Cmdr. Rosemary Conatser Mariner is the first woman to head an operational flying squadron (in the navy); Lt. Col. Teresa Marné Peterson is the first woman to command an air force flying training squadron; and Lt. Cmdr. Darlene Iskra is the first woman to command a navy ship, the salvage ship USS Opportune, with long assignments at sea.

—1991 Juliane Gallina is the first female midshipman captain at the U.S. Naval Academy.

—In 1995 Lt. Rebecca Marier is the first female at the top of her class at the West Point academy. "I'm just glad to be part of the progress women are making all over the country," she says.

do she and her battalion achieve their objective. Later, however, Bray resigns due to negative responses by other army officers. Two other women, helicopter pilots Lisa Kutschera and Debra Mann, also come under heavy fire and receive the Air Medal with a "V" for valor in 1990.

During the 1991 Persian Gulf War up to 40,000 U.S. military women serve in the combat area, flying in troops and supplies, maintaining equipment, running communications systems, firing Patriot missiles, and performing other "noncombat" jobs. Eleven women are killed in the war, and two, Maj. Rhonda Cornum (an army physician) and Sp4c. Melissa Rathbun-Nealy (an army truck driver), are taken prisoner.

Passed late in 1991, Public Law 102-190 lifts the ban on women flying combat planes in the air force and navy. It also sets up a commission to study an end to other restrictions and allows the defense secretary to waive combat exclusions for test purposes.

After the 1991 annual meeting of the Tailhook Association of navy aviators in Las Vegas, women report being pawed while forced to run a gauntlet, as well as other instances of sexual assault. Frustrated when the navy fails to act on the complaints, Lt. Paula Coughlin brings the scandal to public attention in 1992. The secretary of the navy resigns and a number of officers are reprimanded, but a top admiral who was present retires at full pension. In 1994 Coughlin wins $6.7 million in damages from the Hilton Hotels for inadequate security, but she finds it impossible to continue her career in the navy.

Col. Margarethe Cammermeyer, chief nurse in the Washington National Guard and a Bronze Star Vietnam War vet, is dismissed in 1992 because she is a lesbian. A federal judge orders her reinstated in 1994.

By 1993 women are almost 12% of the armed forces: 15% of the air force, 12.5% of the army, 10.7% of the navy, 8% of the Coast Guard, and 4.4% of the marines. Almost half are African American.

In 1993 the secretary of defense approves the use of women as combat pilots and aboard combat ships. The USS *Eisenhower* is the first navy warship to take on a mixed crew, in 1994.

Sheila Widnall is the first female secretary of the air force in 1993.

The memorial for female Vietnam War veterans, designed by Glenna Goodacre, is unveiled in 1994.

The navy and air force assign their first female combat pilots in 1994; the army assigned its first in 1993.

In 1994 Congress approves a Women's Center in the Department of Veterans Affairs.

In 1995, after a long court fight, Shannon Faulkner is the first woman to enter The Citadel, a 152-year-old South Carolina military college. Although she—along with several male cadets—drops out in the first week, another young woman, Nancy Mellette, vows to take her place.

Exploration and Adventure

Mazamas, a climbing club, ascending Mt. Hood in 1913 (Angelus Studio Collection #1094, Special Collections, University of Oregon Library, Eugene)

Two Native Women on Expeditions

In 1805 Sacagawea and her newly born son travel with the Lewis and Clark expedition from North Dakota to the Pacific. Not only does she help Toussaint Charbonneau (the French-Canadian who had purchased her as a wife) in his work as interpreter and guide, but she also obtains needed horses from her brother, a Shoshone leader; rescues important equipment when a canoe overturns; and on the return trip shows the group a shortcut through the Big Hole (Bozeman Pass). Her very presence helps ensure the group's peaceful passage through Native lands.

In 1811–12 Marie Dorion (later LaGuivoise, c. 1790–c. 1850), an Iowa Indian, travels with her two young sons and her husband, an interpreter, on an expedition traveling overland 3,500 miles from St. Louis to Astoria in Oregon. Later, on a bear-hunting trip in 1814, she and her children are the only ones to survive an Indian attack. She sets out for Astoria but is trapped in a snowstorm. Building a shelter with branches and snow, she and her sons survive for 53 wintry days, eating their horse for food. After further difficulties, she finally makes it to a Wallawalla village.

1500s–1700s

In 1540 Big Eyes, a Wichita woman who was a slave of the Tiguex in Arizona, is captured by the Spanish and becomes part of the Coronado expedition. When the Spanish reach her Texas panhandle homeland in 1541, she escapes to her people. The next year, when Hernando de Soto questions her about her travels with Coronado, she draws a map in the dirt, which is copied and sent to European mapmakers.

The first white woman in North America is Francesca Hinestrosa, killed in a Chickasaw attack on de Soto's group in Florida in 1541.

In 1587 Virginia Dare is the first English child born in America, on Roanoke Island in Virginia (later North Carolina). Soon after her birth her grandfather, Governor John White, leaves for England, and when he returns in 1591 there is no trace of the settlement.

The first permanent English women settlers arrive in Jamestown, Virginia, in 1607; the first African women arrive there in 1619. By 1620 the Virginia Company is shipping potential wives to the colony. To the north, in Massachusetts, Mary Chilton is the first Pilgrim woman to step ashore at Plymouth Rock in 1620. Quaker women missionaries travel through the colonies beginning in the 1650s (see "Religion").

An early travel diary comes from Sarah Kemble Knight (1666–1727), who sets out on horseback from Boston to New York in 1704.

Possibly the first white woman to see the Ohio River is Mary Draper Ingles, captured by Indians in 1755. She escapes, taking a knife, tomahawk, and blanket, and travels 700 miles to her West Virginia home.

In 1775 the recently widowed María Feliciana Arballo y Gutiérrez joins an expedition from Tubac, Arizona, across the desert 1,600 miles to San Gabriel, California (where she remarries and stays).

1800–49

In 1825 Madame Johnson is the first known woman balloonist in America, taking off in New York and landing in a New Jersey marsh.

Eliza Hart Spalding (1807–51) and Narcissa Prentiss Whitman (1808–47), Presbyterian missionaries traveling with their husbands to Oregon, are the first white women to cross the continental divide, at South Pass, Wyoming, in 1836. They ride sidesaddle much of the trip. The Spaldings start a mission among the Nez Perce in Idaho; the Whitmans try to convert the Cayuse in Washington but are later killed by them.

In the 1840s and 1850s, many women traveling overland to California and Oregon record their experiences in diaries (see sidebar opposite). Often women give birth on the journey, and many die en route.

1850–99

After living alone for 18 years on San Nicholas Island off the California coast, Juana Maria (c. 1815–53) is "rescued" by some hunters. Her people were brought to the mainland by Father Junipero Serra in 1835, but she was left behind. When she arrives at the Santa Barbara mission, no one understands her language, and she soon dies of dysentery.

In 1856, sailing from New York around Cape Horn to San Francisco, Mary Ann Patten (1837–61) takes command of her husband's clipper ship when he becomes ill and uses the skills she has learned on a previous trip to safely plot its course. She is pregnant at the time.

Wearing bloomers, Julia Archibald Holmes (1838–87) climbs the 14,110-foot Pikes Peak in Colorado with her husband and two other men in 1858. She writes to her mother: "In all probability I am the first woman who has ever stood on the summit of this mountain and gazed upon this wondrous scene, which my eyes now behold."

When the 1862 Homestead Act gives land in the West to anyone who clears and settles on it, some women make claims.

In 1865 Elizabeth Cary Agassiz joins the Thayer Expedition to Brazil. She is just one example of the women in the sciences who travel into wilderness areas (see "Science").

In 1867 Frances S. Case and Mary Robinson, climbing with men, are the first white women to ascend the 11,235-foot Mt. Hood in Oregon.

Addie Alexander is the first white woman to climb the 14,256-foot Longs Peak in Colorado, in 1871. Two years later the well-known orator Anna Dickinson rides most of the way to the top.

When the Appalachian Mountain Club forms in 1876, 10% of its members are female. Similar clubs also welcome women, such as the Sierra Club in California (1892) and the Mazamas in Oregon (1895).

In 1875, dressed in men's clothes, "Calamity Jane," or Martha Canary (later Burk, c. 1852–1903), leaves her brothel to join a geological expedition to the Black Hills. She later hangs out with "Wild Bill" Hickok and becomes famous in dime novels, as the fictionalized daring partner of "Deadwood Dick." Her real exploits are hard to pin down. She probably helps drive ox teams and nurses miners in a smallpox epidemic, but it is unlikely that she fights Indians or drives a stagecoach, as she claims.

Starting in 1877, Carrie Green Strahorn travels through the West with her husband as he gathers information for promotional booklets for the railroad. She describes her experience in *Fifteen Thousand Miles by Stage: A Woman's Unique Experience during Thirty Years of Path Finding and Pioneering from Missouri to the Pacific and from Alaska to Mexico* (1911).

On her first balloon ascent in 1880, in Little Falls, New York, Mary ("Carlotta") Breed Hawley Myers releases homing pigeons to indicate her flight's progress. In the next 10 years she sets a record for ascents.

In 1883 Eliza Ruhamah Scidmore travels on the first passenger ship in what is now Glacier Bay National Park, where the Scidmore Glacier is named after her. She later writes a guidebook and is the first woman on the board of management of the National Geographic Society.

"A Frightful Place"

"I've often been asked if we did not suffer with fear in those days but I've said we did not have sense enough to realize our danger we just had the time of our lives but since I've grown older and could realize the danger and the feelings of the mothers, I often wonder how they really lived through it all and retained their reason."
    —Nancy Hembree Snow Bogart

"[Here is] a worse place than we ever had before us to be crossed, called Bridge Creek. I presume it takes its name from a natural bridge which crosses it. This bridge is only wide enough to admit one person at a time. A frightful place, with the water roaring and tumbling ten or fifteen feet below it. This bridge is composed of rocks, and all around us, it is nothing but a solid mass of rocks, with the water ripping and tearing over them. Here we have to unload all the wagons and pack everything by hand, and then we are only on an island. There is a worse place to cross yet. . . ."
    —Amelia Stewart Knight; both in Lillian Schlissel, *Women's Diaries of the Westward Journey* (New York: Schocken Books, 1982)

Two Mountaineers

Fanny Bullock Workman (1859–1925) and her husband, William, start with biking trips, touring Algeria in 1895, then Ceylon and Southeast Asia, as well as 14,000 miles in India (described in her book Through Town and Jungle*). In 1899 they begin a series of expeditions to map the unexplored Karakorum range in the northwest Himalayas. Workman sets an altitude record for women by climbing the 21,000-foot Mt. Koser Gunga in 1903 and another in 1906, when she ascends a 23,300-foot peak in the Nun Kun range in the Himalayas. This record stands until 1934. She details her observations in books such as* Peaks and Glaciers of Nun Kun.*

Annie Smith Peck (1850–1935) gains attention in 1895 when she wears knickerbockers rather than long skirts to climb the Matterhorn in Switzerland. She sets an altitude record in the Americas in 1897, as the first woman to climb 18,314-foot Mt. Orizaba in Mexico. In 1908 she is the first to scale the north peak of Mt. Huascarán in the Peruvian Andes; this peak is named Cumbre Aña Peck in her honor. She believes she has set an altitude record, but Fanny Workman sends scientists to triangulate the peak, which is 21,812 feet (under Workman's record). In 1911, at the age of 61, Peck is the first to climb Peru's 21,250-foot Mt. Coropuna, where she places a pennant: "Votes for women."

Annie Oakley (Phoebe Ann Moses, 1860–1926) tours with Buffalo Bill Cody's Wild West Show beginning in 1885. Known as "Peerless Lady Wing-Shot," she fires at dimes thrown in the air, blasts a cigarette from her husband's mouth, shoots out candle flames as she races past standing on her horse, and riddles a playing card before it reaches the ground (punched-out tickets are thus called "Annie Oakleys").

Journalist "Nellie Bly" gains attention for going around the world in under 80 days in 1889–90 (see "Journalism").

In 1890 Fay Fuller, climbing with four men, is the first known woman atop 14,410-foot Mt. Rainier (then Mt. Tacoma) in Washington. "I expect to have my example followed by a good many women," she says.

In 1890 Harriet Chalmers Adams (1875–1937) takes the first of many trips through Central and South America, often going where no white woman has been before. During her lifetime she travels some 100,000 miles, from Alaska to Tierra del Fuego, making a number of trips alone. From 1907 she describes her expeditions in *National Geographic*.

In 1891, carrying a banner *"Noli me tangere,"* May French Sheldon (1847–1936) leads her own expedition from Mobasa to Kilimanjaro in East Africa. She later describes her trip in *Sultan to Sultan* (1892).

When Mary Bong (1880–1958) arrives is Sitka, Alaska, in 1895, she is probably the first Chinese woman in the territory. Later she becomes the area's first woman troller, operating her 18-foot salmon boat alone.

1900–19

To win a reward and save her Texas ranch, Anna Edson Taylor is the first woman to survive going over Niagara's Horseshoe Falls alone in a barrel, in 1901.

In 1909, with three female passengers, Alice Huler Ramsey is the first female to drive a car cross-country, from New York to San Francisco, in 41 days with 11 tire changes. Also, the Woman's Motoring Club holds the first all-female auto race, from New York to Philadelphia and back.

Mary Blair Rice Beebe (later Blair Niles, 1880–1959) and her husband, C. William, coauthor *Our Search for a Wilderness* (1910), on their trips to Venezuela and British Guiana. She then goes to the Far East and in 1927 is the first white woman to visit the penal colony Devil's Island.

Nan Jane Aspinall is the first known woman to ride across the country alone on horseback, from San Francisco to New York, in 1910–11.

Millionaire Margaret ("Molly") Brown becomes a national hero when, as the *Titanic* sinks in 1912, she hurries children and women into lifeboats, gives most of her voluminous layers of clothing to freezing passengers, and bullies the crew and others into rowing (she helps as well).

In 1912 Osa Leighty Johnson (1894–1953) joins her husband, Martin, on the first of many trips to the Pacific islands to film native people. Later they travel to Africa to film wildlife (see 1940).

"To go whither we knew not"—Mary Lee Jobe

Mary Lee Jobe (later Akeley, 1878–1966) explores and helps map the Canadian Rockies from 1913 to 1918. A peak in the area is later named Mount Jobe in her honor (see also 1926).

In 1913 Georgia ("Tiny") Broadwick is the first person to parachute freefall from an airplane, near San Diego.

Two sisters, Adeline and Augusta Van Buren, are the first women to ride motorcycles across the country, from Brooklyn to San Francisco, in 1916. Their intent is to show that women are fit enough to serve in the armed forces should the United States enter World War I.

1920–39

In 1921 Bessie Coleman (1893–1926), unable to earn a U.S. license because she is African American, is the first U.S. woman to qualify for an international pilot's license, from the Fedération Aéronautique Internationale in 1921. Later, as a popular barnstormer in U.S. airshows, she insists on performing for desegregated audiences. Flying without a seatbelt, she is thrown from her plane at 2,000 feet in 1926 and dies.

Phoebe Fairgrave (later Omlie, 1902–75) is in 1921 the first woman to do a double parachute jump, opening one chute, cutting loose, then opening another. In 1922 she sets an altitude record when she jumps from 15,200 feet during an airshow (see also sidebar, next page).

Grace Gallatin Thompson Seton (1872–1959) describes her travels and the women she encounters in *A Woman Tenderfoot in Egypt* (1923) and *Chinese Lanterns* (1924). Subsequent trips take her to India, then Brazil. In *Magic Words* (1933) she details her journey alone from Brazil to Peru, Bolivia, and the western coast. She next travels to Southeast Asia.

After being imprisoned in Russia as a spy (p. 261), Marguerite Baker Harrison in 1924 helps make the documentary *Grass*, following the Bakntiari tribe as they move from their winter to their summer grazing grounds in Persia. She later describes her adventures in *There's Always Tomorrow: The Story of a Checkered Life* (1935).

In 1924 Delia J. Denning Akeley (1875–1970), who has traveled extensively in Africa with her ex-husband Carl Akeley, is the first woman to lead a museum-sponsored trip to collect animal specimens in Africa. Employed by the Brooklyn Museum, she crosses Kenya and the Somali desert, then lives several months with the Pygmies in the Congo.

Harriet Chalmers Adams, Marguerite Harrison, Blair Niles, and Grace Seton set up the Society of Women Geographers in 1925.

When Carl Akeley dies on an expedition to Africa in 1926, Mary Jobe Akeley, his second wife, takes charge, photographing animals and helping to map parts of Kenya, Tanganyika, and the Congo. Later, in 1935, she leads her own expedition to Africa for New York's Museum of Natural History; she crusades for wildlife preserves in Africa.

Some of the Early Aviators

Among the first women aviators are the following:

—Bessica Raiche, the first woman to fly solo, in 1910 in a plane built of bamboo, wire, and silk by her husband.

—Journalist Harriet Quimby, the first U.S. woman to receive a pilot's license, in 1911; in 1912 she is the first woman to fly across the English Channel but is later killed at a Boston flying meet, when she is thrown from her plane at 6,000 feet.

—Blanche Scott, who flies cross-country in 69 days in 1912 and joins the barnstorming circuit as a stunt pilot, diving 4,000 feet before leveling out at 200 feet or flying upside down at 20 feet.

—Katherine Stinson (later Otero) and her sister Marjorie, who teach pilots at the family flying school in San Antonio, Texas, in 1915; Katherine gives flight demonstrations in China and Japan in 1917.

—Anna Low, the first Chinese American woman aviator, flying in San Francisco in 1919; the first to earn her pilot's license, however, is Kathryn Cheung, in 1931.

Early Air Races

Here are a few of the first races:

—The first cross-country women's air derby, sometimes called the powder puff derby, is held in 1929. The women fly solo, without mechanics, 2,350 miles from Santa Monica to Cleveland. The winner in the heavier-plane class is Louise McPhetridge Thaden (c. 1905–79), who already holds the women's altitude, speed, and endurance records. Her flying time is just over 20 hours 19 minutes. The winner in the light-plane class is Phoebe Omlie, with a flying time of 24 hours, 12 minutes. Of the 20 who enter, 15 finish, but Marvel Crosson dies when her parachute fails to open.

—In 1931 Phoebe Omlie scores the highest points in the first air race between women and men, in Cleveland.

—In 1935 Jacqueline Cochran (c. 1910–80) is the first woman to enter the Bendix Transcontinental Air Race, from Los Angeles to New York, and in 1936 Louise Thaden and her copilot, Blanche Noyes, are the first women to win the race. Cochran wins in 1938 and sets over 200 flying records in her lifetime (see also 1953).

Miriam O'Brien (later Underhill) is, in 1927, the first person to traverse the pass now called the Via Miriam in the Dolomites. In 1929 she leads the first traverse of the Aiguille de Grépon in France; in 1931 she and a European woman make the first all-female ascent of the Matterhorn.

After a failed attempt by Ruth Elder in 1927, Amelia Earhart (later Putnam, 1897–1937) is in 1928 the first woman to fly, with two men, across the Atlantic. An instant hero, she is given a ticker-tape parade on her return, although she insists that she just kept the log.

In 1929 women pilots form the Ninety-Nines Club, with Amelia Earhart as president. The name comes from the 99 of the 126 licensed U.S. women pilots who join. By 1994 the club has 6,400 members.

Florence ("Pancho") Lowe Barnes (1901–75) is a stunt pilot for the movie *Hell's Angels* (1929); in 1930 she sets a women's speed record, flying just over 196 mph.

1930–49

In 1930 Anne Spencer Morrow Lindbergh is the first woman to gain a glider's license. Flying with her husband, Charles, and making only one stop, she helps set a transcontinental speed record, from California to Long Island, in 1930. Later, in 1934, she receives a gold medal from the National Geographic Society after she and her husband fly 40,000 miles over five continents to map out air routes.

In a bathysphere in 1931, Gloria Hollister (later Anable, 1903–88) descends 1,208 feet underwater, a record for women. In 1936, flying a light plane in British Guiana, she finds 43 uncharted waterfalls.

In 1931 heiress Louise Arner Boyd (1887–1972), on her third Arctic trip, sights an area of Greenland later named after her. Increasingly interested in the scientific exploration, she heads her own expeditions, conducts observations, and is the first woman to receive the Cullum Medal of the American Geographical Society, in New York in 1938.

Amelia Earhart is the first woman to fly solo across the Atlantic in 1932. Piloting a Lockheed Vega monoplane, she flies from Newfoundland to Ireland in just under 15 hours. Congress awards her the Distinguished Flying Cross. Three years later, in 1935, she makes the first solo flight from Hawaii to the U.S. mainland, as well as the first nonstop flight from Mexico City to Newark, New Jersey.

Balloon pilot Jeannette Piccard and her huband, Jean, ascend to the stratosphere, reaching a record of nearly 57,600 feet, in 1934. Later, in 1974, she is one of the first female Episcopal priests (see "Religion").

Attempting a round-the-world flight in 1937, Amelia Earhart and her navigator, Freddie Noonan, disappear on the leg between New Guinea and Howland Island. Neither the plane nor the passengers are found.

In *Enchanted Vagabonds* (1938), Ginger and Dana Lamb describe a 1,600-mile canoe trip from San Diego to the Panama Canal.

In her best-selling autobiography, *I Married Adventure* (1940), Osa Johnson describes her adventures first in the South Seas and then in Africa, where she and her husband made such films as *Wonders of the Congo* (1931). In 1941 she makes the film *African Paradise*.

In 1941 Elizabeth ("Betsy") Strong Cowles (later Partridge, 1902–74) is in the first group to climb several peaks in the Santa Marta range in northern Columbia, including La Reina (over 18,000 feet).

As a women's auxiliary pilot during World War II, Ann Baumgartner (later Carl) is the first woman to fly an experimental jet plane, reaching 350 mph at 35,000 feet, in 1944.

In 1947 Ann Shaw Carter is the first woman licensed to fly a helicopter. She becomes one of 13 founding members of the first association of female helicopter pilots, the Whirly Girls, in 1955.

1950–69

Jacqueline Cochran is the first woman to break the sound barrier, in 1953. She also sets new speed records for the 15-km, 100-km, and 500-km courses. Later records include an altitude record of 55,253 feet in 1961 and a women's speed record of 1,429 mph in 1964.

Chartering a plane, Louise Boyd is the first woman to fly over the North Pole, in 1955.

In 1960 Jerrie Cobb passes all 75 qualifying tests for the astronaut progam but is rejected by the National Aeronautics and Space Administration (NASA), which is not ready for female astronauts. Cobb holds several women's records, including longest nonstop flight, from Guatemala City to Oklahoma City (1957), and highest altitude at 37,010 feet (1960), although Jacqueline Cochran surpasses this in 1961.

Jerrie Mock (born Geraldine Fredritz) is the first woman to fly solo around the world, in 1964. In 29½ days, with 21 stopovers, she flies almost 22,860 miles.

In 1968 Jeanne Gurnee is the only woman on an expedition that uncovers an ancient Mayan ceremonial cave in Guatemala. In 1992 she is the first woman president of the National Speleological Society.

When Sharon Sites Adams sails the 31-foot *Sea Harp* from Yokohama, Japan, to San Diego in 1969, she is the first woman to sail solo across the Pacific. It takes nearly 75 days.

1970–95

In 1970 Grace Hoeman, Arlene Blum, and four other women are the first all-female team to reach the top of 20,320-foot Mt. McKinley (Denali) in Alaska.

Kitty O'Neil, a top Hollywood stunt person who is totally deaf, sets a 1976 land speed record for women, traveling 322 mph in a rocket-powered three-wheel vehicle. Earlier she set a waterskiing speed record, going almost 105 mph in 1970.

Records in the Air

These are some 1930s records:

—Ruth Nichols (1901–60), the first woman with an international hydroplane license (1924), makes a record-breaking cross-country flight in 1930, shaving almost four hours off the previous women's record with a flying time of just under 17 hours. On the return flight, with 13 hours 22 minutes in the air, she averages almost 200 mph. In 1931 she sets a women's altitude record of 28,743 feet, speed record of 210.7 mph, and distance record, flying nonstop from Oakland, California, to Louisville, Kentucky.

—Florence Gunderson Klingensmith flies through 1,078 loops nonstop in 4.5 hours in 1931. Two years later she is killed in an air race when she stays with her failing plane, steering it away from a crowd below, rather than parachuting to safety.

—In 1933 Helen Richey and Frances Marsalis fly continuously (with refueling) for almost 10 days. In 1934 Richey is the first U.S. woman to fly as an airmail courier, although she resigns when she is limited to fair-weather flying.

—In 1935 Laura Ingalls, who initially earned notice as a stunt pilot, is the first woman to fly across the country nonstop east to west, from Brooklyn to Burbank. Later she is convicted of being a Nazi agent.

Women in Space

NASA accepts its first six women for astronaut training in 1978: physician Anna L. Fisher, biochemist Shannon W. Lucid, electrical engineer Judith A. Resnik, physicist Sally K. Ride, physician Margaret Rhea Seddon, and geologist Kathryn D. Sullivan.

In 1983 Sally K. Ride is the first woman in space, spending six days aboard the Challenger.

In 1984 Kathryn Sullivan is the first woman to walk in space. Also in 1984 Judith Resnik is mission specialist on the first flight of the orbiter Discovery, and Anna L. Fisher is the first mother in space.

Margaret Seddon makes her first space flight in 1985.

In 1986 the space shuttle Challenger explodes about a minute after liftoff, killing all seven astronauts, including Judith Resnik and schoolteacher Christa McAuliffe, chosen as the first civilian in space.

Physician Mae C. Jemison, who qualifies as an astronaut in 1988, is the first African American woman in space, in 1992.

Physicist Ellen Ochoa, who qualifies as an astronaut in 1990, is the first Latina in space, in 1993.

In 1995 Eileen M. Collins, who qualifies as a space-shuttle pilot in 1990, is the first female to pilot a spacecraft.

In 1978 Arlene Blum leads the first all-woman and first U.S. team to climb the 26,540-foot Annapurna in the Himalayas. At the summit Irene Miller and Vera Komarkova stick a banner claiming: "A woman's place is on top." Unfortunately, two women, Alison Chadwick and Vera Watson, die in a fall at the last stage. Blum describes the trip in *Annapurna: A Woman's Place* (1980).

In 1980 Janice Brown flies the first solar-powered plane, *Solar Challenger*, six miles in 22 minutes in Arizona.

Eleanor Conn and her husband, Sidney, are the first to fly a hot-air balloon, *Joy of Sound*, over the North Pole, in 1980.

In 1981 the 76-year-old Explorers Club admits its first women: astronaut Kathryn Sullivan, and record-holding deep-sea diver Sylvia Earle.

Alice Hager, a 63-year-old Nisei nurse, sails solo from the West Coast to Japan in 1984 after a practice run to Hawaii in 1983.

Ann Bancroft, on an expedition with five men, is the first woman to reach the North Pole without mechanical support, in 1986. The group skis and uses dog sleds for the 1,000 miles from Ward Hunt Island.

In 1986 Jeana Yeager and copilot Dick Rutan are the first to fly around the world without stopping or refueling. It takes just over nine days to cover the 26,000 miles in the *Voyager*, a specially designed plane, lighter than a car but with a wing span wider than that of a Boeing 727.

After a two-year trip Tania Aebi is the first U.S. woman to sail solo around the world, in 1987. At one point she collided with a freighter.

Accompanied only by her dog, Charlie, Helen Thayer is the first woman to ski solo to the North Magnetic Pole, in 1988. She covers 345 miles in 27 days and survives temperatures of −48°F.

In 1988 stunt pilot Joann Osterud sets a record, flying in continuous loops for two hours. In 1991 she flies upside down for four hours.

Stacy Allison is the first U.S. woman to reach the top of the 29,028-foot Mt. Everest, in 1988.

In 1989, with nine others, Victoria Murden and Shirley Metz ski 740 miles in 51 days to become the first women and first Americans to reach the South Pole overland.

On a 1992 U.S. women's trans-Antarctic venture, Ann Bancroft, Sue Geller, Anne Dal Vera, and Sunniva Sorby don't make it across but do trek 660 miles to the South Pole without using motor vehicles or dogs.

In 1993, at age 11, Vicki Van Meter is the youngest female to fly cross-country, but her record is broken in 1994 by Rachel Carter, age 9. Van Meter is the youngest female to fly across the Atlantic, in 1994.

Merrick Johnston, age 12, is the youngest girl to climb Mt. McKinley, in 1995, beating Tara Genet's 1991 record by a few months.

Sports

Mildred ("Babe") Didrikson (UPI/Bettmann)

Early Recreation

One of the first to advocate some form of physical education for girls is Catharine Beecher (p. 170), who introduces calisthenics in the mid-1820s. In the 1850s the main recreational activity for middle- to upper-class women is riding, with the emphasis on grace and elegance, as set forth in The Lady's Equestrian Manual (1854). By 1859 ice skating is a popular sport for both women and men, with crowds of up to 50,000 congregating in New York's Central Park, for example. In the 1860s croquet becomes a popular game.

Later, in the 1880s and 1890s, bicycling becomes a major fad. In A Wheel within a Wheel (1895), WCTU leader Frances E. Willard (p. 147) describes learning to ride a bicycle at age 53. "The bicycle meets all the conditions [of congenial exercise] and will ere long come within the reach of all," she writes. "Therefore, in obedience to the laws of health, I learned to ride. I also wanted to help women to a wider world, for I hold that the more interests women and men have in common, in thought, word, and deed, the happier will it be for the home."

1860–99

Gymnastics lessons are given by Miss Evans at Mount Holyoke Seminary in 1862, and in 1866 Vassar women start two baseball clubs. The Vassar prospectus lists calisthenics, swimming, skating, and gardening as part of its physical education curriculum.

Possibly the first American ski races for women and girls are held in the California Sierras in 1867.

In 1874, after learning tennis on a trip to Bermuda, Mary Ewing Outerbridge brings back the necessary equipment—balls, rackets, nets, and rules—and sets up the first court in Staten Island. In 1881 the U.S. Lawn Tennis Association (USLTA) is organized.

The first "professional" (paid) women's baseball game is held between the Blondes and Brunettes in Springfield, Illinois, in 1875. Also called the Reds and Blues, they tour and entertain spectators for 10 years.

Wellesley College introduces rowing as a sport in 1875, but there is no real competition among women until 1938.

In the 1880s women's archery clubs are started. In 1882 Lydia Scott Howell wins the first of her 17 national archery championships.

The first known track and field events for women are in 1882 by the Boston YWCA. Vassar introduces the first college field day in 1895.

Ellen Forde Hansell wins the first USLTA women's singles tennis championship in 1887. Bertha Townsend wins in 1888 and 1889.

The first mention of U.S. women playing golf is in 1889; by 1895 there are at least 100 women golfers, and the U.S. Golf Association sponsors the first women's national tournament in Long Island. Mrs. Charles Brown wins with a score of 132 for 18 holes.

Physical education instructor Senda Berenson introduces basketball at Smith College in 1892 and prepares the official rule book in 1899. Designed to limit women's physical exertion, her rules confine each player to a third of the court. Although this extended to half the court in 1914, not until the 1970s do women play full-court basketball.

One of the first "bloomer girls" baseball teams starts in Wapakoneta, Ohio, in 1892. These barnstorming teams tour the country, challenging local men's teams. Occasionally they play each other.

Stanford beats the University of California, Berkeley, in the first intercollegiate women's basketball game, in 1896. No men can watch.

Elizabeth H. Moore wins the first of four national women's singles tennis championships (1896, 1901, 1903, 1905).

1900–19

At the first Olympics to include women athletes, in 1900, Margaret Abbot wins a gold medal for the United States in golf, a sport that is discontinued in the Olympics after 1904.

British-born Constance M. K. Applebee introduces field hockey to U.S. women's colleges in 1901, and the first field hockey club is started in Philadelphia.

At the 1904 Olympics in St. Louis, Lydia Scott Howell wins three gold medals in archery (an unofficial sport).

Amanda Clement is a paid umpire for men's semiprofessional baseball in Iowa in 1904. She works in several states for the next four years.

British-born May Sutton (later Bundy, 1887–1975), raised in California, wins the women's singles title at Wimbledon in 1905, when she also wins the USLTA women's singles.

In 1906 Ada Evans Dean takes her jockey's place and rides her horse to a first-place finish in Liberty, New York; in 1907 Dorothy Tyler rides her horse to victory in a race in Joplin, Missouri.

For three years straight (1909–11) tennis star Hazel Hotchkiss (later Wightman, 1886–1974) wins the USLTA women's singles and doubles tournaments; she also wins the mixed doubles in 1909–11. She wins the singles again in 1919 and the doubles in 1915, 1924, and 1928.

Mary K. Browne wins three USLTA tennis singles titles (1912–14).

The first national fencing championship for women is in 1912.

In 1914 the first national figure-skating championships are held, with Theresa Weld (later Blanchard) winning six singles and nine pairs titles between 1914 and 1927; she also wins a bronze at the 1920 Olympics.

The Amateur Athletic Union (AAU) lets women register in swimming in 1914. The first national swim championships include the 100-, 220-, 440-, and 880-yard and 1-mile freestyle. By 1920 breaststroke and backstroke events are added. The butterfly is only introduced in 1954.

In 1915 Molla Bjurstedt (later Mallory) wins the first of eight U.S. national tennis singles championships (1915–18, 1920–22, 1926).

In St. Louis 40 women start the Women's International Bowling Congress (WIBC) in 1916, and 100 women compete in its first bowling tournament in 1917. By the mid-1920s there are almost 5,000 members; by 1965 there are 3 million.

In 1917 Lucy Diggs Slowe (1885–1936) wins the first national women's singles tennis tournament of the American Tennis Association, formed in 1916 for black players, who are excluded from the USLTA.

1920–29

At the 1920 Olympics, 14-year-old Aileen Riggin wins the first women's springboard diving event; Helen Wainwright and Thelma Payne take the silver and bronze. Ethelda Bleibtrey, who started swimming after a bout of polio, earns gold medals in the 100-m, 400-m, and relay freestyle events, setting a world record in the 100-m. Her relay partners Irene Guest and Frances Schroth win silver and bronze in the 100-m,

Early Baseball Stars

Described as a "phenomenal pitcher" by the Oregonian *in 1897, Maud Nelson (later Olson, then Dellacqua, 1881–1944), born Clementina Brida, is the starting pitcher for the Boston Bloomer Girls and also plays third base. In 1908 she plays with men on the Cherokee Indian Base Ball Team. In 1911 she forms the Western Bloomer Girls with six women and three men. She and co-owner Kate Becker share the pitching. Once the team is successful, she sells her share to Becker and starts another team, building up several women's baseball teams.*

At age 22, Elizabeth Stride, known as Lizzie Arlington, pitches for the Philadelphia Reserves and is the first woman signed to a minor league contract. She is soon dismissed, however, when she fails to draw large crowds. She then plays on a bloomer team.

Alta Weiss (1890–1964) joins the semiprofessional Vermilion Independents in Ohio as the pitcher. In 1908 she is the main attraction of the Weiss All-Stars, owned by her father.

Mary Elizabeth ("Lizzie") Murphy (1894–1964) signs up as first baseman on Ed Carr's All-Stars of Boston in 1918. Her name is printed in big letters on her uniform so fans can't miss it. In 1928 she is the first woman to play against a major league team, in an exhibition game.

At the 1924 Olympics gold medals go to Ethel Lackie in the 100-m freestyle, Martha Norelius in the 400-m freestyle, Sybil Bauer in the 100-m backstroke, Elizabeth Becker in the springboard dive, and Caroline Smith in the platform dive. The U.S. team of Gertrude Ederle, Euphrasia Donnelly, Ethel Lackie, and Mariechen Wehselau also wins the freestyle relay. In addition, Ederle wins bronzes in the 100-m and 400-m freestyle; Aileen Riggin, a silver in springboard dive and a bronze in the 100-m backstroke; and Elizabeth Becker a silver in the platform dive. Helen Wills wins the tennis singles and doubles, with Hazel Hotchkiss Wightman; Wightman also wins the mixed doubles.

At the 1928 Olympics, Elizabeth ("Betty") Robinson takes the first 100-m dash event in 12.2 seconds. Martha Norelius is the first woman to win back-to-back golds, in the 400-m freestyle. Albina Osipowich wins the 100-m freestyle, Helen Meany the springboard dive, Elizabeth Becker the platform dive, and Osipowich, Norelius, Eleanor Garratti, and Adelaide Lambert the freestyle relay.

as do Margaret Woodbridge and Schroth in the 400-m. In the winter events Theresa Weld's bronze is the first U.S. figure-skating medal.

The National Women's Athletic Association is organized in 1921, and in 1922 the AAU adds track and field events for women. Other AAU sports open to women in 1923.

The star of the new Philadelphia Bobbies, formed by Mary O'Gara in 1922, is 10-year-old shortstop Edith Houghton.

Sybil Bauer breaks both the men's and women's world records in the 440-yd backstroke in 1922. By 1924 she sets 21 records for women.

The U.S. Field Hockey Association is established in 1922.

Glenna Collett (later Vare) wins the first of six U.S. women's amateur golf championships in 1922. The Vare Trophy, started in 1953 for the woman with the lowest average score in official Ladies Professional Golf Association events, is named in her honor.

Hazel Hotchkiss Wightman and her husband establish the Wightman Cup in 1923. Intended as a counterpart to the Davis Cup for men, it is awarded to the winning team in matches between U.S. and British players. The Americans (with Wightman) win the first tournament.

Helen Wills (later Moody, then Roark) earns the first of seven USLTA women's singles titles (1923–25, 1927–29, 1931). She also gains seven Wimbledon singles titles (1927–30, 1932–33, 1935, 1938) and four French singles titles, plus four U.S., three Wimbledon, and two French doubles events. She also earns gold at the 1924 Olympics (see sidebar).

In 1924 Ora Washington wins the first of 12 successive women's singles titles in the American Tennis Association competitions. She challenges white champion Helen Wills to a game, but Wills refuses.

The Amateur Skating Union sponsors the first national speed-skating championships for women in 1926. Also, the AAU holds the first national basketball tournament for women, with six teams.

In 1926 Gertrude Ederle is the first woman to swim the English Channel. Starting near Calais in France, she battles stormy seas and a strong tide to reach Dover, England. The battering waves, in fact, cause some permanent hearing loss. Ederle's time of 14½ hours shaves almost 2 hours off the previous (man's) record. On her return to New York, she is greeted by a huge ticker-tape parade.

In 1928 Eleanora Sears, a former tennis champion, wins the first U.S. squash racquets tournament, in which 40 women participate.

Maribel Vinson (later Owen) wins the first of nine U.S. singles figure-skating titles in 1928; she also wins six pairs titles from 1928 to 1937.

1930–39
From 1931 to 1940 the *Philadelphia Tribune* basketball team, organized by tennis champion Ora Washington, is the top U.S. women's team.

Already a basketball star, Mildred ("Babe") Didrikson (later Zaharias, c. 1911–56) dominates the 1932 AAU track and field competitions; she wins 5 of the 10 events and ties in another. She then wins two golds and a silver at the 1932 Olympics (below) and is named woman athlete of the year by Associated Press. After her photo is used for a car ad, she is banned from amateur events. She then joins a barnstorming baseball team (earning the nickname "Babe") and later is a golf champion.

At the 1932 Winter Olympics, where speed skating is a demonstration sport, Elizabeth Dubois and Kit Klein win at 1,000 m and 1,500 m respectively. In the summer games Babe Didrikson wins the javelin and 80 m hurdles, her record high jump, using a western roll (or "Fosbury Flop"), is disqualified, so she gets the silver and her teammate Jean Shiley wins the gold. Other gold medalists are Lillian Copeland (discus throw), Georgia Coleman (springboard dive), Dorothy Poynton (later Hill, platform dive), Helene Madison (100-m and 400-m freestyle), and Eleanor Holm (100-m backstroke). Madison sets 17 world records in her freestyle career and is the first woman to swim the 100-yd freestyle in a minute. Louise Stokes and Tydie Pickett are the first two African American women to qualify for the Olympic team, but they are replaced by white women in the games.

The Amateur Softball Association forms in 1932 and holds its first national championships in 1933. The U.S. Women's Lacrosse Association is also started in 1932 and holds its first tournament in 1933.

Former golf champions Harriot and Margaret Curtis establish the Curtis Cup for golf matches between U.S. and British women in 1932.

Helen Hull Jacobs wins her first of four straight U.S. tennis singles at Forest Hills (1932–35). In 1936 she wins at Wimbledon.

Maud Nelson's All Star Ranger Girls, with Margaret Gisolo, Rose Gacioch, Beatrice ("Peanut") Schmidt, and other stars, play their last games in 1934, as softball replaces women's baseball.

Mary Hirsch is the first female licensed trainer of thoroughbreds, in 1934. Her horse "No Sir" races in the Kentucky Derby in 1937.

Although she never wins a singles title, Elizabeth Ryan gains her 19th Wimbledon doubles victory in 1934, a record that holds for 45 years.

Alice Marble gains her first tennis singles title at Forest Hills in 1936; she wins again in 1938–40 and also wins the singles, doubles, and mixed doubles at Wimbledon in 1939.

The Red Heads (named for their red wigs) form as a barnstorming basketball team in 1936. By 1947 they play 180 games a season, traveling 30,000 miles. In 1971 they beat 169 men's teams, using men's rules.

Ruth Hughes Aarons is the first American to win the world singles title in table tennis, in 1936. She also wins mixed doubles in 1934–37.

At the 1936 Olympics, Helen Stephens takes golds in the 100-m dash

Jackie's Coup

Pitcher Virne Beatrice ("Jackie") Mitchell is the second woman to sign a minor league contract, in 1931 for the Chattanooga Lookouts. In a 1931 exhibition game against the New York Yankees, the 17-year-old strikes out Babe Ruth and Lou Gehrig in succession. Soon afterward the U.S. baseball commissioner cancels Mitchell's contract, claiming that the sport is "too strenuous" for women. She continues on the Junior Lookouts and later as a barnstormer.

Jackie Mitchell with Babe Ruth and Lou Gehrig (Chattanooga Regional History Museum)

All-American Girls

In 1943 Philip K. Wrigley starts the All-American Girls Softball (later Baseball) League with four teams (later 10). The league lasts until 1954 and involves about 600 women (African American players are excluded). The women are required to attend charm school, put on makeup, and wear short skirts (hardly conducive to sliding into a base), as depicted in the later film A League of Their Own (1992). A few of the players who stand out are Dorothy Kamenshek, first baseman and star hitter of the Rockford Peaches; Rose Gacioch, a Rockford Peaches outfielder and pitcher who is an old-timer, having played on a bloomer girls team earlier; Sophie Kurys, second baseman for the Racine Belles and top base stealer in the league (stealing 1,114 bases in her eight years at play); Jean Faut, South Bend Blue Sox pitcher, with two perfect games to her credit; and Isabel Alvarez, who played with the Estrellas Cubanas (Cuban Stars) before coming to the United States to play for the Fort Wayne Daisies.

and as part of the relay team. Dorothy Poynton Hill wins the platform dive, and 13-year-old Marjorie Gestring the springboard event.

After Esther Williams wins the 1939 national 100-m freestyle championship, she popularizes synchronized swimming in the movies.

1940–49

Pauline Betz wins the U.S. tennis singles at Forest Hills in 1942–44; in 1946 she wins both at both Forest Hills and Wimbledon (which was not held during World War II). Also, Louise Brough (later Clapp) and Margaret Osborne (later du Pont) begin their winning streak as doubles champions at Forest Hills (1942–50; also 1955–57). Brough wins the U.S. singles in 1947 and Wimbledon in 1948–50 and 1955. Osborne wins singles at Wimbledon in 1947 and Forest Hills in 1948–50.

In 1944 Ann Curtis, with 18 U.S. swimming records, is the first woman to win the AAU Sullivan Award for the year's outstanding athlete.

In 1946 Edith Houghton, a baseball star of the 1920s, is the first woman scout for a major league team, the Philadelphia Phillies.

When the newly formed Women's Professional Golf Association holds its first national tournament in 1946, Patty Berg is the first champion. In 1948, led by Babe Didrikson Zaharias, the group is reformed as the Ladies Professional Golf Association (LPGA).

At the 1948 winter games Gretchen Fraser is the first U.S. skier to win at the Olympics. She gains the gold in the slalom and the silver in the alpine combined event; she also wins the world slalom championship.

In the summer games Alice Coachman is the first black woman to win gold, in the high jump. Ann Curtis gains golds in the 400-m freestyle and as part of the relay team. Victoria ("Vickie") Draves is the first woman to win both the platform and springboard diving events.

1950–59

Marian Ladewig is bowler of the year for the first of nine times (1950–54, 1957–59, 1963). Also, in 1950 she wins the second of nine all-star championships and the Women's International Bowling Congress.

Babe Didrikson Zaharias is named woman athlete of the half-century in an Associated Press poll in 1950. The leading LPGA money winner in 1949–51, she wins the U.S. Women's Open three times.

Althea Gibson is the first African American of either sex to play at the U.S. Open at Forest Hills, in 1950. In 1951 she integrates Wimbledon.

In the American Softball Association, "Blazing Bertha" Tickey strikes out 20 players in a seven-inning game in 1950. In her 23-year career, ending in 1968, she pitches 757 winning games and loses only 88.

After beating Gertrude Ederle's record for the France to England channel swim in 1950, Florence Chadwick is the first female to swim against the tide from England to France, in 1951. She finishes in 16 hours 22 minutes; on her third swim in 1955, she shaves this time to 13 hours 55 minutes. In 1953 she sets records on four crossings: England to France, the Strait of Gibraltar, the Bosphorus (round trip), and the Dardanelles.

In 1951 golfer Elizabeth ("Betsy") Earle Rawls wins her first U.S. Open (also 1953, 1957, 1960); she later wins two LPGA championships.

Tenley Albright, who had polio at age nine, wins the first of four U.S. figure-skating titles (1952–56). In 1953 she is the first U.S. skater to gain the world title, which she wins again in 1955. She takes the Olympic silver in 1952 and the gold in 1956.

At the 1952 winter games, Andrea Mead Lawrence is the first U.S. skier to win two golds in one Olympics, in the slalom and giant slalom (she also holds the world championships in both events). In the summer games Patricia Keller McCormick wins the platform and springboard diving events. The U.S. track relay team also wins.

After winning Forest Hills in 1951 and both Forest Hills and Wimbledon in 1952, Maureen ("Little Mo") Connolly (later Brinker, 1934–69) is the first woman to win the tennis grand slam, taking the French, Wimbledon, U.S., and Australian titles for 1953. She wins Wimbledon again in 1954 but then damages her leg in a riding accident.

"I come to play ball"—Toni Stone

As "Toni Stone," Marcenia Lyle (later Alberga) is the first woman to play baseball in a major league, as second baseman for the Indianapolis Clowns in the Negro American League in 1953. "Big Mo" Aldredge is the first black woman on the national AAU basketball team, in 1953.

In 1954 Judith Devlin Hashman wins the first of 11 U.S. singles badminton titles and the first of 10 All-England titles. With her sister Susan Devlin Peard, she wins 10 U.S. and 6 All-England doubles titles.

After winning the Wimbledon singles in 1951, Doris J. Hart wins the U.S. singles, doubles (with Shirley Fry), and mixed doubles. She wins the U.S. singles again in 1955. Her doubles partner, Shirley Fry, takes both the U.S. and Wimbledon singles in 1956.

In 1955 Willa Worthington McGuire wins a record third world waterskiing overall title (1949–50, 1955) and her eighth overall U.S. title.

Carol Heiss begins her reign as world figure-skating champion (1956–60), following with the U.S. title (1957–60) and Olympic gold (1960).

At the 1956 winter Olympics, Tenley Albright wins the first gold for U.S. figure skater in the women's singles. In the summer games Patricia McCormick wins double golds in springboard and platform diving for the second time—the first woman to do so. Shelley Mann takes the first 100-m butterfly. Mildred McDaniel wins the one track-and-field gold, in the high jump. Nell Cecilia Jackson, a member of the 1948 Olympic team, is the first black coach of the women's track team.

In 1958 Mary Kathryn ("Mickey") Wright wins the first of four LPGA

Althea Gibson (Library of Congress)

Olympics 1968

At the 1968 Winter Olympics, Peggy Fleming wins the figure-skating gold.

At the summer games the first woman to carry the U.S. flag is Janice Lee York Romary, a fencer and Olympic team member from 1948 to 1968. A major star is Wyomia Tyus, the first person to win successive golds in the 100-m dash (she also wins a gold as part of the relay team). Madeline Manning Jackson wins the 800-m run in record time. U.S. swimmers take all three medals in the 100-m freestyle (gold: Jan Henne), 200-m freestyle (gold: Debbie Meyer), and 200-m individual medley (gold: Claudia Kolb). Kolb takes the 400-m individual medley; Kaye Hall the 100-m backstroke; Lillian ("Pokey") Watson the first 200-m backstroke; and Sharon Wichman the 200-m breaststroke. Meyer, who wins the 400-m and first 800-m freestyle in addition to the 200-m, is the first woman to win three individual golds in the same Olympics. U.S. teams win the medley and freestyle relays, and Sue Gossick takes the springboard dive.

championships (1958, 1960–61, 1963) and the first of four U.S. Opens (1958–59, 1961, 1964).

Golfer Patty Berg, the first winner of the U.S. Women's Open in 1946, is the first woman to hit a hole-in-one in the tournament, in 1959. She wins 10 titles plus the Vare Trophy in 1959.

1960–69

At the 1960 Olympics, Carol Heiss wins the figure-skating gold. In the summer Wilma Rudolph, who had polio as a child, is the first U.S. woman to win three gold medals: in the 100-m and 200-m sprints and on the relay team. Lynn Burke wins the 100-m backstroke, Chris von Saltzka the 400-m freestyle, and Carolyn Schuler the 100-m butterfly; U.S. swimmers also win the medley and freestyle relays.

Darlene Hard wins the tennis title at Forest Hills in 1960 and 1961.

In 1961 Mickey Wright is the first woman to win a golf grand slam, taking the LPGA championship, U.S. Open, and Titleholders tournament. She also wins the second of five Vare Trophies (1960–64).

The National Women's Rowing Association is organized in 1962.

Peggy Fleming wins her first of five U.S. figure-skating titles (1964–68); she then wins three world titles (1966–68) and an Olympic gold (1968).

At the 1964 Summer Olympics, Wyomia Tyus wins the 100-m dash, Edith McGuire the 200-m run, Lesley Bush the platform dive, Virginia ("Ginny") Duenkel the 400-m freestyle, Cathy Ferguson the 100-m backstroke, Sharon Stouder the 100-m butterfly, and Donna de Varona the first 400-m individual medley. U.S. swimmers also win both relays. De Varona, with 37 U.S. championships in freestyle, backstroke, and breaststroke by 1965, is the first woman sportscaster on national TV.

Kathryne ("Kathy") Whitworth is the leading LPGA money winner in 1965 and again in 1967–73. She also wins her first of seven Vare Trophies (1965–67, 1969–72). The first LPGA Player of the Year in 1966, she is selected six more times (1967–69, 1971–73).

In 1966 Billie Jean Moffitt King wins her first Wimbledon singles. In 1967 she wins both the U.S. and Wimbledon singles, doubles, and mixed doubles—the first such sweep since 1938. In all she wins 20 Wimbledon titles during her career (6 singles, 10 doubles, and 4 mixed doubles). Her main doubles partner is Rosemary Casals.

In 1967 German-born K. Switzer secretly enters the Boston Marathon. When an official realizes that "K" stands for "Kathrine," he tries to tear off her number, but she avoids him and finishes the race.

In 1968 Kathy Kusner is the first female jockey licensed to race thoroughbreds at major tracks. In her first race, in 1969, she finishes third. On the equestrian jumping team, she gains silver at the 1972 Olympics.

Janet Lynn wins her first of five U.S. figure-skating titles (1969–73).

In 1969 Diane Crump is the first female jockey at the Hialeah Pari-mutuel Race; in 1970 she is the first female jockey in the Kentucky Derby (the next is not until 1984). Barbara J. Rubin is the first to win on a thoroughbred racetrack, in 1969 at Charles Town, West Virginia.

1970–79

Angry at the much larger prizes given to male players, Billie Jean King, Rosemary Casals, and others call for reform and, when the USLTA ignores them, join Gladys Heldman in setting up the first Virginia Slims Invitational in 1970, which Casals wins.

Cathy Rigby (later McCoy) is the first American to medal (silver on the balance beam) at the World Gymnastics Championship, in 1970.

In 1971 Billie Jean King is the first female athlete to win $100,000; the top male tennis player, however, earns almost three times as much. She wins the U.S. Open in 1971–72 and Wimbledon in 1972–73.

Title IX of the Educational Amendments (1972) forbids sex discrimination in federally funded education programs. It thus calls for relative equalization of women's chances to participate in sports, gain scholarship money, and enjoy adequate facilities and support services.

The 1972 international surfing champion, Laura Blears Ching, is the first female to go against men in a surfing meet, in Hawaii in 1973.

In 1973 jockey Robyn Smith, the first female to race at Saratoga, in 1970, is the first to win a major stakes race, taking in $27,450 in the Paumanauk Handicap at New York's Aqueduct racetrack.

In the highly publicized "Battle of the Sexes" in 1973, Billie Jean King plays Bobby Riggs, the 1939 Wimbledon champion, in the Houston Astrodome. She beats him decisively 6–4, 6–3, 6–3. In the same year the prizes for women and men at the U.S. Open are equalized.

In 1973 Linda Meyers is the first U.S. world champion in archery.

After losing a sex discrimination suit in New Jersey and facing many more, Little League Baseball allows girls to play on its teams in 1974. That year Bunny Taylor, age 11, is the first to pitch a no-hitter.

The seven teams in the first women's professional football league in 1974 are the California Mustangs, Columbus (Ohio) Pacesetters, Dallas Bluebonnets, Detroit Demons, Fort Worth (Texas) Shamrocks, Los Angeles Dandelions, and Toledo (Ohio) Troopers.

Dorothy Hamill wins her first of three U.S. figure-skating titles (1974–76). In 1976 she also wins both the world title and Olympic gold.

In a 56-match winning streak, Christine ("Chris") Evert (later Lloyd) wins the French and Italian titles as well as her first Wimbledon singles in 1974. She then wins the U.S. Open four years running (1975–78), as well as Wimbledon in 1976.

After 20 years in amateur softball, pitcher Joan Joyce, 18-time All-

Olympics 1972

At the 1972 Winter Olympics, Barbara Ann Cochran wins the first gold for U.S. women skiers in 20 years, in the slalom. Speed skaters Annie Henning in the 500-m and Dianne Holum in the 1,500-m race win the first official U.S. women's speed-skating golds (see 1932).

In the summer games Doreen Wilber wins the gold in the first individual archery championship. Also, Sandra Neilson wins the 100-m freestyle, Keena Rothhammer the 800-m freestyle, Melissa Belote the 100-m and 200-m backstroke, Catherine Carr the 100-m breaststroke, Karen Moe the 200-m butterfly, and Maxine ("Micki") King the springboard dive. The relay swim teams also win their events.

Greenwood, Mississippi, proclaims "Willye B. White Day" to honor its five-time Olympian (1956–72), silver medalist in the 1956 long jump and on the 1964 relay team. White holds 17 national track titles by 1972.

Firsts for the 1970s

These are firsts for the later 1970s:

—In 1975 Diana Nyad is the first person to cross Lake Ontario. In 1979 she is the first to brave shark-infested waters and swim from the Bahamas to Florida.

—In 1975 Shirley Maldowney is the first woman to qualify for the top dragster category in the U.S. National Hot Rod Association. In 1976 she is the first woman to win the spring nationals, with the lowest time and fastest speed; she repeats this in 1977.

—In 1975 Marion Bermudez is the first U.S. woman to fight against men at the Golden Gloves boxing tournament in Mexico City. She wins her first match.

—In 1975 Margo Oberg wins the first professional women's surfing contest, the Hang Ten International in Malibu.

—In 1976 Natalie Dunn is the first U.S. woman to win the world figure roller-skating title; she also wins in 1977.

—In 1976 Lucy Giovinco is the first American to win the Women's Bowling World Cup.

—In 1977 Janet Guthrie is the first female driver in the Indianapolis 500. Car problems force her to withdraw, but in 1978 she finishes the race in eighth place.

—In 1978 Marcia Frederick is the first U.S. female gymnast to win a gold (on the uneven bars) in a world competition.

American, retires in 1975. She has pitched 509 winning games, including 105 no-hitters and 33 perfect games; she has lost only 33.

In 1975 Liz Allan Shetter ties Willa McGuire's record with three world waterskiing titles (1965, 1969, 1975) and eight U.S. titles (1968–75).

One of the first female Little League players in 1974, Amy Dickinson, age 11, wins a place on the All-Star team for the third year in 1976.

In 1976 Judy Torloemeke Rankin, LPGA Player of the Year, is the first woman golfer to earn more than $100,000 in a year.

In 1976 Caroline Svendsen knocks out Jean Lange in the first professional boxing bout for U.S. women. Also, Cathy Ann ("Cat") Davis sues when she is denied a New York boxing license and later wins.

At the 1976 Winter Olympics, Dorothy Hamill, using the new Hamill camel, takes the gold in figure skating. Sheila Young (later Ochowicz), a world sprint champion in both skating and cycling, wins the 500-m speed skating, with a silver in the 1,500-m and a bronze in the 1,000-m races. In the summer games Mary Anne Tasukey wins a gold as part of the three-day equestrian team event. Margaret Murdock is the first markswoman to beat men for a medal (silver in the small-bore rifle, three-position event). U.S. swimmers win the freestyle relay, and Shirley Babashoff wins four individual silvers as well as a gold on the relay. Springboard diver Jennifer Chandler wins gold. The first U.S. single sculling medal (a silver) is won by Joan Lind, five-time national champ.

Linda Fratianne wins both the U.S. and world figure-skating titles in 1977, repeating this in 1979 and winning silver at the 1980 Olympics.

In 1977 Lusia Harris is the first African American woman picked by a National Basketball Association team; she turns down two offers from the New Orleans Jazz and the Milwaukee Bucks.

Penny Dean, age 13, sets a England–France channel crossing record of 7 hours 40 minutes in 1978.

Carol ("Blaze") Blazejowski of Montclair (New Jersey) State College wins the first Margaret Wade Trophy for best female collegiate basketball player in 1978. In one game she scores 52 points.

In 1978, her first year as a professional golfer, Nancy Lopez wins a record five successive LPGA tournaments (plus four more), the LPGA championship, and more money than any other rookie of either sex. Named LPGA Player of the Year four times (1978–79, 1985, 1988), she wins the LPGA championship again in 1985 and 1989.

Swimmer Tracy Caulkins wins five golds and one silver at the world championships in 1978 and receives the Sullivan Award. During her career she sets 61 U.S. and 5 world records.

Donna Adamek is named Bowler of the Year for the first of four years (1978–81). She is the first woman to bowl six 300 games.

At age 16, Tracy Austin wins both the U.S. and Italian Opens in 1979, but by 1981 (when she wins again) she is plagued by injuries. Czech-born Martina Navratilova, later a U.S. citizen, wins the second of her record nine Wimbledon singles titles (1978–79, 1982–87, 1990), and Billie Jean King wins her 20th Wimbledon championship (in doubles).

Joan Benoit (later Samuelson) runs her first Boston Marathon in 1979 and is the first woman at the finish, repeating this in 1981.

1980–89

Martina Navratilova and Chris Evert Lloyd dominate tennis for much of the 1980s. Evert Lloyd wins U.S. (1980, 1982), Wimbledon (1981), French (1980, 1983, 1985–86), and Australian (1982, 1984) singles titles; Navratilova U.S. (1983–84, 1986–87), Wimbledon (1982–87), French (1982, 1984), and Australian (1985) wins. Navratilova wins 74 straight matches in 1984; she and her doubles partner, Pam Shriver, win a record of 20 Grand Slam doubles titles in 1982–89.

In 1980 Beth Heiden not only takes a bronze in the 3,000-m speed-skating event at the Winter Olympics but also wins three cycling titles: the world and national road races and the Coors International Classic.

Still an apprentice jockey, Melinda Spickard rides three winners on the same day at Churchill Downs in 1981.

Kathy Arendsen, a softball pitcher for the Hi-Ho Brakettes, strikes out Reggie Jackson on three separate occasions in 1981.

After setting world records in the 5,000-m and 10,000-m runs, Mary Decker is the first woman to receive the Jesse Owens Award, in 1982. She wins the world titles in the 1,500-m and 3,000-m in 1983, but can't finish her race in the 1984 Olympics after a controversial collision with white South African runner Zola Budd.

Baseball umpire Pam Postena gains a spot in the Triple-A Pacific Coast League, a step away from the majors in 1983, but is not promoted, despite an excellent record. She describes the sexism she faces in *You've Got to Have Balls to Make It in This League* (1992).

At the 1984 Winter Olympics, Deborah ("Debbie") Armstrong wins a gold in the giant slalom, with Christin Cooper taking the silver. In the summer games in Los Angeles (which the Soviets boycott), U.S. women dominate. Joan Benoit wins the first women's marathon in 2 hours 24 minutes 52 seconds. Evelyn Ashford takes the 100-m dash, Valerie Brisco-Hooks the 200-m and 400-m races (the first Olympian to win both), and Benita Fitzgerald-Brown the 100-m hurdles. U.S. women also win the 4x100 and 4x400 track relays. Pat Spurgin wins the women's air rifle event. Leslie Burr and Melanie Smith are part of the gold-winning equestrian jumping team, and Karen Stives is the first U.S. female equestrian to earn an individual medal, a silver in the three-day event. In cycling Connie Carpenter-Phinney gains gold in the 79-km road race (not only has she won four world titles and three Coors

Here are firsts from the late 1970s and early 1980s:

—In 1979 Lyn Lemaire is the first woman to finish the Hawaii Ironman Triathlon, which includes a 2.4-mile swim, 112-mile bike ride, and 26.2-mile marathon.

—In 1979 Evelyn Ashford is the first woman to run the 100-m dash in less than 11 seconds.

—In 1980 Karen Rogers is the first female jockey to win the daily double at New York's Aqueduct racetrack.

—In 1980 Crystal Fields, age 11, bests seven boys in the 9–12 age group and is the first girl to win the U.S. Pitch, Hit, and Run Championship.

—In 1982 Shirley Muldowney is the first person to win three National Hot Rod Association World Championships (1977, 1980, 1982). She is also the first to win the top drag-racing event, the Winston World Championship, three times (1977, 1980–81).

—In 1983 Tamara McKinney is the first U.S. skier to win the World Cup overall. She is also a top equestrian.

—In 1983 about 630 women enter the first all-female triathlon in California.

—In 1983 the first Naismith Trophy in college basketball goes to Anne Donovan. Cheryl Miller then wins for three years straight (1984–86).

Firsts for the 1980s

These are firsts for the later 1980s:

—In 1985 Libby Riddles is the first woman to win the Iditarod Trail Sled Dog Race, driving 13 dogs over 1,100 miles of Alaska wilderness from Anchorage to Nome in just over 17 days.

—In 1985 Tiffany Chin is the first Asian American to win the U.S. figure-skating championship.

—In 1985 Lynnette Woodard and Jackie White win a competition and are the first two women signed on by the previously all-male professional basketball team the Harlem Globetrotters.

—In 1986 Nancy Lieberman signs on with the Springfield Fame in Massachusetts and becomes the first woman to play in the U.S. Basketball League. In 1987 she switches to the Washington Generals, a frequent opponent of the Harlem Globetrotters.

—In 1986 Debi Thomas is the first African American to win first the U.S. and then world figure-skating singles titles, in 1986.

—In 1989 cyclist Susan Notorangelo is the first woman finisher and seventh overall in the Race Across America. Her time is better than that of the first-place male finisher in 1987.

—In 1989 Ann Trason is the first female runner to win a mixed-sex national race, the 143-mile Sri Chimnoy TAC/USA 24-Hour Race. The fourth finisher is also a woman, Sue Ellen Trapp.

International Classics, but she is also a top speed skater). Just a hair behind her is Rebecca Twig (who in 1982 was the first American to win gold in the world 3-km pursuit race). U.S. scullers win the eight oars event, and captain Lynette Woodard (four-time All-American) and top-scorer Cheryl Miller (also a four-time All-American) lead the basketball team to a gold. Mary Lou Retton wins gold in the all-around competition with two perfect (10) vaults; she also wins a silver (vault) and two bronzes (uneven bars and floor exercises). Julianne McNamara ties for the gold on the uneven bars and wins a silver in floor exercises. In the first Olympic synchronized swimming events, Tracie Ruiz (later Conforto) takes the individual gold as well as the duet, with Candy Costie (her partner since 1975). In swimming Carrie Steinseifer and Nancy Hogshead tie for the 100-m freestyle; Mary Wayte takes the 200-m freestyle; Tiffany Cohen the 400-m and 800-m freestyle; Theresa Andrews the 100-m backstroke; Tracy Caulkins the 200-m and 400-m individual medleys; Mary T. Meagher the 100-m and 200-m butterfly. The U.S. swimmers also win both relays.

"Alaska: Where men are men and women win the Iditarod"—T-shirt slogan

A competitor since 1978, Susan Butcher wins the first of four Iditarod Trail Dog Sled races (1986–88, 1990). "We don't need to ask men to move over," she later says. "We're just there."

Pat Bradley is the first woman golfer to earn over $2 million in a year, in 1986. She wins the LPGA championship and is the first woman to win three du Maurier Classic championships (1980, 1985–86).

Bowler Jeanne Maiden sets two records in 1986: 40 consecutive strikes and an 864 score for three games during the Women's International Bowling Congress.

In the 1988 Olympics, Debi Thomas is the first African American to win a medal in the winter games, a bronze in figure skating. Speed skater Bonnie Blair wins her first gold, in the 500-m race. In the summer games Jackie Joyner-Kersee wins the long jump as well as the heptathlon (a 1984 silver medalist in this event, she was the first woman to break the 7,000 mark, in 1986). Her sister-in-law Florence Griffith Joyner takes both the 100-m and 200-m sprints and gains another gold as part of the 4x100-m relay team. Louise Ritter wins the high jump. In swimming Janet Evans is the only gold medalist, taking the 400-m and 800-m freestyle and the 400-m individual medley. The U.S. basketball team wins, and Zina Garrison and Pam Shriver take the doubles gold in tennis.

Sarah Covington-Fulcher runs 11,134 miles around the United States in 1988, setting a record for the longest run by any person.

Frieda Zamba wins a record fourth title in the world's professional surfing championship (1984–86, 1988).

Julie Croteau is the first known woman to play on an otherwise-male college varsity baseball team, as first baseman for the Seahawks of St. Mary's College in Maryland.

1990–95

Although women's participation in sports has greatly increased since passage of Title IX in 1972, the percentage of women coaches at colleges has sharply declined by 1990. However, Bernadette Locke (later Mattox) scores a first: as assistant coach for the men's basketball team at the University of Kentucky, she is the first female coach in the National College Athletic Association Division I of men's basketball. By 1992 Amy Machin-Ward is coaching men's soccer at Regis University in Denver and Barbara Hedges runs the athletic department at the University of Washington in Seattle, which has an NCAA Division I-A football team.

At the first all-female triathlon, in 1990 in Long Beach, California, more than 2,000 women enter. Lisa Lahti wins.

Jill Trenary wins the world figure-skating title in 1990, after winning the U.S. title three times (1987, 1989–90).

Golfer Betsy King wins her second straight U.S. Open in 1990 as well as the Nabisco Dinah Shore title. In 1992 she wins the LPGA title.

In 1991 Judy Sweet, athletic director at the University of California, San Diego, is the first woman president of the National College Athletic Association.

Susan O'Malley, in 1991, is the only female president of a National Basketball Association team, the Washington Bullets.

The U.S. women's soccer team wins the first World Cup trophy for women in 1991 by beating Norway. Carin Jenning is the competition's most valuable player.

Kim Zmeskal is the first U.S. woman to win the all-around title at the world gymnastics championships, in 1991. At the 1991 figure-skating world championships, for the first time three women from one country—the United States—sweep their event. Kristi Yamaguchi places first, Tonya Harding second, and Nancy Kerrigan third.

In 1991 college basketball star Dawn Staley wins the Broderick Award and Naismith Trophy; she repeats this in 1992.

Kristen Somogyi takes over as New Jersey's all-time top-scoring high school basketball player in 1992, when she bests the record set by her father 24 years ago.

On her first Indianapolis 500 race in 1992, Lyn St. James places 11th, the top rookie finisher. Earlier, she was the first woman to win the International Motor Sport Association's Camel GTO series.

In 1993 number-one female jockey Julie Krone, riding "Colonial

Olympics 1992

At the 1992 Winter Olympics Kristi Yamaguchi is the first Asian American to win a gold in figure skating. Donna Weinbrecht wins the gold in the first women's freestyle skiing event (moguls). Speed skater Bonnie Blair is the first woman to win two consecutive golds in the 500-m race; she also captures a gold in the 1000-m event. Cathy Turner takes the gold in the first 500-m short-track speed-skating event.

At the summer games the tennis singles gold goes to Jennifer Capriati and the doubles to Gigi Fernández (the first Puerto Rican woman to win a gold) and Mary Joe Fernández (not related). Jackie Joyner-Kersee gains her second gold in the heptathlon. Gail Denvers takes the 100-m dash and Gwen Torrence the 200-m event; the U.S. women also win the 4x100 relay. Launi Meili wins the three-position rifle. In swimming Janet Evans earns her second gold in the 800-m freestyle; Nicole Haislett wins the 200-m freestyle, and Summer Sanders the 200-m breaststroke. The U.S. women also take both relays. Kristen Babb-Sprague wins the solo synchronized swimming, and Karen and Sarah Josephson the duet. Even though she does not win gold, gymnast Shannon Miller brings home the most U.S. medals (two silvers and three bronzes).

Olympics 1994

Coverage of the 1994 Winter Olympics is dominated by the battle between figure skaters Nancy Kerrigan and Tonya Harding, after Kerrigan is attacked and injured at the 1994 national championships by associates of Harding. Kerrigan makes a complete comeback from her injury and takes the silver, losing the gold by the smallest margin in Olympic history.

In alpine skiing, Diann Roffe-Steinrotter wins gold in the super giant slalom, and Picabo Street earns a silver in the downhill. In freestyle skiing Liz McIntyre gets a silver in moguls. Bonnie Blair is first in both the 500-m (for the third time) and 1,000-m speed skating (for the second time). She thus ties Eric Heiden's record for the most U.S. golds (five) in the winter games and sets a record for U.S. women. In the 500-m short-track speed skating, Cathy Turner takes gold (her second) and Amy Peterson bronze.

Affair," is the first woman to win a Triple Crown horse race, New York's Belmont Stakes.

Patty Sheehan wins her third LPGA championship (1983–84, 1993).

The Colorado Silver Bullets, the first all-female professional baseball team to compete against men, take to the field in 1994. They win 6 of 44 games in their first season.

When Martina Navratilova retires from tennis in 1994, she has won more than 1,400 matches.

Dominique Dawes is the first to win all five events at the U.S. gymnastics championship, in 1994. She is also the first African American to hold the title. In 1995 Dominique Moceanu, age 13, is the youngest all-around national gymnastics champion.

Cassie Clark and Stephanie Brody are the first two women on a men's national junior weightlifting squad, in 1994.

In 1995 Yugoslavian-born tennis champion Monica Seles, winner of the 1991–92 U.S. Open titles, makes a comeback after being stabbed in 1993 and put out of action for two years by a fan of top German player Steffi Graff. Seles beats Martina Navratilova, then loses a close match with Graff at the U.S. Open (Seles actually wins more sets).

In 1995 America's *Mighty Mary* is the first boat to enter the America's Cup trials with an all-female crew, but a male tactician is added at the last minute. Although Dennis Connor and his crew win the last race, the women are ahead for five of the six legs.

Led by forward Rebecca Lobo, the University of Connecticut basketball team has an undefeated season and wins the 1995 National College Athletic Association championship. Lobo is every organization's pick for player of the year.

In 1995 Rutgers University hires Vivian Stringer to coach its women's basketball team and signs her on at a higher base salary than that of the men's basketball coach.

Picabo Street is the first U.S. woman to win the World Cup downhill title, in 1995.

Journalism

Photograph of cotton-picker child at strike meeting
by Dorothea Lange (Library of Congress)

In the colonies 16 of 78 papers are edited by women (see sidebar). By 1820 at least 32 women have published papers. An early columnist is Judith Sargent Murray (p. 306), who writes a monthly column, "The Gleaner," for *Massachusetts Magazine* from 1792 to 1794. In it she discusses political issues and propounds equal education for women.

1800–49

In 1826 Lydia Maria Francis (later Child) starts *Juvenile Miscellany*, the first U.S. children's magazine, but circulation drops after her 1833 antislavery tract (p. 17). She later edits the *National Anti-Slavery Standard*.

Elizabeth Margaret Chandler (1807–34) begins writing for the abolitionist paper *Genius of Universal Emancipation* in 1826. She urges women not to buy anything produced by slave labor.

In Boston in 1828 Sara Josepha Buell Hale (1788–1879) edits the new *Ladies' Magazine* (later *American Ladies' Magazine*). Although she advocates education for women, she sees women's proper "sphere" as the home and criticizes those who speak in public. In 1837 her magazine merges with *Godey's Lady's Book,* which she edits for 40 years, increasing the circulation from 10,000 to 150,000 by 1860. The 100-page monthly mixes fashion, fiction, poetry, homemaking tips, recipes, and health advice but steers clear of politics, never even mentioning the Civil War.

In 1828 Frances Wright (p. 16) and Robert Dale Owen start the *New-Harmony Gazette* in Indiana. In 1829 in New York, they put out the *Free Enquirer,* advocating abolition, women's rights, and other causes.

After publishing a series of travel sketches, Anne Newport Royall (1769–1854) settles in Washington, D.C., and offers gossip and pointed commentary in her weekly, *Paul Pry,* in 1831. She starts the *Huntress* in 1836, relentlessly exposing corruption wherever she finds it.

In 1832 Caroline Howard Gilman (1794–1888) starts *Rose-Bud, or Youth's Gazette;* in 1835 she renames it *Southern Rosebud* and extends its appeal to the whole family.

In 1840 Margaret Fuller (p. 20) edits the Transcendentalist magazine, the *Dial*. She is the first literary critic for the *New York Tribune,* in 1844, and also writes general new stories. After leaving for Europe in 1846, she sends "letters" describing encounters with George Sand and others.

From 1842, Ann S. Stephens (1810–86) coedits *Peterson's Ladies' Magazine,* a rival of *Godey's Lady's Book,* and prints her popular serials in it.

Windham Country Democrat editor Clarina Howard Nichols (1810–85) helps secure Vermont laws granting property rights to married women with her 1847 editorials.

In 1849 Amelia Jenks Bloomer (1818–94) starts *Lily,* the first woman-run paper for women, put out by female typesetters. In its columns she advocates women's rights, temperance, and dress reform.

Early Publishers

Among publishers in the 1770s:

—Anna Zenger takes charge of the New York Weekly Journal *when her husband, John Peter, is arrested for criticizing the government in a famous freedom-of-the press case (1734–35).*

—Elizabeth Timothy, the first female editor in the South, puts out the South-Carolina Gazette *after her husband dies in 1738. Her daughter-in-law, Ann Donovan Timothy (c. 1727–92), takes over in 1783.*

—In Philadelphia, Cornelia Smith Bradford takes control of the American Weekly Mercury *in 1742, after her husband's death, and is its sole editor and publisher from 1744 to at least 1746.*

—From 1765 to 1768 Mary Katherine Goddard (1738–1816) and her mother, Sarah Updike Goddard (c. 1700–70), publish the weekly Providence Gazette *in Rhode Island. In 1774 she publishes the* Maryland Journal *and prints the first signed copy of the Declaration of Independence.*

—Clementina Rind (c. 1740–74) runs the Virginia Gazette *after her husband's death in 1773. Its motto is "Open to ALL PARTIES but Influenced by NONE."*

—Anne Hoof Green (c. 1720–75) runs the Maryland Gazette *after her husband dies in 1767. As the colony's only paper until 1773, it is a key source of imformation on events leading up to the Revolutionary War.*

1850–59

Elizabeth Oakes Prince Smith (1806–93) pens an 1850 series on women's rights for the *New York Tribune;* it is then published as *Women and Her Needs* (1851).

Writing as "Grace Greenwood," Sara Clarke (later Lippincott, 1823–1904) begins her "Washington Letters" for the *Saturday Evening Post* in 1850, voicing strong support for women's rights and abolition. In the 1870s her column appears in the *New York Times* and other papers.

Mary Ann Shadd (later Cary, p. 22) is the first African American woman editor, cofounding the *Provincial Freeman* in Canada in 1853. Its motto is "Self-Reliance Is the Fine Road to Independence."

Sara Payson Willis (later Parton, 1811–72), publishes a collection of her magazine writings as "Fanny Fern" in *Fern Leaves from Fanny's Porfolio* (1853), a best-seller. In 1855 the *New York Ledger* hires her as one of the first women columnists. Using satire, she addresses contemporary issues, including women's status and the plight of the poor.

Several women's publications appear. Women's rights activist Paulina Kellogg Wright Davis (1813–76) puts out *Una* from 1853 to 1855. In 1855, with an all-woman staff and female typesetters, Anne Elizabeth McDowell (1826–1901) starts the weekly *Woman's Advocate* in Philadelphia. In 1856, as editor of the biweekly *Sibyl*, Lydia Sayer (later Hasbrouck) promotes dress reform.

As "Jennie June," Jane Cunningham Croly (1829–1901) sells her column "Parlor and Side-walk Gossip," to papers in several cities in 1857. She soon edits the woman's page for *New York World*.

In 1859 actress Ada Clare (Jane McElhenney, c. 1836–74) begins her wide-ranging column for the New York weekly *Saturday Press*.

1860–69

With her husband, William, Ellen Curtis Demorest (1824–98) starts the quarterly *Mme. Demorest's Mirror of Fashions* in 1860. After seeing her black maid use a brown-paper pattern to cut out a dress, she mass-produces tissue-paper patterns and includes one with each issue. Soon the magazine and pattern business employ more than 200 women.

After a letter defending women as government clerks, Emily Edson Briggs (1830–1910) is hired in 1861 as a daily columnist ("Olivia") for the jointly owned *Philadelphia Press* and *Washington Chronicle*. She is the first woman to report regularly on White House news.

In 1863 Miriam Folline Squier (later Leslie, 1836–1914) edits *Lady's Magazine,* published by Frank Leslie. In 1865 she helps him launch a family magazine, *Frank Leslie's Chimney Corner,* and in 1871 edits *Frank Leslie's Lady's Journal,* a fashion magazine. After Leslie's death in 1880, she takes over the business, managing 400 employees at such publications as *Frank Leslie's Illustrated Newspaper* and *Frank Leslie's Popular Monthly,* which have a total circulation of 250,000.

A Crusading Editor

In Pittsburgh in 1848, Jane Grey Cannon Swisshelm (1815–84), an ardent abolitionist and proponent of women's rights, starts the Saturday Visiter (the spelling she prefers). In four years she builds up a circulation of 6,000, and her articles are widely reprinted. Later, in 1857, she moves and begins a new paper, the St. Cloud Visiter, in Minnesota. Her strong antislavery views and criticisms of the local Democratic Party boss lead to a vigilante attack in which her press is destroyed. But she remains defiant and remounts her attacks; when threatened with a libel suit, she agrees not to say any more in the St. Cloud Visiter, folds her paper, and starts up the St. Cloud Democrat. Despite her strong abolitionist stance, she is a fervent opponent of the Sioux and demands federal action against them.

Susan B. Anthony and Elizabeth Cady Stanton start their women's rights weekly, the Revolution, *in 1868 (see p. 26). Another new suffragist paper is the* Agitator, *put out by Mary Ashton Livermore, which folds into the* Woman's Journal *in 1870.*

Victoria Woodhull (p. 28) and her sister Tennessee Calflin launch Woodhull and Claflin's Weekly *in 1870 to put forward their views on women's rights, free love, and other causes. They are the first to publish the* Communist Manifesto *in America, in 1871, but Woodhull loses support when she prints an 1872 article accusing Henry Ward Beecher of an affair with Elizabeth Tilton, a married woman.*

In 1870 Lucy Stone starts the Woman's Journal *as the organ of the American Woman Suffrage Association (p. 27) and later National American Woman Suffrage Association. Edited for the first two years by Mary A. Livermore, it continues until 1917 under the direction of Stone and her husband, Henry Blackwell, and later their daughter, Alice Stone Blackwell (1857–1950). Although the paper pushes for women's rights, it does not support labor unions and strikes.*

In Portland, Oregon, Abigail Scott Duniway (1834–1915) starts the suffragist paper New Northwest *in 1871.*

Writing for the *Independent,* a New York weekly, Mary E. Clemmer Ames (1831–84) includes political commentary in her "Woman's Letter from Washington," beginning in 1866.

Mary Louise Booth (1831–89) edits the new *Harper's Bazar* in 1867 and helps it acquire 80,000 readers in 10 years by combining fashion, fiction, and household advice.

1870–79

Ida A. Husted Harper (p. 39) begins her long journalistic career in 1872, writing under a male pseudonym for the *Terre Haute Saturday Evening Mail* in Indiana. In 1890 she becomes the paper's editor-in-chief; she later writes a women's column for the *New York Sunday Sun* (1899–1903) and edits the woman's page in *Harper's Bazaar* (1909–13).

Mary Mapes Dodge (1831–1905) edits the new *St. Nicholas Magazine* in 1873 and establishes high standards for fiction and illustrations in children's magazines. She personally answers the hundreds of letters she receives from young readers.

After her husband's death in 1876, Eliza Jane Poitevent Holbrook (later Nicholson, 1849–96) publishes the daily *New Orleans Picayune.* By adding women's and children's features, she increases the readership.

1880–89

The Woman's National Press Association forms in 1882 with Emily Edson Briggs as its first president.

In 1883 in Nebraska, Clara Bewick Colby (1846–1916) starts the weekly *Woman's Tribune,* soon the official paper of Susan B. Anthony and Elizabeth Cady Stanton's National Woman Suffrage Assocation.

In the first issue of the *New York Freeman* in 1885, Gertrude Bustill Mossell (1855–1948) publishes "Woman's Suffrage" in a column to "promote true womanhood, especially that of the African race."

In 1889 Ida B. Wells (later Barnett, 1862–1931), who often uses the pen name "Iola," acquires a share of the *Memphis Free Speech and Headlight* (later just *Free Speech*). To make sure readers know they are getting the right paper, she prints it on pink paper. Unafraid of controversial issues, she criticizes school conditions for black children in 1891 and promptly loses her own teaching contract. After her strongly worded attack on lynching in 1892, her office is destroyed (see "Politics").

In 1889 the *Journalist* features biographies of 40 white and 10 black women reporters. About 200 female journalists, including Nellie Bly (see sidebar opposite), work in New York alone at the time.

1890–99

Journalist Kate Field (1838–96) starts *Kate Field's Washington,* a 16-page weekly, in 1890.

In 1890 Elizabeth Garver Jordan (1865–1947) of the *New York World* scoops other reporters by interviewing First Lady Caroline Scott Harrison. She then embellishes one-line police-blotter-type dramas into "True Stories of the News." Her book *Tales of the City Room* (1895) inspires women journalists. Later, in 1900, she edits *Harper's Bazar.*

Writing as "Annie Laurie," Winifred Sweet Black (later Bonfils, 1863–1936) joins the *San Francisco Examiner* in 1890. Her first major scoop is in 1892, when she gains an interview with President Benjamin Harrison by sneaking onto his campaign train and hiding under a table.

The *Union Signal,* put out by the WCTU, is the largest women's paper in 1890, with a circulation of 100,000.

Julia Ringwood Coston initiates the first illustrated paper for black women, *Ringwood's Afro-American Journal of Fashion,* in 1891.

Rosa Sonneschein launches the *American Jewess* in reponse to the 1893 Congress of Jewish Women (see "Religion").

Josephine St. Pierre Ruffin edits the monthly *Woman's Era,* begun in 1894, with news of the growing black club movement.

"Dorothy Dix" (Elizabeth Meriwether Gilmer, 1861–1951) begins her advice column at the *New Orleans Daily Picayune* in 1896. William Randolph Hearst hires her for his *New York Journal* in 1901, and she joins other women in covering the sensational murder trials of the day. In 1917, however, she returns to New Orleans and syndicates her column, which is carried in 273 papers by 1940.

In 1898 Mexican American rights activist Sara Estela Ramírez (1881–1910) starts publishing in *La Crónica* and *El Demócrata Fronterizo.*

"Beatrice Fairfax" (Marie Manning, c. 1873–1945) initiates an advice column for the lovelorn, at the *New York Evening Journal* in 1898.

1900–9

Disguised as a boy, "Annie Laurie" (Winifred Black) slips behind police lines after a tidal wave kills 7,000 in Galveston, Texas, in 1900. She is the first outside reporter on the scene.

An early photojournalist, Jessie Tarbox Beals (1870–1942) starts with a photo of a local fair in a Brattleboro, Vermont, paper in 1900. In 1904 she spends six months carrying 30 pounds of equipment to cover the St. Louis World's Fair. Another early documentary photographer is Frances Benjamin Johnston (1864–1952), best known for her record of the Hampton Normal and Agricultural Institute in 1899 to 1900.

The first major female art critic is Leila Mechlin (1874–1949), at the *Washington Evening Star* and *Sunday Star* in 1900. In 1909 she starts *Art and Progress,* the magazine of the American Federation of Arts.

In 1903 Leonel Campbell (later O'Bryan, 1857–1938) starts her own 20-page weekly, using her pen name as its title, *Polly Pry.* The paper claims "To hold as 'twere the Mirror up to Nature" and offers a gossip column called "Tell Truth and Shame Devil."

Nellie Bly

In 1887 New York World *reporter Elizabeth Cochrane (later Seaman, 1867–1922), writing as "Nellie Bly," fakes insanity, is sent to an asylum, and provokes a grand jury investigation with her reports (in the paper and* Ten Days in a Mad House*). Other exposés involve a job in a sweatshop and jail time for shoplifting. In 1889 she challenges the record of the fictional Phineas Fogg in Jules Verne's* Around the World in 80 Days. *Setting off in November, she races across the Atlantic, around to Tokyo, San Francisco, and back to New York, cabling stories that make the front page every day. On her arrival home in January 1890, after 72 days, 6 hours, 11 minutes, cannons are fired.*

Nellie Bly (Library of Congress)

Taking Up Causes

During the Progressive era women reporters champion a variety of causes. A well-known "muckraking" journalist is Ida Tarbell (1857–1944). In 1902 she starts a 19-article series in McClure's *magazine exposing the unethical rise to power of the Standard Oil Company (published in book form in 1904). Her probe fuels the drive for antitrust laws. In 1906 she becomes a co-owner and associate editor of* American Magazine, *for which she writes the articles published in the book* The Tariff in Our Times *(1911).*

Other women espouse radical causes. Emma Goldman cofounds the anarchist journal Mother Earth *in 1906. Theresa Malkiel and Josephine Conger-Kaneko edit the Socialist weekly* Progressive Woman *around 1912. Mary Heaton Vorse (1882–1966) covers the 1912 Lawrence, Massachusetts, strike and other labor disputes. She and such women as Inez Haynes Gilmore, Elsie Clews Parsons, and Crystal Eastman, write for the* Masses. *Consuelo Kanaga photographs for leftist publications.*

Another outlet is suffragist publications. In 1914 Rheta Childe Dorr (1866–1948), former New York Evening Post *woman's editor and author of* What Eight Million Women Want *(1910), edits the* Suffragist *for the Congressional Union (later National Woman's Party), led by Alice Paul.*

Four women journalists—Winifred Black Bonfils, Nixola Greeley-Smith, Ada Patterson, and "Dorothea Dix"—earn the epithet "sob sisters" for their support of Evelyn Nesbit Thaw at her husband's 1907 trial for the murder of architect Stanford White. Bonfils resents the label: "I'm not a sob sister or special writer. I'm just a plain, practical, all-around newspaper woman. That's my profession, and that's my pride."

Isidra T. Cárdenas publishes the paper *La voz de la mujer* (Woman's Voice) in El Paso, Texas, in 1907. Another early Latina paper is Blanca de Moncaleano's *Plume Roja* (Red Pen) in 1913 Los Angeles; she champions education for women and other issues.

Taking over as editor-in-chief in 1912, Gertrude Battles Lane (1874–1941) turns *Woman's Home Companion* into the top U.S. women's magazine by 1937. In addition to practical tips for homemakers, she offers articles on women's new roles and high-quality fiction.

In 1912 Charlotta Spears Bass (c. 1880–1969) and her husband, Joseph, take over the *California Eagle* and turn it into a major voice for the rights of African Americans.

In 1914 Louella Oettinger Parsons (c. 1881–1972) is the first U.S. movie columnist, in the *Chicago Record-Herald.* She later adds gossip and syndicates her column in the Hearst papers, reaching more than 2 million readers. She also hosts a radio interview show in 1934.

From 1914 to 1952 Edna Woolman Chase (1877–1957) is editor-in-chief of *Vogue* and becomes a major influence on U.S. fashion.

Mary Roberts Rinehart (1876–1958) goes to Europe in 1915 to cover World War I for the *Saturday Evening Post* and is thus the first female foreign war correspondent. She also is the first reporter to gain an interview with Queen Mary of England.

In 1916 Zitkala-Sa (Gertrude Simmons Bonnin, p. 46) edits the *American Indian Magazine* for the Society of American Indians.

A number of women journalists try to cover World War I after the U.S. entry in 1917. Because they are not allowed near U.S. troops, Rheta Childe Dorr of the *New York Mail,* Bessie Beatty of the *San Francisco Bulletin,* and Louise Bryant of Bell Syndicate cover the Russian front and later the Russian Revolution. Beatty and Dorr, for example, report on the Women's Death Battalion, a troop of Russian women. In 1918 Beatty publishes *The Red Heart of Russia* and Bryant (married to John Reed) comes out with *Six Red Months in Russia.*

In 1918 Henrietta ("Peggy") Goodnough Hull (1889–1967) is accredited as a war reporter; she is the one woman to cover both world wars.

1920–29

Chicago Tribune reporter Genevieve Forbes (latter Herrick, 1894–1962) disguises herself as an immigrant and exposes conditions on Ellis Island in 1921, leading to a congressional investigation.

Lila Bell Acheson Wallace (1899–1984) and her husband, DeWitt, select the best magazine articles and condense them for their new *Reader's Digest* magazine in 1922.

In 1922 Judith Cary Waller (1889–1973) is one of the first radio station managers in Chicago. A trailblazer, she airs the first play-by-play college football game in 1924 and both parties' political conventions.

May Adams Craig (1889–1975) begins her 40-some-year journalistic career in Washington in 1924 as a correspondent for Maine papers. She becomes known for her sharp questioning of politicians and her flowery hats (easy to spot at press conferences).

In 1925 Sigrid Schultz (1893–1980) is named chief of the Berlin bureau for the *Chicago Tribune;* soon afterward Dorothy Thompson (1893–1961) is appointed Central European bureau chief, based in Berlin, for the *Philadelphia Public Ledger* and *New York Evening Post.*

At the new *New Yorker* magazine in 1925, Katharine White is the first fiction editor. Also, Janet Flanner (1892–1978) begins her biweekly "Paris Letter" using the pen name Genêt; she later writes letters from other cities and profiles such major figures as Edith Wharton and Pablo Picasso. She continues her letters for just short of 50 years.

Louise Larson is the first Chinese American woman reporter on a city newspaper, in 1926.

Working for Associated Press, Bess Furman (1894–1969) is, in 1929, the first woman reporter to cover Congress regularly for a news service. After 1932 her main assignment is First Lady Eleanor Roosevelt.

1930–39

First Lady Eleanor Roosevelt begins regular Monday morning press conferences in 1933. Only women reporters are invited, forcing editors to keep women on staff during the Depression; some papers even hire their first female reporters to attend. Reporter Esther Van Wagoner Tufty later says that Eleanor Roosevelt "caused more to be written by women, for women, about women, than any other First Lady or maybe any other American woman." Some journalists, such as Associated Press reporter Lorena A. Hickok, become close friends of the First Lady.

In 1933 Dorothy Day (p. 156) starts publishing the *Catholic Worker,* which calls for social justice and an end to war. It sells for just a penny a copy and gains 150,000 readers in three years.

Although when she first meets Adolf Hitler she thinks he is insignificant, Dorothy Thompson soon changes her mind and is expelled from Germany in 1934 for her anti-Nazi reports. In 1936 she warns against Hitler in her column, "On the Record," which runs three times weekly in the *Herald Tribune* and is soon syndicated in 170 papers. After the war her anti-Zionist stance causes several papers to drop her column.

In 1934 radio WOR in New York hires Mary Margaret McBride

Women at the Top

After starting to work for her husband's New York Tribune *in 1918,* Helen Rogers Reid *(1882–1970) assumes the vice presidency of the newly merged* New York Herald Tribune *in 1924. She encourages women reporters, such as foreign correspondent Dorothy Thompson and book review editor Irita Bradford Van Doren, and by the 1940s the* Tribune *employs more women than any other U.S. daily.*

Editor Eleanor ("Cissy") Medill Patterson *(1881–1948) brings new life to the* Washington Herald *in 1930 and surrounds herself with strong women writers (she also does stories herself). Later, in 1939, she buys the* Herald *and the* Washington Times, *creating the* Washington Times-Herald, *a six-edition daily that within four years is the capital's biggest circulation paper.*

After joining the Nation *in 1918,* Freda Kirchwey *(1893–1976) beomes managing editor in 1922 and editor in 1933 (until 1955). For 10 years (1937–47) she also owns the journal.*

Reporting on China

Anna Louise Strong (1885–1970) first gains attention with a rousing editorial calling for the 1919 Seattle General Strike. Excited by the Russian Revolution, she goes to Moscow and writes The First Time in History *(1924) in defense of Communist policies. In 1925 she travels to China and later writes* China's Millions *(1928). In the 1930s she reports on Russia and China, as well as the Spanish Civil War. During the Chinese revolution in 1946, Strong manages to interview Mao Tse-Tung in a cave in China. In 1949 she is kicked out of the Soviet Union for her Chinese sympathies. In the late 1950s she moves to China and in 1962 issues a newsletter,* Letter from China. *When she dies, she is buried in Beijing's National Memorial Cemetery of Revolutionary Martyrs (near Agnes Smedley).*

Agnes Smedley (c. 1894–1950) initially goes to China in 1928 for a German paper and publishes Chinese Destinies *(1933) and* China's Red Army Marches *(1934). After joining up with the Chinese army at the battlefront during the Sino-Japanese War, she describes her experience in* China Fights Back: An American Woman with the Eighth Route Army *(1938). Continuing to travel with guerrilla forces, she sends reports to England and later writes* Battle Hymn of China *(1943).*

(1899–1976) to give grandmotherly advice to women as the endearing "Martha Deane." McBride, however, soon tells her audience that she's just playing a part. In 1937 she starts her own weekly CBS (later NBC) radio program mixing commentary and interviews in an early talk show format. She has millions of listeners and by 1950 runs daily.

In 1934 Martha Gellhorn of *Collier's* reports on the Spanish Civil War; she later covers the Russian invasion of Finland, the Japanese invasion of China, and the American forces in Europe.

In the mid-1930s, with her coverage of the Lindbergh kidnapping trial, Senator Huey Long's assassination, and the abdication of Edward VIII, Adela Rogers St. Johns is one of the best-known U.S. reporters.

Sylvia Field Porter (1913–91) begins her financial column for the *New York Post* as the nonthreatening "S. F. Porter" in 1935; by 1938 it is running daily. She not only provides financial tips but also exposes unethical practices in the financial world. Later she becomes known for such popular books as *Sylvia Porter's Money Book* (1975).

After editing the Sunday magazine for the *New York Herald Tribune* since 1926, Marie Mattingly Meloney (1878–1943) takes charge of the supplement *This Week,* which she builds to a circulation of 6 million.

Eleanor Roosevelt starts her syndicated newspaper column, "My Day," in 1936. To support women workers, she insists on being paid for her writing. In 1939 she starts 15-minute "My Day" radio broadcasts.

Several women photographers document conditions for the Farm Security Administration during the mid-1930s. The most famous is Dorothea Lange, whose 1936 photo *Migrant Mother, Nipomo, California,* comes to symbolize the Depression. Other FSA photographers are Esther Bubley, Marjory Collins, Pauline Ehrlich, Martha McMillan Roberts, Marion Post Wolcott, Ann Rosener, and Louise Rosskam.

Already known for her photographs in *Fortune* magazine and her book *Eyes on Russia* (1931), Margaret Bourke-White (1906–71) does the cover photograph (of the massive Fort Peck dam in Montana) and lead article for the first issue of *Life* magazine in 1936. She also travels with Erskine Caldwell throughout the South to take photographs of sharecroppers for their book, *Have You Seen Their Faces?* (1936).

"Hedda Hopper" (Elda Furry, 1890–1966) starts broadcasting Hollywood gossip in 1936 and in 1938 adds a syndicated column, becoming the archrival of Louella Parsons.

In 1936 news commentator Kathryn Cravens is the first woman radio broadcaster to be carried on stations across the country by CBS.

New York Herald Tribune reporter Ishbel Ross (1895–1975) describes many top women journalists in her book *Ladies of the Press* (1936), including Lorena Hickok, Bess Furman, Ruby Black, Grace Robinson, Marjorie Driscoll, Elinore Kellogg, and Genevieve Forbes Herrick.

Another 1936 book that popularizes the life of women reporters is *Peggy Covers the News,* based on the experiences of its author, *Herald Tribune* reporter Emma Bugbee (1999–1981).

"The face of the world has changed"
—Anne O'Hare McCormick

After reporting on the rise of Benito Mussolini and fascism in Italy, Anne O'Hare McCormick (1880–1954) is the first woman on the editorial board of the *New York Times,* in 1936. The next year, in 1937, she is the first woman to win the Pulitzer Prize for foreign correspondence, based on the body of her work rather than just one article.

In 1938 Dorothy Kilgallen (1913–65) starts her column, "The Voice of Broadway," for the *New York Journal-American,* which is soon syndicated. In 1941 she also broadcasts a weekly radio show.

Dorothy Schiff buys the controlling interest in the *New York Post* in 1939, taking on the title of publisher in 1942 (until 1977).

After coediting the influential *Whitehall News* to alert Western leaders to the impending war, Helen Kirkpatrick (later Milbank) is hired by the *Chicago Daily News* as its first female foreign correspondent in 1939. "If they wanted me they had to change their policy [against women on staff] since I wouldn't change my sex!" she recalls.

One of the first to announce the outbreak of war on radio in 1939 is Sigrid Schultz. Another female radio broadcaster at the time is Mary Marvin Breckinridge, who is the first female foreign correspondent on CBS radio. In early 1940 she broadcasts from Berlin; when she marries a diplomat, however, she has to resign.

1940–49

In 1940 Alicia Patterson (1906–63) and her husband start *Newsday,* which she edits and publishes. It becomes Long Island's largest daily.

Daisy Lee Gatson Bates (p. 188) and her husband start the weekly *State Press* in Arkansas in 1941 and expose police brutality and other injustices to African Americans.

During the war women serve not only as reporters (see sidebar) but also as photojournalists. Expatriate Thérèse Bonney (1894–1978) covers the Russo-Finnish War in 1939–40 and is one of the few to photograph the Battle of France; she is best known, however, for her moving pictures of displaced children, shown in her books *War Comes to the People* (1940) and *Europe's Children* (1943). Toni Frissell (1907–88) documents the U.S. Army Air Corps in England and does volunteer photography for the Red Cross; Elizabeth ("Tex") Williams works for the Women's Army Auxiliary Corps, beginning in 1944, and is one of the few African American women photographers. Margaret Bourke-White is the first female photographer accredited as a war correspondent. Torpedoed when she first ships out to Algiers, she later joins a

War Reporters

Wartime journalists include Russian-born Sonia Tomara, a New York Herald Tribune *reporter, who is in Warsaw when the war breaks out in 1939. She later reports the fall of France and in 1942 goes on a bombing mission while covering the China-Burma-India theater.*

Helen Kirkpatrick spends six months covering the Algerian campaign in 1943 and helps plan the press coverage of the Normandy invasion in 1944. She is one of the first correspondents in France on Liberation Day.

Ruth Cowan of Associated Press (AP) also travels to Algiers, with the first WAAC companies, and then covers the front in France. In 1944 Lee Carson of the International News Service (INS) witnesses D-Day from the air and later follows the tanks entering Paris on Liberation Day. Ann Stringer of United Press (UP) scoops all other reporters on the Russian arrival at the Elbe to meet U.S. forces in 1945, flying back to Paris with her story.

Other war correspondents in Europe include May Craig, Esther Tufty, and Doris Fleeson. Among the female correspondents on the Pacific front are Patricia Lockridge of Woman's Home Companion *and Charlotte Ebener, a stringer for INS and* Newsweek.

Reporting Firsts

Some firsts in the 1940s include:

—In 1945 Doris Fleeson (1901–70), who began reporting from the capital in the early 1920s and covered the war for Woman's Home Companion, *is the first woman to write a syndicated political column. She exposes fraud and corruption and takes presidents to task.*

—In 1946 Alice Allison Dunnigan (1906–83) is the first African American woman journalist to get her White House credentials, and in 1948 she travels with President Harry Truman on his cross-country whistle-stop campaign. Later she tackles President Dwight David Eisenhower on racial discrimination. "I always felt that a journalist should be a crusader," she says.

—Agnes Wilson Underwood is the first female city editor of a major daily, at the Los Angeles Evening Herald *(later* Herald-Examiner*) in 1947.*

—Pauline Frederick (1906–90), one of the first women news analysts on radio in 1939, is the first woman news reporter on television, covering the 1948 political conventions for ABC in order to get interviews with Helen Gahagan Douglas as well as the candidates' wives. In the early 1950s she becomes NBC's UN correspondent.

bombing mission and is with General Patton's troops when they cross the German border. In 1945 her photographs show the world the horrors of the Buchenwald concentration camp when it is liberated. Lee Miller (1907–77), known as a fashion photographer, is also an official war correspondent for the U.S. forces in Europe; Georgette ("Dickey") Meyer Chapman (1920–65) photographs the wounded at Iwo Jima in 1945.

In California in 1947, Marie Potts (1895–1978) starts *Smoke Signal,* an intertribal bimonthly that focuses on Indian rights.

1950–59

Marguerite ("Maggie") Higgins (1920–66), made Tokyo bureau chief for the *New York Herald Tribune* in 1950, is one of the first reporters on the scene when the Korean War breaks out in 1950 and persuades army officers to let her stay when they try to kick her out. For her reporting, she is the first woman to receive the Pulitzer Prize for international reporting, sharing it with five men. Her *War in Korea* (1951) is a best-seller.

In 1951 *Look* magazine hires Charlotte Brooks as its first woman staff photographer, and Eve Arnold is the first U.S. woman photographer represented by the photo agency Magnum.

In 1953 Ethel Lois Payne (1911–90) beomes the *Chicago Defender*'s only Washington correspondent. She makes front-page news when she confronts President Eisenhower on segregation and covers the civil rights movement as both a reporter and a demonstrator.

In 1954 Virginia M. Schau is the first woman to win the Pulitzer for spot news photography.

Mary McGrory gets her break when she covers the Army-McCarthy hearings in 1954 and then starts a three-times-weekly syndicated column at the *Washington Star-News* and later the *Washington Post.*

In 1955 Esther Pauline Friedman Lederer starts writing her advice column as "Ann Landers" for the *Chicago Sun-Times.* In 1956 her twin sister, Pauline Friedman Phillips, first publishes her "Dear Abby" column in the *San Francisco Chronicle.*

In 1955 Caro Brown is the first woman to win a Pulitzer Prize for local reporting, for braving threats to expose political corruption in Texas for the *Alice Daily Echo.*

The National Press Club first allows women reporters at its luncheons for celebrities in 1955, but they are confined to a small balcony above the dining room and cannot ask any questions.

Daughters of Bilitis publishes the *Ladder,* a pioneering lesbian magazine, in 1956.

Flora Lewis is the *Washington Post*'s first female foreign correspondent in 1958. In 1972 she joins the *New York Times* to head its Paris bureau.

For 12 weeks in 1959, Marya Mannes has her own interview program, *I Speak for Myself,* on WNEW-TV in New York.

Mary Lou Werner (later Forbes) of the *Washington Evening Star* shares the 1959 Pulitzer Prize for local reporting, for her coverage of school integration in Virginia.

In 1959 Marie Torre, a television columnist for the *New York Herald Tribune,* refuses to divulge her source for a derogatory remark about Judy Garland by a CBS executive and is the first newswoman to be jailed for contempt, serving 10 days in New Jersey.

1960–69

Miriam Ottenberg of the *Washington Evening Star* gains a 1960 Pulitzer for local reporting, for revealing unethical used-car dealers. Her other exposés include adoption fraud and bogus marriage counselors.

Nancy Conners Hanschmann (later Dickerson) is the first female TV news correspondent for CBS, in 1960. In 1963, now with NBC, she is the first woman to have her own news broadcast, *Nancy Dickerson with the News,* during daytime hours.

Heloise Bowles first syndicates her household tips column, "Hints from Heloise," in 1961. An offer of a free pamphlet on "whiter" laundry draws 100,000 requests in five days, overwhelming her post office.

Working for the Hearst papers, Marianne Means is, in 1961, the first woman assigned full-time to the White House. She publishes *The Woman in the White House* (1963).

After serving as fashion editor at *Harper's Bazaar* for two decades, Diana Dalziel Vreeland (c. 1903–89) joins *Vogue* in 1962 and is its editor-in-chief in 1963. She helps create the mystique of "Beautiful People."

Art critic Aline Bernstein Louchheim Saarinen (1914–72) joins NBC News in 1964 as its third female reporter; she also moderates the panel show *For Women Only.* In 1971 she heads the network's Paris bureau, the first woman to run an overseas bureau for a major TV network.

Shana Alexander first gains attention as a reporter with her column, "The Feminine Eye," at *Life* in 1964.

"Sheilah Graham" (Lily Sheil) is the top-ranking Hollywood gossip columnist in 1964, surpassing Louella Parsons and Hedda Hopper.

Lillian Wiggins begins editing the *Washington Afro-American Newspaper* in 1964. Also during the 1960s Dorothy Gillam is the first black woman editor on the *Washington Post,* in charge of the style section.

In 1964 Hazel Brannon Smith, owner of four local Mississippi papers, is the first woman to win a Pulitzer Prize for editorial writing, for her column, "Through Hazel Eyes," in the *Lexington Advertiser.* She has faced cross burnings and firebombings for her stance against racism.

On ABC-TV in 1964, reporter Marlene Sanders is the first woman to

Starts in the 1960s

Several women who have a strong impact on journalism get their start in the 1960s, including:

—Katherine ("Kay") Meyer Graham, who assumes control of the Washington Post *after her husband's death in 1963. She builds it into a major national paper with strong investigative reporting and backs her staff in exposing the Watergate scandal of the 1970s.*

—Ada Louise Landman Huxtable, who is the first full-time architecture critic at the New York Times *in 1963. She becomes a key proponent of historic preservation. In 1970 she is awarded the first Pulitzer Prize for distinguished criticism.*

—Barbara Walters, who gains a reporting spot on NBC's Today Show *in 1963, after working as a scriptwriter. She moves up to co-host in 1974 and in 1976 anchors ABC's evening news (see p. 301).*

— Judith Klein Crist, who becomes the movie reviewer for NBC's Today Show, *as well as movie critic for the* New York Herald Tribune *in 1963.*

—Pauline Kael, who publishes I Lost It at the Movies *(1965) and in 1968 becomes the* New Yorker *movie critic.*

Women's Liberation activists begin their own publications in 1968, such as Voice of the Women's Liberation Movement, *edited by "Joreen" (Jo Freeman) and other Chicago women;* Notes from the First Year, *put out by New York Radical Women; and* No More Fun and Games: A Journal of Female Liberation, *by Boston's Female Liberation Front. In 1970* off our backs *is started by Marilyn Saltzman Webb and others in Washington, D.C. Many more women's publications are established in the 1970s, including* Encuentro feminil *(1973),* Quest *(1973),* Sinister Wisdom *(1976),* Conditions *(1977), and* Heresies *(1977).*

Activists also tell their story in the mainstream media. Led by Susan Brownmiller, a coalition of 100-some women stages an 11-hour sit-in at Ladies' Home Journal *in 1970 to protest its stereotyped portrayal of women and demand better working conditions for its female staff. The group is "invited" to put out a special eight-page supplement to the August issue, which includes articles like "Help Wanted: Female, 99.6 Hours a Week, No Pay, Bed and Bored, Must Be Good with Children," as well as a list of feminist groups.*

anchor an evening news broadcast, but only as a substitute. She later anchors the weekend evening news.

Photojournalist Dickey Chapelle, author of *What's a Woman Doing Here* (1961), is killed while covering Vietnam when she steps on an antipersonnel mine. Other women who report on the Vietnam War include Liz Trotta for NBC-TV; Gloria Emerson of the *New York Times*, who later writes *Winners and Losers* (1978); Frances FitzGerald, whose articles appear in *Atlantic* and her award-winning book *Fire in the Lake* (1972); Maggie Higgins, who publishes *Our Vietnam Nightmare* (1965).

Helen Gurley Brown, author of the best-selling *Sex and the Single Girl* (1962), takes over as editor of the foundering *Cosmopolitan* magazine in 1965 and turns it into a top-selling publication.

Erma Bombeck begins her humorous column about housekeeping, "At Wit's End," a Dayton, Ohio, paper in 1965 and by 1968 it is carried in more than 200 other papers. Her books, such as *The Grass Is Always Greener Over the Septic Tank* (1976), are best-sellers.

In 1965 Joan Murray is the first black woman journalist hired by a major TV news station, WCBS in New York.

One of the first U.S. reporters to cover the unrest in Central America, Georgie Ann Geyer is the first to interview guerrilla leader César Montes in Guatemala in 1967; she also interviews Fidel Castro.

Helen Marmor is NBC's first woman news manager, in 1967.

Meg Greenfield joins the *Washington Post* in 1968, is the first woman on its editorial board, and in 1978 wins a Pulitzer Prize for editorial writing. From 1974 she also writes a regular column in *Newsweek*.

Elizabeth Betita Martinez and Enriqueta Longauex y Vasquez edit *El Grito del Norte* (The Cry of the North) in New Mexico (1968–73).

1970–79

In 1970, on the day that *Newsweek* comes out with a cover story on the women's movement, 46 female staff members tell the press they are filing sex discrimination charges. Only one of 52 writers is a woman, and there are no female executives. Women at *Time* file similar charges.

In 1971, after ongoing protests by women journalists, the National Press Club finally admits women as full members; Esther Van Wagoner Tufty is its first female member.

After adding "sex" to its antidiscrimination provisions in 1969, the Federal Communications Commission (FCC) requires TV stations to adopt affirmative action plans for women in 1971. NOW and other groups draw attention to inequities by challenging two stations when they try to renew their licenses.

In 1971 Marcia Ann Gillespie takes over as editor of *Essence* magazine (started 1970) and makes it a success. Susan Taylor follows her in 1981.

In 1971 Lucinda Franks is the first woman to win a Pulitzer Prize for national reporting. She shares the prize with Thomas Powers for a five-article series, "The Making of a Terrorist," on Diana Oughton (p. 80).

In 1972 Susan Stamberg is the first woman news anchor on a radio network, for National Public Radio's *All Things Considered*.

Ms. magazine premieres in 1972 and gains a circulation of 350,000 by 1973. Patricia Carbine, formerly executive editor of *Look* and then editor of *McCall's*, is the publisher, and activist Gloria Steinem, known for her 1963 exposé of Playboy bunnies and contributions to *New York* magazine, is the editor. In 1974 *Ms.* sponsors a documentary series for public television, *Woman Alive*, produced by Joan Shigekawa.

The Women's Institute for Freedom of the Press is formed in 1972. "For the right to 'freedom of the press' to be meaningful," it points out, "there must be a realistic means of exercising it."

Helen Copley takes charge of Copley Newspapers, publishers of 9 daily and 24 weekly papers in California, in 1973.

Helen Thomas becomes the first woman to head the White House bureau of United Press International, in 1974. She becomes the first woman president of the White House Correspondents Association in 1975 and the first female head of the Gridiron Club of journalists.

Mary Sullivan Simons becomes the first woman senior editor at the Sunday *New York Times Magazine* in 1974. In the same year Charlotte Curtis is the first woman on the *New York Times* masthead, as associate editor of the paper and editor of the Op-Ed page.

Carol Sutton (1933–85) is the first female managing editor of a major city daily, the *Louisville Courier-Journal*, in 1974. She later, in 1979, becomes senior editor of that paper and the sister *Louisville Times*.

"*Women . . . banded together*"—*Nan Robertson*

In 1974 seven women at the *New York Times* file a sex discrimination suit, *Elizabeth Boylan et al.* v. *The New York Times*, charging inequities in hiring, promotion, and pay. The suit, expanded into a class action for 550 female employees, is settled in 1978 in their favor. Later Nan Roberston describes the case in *The Girls in the Balcony* (1992).

As editor-in-chief of the *Pittsburgh Courier*, Hazel Garland is, in 1974, the first woman at the helm of a nationally circulated black newspaper.

Art critic Emily Genauer, initially at the *New York Herald Tribune* and later at *Newsday*, wins the Pulitzer Prize for criticism in 1974. In 1975 Mary McGrory, writer of the syndicated column "Point of View," is the first woman to receive the Pulitzer for commentary, for her 20 years of work, especially her coverage of the Watergate hearings.

Known for her incisive interviews, Barbara Walters, cohost of NBC's *Today Show*, is signed on by ABC in 1976 as the first woman to

Gains in the 1970s

TV firsts for the 1970s include:

—Barbara Tanabe is the first Asian American TV local news reporter, on KOMO-TV in Seattle in 1971. In the same year, after the FCC ruling, Constance ("Connie") Yu-Hwa Chung is one of four women hired by the CBS Washington bureau.

—Norma R. Quarles is both the first woman and the first African American woman to coanchor the evening news on a New York station, for WNBC-TV in 1971.

—In 1972, for NBC, Catherine Mackin is the first woman to cover both national conventions as a floor reporter.

—Alicia Weber is the first camerawoman on a TV network, NBC, in 1972. Risa Korris is the first at CBS News, in 1973.

—Canadian-born Hilary Brown is the first female TV foreign correspondent, for ABC in 1973.

—Lesley Stahl becomes the first regional anchor for CBS News in 1974 and in 1976 helps Walter Cronkite cover the California vote on election night.

—In 1974 Susan Peterson is the first female CBS TV foreign correspondent, although she isn't given a proper office when she first arrives at the London bureau.

Photographing the Story

A number of women gain prominence as photojournalists starting in the 1970s and 1980s:

—In 1970 Mary Ellen Mark publishes her startling photos of heroin users in Look *magazine. She later documents women in a mental institution (*Ward 81, *1979),* Mother Teresa *(*Life, *1980), street kids in Seattle (*Streetwise, *1988), and other subjects.*

—In 1973 Annie Leibovitz, known for her celebrity portraits, becomes the chief photographer for Rolling Stone *magazine; in 1983 she is the first contributing photographer to* Vanity Fair.

—Beginning in 1978 Susan Meiselas's photographs of the Nicaraguan Revolution are published in various magazines (also in her book Nicaragua, *1981).*

—In 1986 the Philadelphia Inquirer *publishes Donna Ferrato's series of photos on domestic violence (later in her book* Living with the Enemy, *1991).*

—Maggie Steber begins photographing Haiti in 1986; her work appears in magazines and her book Dancing on Fire *(1992).*

—Coreen Simpson photographs New York lifestyles for the Village Voice, Essence, Encore, *and other publications in the 1980s. She also begins her large portrait series of African American and Latino youth.*

coanchor a major network's evening news program. However, after constant friction with her coanchor, Harry Reasoner, she leaves in 1978 and starts co-hosting *20/20* in 1979. Jane Pauley takes Walters's place on the *Today Show* (without the cohost title).

In 1976 Marlene Sanders is named ABC vice president and director of documentaries, becoming the first female news vice president in TV. Joan Richman is executive producer of the CBS Weekend News. Pauline Frederick is the first woman to moderate a televised presidential debate, between Jimmie Carter and Gerald Ford.

Cynthia Tucker is the first African American woman editor of a major daily, the *Atlanta Constitution,* in 1976.

In 1977 both NBC and *Reader's Digest* settle sex discrimination suits with large back-pay awards and future improvements.

Margo Huston of the *Milwaukee Journal* receives the 1977 Pulitzer for local reporting for her exposé on the neglected elderly: "I'll Never Leave My Home, Would You?"

In a case brought by Melissa Ludtke Lincoln of *Sports Illustrated,* U.S. District Court judge Constance Baker Motley rules in 1978 that women sportswriters must be given equal access to baseball team locker rooms to conduct after-game interviews.

Charlayne Hunter-Gault (p. 189) joins the *MacNeil/Lehrer Report* on PBS in 1978 and in 1983 becomes a national correspondent when the show is expanded.

1980–89

Ellen Holtz Goodman, syndicated columnist at the *Boston Globe,* wins the 1980 Pulitzer Prize for commentary. "I worry about my weight and the bomb," she comments at one point. Another Pulitzer Prize winner in 1980 is Madeleine Blais of the *Miami Herald,* for feature writing. Indeed, women dominate the feature writing awards in the next five years, with Teresa Carpenter of the *Village Voice* in New York winning in 1981, Nan Robertson of the *New York Times* in 1983, and Alice Steinbach of the *Baltimore Sun* in 1985. Also, Shirley Christian wins the 1981 Pulitzer for international reporting for her coverage of Latin America for the *Miami Herald,* and Karen Elliot House of the *Wall Street Journal* wins the 1984 award.

In 1982 the percentage of female local TV news anchors has more than tripled since 1972, from 11% to 36%.

Lesley Stahl, later the second *60 Minutes* female reporter, begins hosting *Face the Nation* on Sunday CBS in 1983.

Former KMBC-TV (Kansas City) news anchor Christine Craft sues for sex discrimination in 1983, pointing to unequal pay and claiming she was fired because she was not attractive enough. Two juries find in her favor, but the judge overrules them, as does the appeals court.

In 1984, of 24 reporters at National Public Radio, 11 are women, including Susan Stamberg (coanchor of *All Things Considered*), Linda Wertheimer, Nina Totenberg, and Cokie Boggs Roberts.

As coanchor of the evening news for WNBC-TV in New York, Pat Harper shares in five Emmy awards for newscasts in 1984–89. She also receives an Emmy for her piece on the homeless.

Diane Sawyer becomes the first woman reporter on CBS's *60 Minutes* in 1984. She leaves in 1989 to coanchor ABC's *Prime Time Live*.

In 1984 Cathleen Black, former associate publisher of *Ms.*, becomes publisher of *USA Today*, the third largest U.S. daily.

Only in 1986 does the *New York Times* agree to use the term "Ms."

Four women receive Pulitzer Prizes in 1986: Edna Buchanan of the *Miami Herald* wins for general news reporting; Mary Pat Flaherty of the *Pittsburgh Press* shares the prize for specialized news reporting; Katherine Ellison shares the prize for international reporting, and Carol Guzy of the *Miami Herald* shares the prize for spot news photography (she wins a second prize in 1995).

NBC news broadcaster Linda Ellerbee publishes her witty account *"And So It Goes": Adventures in Television* (1986).

In 1987 all the coverage of the Iran Contra hearings in Congress for the *MacNeil/Lehrer News Hour* is done by women. Judy Woodruff and Elizabeth Drew coanchor the reports, with Cokie Roberts providing occasional floor interviews.

In a 1987 study of 239 network reporters, no women rank in the 10 with the most air time. The top female is Rita Braver (13th), followed by Susan Spencer (23rd).

Carole Simpson, who was the first black newsperson on Chicago TV in 1970, anchors *ABC's World News Saturday* in 1988, as well as appearing regularly on *Nightline* and *20/20*.

Jane E. Healey of the *Orlando Sentinel* wins the 1988 Pulitzer for editorial writing, and Lois Wille of the *Chicago Tribune* the 1989 award. Jacqui Banaszynski of the *St. Paul Pioneer Press and Dispatch* wins in 1988 for feature writing.

After being replaced as editor of *Vogue*, Grace Mirabella starts her own magazine, *Mirabella*, in 1989.

1990–95

Answering an appeal by *Des Moines Register* editor Geneva Overholser, rape survivor Nancy Ziegenmeyer agrees to use her name in a 1990 story by reporter Jane Schorer in an attempt to end the secrecy and consequent stigma attached to rape. Yet in 1991 the *New York Times* doesn't bother to ask permission before using the name and attacking the character of a woman who has accused William Kennedy Smith of

Filming Documentaries

Women documentary filmmakers abound from the late 1970s on:

—Barbara Kopple's Harlan County USA *wins the 1976 Academy Award for best documentary. She wins a second Oscar for* American Dreams *(1990).*

—In 1977 Perry Miller Adato is the first woman to win an award from the Directors Guild of America, for her documentary on Georgia O'Keeffe. Also in 1977, Union Maids, *coproduced by Julia Reichert, is nominated for an Academy Award.*

—A few other documentaries by women include Lee Grant's Oscar-winning Down and Out in America *(1985), Sylvia Morales's* Chicana *(1979), Sandra Osawa and Peggy Barnett's* The Black Hills Are Not for Sale, *Michele Citron's* What You Take for Granted *(1983), Renie Tajima and Christine Choy's* Who Killed Vincent Chin? *(1988), Ginny Durrin's* Promises to Keep *(1988), Judith Montell's* Forever Activists *(1990), Debra Chasnoff's Oscar-winning* Deadly Deception *(1991), Jennie Livingston's* Paris Is Burning *(1991), Diana Reyna's* Surviving Columbus *(1992), Deborah Hoffman's* Complaints of a Dutiful Daughter *(1994), Connie Field and Marilyn Mulford's* Freedom on My Mind *(1994), and Freida Lee Mock's Oscar-winning* Maya Lin *(1994).*

rape. Outrage expressed by readers and female employees leads the *Times* to print an apology.

Caryle Murphy of the *Washington Post* receives a 1990 award from the International Women's Media Foundation for courageous reporting from Kuwait City during the Iraqi invasion (see also sidebar). Christiane Amanpour of CNN also gains attention for coverage of Kuwait and later receives an Emmy for her reporting on the Bosnian war.

Victoria Corderi receives a 1990 Emmy for her report "Women Doing Time" on *48 Hours*. She also is the first Latina to coanchor a national network news program, at CBS *Morning News*.

Mónica Cecilia Lozano becomes editor of *La Opinión*, the nation's largest Spanish-language daily, in 1991.

Elizabeth P. Valk is the first woman publisher of *Time*, in 1991.

Pearl Stewart is the second black woman to head a major city daily, as editor of the *Oakland Tribune* in California in 1992.

Giselle Fernandez, former coanchor of CBS *This Morning*, becomes a correspondent for the CBS Evening News in 1992 and later anchors some of the weekend editions. Jackie Nespral hosts weekend editions of the *Today Show*.

Deb Price of the *Detroit News* is the first to syndicate an openly gay column, in 1992. She later publishes *And Say Hi to Joyce: America's First Gay Columnist Comes Out* (1995).

After turning *Vanity Fair* into a success, British-born Tina Brown is named the first woman editor of the *New Yorker*, in 1992.

After winning the 1992 Pulitzer (see sidebar), Anna Quindlen of the *New York Times* publishes a collection of her Op-Ed columns, *Thinking Out Loud*, in 1993. (Her 1988 collection, *Living Out Loud*, featured her syndicated "Life in the 30's" columns.)

In 1993 Connie Chung follows in Barbara Walters's footsteps and is the second woman to coanchor an evening news broadcast on national network television, for CBS. However, tensions develop with her coanchor, Dan Rather, and she is forced out in 1995.

Literature and
Other Writings

Toni Morrison after learning she won the 1993
Nobel Prize for Literature (AP/Wide World Photos)

The First Poets

In 1650 the brother-in-law of Anne Bradstreet takes her poems to London and has them published, without her permission, in The Tenth Muse Lately Sprung Up in America, *the first published work by an American woman writer. The mother of eight children, she continues writing, and a revised, expanded edition is published posthumously,* Several Poems Compiled with Great Variety of Wit and Learning *(1678). In one poem, to her husband, she writes: "If ever two were one, then surely we./If ever man were loved by wife, then thee."*

The first known poem by an African American writer is "Bars Fight," written in 1746 by Lucy Terry (later Prince, p. 15) about an Indian raid in Deerfield, Massachusetts. It is not, however, published until 1855.

1600s

Anne Dudley Bradstreet (1612–72) is the first published American woman writer (see sidebar). Some of the early Quaker missionaries, such as Mary Dyer, leave writings (see "Religion"). A different document comes from Mary White Rowlandson. Captured by the Indians in the mid-1670s, she describes her 83 days as a prisoner, mostly in Weetamoo's household, in one of the first captivity narratives, published in 1682.

1700s

In 1704 Sarah Kemble Knight (p. 268) recounts her experiences riding on horseback from Boston to New York and back in her diary, published posthumously in 1825 as *The Journal of Madam Knight.*

Esther Edwards Burr (1732–58) is one of many women whose journals are an important source of information on daily American life in the mid-1700s. Another is Elizabeth Sandwich Drinker (1734–1807), whose journal is published much later as *Not So Long Ago* (1937).

Martha Wadsworth Brewster of Lebanon, Connecticut, publishes her *Poems on Divers Subjects* in 1757.

Mercy Otis Warren (1728–1814) publishes her first satirical play, *The Adulateur,* anonymously in the *Massachusetts Spy* in 1772. Other dramas of political satire, intended to be read rather than performed, include *The Defeat* (1773) and *The Group* (1775).

Phillis Wheatley (c. 1753–84) is the first African American to publish a poetry collection, *Poems on Various Subjects, Religious and Moral* (1773). She is legally freed from slavery only after the book's publication and later writes a friend, "In every human Breast, God has implanted a Principle, which we call Love of Freedom; it is impatient of Oppression, and pants for Deliverance."

Writing as "Constantia," Judith Sargent Stevens (later Murray, 1751–1820) publishes her first essay, "Desultory Thoughts upon the Utility of Encouraging a Degree of Self-Complacency, Especially in Female Bosoms." She later writes a regular column of commentary (p. 290) and publishes three volumes of her essays, *The Gleaner* (1798). Her "On the Equality of the Sexes" (1790) is an important feminist document (see p. 14). She also writes plays and poems.

The first woman to earn her livelihood from writing is Hannah Adams (1755–1831), who publishes *An Alphabetical Compendium of Various Sects* in 1784, as well as other historical works.

After contributing poems by "Philenia" to magazines, Sarah Wentworth Apthorp Morton (1759–1846) publishes her long poem *Ouâbi: or The Virtues of Nature* (1790), followed by *Beacon Hill* (1797).

The poems and prose works of Ann Eliza Bleecker (1752–83), published posthumously in 1793, include a depiction of frontier life during the Revolutionary War.

1800–19

The first major history by a U.S. woman is Mercy Otis Warren's three-volume *History of the Rise, Progress and Termination of the American Revolution* (1805), which includes her own opinions of the events.

Essayist Hannah Mather Crocker publishes *Observations on the Real Rights of Women* in 1818 (see p. 15).

1820–39

Scottish-born Frances ("Fanny") Wright publishes letters from her first U.S. trip in *View of Society and Manners in America* in 1821 (see p 16).

Catharine Maria Sedgwick (1789–1867) anonymously publishes her anti-Calvinist novel, *A New-England Tale* (1822). She portrays a wily spinster in *Redwood* (1824) and depicts relations between whites and Native Americans in the historical romance *Hope Leslie* (1827).

Lydia Maria Francis (later Child) publishes the novel *Hobomok* (1824) and *The Rebels, or Boston before the Revolution* (1825). Her guide *The Frugal Housewife* (1829) is a popular success, but she is best known for her abolitionist writings in the 1830s (see p. 17).

In 1824 Mary Jemison describes her life with the Seneca (see p. 109).

Magazine editor Sara Josepha Hale (p. 290) authors *Poems for Our Children* (1830), which includes "Mary Had a Little Lamb."

Published in London in 1831, Mary Prince's account of her ordeal as a slave in Bermuda is the first slave narrative by a woman and serves as an important model for later accounts.

Widely read in her time, Lydia Huntley Sigourney (1791–1865) writes *Letters to Young Ladies* (1833), *Poems* (1834), and other works.

Angelina and Sarah Grimké publish several important abolitionist tracts in the mid-1830s (see pp. 18–19).

Eliza Leslie (1787–1858) writes children's stories, collected in *Atlantic Tales* (1833), as well as cookbooks and an etiquette manual (1853).

Poet Maria Gowen Brooks (c. 1794–1845) publishes *Zóphiël; or, the Pride of Seven* (1833) and the autobiographical *Idomen; or the Vale of Yumuri* (1838).

After starting a children's magazine (p. 290), Caroline Howard Gilman writes *Recollections of a Housekeeper* (1834) and later *Recollections of a Southern Matron* (1838).

Elleanor Eldridge (1784–c. 1845) publishes her *Memoirs* (1838), an early narrative by a free black woman in New England.

In 1838 Frances Sargent Locke Osgood (1811–50) publishes her first two poetry volumes, *Casket of Fate* and *A Wreath of Wild Flowers from New England*.

Caroline Stansbury Kirkland (1801–64) writes her autobiographical

Early Novelists

American Susanna Haswell Rowson (c. 1762– 1824) publishes her novel Charlotte; a Tale of Truth *(based on a seduction scandal) in London in 1791; reprinted as* Charlotte Temple *in 1794 in Philadelphia, it is America's first best-seller. Rowson takes to the stage, performing in several of her own works, and then sets up a school.*

In 1797 Hannah Webster Foster (1758–1840) writes The Coquette; or The History of Eliza Wharton, *a fictionalized account of the seduction, affair, and tragic death of Elizabeth Whitman.*

Julia and the Illuminated Baron (1800) is the first novel by Sarah Sayward Barrell Keating (later Wood, 1759–1854), who calls herself the "Lady of Maine."

In 1801 Tabitha Gilman Tenney (1762–1837) publishes her two-volume satirical novel, Female Quixotism: Exhibited in the Romantic Opinions and Extravagant Adventures of Dorcasina Sheldon.

Rebecca Rush publishes her one known novel, Kelroy, *in 1812.*

novel, *A New Home—Who'll Follow?* (1839), offering realistic descriptions of life on the Michigan frontier.

1840–49

In the early 1840s Lowell, Massachusetts, mill workers publish their writings in the *Lowell Offering* (see "Work").

In 1840 Elizabeth Palmer Peabody runs a Boston bookshop, a gathering place for Transcendentalists, and is probably the first U.S. female book publisher, issuing children's books by Nathaniel Haw-thorne and translations by Margaret Fuller.

Educator Catharine Beecher offers practical housekeeping and childcare advice in *A Treatise on Domestic Ecomony* (1841) and *The Domestic Receipt Book* (1846). Later she coauthors *The American Woman's Home* (1869) with her sister, Harriet Beecher Stowe.

Essays (1841) by Ann Plato is the first book of essays by an African American; it also includes poems and biographies.

In *Flowers to Children* (1844), Lydia Maria Child includes her poem beginning "Over the river and through the woods."

In 1845 Margaret Fuller publishes her seminal *Woman in the Nineteenth Century* (see sidebar and p. 20).

After publishing two novels and various poems and essays, Anna Ogden Mowatt (1819–70) turns to drama. Her satirical comedy *Fashion; or, Life in New York* (1845) is a hit.

In 1845 Frances Manwaring Caulkins (1795–1869) writes a detailed history of Norwich, Connecticut, and is the first woman elected to the Massachusetts Historical Society, in 1849.

Starting in 1846, Miriam Berry Whitcher (1811–52) writes amusing satirical sketches in popular magazines. One series offers the ramblings of "The Widow Bedott"; another relates "Aunt Magwire's Experience."

Elizabeth Lummis Ellet (c. 1812–77) authors the three-volume *The Women of the American Revolution* (1848–50), *Domestic History of the American Revolution* (1850), and *Pioneer Women of the West* (1852).

E.D.E.N. (Emma Dorothy Eliza Nevitte) Southworth (1819–99) publishes her first novel, *Retribution* (1849), and writes more than 60 other popular romances and melodramas (see 1859).

1850–59

The Narrative of Sojourner Truth (which is written down by Olive Gilbert) is published in 1850 (see also p. 22).

New feminist works include *Discourse on Women* (1850) by Lucretia Mott (p. 17) and *Woman and Her Needs* (1851) by Elizabeth Oakes Prince Smith (1806–93), who also publishes several poems and stories.

The Wide, Wide World (1851), a sentimental tale by Susan Bogert

Warner (1819–85), is the first U.S. book to pass the million mark in sales. Warner's other works include *Queechy* (1852).

Sarah Tittle Barrett Bolton (1814–93) is best known for her poem "Paddle Your Own Canoe" (1851).

In 1852 Harriet Beecher Stowe (p. 22) publishes her top-selling antislavery novel, *Uncle Tom's Cabin; or, Life Among the Lowly*, first serialized in the *National Era*. To counter vociferous attacks on her book, Stowe puts out *A Key to Uncle Tom's Cabin*, documenting the abuses her critics claim she made up. Later she writes another antislavery novel, *Dred: A Tale of the Great Dismal Swamp* (1856). Many southern writers respond to Stowe's work with defenses of slavery, including Mary Henderson Eastman (1819–87) with *Aunt Phillis's Cabin; or, Southern Life as It Is* (1852), and Caroline Lee Whiting Hentz (1800–56) with *The Planter's Northern Bride* (1854).

Sara Josepha Hale's *Woman's Record* (1853) includes biographical sketches of more than 2,500 women from antiquity to 1850.

Already known as an abolitionist lecturer, Frances Ellen Watkins (later Harper, p. 23) publishes *Poems on Miscellaneous Subjects* (1854), including such works as "The Slave Mother." Her tale "The Two Offers" is the first known short story printed by an African American, in the *Anglo-African Magazine* in 1859.

Harriet E. Adams Wilson publishes the first known novel by an African American woman, *Our Nig; or, Sketches from the Life of a Free Black, in a Two-Story White House, North. Showing That Slavery's Shadows Fall Even There* (1859). Abolitionists, however, do not highlight her work, as it focuses on northern racism rather than southern slavery.

Many women in the mid-19th century keep journals that detail the daily life of the time. Women traveling west, for example, record their impressions and activities (see p. 269).

Additional prose pieces of the 1850s include *Greenwood Leaves* (1850), a collection of magazine sketches, and *Haps and Mishaps of a Tour in Europe* (1854) by "Grace Greenwood" (Sara Jane Clarke Lippincott, p. 291); *Rural Hours* (1850), a year-long nature diary by Susan Fenimore Cooper (1813–94); and *This, That, and the Other* (1854), with sketches and poems by Ellen Louise Chandler (later Moulton, 1835–1908).

1860–69

Ann Stephens's *Malaeska: The Indian Wife of the White Hunter* (1860) is the first of Beadle's dime novels and quickly sells a half-million copies. Other dime novel writers include Metta Victoria Fuller Victor (1831–85) and Mary Ann Andrews Denison (c. 1826–1911).

Works by feminist Caroline Wells Healey Dall (1822–1912) include *Woman's Right to Labor* (1860) and *The College, the Market, and the Court* (1867). She argues for equal educational opportunities, an end to legal restrictions, and equal pay.

Fiction of the 1850s

In addition to the novels cited in the text, new works include The Red Hand of Ulster *(1850) and* Alice Riordan *(1851) by Irish-born Mary Anne Madden Sadlier (1820–1903), who writes some 60 other popular pro-Catholic novels;* The Conspirator *(1850) by Eliza Ann Dupuy (1814–80), a writer of romantic novels and thrillers;* The Sunny Side; or, The Country Minister's Wife *(1851), a religious novel by Elizabeth Wooster Stuart Phelps (1815–52);* Clovernook, or Recollections of Our Neighborhood in the West *(1852) by Alice Cary (1820–71);* Ida May *(1854), a best-seller about white slavery, by Mary Hayden Green Pike (1824–1908);* Fashion and Famine *(1854) and* The Old Homestead *(1855), two of many popular novels by Ann Sophia Winterbotham Stephens (1810–86);* Lena Rivers *and other domestic tales by Mary Jane Hawes Holmes (1825–1907);* The Lamplighter *(1854), a best-seller about an orphan, by Maria Susanna Cummins (1827–66);* Alone *(1856) and other romances by "Marion Harland" (Mary Hawes Terhune, 1830–1922); the lead story in the first* Atlantic Monthly *(1857), by Rose Terry Cooke (1827–92), a forerunner of the local-color realists; and* The Hidden Hand *(1859), the most popular work of E.D.E.N. Southworth.*

Rebecca Blaine Harding (later Davis, 1831–1910) anonymously publishes her short novel *Life in the Iron Mills* (1861), offering a naturalistic picture of the grim life of mill workers. Her second book, *Margret Howth* (1862), extends this theme. Other stories depict the horrors of war, and the novel *Waiting for the Verdict* (1868) concerns race relations.

Harriet Ann Jacobs (1813–97), as "Linda Brent," publishes the autobiographical *Incidents in the Life of a Slave Girl: Written by Herself* (1861), describing the abuse and torture she escaped from and her seven years living in a crawlspace.

Julia Ward Howe (1819–1910) writes her most famous poem, "The Battle Hymn of the Republic" (1862), which is set to music and becomes the anthem of the Union army during the Civil War.

In *Journal of a Residence on a Georgian Plantation* (1863), British actress Fanny Kemble (1809–93) details her horror at the slavery on her husband's plantation in an effort to turn England against the Confederacy.

A prolific writer of potboilers and thrillers, Louisa May Alcott (1832–88) first gains attention with *Hospital Sketches* (1863), on her experiences as a Civil War nurse. Asked to write a popular girls' story, she pens the classic, semiautobiographical *Little Women; or Meg, Jo, Beth, and Amy* (1868–69), which is an immediate hit (see also 1870s).

Prison reformer Eliza Wood Burhans Farnham writes *Woman and Her Era* (1864), celebrating woman's moral superiority over man.

Mary Mapes Dodge (p. 292) writes her classic children's tale, *Hans Brinker; or the Silver Skates* (1865).

Elizabeth Hobbs Keckley (c. 1818/24–1907) publishes her autobiography, *Behind the Scenes; or Thirty Years a Slave and Four Years in the White House* (1868), which creates controversy over her portrayal of Mary Todd Lincoln, for whom she worked as a dressmaker.

Scenes in the Life of Harriet Tubman, as told to Sarah Hopkins Bradford, appears in 1869 (expanded in 1886 as *Harriet Tubman: The Moses of Her People*).

Louisa May Alcott (Library of Congress)

Additional 1860s fiction includes the top-selling *Rutledge* (1860), a gothic romance by Miriam Coles Harris (1834–1925), whose works generally involve the humbling of a rebellious heroine; *Faith Gartney's Girlhood* (1863) and other didactic novels by Adeline Dutton Train Whitney (1824–1906); *The Amber Gods* (1863), the first short story collection by Harriet Prescott (later Spofford, 1835–1921), a popular magazine fiction writer in the period 1868–90; the pro-Confederacy *Macaria; or, Atlas of Sacrifice* (1864) and top-selling *St. Elmo* (1866) by Augusta Evans (later Wilson, 1835–1909); *The Gates Ajar* (1868), a highly popular spiritual novel by Elizabeth Stuart Phelps (later Ward, 1844–1911); and *Stepping Heavenward* (1869), a top-selling autobiographical tale revealing a young girl's emotions, by Elizabeth Payson Prentiss (1818–78), who is already a popular children's book author.

Juvenile books include the Prudy Parlin series (1863–65) and Dotty Dimple stories (1867–69), featuring mischievous children, by "Sophie May" (Rebecca Sophia Clarke, 1833–1906); and *Elsie Dinsmore* (1867), the first of a 28-volume series by Martha Finley (1828–1909);

Additional poetry includes "Rock Me to Sleep" (1860), used as a campfire song during the Civil War, by Elizabeth Chase Akers (later Allen, 1832–1911), and "The Picket Guard" (1861), with its famous opening line "All quiet along the Potomac tonight," by Ethel Lynn Eliot Beers (1827–79).

Diarists include Mary Boykin Miller Chesnut (1823–86), the wife of a prominent Confederate, who begins her conscious record of events in the South around 1860, later published as *A Diary from Dixie* (1905), and Eliza Frances Andrews (1840–1931), who in 1864 starts the diary later published as *The War-Time Journal of a Georgia Girl* (1908). A different perspective is given by Charlotte Forten Grimké in her descriptions of teaching freedmen in the Sea Islands (see "Education").

1870–79

Louisa May Alcott publishes almost a book a year, including *An Old-Fashioned Girl* (1870), *Little Men* (1871), *Eight Cousins* (1875), and *Rose in Bloom* (1876). Her final sequel to *Little Women* is *Jo's Boys* (1886).

Rose Hartwick (later Thorpe, 1850–1939) publishes "Curfew Must Not Ring Tonight" (1870) without a copyright, so she does not benefit from its popularity. Later she writes "Remember the Alamo."

In her satirical novel *Who Would have Thought It?* (1872), María Ampara Ruiz de Burton (1832–95) attacks the racism of New England.

Humorist Marietta Holley (1836–1926) publishes *My Opinion and Betsy Bobbet's* (1873), the first in a series using the common-sense voice of a hard-working country wife, "Samantha Allen," to expose the ridiculousness of other characters who oppose women's rights.

Lucy Larcom (1824–93), a former mill worker, writes *An Idyl of Work* (1875), a narrative in blank verse.

Anna Katherine Green (1846–1935) pens one of the earliest detective stories, and the first by a woman, *The Leavenworth Case* (1878) with Detective Ebenezer Gryce and his assistant, Amelia Butterworth. Her 40 or so books help set the formula for the detective novel.

Pauline Hopkins (1859–1930) writes *Slaves' Escape; or, the Underground Railroad* (1879), the first known play by an African American woman. It is staged in Boston by a family troupe in 1880.

Books on women's issues in the 1870s include *Woman in American Society* (1873) by dress reformer Abba Goold Woolson (1838–1921); *The Sexes Throughout Nature* (1875) by Antoinette Brown Blackwell (p. 203), who uses Darwin's ideas to argue for female emancipation; and *American Women* (1877), two volumes of biographical sketches by

More from the 1870s

Fiction includes Fettered for Life; or Lord and Master *(1874), a feminist novel by suffragist Lillie Devereux Blake;* A Family Secret *by Eliza Frances Andrews;* Deephaven *(1877), the first collection of sketches by Sarah Orne Jewett (1849–1909); and* That Husband of Mine *(1877), a best-seller by Mary Ann Andrews Denison.*

Juvenile literature includes The William Henry Letters *(1870) and* Lucy Maria *(1874) by Abby Morton Diaz (1821–1904) and* What Katy Did, *the first in a five-volume series by Susan Coolidge (Sarah Chauncey Woolsey, 1835–1905).*

Nonfiction includes The River of the West *(1870), the story of a mountain man, and historical writings by Frances Fuller Victor (1826–1902);* Among the Isles of Shoals *(1872) by Celia Laighton Thaxter (1835–94), also a poet;* History of the City of New York *(two volumes, 1877, 1881) by Martha Reade Nash Lamb (1826–93); and* A Year of American Travel *(1878), the first of several collections of articles by Jessie Benton Frémont (1824–1902).*

Fiction of the 1880s

Fiction includes Anne *(1882), a mystery thriller, and* For the Major *(1883) by Constance Fenimore Woolson (1840–94);* Somebody's Neighbors *(1881), short stories by Rose Terry Cooke (1827–92);* A Fatal Wooing *(1883) and other escapist melodramas for young working women by Laura Jean Libbey (1862–1924);* The Led-Horse Claim: A Romance of a Mining Town, *written and illustrated by Mary Hallock Foote;* In the Tennessee Mountains *(1884), a short story collection, and several novels by "Charles Egbert Craddock," later revealed as Mary Noailles Murfree (1850–1922);* Guenn: A Wave on the Breton Coast *(1884) and other romantic fiction by Blanche Willis Howard (1847–98); the novel* A Country Doctor *(1884) and* A White Heron, and Other Stories *(1886) by Sarah Orne Jewett; historical romances such as* The Bow of Orange Ribbon *(1886) and* Remember the Alamo *(1888) by Amelia Huddleston Barr (1831–1919);* Samantha at Saratoga; or, Racin' After Fash-ion *(1887) by Marietta Holley;* John Ward, Preacher *(1888), the first of several best-sellers by Margaret Wade Campbell Deland (1857–1945);* The Romance of Dollard *by Mary Hartwell Catherwood (1847–1902).*

Frances E. Willard (revised with Mary A. Livermore in 1893), although no African American women are included.

The autobiographies of about 15 Mexican American women in early California are transcribed in the late 1870s by Hubert Bancroft, including María Inocenta Avila's *Cosas de California (Things of California)*, Apolinaria Lorenzana's *Memorias de la beata (Memories of a Pious Woman)*, and Euralia Pérez's *Una viega y sus recuerdos (An Old Woman and Her Memories)*.

1880–89

Several juvenile classics appear in the 1880s. Lucretia Peabody Hale (1820–1900), who first introduced the mishap-prone Peterkin family in an 1868 story, publishes *The Peterkin Papers* (1880) and *The Last of the Peterkins* (1886). Writing as "Margaret Sidney," Harriet Mulford Stone (later Lothrop, 1844–1924) publishes *Five Little Peppers and How They Grew* (1880), followed by 11 more tales about the Pepper family as well as many other books. British-born Frances Hodgson Burnett (1849–1924) writes *Little Lord Fauntleroy* (1886), which she later dramatizes, and *Sarah Crewe* (1888). Louisa May Alcott's *Jo's Boys* appears in 1886.

Laura Elizabeth Howe Richards (1850–1943) publishes *Sketches and Scraps* (1880), the first U.S. book of nonsense rhymes, as well as a story collection, *Five Mice in a Mouse-trap* (1880).

In 1881 Jeanette Leonard Gilder (1849–1916) and her brother start the *Critic*, an important literary criticism magazine. In 1889 Helen Archibald Clarke (1860–1926) and Charlotte Endymion Porter (1857–1942) start *Poet Lore*, a monthly with mostly European works.

The first three volumes of *The History of Woman Suffrage* appear (1881, 1882, 1886; see "Politics").

"Your huddled masses yearning to be free"
—Emma Lazarus

In 1882 Emma Lazarus (1849–87) publishes *Songs of a Semite*, which includes the play *The Dance of Death* and several poems. "The Banner of the Jew" (1882) is a militant call to action against oppression. In 1883 she writes her best-known poem, "The New Colossus," which is inscribed at the base of the Statue of Liberty, with the lines above.

Poems of Passion (1883) by Ella Wheeler (later Wilcox, 1850–1919) is a top-selling collection.

After publishing *A Century of Dishonor* (1881; see p. 32), outlining government injustices to Native Americans, Helen Fiske Hunt Jackson (1830–85) writes the sentimental novel *Ramona* (1884) to further the crusade for Indian rights. A more direct appeal is made by Sarah Winnemucca in *Life Among the Piutes* (see p. 32).

Nonfiction of the 1880s includes *The Problem of the Poor* (1882) and

Prisoners of Poverty (1887), the latter about the exploitation of women workers, by Helen Stuart Campbell (1839–1918); *The Life of Mary Wollstonecraft* (1884) by Elizabeth Robins Pennell (1855–1936), as well as a travel book, *A Canterbury Pilgrimage* (1885), illustrated by her husband, Joseph; *Some Successful Women* (1888), the first of several biographical studies by Sarah Knowles Bolton (1841–1916); *Books and Men* (1888), the first of several essay collections by Agnes Repplier (1855–1950); and *A New England Girlhood* (1889), an autobiographical account of Lucy Larcom's experience in the Lowell mills.

1890–99

Although seven poems were published, without her consent, during her lifetime, most of the work of Emily Dickinson (1830–86) is found, in neatly wrapped bundles, by her sister, Lavinia, after her death. The first collection is published posthumously in 1890, followed by two more, in 1891 and 1896. Over time Dickinson's 1,775 poems, highly concise and often with unusual phrasing, earn her a reputation as one of America's greatest poets. She also leaves a voluminous correspondence, which was her main link to the outside literary world during her reclusive life.

Octavia Victoria Rogers Albert's collection of stories from former slaves, *The House of Bondage*, is published posthumously in 1890.

Among the first novels by African American women are Emma Dunham Kelley's *Megda* (1891), Frances Ellen Watkins Harper's *Iola Leroy, or, Shadows Uplifted* (1892) and social reformer Victoria Earle Matthew's *Aunt Lindy* (1893). An earlier novel by Harper, *Minnie's Sacrifice*, was serialized in the *Christian Recorder* in 1869.

The first known Native American woman's novel is *Wynema: A Child of the Forest* (1891) by Creek writer and teacher Sophia Alice Callahan (1868–94), who protests government policies against Indians.

Charlotte Perkins Stetson (later Gilman) publishes her short story "The Yellow Wallpaper" (1892), a graphic depiction of a young wife's mental breakdown, based on her own experience. She later publishes a major feminist plea, *Women and Economics* (1898; see p. 38).

Kate O'Flaherty Chopin (1851–1904) publishes a number of short stories, including the collection *Bayou Folk* (1894), and her novel *The Awakening* (1899), which is condemned by critics for its description of a young woman's sexual desires.

Inspired by the view on top of Pikes Peak in Colorado, Katharine Lee Bates (1859–1929) writes her most famous poem, "America the Beautiful" (1895), which is later set to music.

In *From Plotzk to Boston* (1899), Mary Antin (1881–1949) translates the letters she wrote in Yiddish to her uncle in Russia describing her journey to America.

The first Chinese American women fiction writers are two sisters: Winnifred Eaton (later Babcock, c. 1877–1954), using the Japanese

Fiction of the 1890s

In addition to the works cited in the text, fiction includes Is This Your Son, My Lord? *(1890), critiquing the double moral standard, and* Pray You, Sir, Whose Daughter? *(1892), attacking the restrictions on married women, by Helen Hamilton Gardener (legally changed from Alice Chenoweth Smart, 1853–1925);* Jerry *(1891), an early realist novel by Sarah Barnwell Elliott (1848–1928);* Pembroke *(1894), a novel, as well as local-color stories by Mary Eleanor Wilkins (later Freeman, 1852–1930);* Meadow-Grass *(1895) and* Tiverton Tales *(1899), local-color stories by Alice Brown (1856–1948);* The Country of the Pointed Firs *(1896), considered the major work of Sarah Orne Jewett;* The Descendant *(1897), the first novel (published anonymously) by Ellen Glasgow (1873–1945); short story collections such as* A Slave to Duty and Other Women *and* The Heart of Toil *(both 1898) by Alice French (1850–1934);* Prisoners of Hope *(1898), a best-seller by Mary Johnston (1870–1936);* Patience Sparwhawk and Her Times *(1897),* The Californians *(1898), and other novels by Gertrude Franklin Horn Atherton (1857–1948);* The Goodness of St. Rocque and Other Stories *(1899) by Alice Moore Dunbar (later Nelson, 1875–1935), also known for her journalistic coverage of race relations for African American papers.*

pseudonym "Onoto Watanna," and Edith Maud Eaton (1867–1915), writing as "Sui Sin Far." Winnifred publishes the first of 17 books, the novel *Miss Nume of Japan* (1899) and Edith writes her short story "A Chinese Ishmael" (1899).

Juvenile literature of the 1890s includes *Captain January* (1890) by Laura Howe Richards, also the author of two popular series beginning with *Queen Hildegarde* (1889) and *Three Margarets* (1897), and *The Little Colonel* (1896), later a famous Shirley Temple movie, by Annie Fellows Johnston (1863–1931).

Historical works include *The Sabbath in Puritan New England* (1891), *Margaret Winthrop* (1895), *Home Life in Colonial Days* (1898), and other works by Alice Morse Earle (1851–1911); and Ida A. Husted Harper's first two volumes of *Life and Work of Susan B. Anthony* (1898; third volume 1908).

Nonfiction includes *A Voice from the South by a Black Woman of the South* (1892) by Anna J. Cooper (see p. 35); *Women Wage-Earners* (1893) by Helen Stuart Campbell; *English Cathedrals* (1892), the most popular art book of Mariana Alley Griswold Van Rensselaer (1851–1934); *Shelf of Old Books* (1894) and *Authors and Friends* (1896), literary memoirs, by Annie Fields (1834–1915); and *The Woman's Bible* (1895; see "Religion") and *Eighty Years and More* (1898) by Elizabeth Cady Stanton.

Additional poetry includes *An Irish Wild-Flower* (1891) and other works by Sarah Morgan Bryan Piatt (1836–1919) and Henrietta Cordelia Ray's *Sonnets* (1893).

1900–9

Pauline Elizabeth Hopkins (1859–1930) publishes her first novel, *Contending Forces: A Romance Illustrative of Negro Life North and South* (1900). Her next three novels are serialized in the *Colored American* magazine, which she helps found.

Zitkala-Sa, or Gertrude Simmons (later Bonnin, p. 46), translates traditional Sioux stories in *Old Indian Legends* (1901), illustrated by Angel De Cora (Hinookmahiwi-Kilinaka). She also writes short stories and autobiographical sketches for *Atlantic Monthly* and *Harper's* in the early 1900s, later published in *American Indian Legends* (1921).

Edith Wharton (born Edith Newbold Jones, 1862–1937) gains acclaim for her first novel of New York manners, *The House of Mirth* (1905).

Willa Cather (1873–1947) publishes her first collection of short stories, *The Troll Garden* (1905) and gains a job at *McClure's* magazine.

From about 1906, Gertrude Stein (1874–1946) runs one of the key artistic salons in Paris, and in 1909 she publishes her first book, *Three Lives*, with its experimental use of language.

Rachel Crothers (1870–1958) begins her long career as a successful Broadway playwright in the early 1900s. *The Three of Us* (1906) and *A*

Zitkala-Sa (photograph by Gertrude Käsebier, Smithsonian Institution, photo #85-7209)

Man's World (1909) both have strong female leads. Another playwright is Josephine Preston Peabody (1874–1922), whose verse drama *The Piper* (1909) is performed in England and New York.

Mary Roberts Rinehart (1876–1958) publishes her first mysteries: *A Circular Staircase* (1908) and *The Man in Lower Ten* (1909), which causes its readers to stay away from that railroad bunk for years.

Juvenile literature of the decade includes *The Book of Saints and Friendly Beasts* (1900), *In the Days of the Giants* (1902), and many others by Abbie Farwell Brown (1871–1927); *Rebecca of Sunnybrook Farm* (1903), an adult and juvenile best-seller by former kindergarten teacher Kate Douglas Smith Wiggin (1825–1923), who later adapts it for the stage; and *A Little Princess* (1905), later a Shirley Temple film, by Frances Hodgson Burnett.

Nonfiction includes *The Land of Little Rain* (1903), nature essays by Mary Hunter Austin (1868–1934); *The Story of My Life* (1902) by Helen Keller; and *Democracy and Social Ethics* (1902), essays by social reformer Jane Addams.

1910–19

As editor of her own monthly magazine, *Forerunner*, Charlotte Perkins Gilman serializes many of her works, including *The Man-Made World* (1911), in which she contrasts male and female natures, and the utopian fantasy *Herland* (1915).

Willa Cather's first novels are *Alexander's Bridge* (1912), *O Pioneers!* (1913), *The Song of the Lark* (1915), and *My Ántonia* (1918).

In 1912 poet Harriet Monroe (1860–1936) starts *Poetry: A Magazine of Verse*, which she edits for 24 years and turns into the leading journal for poems in English. One of the poets she introduces, in 1913, is H.D. (Hilda Doolittle, 1886–1961). Monroe and Alice Henderson edit *The New Poetry: An Anthology of Twentieth-Century Verse in English* (1917).

Amy Lowell (1874–1925) publishes several poetry collections: *A Dome of Many-Colored Glass* (1912); *Sword Blades and Poppy Seeds* (1914), with her first experiments in free verse and imagism; *Men, Women, and Ghosts* (1916); and *Pictures of the Floating World* (1919). She also edits the three-volume anthology *Some Imagist Poets* (1915–17).

Already known for her Florence salon, Mabel Dodge (later Luhan, 1879–1962) sets up a literary salon in New York in 1912, attracting Emma Goldman, Margaret Sanger, Alfred Stieglitz, and others. In 1923 she moves with her husband to Taos, where she invites such artists and writers as Georgia O'Keeffe and D. H. Lawrence.

In 1914 Margaret Anderson starts *Little Review*, an experimental literary magazine, and is later assisted by Jane Heap. When she serializes James Joyce's *Ulysses* in 1918, the U.S. Post Office seizes and burns four issues as "obscene." At one point, when nothing seems experimental enough, she publishes 64 blank pages.

Fiction: 1900–9

In addition to the works noted in the text, fiction includes the best-selling historical romance To Have and to Hold *(1900), about women colonialists in Jamestown, by Mary Johnston;* The Voice of the People *(1900) by Ellen Glasgow; the best-selling* Mrs. Wiggs of the Cabbage Patch *(1901), about a widow and her family in the industrial slum area of Louisville, by Alice Caldwell Hegan (later Rice, 1870–1942), adapted for the stage by Anne Crawford Flexner in 1904;* A Japanese Nightingale *(1901) and others by Onoto Watanna (Winnifred Eaton);* The Conqueror *(1902), a fictionalized biography of Alexander Hamilton, introducing a new genre, by Gertrude Atherton;* Lavender and Old Lace *(1902) and other works by Myrtle Reed (1874–1911);* Emmy Lou: Her Book and Heart *(1902), stories by George (Georgia May) Madden Martin (1866–1946); the best-selling* Freckles *(1904) and* A Girl of Limberlost *(1909) by Gene (Geneva) Stratton Porter (1863–1924);* Renegades and Other Stories *(1905), about Jewish women, by Martha Wolfenstein (1869–1905);* The Awakening of Helena Richie *(1906) by Margaret Deland; and* Marcia Schuyler *(1908), the first big hit by popular romance writer Grace Livingston Hill (1865–1947), who writes almost 80 novels in her lifetime.*

Fiction of the 1910s

In addition to the works cited in the text, fiction includes Ethan Frome *(1911),* The Custom of the Country *(1913),* Xingu *(short stories, 1916), and other works by* Edith Wharton; The Amazing Letitia Carberry *(1911), the start of a humorous series by Mary Roberts Rinehart;* Mother *(1911), the first of many Irish-American novels by Kathleen Thompson Norris (1880–1969);* Tante *(1911), a best-seller by Anne Sedgwick (1873–1935);* Mrs. Spring Fragrance *(1912), stories by Sui Sin Far (Edith Eaton);* A Woman of Genius *(1912) by Mary Austin; the best-selling* Daddy-Long-Legs *(1912), later adapted for stage and film, and* Dear Enemy *(1914) by Jean Webster (1876–1916);* Virginia *(1913) and* Life and Gabriella: The Story of a Woman's Courage *(1916) by Ellen Glasgow;* The Girl from Amshit *(1913), an autobiographical novel by Lebanese-born Afifa Karam (1883–1914);* The Bent Twig *by Dorothy Canfield Fisher (1879–1958); and* Shadows of Flames *(1915), a realistic depiction of morphine addiction, by Amélie Rives (1863–1945).*

Sisters Maude Howe Elliott (1854–1948) and Laura Howe Richards (1850–1943) publish a 1915 biography of their mother, *Julia Ward Howe, 1819–1910.* With this book, they are the first winners of the Pulitzer Prize for biography, in 1917.

Expatriate Sylvia Woodbridge Beach (1887–1962) opens her Paris bookshop, Shakespeare and Company, in 1919. In 1922 she is the first to publish James Joyce's complete, uncensored *Ulysses.*

Juvenile literature of the decade includes *Maida's Little Shop* (1910), the first in a series by suffragist Inez Haynes Gillmore (later Irwin, 1873–1970); *The Secret Garden* (1911) by Frances Hodgson Burnett; *The Dutch Twins* (1911), the first in a series written and illustrated by Lucy Fitch Perkins (1865–1937); *Pollyanna* (1913), which inspires "glad" clubs (emphasizing an optimistic outlook), by Eleanor Hodgman Porter (1868–1920); *Understood Betsy* (1917) by Dorothy Canfield Fisher; *Come Out of the Kitchen* (1916), later dramatized for Broadway, by Alice Duer Miller (1874–1942). Also Louise Seaman organizes the first U.S. children's book publishing department, at Macmillan.

Nonfiction includes *Twenty Years at Hull-House* (1910) by Jane Addams; *Anarchism and Other Essays* (1911) by Emma Goldman; *The Promised Land* (1912), recollecting her childhood immigration experience, and *They Who Knock at Our Gates* (1914), defending immigrants, by Mary Antin; *Mothers Who Must Earn* (1914) by Katharine Susan Anthony (1877–1965), who later writes several biographies of women, including her aunt, Susan B. Anthony; and *The Negro Trail-Blazers in California* (1919) by Delilah Leontiu Beasley (1872–1934).

Additional poetry includes *Helen of Troy and Other Poems* (1911), *Rivers to the Sea* (1915), and *Love Songs* (1917), winner of the top poetry prize (the predecessor of the Pulitzer), all by Sara Teasdale (1884–1933); the posthumously published *Verse* (1915), with the new cinquain form invented by Adelaide Crapsey (1878–1914); *Sea Garden* (1916) by H.D.; *Renascence and Other Poems* (1917), the first collection of Edna St. Vincent Millay (1892–1950); *Old Road to Paradise* (1918), a pre-Pulitzer award winner, by Margaret Widdemer; *The Heart of a Woman and Other Poems* (1918), the first collection of Georgia Douglas Camp Johnson (1877–1966); and *The Ghetto* (1918), the first collection of leftist poet Lola Ridge (1873–1941).

Drama (see also "Entertainment") includes *Rachel* by Angelina Weld Grimké (1880–1958), which is the first full-length play by a black woman to be staged (in 1916); *Trifles* (1916), a feminist classic, and *Woman's Honor* (1918) by Susan Keating Glaspell (c. 1876–1948), cofounder of the Provincetown Players; and *The Magical City* (1916), a vers libre drama, and *Déclassée* (1919) by Zoë Akins (1886–1958).

1920–29

With *Age of Innocence* (1920), Edith Wharton is the first woman to win the Pulitzer Prize for fiction, in 1921. Her other works of the

1920s include *The Mother's Recompense* (1924) and the best-selling *Twilight Sleep* (1927). In 1923 Willa Cather wins the Pulitzer for *One of Ours* (1922); she also writes *A Lost Lady* (1923) and *Death Comes for the Archbishop* (1927). The third woman to win the Pulitzer for fiction is Edna Ferber, for *So Big* (1924); she also publishes *Show Boat* (1926), which is adapted into a popular musical, and begins collaborating on plays with George S. Kaufman. Also Julia Peterkin (1880–1961) wins for the best-selling *Scarlet Sister Mary* (1928).

"My candle burns at both ends"
—Edna St. Vincent Millay

Edna St. Vincent Millay is the first woman to win the Pulitzer Prize for poetry, in 1923, for *A Few Figs from Thistles* (1920), *Ballad of the Harper-Weaver* (1923), and other works. She also writes the libretto for the opera *The King's Henchman* (1927). Two other women win the poetry Pulitzer: Amy Lowell for *What O'Clock* in 1926 and Leonora Speyer for *Fiddler's Farewell* in 1927.

Anzia Yezierska (c. 1880–1970) publishes her short stories about the immigration experience in *Hungry Hearts* (1920), which is made into a movie in 1922. During the 1920s she averages a book a year, including her fictionalized autobiography, *Bread Givers* (1925), which details the struggle between a daughter and her Old World Jewish father.

After Zona Gale (1874–1938) publishes the witty short novel *Miss Lulu Brett* (1920), she dramatizes it for Broadway and is the first woman to win the Pulitzer for drama, in 1921. Her other novels include *Faint Perfume* (1923) and *Preface to a Life* (1926).

After publishing several short story collections, social activist Fannie Hurst (1889–1968) pens the novels *Stardust* (1921), *Lummox* (1923), and more. By 1940 she is probably the most highly paid U.S. writer.

A number of women are prominent in the Harlem Renaissance in the 1920s, including Georgia Douglass Johnson, who publishes the poetry collections *Bronze* (1922) and *An Autumn Love Cycle* (1928), as well as *Plumes* (1927) and other plays. Novelist Jessie Redmon Fauset (c. 1882–1961), literary editor of the *Crisis*, writes *There Is Confusion* (1924) and *Plum Bun* (1929). Nella Larsen (1891–1964) publishes the novels *Quicksand* (1928) and *Passing* (1929). Alice Dunbar-Nelson, also a major figure, keeps a diary during this period that is published much later, as *Give Us Each Day* (1984). Zora Neale Hurston (c. 1891–1960) is a central figure, but her major works are in the 1930s. Other writers include Gwendolyn Bennett, Marita Bonner, Helene Johnson, and Anne Spencer. A'Leila Walker (1885–1931), the daughter of Madame C.J. Walker, runs a literary salon, Dark Tower, in 1927.

Expatriate Natalie Clifford Barney (1876–1972) runs an important literary salon in Paris in the 1920s and 1930s; she also publishes many novels about her lesbian love affairs.

Fiction of the 1920s

In addition to the works noted in the text, fiction includes Dorothy Canfield Fisher's The Brimming Cup *(1921) and* The Home-Maker *(1926);* Mavis of Green Hill *(1921), the first of many popular novels by Faith Baldwin (1893–1978); Gertrude Atherton's best-selling* Black Oxen *(1923); Anne Sedgwick's best-selling* The Little French Girl *(1924); Ellen Glasgow's* Barren Ground *(1925) and* They Stooped to Folly *(1929); Gertrude Stein's* The Making of Americans *(1925);* Gentlemen Prefer Blondes *(1925), also dramatized, and its sequel* But Gentlemen Marry Brunettes *(1928) by Anita Loos (1893–1981), who later writes Hollywood screenplays;* Iowa Interiors *(1926), stories by Ruth Suckow (1892–1960);* The Hard-Boiled Virgin *(1926), banned in Boston, by Frances Newman (1883–1928);* The Time of Man *(1926) and* My Heart and My Flesh *(1927) by Elizabeth Madox Roberts (1881–1941);* Cogewea, the Half-Blood *(1927) by Mourning Dove (Christal Quintasket Galler, 1888–1936), edited by Lucullus V. McWhorter;* A Lantern in Her Hand *(1928) by Bess Streeter Aldrich (1881–1954);* Ryder *(1928), which is censored, by Djuna Barnes (1892–1982);* HERmione *(1928) by H.D.;* Nothing Is Sacred *(1928) by Josephine Herbst (1897–1969); and* The Patient in Room 18 *(1929), the first of many mysteries by Mignon Good Eberhart.*

In addition to the works cited in the text, poetry includes Sara Teasdale's Flame and Shadow *(1920) and* Dark of the Moon *(1926);* Nets to Catch the Wind *(1921) by Elinor Wylie (1885–1928);* For Eager Lovers *(1922),* Hawaiian Hilltop *(1923), and* Words for the Chisel *(1926) by socialist Genevieve Taggard (1894–1948);* Body of This Death *(1923), the first collection of Louise Bogan (1897–1970);* Lunar Baedeker *(1923) by Mina Loy (1882–1966); the much-acclaimed* Observations *(1924) by Marianne Craig Moore (1887–1972), who edits the literary magazine the* Dial *from 1925 to 1929;* Honey Out of the Rock *(1925) by Babette Deutsch (1895–1982); H.D.'s* Collected Poems *(1925);* The Close Chaplet *(1926) by Laura Riding (later Jackson, 1901–91; born Laura Reichenthal); Lola Ridge's* Red Flag and Other Poems *(1927); and* Sonnets from a Lock Box *(1929) by Anna Hempstead Branch (1875–1937).*

Dorothy Rothschild Parker (1893–1967), a regular at the "Round Table" literary luncheons at New York's Algonquin Hotel, publishes her two best-selling books of short, witty verse, *Enough Rope* (1926) and *Sunset Gun* (1928). She also wins the O. Henry prize for her short story "Big Blonde" (1929).

Mary Ritter Beard (1876–1958) coauthors *The Rise of American Civilization* (1927) with her husband, Charles.

Juvenile literature of the 1920s includes *The Velveteen Rabbit* (1922) and other works by Margery Williams Bianco (1881–1944); *Millions of Cats* (1928), a picturebook by Wanda Gág, and *Hitty, Her First Hundred Years* (1929), a 1930 Newberry Medal winner, by Rachel Lyman Field, with illustrations by Dorothy Lathrop. Also, May Massee sets up the second children's book publishing department, at Doubleday in 1922, and Bertha Mahony (later Miller) and Elinor Whitney start the *Horn Book Magazine,* to review children's books, in 1924.

Drama (see also "Entertainment") includes Susan Glaspell's *The Inheritors* and *The Verge* (both 1921); Zoë Akins's *Daddy's Gone A-Hunting* (1921) and many others; Rachel Crothers's *Nice People* (1921), *Mary the Third* (1923), and *Let Us Be Gay* (1929); Gladys Li's *The Submission of Rose Moy* (1928); and *The Purple Flower* (1928), about race relations, by Marita Bonner (later Occomy, 1899–1971).

Feminist writing includes Harriot Stanton Blatch's *A Woman's Point of View* (1920), an argument against war; Inez Irwin's *Story of the Woman's Party* (1921); Carrie Chapman Catt and Nettie Rogers Shuler's *Woman Suffrage and Politics* (1923); Charlotte Perkins Gilman's *His Religion and Hers* (1923); *Homespun Heroines and Other Women of Distinction,* compiled by Hallie Quinn Brown (c. 1845–1949); Alice Beal Parsons's *Woman's Dilemma* (1926); and Suzanne La Follette's *Concerning Women* (1926).

Autobiography includes *Waheenee: An Indian Girl's Story* (1921) by Buffalo Bird Woman, as told to Gilbert Wilson; *A Woman of Fifty* (1924) by journalist and suffragist Rheta Childe Dorr; *A Daughter of the Samurai* (1925) by Etsu Inagaki Sugimoto; *The Autobiography of Mother Jones* (1925) by Mary Harris Jones; and *Life of an Ordinary Woman* (1929) by Anne Ellis, who describes a western mining town.

1930–39

Several women win the Pulitzer Prize. In drama Susan Glaspell's *Alison's House* (1930), based on the life of Emily Dickinson, wins the 1931 Pulitzer, and Zoë Akins's *The Old Maid* (1934), a dramatization of an Edith Wharton novella, wins the 1935 Pulitzer.

In fiction Margaret Ayer Barnes (1886–1967) wins in 1931 for *Years of Grace* (1930); her other works include *Westward Passage* (1931) and *Wisdom's Gate* (1938).

After her first book, *East Wind: West Wind* (1930), is finally published after many rejections, Pearl Sydenstricker Buck (1892–1973) writes *The Good Earth* (1931), set in China, where she grew up. It wins the 1932 Pulitzer. Her next works include *The Mother* (1934) and two biographies of her parents, *The Exile* and *The Fighting Angel* (both 1936). In 1938 she becomes the first U.S. woman to receive the Nobel Prize for Literature.

Caroline Pafford Miller wins the Pulitzer for fiction for *Lamb in His Bosom* (1933), and Josephine Winslow Johnson for *Now in November* (1934), her first novel. Margaret Munnerlyn Mitchell (1900–49) finally stops revising and publishes her only novel, *Gone with the Wind* (1936), which quickly breaks all sales records and wins the Pulitzer in 1937. After winning the 1933 O. Henry award for her story "Gal Young Un," Marjorie Kinnan Rawlings (1896–1953) publishes her classic, *The Yearling* (1938), which wins the 1939 Pulitzer.

Poetry Pulitzers go to Audrey Wurdemann for *Bright Ambush* (1934) and Marya Zaturenska for *Cold Morning Sky* (1937).

Beginning in 1930, Harriet Stratemeyer Adams (1892–1982), writing as "Carolyn Keene," pens 56 Nancy Drew mysteries and 32 books in the Dana Girls series. Under other pseudonyms, she writes Hardy Boys, Tom Swift, and Bobbsey Twins books. Before Adams, Mildred Wirt Benson wrote many of the first Nancy Drew stories.

The Harlem Renaissance continues in the 1930s. Jessie Redmon Fauset writes two new novels, *The Chinaberry Tree* (1931) and *Comedy: American Style* (1933). Zora Neale Hurston, trained as an anthropologist, publishes her first novel, *Jonah's Gourd Vine* (1934); two collections of folklore, *Mules and Men* (1935) and *Tell My Horse* (1938); her masterpiece *Their Eyes Were Watching God* (1937); and *Moses, Man of the Mountain* (1939). Dorothy West starts *Challenge*, a literary magazine, in 1934 and also publishes her own stories.

Proletarian novels during the 1930s include Mary Heaton Vorse's *Strike!* (1930), Grace Lumpkin's *To Make My Bread* (1932), Lauren Gilfallen's *I Went to Pit College* (1934), and Clara Weatherwax's *Marching! Marching!* (1935). Meridel LeSueur writes *The Girl* in 1932, although it is not published until 1978.

Other fiction of the 1930s includes the story collections *Flowering Judas* (1930) and *Pale Horse, Pale Rider* (1939) by Katherine Ann Porter (1890–1980); Edna Ferber's *Cimarron* (1930); Dorothy Parker's stories *Laments for the Living* (1930); Willa Cather's *Shadows on the Rock* (1931) and stories *Obscure Destinies* (1932); Bess Aldrich's *A White Bird Flying* (1931) and *Miss Bishop* (1933); *Penhally* (1931) and *None Shall Look Back* (1937) by Caroline Gordon (1895–1981); *Plagued by the Nightingale* (1931), the first of many novels by Kay Boyle (1902–92), who wins the 1935 O. Henry Prize for her story "The White Horses of Vienna"; Fannie Hurst's *Back Street* (1931) and *Imitation of Life* (1933), both made into popular movies; Ellen Glasgow's *The Sheltered Life* (1932) and well-received *Vein of Iron* (1935); *Save Me the Waltz* (1932), the autobiographical novel of Zelda Sayre Fitzgerald

Books for the Young

Women write many children's classics during the 1930s. In fact, the American Library Association's Newberry Medal goes to a woman in each year. Rachel Field, who wins in 1930 for Hitty, Her First Hundred Years (1929), also writes Calico Bush (1931) and Hepatica Hawks (1932). Elizabeth Coatsworth wins in 1931 for The Cat Who Went to Heaven; Laura Adams Arrner in 1932 for Waterless Mountain; Elizabeth Foreman Lewis in 1933 for Young Fu of the Upper Yangtze; Cornelia Meigs in 1934 for Invincible Louisa, about Louisa May Alcott; Monica Shannon in 1935 for Dobry; Carol Ryrie Brink in 1936 for Caddie Woodlawn; Ruth Sawyer in 1937 for Roller Skates, an autobiographical story about a girl exploring New York on her own; Kate Seredy in 1938 for The White Stag; and Elizabeth Enright in 1939 for Thimble Summer.

In 1932 Laura Ingalls Wilder (1867–1957) publishes Little House in the Big Woods, the first in her much-loved series of eight books based on her childhood experiences as a pioneer.

In 1939 Margaret Wise Brown (1910–50) publishes Noisy Book, one of her 100 or so children's books. Also in 1939 Virginia Lee Burton writes Mike Mulligan and His Steam Shovel.

Poetry of the 1930s

In addition to the Pulitzer Prize winners, poetry includes Babette Deutsch's Epistle to Prometheus *(1930); Sara Teasdale's* Stars To-night *(1930) and posthumous* Strange Victory *(1933); Dorothy Parker's* Death and Taxes *(1931) and* Not So Deep as a Well *(1936); On the Contrary (1934), the first volume by Phyllis McGinley (1905–78); Edna St. Vincent Millay's* Wine from These Grapes *(1934); Marianne Moore's* Selected Poems *(1935); Theory of Flight (1935), the first volume by Muriel Rukeyser (1913–80); Louise Bogan's* The Sleeping Fury *(1937); Jessie Sampter's* Brand Plucked from the Fire *(1937); Laura Riding's* Collected Poems *(1938); Lines at Intersections (1939), the first volume of Josephine Miles (1911–85); and Canción de la Verdad Sencilla (Song of the Simple Truth, 1939) by Julia de Burgos (c. 1914–53), a Puerto Rican poet who works for* Pueblos Hispanos *in New York in the 1940s and influences many U.S.-based poets.*

(1900–48); Dorothy Canfield Fisher's *Bonfire* (1933) and *Seasoned Timber* (1939); Mourning Dove's *Coyote Stories* (1933), based on Okanogan tales; Josephine Herbst's trilogy *Pity Is Not Enough* (1933), *The Executioner Waits* (1934), and *Rope of Gold* (1939); *A Watch in the Night* (1933) by Helen Constance White (1896–1967); Ruth Suckow's *The Folks* (1934); Bessie Brauer's *Memory of Love* (1934) and *The Daughter* (1938); Tess Slesinger's *The Unpossessed* (1934) and *On Being Told That Her Second Husband Has Taken His First Lover and Other Stories* (1935); Djuna Barnes's acclaimed *Nightwood* (1936); *The House of Incest* (1936), the first novel, published in France, by Anaïs Nin (1903–77); *Honor Bright* (1936), the first best-selling romance by Frances Parkinson Wheeler Keyes (1885–1970), who writes many more; *Dynasty of Death* (1938), the first of many novels by (Janet) Taylor Caldwell (1900–85); and *Escape* (1939), a best-seller by Grace Zaring Stone (1896–1991), writing as "Ethel Vance."

In drama Lillian Hellman (1905–84) writes two Broadway plays: *The Children's Hour* (1934), about two teachers accused of lesbianism, and *Little Foxes* (1939), about a greedy southern family. Clare Boothe Luce (1903–87) also has successful Broadway plays: *Abide with Me* (1935), *The Women* (1936), and *Kiss the Boys Goodbye* (1938). Josefina Niggli writes folk plays, such as *Tooth or Shave* (1935), and one-act plays, such as *Soldadera* (1937).

Nonfiction includes *The Greek Way* (1930) and *The Roman Way* (1932), interpreting the classical world to a general audience, by Edith Hamilton (1867–1963); *The Practice of Philosophy* (1930) by Susanne Knauth Langer (1895–1985); *American Humor: A Study of the National Character* (1931) by Constance Mayfield Rourke (1885–1941); Mabel Dodge Luhan's *Winter in Taos* (1935); Mari Sandoz's *Old Jules* (1935), depicting her father's life as a pioneer miner; Anne Spencer Morrow Lindbergh's *North to the Orient* (1935), describing a flight with her husband, Charles; and *Serve It Forth* (1937), on food and cooking, by M.F.K. (Mary Frances Kennedy) Fisher (1908–92).

Books on women include Mary Ritter Beard's *On Understanding Women* (1931) and *Laughing Their Way: Women's Humor in America* (1934); sociologist Margaret Jarman Hagood's *Mothers of the South* (1937), based on 240 interviews; and Mary Inman's *In Woman's Defense* (1939).

Autobiographical works include exiled Emma Goldman's *Living My Life* (1931); Pretty-Shield, *Pretty-Shield: Medicine Woman of the Crows* (1932), as told to Frank B. Linderman (see p. 260); Gertrude Stein's *The Autobiography of Alice B. Toklas* (1932), in which her longtime companion supposedly recounts her life with Stein; *The Autobiography of a Papago Woman* (1936) by Maria Chona, as told to Ruth Underhill; and Eleanor Roosevelt's *This Is My Story* (1937).

1940–49

Ellen Glasgow receives the 1942 Pulitzer Prize for fiction for *In This Our Life* (1941) and implicitly for her earlier work.

In history Margaret Kernochan Leech (1893–1974) is the first woman to receive the Pulitzer Prize, in 1942, for her best-selling *Reveille in Washington* (1941), about the capital during the Civil War. She later wins a second Pulitzer (see 1960). In 1943 Esther Forbes (1891–1967) wins for *Paul Revere and the World He Lived In* (1942).

In biography Ola Elizabeth Winslow wins the 1941 Pulitzer for *Jonathan Edwards* (1940), and Margaret Clapp (1910–74) receives the 1948 prize for *Forgotten First Citizen, John Bigelow* (1948).

In drama Mary Chase earns the 1945 Pulitzer for *Harvey* (1944).

In poetry Gwendolyn Brooks publishes her vignettes of a Chicago neighborhood, *A Street in Bronzeville* (1945), followed by a second collection, *Annie Allen* (1949), which wins the 1950 Pulitzer. She is the first African American to win this poetry award.

Lillian Smith (1897–1966) stirs up controversy with her novel about interracial love, *Strange Fruit* (1944), which the Post Office tries to bar until Eleanor Roosevelt intervenes. In *Killers of the Dream* (1949), she attacks segregation.

Anthropologist Ella Cara Deloria (1889–1971) first finishes her novel *Waterlily*, about a Teton Sioux woman, in 1944; she later revises it, and it is not published until 1988.

"In the quiet, secret night she was by herself again"—
Carson McCullers

Additional fiction includes *The Heart Is a Lonely Hunter* (1940), *Reflections in a Golden Eye* (1941), "The Ballad of the Sad Café" (1944), and *Member of the Wedding* (1946; later dramatized) by Carson McCullers (born Lulu Carson Smith, 1917–67); Alice Duer Miller's popular *White Cliffs* (1940); Kay Boyle's novella *Crazy Horse* (1940) and several novels; Eudora Welty's stories *A Curtain of Green* (1941) and novels *The Robber Bridegroom* (1942) and *Delta Wedding* (1946); Han Suyin's *Destination Chung-king* (1942); *The Company She Keeps* (1942), the first novel of Mary McCarthy (1912–89); *Meet Me in St. Louis* (1942), stories later made into a movie, by Sally Benson (1900–72), an earlier O. Henry prize winner; *The Water Carrier's Secret* (1942) by María Cristina Mena (1893–1965); Gertrude Atherton's *The Horn of Life* (1942); Tai-Yi Lin's *War Tide* (1943); *A Tree Grows in Brooklyn* (1943) by Betty Wehner Smith (1904–72); *The Fountainhead* (1943), the best-seller by Ayn Rand (1905–82), whose philosophy of objectivism puts self-interest over altruism; *Two Serious Ladies* (1943) by Jane Auer Bowles (1917–73); Helena Kuo's *Westward to Chung-king* (1944); *Boston Adventure* (1944) and *The Mountain Lion* (1947) by Jean Stafford (1915–79); Josefina Niggli's *Mexican Village* (1945); Elizabeth Hardwick's first novel, *The Ghostly Lover* (1945); Jessamyn West's stories about two Quakers, *The Friendly Persuasion* (1945), which she later adapts for film; Taylor Caldwell's *This Side of Innocence* (1946); Ann Lane Petry's best-selling *The Street* (1946); Pearl S. Buck's *The*

Biography in the 1940s

In addition to the Pulitzer Prize winners, biographies include Alma Lutz's Created Equal: A Biography of Elizabeth Cady Stanton *(1940); Marl Sandoz's* Crazy Horse *(1942); Yankee from Olympus: Justice Holmes and His Family *(1944), the first in a series of partly fictionalized biographies, by Catherine Drinker Bowen (1897–1973); and* Paul Robeson: Citizen of the World *(1946), the first of 13 biographies by Shirley Graham (later Du Bois, 1907–77).*

Autobiographical works include Zora Neale Hurston's partly fictionalized Dust Tracks on a Road *(1942);* Our Hearts Were Young and Gay *(1942) by Emily Kimbrough and Cornelia Otis Skinner; Marjorie Kinnan Rawlings's* Cross Creek *(1942); labor organizer Rose Pesotta's* Bread Upon the Waters *(1944); Santha Rama Rau's* Home to India *(1945);* The Egg and I *(1945) by humorist Betty Bard MacDonald (1908–58); Jade Snow Wong's* Fifth Chinese Daughter *(1945); and Eleanor Roosevelt's* This I Remember *(1949).*

Children's Books of the 1940s

Juvenile literature of the decade includes the last volumes in Laura Ingalls Wilder's series (see 1930s); Dorothy Kunhardt's Pat the Bunny *(1940), the first tactile picture book; Mary O'Hara's* My Friend Flicka *(1941); Margaret Rey's* Curious George *(1941); Virginia Burton's illustrated* The Little House *(1942), for which she wins a Caldecott Medal; Esther Forbes's* Johnny Tremain *(1943), a Newberry Medal winner; Lois Lenski's* Strawberry Girl *(1945), also a Newberry Medal winner; Betty MacDonald's* Mrs. Piggle-Wiggle *(1947), the first in a series; Margaret Wise Brown's* Goodnight Moon *(1947); and Marguerite Henry's* King of the Wind *(1948), a Newberry Medal winner. Also, librarian Charlemae Hill Rollins (1897–1979) publishes* We Build Together *(1941), a bibliography of children's books with realistic images of African Americans.*

Pavilion of Women (1946); *Gentleman's Agreement* (1947), a best-selling exposé of anti-Semitism, by Laura Zametkin Hobson (1900–86); Dorothy West's satire *The Living Is Easy* (1948); and "The Lottery" (1948), an eerie short story by Shirley Hardie Jackson (1916–65).

Mysteries and romances of the decade include Helen Clark MacInnes's first suspenses, *Above Suspicion* (1941) and *Assignment in Brittany* (1942); Gypsy Rose Lee's best-selling *The G-String Murders* (1941); *A Place for Ann* (1941), the first of many, mostly romance mysteries by Phyllis Ayame Whitney; *Lay On, MacDuff!* (1942), the first of many mysteries by Charlotte Armstrong (1905–69); *A Compound for Death* (1943), the first of many mysteries by Doris Miles Disney (1907–76); *Forever Amber* (1944), a best-seller by Kathleen Winsor, which is banned in places because of the sexual heroine; and *Dragonwyck* (1944), one of many Gothic romances by Anya Seton.

In addition to Gwendolyn Brooks's work, poetry includes *For My People* (1942) by Margaret Walker (later Alexander), which is the first book by an African American selected for the Yale Younger Poets series; Muriel Rukeyser's *Beast in View* (1944); H.D.'s *Trilogy* (*The Walls Do Not Fall, Tribute to Angels,* and *The Flowering of the Rod*, 1944–46); *Family Circle* (1946) by Eve Merriam (1918–92); Josephine Miles's *Local Measures* (1946); and *North and South* (1946), the first volume by Elizabeth Bishop (1911–79).

Drama (see also "Entertainment") includes Lillian Hellman's *Watch on the Rhine* (1941), Gypsy Rose Lee's *The Naked Genius* (1943); and Rose Franken's *Outrageous Fortune* (1943).

Nonfiction includes anthropologist Ruth Benedict's *Race: Science and Politics* (1940) and *The Chrysanthemum and the Sword: Patterns of Japanese Culture* (1946); Susanne K. Langer's influential *Philosophy in a New Key: A Study in the Symbolism of Reason, Rite, and Art* (1942); Mary Beard's *Woman as Force in History* (1946); and *The Modern Woman: The Lost Sex* (1947), an influential antifeminist tract by psychoanalyst Marynia Farnham and Ferdinand Lundberg.

1950–59

In poetry the 1950 Pulitzer Prize goes to Gwendolyn Brooks (see 1940s). Marianne Moore publishes her *Collected Poems* (1951), which wins the 1952 Pulitzer; she is also the first woman (and third poet) to be awarded the prestigious Bollingen Prize, in 1952. In 1956 Elizabeth Bishop wins the Pulitzer Prize for her *North and South* and *A Cold Spring* (1955), an expanded version of her 1946 collection.

In biography Margaret Louise Coit wins the 1951 Pulitzer for *John C. Calhoun: American Portrait,* and Mary Wells Ashworth shares the 1958 prize as coauthor of volume 7 of *George Washington.*

In drama Frances Goodrich shares the 1956 Pulitzer Prize as coauthor of the stage version of *The Diary of Anne Frank.*

French writer Marguerite Yourcenar (born de Crayencour, 1903–87), a

U.S. citizen since 1947, publishes her best-known historical novel, *The Memoirs of Hadrian* (in French 1951, in English 1954). She is later (in 1980) the first woman in the French Academy, founded in 1635.

Fiction of the decade includes Kay Boyle's *The Smoking Mountain: Stories of Germany During the Occupation* (1951); Shelley Ota's *Upon Their Shoulders* (1951), about Japanese American immigration; Caroline Gordon's *The Strange Children* (1951) and *The Malefactors* (1956); Hortense Calisher's first short story collection, *In the Absence of Angels* (1951); Edna Ferber's *Giant* (1952); Jean Stafford's *The Catherine Wheel* (1952); the short novel *Wise Blood* (1952), *A Good Man Is Hard to Find and Other Stories* (1955), and *The Violent Bear It Away* (1959) by Flannery O'Connor (1925–64); Mary McCarthy's *The Groves of Academe* (1952); physician Han Suyin's *A Many Splendored Thing* (1952), made into a movie; Elizabeth Spencer's *The Crooked Way* (1952) and *The Voice at the Back Door* (1956); Gwendolyn Brooks's *Maud Martha* (1953); Ann Petry's *The Narrows* (1953); Fabiola Cabeza de Baca's *We Fed Them Cactus* (1954), a mix of fiction, folklore, and history; Harriette Simpson Arnow's *The Dollmaker* (1954); Eudora Welty's novella *The Ponder Heart* (1954) and stories *The Bride of the Innisfallen* (1955); Taylor Caldwell's *Never Victorious, Never Defeated* (1954); Shirley Ann Grau's *The Black Prince and Other Stories* (1955); Eileen Chang's *The Rice Sprout Song* (1955) and *The Naked Earth* (1956); *The Changeling* (1955) by Jo Sinclair (Ruth Seid); Tillie Lerner Olsen's story "Tell Me a Riddle" (1956), which wins the O. Henry award; Grace Metalious's best-selling *Peyton Place* (1956); Diana Chang's first novel, *The Frontiers of Love* (1956); Ayn Rand's best-selling *Atlas Shrugged* (1957); Shirley Jackson's *The Sundial* (1958) and *The Haunting of Hill House* (1959); Grace Paley's first short story collection, *The Little Disturbances of Man* (1959); and *Brown Girl, Brownstones* (1959) by Paule Marshall (born Valenza Pauline Burke).

New mystery writers include Patricia Highsmith, whose *Strangers on a Train* (1950) is made into an Alfred Hitchcock movie. She also writes the best-selling lesbian novel *The Price of Salt* (1952) under the name "Claire Morgan."

Drama (see also "Entertainment") includes Carson McCullers's stage adaptation of *The Member of the Wedding* (1950); Lillian Hellman's *The Autumn Garden* (1951); *King of Hearts* (1954) by Jeanne Collins Kerr and Eleanor Brooke; and Alice Childress's *Trouble in Mind* (1955), for which she is the first black woman to receive an Obie (off-Broadway) award. *A Raisin in the Sun* (1959) by Lorraine Hansberry (1930–65) is the first play by a black woman to be staged on Broadway and wins the New York Drama Critics' Circle Award.

Autobiographical writings include social activist Dorothy Day's *The Long Loneliness* (1952); Monica Sone's *Nisei Daughter* (1953); *The Alice B. Toklas Cookbook* (1954), with reminiscences and recipes, by Alice B. Toklas (1877–1967); *Romance of a Little Village Girl* (1955) by Cleofas

Poetry of the 1950s

In addition to the Pulitzer Prize winners, poetry includes Adrienne Rich's first collections, A Change of World *(1951) and* The Diamond Cutters *(1955), Louise Bogan's* Collected Poems, 1923–53 *(1954), a winner of the Bollingen Prize; Babette Deutsch's* Animal, Vegetable, Mineral *(1954);* Another Animal *(1954) and* Cage of Spires *(1958) by May Swenson (1919–89); British-born Denise Levertov's* Here and Now *(1957) and* Overland to the Islands *(1958); Muriel Rukeyser's* Body of Waking *(1958);* Angeles de ceniza *(Angels of Ashes, 1958) by Diana Ramírez de Arellano, who is named poet laureate of Puerto Rico;* Mona Van Duyn's *Valentines to the Wide World (1959); and* This Kind of Bird Flies Backwards *(1959) by Diane Di Prima, one of the few women among the Beat poets.*

Nonfiction includes The Origins of Totalitarianism *(1951) and* The Human Condition *(1958) by political philosopher and Nazi refugee Hannah Arendt (1906–75); Rachel Carson's* The Sea Around Us *(1951) and* The Edge of the Sea *(1955); Susanne K. Langer's* Feeling and Form *(1953); Mirra Komarovsky's* Women in the Modern World *(1953); Mari Sandoz's* Buffalo Hunters *(1954);* Proud Shoes: The Story of an American Family *(1956) by Pauli Murray (p. 73); Anne Morrow Lindbergh's essays* Gift from the Sea *(1955); Mary McCarthy's* Venice Observed *(1956) and* The Stones of Florence *(1959); play-wright Jean Kerr's essays* Please Don't Eat the Daisies *(1957); Catherine Drinker Bowen's biography of Sir Edward Coke,* The Lion and the Throne *(1957); Aline Saarinen's portrayal of American art collectors,* The Proud Possessors *(1958); Marya Mannes's* More in Anger *(1958), essays critiquing U.S. mores; and Eleanor Flexner's seminal history of women's rights,* Century of Struggle *(1959).*

Martínez Jaramillo (1878–1956); Marian Anderson's *My Lord What a Morning* (1956); Billie Holiday's *Lady Sings the Blues* (1956); Mary McCarthy's *Memories of a Catholic Girlhood* (1957); and Eleanor Roosevelt's *On My Own* (1958).

Juvenile literature includes Elizabeth Yates's *Amos Fortune, Free Man* (1950), a Newberry Medal winner; Dorothy Sterling's *Freedom Train: The Story of Harriet Tubman* (1954); singer and radio celebrity Kay Thompson's *Eloise* (1955), a best-seller about a six-year-old terror in New York's Hotel Plaza; and Elizabeth George Speare's *The Witch of Blackbird Pond* (1958), a Newberry Medal winner.

1960–69

In fiction Harper Lee publishes her best-selling novel about racial intolerance, *To Kill a Mockingbird* (1960), which wins the 1961 Pulitzer. Shirley Ann Grau's *Keepers of the House* (1964) earns the 1965 prize, followed by Katherine Anne Porter's *Collected Stories* in 1966. Porter also publishes her only full-length novel, the best-selling *Ship of Fools* (1961), which she has worked on for 20 years. Jean Stafford puts out her *Collected Stories* (1969), which receives the 1970 Pulitzer.

In poetry Phyllis McGinley publishes *Times Three: Selected Verse from Three Decades* (1960), which wins the 1961 Pulitzer Prize; she also releases *Sixpence in Her Shoe* (1964). Anne Harvey Sexton (1928–74) puts out the collections *To Bedlam and Part Way Back* (1960), *All My Pretty Ones* (1962), and *Live or Die* (1966), for which she receives the 1967 Pulitzer.

In history Margaret Leech wins her second Pulitzer Prize in 1960, for *In the Days of McKinley*, which also wins the prestigious Bancroft Prize. Constance McLaughlin Green wins in 1963 for *Washington, Village and Capital, 1800–1878*, which she follows with two more volumes tracing the city's history through the civil rights movement.

In general nonfiction Barbara Wertheim Tuchman (1912–89) writes *The Guns of August* (1962), tracing diplomatic and military activities at the start of World War I. She is the second person and first woman to win the Pulitzer Prize in this new category, in 1963 (she wins again in 1972). Later, she writes *The Proud Tower* (1966), of the decades before the war. Ariel Durant shares the 1968 prize with her husband, Will, for their *Rousseau and Revolution*.

"All I could see were question marks"—Sylvia Plath

Additional fiction includes Tillie Olsen's story collection *Tell Me a Riddle* (1961); May Sarton's *The Small Room* (1961) and *Mrs. Stevens Hears the Mermaids Singing* (1965); Shirley Jackson's *We Have Always Lived in the Castle* (1962); Alison Lurie's *Love and Friendship* (1962), *Imaginary Friends* (1967), and *Real People* (1969). Sylvia Plath's autobiographical novel, *The Bell Jar* (1963); Hortense Calisher's novel *Textures of Life* (1963) and stories *The New Yorkers* (1969); Joan Didion's *Run River* (1963); Mary McCarthy's *The Group* (1963), about eight Vassar women; Joyce Carol Oates's first story collection, *By the North Gate*

(1963) and first novel, *With Shuddering Fall* (1964), as well as *Expensive People* (1967) and the award-winning *them* (1969); Susan Sontag's novels *The Benefactor* (1963) and *Death Kit* (1967); Anne Tyler's *If Morning Ever Comes* (1963) and *The Tin Can Tree* (1965); Kristin Eggleston Hunter's *God Bless the Child* (1964); *I Never Promised You a Rose Garden* (1964) by Hannah Green (Joanne Goldenberg Greenberg); Bel Kaufman's *Up the Down Staircase* (1964); Taylor Caldwell's *A Pillar of Iron* (1965); Flannery O'Connor's posthumously published stories, *Everything That Rises Must Converge* (1965); Jane Bowles's stories *Plain Pleasures* (1966); Doris Betts's *The Astronomer and Other Stories* (1966); Cynthia Ozick's first novel, *Trust* (1966); Margaret Walker's *Jubilee* (1966), a fictionalized account of her grandmother's life from slavery to Reconstruction; Jacqueline Susann's best-selling *The Valley of the Dolls* (1966) and *The Love Machine* (1969); Sue Kaufman's *The Diary of a Mad Housewife* (1967); Anna Moore Shaw's *Pima Legends* (1968); Chang Hua's *Crossings* (1968); Marge Piercy's *Going Down Fast* (1969); *A Place for Us* (1969, later called *Patience and Sarah*) by Isabel Miller (Alma Routsong); Paule Marshall's *The Chosen Place, the Timeless People* (1969); and Sarah Elizabeth Wright's *This Child's Gonna Live* (1969).

Mysteries and science fiction include Andre Norton's *Witch World* (1964) with the female hero Jaelithe; Marion Zimmer Bradley's first volume in the *Darkover* series (1964); the first Kate Fansler mystery, *In the Last Analysis* (1964), by Amanda Cross (Carolyn Gold Heilbrun); *Death Shall Overcome* (1966) and others by Emma Lathen (Mary J. Latis and Marha Hennisart); Ursula Kroeber LeGuin's *Rocannon's World* and *Planet of Exile* (both 1966), *A Wizard of Earthsea* (1968), and *Left Hand of Darkness* (1969); and Dorothy Uhnak's *The Bait* (1968) with policewoman Christie Opara.

Drama (see also "Entertainment") includes Lillian Hellman's *Toys in the Attic* (1960); Jean Kerr's *Mary, Mary* (1961) and *Poor Richard* (1964); Adrienne Kennedy's *Funnyhouse of a Negro* (1964), which wins an Obie, and *The Owl Answers* (1965); Lorraine Hansberry's *The Sign in Sidney Brustein's Window* (1964) and her posthumous *To Be Young, Gifted and Black* (1969); Roxanne Drexler's *Home Movies* (1964), which wins an Obie, and *The Investigation* (1966); Maria Irene Fornes's Obie-winning *Successful Life of Three* and *Promenade* (both 1965); Megan Terry's *Viet Rock: A Folk War Movie* (1966) and *Calm Down Mother* (1966); Barbara Garson's *MacBird* (1967); Rochelle Owens's *Futz* (1968); and Alice Childress's *Wine in the Wilderness* (1969).

Poetry includes Gwendolyn Brooks's *Bean Eaters* (1960), *In the Mecca* (1968), and *Riot* (1969); *The Colossus* (1960), the first volume by Sylvia Plath (1932–64), as well as the posthumous *Ariel* (1965); Maxine Winokur Kumin's *Halfway* (1961) and *Privilege* (1965); Carolyn Kizer's *The Ungrateful Garden* (1961) and *Knock Upon Silence* (1965); H.D.'s *Helen in Egypt* (1961); Muriel Rukeyser's *Waterlily Fire* (1962) and *The Speed of Darkness* (1968); Diane Wakoski's *Coins and Coffins* (1962) and

Some Nonfiction of the 1960s

Nonfiction includes Jean Kerr's The Snake Has All the Lines *(1960);* The Death and Life of Great American Cities *(1961) by Jane Butzner Jacobs, senior editor of* Architectural Forum; *Santha Rama Rau's* Gifts of Passage *(1961); Helen Gurley Brown's* Sex and the Single Girl *(1962); Rachel Carson's* Silent Spring *(1962, p. 158); Betty Friedan's seminal* The Feminine Mystique *(1963, p. 71); British-born Jessica Mitford's* The American Way of Death *(1963); Hannah Arendt's controversial* Eichmann in Jerusalem: A Report on the Banality of Evil *(1964); Eve Merriam's* After Nora Slammed the Door: American Women in the 1960s, the Unfinished Revolution *(1964); Aileen Kraditor's* Ideas of the Woman Suffrage Movement *(1965); Susan Sontag's essays* Against Interpretation *(1966); Hortense Powdermaker's* Stranger and Friend: The Way of an Anthropologist *(1966); Gerda Lerner's* The Grimké Sisters from South Carolina *(1967); Susanne K. Langer's three-volume* Mind: An Essay on Human Feeling *(1967, 1973, 1982); Joan Didion's essays* Slouching Towards Bethlehem *(1968); Caroline Bird's* Born Female: The High Cost of Keeping Women Down *(1968); and Mary Ellman's* Thinking About Women *(1968), an indictment of academia.*

Feminist Publishers

Beginning in 1969, women found their own publishing houses to promote women's writings. Poet Alta starts Shameless Hussy Press in 1969 in the San Francisco Bay area and prints not only her own work but also that of Susan Griffin, Ntozake Shange, and others. In Pittsburgh 19 NOW members begin Know, Inc., and publish nonfiction. Florence Howe co-founds the Feminist Press in 1970 and reprints many women's classics as well as new work.

Other early publishers include the Women's Press Collective (1970) in Oakland, California; Aunt Lute Book Company, which begins as the Iowa City Women's Press (1972) and later moves to the Bay area; Diana Press (1972), which starts in Baltimore and later shifts to Oakland; Daughters, Inc. (1972), founded in Vermont to publish lesbian novels; Naiad Press (1973), a lesbian press; Persephone Press (1976), near Boston; and Spinsters, Inc. (1978).

In the 1980s a number of other important presses start, including Kitchen Table: Women of Color Press and Cleis Press in 1981 and Firebrand Press and Calyx Books in the mid-1980s.

Inside the Blood Factory (1968); Mona Van Duyn's *A Time of Bees* (1964); Elizabeth Bishop's *Questions of Travel* (1965) and *Complete Poems* (1969); Margaret Walker's *Ballad of the Free* (1966); Adrienne Rich's *Necessities of Life* (1966); Nikki Giovanni's first two collections, *Black Feeling, Black Talk* (1967) and *Black Judgement* (1968); Josephine Miles's *Bent* (1967); Denise Levertov's *The Sorrow Dance* (1967); May Swenson's *Half Sun Half Sleep* (1967); *The First Cities* (1968), the first collection of Audre Lorde (1934–92); Mari Evans's *Where Is All the Music?* (1968); Jane Cooper's first volume, *The Weather of Six Mornings* (1968); Margaret Taylor Goss Burroughs's *What Shall I Tell My Children Who Are Black?* (1968); Marge Piercy's first volume, *Breaking Camp* (1968); and Louise Bogan's *The Blue Estuaries* (1968). In 1969 a number of poets' first volumes come out, including June Jordan's *Who Look at Me*, Sonia Sanchez's *Homecoming*, Lucille Sayles Clifton's *Good Times*, Jayne Cortez's *Pissstained Stairs and the Monkey Man's Wares*, and *Freedom's in Sight* by Alta (Gerrey).

Autobiographical works include Eleanor Roosevelt's *You Learn by Living* (1960) and *Autobiography* (1961); Kay Curley Bennett's *Kaibah: Recollections of a Navajo Girlhood* (1964); *No Turning Back: A Hopi Indian Woman's Struggle to Live in Two Worlds* (1964) by Polingaysi Qoyawayma (Elizabeth Q. White, c. 1892–1990); Barbara Deming's *Prison Notes* (1966); *Mountain Wolf Woman, Sister of Crashing Thunder* (1966) by Mountain Wolf Woman (1884–1960), edited by anthropologist Nancy Ostreich Lurie; Anaïs Nin's *Diary*, which begins publication (1966–77); labor organizer Rose Schneiderman's *All for One* (1967); *The Autobiography of Delfina Cuero* (1968) by Delfino Cuero (c. 1900–72), edited by Florence Shipek; May Sarton's journal *Plant Dreaming Deep* (1968); Anne E. Moody's *Coming of Age in Mississippi* (1968, p. 68); Lucille Jerry Winnie's *Sah-Gan-De-Oh, The Chief's Daughter* (1969); Lillian Hellman's *An Unfinished Woman* (1969); Diane Di Prima's *Memoirs of a Beatnik* (1969); and Coretta Scott King's *My Life with Martin Luther King, Jr.* (1969).

Juvenile literature includes Madeline L'Engle's *A Wrinkle in Time* (1962), which wins the Newberry Medal; Louise Fitzhugh's *Harriet the Spy* (1964); Kristin Hunter's *The Soul Brothers and Sister Lou* (1968); and Eve Merriam's provocative *The Inner City Mother Goose* (1969).

1970–79

The year 1970 brings major publications by women writers. Influential feminist works (see also p. 79) include Kate Millett's *Sexual Politics*, Shulamith Firestone's *The Dialectic of Sex*, and the anthologies *Sisterhood Is Powerful*, edited by Robin Morgan, and *The Black Woman*, edited by Toni Cade (later Bambara). In particular, African American women's writings stand out, including *The Bluest Eye*, the first novel by Toni Morrison (Chloe Anthony Wofford); Alice Walker's first novel, *The Third Life of Grange Copeland*; Louise Meriwether's first novel, *Daddy Was a Number Runner*; *I Know Why the Caged Bird Sings*, the first in an autobiographical series by Maya Angelou (born Marguerite

Johnson); Nikki Giovanni's reissue of her two earlier poetry collections (see 1960s) and *Re-Creation;* Mari Evans's poems *I Am a Black Woman;* Audre Lorde's poems *Cables to Rage;* Sonia Sanchez's poems *We a BaddDDD People;* Margaret Walker's poems *Prophets for a New Day;* and Shirley Chisolm's autobiography *Unbought and Unbossed.*

Additional fiction includes Gail Godwin's *The Perfectionist* (1970) and *The Odd Woman* (1974); Joan Didion's *Play It as It Lays* (1970) and *A Book of Common Prayer* (1977); May Sarton's *Kinds of Love* (1970) and *A Reckoning* (1978), Bharati Mukherjee's first novel, *The Tiger's Daughter* (1971); Joyce Carol Oates's *Wonderland* (1971) and *The Assassins* (1975); Shirley Ann Grau's *The Condor Passes* (1971); Toni Cade Bambara's stories *Gorilla, My Love* (1972); Alix Kates Shulman's *Memoirs of an Ex-Prom Queen* (1972); Lois Gould's *Necessary Objects* (1972) and *Final Analysis* (1974); Marge Piercy's *Small Changes* (1973) and *Woman on the Edge of Time* (1976); Alice Walker's *Meridian* (1973); Toni Morrison's *Sula* (1973) and award-winning *Song of Solomon* (1977); *I Heard the Owl Call My Name* (1973), the first novel by Margaret Craven (1901–80); Erica Jong's *Fear of Flying* (1973), with its heterosexual escapades, and Rita Mae Brown's *Rubyfruit Jungle* (1973), with its lesbian escapades; Nicholasa Mohr's illustrated novel *Nilda* (1973), for juveniles and adults, and her stories *El Bronx Remembered* (1975), told from a child's point of view; Susan Fromberg Schaeffer's *Anya* (1974); Tillie Olsen's *Yonnondio* (1974); Ann Allen Schockley's *Loving Her* (1974); Anne Tyler's *Celestial Navigation* (1974) and *Earthly Possessions* (1977); Alison Lurie's *The War Between the Tates* (1974); Grace Paley's stories *Enormous Changes at the Last Minute* (1974); Kate Millett's *Sita* (1974); Alice Adams's *Families and Survivors* (1974); Lisa Alther's *Kinflicks* (1975); Sara Davidson's *Loose Change* (1975); Judith Rossner's *Looking for Mr. Goodbar* (1975); Gayl Jones's *Corrigedora* (1975) and *Eva's Man* (1976); Ann Beattie's first novel, *Chilly Scenes of Winter* (1976), and stories *Distortions* (1976); Judith Guest's *Ordinary People* (1976); Francine du Plessix Gray's *Lovers and Tyrants* (1976); Rosellen Brown's first novel, *The Auotbiography of My Mother* (1976); Anne Rice's *Interview with a Vampire* (1976); Renata Adler's stories *Speedboat* (1976); Leslie Marmon Silko's highly acclaimed first novel, *Ceremony* (1977); Marilyn Edwards French's *The Women's Room* (1977); Ntozake Shange's novella *Sassafrass* (1977); Alice Hoffman's first novel, *Property Of* (1977); Mary Lee Settle's award-winning *Blood Tie* (1977); Hortense Calisher's *On Keeping Women* (1977); the novel *Happy All the Time* (1978) by Laurie Colwin (1944–92); Mary Gordon's *Final Payments* (1978); E. M. (Esther Masserman) Broner's *A Weave of Women* (1978); Elizabeth Hardwick's *Sleepless Nights* (1979); and Barbara Chase-Riboud's *Sally Hemings* (1979), about Thomas Jefferson's slave and mistress.

New top-selling romance writers include Danielle Fernande Steel, whose first book of many books is *Going Home* (1973), and Judith Tarcher Krantz, who publishes *Scruples* (1978). Mary Higgins Clark writes her first successful suspense, *Where Are the Children?* (1975).

Pulitzer Winners in the 1970s

Despite the huge upsurge in women's writing in the 1970s, very few Pulitzer Prizes are awarded to women. Jean Stafford wins the 1970 fiction award for her Collected Stories *(1969); Eudora Welty receives the 1973 prize for* The Optimist's Daughter *(1972), after also writing* Losing Battles *(1970). There are no drama, history, or biography awards to women.*

In poetry Maxine Kumin wins the 1973 prize for Up Country: Poems of New England *(1972), after also publishing* The Nightmare Factory *(1970).*

Under general fiction Barbara W. Tuchman wins her second award, in 1972 for Stilwell and the American Experience in China *(1971); she also writes the bestselling* A Distant Mirror *(1978). In 1973 Frances FitzGerald shares the prize for her book on Vietnam,* Fire in the Lake, *and in 1975 Annie Dillard wins for her essays* Pilgrim at Tinker Creek *(1974).*

Science Fiction by Women

In the 1970s there is an upsurge of science fiction writing by women. Ursula K. LeGuin continues her Earthsea trilogy with The Tombs of Atuan *(1971) and* The Farthest Shore *(1972); in addition, she writes* The Dispossessed *(1974).*

Joanna Russ introduces a female hero, Jael, in The Female Man *(1975), and Marion Zimmer Bradley features Jaelle in* The Shattered Chain *(1976). Marge Piercy's* Woman on the Edge of Time *(1976) also classifies as science fiction.*

Octavia E. Butler pens Patternmaster *(1976) and other works in her Patternist series; she also writes* Kindred *(1979). The first prominent African American woman science fiction writer, she later receives multiple awards for* Bloodchild *(1984).*

Other works include Motherlines *(1978) by Suzy McKee Charnas,* Up the Walls of the World *(1978) by James Tiptree, Jr. (Alice Sheldon), and* The Wanderground *(1979) by Sally Miller Gearhart.*

In poetry Mona Van Duyn's *To See, To Take* (1970) wins the National Book Award, and in 1971 she is the first woman in 17 years to receive the Bollingen Prize; she also writes *Bedtime Stories* (1972) and *Merciful Disguises* (1973). Additional poetry includes Laura Riding Jackson's *Selected Poems* (1970); Denise Levertov's *Relearning the Alphabet* (1970), *The Freeing of the Dust* (1975), and *Life in the Forest* (1978); Maya Angelou's *Just Give Me a Cool Drink of Water 'fore I Diiie* (1971); Maggie Ann Culver Fry's *The Umbilical Cord* (1971); *Child of Myself* (1971) by Pat Parker (1944–89); Erica Jong's first volume, *Fruits and Vegetables* (1971); Diane Wakoski's *The Motorcycle Betrayer Poems* (1971); Carolyn Kizer's *Midnight Was My Cry* (1971); Adrienne Rich's *The Will to Change* (1971), award-winning *Diving into the Wreck* (1973), and *The Dream of a Common Language* (1978); Dolores Prida's *Women of the Hour* (1971); Ruth Stone's *Topography and Other Poems* (1971); Mary Oliver's *The River Styx, Ohio and Other Poems* (1972) and *Twelve Moons* (1979); Anne Sexton's *Transformations* (1972), *The Death Notebooks* (1974), and several posthumous volumes; Nikki Giovanni's *My House* (1972) and *The Women and the Men* (1975); Naomi Long Madgett's *Pink Ladies in the Afternoon* (1972); Audre Lorde's *From a Land Where Other People Live* (1973) and *The Black Unicorn* (1978); Jayne Cortez's *Scarifications* (1973); Muriel Rukeyser's *Breaking Open* (1973); Lucille Clifton's *An Ordinary Woman* (1974); Sonia Sanchez's *A Blues Book for Blue Magic Women* (1974); Leslie Marmon Silko's *Laguna Woman* (1974); Jane Cooper's *Maps and Windows* (1974); Marilyn Hacker's award-winning *Presentation Piece* (1974); *Song to San Juan, Puerto Rico and Other Poems* (1974) by Amelia Agostini de Del Río (1896–1980); Louise Glück's *The House on Marshland* (1975) and *The Garden* (1976); Sherley Anne Williams's *The Peacock Poems* (1975); Diane Di Prima's *Selected Poems* (1975); Josephine Miles's *Coming to Terms* (1975); Joy Harjo's first volume, *The Last Song* (1975); Maxine Kumin's *House, Bridge, Fountain, Gate* (1975); Angela de Hoyos's first works, *Arise Chicano* and *Chicano Poems for the Barrio* (both 1975); Tess Gallagher's *Instructions to the Double* (1976) and *Under Stars* (1978); Elizabeth Bishop's award-winning *Geography III* (1976); Carolyn Forché's first volume, *Gathering the Tribes* (1976); Mitsuye Yamada's *Camp Notes* (1976); Carolyn M. Rodgers's *How i got ovah* (1976); Nellie Wong's *Dreams in Harrison Railroad Park* (1977); Alma Luz Villanueva's *Bloodroot* and *Poems* (both 1977); June Jordan's *Things I Do in the Dark* (1977); Ntozake Shange's *Nappy Edges* (1978); Marilou Awiakta's *Abiding Appalachia: Where Mountains and Atom Meet* (1978); Janice Mirikitani's *Awake in the River* (1978, includes prose); Pinkie Gordon Lane's *Mystic Female* (1978); Luz María Umpièrre, *A Puertorriqueña in Penn* (1978), and Linda Hogan's first volume, *Calling Myself Home* (1979).

Drama (see also "Entertainment") includes Momoko Iko's *Gold Watch* (1970); Susan Yankowitz's *Slaughterhouse Play* (1971); Clare Boothe Luce's *Slam the Door Softly* (1971); Estela Portillo-Trombley's *The Day of the Swallows* (1971); Sonia Sanchez's poem plays such as *Sister Son/ji* (1972); Megan Terry's *Babes in the Bighouse* (1974); Wakako

Yamauchi's *And the Soul Shall Dance* (1974); *For colored girls who have considered suicide/when the rainbow is enuf* (1975; staged on Broadway in 1976) by Ntozake Shange (born Paulette Williams); Tina Howe's *Museum* (1976) and *The Art of Dining* (1979); María Irene Fornes's *Fefu and Her Friends* (1977); Marsha Norman's *Getting Out* (1977); Eve Merriam's *The Club* (1977); Susan Miller's *Nasty Rumors* and *Final Remarks* (both 1978); Jessica Tarahata Hagedorn's *Mango Tango* (1978); Wendy Wasserstein's *Uncommon Women and Others* (1978); Beth Henley's *The Miss Firecracker Contest* (1979); and Joan Schenkar's *Signs of Life* (1979).

"We who write are survivors"—Tillie Olsen

Books on women's issues include *Woman in Sexist Society* (1971), edited by Vivian Gornick and Barbara K. Moran; Elizabeth Janeway's *Man's World, Woman's Place: A Study in Social Mythology* (1971) and *Women: Their Changing Roles* (1973); the three-volume biography *Notable American Women* (1971), edited by Edward and Janet Wilson James, with entries for more than 1,350 women; Juanita Kreps's *Sex in the Marketplace: American Women at Work* (1971); Elizabeth Gould Davis's *The First Sex* (1971); Phyllis Chesler's *Women and Madness* (1972); conservative Midge Decter's *The New Chastity and Other Arguments Against Women's Liberation* (1972); the anthology *Black Women in White America* (1972), edited by Gerda Lerner; Susan Rennie and Kirsten Grimstad's *The New Woman's Survival Catalogue* (1973); Jill Johnston's *Lesbian Nation: The Feminist Solution* (1973); *Clio's Consciousness Raised* (1973), edited by Mary Hartman and Lois Banner; Andrea Dworkin's *Woman Hating* (1974); *Seduction and Betrayal: Women and Literature* (1974) by Elizabeth Hardwick, founder of the *New York Review of Books;* Molly Haskell's *From Reverence to Rape: The Treatment of Women in the Movies* (1974); Ti-Grace Atkinson's *Amazon Odyssey* (1974); Susan Brownmiller's *Against Our Will: Men, Women and Rape* (1975); Nora Ephron's *Crazy Salad: Some Things about Women* (1975); Adrienne Rich's *Of Woman Born: Motherhood as Experience and Institution* (1976) and *On Lies, Secrets, and Silence* (1979); Jean Baker Miller's *Toward a Psychology of Women* (1976); Dorothy Dinnerstein's *The Mermaid and the Minotaur* (1976); Del Martin's *Battered Wives* (1976); Betty Friedan's *It Changed My Life* (1976); Shere Hite's *The Hite Report* (1977, p. 235); Elaine Showalter's *A Literature of Their Own* (1977); Nancy Friday's *My Mother/My Self* (1977); Tillie Olsen's *Silences* (1978); Susan Griffin's *Woman and Nature: The Roaring Inside Her* (1978); Nancy Chodorow's influential *The Reproduction of Mothering: Psychoanalysis and the Sociology of Gender* (1978); Barbara Ehrenreich and Deirdre English's *For Her Own Good: 150 Years of the Experts' Advice to Women* (1978); Sandra Gilbert and Susan Gubar's *The Madwoman in the Attic* (1979); Michele Wallace's *Black Macho and the Myth of the Superwoman* (1979); and Carolyn Heilbrun's *Reinventing Womanhood* (1979).

Additional nonfiction includes M.F.K. Fisher's *Among Friends* (1971);

"A Culture of Our Own"

"Women's culture . . . is active: women have been the truly active people in all culture, without whom human society would long ago have perished, though our activity has most often come on behalf of men and children. Today women are talking to each other, recovering an oral culture, telling our life-stories, reading aloud to one another the books that have moved and healed us, analyzing the language that has lied about us, reading our own words aloud to each other. But to name and found a culture of our own means a real break from the passivity of the twentieth-century Western mind."
—Adrienne Rich, *On Lies, Secrets, and Silence: Selected Prose, 1966–1978* (New York: W.W. Norton, 1979)

Jessica Mitford's *Kind and Unusual Punishment: The Prison Business* (1973); *The War Against the Jews* (1975) by Lucy S. Dawidowicz (1915–90); Gail Sheehy's *Passages: Predictable Crises of Adult Life* (1976); Susan Sontag's *On Photography* (1977) and *Illness as Metaphor* (1978); Fran Lebowitz's *Metropolitan Life* (1978); Maureen Howard's award-winning *Facts of Life* (1978); and Ann Douglas's *The Feminization of American Culture* (1978).

Autobiographical and diaristic writings include Anne Morrow Lindbergh's *Bring Me a Unicorn* (1972); Lillian Hellman's *Pentimento: A Book of Portraits* (1973) and *Scoundrel Time* (1976); Jeanne Wakatsuki Houston's *Farewell to Manzanar* (1973); Angela Davis's *An Autobiography* (1974); Anna Moore Shaw's *A Pima Past* (1974); Maxine Hong Kingston's award-winning *The Woman Warrior: Memoirs of a Girlhood among Ghosts* (1976); Jade Snow Wong's *No Chinese Stranger* (1976); Robin Morgan's *Going Too Far: The Personal Chronicles of a Feminist* (1977); and May Sarton's *A House by the Sea* (1977).

Juvenile literature includes Betsy Byars's award-winning *Summer of the Swans* (1970); Judy Blume's *Otherwise Known as Sheila the Great* (1972), *Forever* (1976), and many others; Jean George's award-winning *Julie of the Wolves* (1972); Alice Childress's *A Hero Ain't Nothing But a Sandwich* (1973); Paula Fox's award-winning *The Slave Dancer* (1973); Janet Camp-bell Hale's *The Owl's Song* (1974); Rosa Cuthbert Guy's *The Friends* (1974); Virginia Esther Hamilton's award-winning *M.C. Higgins, the Great* (1974); Susan Cooper's award-winning *The Grey King* (1975); Natachee Scott Momaday's *Owl in the Cedar Tree* (1975); Mildred Taylor's award-winning *Roll of Thunder, Hear My Cry* (1976); Katherine Paterson's award-winning *Bridge to Terbithia* (1977); Judith Viorst's *Alexander and the Terrible Horrible No Good Very Bad Day* (1977); and Ellen Raskin's award-winning *The Westing Game* (1978).

1980–89

In fiction Alice Walker is the first African American woman to receive the Pulitzer Prize in fiction, in 1983 for *The Color Purple* (1982), later made into a film; Walker later writes *The Temple of My Familiar* (1989). Alison Lurie receives the 1985 prize for *Foreign Affairs* (1984). Toni Morrison wins in 1988 for *Beloved* (1987), inspired partly by the story of Margaret Garner, a fugitive slave who tried to kill her children rather than have them face recapture; Morrison also writes *Tar Baby* (1981). Anne Tyler is awarded the 1989 prize for *Breathing Lessons* (1988); her other books include *Dinner at the Homesick Restaurant* (1982) and *The Accidental Tourist* (1985).

In drama as many women win the Pulitzer in the 1980s as in all the past years. Beth Henley wins the 1981 Pultizer for *Crimes of the Heart* before it even opens on Broadway; her other plays include *The Wake of Jamey Foster* (1982) and *The Debutante Ball* (1985). In 1983 Marsha Norman receives the award for *'night Mother* (1982); she also writes *The Holdup* (1983) and *Sarah and Abraham* (1988). Wendy Wasserstein wins in 1989 for *The Heidi Chronicles*, which also receives a

Tony Award for best play. Wasserstein's other works include *Isn't It Romantic?* (1983).

In poetry a posthumous Pulitzer Prize is given in 1982, for Sylvia Plath's *Collected Poems* (1981). Mary Oliver wins in 1984 for *The American Primitive* (1983). Carolyn Kizer is awarded the 1985 prize for *Yin* (1984); she also publishes *Mermaids in the Basement: Poems for Women* (1984). Rita Dove receives the 1987 award for *Thomas and Beulah* (1986), about her grandparents; her other works include *The Yellow House on the Corner* (1980), *Museum Pieces* (1983), and *Grace Notes* (1989). In addition, May Swenson shares the 1981 Bollingen Prize for Poetry.

In biography Elizabeth Frank wins the 1986 Pulitzer for *Louise Bogan: A Portrait* (1985). Under general nonfiction Susan Sheehan receives the 1983 Pulitzer for *Is There No Place on Earth for Me?* (1982), chronicling the life of a schizophrenic woman.

Other fiction includes Toni Cade Bambara's award-winning *Salt Eaters* (1980); Joyce Carol Oates's *Bellefleur* (1980), *A Bloodsmoor Romance* (1981), *Marya, A Life* (1986), and *You Must Remember This* (1987); Shirley Hazard's award-winning *The Transit of Venus* (1980); Jean Auel's *The Clan of the Cave Bear* (1980), the first in a series; Ann Beattie's *Falling in Place* (1980); Marge Piercy's *Vida* (1980); Marilynne Robinson's *Housekeeping* (1980); Marilyn French's *The Bleeding Heart* (1980) and *Her Mother's Daughter* (1987); Jane Smiley's *Barn Blend* (1980) and *The Greenlanders* (1987); Mary Gordon's *The Company of Women* (1981) and *Men and Angels* (1985); Lisa Alther's *Original Sins* (1981); Ruthann Lum McCunn's *Thousand Pieces of Gold* (1981); Ellen Gilchrist's stories *In the Land of Dreamy Dreams* (1981), award-winning *Victory over Japan* (1984), and novel *The Anna Papers* (1988); Bette Bao Lord's *Spring Moon: A Novel of China* (1981); Clara Mitsuko Telsma's *Teapot Tales and Other Stories* (1981); Jessica Hagedorn's award-winning novella *Pet Food and Tropical Apparitions* (1981); Laurie Colwin's *The Lone Pilgrim and Other Stories* (1981); Bobbie Ann Mason's *Shiloh and Other Stories* (1982), *In Country* (1985), and *Spence and Lila* (1988); Ntozake Shange's *Sassafrass, Cypress and Indigo* (1982); Gloria Naylor's award-winning *The Women of Brewster Place* (1982), *Linden Hills* (1985), and *Mama Day* (1989); Cynthia Ozick's *Levitation: Five Fictions* (1982) and *The Messiah of Stockholm* (1987); Gail Godwin's *A Mother and Two Daughters* (1982) and *The Finishing School* (1985); Alice McDermott's *A Bigamist's Daughter* (1982); Paula Gunn Allen's *The Woman Who Owned the Shadows* (1983); Nora Ephron's *Heartburn* (1983); Judith Rossner's *August* (1983); Wendy Law-Yone's *The Coffin Tree* (1983); Rebecca Goldstein's *The Mind-Body Problem* (1983); Paule Marshall's *Praisesong for the Widow* (1983); Lee Smith's *Oral History* (1983); Michelle Cliff's *Abend: A Novel* (1984); Josephine Humphreys's *Dreams of Sleep* (1984) and *Rich in Love* (1988); Harriet Doerr's award-winning *Stones for Ibarra* (1984); Joan Didion's *Democracy* (1984); Alice Adams's *Superior Women* (1984) and *Second Chances* (1988); Louise Erdrich's award-winning *Love Medicine* (1984) and related *The Beet*

Female Sleuths

During the 1980s an increasing number of women mystery writers use female detectives. In 1982, for example, Sara Paretsky introduces V. I. Warshawski in Indemnity Only *and* Sue Grafton presents Kinsey Millhone in "A" Is for Alibi. Amanda Cross (Carolyn Heilbrun) continues the exploits of English professor Kate Fansler. In addition to detective Sharon McCone, who first appeared in Edwin of the Iron Shoes *(1977)*, Marcia Muller offers museum curator Elena Olivarez, starting in The Tree of Death *(1983). A few of the many other female sleuths are Susan Dunlap's Veejay Haskell and Jill Smith, Patricia Cornwell's Dr. Kay Scarpetta, and Julie Smith's Skip Langdon.*

Drama of the 1980s

In addition to the Pulitzer Prize winners, some of the many plays by women are Jane Chambers's Last Summer at Blue-Fish Cove *(1980); Emily Mann's* Still Life *(1980) and* Execution of Justice *(1983); Wendy Kesselman's* My Sister in This House *(1981); Laura Farabough's* Femme Fatale: The Invention of Personality *(1981); Lynne Alvarez's* Gracilla, Latinos, Mundo *(1982); Tina Howe's* Painting Churches *(1983) and* Coastal Disturbances *(1986); Sally Nemeth's* Holy Days *(1983); María Irene Fornes's* Mud *(1983) and* The Conduct of Life *(1985); Velena Hasu Houston's* Tea, American Dreams, *and* Amerasian Girls *(all 1983); Susan Yankowitz's* A Knife in the Heart *(1983); Estela Portillo-Tramblay's* Sor Juana and Other Plays *(1983); Barbara Lebow's* A Shayna Maidel *(1984); Rosalyn Drexler's* Transients Welcome *(1984), an Obie winner; Milcha Sanchez-Scott's* Dog Lady *(1984) and* Roosters *(1987); Sybille Pearson's* Sally and Marsha *(1985); Mary Gallagher's* How to Say Goodbye *(1986); Cherríe Moraga's* Giving Up the Ghost *(1986); Wakako Yamauchi's* The Memento *(1986); Marlane Meyer's* Etta Jenks *(1987); Ellen McLaughlin's* A Narrow Bed *(1987); Megan Terry's* Walking through Walls *(1987); and Suzan-Lori Parks's* Imperceptible Mutabilities in the Third Kingdom *(1989), an Obie winner. (See also "Entertainment.")*

Queen (1986) and *Tracks* (1988); Sandra Cisneros's award-winning *The House on Mango Street* (1984); *Annie John* (1985) by Jamaica Kincaid (born Elaine Potter Richardson); May Sarton's *The Magnificent Spinster* (1985); Beth Brant's stories *Mohawk Trail* (1985); Helena María Viramontes's *The Moths and Other Stories* (1985); Grace Paley's stories *Later the Same Day* (1985); Lore Groszmann Segal's *Her First American: A Novel* (1985); Anna Lee Walters's stories *The Sun Is Not Merciful* (1985); Nicholasa Mohr's stories *Rituals of Survival: A Woman's Portfolio* (1985); Janet Campbell Hale's *The Jailing of Cecilia Capture* (1985); Alice Hoffman's *Fortune's Daughter* (1985) and *Illumination Night* (1987); Anne Rice's *The Vampire Lestat* (1985) and *Queen of the Damned* (1988); Carolyn Chute's *The Beans of Egypt, Maine* (1985); Maureen Howard's *Expensive Habits* (1986); Sherley Anne Williams's *Dessa Rose* (1986); Ana Castillo's award-winning *The Mixquiahuala Letters* (1986); Mona Simpson's *Anywhere But Here* (1986); Marita Golden's *A Woman's Place* (1986); Denise Chávez's stories *The Last of the Menu Girls* (1986); Susan Minot's *Monkeys* (1986); Tama Janowitz's stories *Slaves of New York* (1986) and *A Cannibal in Manhattan* (1987); Carolyn See's *Golden Days* (1987); Diane Johnson's *Persian Nights* (1987); Terry McMillan's *Mama* (1987) and *Disappearing Acts* (1989); Fanny Flagg's *Fried Green Tomatoes at the Whistle Stop Café* (1987); Anne Roiphe's *Loving Kindness* (1987); *Clay Walls* (1987) by Ronyoung Kim (1926–87); Bharati Mukherjee's award-winning *The Middleman and Other Stories* (1988) and novel *Jasmine* (1989); Ninotchka Rosca's *State of War* (1988); Hisaye Yamamoto's *Seventeen Syllables and Other Stories* (1988); Lynda Barry's *The Good Times Are Killing Me* (1988), also dramatized; Barbara Kingsolver's *The Bean Trees* (1988); Amy Tan's *The Joy Luck Club* (1989); Mary Morris's *The Waiting Room* (1989); Marianne Wiggins's *John Dollar* (1989); Jane Hamilton's *The Book of Ruth* (1989); Carmen de Monteflores's *Singing Softly/Cantando Bajito* (1989); Rita Mae Brown's *Six of One* (1989); and Judith Ortiz Cofer's *The Line of the Sun* (1989);

Experimental works include Leslie Marmon Silko's *Storyteller* (1981), mixing stories and poems; *DICTEE* (1982) by performance and video artist Theresa Hak Kyung Cha (1951–82); and Kathy Acker's *Hello, I'm Erica Jong* (1982) and other works.

Additional poetry includes Sandra María Esteves's *Yerba Buena* (1980), and *Tropical Rains* (1984); Michelle Cliff's *Claiming an Identity They Taught Me to Despise* (1980); Wendy Rose's *Lost Copper* (1980) and *Halfbreed Chronicles* (1985); Lucille Clifton's *Two-Headed Woman* (1980); Naomi Shihab Nye's *Different Ways to Pray* (1980); Judy Grahn's *The Work of a Common Woman* (1980); Adrienne Rich's *A Wild Patience Has Taken Me This Far* (1981) and *Your Native Land, Your Life* (1986); Lorna Dee Cervantes's award-winning *Emplumada* (1981); Gayl Jones's *Song for Anninho* (1981); Carolyn Forché's *The Country Between Us* (1981); Audre Lorde's *Chosen Poems: Old and New* (1982) and *Our Dead Behind Us* (1986); Katha Pollitt's award-winning *Antarctic Traveller* (1982); Mona Van Duyn's *Letters from a Father and Other Poems*

(1982); Marge Piercy's *Circles on the Water* (1982) and *Available Light* (1988); Cheryl Clarke's *Narratives: Poems in the Tradition of Black Women* (1982); Paula Gunn Allen's *Shadow Country* (1982); Jayne Cortez's *Firespitter* (1982) and *Coagulations* (1985); Susan Howe's *Pythagorean Silence* (1982); Denise Levertov's *Candles in Babylon* (1982); Ntozake Shange's *A Daughter's Geography* (1983) and *Nappy Edges* (1987); Amy Clampitt's *The Kingfisher* and *The Summer Solstice* (both 1983); Kitty Tsui's *The Words of a Woman Who Breathes Fire* (1983); Joy Harjo's *She Had Some Horses* (1983); Cathy Song's award-winning *Picture Bride* (1983); Cherríe Moraga's prose poem *Loving in the War Years: Lo que nunca paso por sus labios* (1983); Sonia Sanchez's *Home Girls and Handgrenades* (1984) and *Under a Soprano Sky* (1987); Ana Castillo's *Women Are Not Roses* (1984); Sharon Olds's award-winning *The Dead and the Living* (1984); Diane Wakoski's *The Collected Greed* (1984) and *Emerald Ice* (1988); Diane Glancy's *Wolf Leaves the Res* (1984); Pat Mora's *Chants* (1984); Linda Hogan's award-winning *Seeing through the Sun* (1985); Pat Parker's *Jonestown and Other Madness* (1985); Marilyn Hacker's *Assumptions* (1985) and *Love, Death and the Changing of the Season* (1986), a verse novel; Louise Glück's award-winning *The Triumph of Achilles* (1985); Anne Winters's award-winning *The Key to the City* (1985); Tess Gallagher's *Willingly* (1985); June Jordan's *Living Room* (1985) and *Naming Our Destiny* (1989); Wendy W. Larsen and Tran Thi Nga's *Shallow Graves: Two Women and Vietnam* (1986); Janice Mirikitani's *Shedding Silence* (1987, with prose); Luz María Umpièrre's *The Margarita Poems* (1987); May Swenson's *In Other Words* (1987); Elizabeth Woody's award-winning *Hand into Stone* (1988); Nikki Giovanni's *Sacred Cows and Other Edibles* (1988); Mitsuye Yamada's *Desert Run* (1988, with stories); Kimiko Hahn's *Air Pocket* (1989); and Margaret Walker's *This Is My Country* (1989).

"I have dreamed of a bridge"—Cherríe Moraga

Books on women's issues include *This Bridge Called My Back: Writings by Radical Women of Color* (1981), edited by Cherríe Moraga and Gloria Anzaldúa; Angela Davis's *Women, Race, and Class* (1981) and *Women, Culture and Politics* (1989); Betty Friedan's *The Second Stage* (1981); bell hooks's *Ain't I a Woman: Black Women and Feminism* (1981) and *Talking Back: Thinking Feminist, Thinking Black* (1989); Andrea Dworkin's *Pornography* (1981) and *Right-wing Women* (1983); Carol Gilligan's *In a Different Voice* (1982), proposing a distinct route of moral development for women; *But Some of Us Are Brave* (1982), a black women's studies anthology edited by Gloria T. Hull, Patricia Bell Scott, and Barbara Smith; Alice Walker's essays *In Search of Our Mothers' Gardens* (1983); Gloria Steinem's essays *Outrageous Acts and Everyday Rebellions* (1983); *A Gathering of Spirit: A Collection by North American Indian Women* (1984/1988), edited by Beth Brant; Audre Lorde's essays *Sister Outsider* (1984); *Sisterhood Is Global* (1984) by Robin Morgan; Paula Gidding's history of African American women, *When and Where I Enter* (1984); Paula Gunn Allen's *The Sacred Hoop*

"My Mother's Stories"

". . . so many of the stories that I write, that we all write, are my mother's stories. Only recently did I fully realize this: that through years of listening to my mother's stories of her life, I have absorbed not only the stories themselves, but something of the manner in which she spoke, something of the urgency that involves the knowledge that her stories—like her life—must be recorded."
—Alice Walker, "In Search of Our Mothers' Gardens," in *In Search of Our Mothers' Gardens* (New York: Harcourt Brace and Company, 1984)

Personal Stories

Autobiographical and diaristic works from the 1980s include Maxine Hong Kingston's China Men *(1980); Audre Lorde's* The Cancer Journals *(1980) and* Zami: A New Spelling of My Name *(1982); Kate Millett's* The Loony-Bin Trap *(1980); Maya Angelou's* The Heart of a Woman *(1981) and* All God's Children Need Traveling Shoes *(1986); Maggie Ann Culver Fry's* Sunrise over Red Man's Land *(1981); Kim Chernin's* In My Mother's House *(1983); Shirley Abbott's* Womenfolks: Growing Up Down South *(1983); Eudora Welty's* One Writer's Beginning *(1984); May Sarton's* At Seventy *(1984); Aurora Levins Morales and Rosario Morales's* Getting Home Alive *(1986); Vivian Gornick's* Fierce Attachments *(1987); Joan Nestle's* A Restricted Country *(1987); Pauli Murray's posthumously published* Song in a Weary Throat *(1987); Mary Morris's* Nothing to Declare: Memoirs of a Woman Traveling Alone *(1988); and Eva Hoffman's* Lost in Translation: Life in a New Language *(1989).*

(1986); *Women's Ways of Knowing* (1986) by Mary Field Belenky, Blythe McVicker Clinchy, Nancy Rule Goldberger, and Jill Mattuck Tarule; Gerda Lerner's *The Creation of Patriarchy* (1986); Carolyn Heilbrun's *Writing a Woman's Life* (1988); two 1989 anthologies of Asian American women's writings, *Making Waves* (edited by Asian Women United) and *The Forbidden Stitch* (edited by Shirley Geok-lin Lim, Mayumi Tsutakawa, and Margarita Donnelly); and filmmaker Trinh T. Minh-ha's *Woman, Native, Other: Writing Postcoloniality and Feminism* (1989).

Other nonfiction includes Florence Rush's *The Best Kept Secret: The Sexual Abuse of Children* (1980); June Jordan's essays *Civil Wars* (1981) and *On Call* (1985); Annie Dillard's *Living by Fiction* (1982) and *Writing Life* (1989); Joan Didion's *Salvador* (1982) and *Miami* (1987); M.F.K. Fisher's *As They Were* (1982) and *Sister Age* (1984, with stories); Cynthia Ozick's *Art and Ardor* (1983) and *Metaphor and Memory* (1989); Barbara Ehrenreich's *The Hearts of Men* (1983) and *Fear of Falling: The Inner Life of the Middle Class* (1989); Judith Viorst's *Necessary Losses* (1986); Sue Hubbell's *A Country Year: Living the Question* (1986); Gloria Anzaldúa's *Borderlands/La Frontiera: The New Mestiza* (1987); Lucy S. Dawidowicz's *From That Place and Time* (1989); Mary Catherine Bateson's *Composing a Life* (1989); and Susan Sontag's *AIDS and Its Metaphors* (1989).

1990–95

In 1993, after her novel *Jazz* (1992), Toni Morrison is the second U.S. woman (after Pearl Buck) and first African American to receive the Nobel Prize for Literature. She later says, "I felt a lot of 'we' excitement. It was as if the whole category of 'female writer' and 'black writer' had been redeemed. I felt I represented a whole world of women who either were silenced or who had never received the imprimatur of the established literary world."

A number of women receive the Pulitzer Prize in the early 1990s. In fiction Jane Smiley wins the 1992 Pulitzer for *A Thousand Acres* (1991); she later writes the satirical *Moo* (1995). E. (Edna) Annie Proulx receives the 1994 award for *The Shipping News* (1993); she also writes *Postcards* (1992). U.S.-born Canadian novelist Carol Shields wins the 1995 prize for *The Stone Diaries* (1994).

In poetry Mona Van Duyn receives the 1991 Pulitzer Prize for *Near Changes* (1990). Van Duyn is also named the sixth, and first woman, U.S. poet laureate in 1992. In 1993 she is succeeded by the second woman and first African American, Rita Dove, who publishes *Through the Ivory Gate* (1993). In 1993 Louise Glück wins the poetry Pulitzer, for *The Wild Iris* (1992); she also writes *Ararat* (1990). Another major poetry award, the Bollingen Prize, is shared by Laura Riding Jackson in 1991.

In history the 1991 Pulitzer Prize goes to Laurel Tatcher Ulrich for *A Midwife's Tale: The Life of Martha Ballard, based on her diary, 1785–1812.* In 1995 the prize is awarded to Doris Kearns Goodwin for *No Ordinary Time: Franklin and Eleanor Rooosevelt: The Home Front in*

World War II. Joan D. Hedrick receives the 1995 biography Pulitzer for *Harriet Beecher Stowe: A Life.*

In 1993 Maya Angelou reads her poem "On the Pulse of the Morning" at the inauguration of President Bill Clinton. She also writes the best-selling *Wouldn't Take Nothing for My Journey Now* (1993). "Women should be tough, tender, laugh as much as possible, and live long lives," she asserts.

Other fiction includes Jessica Hagedorn's *Dogeaters* (1990); Linda Hogan's *Mean Spirit* (1990) and *Solar Storms* (1994); Erica Jong's *Any Woman's Blues* (1990); Joyce Carol Oates's *Because It Is Bitter, and Because It Is My Heart* (1990) and *Foxfire: Confessions of a Girl Gang* (1993); Maxine Hong Kingston's *Tripmaster Monkey* (1990); Diane Glancy's stories *Trigger Dance* (1990); Jamaica Kincaid's *Lucy* (1990); Barbara Kingsolver's *Animal Dreams* (1990) and *Pigs in Heaven* (1993); Elizabeth Cook-Lynn's *The Power of Horses and Other Stories* (1990); Ann Beattie's *Picturing Will* (1990); Sue Miller's *Family Pictures* (1990); Anne Tyler's *Saint Maybe* (1991) and *Ladder of Years* (1995); Leslie Marmon Silko's *Almanac of the Dead* (1991); *The Crown of Columbus* (1991) by Louise Erdrich with her husband, Michael Dorris; Grace Paley's *Long Walks and Intimate Talks* (1991); Mona Simpson's *The Lost Father* (1991); Sandra Cisneros's *Woman Hollering Creek and Other Stories* (1991); Meena Alexander's *Nampally Road* (1991); Amy Tan's *The Kitchen God's Wife* (1991) and *The Hundred Secret Senses* (1995); Julia Alvarez's *How the Garcia Girls Lost Their Accents* (1991) and *In the Time of the Butterflies* (1994); Paule Marshall's *Daughters* (1991); Blanche Boyd's *The Revolution of Little Girls* (1991); Jessica K. Saki's *From Lanai and Other Stories* (1991); Alice Adams's *Caroline's Daughters* (1991) and *Almost Perfect* (1993); Terry McMillan's best-selling *Waiting to Exhale* (1992); Dorothy Allison's *Bastard Out of Carolina* (1992); Susan Sontag's *The Volcano Lover* (1992); Anne Rice's *The Tale of the Body Thief* (1992); Gloria Naylor's *Bailey's Cafe* (1992); Alice Hoffman's *Seventh Heaven* (1990) and *Turtle Moon* (1992); Rosellen Brown's *Before and After* (1992); Anne Roiphe's *The Pursuit of Happiness* (1992); Annie Dillard's *The Living* (1992); Thulani Davis's *1959* (1992); Alice Walker's *Possessing the Secret Joy* (1992); Donna Tartt's *The Secret History* (1992); Cristina Garcia's *Dreaming in Cuban* (1992); Michelle Cliff's *Free Enterprise* (1993); Ana Castillo's *So Far from God* (1993); Fae Myenne Ng's *Bone* (1993); Susan Power's *The Grass Dancer* (1994); and Julie Shige Kuni's *A Bridge Between Us* (1995)

Other poetry includes Pat Parker's posthumous *Collected Poetry* (1990); Sandra María Esteves's *Bluestown Mockingbird Mambo* (1990), Joy Harjo's award-winning *In Mad Love and War* (1990); Amy Gerstler's award-winning *Bitter Angel* (1990); Susan Howe's *The Europe of Trusts* (1990); Irene Klepfisz's *A Few Words in the Mother Tongue* (1990); Mary TallMountain's *The Light on the Tent Wall* (1990); Adrienne Rich's *An Atlas of the Difficult World* (1991) and *Dark Fields of the Republic* (1995); Ntozake Shange's *The Love Space Demands* (1991); Linda

"Power Resides Within Certain Stories"

"Yoeme had made margin notes after the pages describing her deliverance. Yoeme had believed power resides within certain stories; this power ensures the story to be retold, and with each retelling a slight but permanent shift took place. Yoeme's story of her deliverance changed forever the odds against all captives; each time a revolutionist escaped death in one century, two revolutionists escaped certain death in the following century even if they had never heard such an escape story. Where such miraculous escape stories are greatly prized and rapidly circulated, miraculous escapes from death gradually increase."
—Leslie Marmon Silko, *Almanac of the Dead: A Novel* (New York: Penguin Books, 1991)

Books on Women's Issues for the 1990s

A few of the many new books on women's issues are Deborah F. Tannen's best-selling You Just Don't Understand: Women and Men in Conversation *(1990); Susan Faludi's* Backlash: The Undeclared War on Women *(1991); Naomi Wolf's* The Beauty Myth *(1991) and* Fire with Fire: The New Female Power *(1993); Letty Cottin Pogrebin's* Deborah, Golda and Me *(1991); Gloria Steinem's* Revolution from Within: A Book of Self-Esteem *(1991); Clarissa Pinkola Estés's best-selling* Women Who Run with the Wolves: Myths and Stories of the Wild Woman Archetype *(1992); Carol Tavris's* The Mismeasure of Woman *(1992); Katie Roiphe's* The Morning After: Sex, Fear, and Feminism *(1993); Betty Friedan's* The Fountain of Age *(1993); Gerda Lerner's* The Creation of Feminist Consciousness *(1993); Katha Pollitt's* Reasonable Creatures: Essays on Women and Feminism *(1994); and Ana Castillo's* Massacre of the Dreams: Essay on Xicanisma *(1995). Several other books are discussed in the sections on education and religion.*

McCarriston's *Eva–Mary* (1991); Ruth Stone's *Who Is the Widow's Muse?* (1991); Lorna Dee Cervantes's *From the Cables of Genocide* (1991); Alice Walker's *Her Blue Body Everything We Know* (1991); Jayne Cortez's *Poet Magnetic* (1991); Mary Oliver's award-winning *New and Selected Poems* (1992); and Patricia Spears Jones's *The Weather That Kills* (1995).

Additional drama (see also "Entertainment") includes Beth Henley's *Abundance* (1990); Wendy Kesselman's *Olympe and the Executioner* (1990); Sally Nemeth's *Mill Fire* (1990); Suzan-Lori Parks's *The Death of the Last Black Man in the Whole Entire World* (1991); Cheryl L. West's *Before It Hits Home* (1991) and *Jar the Floor* (1992); Therese Rebeck's *Spike Heels* (1992) and *The Family of Mann* (1994); Catherine Butterfield's *Joined at the Head* (1992); Wendy Wasserstein's *The Sisters Rosensweig* (1992); Paula Vogel's *The Baltimore Waltz* (1992), an Obie winner, and *Hot 'N' Throbbing* (1994); Anna Deavere Smith's *Fires in the Mirror* (1992) and *Twilight Los Angeles, 1992* (1994), an Obie winner; Joan Ackerman's *Off the Map* (1994); and Emily Mann's adaptation of the Delany sisters' book (below), *Having Our Say* (1995).

Additional nonfiction includes Diane Ackerman's *A Natural History of the Senses* (1990); Camille Paglia's *Sexual Personae* (1990); Melissa Fay Greene's *Praying for Sheetrock* (1991); Patricia Williams's *The Alchemy of Race and Rights* (1991); Susan Griffin's *A Chorus of Stones: The Private Life of War* (1992); June Jordan's essays *Technical Difficulties* (1992); Sue Halpern's *Migrations to Solitude* (1992); and Tina Rosenberg's *The Haunted Land: Facing Europe's Ghost after Communism* (1995).

Autobiographical writings include Mary Paik Lee's *Quiet Odyssey: A Pioneer Korean Woman in America* (1990); *Lakota Woman* (1990) and *Ohitka Woman* (1993) by Mary Crow Dog (later Mary Brave Bird), with Richard Erdoes; Judith Ortiz Cofer's *Silent Dancing: A Partial Remembrance of a Puerto Rican Childhood* (1990); Lorene Cary's *Black Ice* (1991); Elmaz Abinader's *Children of the Roojme* (1991); Donna Williams's *Nobody Nowhere* (1992), describing the world of autism; May Sarton's *Encore: A Journal of the Eightieth Year* (1993); Janet Campbell Hale's *Bloodlines: Odyssey of a Native Daughter* (1993); Sarah L. and A. Elizabeth Delany's best-selling *Having Our Say* (1993), with Amy Hill Hearth; Elaine Brown's *A Taste of Power* (1993); and Kate Millett's *A.D.* (1995).

Entertainment and Performing Arts

Meredith Monk's *Education of the Girlchild,* with (left to right) Meredith Monk, Blondell Cummings, Coco Pekeys, Lee Nagrin, Monica Moseley, and Lanny Harrison (courtesy © Peter Moore)

Performers in the 1700s include:

—British-born Mrs. Lewis Hallam, a member of a traveling theater company and one of the first actresses in America. She performs as Portia in The Merchant of Venice *in Williamsburg, Virginia, in 1752 and then tours other cities. Margaret Cheer takes over the female leads in the Hallam Company's performances in 1766; Nancy Hallam succeeds her in 1769, playing Juliet in* Romeo and Juliet, *Polly in* Beggar's Opera, *and other roles.*

—Suzanne Theodore Vaillande (later Douvillier, 1778–1826), who, using the name "Madame Placide," stars in the first U.S. ballet performance, in New York in 1792. She later choreographs her own pieces and, beginning in 1813, is the first female set designer in America.

—British-born Elizabeth Morris (c. 1753–1826), who is arrested in Boston in 1792 for appearing in School for Scandal, *but soon moves to Philadelphia, where she is considered a major actress.*

—British actress Ann Brunton Merry (1769–1808), who debuts in Romeo and Juliet *in Philadelphia in 1796 and is the undisputed leading tragic actress of the day.*

—Catherine Graupner, an early vocal soloist, who performs in Boston in 1798.

1700s

In the 1700s American women emerge as both performers (see sidebar) and creators. In 1766, for example, the Ephrata sisters in Pennsylvania begin composing their own hymns, some of the first music by American women (see "Religion"). In 1794 Anne Julia Hatton (c. 1757–96) writes the libretto for the opera *Tammany; or, The Indian Chief.* In the same year Susanna Rowson (c. 1762–1824) acts in one of her own plays, *Slaves in Algiers, or a Struggle for Freedom.*

1800–39

Theater: Mary Anne Dyke (1794–1857) is first acclaimed as Juliet in Boston in 1818. Playing mostly Shakespearean tragic roles, she is the lead performer of her day. Performing in New York in 1820, the African Company includes some of the first African American female performers. In 1825 Frances Ann Denny Drake (1797–1875), already a star on the New York stage, travels west, where she reigns as the "tragedy queen." When British actress Clara Fisher (1811–98) opens in New York in 1827, she is such a success that people name everything from babies to steamboats after her. For the next seven years she plays both male and female leads, from Shylock to Juliet, in the United States. British actress Fanny Kemble (1809–93) debuts in New York in 1832 as Bianca in *Fazio.* After performing for two years, she marries Pierce Butler, a slave owner, and describes her horror at slavery in a published journal (see "Literature").

Music: After making her debut as a pianist in 1807 at age seven, Sophia Hewitt (later Ostinelli) is the first and only woman asked to play the organ for the Handel and Haydn Society in Boston, in 1820.

1840–49

Theater: After her acting debut as Lady Macbeth in New Orleans and New York in 1836, Charlotte Saunders Cushman (1816–76) manages the Walnut Street Theatre in Philadelphia in 1842. She commutes between Philadelphia and New York on alternate nights to play Lady Macbeth opposite British actor William Macready in 1843. In 1844 she achieves her first major success in London, starring opposite Edwin Forrest in the romantic tragedy *Fazio.* In 1845 she plays Romeo to the Juliet of her sister, Susan. Acclaimed as one of the greatest actresses of the day, she performs before Queen Victoria in 1848 and tours the United States in 1849–1852.

After a successful three-week run of her satire *Fashion* (1845) in New York, Ana Ogden Mowatt takes up an acting career. In *Autobiography of an Actress* (1854) she describes the theater world of her day.

Music: In 1842 Abigail Jemima Hutchinson (1829–92) tours the country with her brothers, both as a soloist and part of a quartet. She sometimes sings at abolitionist rallies.

Dance: Ballerina Augusta Maywood (1825–76) makes her highly successful New York debut in 1837 and is equally acclaimed at the Paris Opérà in 1839, the first U.S. ballerina to gain international fame. A scandal forces her to leave Paris, but she continues her success in Italy. In 1849 La Scala in Milan proclaims her *prima donna assoluta*.

After sudying in Paris, Mary Ann Lee (c. 1824–99) introduces the ballet *Giselle* to U.S. audiences in 1846. After starring in the *Naiad Queen*, Julia Anna Turnbull (1822–87) also dances *Giselle*, in New York in 1847, to much acclaim.

1850–59

Theater: After her 1852 debut, Caroline Chapman (c. 1818–76) is the leading actress of the decade in San Francisco. British-born Agnes Kelly Robertson (1833–1916) debuts in New York in 1853 by playing six characters in a farce, *The Young Actress,* written by her husband. Called the "fairy star" for her petite size, she is one of the most popular touring stars of the decade. In 1853 British-born actress Laura Keene (c. 1820–73) takes over as manager of the Charles Street Theatre in Baltimore; she moves to New York in 1856 and builds Laura Keene's Theater. The first major U.S. woman theater producer, she stars in the company's productions, designs costumes and scenery, instructs actors, and puts together scripts. In 1855 actress Julia Dean (1830–68), known for her performances as Jula in *The Hunchback* and Juliet, stars in her own play, *Mary of Mantua.* In 1857 in New York, Matilda Agnes Heron (1830–77) plays the title role in *Camille,* her own translation of Alexandre Dumas's *La Dame aux Camélias;* her next vehicle is her own translation of *Medée.*

Dance: In 1852 Irish-born dancer and beauty Lola Montez (Eliza Gilbert, 1818–61) arrives in New York and tours the country, entrancing San Francisco audiences with her *Spider Dance* in 1853. She marries and holds sway in a mining camp, where she teaches Lotta Crabtree (see below).

1860–69

Theater: Adah Isaacs Menken (c. 1835–68) achieves instant fame in 1861 when she appears in a skin-colored body stocking, strapped to a horse, in the climactic scene of *Mazeppa,* adapted from Lord Byron's poem. Maggie Mitchell (1832–1918) first stars in *Fanchon, the Cricket* in New Orleans in 1861 and continues to entrance audiences in the role of this spritelike girl for two decades. In 1861 actress Louisa Lane Drew (1820–97) is the new manager of Philadelphia's Arch Street Theatre, which she builds into a major repertory company. She is best known for playing Mrs. Malaprop in *The Rivals.* In 1862 Kate Josephine Bateman (1842–1917) is a hit in the title role of *Leah the Forsaken* in Boston, New York, and London. After first introducing *Our American Cousin* in 1858, Laura Keene produces it at Ford's Theatre in 1865. When John Wilkes Booth assassinates President Abraham Lincoln during a performance, she identifies the murderer and tends to his victim. Character actress Anne Jane Harley Gilbert (1821–1904) is a hit as the Marquise de St. Maur in the comedy *Caste,* in New York in 1867. Taught by Lola Montez in a California mining camp, Lotta Crabtree (1847–1924) has her first hit in *Little Nell and*

Top singers of the 1850s include:

—Swedish soprano Jenny Lind, who arrives in New York in 1850 for a tour sponsored by P. T. Barnum. Some 40,000 people welcome her at the docks. She gives much of the money from her two-year tour to charity.

—Elizabeth Taylor Greenfield (c. 1819–76), the first African American concert singer, who debuts in Buffalo in 1851. Dubbed the "Black Swan" by the press, she sings before an all-white audience of 4,000 in New York's Metropolitan Hall in 1853 and later holds a benefit concert at a black old-age home and orphan asylum. In 1854, while studying in Europe, she gives a command performance for Queen Victoria.

—Coloratura soprano Adelina Patti (1843–1919), who makes her operatic debut in New York in 1859. She is an immediate sensation when she sings La Somnambula at Covent Garden in London in 1861. Considered one of the greatest voices of the day, she builds a repertoire of 42 operas, performing mostly in Europe. In 1881 she begins yearly U.S. tours, ending her programs with "Home Sweet Home."

Acting in the 1870s

Some notable actresses are:
—Kate Claxton (Kate Eliza Cone, 1848–1924), famed for her portrayal of a blind girl in The Two Orphans (1874).
—Charlotte Cushman, whose 25,000 fans applaud her in front of her hotel after her farewell performance in New York in 1874.
—Sisters Anna and Emma Hyers, who tour as the stars of such musicals as Out of Bondage (1875) and The Underground Railroad (1879), portraying the African American experience.
—Clara Morris (1847–1925), who plays the suffering melodramatic heroine and has her biggest hit in Miss Multon (1876).
—Mary Anderson (1859–1940), who makes her New York debut in The Lady of Lyons in 1877. She later tours with her own arrangement of The Winter's Tale (1888).
—Polish-born Helena Modjeska (Jadwiga Opid, 1840–1909), who has her U.S. debut in 1877 in Adrienne Lecouvreur and Camille. Later, in 1889–90, she stars opposite Edwin Booth in many of the great Shakespearean roles.
—Rose Eytinge (1835–1911), who plays one of her most memorable roles as Cleopatra in Shakespeare's tragedy in 1877.
—Rose Coghlan, who is the leading lady in Lester Wallach's New York stock company in 1877 and stars in The School for Scandal and other comedies.

the Marchioness, a play written for her, in 1867 in Chicago. By 1870 the popular actress is touring with her own company, with a repertoire of plays to showcase her comic talent.

Opera: Soprano Clara Louise Kellogg (1842–1916) gains acclaim in New York in 1863, when she is the first woman to sing Marguerite in Gounod's *Faust.* For almost 25 years she is feted in this part.

Music: Venezuelan-born Teresa Carreño (1853–1917), a child prodigy, debuts as a pianist in New York in 1862 and in 1863 performs two of her own compositions at a Boston concert. She soon goes to Europe to study. French-born violinist Camilla Urso (1842–1902), who first gained acclaim at age 11, plays in Boston and then with the New York Philharmonic in 1863. One of the top violinists of the time, she begins touring and soon forms her own concert company. Constance Faunt Le Roy Runcie (1836–1911) composes her first hymn, "There Is a Land of Pure Delight" in 1863. Her other works include a cantata and an opera, as well as more hymns.

Dance: Italian-born ballerina Marie Bonfanti (c. 1847–1921) stars in possibly the first musical comedy, *The Black Crook,* in New York in 1866. It runs for two years. Another Italian-born dancer, Giuseppina Morlacchi (1836–86), draws audiences to the spectacle *The Devil's Auction* in 1867 in New York and Boston.

1870–79

Opera: Contralto Annie Louise Cary (1841–1921) is the first U.S. Wagnerian heroine, in *Lohengrin* in New York in 1874; she also sings in the first U.S. performance of Verdi's *Requiem* (1874). Singer Emma Abbott (1850–91) is the first woman to form her own opera company, the Emma Abbott English Opera Company, in 1878. She helps to popularize opera by producing abridged versions of such pieces as *The Daughter of the Regiment.*

Concert Singers: The Fisk University Jubilee Singers form in 1871 with seven women, including Ella Sheppard (later Moore) and Maggie L. Porter, and four men. Singing slave songs as well as white music, they tour the United States and Europe to raise money for the college. Emma Cecilia Thursby (1845–1931) first gains attention as a singer in 1874, with Patrick Gilmore's 22d Regiment Band in Philadelphia.

Musicians: Maud Morgan (1864–1941) debuts as a classical harpist in 1874 and continues to perform successfully for 50 years. At her 1875 debut with the New York Philharmonic, pianist Julie Rivé-King (1854–1937) plays her teacher Franz Liszt's Concerto in E Flat and a difficult Schumann work. By 1899 she has performed in 4,000 concerts, playing both European and American composers. She also composes some of her own pieces, such as *Polonaise Héroïque.*

1880–89

Theater: Effie Ellsler (c. 1854–1942) stars in *Hazel Kirke* (1880), a role she plays 1,500 times. Annie Russell (1864–1936) is a hit in *Esmeralda*

(1881), coauthored by Frances Hodgson Burnett; her successor in this role, Viola Emily Allen (1867–1948), is also acclaimed. Fanny Davenport (1850–98) is a hit in *Féodora* in New York, in the role Sarah Bernhardt made famous. Agnes Booth (c. 1841–1910) has her greatest triumph in the melodrama *Jim, the Penman* in New York in 1886. Ada Rehan (Ada Crehan, 1857–1916), who first appeared in New York in 1879, is memorable as Katherine in *The Taming of the Shew* in 1887.

Musical comedy: Lillian Russell (Helen Louise Leonard, 1861–1922) first gains popularity as D'Jemma in *The Snake Charmer* (1881).

Concert Singers: In 1885 Flora Batson (1864–1906) is celebrated for her baritone to soprano range. Another major African American singer, Sissieretta Joyner Jones (1868–1933) debuts in New York in 1888; she is soon called "Black Patti" (after the top opera singer Adelina Patti).

Musicians: A top pianist of the day, Teresa Carreño introduces Grieg's Piano Concerto to U.S. audiences in 1883 and also performs her own works, such as the Teresita Waltz; she is also feted in Europe. Another celebrated pianist, Fannie Bloomfield-Zeisler (c. 1863–1927), has her New York debut in 1885 and in 1891 begins yearly appearances with the Chicago Symphony Orchestra. In 1885 violinist Maud Powell (1868–1920) debuts with the Berlin Philharmonic and then the New York Philharmonic Society; in 1889 she is one of the first Americans to perform Tchaikovsky's Violin Concerto, and she later introduces works by such composers as Sibelius and Saint-Saëns. Violinist Caroline Nichols (1864–1939) starts a successful all-woman orchestra, the Fadettes, in Boston in 1888, expanding from 6 to 15 players by 1890.

Other Performers: Annie Oakley joins Buffalo Bill Cody's Wild West Show in 1885 (see p. 270).

1890–99

Theater: In 1890 Georgiana Emma Drew Barrymore (1854–93) is a hit in the comedy *The Senator.* Sara Adler is a major star in New York Yiddish theater in the 1890s; another is Bertha Kalich (1874–1939). Julia Arthur (Ida Lewis, 1869–1950) stars as Queen Fortunetta in *The Black Masque* (adapted from a Edgar Allen Poe story) in 1891 and in the title role of Oscar Wilde's *Lady Windemere's Fan,* opposite Maurice Barrymore, in 1893. Caroline Dudley Carter (1862–1937), known as Mrs. Leslie Carter, has her first of several hits in David Belasco's *The Heart of Maryland* (1895). Maude Adams (1872–1953) gains fame in James Barrie's *The Little Minister* (1897) and continues to star in his plays. Amelia Smiley Bingham (1869–1927), star of such plays as *Captain Impudence,* is voted the most popular actress in an 1897 newspaper poll. Minnie Maddern Fiske (1865–1932) is a success starring in *Tess of the d'Ubervilles* (1897) and *Becky Sharp* (1899); she also helps introduce Henrik Ibsen's plays to U.S. audiences. Viola Allen is a hit in Hall Caine's *The Christian* (1898).

Opera: Lillian Nordica begins singing regularly at the Metropolitan

Opera in the 1880s

Opera events include:
    —*Polish-born Marcella Sembrich (Praxede Marcellina Kochanska, 1858–1935) debuts at New York's Metropolitan Opera in* Lucia di Lammermoor *in 1883. The next year, at an 1884 concert, she not only sings but also plays the piano and violin.*

    —*After acquiring fame in Europe, U.S.-born soprano Lillian Nordica (Lillian Norton, 1857–1914) debuts in New York as Marguerite in Gounod's* Faust *in 1883.*

    —*At the peak of her career, U.S.-born soprano Marie Van Zandt (1858–1919) creates the lead in* Lakmé *(1883), supposedly written for her, at the Paris Opéra-Comique. In 1884, however, she loses her voice on stage and drops out of favor.*

    —*Soprano Emma Nevada (Emma Wixom, 1859–1940), already a success in Europe, makes her New York debut in* La Sonnambula *in 1884.*

    —*In 1889 U.S.-born soprano Sibyl Swift Sanderson (1865–1903) debuts in Paris in* Esclarmonde, *one of several operas, including* Thaïs, *written specifically for her by Jules Massenet.*

    —Fleurette, *a light opera by conductor and composer Emma Steiner (c. 1850–1928), opens in San Francisco in 1889 and New York in 1891.*

In 1890 in New York, Lillian Russell sings one of the numbers from her starring role in Offenbach's The Grand Duchess *over the new long-distance phone, to show its capabilities to President Harrison and others in Washington, D.C. In 1891 she forms her own light opera company.*

One of the first Irish comedy singers, Maggie Cline (1857–1934) delights audiences with her rendition of "Throw 'Em Down, McCloskey" in 1890.

Della May Fox (1870–1913) is at the height of her career in the 1890s in such hits as The Wedding Day *(1897, with Lillian Russell) and* The Little Host *(1898).*

U.S.-born Ellen Beach Yaw (1868–1947), dubbed "Lark Ellen," stars in Sir Arthur Sullivan's The Rose of Persia, *written for her, in London in 1896 (she later sings grand opera roles).*

Alice Nielsen (c. 1870–1943) establishes her own comic opera company in 1897 and is a hit in Victor Herbert's The Fortune Teller *(1898) and* The Singing Girl *(1899).*

Already a star outside New York, Fay Templeton (1865–1939) performs in Joe Weber and Lew Fields's burlesque Hurly Burly *(1898) and other shows.*

Opera in 1893 and soon is famed for her Wagnerian roles. In 1898 Marcella Sembrich returns from Europe and performs regularly at the Met, starring opposite Enrico Caruso in such operas as *Rigoletto*. Austrian-born contralto Ernestine Schumann-Heink (1861–1936), known for her Wagnerian roles, debuts with the Metropolitan Opera in 1898. Mezzo-soprano Eleonora Broadfoot (later de Cisneros, 1878–1938) is the first U.S.-trained singer hired by the Met, in 1899.

Other Singers: Sissieretta Jones gives a command performance for President Benjamin Harrison in 1892 and in 1896 begins touring with the Black Patti Troubadors. Not allowed to perform with the opera companies because of her race, she sings major operatic scenes for her audiences. In 1896 she joins Flora Batson and Marie Smith Selika (c. 1849–1937), the two other great black concert singers of the day, for a concert at Carnegie Hall in New York.

Classical Music: Violinist Geraldine Morgan (1868–1918) debuts with the New York Symphony in 1892. Composer Amy Marcy Cheney Beach (1867–1944), known as Mrs. H.H.A. Beach, has her first major work, the Mass in E-flat Major, performed by the Handel and Haydn Society in Boston in 1893. She writes *Festival Jubilante* for the dedication of the Woman's Building at the 1893 World's Columbian Exposition in Chicago, and in 1896 her *Gaelic Symphony* is premiered by the Boston Symphony Orchestra. Even before Beach, in 1893, Margaret Ruthven Lang (1867–1972) has her *Dramatic Overture* performed by the Boston Symphony; her overture *Witichis* also premieres in Chicago. Several all-woman orchestras form, including the Ladies Philharmonic Orchestra of Boston (1892), the Los Angeles Woman's Symphony (1893), and the Women's String Orchestra of New York (1896). Violinist Maud Powell forms her own string quartet in 1894.

Popular Music: In 1893 organist Mildred J. Smith composes the music and her sister, educator Patty Smith Hill, writes the lyrics for "Good Morning to All," later reworked as "Happy Birthday to You." Maude Nugent first performs her song "Sweet Rosie O'Grady" in 1896. Female ragtime composers include Sadie Koninsky with "Eli Green's Cakewalk" (1897). In 1898 Liliuokalani (p. 35) writes the lyrics and music to her most famous song, "Aloha Oe" ("Farewell to Thee").

Dance: In 1892, with her gauzy, flowing skirt and dramatic lighting, Loie Fuller (1862–1928) is an overnight sensation with her "Serpentine Dance" in the New York revue *Uncle Celestin*. She soon stages her own show at Madison Square Garden and later, in Paris, creates her celebrated "Fire Dance," dancing on glass that is lit from below.

1900–9

Theater: Minnie Maddern Fiske stars in Anne Crawford Flexner's play *Miranda of the Balcony* (1901), which opens the Manhattan Theater; in 1903 she plays in Ibsen's *Hedda Gabler*. Ethel Barrymore (1879–1959) has her first hit in *Captain Jinks of the Horse Marines* (1901). After gaining attention in *Mistress Nell* (1900), Henrietta Foster Crosman

(1861–1944) is a smash in David Belasco's *Sweet Kitty Bellairs* (1903). Marguerite Clark (1883–1940) has her first stage hits in *Mr. Pickwick* (1903) and *Happyland* (1905). Maxine Elliott (Jessie Carolyn Dermot, 1868–1940) stars in Clyde Fitch's *Her Own Way* (1903), the first of several hits. After her success in such plays as Clyde Fitch's *Barbara Frietchie* (1899), Julia Marlowe (Sarah Frances Frost, 1866–1950) joins Edward H. Sothern to perform Shakespearean dramas, beginning with *Romeo and Juliet* in 1904. Character actress Anne Gilbert stars in Clyde Fitch's *Granny* (1904), adapted especially for her comic talents. In 1905 Mary G. Shaw (1859–1929) leads the first New York production of George Bernard Shaw's *Mrs. Warren's Profession,* which is shut down for "indecency" (later overturned by the Supreme Court); she also stars in Elizabeth Robins's play *Votes for Women* (1909) at Wallack's Theatre in New York. Blanche Lyon Bates (1873–1941) is a hit as Minnie Smith, a role written for her, in Belasco's *The Girl of the Golden West* (1905). Designing her own costume with its popular round collar, Maude Adams opens in the title role of James M. Barrie's *Peter Pan* in 1905 and plays the part 1,500 more times. After creating the lead in Shaw's *Major Barbara* in London in 1905, Annie Russell (1864–1936) returns to New York to play Puck in *A Midsummer Night's Dream* in 1906; she later forms her own company to promote high-quality comedy. Rachel Crothers (1870–1958) opens her play *The Three of Us* on Broadway in 1906, and she writes, produces, and directs about a play a year for the next 30 years, including *Myself–Bettina* (1908) with Maxine Elliott. After many years as a comic character actress, May Robson (Mary Jeannette Robison, 1858–1942) is a major hit in *The Rejuvenation of Aunt Mary* (1907). In 1909 in New York *The Goddess of Reason* by Mary Johnston (1870–1936) opens with Julia Marlowe; another new play is *Seven Days,* coauthored by Mary Roberts Rinehart.

Opera: Contralto Louise Dilworth Beatty Homer (1871–1947) debuts with the Met, singing Amneris in *Aïda,* in 1900 and in 1902 records duets with Alma Gluck, Enrico Caruso, and others for Victor Talking Machine Company. Soprano Mary Garden (1874–1967) premieres the lead in Claude Debussy's *Pelléas et Mélisande* in Paris in 1902 and debuts in New York in Jules Massenet's *Thaïs* in 1907. Already an opera star in Europe, soprano Geraldine Farrar (1882–1967) is a hit as Cio-Cio-San in Puccini's *Madama Butterfly* at the Met in 1907.

Concert and Choral Singers: Corinne Rider-Kelsey (1877–1947) first sings with the New York Oratorio Society in *The Messiah* and with the New York Symphony Orchestra in *Elijah* in 1904; she later is the first U.S.-trained singer to star with the Royal Opera in London, in 1908, but prefers concert singing. Azalia Singer Smith Hackley (1867–1922) forms the 100-voice People's Chorus in Philadelphia in 1904 and does much to encourage black musicians.

Classical Music: Violinist Leonora Jackson (1879–1969) makes her New York debut in 1900. In 1904 pianist Hazel Lucile Harrison (1883–1969) performs as a soloist with the Berlin Philharmonic Orchestra;

Musicals and Vaudeville: 1910–19

Comedian Fannie Brice (Fannie Borach, 1891–1951) is first a hit in the Ziegfeld Follies of 1910. Marie Dressler (Leslie Marie Koerber, 1869–1934) has her biggest stage hit in Tillie's Nightmare in 1910; she later stars in such films as Tillie's Punctured Romance (1914), with Charlie Chaplin and Mabel Normand. Sophie Tucker (Sophie Kalish, 1884–1966), on the vaudeville circuit for 20 years, writes and sings her trademark song, "Some of These Days," in 1911. Russian-born Alla Nazimova (Alla Leventon, 1878–1945) tours the vaudeville circuit in 1915 in a pacifist work, War Brides (filmed in 1916). Mae West (1892–1980) is a hit singing "Any Kind of Man" in Sometime (1918). Other Broadway musical stars include Ann Pennington, Marilyn Miller, Ina Claire (Ina Fagan), Louise Dresser, Peggy Wood, Marion Davies, Edna May Oliver, Hazel Dawn, Vivienne Segal, and Edith Day.

Rida Johnson Young writes the book and lyrics for Victor Herbert's musical Naughty Marietta (1910) and later collaborates with Sigmund Romberg on Maytime (1917). Another female writer, Fred de Gresac, collaborates with Herbert on The Enchantress (1911) and Sweethearts (1913). Anne Caldwell (1867–1936) writes the book and lyrics for Jerome Kern's She's a Good Fellow (1919), as well as later musicals.

she performs in U.S. concert halls but is not invited to play with any major orchestras because she is African American. Maud Powell is the first violinist to make a phonograph recording, in 1904. Scottish-born composer and pianist Helen Hopekirk (1856–1945) performs her Concertstück (composed in 1894) with the Boston Symphony in 1904. Using all her savings, pianist Olga Samaroff (Lucy Mary Olga Agnes Hickenlooper, 1882–1948) hires Walter Damrosch and the New York Symphony for her debut at New York's Carnegie Hall in 1905 and is soon invited to play with most major U.S. orchestras.

Popular Music: Carrie Jacobs Bond (1862–1946) publishes *Seven Songs as Unpretentious as the Wild Rose* (1901), including such popular tunes as "I Love You Truly." "Ma" (Gertrude Pridgett) Rainey (1886–1939) begins singing blues in tent shows in the South in the early 1900s. Adaline Shepherd (later Olson, 1883–1950) composes the ragtime hit "Pickles and Peppers" (1906); other female ragtime composers include May Frances Aufderheide (later Kaufman) and Julia Lie Niebergall.

Dance: In Europe during the early 1900s innovative U.S.-born dancer Isadora Duncan (1878–1927) emphasizes the body's fluid, expressive powers in her solos, which she performs barefoot in loose robes. Ruth St. Denis (c. 1878–1968) first performs her dance *Radha*, with its theme of a female deity and stylized movements, in 1906 in New York.

Film: Florence E. Turner (c. 1888–1946), the first actor given a contract by Vitagraph, in 1907, appears as "The Vitagraph Girl" in films until 1910, when she receives name billing.

1910–19

Theater: Rachel Crothers's new plays include *He and She* (1911). In 1912 in New York, Jessie Bonstelle (1871–1932) directs Alice Brady (1892–1939) in *Little Women,* adapted for the stage by Marian de Forest; in 1919 she directs Katharine Cornell (1893–1974) in the London production. Laurette Taylor (Loretta Cooney, 1884–1946) is a hit in *Peg o' My Heart* (1912), written for her as an engagement gift by J. Hartley Manners. Jane Cowl (Grace Bailey, 1883–1950) stars in *Within the Law* on Broadway in 1912; another hit is the 1919 play *Smilin' Through* by "Alan Langdon Martin" (a pseudonym she and Jane Murfin use to get past audience's prejudices). Among actress Ethel Barrymore's successes are *Tante* (1913); *Our Mrs. McChesney* (1915), a dramatization of Edna Ferber's stories; *The Lady of the Camellias* (1917); and Zoë Akins's *Déclassé* (1919). Known for her ability to make offstage characters real, Ruth Draper (1884–1956) premieres her monologues in 1915 but does not gain major recognition until her 1920 London debut. In 1915 actress Anita Bush (c. 1883–1974) founds the Anita Bush (later Lafayette) Players, a stock company that trains more than 300 African American performers and takes some 250 dramas to 25 cities. Susan Glaspell helps her husband, George Cram Cook, start the Provincetown Players in 1915; she and Eugene O'Neill are the main playwrights for the group. Helen Hayes (1900–93) debuts on Broadway in *Pollyanna* in 1916. Alice Brady is a hit in the Broadway comedy *Forever After* (1918). Berta Gersten (Berta Gerstenman, c. 1896–1972) begins her long career as a star in the Yiddish theater in 1918.

Opera: In 1910 Geraldine Farrar is the first to sing the Goose Girl in Engelbert Humperdinck's *Königskinder.* In 1912 Mary Carr Moore (1873–1957) sees her first opera, *Narcissa,* based on the story of Narcissa Whitman, performed in Seattle. Soprano Rosa Melba Ponselle (1897–1981) debuts opposite Enrico Caruso in *La Forza del Destino* at the Met in 1918. She is the first Met star without European training.

Concert Singers: Soprano Alma Gluck (Reba Fiersohn, 1884–1938) is one of the most popular singers of the decade, giving as many as 100 recitals a year; she also records folk ballads, such as "Carry Me Back to Old Virginny." After several years at the Met, contralto Sophie Braslau (1888–1935) begins a successful career as a concert singer in 1915.

Classical Music: Mary Davenport Engberg, probably the first female symphony conductor, starts an orchestra in Bellingham, Washington, in 1911 and by 1916 is conducting 80 players, about half female. In 1913 Marion Eugénie Bauer (1882–1955) composes *Up the Ocklawaha,* a tone poem for piano and violin, and *Fair Daffodils,* a trio for female voices. Mabel Wheeler Daniels (1877–1971) conducts her cantata *The Desolate City* at the MacDowell Colony in 1913 and her prelude *Deep Forest* with the Chicago Symphony in 1915. Pianist Hazel Harrison (1883–1969) features contemporary African American composers as well as traditional works in her concert tours beginning 1914.

Popular Music: Carrie Jacobs Bond composes the most popular of her 400-some songs, "A Perfect Day" (1910).

Film Performances: With a publicity campaign orchestrated by Independent Motion Picture Company, Florence Bridgewood Lawrence (1886–1938)—"the IMP Girl"—is an early movie star, in 1910. Another box office draw is Canadian-born Mary Pickford (Gladys Mary Smith, 1893–1979), with such films as *The Informer* (1912) to her credit (see also sidebar). Both Lillian Gish (1893–1993) and her sister Dorothy (1898–1968) first appear in D. W. Griffith's *An Unseen Enemy* (1912), as well as later in *Sisters* (1914) and *Hearts of the World* (1918). Comedian Mabel Normand (1894–1930) directs all her own films after 1913, including *Mickey* (1918). A Pickford rival, Marguerite Clark makes her first film, *Wildflower* (1914), and then averages seven a year. Pearl White (1889–1938), who does many of her own stunts, is a sensation in the 20-episode cliff hanger *The Perils of Pauline* (1914); a similar 1914 serial is *The Hazards of Helen,* featuring Helen Holmes (1892–1950) and later Helen Gibson (Rose Helena Wenger, 1894–1977). In 1915, wearing special eye makeup created by Helena Rubinstein, Theda Bara (Theodosia Goodman, 1885–1955) establishes the image of the "vamp" in *A Fool There Was* (1915). Lillian Gish and Mae (Mary) Marsh (1895–1968) star in D.W. Griffith's 1915 film *The Birth of a Nation,* which is strongly protested by the NAACP for its negative

A Rising Star

Promoted as "America's Sweetheart," Mary Pickford is a major hit in Tess of the Storm Country *(1914, remade in 1922); other films include* The Poor Little Rich Girl *and* Rebecca of Sunnybrook Farm *(both 1917) and* Stella Maris *(1918), the scripts for which are all written or adapted by Frances Marion (1887–1973), a major screenwriter of the day. In 1919 Pickford cofounds United Artists with D. W. Griffith, Charlie Chaplin, and her future husband, actor Douglas Fairbanks. Although she avoids credit on the screen, she often directs her performance.*

Mary Pickford (Library of Congress)

Early Directors

French-born Alice Guy Blaché (1875–1968), probably the first person to direct a narrative film (in France in 1896), sets up her studio in New Jersey in 1912 and directs such silents as In the Year 2000 (1912) and The Tigress (1914).

Starting in 1913, Lois Weber (1882–1939) directs numerous films with a message, including Hypocrites (1914), which creates a sensation for showing a nude woman as a statue of "Naked Truth"; Where Are My Children? (1916), which is banned in Philadelphia for its pro–birth control stance; and Shoes (1916), condemning child labor. Weber also makes the only feature starring Anna Pavlova, The Dumb Girl of Portici (1916).

Canadian-born Nell Shipman (1892–1970) writes, directs, and stars in the first wildlife adventure feature, God's Country and the Woman (1916). She trains the animal "actors" in her films.

Actress Cleo Madison (1883–1964) directs the suffragist classic Her Bitter Cup (1916).

Other films by women include Ruth Ann Baldwin's The Black Box (1915) and Retribution (1916), Marguerite Bertsch's The Law Decides (1916), actress Lule Warrenton's A Bit O' Heaven (1917), and Ida May Park's Fires of Rebellion (1917) and Bread (1918).

racial stereotypes. Constance Talmadge joins Gish and Marsh in Griffith's *Intolerance* (1916). Alice Brady (1892–1939) stars in *La Bohème* (1916) and *Besty Ross* (1917). Evelyn Preer (1896–1932) appears in *The Homesteader* (1917), the first silent film by African American director Oscar Micheaux, as well as later films such as *The Conjure Woman* (1926). Marion E. Wong, president of the Mandarin Film Company in Oakland, California, stars in *The Curse of Quon Qwon* (1917) with her sister. Gloria Swanson (Gloria Swenson, 1899–1983) has her first major hit in Cecil B. De Mille's *Male and Female* (1919).

Film Writing and Editing: Anita Loos (p. 317) writes 105 film scripts between 1912 and 1915, including *The New York Hat* (1912), starring Mary Pickford. Grace Cunnard (Harriet Mildred Jeffries, 1893–1967) writes and acts in the serial *Lucille Love, Girl of Mystery* (1914) and creates about 400 scenarios for cliff-hanger serials. Frances Marion begins her prolific scriptwriting career in 1915 (see sidebar, p. 345). Among the first women film editors are Viola Lawrence (1895–1973) and Anne Bauchens (c. 1881–1967), who edits all of Cecil B. De Mille's films beginning in 1918.

Dance: During the decade Irene Foote Castle (1893–1969) and her husband, Vernon, popularize such dances as the Turkey Trot, Castle Polka, Tango, and Castle Waltz; they also star in *Watch Your Step* (1914), written for them by Irving Berlin, and in the film *The Whirl of Life* (1915). Ruth St. Denis and her husband, Ted Shawn, start their own dance school, the Denishawn School, in Los Angeles in 1915. Their pupils later include Martha Graham and Doris Humphrey. Adele Astaire (Adele Austerlitz) dances with her brother, Fred, in the Broadway revue *Over the Top* (1917).

1920–29

Theater: Effie Ellsier stars in *The Bat* (1920), based on Mary Roberts Rhinehart's mystery *The Circular Staircase*. Carroll McComas is the lead in Zona Gale's hit *Miss Lulu Bett* (1920). Rachel Crothers's plays include *Nice People* (1921), *Mary the Third* (1923), and *Let Us Be Gay* (1929). Katharine Cornell makes her name in New York in *A Bill of Divorcement* (1921), followed by *Candida* (1924). Pauline Lord (1890–1950) is a success as the lead in Eugene O'Neill's *Anna Christie* (1921), as well as in Sidney Howard's *They Knew What They Wanted* (1924). Actress Marita Reed forms her own company in 1922 and is one of the leading actors and directors of Hispanic theater for three decades. Jeanne Eagels (1890–1929) gains fame as Sadie Thompson in *Rain* (1922). Anne Nichols's play *Abie's Irish Rose*, starring Marie Carroll, runs for a record 2,500-some performances on Broadway in 1922; Zoë Akins's *The Texas Nightingale* is also staged in New York. After writing and staging the one-act play *Overtones* (1915), Alice Gerstenberg (1885–1972) founds the Playwrights' Theatre of Chicago in 1922. Lynn Fontanne first appears with her husband, Alfred Lunt, in *The Guardsman* (1924), and they continue to star together in Noël Coward comedies and other works. Helen Hayes stars in Shaw's *Caesar and*

Cleopatra (1925) and James Barrie's *What Every Woman Knows* (1926). Jessie Bonstelle founds the Bonstelle Playhouse in Detroit in 1925. During the 1920s Irene and Alice Lewisohn produce many experimental plays at their Neighborhood Playhouse, opposite the Henry Street Settlement House in New York. Theresa Helbrun (1887–1959) is executive director of New York's Theatre Guild and produces 14 hits in the period 1926–28. Eva Le Gallienne starts the Civic Repertory Theatre in New York in 1926; she both directs and stars in many of the productions. Considered the leading African American dramatic actress, Rose McClendon (Rosalie Scott, 1884–1936) appears in *Deep River* (1926), with Ethel Barrymore, and the Pulitzer Prize–winning drama *In Abraham's Bosom* (1926), with Abbie Mitchell (1884–1960). June Walker stars in *Gentlemen Prefer Blondes* (1926), adapted by Anita Loos with John Emerson from her novel. Ethel Barrymore opens the theater named after her as Sister García in *The Kingdom of God* (1928). Alla Nazimova has her greatest success in Chekhov's *The Cherry Orchard* (1928). Actress Antoinette Perry (1888–1946) begins directing in 1928 and has a hit with Preston Sturges's *Strictly Dishonorable* (1929).

Comedy: Gracie Allen (1895–1964) first teams up with George Burns in 1922.

Musical Writers: Actress Dorothy Donnelly (1880–1928) writes the book and lyrics for Sigmund Romberg's *Blossomtime* (1921) and *The Student Prince* (1924). Lyricist Dorothy Fields (1905–74) has her first success with *Blackbirds of 1928* (music by Jimmy McHugh), including "I Can't Give You Anything But Love," sung by Adelaide Hall.

Chinese Opera: Kwan Ying Lin is one of the first women to perform in traditional Chinese opera in America, in 1922.

Western Opera: Eleanor Warner Everest Freer's first one-act opera, *Legend of the Red Piper* (1921), is performed in 1924. Mezzo-soprano Tsianina Redfeather Blackstone (c. 1882–1985) sings the title role in Charles Wakefield Cadman's opera *Shanewis: The Robin Woman*, based loosely on her life, in Los Angeles in 1926. Rosa Ponselle is highly acclaimed in *Norma* (1927). Edna St. Vincent Millay writes the libretto for Deems Taylor's *The King's Henchman* (1927) at the Met.

Classical Music: Austrian-born violinist Erica Morini makes her debut at Carnegie Hall at age 17 in 1921. The Society of American Women Composers forms in 1924, with Amy Beach as president. Pianists Mary Carlisle Howe (1882–1964) and Anne Hull give a two-piano recital at New York's Aeolian (later Town) Hall in 1924, and in 1925 Howe's *Chain Gang Song*, for chorus and orchestra, is played by the New York Symphony at the Worcester Festival. A special 1925 program at New York's Metropolitan Opera honors the works of composer Emma R. Steiner. Eva Anderson, Elina Moneak, and Ebba Sundstron all conduct women's orchestras in the mid-1920s. After guest conducting several major European orchestras, British-born pianist and composer Ethel Leginska (Ethel Liggins, 1886–1970) is the first woman to

Entertainers: 1920s

Grace Moore stars in Kitchy-Koo *(1920) and Irving Berlin's* Music Box Review *(1923–24). Florence Mills (1896–1927) is a hit in Noble Sissle and Eubie Blake's* Shuffle Along *(1921), which also features Josephine Baker (Josephine Freda MacDonald, 1906–75). Mills then stars in such other Jazz Age musical comedies as* Dixie to Broadway *(1924) and* Blackbirds of 1926; *Baker establishes her singing and dancing career in Paris with* La Revue Nègre *(1925). In Jerome Kern's* Sally *(1920), Marilyn Miller gains fame singing "Look for the Silver Lining." Fanny Brice first sings her theme song, "My Man," in the* Ziegfeld Follies of 1921. *Adele Astaire and her brother, Fred, star in George and Ira Gershwin's* Lady Be Good *(1924). Mae West leads her own satire,* Sex *(1926), which is promptly closed down for its "corrupting" influence; her next show is* Diamond Lil *(1928). Helen Morgan (Helen Riggins, c. 1900–41) creates the role of Julie in Jerome Kern and Oscar Hammerstein's* Show Boat *(1927), with a book written by Edna Ferber; she then stars in* Sweet Adeline *(1929), written for her by Kern and Hammerstein.*

Blueswomen

In 1920 Mamie Smith (Mamie Gardener, 1893–1946) records "Crazy Blues," which sells almost a million copies; she also records the hits "That Thing Called Love" and "You Can't Keep a Good Man Down." In 1923 Bessie Smith (c. 1894/8–1937), the "Empress of the Blues," records her classic hit "Down-Hearted Blues" (written by Lovie Austin and Alberta Hunter); other recordings include "Jailhouse Blues" (1923, with Fletcher Henderson), "St. Louis Blues" (1925, with Louis Armstrong), and "Backwater Blues" (1927, with James P. Johnson). Ma Rainey, billed as "Mother of the Blues," also cuts her first record in 1923 and makes 90 more by 1928, including "See, See Rider" and "Trust No Man." Among other 1920s hits are "Wild Women Don't Have the Blues" by Ida Cox (Ida Prather, 1896–1967); "Shorty George" and "I'm a Mighty Tight Woman" by Sippie Wallace (Beulah Thomas, 1898–1986), the "Texas Nightingale"; and "Black Market Blues" by Bertha "Chippie" Hill (c. 1900/5–1948).

conduct a major U.S. orchestra, the New York Symphony Orchestra, at Carnegie Hall in 1925. In 1927 she forms the Boston Woman's Symphony Orchestra, which performs some of her works. The New York Symphony Orchestra performs *The Artisan*, a symphonic poem by Harriet Ware (1877–1962), in 1927. Early pieces by Ruth Crawford (later Seeger, 1901–53) include three piano preludes, performed in New York in 1928, and five 1929 songs set to the poems of Carl Sandburg. Gena Branscombe (1881–1977) composes the choral work *Pilgrims of Destiny* (1928), performed in Plymouth, Massachusetts, in 1929.

Other Music: Noted jazz pianist-composers include Lovie Austin (Cora Calhoun, 1887–1972), Lillian ("Lil") Hardin Armstrong (1898–1971), and "Sister" Arizona Juanita Dranes (c. 1905–60). Eva Jessye (1895–1992) forms her professional choir in 1926; she also serves as the music director for King Vidor's all-black film *Hallelujah* (1929). In 1927 Maybelle Addington Carter (1909–78), with her "Carter lick" guitar-playing style, records the first country music album with family members.

Academy Awards: The first Academy Award for Best Actress goes to Janet Gaynor (Laura Gainor, 1906–84) in 1928 for three films: *Seventh Heaven* (1927), *Sunrise* (1927), and *Street Angel* (1928). Mary Pickford receives the 1929 award for her first "talkie," *Coquette* (1929). Josephine Lovett and Bess Meredyth are nominated for writing awards in 1929.

"If I could sell happiness"—Mary Pickford

Other Film Performances: Mary Pickford's hits include the silents *Pollyanna* (1920, script by Frances Marion) and *Little Lord Fauntleroy* (1921). She produces all her own films after 1921. Pauline Frederick (1883–1938) has her greatest film hit in *Madame X* (1920). Anita Bush stars in the first all-black Western, *The Crimson Skull* (1921). Constance Talmadge takes the lead in *A Woman's Place* (1921), written by Anita Loos. Lillian and Dorothy Gish star in D. W. Griffith's *Orphans of the Storm* (1922). Lillian's other films include *La Bohème* (1926), *The Scarlet Letter* (1926, script by Frances Marion), and *The Wind* (1928). Embodying the image of the 1920s flapper, Clara Bow (1905–65) is known as the "It Girl" after appearing in *It* (1927), written for her by Elinor Glyn; her many other silents include *The Plastic Age* (1925), *Wings* (1927), and *Ladies of the Mob* (1928). Swedish-born Greta Garbo (Greta Lovisa Gustafsson, 1905–90) is a sensation in *Flesh and the Devil* and *Love* (1927), paired with her real-life lover, John Gilbert. Mexican-born Dolores Del Río (Lolita Dolores Asúnsolo y López Negrete, 1905–83) stars in the silents *Resurrection* (1927) and *Ramona* (1928). Norma Talmadge plays the lead in *Camille* (1927). After nearly 10 years of typecasting as the "Dragon Lady" in such silents as *The Thief of Bagdad* (1924), Anna May Wong (1905–61) leaves for Europe in 1928, where she stars in several melodramas. Louise Brooks (1906–85) has her most memorable roles in G. W. Pabst's *Pandora's Box* (1928) and *Diary of a Lost Girl* (1929). Joan Crawford (Lucille Le Sueur, 1904–77) scores a hit in *Our Dancing Daughters* (1928).

Radio: In 1920 Vaughan DeLeath (1900–43), crooning "Swanee River," is the first woman broadcast by Lee De Forest. She also composes 500 songs and performs in many Broadway shows. In 1929 Gertrude Edelstein Berg (1899–1966) creates a popular sitcom about a Jewish family, *The Rise of the Goldbergs,* in which she stars as Molly Goldberg.

Dance: Elida Webb is the first African American woman to choreograph a Broadway show, *Runnin' Wild* (1923). Doris Humphrey (1895–1958) experiments with balance and falling in her early 1920s dance; in 1928 she forms her own company with Charles Weidman. Modern dance pioneer Martha Graham (1893–1991) gives her first dance recital in 1926 and forms her school of contemporary dance in New York in 1927. During her life she choreographs more than 160 works.

1930–39

Theater: Susan Glaspell's Pulitzer Prize–winning drama *Alison's House* opens with Eva Le Gallienne in 1930. Cheryl Crawford joins Lee Strasberg and Harold Clurman in founding the Group Theatre in 1931 to promote Stanislavsky's method acting. Katharine Cornell plays her most famous role as Elizabeth Barrett Browning in *The Barretts of Wimpole Street* in 1931; she also plays the title role in Shaw's *Saint Joan* in 1934. Alla Nazimova and Alice Brady star in Eugene O'Neill's *Mourning Becomes Electra* (1931). Rose Franken's *Another Language* (1932) features Margaret Hamilton, Margaret Wycherly, and Dorothy Stickney. Edna Ferber collaborates with George S. Kaufman on *Dinner at Eight* (1932) and *Stage Door* (1936), with Margaret Sullavan. Rachel Crothers's plays include *When Ladies Meet* (1932) and *Susan and God* (1937). Eva Le Gallienne and Frieda Friebus adapt Lewis Carroll's *Alice in Wonderland* and *Through the Looking Glass* to the stage in 1932, with Le Gallienne playing the part of the White Queen. Helen Hayes stars in Maxwell Anderson's *Mary of Scotland* (1933–34), written for her, and Laurence Housman's *Victoria Regina* (1935–39). Lynn Fontanne and Alfred Lunt are in Noël Coward's *Design for Living* (1933), *Taming of the Shrew* (1935), and Robert Sherwood's *Idiot's Delight* (1936). Lillian Hellman's *The Children's Hour* (1934) features Katherine Emery, Anne Revere, and Florence McGee. In 1935 Rose McClendon stars in Langston Hughes's *Mulatto* and helps found the Negro People's Theatre in Harlem. Stella Adler appears in Clifford Odet's *Awake and Sing!* (1935), and Margo (Maria Marguerita Guadelupe Boldao y Castella) is in Maxwell Anderson's *Winterset* (1935). Australian-born Judith Anderson and Helen Menken star in Zoë Akins's Pulitzer Prize–winning *The Old Maid* (1935). Producer and director Margo Jones (1912–55) starts the Houston Community Players in 1936. *The Women* (1936) by Clare Boothe (later Luce) has an all-woman cast. Margaret Webster (1905–72) directs *Richard II* in 1937 and other Shakespeare plays starring British actor Maurice Evans. Antoinette Perry directs *Kiss the Boys Goodbye* (1938) by Clare Boothe (Luce). Katharine Hepburn appears on stage, with Shirley Booth (1907–92) and Lenore Lonergan, in *The Philadelphia Story*

Women continue to be important as film directors, writers, and editors in the 1920s. Lois Weber's most successful film is The Blot *(1921). June Mathis writes the script for such films as* The Sheik *(1921) and* Blood and Sand *(1922). Actress Margery Wilson (Sara Strayer, 1898–1986) directs and writes* Insinuation *(1922). Some other early films directed by women include Ida May Parks's* The Butterfly Man *(1920), Vera McCord's* Good Bad Wife *(1920), Ruth Ann Baldwin's* Puppets of Fate *(1921), Mrs. George Randolph Chester's* The Sons of Wallingford *(1921), Frances Marion's* The Love Light *(1921, starring Mary Pickford), Nell Shipman's* Neptune's Daughter *(1922), and May Tully's* Our Mutual Friend *(1922). Dorothy Davenport Reid (1895–1977) produces and stars in* Human Wreckage *(1923), an antidrug film, and* The Red Kimono *(1926), based on a story by Adela Rogers St. John, with a screenplay by Dorothy Arzner (1900–79). After editing such films as* Blood and Sand *(1922), Arzner begins directing in 1927, with the silents* Fashions for Women *and* Get Your Man *(starring Clara Bow). In 1929 she makes Paramount's first talking picture,* The Wild Party *(again with Clara Bow).*

Opera Creators

Several women either compose or write the libretto for operas in the 1930s:

—Mary Carr Moore's operas Los Rubios *and* Davide Rizzio *receive premieres in 1931 and 1932 respectively.*

—Mabel Wheeler Daniels's Exultate Deo *(composed in 1929) is performed by the Boston Symphony in 1932.*

—Shirley Graham (later Du Bois, 1896–1977) *writes and produces* Tom-Toms: An Epic of Music and the Negro *(1932), which has a cast of 500 at the Cleveland Opera.*

Gertrude Stein writes the libretto for Virgil Thomson's Four Saints in Three Acts, *performed in 1934 with the Eva Jessye Choir and with sets and costumes by Florine Stettheimer (1871–1944).*

—Ethel Leginska *conducts the Chicago City Opera in the premiere of her one-act opera* Gale *in 1935; she also composes* The Rose and the Ring *(1932), which is not performed until 1957.*

(1939), as well as in the 1940 film. As Hagar in *Mamba's Daughters* (1939), Ethel Waters (1896–1977) is the first black woman to star in a nonmusical Broadway show. After establishing herself on the London stage in the 1920s, Tallulah Bankhead (1903–68) returns to America in the 1930s and has her most memorable role as Regina Giddens in Lillian Hellman's *Little Foxes* (1939), with sets and costumes by Aline Bernstein. Dorothy Stickney stars in *Life with Father* (1939).

Musicals and Vaudeville: Ethel Merman (Ethel Zimmerman, 1909–84) launches many hit songs with her performances, including "I've Got Rhythm" in Gershwin's *Girl Crazy* (1930) and "Life Is Just a Bowl of Cherries" from *George White's Scandals* (1931); she also stars in both the stage (1934) and film (1936) versions of Cole Porter's *Anything Goes.* Kay Swift (1897–1993) composes the music and her husband, Paul James (James Paul Warburg), the lyrics for *Fine and Dandy* (1930). In *Sweet and Low* (1930) and on the radio in 1936 Fanny Brice popularizes the character of "Baby Snooks," first introduced in 1921; later, in 1944, she has her own "Baby Snooks" radio show. Burlesque queen Gypsy Rose Lee (Rose Louise Hovick, 1914–70) first appears in New York clubs in 1931 and is featured in the *Ziegfeld Follies* of 1936. Ethel Waters sings "Heat Wave" in Irving Berlin's *As Thousands Cheer* (1933), which also stars Marilyn Miller. Eva Jessye helps George Gershwin with the music for *Porgy and Bess* (1935) and directs her choir in the performance. The libretto is written by DuBose and Dorothy Heyward; performers include Anne Wiggins Brown as Bess. In 1935, under the Works Progress Administration, Hallie Ferguson Flanagan (1890–1969) heads the Federal Theater Project, bringing plays to more than 25 million people across the country. ILGWU garment workers mount *Pins and Needles* (1937), which runs for several years. Sophie Tucker stars in Cole Porter's *Leave It to Me!* (1938), which also features Mary Martin (1913–90) singing "My Heart Belongs to Daddy."

Opera and Concert Singers: French-born coloratura soprano Lily Pons (1904–76) debuts at the Met in *Lucia di Lammermoor* in 1931 and also appears in such films as *That Girl from Paris* (1936). Caterina Jarboro (Catherine Yarboro, 1903–86) performs the title role of *Aïda* as the first black soloist with the Chicago Opera Company, in 1933. Refusing to comply with Nazi requests, Lotte Lehmann (1888–1976) leaves Germany and opens at the Met in *Die Walküre* in 1934; she continues as the main lyric-dramatic soprano until 1946. Russian-born mezzo-soprano Jennie Tourel (Jennie Davidson, c. 1900–73) debuts at the Met in *Mignon* in 1937 and later is known as a concert singer; soprano Helen Traubel (c. 1900–72) also makes her Met debut in 1937.

Not allowed to perform with most U.S. opera companies, African American singers give recitals. Lyric soprano Lillian Evans Evanti (1890–1967), for example, debuts at Town Hall in 1932. After winning acclaim in Europe, where Jean Sibelius composes *Solitude* for her, contralto Marian Anderson (1902–93) debuts at Town Hall in 1935. In 1939, when the DAR refuses to rent Constitution Hall to her because she is African American, Eleanor Roosevelt is outraged and helps arrange for her performance on the steps of the Lincoln Memorial on Easter Sunday. A crowd of 75,000 gathers for this historic concert.

Classical Music: In 1930 Antonia Brico makes her conducting debut with the Berlin Philharmonic, followed by the Los Angeles and San Francisco symphonies; in 1935 she forms her own New York Women's Symphony, which performs at Carnegie Hall. Harpist Edna Phillips is the first female member of the Philadelphia Orchestra; cellist Elsa Hilger joins her in 1936. The Chicago Symphony Orchestra features its first black soloist in 1933, pianist-composer Margaret Bonds (Margaret Majors, 1913–72). Rosalyn Tureck gives a six-concert series of Bach's work, on the piano and harpsichord, at New York's Town Hall in 1937. The Women's Symphony of Boston, formed in 1939, includes at least one woman's work in each performance.

Gospel: Mahalia Jackson (1911–72) begins singing with the Johnson Gospel Singers in 1930 and by mid-decade is in demand in churches from coast to coast. "Gospel songs are the songs of hope," she says. "When you sing them you are delivered of your burden." Sallie Martin (1895–1988) and Willie Mae Ford Smith cofound the National Convention of Gospel Choirs and Choruses with Thomas A. Dorsey in 1932; Martin also forms one of the first all-female gospel groups, the Sallie Martin Singers. Roberta Martin (1907–69) forms her distinctive Roberta Martin Singers in 1935. Sister Rosetta Tharpe (c. 1915–73) is the first gospel singer to record with a major label, in 1938.

Jazz and Blues: Josephine Baker introduces her theme song, "J'ai Deux Amours," during a 1930 revue in Paris. Lillian Armstrong forms the Harlem Harlicans, an all-woman swing band, in 1932. Ethel Waters introduces "Stormy Weather" in 1933 at the Cotton Club. Ella Fitzgerald, later called the "First Lady of Jazz," wins a talent contest at the Apollo Theatre in 1934 and records her hit record "A-tisket, A-tasket" with William "Chick" Webb in 1938. Billie Holiday (Eleanora Fagan, c. 1915–59), later nicknamed "Lady Day," first gains recognition at the Apollo Theatre in 1935 and soon records her interpretations of "God Bless the Child," "Strange Fruit," and other songs. Pianist-composer Mary Lou Williams (Mary Elfreida Scruggs, 1910–81) scores a hit with "Froggy Bottom" (1936). International Sweethearts of Rhythm, an all-female swing band, forms in 1938.

Other Music: The Andrews Sisters—La Verne, Maxene, and Patty—form their trio in 1932 and have their first big hit with "Bei Mir Bist Du Schön" (1937). Lydia Mendoza records "Mal hombre" in 1934 and is soon known as "La alondra de la frontera" ("the lark of the border"). María Grever (Maria de la Portilla, 1894–1951) composes one of the most popular of her hundreds of songs, "What a Difference a Day Makes" ("Cuando Vuelva a Tu Lado"), in 1934. With "I Want to Be a Cowboy's Sweetheart" (1935), Patsy Montana (Rubye Blevins) is the first female country music singer to top a million in record sales.

Classical Composers

Ruth Crawford (Seeger) is the first woman to receive a Guggenheim fellowship for composing, in 1930; she composes the songs "Chinaman, Laundryman" and "Sacco, Vanzetti" in 1932, and in 1935 her string quartet is performed in New York. Radie Britain's orchestral piece Heroic Poem *wins the 1930 International Hollywood Bowl Prize;* Light *is performed in 1935 by women's symphonies in Boston and Chicago. Amy Beach's* The Canticle of the Sun *is performed at the 1931 Worcester Festival. Florence Smith Price (1888–1953) is the first African American woman composer to have a work performed by a major orchestra, when the Chicago Symphony Orchestra plays her Symphony in E Minor at the 1933 World's Fair. After Frederique Joanne Petrides forms the Orchestrette Classique of New York, a 30-woman chamber group, in 1933, it premieres* American Dance Suite *by pianist Julia Smith (1911–89) at Aeolian (Town) Hall in New York in 1936.* The Harp Weaver *by Elinor Remick Warren (1906–91) is premiered by Antonia Brico and the New York Women's Symphony in 1936.*

Best actress winners are Norma Shearer (1900–83) in The Divorcée (1930), Marie Dressler in Min and Bill (1931), Helen Hayes in The Sin of Madelon Claudet (1932), Katharine Hepburn in Morning Glory (1933), French-born Claudette Colbert in It Happened One Night (1934), Bette Davis (Ruth Elizabeth Davis, 1908–89) in Dangerous (1935) and Jezebel (1938), Austrian actress Luise Rainer for The Great Ziegfeld (1936) and The Good Earth (1937), and British actress Vivien Leigh for Gone with the Wind (1939). Best supporting actress winners include Alice Brady in In Old Chicago (1937) and Hattie McDaniel (1895–1952), the first African American to earn an Academy Award, for her role as "Mammy" in Gone with the Wind (1939). Frances Marion is the first woman to win for writing, for The Big House (1930); she also wins for original story, for The Champ (1932); other screenwriting awards go to Sarah Y. Mason for cowriting Little Women (1933) and Eleanore Griffin and Dore Schary for Boys Town (1938). Child star Shirley Temple (later Black) receives a special Oscar as "outstanding personality of 1934" Lyricist Dorothy Fields shares an Academy Award with composer Jerome Kern for the song "The Way You Look Tonight" in the Ginger Rogers–Fred Astaire film Swing Time (1936).

Film Performances: Greta Garbo's first talkie is Anna Christie (1930, script by Frances Marion); others include Mata Hari (1931), Anna Karenina (1935), and Camille (1936, script by Frances Marion). German-born Marlene Dietrich (1901–92) gains acclaim for Blue Angel (1930), followed by Blonde Venus (1932), The Devil Is a Woman (1935), and Destry Rides Again (1939). Jean Harlow (Harlean Carpenter, 1911–37) is called the "Blonde Bombshell" from Hell's Angels (1930); after scoring hits in Red-Headed Woman (1932, script by Anita Loos) and Red Dust (1932), she pokes fun at her sex goddess image in Bombshell (1933) and stars in Dinner at Eight (1933, script by Frances Marion). Mae West creates I'm No Angel (1933) and She Done Him Wrong (1933), a film version of her stage show Diamond Lil, with her much-quoted line to Cary Grant, "Why don't you come up and see me sometime?" Louise Beavers (1908–62) plays West's feisty black maid, Pearl, and the costumes are among the first designed by Edith Head (1907–81), who is the first female chief designer at a major studio (Paramount), in 1938. In 1933 Ginger Rogers (1911–95) has her first hits in 42nd Street (also featuring Ruby Keeler and Bebe McDaniels) and Gold Diggers of 1933 (with Keeler and Joan Blondell); she then joins Fred Astaire for the first of nine tap-dancing films, in Flying Down to Rio (1933, also starring Delores Del Rio). After costarring with Maurice Chevalier in such films as The Merry Widow (1934), Jeanette MacDonald (c. 1903–65) hits her stride with Nelson Eddy in Naughty Marietta (1935), Rose Marie (1936), and Maytime (1937). A hit film of 1934 is Imitation of Life, in which a white mother (Claudette Colbert) sells the pancake recipe of her black maid (Louise Beavers) and becomes a millionaire. It also features Fredi Washington as the maid's mulatto daughter. Stage Door (1937), with Katharine Hepburn, Andrea Leeds, Ginger Rogers, and Lucille Ball, centers on rivalries among women actresses. Offering seasoned actress Anna May Wong only a villainous role (which she declines), Hollywood casts The Good Earth (1937) with all-white leads. Wong has her most sympathetic role in Daughter of Shanghai (1937). In Gone with the Wind (1939) and other films, Academy Award winner Hattie McDaniel and Butterfly (Thelma) McQueen are confined to roles as stereotyped black characters. Judy Garland (Frances Gumm, 1922–69) stars in The Wizard of Oz (1939), singing "Somewhere Over the Rainbow," and wins a special Academy Award for her performance. The Women (1939), from Clare Boothe's stage play, features Norma Shearer, Joan Fontaine, Joan Crawford, Paulette Goddard, Rosalind Russell (1908–76), and Donna Reed (Donna Belle Mullenger, 1921–86).

Other performances include the Oscar winners (see sidebar) and Sylvia Sidney (Sophia Kosow) in An American Tragedy (1931), Jennie Gerhardt (1933), and Dead End (1937); Irene Dunne (1898–1990) in Cimarron (1931), Theodora Goes Wild (1936), and Show Boat (1936, with Helen Morgan and Paul Robeson); Janet Gaynor in Daddy Long Legs (1931), A Star Is Born (1937, script by Dorothy Parker), and Young in Heart (1938), as well as films with Charles Farrell; Gracie Fields in

Sally in Our Alley (1931); Joan Crawford in *Grand Hotel* (1932), *Rain* (1932), *Today We Shall Live* (1933), and *Dancing Lady* (1933); Katharine Hepburn in *Bill of Divorcement* (1932), *Little Women* (1933), and *A Woman Rebels* (1936); Dolores Del Río in *The Girl of Rio* (1932), banned in Mexico as anti-Mexican, and *Bird of Paradise* (1932); Fay Wray in *King Kong* (1933); Shirley Temple in *Stand Up and Cheer* (1934), *Little Miss Marker* (1934), *The Little Colonel* (1935), *Curly Top* (1935), *Captain January* (1936), and *Dimples* (1936); Bette Davis in *Of Human Bondage* (1934) and *Dark Victory* (1939); Myrna Loy (Myrna Williams, 1905–93) in *The Thin Man* (1934); Carole Lombard (Jane Alice Peters, 1908–42) as a screwball comedian in *My Man Godfrey* (1936) and *Nothing Sacred* (1937); and Barbara Stanwyck (Ruby Stevens, 1907–90) in *Stella Dallas* (1937).

Radio: Gracie Allen and George Burns star in *The Adventures of Gracie* on CBS, beginning in 1932. In 1930 Irna Phillips (1901–73) writes her first radio serial drama, *Painted Dreams,* an early soap opera. She also writes *Today's Version* (1932) and coauthors *The Guiding Light* (1937) with Emmons Carlson. One of the most popular radio singers, Kate Smith makes her debut in 1931 with her theme song "When the Moon Comes over the Mountain"; by 1938 she has both daytime and evening shows and is the only one allowed to broadcast Irving Berlin's "God Bless America." Marian Driscoll Jordan and her husband, Jim, star in *Fibber McGee and Molly* on NBC, beginning in 1935.

Dance: Martha Graham's new works include *Lamentation* (1930), *Primitive Mysteries* (1931), and *Frontier* (1935). Katherine Dunham is the main soloist in Ruth Page's *La Guiablesse* at the Chicago Civic Opera Theater in 1934. Doris Humphrey choreographs her celebrated trilogy *Theatre Piece, With My Red Fires,* and *New Dance* (1935–36). Helen Tamiris (Helen Becker, 1905–66) creates *How Long, Brethren?* (1937) and *Adelante* (1939).

1940–49

Theater: Shirley Booth and Jo Ann Sayers are paired in the comedy *My Sister Eileen* (1940). Lillian Hellman's *Watch on the Rhine,* with Mady Christians, earns the New York Drama Critics' Circle Award for 1941; her other plays include *The Searching Wind* (1944) with Cornelia Otis Skinner and *Another Part of the Forest* (1946) with Patricia Neal and Mildred Dunnock. Dorothy McGuire leads in Rose Franken's *Claudia* (1941). Tallulah Bankhead and Florence Eldridge star in Thornton Wilder's *The Skin of Our Teeth* (1942). On Broadway, Margo Jones directs Tennessee Williams's *Glass Menagerie* (1944) with Laurette Taylor and Julie Haydon, Maxine Wood's *On Whitman Avenue* (1946) with Vivian Baber, and Maxwell Anderson's *Joan of Lorraine* (1946); in 1947 she opens a theater in the round in Dallas, which presents some shows that go on to Broadway and inspires other regional theaters. Antoinette Perry directs *Harvey* (1944), the Pulitzer Prize winner by Mary Chase; after Perry's 1946 death the annual Antoinette Perry ("Tony") Awards are established in her honor. Hilda Simms stars in the all-black pro-

Making Movies

Among Dorothy Arzner's 14 sound films of the 1930s are Anybody's Woman *(1930, screenplay by Zoë Akins), with Ruth Chatterton,* Merrily We Go to Hell *(1932), with Sylvia Sidney;* Christopher Strong *(1933, screenplay by Zoë Akins), with Katharine Hepburn;* Nana *(1934) with Anna Sten; and* The Bride Wore Red *(1937), with Joan Crawford. "There should be more of us directing," she says. "Try as any man may, he will never be able to get the woman's viewpoint in directing certain stories."*

One of the few talkies Lois Weber makes is White Heat *(1934), dealing with racism in Hawaii. Mary Ellen Brute's* Rhythm in Light *(1936) is one of the first abstract films.*

In addition to Frances Marion and the other Oscar winners, the many women screenplay writers of the 1930s include Blanche Sewell, Anita Loos, Dorothy Parker, Sonya Levien, Frances Goodrich, Lenore Coffee, and Jane Murfin. Some of the top film editors are Anne Bauchens, Barbara McLean, Margaret Booth, and Viola Lawrence.

Musicals: 1930s

Ethel Waters stars in Cabin in the Sky *(1940), which also features Katherine Dunham and her dancers. Other performances include Vivienne Segal and Canadian-born June Havoc in* Pal Joey *(1940);* Ethel Merman in *Panama Hattie (1940); Eve Arden and Betty Hutton in* Two for the Show *(1940), with lyrics by Nancy Hamilton; Mary Martin in* One Touch of Venus *(1943); and Celeste Holm in* Oklahoma! *(1943). Lyricist Dorothy Fields and her brother, Hubert, write the lyrics for* Annie Get Your Gun *(1946), starring Ethel Merman. Pearl Bailey plays Butterfly in* St. Louis Woman *(1946), opposite Ruby Hill, and receives a Donaldson Award as the most promising new performer. Patricia Morrison and Lisa Kirk star in* Kiss Me, Kate *(1948). Carol Channing is Lorelei Lee in the musical of Anita Loos's* Gentlemen Prefer Blondes *(1949), singing "Diamonds Are a Girl's Best Friend." Mary Martin receives a Tony for her starring role in* South Pacific *(1949), as does Juanita Hall (1901–68) in the supporting role of Bloody Mary, the first African American winner.*

duction of *Anna Lucasta* (1944), which later introduces Ruby Dee (Ruby Ann Wallace). Helen Hayes wins a Tony for her acting in Anita Loos's *Happy Birthday* (1946). With Margaret Webster and Cheryl Crawford, Eva Le Gallienne founds the American Repertory Theatre in New York (1946–47). The Alley Theatre in Houston is started by Nina Vance in 1947. Judith Malina and her husband, Julian Beck, form the experimental troupe the Living Theatre in 1947. British-born Jessica Tandy (1909–94) stars as Blanche DuBois and Kim Hunter (Janet Cole) as Stella Kowalski in Tennessee Williams's *A Streetcar Named Desire* (1947). Gertrude Berg writes and stars in the Broadway show *Me and Molly* (1948), drawing on her successful radio sitcom. Margaret Webster starts her touring Shakespeare company in 1948. Stella Adler founds her school of method acting in 1949.

Opera: Helen Traubel is the top Wagnerian soprano at the Met during the 1940s. Mary Cardwell Dawson (1894–1962) starts the National Negro Opera Company in 1941. Soprano Patrice Munsell debuts at the Met in 1943. Soprano Dorothy Kirstin begins her 30-year career with the Met as Mimi in *La Bohème* in 1945. The first African American woman to perform at the New York City Opera, Camilla Williams sings the title role in *Madama Butterfly* in 1945. Gertrude Stein writes the libretto for Virgil Thomson's opera *Mother of Us All*, and Dorothy Dow plays the lead role of Susan B. Anthony when it is premiered in 1947, after Stein's death.

Classical Music: Mabel Wheeler Daniels's cantata *The Song of Jael* is performed at the 1940 Worcester Festival. The Los Angeles Philharmonic Orchestra premieres Elinor Remick Warren's *The Legend of King Arthur* in 1940. Mary Howe composes songs to Elinor Wylie poems and the string quartet *Three Pieces after Emily Dickinson* (1941). Ruth Crawford (Seeger) creates *Rissolty, Rissolty* (1941); she later publishes her transcriptions of folk songs. Margaret Bonds writes "The Negro Speaks of Rivers" (1941) to a Langston Hughes poem. Louise Talma's *Toccata for Orchestra* is premiered by the Baltimore Symphony in 1945. The New York Philharmonic plays the tone poem *Sun Splendor* by Marion Eugénie Bauer (1887–1955) in 1947. Dika Newlin composes her experimental Chamber Symphony (1947).

Country Music: In 1940 Minnie Pearl (Sarah Ophelia Colley) joins "The Grand Ole Opry" as its only female member. Texas singer Ella Mae Morse's "Cow Cow Boogie" is a hit in 1942. Molly O'Day (LaVerne Williamson, 1923–87) records the country classic "The Tramp on the Street" (1946). Cindy Walker begins writing her 500 country classics during the 1940s, including many of the songs in cowboy films.

Gospel: Roberta Martin composes the first of her more than 100 songs: "Try Jesus He Satisfies" (1943). Pianist Clara Ward (1924–73) debuts with her mother, Gertrude Murphy Ward, and sister Willia at the National Baptist Convetion in 1943; she records such classics as "Surely God Is Able" and "I'm Climbing Higher and Higher" with

Marion Williams, who joins the group in 1947. Margaret Allison, her sister Josephine McDowell, Lucille Shird. and Ella Mae Morris form the Angelic Gospel Sisters in 1944. Mahalia Jackson records "Move On Up a Little Higher" (1946), which sells 8 million copies. Dorothy Vernell Simmons and Doris Akers form the Simmons-Akers Singers in 1947; Akers also publishes her song "A Double Portion of God's Love." Lucie E. Campbell (1885–1963) composes such songs as "There Is a Fountain" (1948) and "Footprints of Jesus" (1949).

Academy Awards: Best actresses include Ginger Rogers in *Kitty Foyle* (1940), Jennifer Jones (Phyllis Isley) in *The Song of Bernadette* (1943), Joan Crawford in *Mildred Pierce* (1945), Loretta (Gretchen) Young in *The Farmer's Daughter* (1947), and Jane Wyman (Sarah Jane Fulks) in *Johnny Belinda* (1948). Best supporting actresses include Mary Astor (Lucille Vasconcellos Langhanke, 1906–87) in *The Great Lie* (1941), Ethel Barrymore in *None But the Lonely Heart* (1944), Anne Baxter (1923–85) in *The Razor's Edge* (1946), and Celeste Holm in *The Gentleman's Agreement* (1947). Editing winners are Anne Bauchens for *Northwest Mounted Police* (1940) and Barbara McLean for *Wilson* (1944).

Other Film Performances: Mae West cowrites and costars with W. C. Fields in *My Little Chickadee* (1940). Betty Grable (1916–73) gains popularity in *Down Argentine Way* and *Tin Pan Alley* (1940), becoming the highest-paid female in the mid-1940s. Rita Hayworth (Margarita Carmen Cansino, 1918–87) costars with Fred Astaire in *You'll Never Get Rich* (1941) and *You Were Never Lovelier* (1942); other films include *Gilda* (1946) and *The Lady from Shanghai* (1948). Mary Astor seals her reputation as a femme fatale opposite Humphrey Bogart in *The Maltese Falcon* (1941). *Woman of the Year* (1942) is Katharine Hepburn's first film with Spencer Tracy; others include *Without You* (1945) and *Adam's Rib* (1949). Carole Lombard's last film is *To Be or Not to Be* (1942). Jean Arthur (Gladys Georgianna Greene, 1908–91) is known for her comic antics in *The Talk of the Town* (1942) and *The More the Merrier* (1943). Dale Evans (Frances Octavia Smith) joins Roy Rogers in *The Cowboy and the Senorita* (1944) and many others. Elizabeth Taylor has her first success in *National Velvet* (1944). Lauren Bacall (Betty Joan Persky) stars opposite Humphrey Bogart in *To Have and Have Not* (1945), *The Big Sleep* (1946), and *Key Largo* (1948). In addition to starring in Mexican films, Dolores Del Río is featured in John Wayne's *The Fugitive* (1947). Jeanne Crain, Ethel Waters, and Ethel Barrymore all gain Oscar nominations for *Pinky* (1949).

Still other performances include Rosalind Russell in *His Gal Friday* (1940), *My Sister Eileen* (1942), and *Sister Kenny* (1946); Bette Davis in *The Man Who Came to Dinner* and *The Little Foxes* (both 1941); Barbara Stanwyck in the comic *The Lady Eve* (1941), *Double Indemnity* (1944), and *Sorry, Wrong Number* (1948); Teresa Wright in *Shadow of a Doubt* (1943) and *The Best Years of Our Lives* (1946); Lena Horne in *Cabin in the Sky,* with Ethel Waters, and *Stormy Weather* (both 1943); Gene Tierney (1920–91) in *Heaven Can Wait* (1943), *Laura* (1944), and *The*

Jazz and Blues: 1930s

New recordings include I See a Million People *(1941) by Una Mae Carlisle (1915–56); Billie Holiday's "God Bless the Child" (1941) and "Lover Man" (1944); Ella Fitzgerald and the Ink Spots' hit "Into Each Life Some Rain Must Fall" (1944); Anita O'Day's "And Her Tears Flowed Like Wine" (1944); "I'll Wait and Pray" (1944), the first record of Sarah Vaughan (1924–91), later called "The Divine," made with Billy Eckstine; also Vaughan's "Lover Man" and "Body and Soul" (both 1946); Helen Humes's 1945 hit "Be Baba Leba"; "Snatch and Grab It" (1946) by pianist-singer Julia Lee (1902–58); and Ruth Brown's "So Long" (1949). Peggy Lee (Norma Egstrom) sings with Benny Goodman's orchestra (1941–43) and later composes such songs as "Mañana" with her husband, David Barbour. Trombonist Melba Liston records with saxophonist Dexter Gordon. Dinah Washington (Ruth Lee Jones, 1924–63), who earns the title "Queen of the Blues," starts recording in 1946, garnering 45 hits in the next 16 years. In 1946 pianist-composer Mary Lou Williams (Mary Elfreida Scruggs, 1910–81) scores three parts of her Zodiac Suite for performance by the New York Philharmonic at Carnegie Hall, a major breakthrough for a black female jazz musician. Bassist Lucille Dixon organizes her own orchestra in 1946, lasting to 1960.*

Choreography: 1940s

Among Martha Graham's noted works are El Penitente *(1940)*, Letter to the World *(1940, about Emily Dickinson),* and Appalachian Spring *(1944).* Based on her Caribbean studies, Katherine Dunham creates Tropics and LeJazz Hot *for* her all-black troupe in 1940 and soon tours the country with such dances as Rites du Passage *and* Bal Nègre. *Agnes de Mille's choreography includes* Rodeo *(1942, to Aaron Copeland's music);* Oklahoma! *(1943),* Carousel *(1945),* and Brigadoon *(1947) on Broadway; and* Fall River Legend *(1948), about Lizzie Borden (danced by Alicia Alonso).* Pearl Primus *choreographs* The Negro Speaks of Rivers *(1943),* to a Langston Hughes poem, as well as such Broadway shows as Show Boat *(1945)* and Emperor Jones *(1947). As artistic director for the José Limon Company, Doris Humphrey creates* Day on Earth *(1947)* and other dances. Additional Broadway choreographers include German-born Hanya Holm with Kiss Me, Kate *(1948),* and Helen Tamiris with Touch and Go *(1949), a Tony Award winner.*

Ghost and Mrs. Muir (1947); Tallulah Bankhead in *Lifeboat* (1944); Judy Garland in *Meet Me in St. Louis* (1944), *The Harvey Girls* (1946), and *Till the Clouds Roll By* (1946); Jennifer Jones in *Duel in the Sun* (1946) and *Portrait of Jennie* (1948); Dorothy McGuire and Joan Blondell in *A Tree Grows in Brooklyn* (1945); Jane Wyman in *The Lost Weekend* (1945) and *The Yearling* (1946); Lana (Julia) Turner in *The Postman Always Rings Twice* (1946); Loretta Young in *The Stranger* (1946); Irene Dunne in *Anna and the King of Siam* (1946) and *I Remember Mama* (1948), with Barbara Bel Geddes; Susan Hayward (Edythe Marrener, c. 1917–75) in *Smash-Up: The Story of a Woman* (1947); and Irish-born Maureen O'Hara (Maureen FitzSimons) and child star Natalie Wood (Natasha Gurdin, 1938–81) in *Miracle on 34th Street* (1947).

Film Directing and Writing: Dorothy Arzner's new films are *Dance, Girl, Dance* (1940) and *First Comes Courage* (1943). Maya Deren (Eleanora Derenkowsky, 1917–61), the "Mother of Underground Film," makes her classic *Meshes of the Afternoon* (1943), *Study in Choreography for Camera (1945), Ritual in Transfigured Time* (1946), and others. In 1947 she is the first woman and first American to receive the prize for avant-garde film at the Cannes Film Festival. Another experimental filmmaker is Marie Menken (1909–70) with *Visual Variations on Noguchi* (1945). British-born actress Ida Lupino (1918–95) directs her first film, *Not Wanted* (1949). Edith Head creates a memorable costume with the peacock train in *Samson and Delilah* (1949), starring Hedy Lamarr (Hedwig Eva Maria Kiesler). Hollywood writers include Dorothy Parker, Lillian Hellman, Sonya Levien, Leigh Brackett, Sally Benson. Frances Goodrich, actress Ruth Gordon (1896–1985), and Virginia Van Upp (1902–70), who is also executive producer at Columbia.

Television: The first woman to win an Emmy is Shirley Dinsdale, for her puppet show, *Judy Splinters,* on KTLA-TV. Molly Berg transfers her radio success to TV with *The Goldbergs* (1949), the first sitcom.

Dancers: Leading ballerinas include Nora Kaye (Nora Koreff), who creates Hagar in Antony Tudor's *Pillar of Fire* (1942); Alicia Alonso, principal dancer with the Ballet Theatre (1943–46), who later forms her own company in Cuba; Ruth Ann Koesun, the first Asian American soloist and principal dancer with a national company, with the American Ballet Theatre (1946–69); Tanaquil Le Clercq, who premieres such George Balanchine ballets as *Four Temperaments* (1946) and *Divertimento* (1947); and Maria Tallchief, another leading Balanchine dancer, creating roles in *Orpheus* (1948 with Le Clercq), *The Firebird* (1949), and others. Also, dancer Lucia Chase begins her reign as managing director of the American Ballet Theatre in 1945.

1950–59

Performer Josephine Baker, honored in France for her work for the Resistance during the war, is denied service at New York's Stork Club in 1951. During her U.S. tour she insists on playing only in integrated theaters and nightclubs, forcing some owners to change their policies.

Theater: Producer-director Zelda Fichlander cofounds the Arena Stage Theater in Washington, D.C., in 1950. Carson McCullers's *The Member of the Wedding* (1950), with Julie Harris and Ethel Waters, wins a New York Drama Critics' Circle Award. Uta Hagen earns a Tony in *The Country Girl* (1950), as does Maureen Stapleton in *The Rose Tattoo* (1951), produced by Cheryl Crawford. Julie Harris and Marian Winters both gain Tonys in *I Am a Camera* (1951); Florence Eldridge and Jane Wyatt star in Lillian Hellman's *The Autumn Garden* (1951). Helen Hayes leads in Mary Chase's *Mrs. McThing* (1952), and Shirley Booth in *Time of the Cuckoo* (1952) wins her second Tony. Jane Bowles's *In the Summerhouse* (1953) features Australian-born actress Judith Anderson. Jean Kerr and Eleanor Brooke's *King of Hearts* opens in 1954, as does *Ladies of the Corridor,* coauthored by Dorothy Parker. In 1955 Kim Stanley stars in *Bus Stop;* Barbara Bel Geddes and Mildred Dunnock in *Cat on a Hot Tin Roof;* and Susan Strasberg in Frances Goodrich and Albert Hackett's *The Diary of Anne Frank,* which wins both a Tony and a Pulitzer. Performances in 1956 include Ruth Gordon in *The Matchmaker* and Florence Eldridge and Katharine Ross in *Long Day's Journey into Night.* Cornelia Otis Skinner coauthors and stars in *The Pleasure of His Company* (1958). Anne Bancroft (Anna Maria Italiano) wins Tonys for her performances in *Two for the Seesaw* (1958) and as Annie Sullivan in *The Miracle Worker* (1959), with Patty Duke as Helen Keller. Lorraine Hansberry's award-winning *A Raisin in the Sun* (1959) casts Ruby Dee as Ruth, Diana Sands (1934–73) as Beneatha, and Claudia McNeil (1917–93) as Lena Younger. Geraldine Page stars in Tennessee Williams's *Sweet Bird of Youth* (1959).

Musicals: In the part inspired by ambassador Perle Mesta in *Call Me Madam* (1950), Ethel Merman wins a Tony; she also plays the title role in *Gypsy* (1959), based on Gypsy Rose Lee's 1957 autobiography. Dorothy Fields writes the lyrics for *A Tree Grows in Brooklyn* (1951), starring Shirley Booth, and the book and lyrics for *Redhead* (1959), in which Gwen Verdon wins a Tony. Eartha Kitt is the star of *New Faces* (1952), with some song lyrics by Jane Carroll. Mary Martin receives a Tony for *Peter Pan* (1954), with lyrics by Carolyn Leigh and the team of Betty Comden and Adolph Green; Martin also leads in *The Sound of Music* (1959). Pearl Bailey, Diahann Carroll (Carol Diann Johnson), and Juanita Hall star in *House of Flowers,* which also features dancer Carmen DeLavallade. Chita Rivera (Dolores Conchita Figuero del Rivero) plays Rita Romano in *Mr. Wonderful* (1956) and Anita in *West Side Story* (1957). As the star of *Jamaica* (1957), Lena Horne insists on the hiring of black stagehands. Mary Rodgers composes the music for *Once Upon a Mattress* (1959), featuring Carol Burnett.

Opera: Soprano Maria Callas (Maria Kalogeropoulos, 1923–77) makes her La Scala debut in 1950 and her U.S. debut at the new Chicago Lyric Opera (founded by Carol Fox) in 1954; she first performs at the Met in *Norma* in 1956. Soprano Phyllis Curtin debuts at the New York City Opera in 1953. Australian-born Peggy Glanville-Hicks (1912–90)

"A Precedent-Shattering Moment"

Marian Anderson's 1939 concert on the steps of the Lincoln Memorial became a powerful symbol for the civil rights movement. In 1955 she creates another "precedent-shattering moment," in the words of Langston Hughes, when she is the first African American singer to perform with the Metropolitan Opera Company. She receives a standing ovation before performing in Verdi's *Un Ballo in Maschera* ("A Masked Ball").

In 1952 Marian Anderson sings at a memorial service for Harold Ickes, former secretary of the interior, who helped set up her historic concert at this site in 1939 (Library of Congress)

composes the opera *The Transposed Heads,* first performed in 1954. Coloratura soprano Beverly Sills (Belle Silverman) debuts as Rosalinda in Strauss's *Die Fledermaus* in 1955 at the New York City Opera. Coloratura soprano Mattiwilda Dobbs, the first African American to sing a principal role at La Scala in Milan, in 1953, makes her debut at the Met in 1956. Although lyric soprano Leontyne Price sings *Tosca* for an NBC-TV production in 1955, she does not make her stage debut until 1957, in the U.S. premiere of Poulenc's *Dialogue of the Carmelites* at the San Francisco Opera. In 1957 conductor Sarah Caldwell starts the Boston Opera Group (later Company), which gives many U.S. premieres. Soprano Anna Moffo debuts at the Met in 1959.

Concert Singers: Soprano Dorothy Maynor is the first black singer allowed to perform at the DAR's Constitution Hall, in 1952.

Classical and Experimental Music: Lucia Dlugoszewski invents the timbre piano in 1951 as well as many different percussion instruments for her music. Ruth Crawford (Seeger) composes Suite for a Wind Quartet (1952). Doriot Anthony Dwyer, the great-grandniece of Susan B. Anthony, is the first woman hired to chair a section in a major orchestra, as principal flutist of the Boston Symphony Orchestra in 1952. Pianist-composer Philippa Duke Schuyler (1931–67) gives a debut recital at New York's Town Hall in 1953. In 1956 electronic music pioneer Bebe Barron (Charlotte Wind) and her husband, Louis, compose music for the film *Forbidden Planet.*

Gospel: Cora Martin-Moore (Cora Bruer) composes "Heaven Sweet Heaven" (1953) and "He'll Wash You Whiter Than Snow" (1954), and Roberta Martin writes "God Is Still on the Throne" (1959).

Academy Awards: Best actress winners include Judy Holliday (1922–65) in *Born Yesterday* (1950), Shirley Booth in *Come Back, Little Sheba* (1952), re-creating her stage success; Belgian-born Audrey Hepburn (Edna Hepburn-Ruston, 1929–93) in *Roman Holiday* (1953), Grace Kelly (1928–82) in *The Country Girl* (1954); Joanne Woodward in *The Three Faces of Eve* (1957); and Susan Hayward in *I Want to Live!* (1958). Best supporting actresses include Kim Hunter (Jane Cole) in *A Streetcar Named Desire* (1951), Donna Reed in *From Here to Eternity* (1953), Eva Marie Saint in *On the Waterfront* (1954), and Shelley Winters (Shirley Schrift) in *The Diary of Anne Frank* (1959).

Additional Film Performances: Grace Kelly is an instant star opposite Gary Cooper in *High Noon* (1952); other films include *Rear Window* (1954) and *To Catch a Thief* (1955). Marilyn Monroe (Norma Jean Mortenson, 1926–62) is the star of the decade, with such films as *Gentlemen Prefer Blondes* (1953), *The Seven Year Itch* (1954), *Bus Stop* (1956), and *Some Like It Hot* (1959). Dorothy Dandridge (1922–65) is the first African American nominated for an Oscar as best actress, in the musical *Carmen Jones* (1954); she also stars in *Porgy and Bess* (1959).

Still other performances include Gloria Swanson (1897–1983) in *Sunset Boulevard* (1950); Bette Davis with Anne Baxter and Celeste

Holm in *All About Eve* (1950); Ava Gardner (1922–90) in *Show Boat* (1951), *Mogambo* (1953), and *The Barefoot Contessa* (1954); Elizabeth Taylor in *A Place in the Sun* (1951), *Cat on a Hot Tin Roof* (1958), and *Suddenly, Last Summer* (1959); Debbie (Mary Frances) Reynolds and Cyd Charisse (Tula Ellice Finklea) in *Singin' in the Rain* (1952); Katharine Hepburn with Humphrey Bogart in *The African Queen* (1951) and with Spencer Tracy in *Desk Set* (1959); Maureen O'Hara in *The Quiet Man* (1952); Audrey Hepburn in *Sabrina* (1954), *Love in the Afternoon* (1957), and *The Nun's Story* (1959); Judy Garland in *A Star Is Born* (1954); Natalie Wood in *Rebel Without a Cause* (1955); Susan Hayward in *I'll Cry Tomorrow* (1956); Doris Day (Doris von Kappelhoff) in *The Pajama Game* (1957); Jennifer Jones in *A Farewell to Arms* (1957); Kim (Marilyn) Novak in *Vertigo* (1958); Rosalind Russell in *Auntie Mame* (1958), re-creating her stage success; Jean Seberg (1938–79) in *Bonjour Tristesse* (1958) and *Breathless* (1959); Lee Remick (1935–91) in *Anatomy of a Murder* (1959); and Eva Marie Saint in *North by Northwest* (1959).

"I didn't want the studios to decide what people should see"—Shirley Clarke

Film Directing and Writing: Ida Lupino directs five films: *Never Fear* (1950), *Outrage* (1950), *Hard, Fast, and Beautiful* (1951), *The Bigamist* (1953), and *The Hitchhiker* (1953). Maya Deren works on *The Very Eye of Night: A Choreography for Cinema* (1952–59). Dancer Shirley Clarke's first films include *A Dance in the Sun* (1953) and *Skyscraper* (1959), a Venice Film Festival winner. Among the women who receive Academy Award nominations are writers Edna Anhalt (who wins as coauthor of *Panic in the Streets* in 1950), Frances Goodrich, Ruth Gordon, Virginia Kellogg, Helen Deutsch, Fay Kanin, and Betty Comden, and editors Anne Bauchens, Adrienne Fazan (who wins for *Gigi* in 1958), Barbara McLean, Dorothy Spencer, Alma Macrorie, and Viola Lawrence. Edith Head earns four costume design Oscars, and Helen Rose two.

Television: Comedian Imogene Coca stars with Sid Caesar in *Your Show of Shows*, beginning in 1950; in 1954 she has her own *Imogene Coca Show*. The series *Beulah* (1950–53) stars Ethel Waters and then Louise Beavers but limits them to a stereotyped black mammy image. Actress Arlene Francis and journalist Dorothy Kilgallen are regular panelists on *What's My Line?*, starting in 1950. Comedian Lucille Ball (1911–89) first stars with her husband, Desi Arnaz, in *I Love Lucy* in 1951. Dinah Shore and Loretta Young have their own successful shows in 1954, as does Donna Reed in 1958.

1960–69

Theater: Maureen Stapleton stars in Lillian Hellman's *Toys in the Attic* (1960); Canadian-born Colleen Dewhurst (1926–91) earns a Tony in *All the Way Home* (1960). Barbara Bel Geddes takes the lead in Jean Kerr's *Mary, Mary* (1961). In 1961 Ellen Stewart starts Café LaMama (later LaMama, Experimental Theatre Company, or LaMama, E.T.C.),

Dance: 1950s

Agnes de Mille's choreography includes the Broadway show Paint Your Wagon *(1951) and the ballet* The Harvest According *(1952). Doris Humphrey choreographs* Ruins and Visions *(1953); her book* The Art of Making Dances *is published posthumously in 1959. In 1955 Ruth Page establishes the Chicago Ballet, which performs her* The Merry Widow. *Anna Sokolow choreographs her classic* Rooms *(1955). Near San Francisco, Ann (later Anna) Halprin forms her Dancers' Workshop in 1955; Trisha Brown, Simone Forti, and Yvonne Rainer all work with her in 1959. Hanya Holm choreographs* My Fair Lady *(1956). Martha Graham choreographs one of her trademark pieces,* Clytemnestra *(1958).*

After joining the Metropolitan Opera ballet in 1951, Janet Collins is its first African American prima ballerina in 1952; in 1956 she is followed by Carmen DeLavallade. Other ballerinas include Melissa Hayden, who debuts with the New York City Ballet in The Duel *in 1950; Lupe Serrano, who becomes a principal dancer for the American Ballet Theatre in 1953; and Patricia McBride, who debuts with the New York City Ballet in 1959.*

Musicals: 1960s

Chita Rivera and Kay Medford star in Bye Bye Birdie *(1960), and Tammy Grimes wins a Tony for creating the lead in* The Unsinkable Molly Brown *(1960). Ossie Davis's* Purlie Victorious *(1961) stars his wife, Ruby Dee, and also features Melba Moore. Diahann Carroll (Carol Diann Johnson) receives a Tony as the star of* No Strings. *Carol Channing wins a Tony for her lead in* Hello, Dolly! *(1964). Dorothy Fields writes the book and lyrics for* Sweet Charity *(1965), starring Gwen Verdon. Barbra Streisand plays Fanny Brice in* Funny Girl *(1964). Mary Rodgers composes the music for* The Mad Show *(1966). Megan Terry's* Viet Rock *(1966), which opens at LaMama, is the first rock musical. Leslie Uggams and Lillian Hayman give Tony-winning performances in* Hallelujah, Baby! *(1967), with lyrics by Betty Comden and Adolph Green (also Tony winners). Gretchen Cryer writes the book and lyrics and Nancy Ford the music for* Now Is the Time for All Good Men *(1967). Pearl Bailey wins a special Tony for her performance as the lead in the all-black production of* Hello, Dolly! *(1968); she also publishes her autobiography,* The Raw Pearl. *Katharine Hepburn returns to Broadway in* Coco *(1969).*

a key New York venue for avant-garde work in the next three decades. "You have to have faith in doing plays whether you have an audience or not," she comments. Uta Hagen in *Who's Afraid of Virginia Woolf?* (1962) and Sandy Dennis in *A Thousand Clowns* (1962) both receive Tonys. Obies for the 1963–64 season go to Rosalyn Drexler's *Home Movies* and Adrienne Kennedy's *Funnyhouse of a Negro*, as well as to Judith Malina for her direction of *Brig*. Diana Sands is the first black actress to play a Broadway role originally written for a white woman, in *The Owl and the Pussycat* (1964); she also stars in Shaw's *Saint Joan* in 1968. Beah Richards plays Sister Margaret Alexander in *The Amen Corner* (1964), and Irene Worth stars in *Tiny Alice* (1964). Women's plays on Broadway in 1964 include Muriel Resnik's *Any Wednesday*, starring Sandy Dennis (who wins a Tony); Lorraine Hansberry's *The Sign in Sidney Brustein's Window*, starring Rita Moreno; and Jean Kerr's *Poor Richard*. Avant-garde plays by women staged in New York in 1965 include Megan Terry's *Calm Down, Mother;* Cuban-born María Irene Fornes's Obie-winning *Successful Life of Three* and *Promenade;* and Rochelle Owens's Obie-winning *Futz*. Ruby Dee is the first African American actress to play leads at the American Shakespeare Festival in Stratford, Connecticut, in 1965; the next year she performs in Alice Childress's *The Wedding Band*. In 1966 Rosemary Harris stars in *The Lion in Winter*, winning a Tony, and Jessica Tandy is in *A Delicate Balance*. In 1967 actress and director Miriam Colón forms the Puerto Rican Traveling Theater in New York, which premieres many works by Latino playwrights. Barbara Garson's *MacBird* (1967) features Stacy Keach. With *Gloria and Esperanza* (1968), Julie Bovasso wins Obies for writing, acting, and directing. Lillian Gish and Teresa Wright star in *I Never Sang for My Father* (1968), and Jane Alexander wins a Tony in *The Great White Hope* (1968). Actress and director Barbara Ann Teer founds the National Black Theatre Company in Harlem in 1968. The Women's Interart Theatre is established in New York in 1969. On stage in 1969 are Tony winner Blythe Danner and Eileen Heckart in *Butterflies Are Free;* Linda Lavin in *Last of the Red Hot Lovers;* and Barbara Baxley and Cicely Tyson in the posthumous production of Lorraine Hansberry's *To Be Young, Gifted and Black*.

Opera: After performing with the San Francisco Opera since 1957, soprano Eileen Farrell debuts in *Alcestis* at the Met in 1960. Internationally acclaimed soprano Leontyne Price finally debuts at the Met in 1961 in *Il Trovatore;* in 1966 she sings Samuel Barber's *Antony and Cleopatra*, written for her, at the opening of the new Metropolitan Opera House in Lincoln Center. Mezzo-soprano Grace Bumbry is the first African American singer at the Wagner Festival in Bayreuth, Germany, in 1961; she has her U.S. debut at the Chicago Lyric Opera in 1963 and at the Met in 1965. In 1962 Louisa Talma is the first U.S. woman composer to have an opera performed at a major European opera house, when *The Alcestiad*, with a libretto by Thornton Wilder, premieres in Germany. Sylvia Regan writes the libretto for the opera *The Golem*, composed by her husband, Abraham Ellstein, and performed at the New York City Opera in 1962. Mezzo-soprano Shirley Verrett debuts at the New York City Opera in 1963 and at the Met in *Carmen* in 1968. Peggy Glanville-Hicks composes *Sappho* (1963) for the San Francisco Opera. Soprano Martina Arroyo first gains acclaim when she substitutes for Birgit Nilsson in *Aïda* at the Met in 1965.

Classical and Experimental Music: Elinor Remick Warren has Los Angeles premieres of her choral work *Abram in Egypt* in 1961 and her Requiem Mass in 1966. Radie Britain composes *Cosmic Mist Symphony* (1962). Marga Richter writes such pieces as *Abyss* (1964) and *Bird of Yearning* (1967–68) for the Harkness Ballet. In 1965 the New York Philharmonic performs *A Short Piece for Orchestra* (1962) by African American composer Julia Amanda Perry (1924–79). Louise Talma completes her 12-tone cantata *All the Days of My Life* (1965). Catharine Crozier is one of the three top organists to give the inaugural organ recital at Lincoln Center's Philharmonic Hall in 1962. Israeli-born composer-pianist Shulamit Ran performs her *Capriccio* in 1963 with the New York Philharmonic. German-born Ursula Mamlok composes the trio *Stray Birds* (1963) and *Haiku Settings* (1967) for soprano and flute. In 1966 double bassist Orin O'Brien is the first regular woman performer with the New York Philharmonic in its 124-year history. Philippa Duke Schuyler's *The Nile Fantasy* is performed posthumously at Town Hall in 1967. Conductor Eve Rabin Queler starts the Opera Orchestra in New York in 1967 to perform unstaged operas; they play *Tosca* at Alice Tully Hall in 1969. Pauline Oliveros composes *In Memoriam Nicola Tesla, Cosmic Engineer* (1968) for the Merce Cunningham Dance Company. Alice Parker writes the cantata *Martin Luther King: A Sermon from the Mountain* (1969).

Folk and Protest Music: Judy Collins's albums include *A Maid of Constant Sorrow* (1961), *In My Life* (1966), and *Who Knows Where the Time Goes* (1968), with the hit "Both Sides Now." Odetta (O. Holmes Felious Gordon) releases *Sometimes I Feel Like Cryin'* (1962) and sings at the 1963 civil rights march. Mary Travers records "Puff the Magic Dragon" and "Blowin' in the Wind" (both 1963) as part of the group Peter, Paul and Mary. Buffie Saint-Marie records her antiwar song "Universal Soldier" (1964). Canadian-born Joni Mitchell (Roberta Joan Anderson) has her first hit with "Clouds" (1969). Yoko Ono and John Lennon record the single "Give Peace a Chance" (1969).

Country: Singers with hits include Skeeter Davis (Mary Fancis Penick) with "The End of the World" (1963); Patsy Cline with the posthumous releases "Sweet Dreams," "Faded Love," and "He Called Me Baby" (all 1963); Dottie West (Dorothy Marie Marsh) with "Here Comes My Baby" (1964), which gains the first Grammy to a female country vocalist; Bobbie Gentry (Roberta Lee Streeter) with "Ode to Billie Joe" (1967, her own composition); Dolly Parton with "Just Because I'm a Woman" (1968); and Tammy Wynette (Virginia Wynette Pugh) with "Stand by Your Man" (1968); she is also the Country Music Association's female vocalist of the year three consecutive times.

Joan Baez (AP/Wide World Photos)

Popular Singers

Connie Frances (Concetta Franco-nero) first tops the charts with "Everybody's Somebody's Fool" (1960); soon after, Brenda Lee (Brenda Mae Tarpley) hits number one with "I'm Sorry" (1960). The Shirelles are the first "girl group" with a number-one single, "Will You Love Me Tomorrow?" (1961), with music by Carole King. Judy Gar-land wins two 1961 Grammys for her Carnegie Hall concert album. Dionne Warwick (Marie Dionne Warrick) has her first hit with "Don't Make Me Over" (1962). Barbra Streisand wins three consecutive Grammys (1963–65) for The Barbra Streisand Album, People, *and* My Name is Barbra. *Mary Wells (1943–92) hits number one with "My Guy" (1964). The Supremes (Diana Ross, Florence Ballard, and Mary Wilson) have the first of 12 number-one hits with "Where Did Our Love Go?" (1964). Cher (Cherilyn Sarkisian LaPierre) is known for "I've Got You Babe" (1965) with Sony Bono. Grace Wing Slick is the lead singer for the Jefferson Airplane in 1966. Janis Joplin (1943–70) is the first female rock superstar after singing "Love Is Like a Ball and Chain" in 1967;* Cheap Thrills *(1968) tops a million. Gladys Knight and the Pips score a hit with "I Heard It Through the Grape Vine" (1967). Roberta Flack's album* First Take *(1969) includes "The First Time Ever I Saw Your Face," which becomes a hit in 1972.*

Gospel: Mahalia Jackson earns her first Grammy with *Every Time I Feel the Spirit* (1961). Right before Martin Luther King, Jr., gives his "I Have a Dream" speech in 1963, she sings "I Been 'Buked and I Been Scorned." Roberta Martin composes "Let It Be" and "Just Jesus and Me" (both 1962). Shirley Caesar forms the Caesar Singers (1966) and has a hit with "Don't Drive Your Mama Away" (1969).

Jazz/Rhythm and Blues: Tina Turner (Annie Mae Bullock) has her first rhythm-and-blues hit with "Fool in Love" (1960). Dinah Washington's biggest hit is "Baby You've Got What It Takes" (1960). Abbey Lincoln (Gaby Lee) records *We Insist! Freedom Now Suite* (1960) with Thelonius Monk, Mal Waldron, and her husband, Max Roach. Valerie Simpson begins her songwriting collaboration with Nicholas Ashford in 1964, creating such hits as Ray Charles's "Let's Go Get Stoned." On her 1967 album, *I Never Loved a Man (the Way I Loved You)*, Aretha Franklin, "Queen of Soul," has two hits: the title song and "Respect." *Lady Soul* (1968) includes "Chain of Fools." Franklin wins the Grammy for the best rhythm-and-blues female vocalist every year from 1967 through 1974. Koko Taylor (Cora Walton) has her first big hit with "Wang Dang Doodle" (1965). Jazz composer Carla Borg Bley begins her opera *Escalator over the Hill* (1967–72). Nina Simone's albums include *Here Comes the Sun* (1967) and *Young, Gifted and Black* (1969). In 1968 Japanese-born jazz composer Toshiko Akiyoshi conducts her first Town Hall concert, with solo, trio, and big-band pieces. Laura Nyro (Laura Nigro) blends jazz with rock in *New York Tendaberry* (1969).

Latin: Vikki Carr (Florencia Bicenta de Casillas Martínez Cardona) releases her top-selling album *It Must Be Him* (1967).

Academy Awards: Best actress winners include Elizabeth Taylor in *Butterfield 8* (1960) and *Who's Afraid of Virginia Woolf?* (1966); Anne Bancroft in *The Miracle Worker* (1962); Patricia Neal in *Hud* (1963); Katharine Hepburn in *Guess Who's Coming to Dinner* (1967) and *The Lion in Winter* (1968), making her the first woman to win three Oscars; and Barbra Streisand (in a tie with Hepburn) in *Funny Girl* (1968). Best supporting actresses include Rita Moreno (Rosa Dolores Alverio) as Anita in *West Side Story* (1961), Patty Duke as Helen Keller in *The Miracle Worker* (1962), Sandy Dennis in *Who's Afraid of Virginia Woolf?* (1966), Ruth Gordon in *Rosemary's Baby* (1968), and Goldie Hawn in *Cactus Flower* (1969). Marilyn and Alan Bergman's "The Windmills of Your Mind" in *The Thomas Crown Affair* (1968) wins an Oscar.

Additional Film Performances: Janet Leigh (Jeanette Morrison) gives a memorable performance in Alfred Hitchcock's *Psycho* (1960). Hong Kong–born Nancy Kwan stars in *The World of Susie Wong* (1960) and *Flower Drum Song* (1961) but is limited to stereotyped images of Asian women. Shirley MacLaine (Shirley MacLean Beatty) receives Oscar nominations for *The Apartment* (1960) and *Irma La Douce* (1963).

Still other performances include Doris Day in *Please Don't Eat the Daisies* (1960); Audrey Hepburn in *Breakfast at Tiffany's* (1961), *My*

Fair Lady (1964), *Two for the Road* (1966), and *Wait until Dark* (1967); Natalie Wood in *Splendor in the Grass* (1961), *West Side Story* (1961), and *Love with the Proper Stranger* (1963); Marilyn Monroe in *The Misfits* (1961); Lee Remick in *Days of Wines and Roses* (1962); Katharine Hepburn in *Long Day's Journey into Night* (1962); Bette Davis in *Whatever Happened to Baby Jane?* (1962), with Joan Crawford, and in *Hush, Hush Sweet Charlotte* (1964); Anne Bancroft and Katharine Ross in *The Graduate* (1967); Faye Dunaway in *Bonnie and Clyde* (1967); antiwar activist Jane Fonda in *Barbarella* (1968) and *They Shoot Horses, Don't They?* (1969); and Mia Farrow in *Rosemary's Baby* (1968).

Film Directing: Shirley Clarke's films include *The Connection* (1961), which wins the Critics' Prize at Cannes, and *The Cool World* (1963). Ida Lupino directs *The Trouble with Angels* (1966).

Television: Shirley Booth is popular in the sitcom *Hazel* (1961–65), and Mary Tyler Moore gains fans on *The Dick Van Dyke Show* (1961–66). Julia Child starts a series called *The French Chef* in 1963. Irna Phillips creates the soap operas *Another World* (1964), *Days of Our Lives* (1965), and *Love Is a Many-Splendored Thing* (1967). From 1964, Elizabeth Montgomery is Samantha on the sitcom *Bewitched*, about a housewife with magical powers. Marlo Thomas stars in the series *That Girl* (1966–71). Carol Burnett begins her 12-year show in 1967. Diahann Carroll is the first African American star of a sitcom, *Julia* (1968). Joan Ganz Cooney produces *Sesame Street* for educational television in 1969.

1970–79

Theater: Megan Terry's *Approaching Simone*, directed by Maxine Klein, wins an Obie for the 1969–70 season. Joan Holden cofounds San Francisco Mime Troupe in 1970 and writes *Independent Female, or A Man Has His Pride!* (1970). JoAnne Akalaitis and Ruth Maleczech are two of the five founders of Mabou Mines in 1970. In Los Angeles in 1970 actress Carmen Zapata, director Margarita Galban, and scenic designer Estela Scarlata start what becomes the Bilingual Foundation for the Arts, presenting Latino works. Maureen Stapleton wins a Tony in *Gingerbread Lady* (1970), and Ruby Dee an Obie in *Boesman and Lena* (1970). Hazel Joan Bryant (1939–83) cofounds New York's Lincoln Center Street Theatre Festival with Mical Whitaker and Geraldine Fitzgerald in 1971, and organizes the first Black Theatre Festival USA in 1979. Susan Yankowitz creates *Terminal* and *Slaughterhouse* (both 1971). Lee Grant (Lyova Haskell Rosenthal) stars in *The Prisoner of Second Avenue* (1971). Jean Kerr's *Finishing Touches* (1973) features Barbara Bel Geddes. Colleen Dewhurst gives a Tony-winning performance in Eugene O'Neill's *A Moon for the Misbegotten* (1973). In 1973 Linda Mussman founds Time and Space Limited and writes and directs such works as *Room/Raum* (1978). In 1974 Megan Terry starts the Magic Theatre in Omaha, Nebraska. Tammy Grimes stars in *California Suite* (1975). When Rita Moreno receives a Tony in *The Ritz* (1975), she is the first woman to receive all four major show business awards: an Oscar, a Tony, a Grammy, and two Emmys. Ellen Burstyn

Dance: 1960s

Martha Graham choreographs Alcestis *(1960)* to music composed by Vivian Fine, as well as Phaedra *(1962)*. Hanya Holm choreographs the Broadway show Carousel *(1960)*. New pieces by Anna Sokolow include Dreams *(1961)* and Steps of Silence *(1967)*. New dancers include Suzanne Farrell (Roberta Sue Flicker), who debuts with the New York City Ballet in 1961 and becomes its principal dancer in 1965; Judith Jamison, who debuts with the Alvin Ailey Dance Theatre in 1965; and Cynthia Gregory, who becomes the American Ballet Theatre's principal dancer in 1967.

The Judson Dance Workshop, which forms in 1962, includes such pioneering choreographers as Yvonne Rainer, Trisha Brown, Elaine Summers, Deborah Hay, Judith Dunn, Lucinda Childs, and later Meredith Monk and Phoebe Neville. Even though she does not join the Judson group, Simone Forti is influential through such early pieces as See-Saw *(1960)*, about balance. Another innovative new dancer is Twyla Tharp, who forms her own dance group in 1965, performing such pieces as Tank Dive. Ann Halprin and her San Francisco dancers perform Parades and Changes *in New York in 1967.*

Musicals: 1970s

Composer Nancy Ford and writer Gretchen Cryer collaborate on their Obie-winning The Last Sweet Days of Isaac *(1970) and* I'm Getting My Act Together and Taking It on the Road *(1978). In 1970 Melba Moore stars in* Purlie; *Lauren Bacall in* Applause, *with a book coauthored by Betty Comden; and Elaine Stritch in* Company. *Margaret Rosezarion Harris conducts* Hair *(1970),* Raisin *(1974), and other Broadway musicals. Micki Grant (Minnie Perkins McCutcheon) composes and stars in the Obie-winning* Don't Bother Me, I Can't Cope *(1972), directed by Vinnette Carroll; among the first African American women composers and directors on Broadway, Grant and Carroll also join forces on Grant's* Your Arm's Too Short to Box with God *(1976), in which Delores Hall wins a Tony. Andrea McArdle stars in* Annie *(1977) with Dorothy Loudon. Writer-composer Elizabeth Swados's* Runaways *(1978), combining monologues and songs, opens in New York. Carole Hall composes the music and lyrics for* Best Little Whorehouse in Texas *(1978). Patti LuPone earns a Tony in* Evita *(1979).*

(Edna Rae Gillooly) earns a Tony as the lead in *Same Time, Next Year* (1975). Three Kuna-Rappahannock sisters, Gloria and Muriel Miguel and Lisa Mayo, form the Spiderwoman Theater in Brooklyn in 1975, performing *Women in Violence* (1976). Also in Brooklyn, Karen Malpede cofounds the New Cycle Theatre in 1976 and puts on *The End of War* (1977). Ntozake Shange (Paulette Williams) stars with six other African American women in her Obie-winning choreopoem *For colored girls who have considered suicide/when the rainbow is enuf* (1976), a Broadway hit. As Emily Dickinson in *The Belle of Amherst* (1976), Julie Harris wins her fifth Tony as best actress, a record. Jessica Tandy receives a Tony in *Gin Game* (1977). María Irene Fornes earns an Obie for her play *Fefu and Her Friends* (1977), as well as a directing award for *Eyes on the Harem* (1979). Tisa Chang founds the Pan Asian Repertory Theatre in New York in 1977 to promote Asian American playwrights and actors. "I was so tired of Westerners using Asianness as an exotic characteristic," she comments. Clare Coss, Sondra Segal, and Roberta Sklar found the Women's Experimental Theatre in 1977 and collaborate on *The Daughters Cycle* (1977–80). Julia Miles starts the Woman's Project at the American Place Theater in New York in 1978. Anne Bogart writes and directs *Inhabitant* and *Hampstadt* (both 1979).

Performance: Among the women who define the hybrid form called performance art, mixing elements from various fields, including the visual arts, are Joan Jonas with *Funeral* (1974), Laurie Anderson with *For Instants* (1976), Julia Heyward with *Shake! Daddy! Shake!* (1976), and Theodora Skipitares with *Venus Cafe* (1977). (See also "Art.")

Opera: Met debuts in 1970 include soprano Judith Blegen, mezzo soprano Friederica Von Stade, and mezzo soprano Marilyn Horne. Alice Parker's first opera, *The Martyr's Mirror,* is premiered in Pennsylvania in 1971. As assistant conductor of the New York City Opera, Judith Somogi is the first woman to conduct Gilbert and Sullivan's *The Mikado,* in 1974. "What we need now is a whole *army* of women pursuing conducting careers," she says. After highly acclaimed debuts in Milan and London, Beverly Sills finally makes her first Met appearance in Rossini's *The Siege of Corinth,* in 1975; in 1979 she becomes director of the New York City Opera. In 1976 Sarah Caldwell is the first woman to conduct the Metropolitan Opera, in a performance of *La Traviata* starring Beverly Sills.

Classical and Experimental Music: Composer and pianist Joan Tower founds the Da Capo Players, a chamber ensemble, in 1970. Margaret Harris is the first African American woman to conduct the Chicago Symphony, in 1971. Pianist Natalie Leota Henderson Hinderas (1927–87) plays music by black composers on her 1971 record. Dika Newlin's *Big Swamp* (1972) uses computer-generated sounds. Timpanist Elayne Jones is the first black woman chair in a major orchestra, the San Francisco Symphony, in 1972, but is later denied tenure in a contested case. Tui St. George composes *Little Piece for Quarter Tone Piano* (1972) as well as recorder pieces. Joyce Mekeel's vocal works include *Corridors of*

Dream (1972) and *Alarums and Excursions* (1975). Nancy Van de Vate starts the International League of Women Composers in 1974, which merges in 1990 with the International Congress on Women in Music (founded in 1977 by Jeannie Pool). Beth Anderson, coeditor of *Ear*, composes her oratorio *Joan* (1974). Suzanne Ciani, a pioneer in work with the Buchla synthesizer, composes *New York, New York* (1974). An example of Joan La Barbara's vocal experiments is her solo *Voice Piece: One-Note Internal Resonance Investigation* (1974). Shulamit Ran's *Ensembles for Seventeen* is performed at the 1975 Berkshire Music Festival. Sarah Caldwell conducts the New York Philharmonic in a "Celebration of Women Composers" (1975), with works by Ruth Crawford (Seeger), Pozzi Escot, and Thea Musgrave (a Scottish composer who has recently moved to America). Computer music pioneer Laurie Spiegel composes such pieces as *The Expanding Universe* (1975). Eve Queler conducts the Philadelphia Orchestra in 1976. Jean Eichelberger Ivey's *Testament of Eve*, written for mezzo-soprano Elaine Bonazzi, is performed by the Baltimore Symphony Orchestra in 1976. The New York Philharmonic plays Barbara Kolb's *Soundings* in 1977. Pauline Oliveros composes her award-winning *Bonn Feier* (1977), a theater piece, and uses the accordion's sustained sounds in *Horse Sings from Cloud* (1977). Women conductors in 1978 include Tania Justina Leon at the Brooklyn Philharmonic and Victoria Bond at the Pittsburgh Symphony.

Country: Skeeter Davis sings "It's Hard to Be a Woman" (1970). Hits by Loretta Lynn (Loretta Webb) include "Coal Miner's Daughter" (1970), "I Wanna Be Free" (1971), and "We've Come a Long Way Baby" (1978). Barbara Mandrell's breakthrough is "The Midnight Oil" (1973). Emmylou Harris's gold albums include *Elite Hotel* (1976) and *Luxury Liner* (1977). Dolly Parton tops country and pop charts in 1977 with "Here You Come Again," composed by Cynthia Weil and Barry Mann.

Folk and Protest Music: New albums include Joni Mitchell's *Blue* (1971) and *Court and Spark* (1974), Joan Baez's *Where Are You Now, My Son?* (1973) and *Diamonds and Rust* (1975), and Judy Collins's *Bread and Roses* (1976). In 1973 Bernice Johnson Reagon forms the all-woman a cappella group Sweet Honey in the Rock, which creates sermon-songs for civil rights and social justice.

Women's Music: Holly Near issues *Hang In There* (1973). Olivia Records, a woman-identified company formed in 1973, releases Meg Christian's *I Know You Know* (1975) and Cris Williamson's *The Changer and the Changed* (1975). The first National Women's Music Festival is in 1974.

Gospel: In 1970 Margaret Pleasant Douroux composes "I'm Glad" (one of many songs) and records *Revival from the Mount*. Shirley Caesar wins a 1971 Grammy for *Put Your Hand in the Hand of the Man from Galilee*.

Jazz/Rhythm and Blues: Mary Lou Williams premieres *Mary Lou Mass* (1971), with choreography by Alvin Ailey. Aretha Franklin wins 1972 Grammys in both rhythm and blues (for the album *Young, Gifted and Black*) and gospel (for the song "Amazing Grace"). Esther Philips's

On the Pop Charts

Diana Ross's first big hit as a solo singer is "Ain't No Mountain High Enough" (1970), written by Valerie Simpson and Nicholas Ashford. Simpson records her own solo album, Exposed, *in 1971. Janis Joplin's posthumous album,* Pearl, *comes out in 1971. Carole King's* Tapestry *(1971), with such songs as "I Feel the Earth Move," wins four Grammys and is the third best-selling album of the decade. Helen Reddy's "I Am Woman" earns her a 1972 Grammy. Bette Midler releases* The Divine Miss M *(1972) and is named best new artist. Roberta Flack is the first to win back-to-back Grammys for record of the year, with "Killing Me Softly with His Song" in 1973.* Imagination *(1973) by Gladys Knight and the Pips offers "Midnight Train to Georgia" and "I've Got to Use My Imagination." Patti LaBelle (Patricia Louise Holte) hits number one with "Lady Marmalade" (1974). Linda Ronstadt's album* Heart Like a Wheel *(1974) is her first million-seller. Releases in 1975 include Patti Smith's* Horses *and Janis Ian's* Between the Lines. *Natalie Cole is the best new artist of 1975. Debbie Harry is the lead singer for the punk– new wave group Blondie, which releases the albums* Blondie *and* Plastic Letters *in 1977. Dionne Warwick has two 1979 Grammy-winning songs: "I'll Never Love This Way Again" and "Déjà Vu."*

Oscars: 1970s

Best actress winners include Jane Fonda in Klute *(1971) and* Coming Home *(1978), Liza Minnelli in* Cabaret *(1972, screenplay by Jay Presson Allen), Ellen Burstyn in* Alice Doesn't Live Here Anymore *(1974), Louise Fletcher in* One Flew over the Cuckoo's Nest *(1975), Faye Dunaway in* Network *(1976), Diane Keaton (Diane Hall) in* Annie Hall *(1977), and Sally Field in* Norma Rae *(1979). Supporting actress winners include Helen Hayes in* Airport *(1970), Cloris Leachman in* The Last Picture Show *(1971), Eileen Heckart in* Butterflies Are Free *(1972), Tatum O'Neal in* Paper Moon *(1973), Lee Grant in* Shampoo *(1975), and Meryl Streep in* Kramer vs. Kramer *(1979). Julia Miller Phillips is the first woman producer to win an Academy Award, as coproducer of* The Sting *(1973); she later writes* You'll Never Eat Lunch in This Town Again *(1990), describing her Hollywood experiences.*

albums include *From a Whisper to a Scream* (1973) and *Alone Again (Naturally)* (1973). Toshiko Akiyoshi, her husband, Lew Tabackin, and band release *Kogun* in 1975. With the introduction of a jazz vocalist category, Ella Fitzgerald wins her first Grammys since 1962, in 1976 and 1979. The first Women's Jazz Festival, held in 1978 in Kansas City, Missouri, features such greats as Mary Lou Williams and Betty Carter; the New York festival also honors women jazz musicians in 1978 with a four-night program. Jazz instrumentalists in the 1970s include tenor saxophonist Willene Barton, trumpeter Clora Bryant, drummers Dottie Dodgson and Paula Hampton, and trombonist Melba Liston.

Latin: Celia Cruz, later called "Queen of Salsa," goes gold with her album *Celia and Johnny* (1974), with Johnny Pacheco.

Film Performances: Bette Davis is the first woman to be gain the American Film Institute's Lifetime Achievement Award, in 1977. Besides the Oscar winners (see sidebar), performances include Carrie Snodgress in *Diary of a Mad Housewife* (1970, screenplay by Eleanor Perry); Karen Black (Karen Ziegler) and Susan Anspach in *Five Easy Pieces* (1970, screenplay by Carole Eastman); Sally Kellerman as "Hot Lips" Houlihan in *M*A*S*H* (1970); Ali McGraw in *Love Story* (1970); Cloris Leachman, Ellen Burstyn, Cybill Shepherd, and Eileen Brennan in *The Last Picture Show* (1971); Jane Fonda in *Klute* (1971) and with British actress Vanessa Redgrave in *Julia* (1977, screenplay by Lillian Hellman); Joanne Woodward in *The Effect of Gamma Rays on Man-in-the-Moon Marigolds* (1971), a Cannes winner; Diana Sands in *Georgia, Georgia* (1971, screenplay by Maya Angelou); Ruth Gordon in *Harold and Maude* (1972); Cicely Tyson in *Sounder* (1972); Diana Ross as Billie Holiday in *Lady Sings the Blues* (1972, screenplay by Suzanne De Passe); Diane Keaton in Woody Allen's *Play It Again, Sam* (1972) and *Sleeper* (1973); Barbra Streisand in *The Way We Were* (1973); Shelley Duvall in *Thieves Like Us* (1974) and with Sissy (Mary Elizabeth) Spacek and Janice Rule in *Three Women* (1977), for which she wins the Cannes best actress award; Gena Rowlands in *A Woman Under the Influence* (1974); Diahann Carroll in *Claudine* (1974); Faye Dunaway in *Chinatown* (1974); Jodie (Alicia) Foster in *Taxi Driver* (1976); Carrie Fisher as Princess Leia in *Star Wars* (1977); Shirley MacLaine in *The Turning Point* (1977), with Anne Bancroft, and in *Being There* (1979); Meryl Streep in *The Deer Hunter* (1978); and Jill Clayburgh in *An Unmarried Woman* (1978), a Cannes winner.

"Being a woman is unexplored territory"
—Barbara Loden

Film Directing and Writing: Elaine May writes, directs, and stars in *A New Leaf* (1971); she also writes and directs *The Heartbreak Kid* (1972), starring her daughter, Jeannie Berlin. Barbara Loden (1932–80) writes, directs, and stars in *Wanda* (1971). The First International Festival of Women's Films takes place in New York in 1972, and the distribution company Women Make Movies forms. Claudia Weill and Joyce Chopra codirect *Joyce at 34* (1972) for public television. Weill also directs the breakthrough *Girlfriends* (1978), starring Melanie Mayron. Dancer Yvonne Rainer makes her first films: *Lives of Performers* (1972), *Film About a Woman Who . . .* (1975), and *Kristina Talking Pictures* (1976). Joan Micklin Silver directs *Hester Street* (1975), starring Carol Kane, and *Between the Lines* (1977), with Lindsay Crouse. Karen Arthur's first feature is *Legacy* (1975), followed by *The Mafu Cage* (1978), with Carol Kane and Lee Grant. Christine Choy, primarily a documentary filmmaker, directs such films as *From Spikes to Spindles* (1976) and *Inside Women Inside* (1978). Other films countering stereotypes of Asians include Renee Cho's *The New Wife* (1978) and Felicia Lowe's *China: Land of My Father* (1979). After writing the screenplays for such Robert Altman films as *Thieves Like Us* (1974) and *Nashville* (1975), Joan Tewkesbury directs her own film, *Old Boyfriends* (1979). Kathleen Collins (Prettyman, 1942–88) films *The Cruz Brothers and Miss Mallory* (1979). Writers nominated for Academy Awards include Gloria Katz, Jay Presson Allen, Nancy Dowd (whose story for *Coming Home* in 1978 wins), and Elaine May. Editors with Oscar nominations include Thelma Schoonmaker, Dorothy Spencer, Marcia Lucas, Dede Allen, Eve Newman, and Verna Fields (who wins for *Jaws* in 1975).

Dance: Tina Ramirez founds the Ballet Hispanico in New York in 1970. Judith Jamison performs *Cry* (1971), choreographed for her by Alvin Ailey to show the strength of African American women. Twyla Tharp creates *Eight Jelly Rolls* (1971) to Jelly Roll Morton's music; she choreographs *Deuce Coupe* (1973, to the Beach Boys' music) and *As Time Goes By* (1973) for the Joffrey Ballet and *Push Comes to Shove* (1976) for the American Ballet Theatre. Meredith Monk creates such performances as *Vessel* (1971, which moves to different locations), *Education of the Girl-child* (1973, see p. 337), and *Quarry* (1976). Other new works include Laura Dean's *Circle Dance* (1972) and *Spinning Dance* (1973); Trisha Brown's *Primary Accumulation* (1972) and *Locus* (1975); Yvonne Rainer's *Story of a Woman Who . . .* (1973), later translated into film; Elaine Summers's filmdances such as *Two Girls Downtown Iowa* (1973); Simone Forti's *Crawling* (1974), based on animal movements; Lucinda Childs's *Calico Mingling* (1974) and *Solo: Character on Three Diagonals* (1976), for the Philip Glass–Robert Wilson opera *Einstein on the Beach;* and Phoebe Neville's *Memory* (1975). Gelsey Kirkland debuts as Mikhail Baryshnikov's partner in 1974. Liz Lerman's new 1975 company ranges in age from 24 to 71. Yvonne Chouteau performs *Indian Trail of Tears* (1976) at the Kennedy Center in Washington, D.C. Pearl Primus choreographs *Michael Row Your Boat Ashore* (1979). Throughout the decade Kei Takei adds new parts with each performance of *Light*.

1980–89

Theater: Marta Montañez Istomin is named artistic director of the Kennedy Center for the Performing Arts in Washington, D.C., at the start of the 1980s. Beth Henley's Pulitzer Prize winner, *Crimes of the*

(1973, see p. 337)

Television: 1970s

Mary Tyler Moore stars in her own show beginning in 1970. The Pearl Bailey Show starts in 1971. Beatrice Arthur premieres in the series Maude (1972). Lin Bolen is the first woman in charge of daytime programming at a major network (NBC), in 1972. Marlo Thomas creates the Emmy-winning children's special Free to Be . . . You and Me (1974). Cicely Tyson wins Emmys for her performance in the TV movie The Autobiography of Miss Jane Pittman (1974), recounting a 110-year-old woman's transition from slavery to civil rights. Mary Hartman, Mary Hartman premieres in 1976, with Louise Lasser in the title role and Mary Kay Place as Loretta Hagers. Lynda Córdoba Carter stars in the new Wonder Woman series (1976). Comedian Gilda Radner (1946–89) earns an Emmy in the 1977–78 season for her work on Saturday Night Live.

Performance: 1980s

Theodora Skipitares's puppet-theater musicals include Micropolis *(1982) and* Defenders of the Code *(1987). Laurie Anderson performs her seven-hour musical-visual theater piece* United States, Parts I–IV *at the Brooklyn Academy of Music's New Wave Festival in 1983; other works include* Talk Normal *(1987) and* Empty Places *(1989). Holly Hughes writes and enacts the humorous* The Well of Horniness *(1983) and* Lady Dick *(1985), about lesbian sexuality. Composer Diamanda Galás begins her* Plague Mass *project in 1984. Jessica Hagedorn, Laurie Carlos, and Robbie McCauley perform together and also individually; McCauley's pieces, for example, include* My Father and the Wars *(1985) and* Indian Blood *(1988). Julie Taymor creates her Obie-winning* Juan Darién: A Carnival Mass *(1988), a theater-opera piece using actors and puppets, in collaboration with composer Elliot Goldenthal. Karen Finley's* The Constant State of Desire *(1988) provokes controversy by promoting female sexuality, and in 1990 the National Endowment for the Arts revokes grants to four solo performers, including Finley and Holly Hughes (they fight in court to get the grants restored). For a few more of the many women in performance, see dance/theater forms and "Art."*

Heart (1981), features Mia Dillon, Holly Hunter, and Lizbeth Mackay. Lois Weaver, Peggy Shaw, and Deb Margolin form the performing group Split Britches in 1981; Weaver and Shaw found the East Village performance venue the WOW cafe in 1982. Elizabeth Ashley, Geraldine Page, and Amanda Plummer star in *Agnes of God* (1982). Ellen Burstyn is the first woman president of Actors' Equity in its 60 years, in 1982. Susan Cooper and Hume Cronyn's *Foxfire* (1982) showcases Cronyn and Jessica Tandy, who wins a Tony. New women's plays in 1983 include Tina Howe's *Painting Churches*, with Marian Seldes and Frances Conroy; Marsha Norman's *'night Mother* with Kathy Bates and Anne Pitoniak, and Wendy Wasserstein's *Isn't It Romantic?* with Lisa Banes and Betty Comden. Whoopi Goldberg (Caryn Johnson) gives a one-woman comedy performance on Broadway in 1984. Glenn Close and Christine Baranski win Tonys in *The Real Thing* (1984); Theresa Merritt stars in *Ma Rainey's Black Bottom* (1984).The only two women directing on Broadway in the 1985–86 season are two playwrights: Emily Mann with her *Execution of Justice* and Jane Wagner with her *The Search for Signs of Intelligent Life in the Universe*, starring Lily Tomlin, who wins a Tony. Off-Broadway, Beth Henley's *The Miss Firecracker Contest* (1984) stars Holly Hunter. María Irene Fornes wins Obies for several plays, including *The Conduct of Life* (1985) and *Abbingdon Square* (1987); other Obies go to Roslyn Dresler's *Transients Welcome* and Lee Nagrin's *Bird/Bear* (1985). Linda Hunt and Kathryn Posson star in *Aunt Dan and Lemon* (1985), and Glenn Close and Mary Beth Hurt in *Benefactors* (1985). Women's theater groups at Boston's 1986 Women in Theater Festival include Thunder Thighs of Baltimore, At the Foot of the Mountain from Minneapolis, and Spiderwoman Theater from New York. In 1986 Tony winner Swoosie Kurtz and Stockard Channing are in *The House of Blue Leaves*, Tony winner Linda Lavin and Phyllis Newman in *Broadway Bound*, Annette Bening and Rosemary Murphy in Tina Howe's *Coastal Disturbances*, and Australian-born Zoë Caldwell in *Lillian*, a one-woman show drawing on Lillian Hellman's autobiographies. Judy Narita stages her one-woman show *Coming into Passion: Song for a Sansei* (1987) in Los Angeles. In New York in 1987 Tony winner Joan Allen stars in *Burn This*, and Lindsay Duncan in *Les Liaisons Dangereuses* (1987). In 1988 Wendy Wasserstein's Pulitzer Prize winner, *The Heidi Chronicles*, starring Joan Allen, opens; Wasserstein is the first woman to win a Tony for an original play (Frances Goodrich won as coauthor of the adaptation *The Diary of Anne Frank*). Writer-director Anne Bogart's many new environmental theater pieces include the Obie-winning *No Plays No Poetry . . .* (1988). Two major women directors during the decade are JoAnne Akalaitis, who wins a 1983–84 Obie for directing *Through the Leaves*, and Elizabeth LeCompte, who mounts innovative and controversial pieces with the Wooster Group.

Dance/Theater Forms: Meredith Monk's *Specimen Days* (1981) and *Turtle Dreams* (1983) combine dance and vocal music. Martha Clarke, a former dancer with Pilobolus, creates her highly acclaimed *The Garden of Earthly Delights* (1984) and her Obie-winning *Vienna: Lusthaus.*

Musicals: Tammy Grimes and Wanda Richert star in *42nd Street* (1980). *Lena Horne: The Lady and Her Music* (1981) breaks records for the longest-running one-woman Broadway show and wins a special Tony. Lauren Bacall and Marilyn Cooper earn Tonys in *Woman of the Year* (1981), as does Jennifer Holliday in *Dreamgirls* (1981). Tony-winning Chita Rivera and Liza Minnelli are in *The Rink* (1984). Bernadette Peters stars in *Sunday in the Park with George* (1984), *Song & Dance*, earning a Tony, and in *Into the Woods* (1987). Debbie Allen is in *Sweet Charity* (1986), with lyrics coauthored by Dorothy Fields. Ruth Brown receives a Tony for her performance in *Black and Blue* (1989), which also features Linda Hopkins and Carrie Smith.

Opera: After singing for 10 years in Europe, soprano Jessye Norman has her U.S. debuts in Stravinsky's *Oedipus Rex* and Purcell's *Dido and Aeneas* at the Opera Company of Philadelphia in 1982; the following year she debuts at the Met. Thea Musgrave composes *Mary, Queen of Scots*, which is performed by the New York City Opera in 1981; she also creates *Harriet, the Woman Called Moses* (1984). In the Grammy-winning filmed opera *Carmen* (1984), Julia Migenes Johnson sings the title role opposite Placido Domingo.

Classical and Experimental Music: In 1980 Miriam Abrams cofounds the Bay Area Women's Philharmonic. Joan Tower composes the orchestral pieces *Sequoia* (1981) and *Silver Ladders* (1986). After Ellen Taaffe Zwillich's Symphony No. 1 is premiered by the American Composers Orchestra in 1982, she is the first woman to receive the Pulitzer Prize for music, in 1983. Shulamit Ran composes her *Amichai Songs* (1985). The Kennedy Center mounts a concert of Pauline Oliveros's works in 1985; she later composes *Portrait of Quintet of the Americas* (1988). Judith Lang Zaimont creates the orchestral work *Chroma: Northern Lights* (1986). Barbara Kolb composes the award-winning *Millefoglie* (1987). In 1987 composer Daria Semegen is the first woman to receive the McKim Commission from the Library of Congress, for *Music for Violin and Piano*. Deborah Borda is the first woman executive director of a major U.S. orchestra, the Detroit Symphony, in 1989; in 1991 she becomes managing director of the New York Philharmonic.

Gospel: Shirley Caesar records the Grammy-winning *Rejoice* (1980). Tramaine Hawkins's albums include *Determined* (1983) and *The Joy That Flooded My Soul* (1988). Amy Grant wins her fourth straight Grammy in 1985 with *Unguarded*.

Country: Roseanne Cash's albums include *Seven Year Ache* (1981) and *King's Record Shop* (1987). In 1984 Naomi (Diana Ellen) Judd and her daughter, Wynonna, win the first of three straight Grammys for best country performance by a duo, with "Mama He's Crazy." Dolly Parton, Linda Ronstadt, and Emmylou Harris release the Grammy-winning album *Trio* (1987). Mary-Chapin Carpenter's album *State of the Heart* (1989) has several hits, including "Never Had It So Good."

Jazz/Rhythm and Blues: Pianists Barbara Carroll, Hazel Scott, and Rose

New Singers: 1980s

Some rising new stars are:

—*Pat Benatar, who wins her fourth rock Grammy in a row with "Love Is a Battlefield" (1983).*

—*Cyndi Lauper, best new Grammy artist in 1984, with her album* She's So Unusual.

—*Madonna (Ciccone), who hits number one in 1984 with "Like a Virgin"; her new album also includes "Material Girl."*

—*Drummer-singer Sheila E. (Sheila Escovedo), with her gold album,* The Glamorous Life *(1984).*

—*Whitney Houston, 1985 Grammy pop vocalist, with "Saving All My Love for You."*

—*Janet Jackson, with five hits on* Control *(1986) and seven on* Rhythm Nation 1814 *(1989).*

—*Salt-N-Pepa (Cheryl James and Sandra Denton), with* Hot, Cool and Vicious *(1986).*

—*Suzanne Vega, with the hit "Luka" on her album* Solitude Standing *(1987).*

—*Tracy Chapman, best new Grammy artist in 1988, with such politically charged songs as "Talkin' 'bout a Revolution."*

—*The Indigo Girls (Amy Ray and Emily Saliers), 1989 Grammy winners for their album* Indigo Girls, *with "Blood and Fire."*

—*Paula Abdul, with her top-selling* Forever Your Girl *(1988).*

—*Michelle Shocked, with* Short Sharp Shocked *(1988).*

—*Queen Latifah (Dana Owens), with her first rap album,* All Hail the Queen *(1989).*

Best actress winners are Sissy Spacek as Loretta Lynn in Coal Miner's Daughter *(1980), Katharine Hepburn—for her fourth Oscar— in* On Golden Pond *(1981), Meryl Streep in* Sophie's Choice *(1982); Shirley MacLaine in* Terms of Endearment *(1983); Sally Field in* Places in the Heart *(1984), Geraldine Page in* The Trip to Bountiful *(1985), Marlee Matlin in* Children of a Lesser God *(1986), Cher in* Moonstruck *(1987), Jodie Foster in* The Accused *(1988), and Jessica Tandy in* Driving Miss Daisy *(1989). Supporting actresses include Mary Steenburgen in* Melvin and Howard *(1980), Maureen Stapleton as Emma Goldman in* Reds *(1981), Jessica Lange in* Tootsie *(1982), Linda Hunt as a man in* The Year of Living Dangerously *(1983), Anjelica Huston in* Prizzi's Honor *(1985), Dianne Wiest in* Hannah and Her Sisters *(1986), Olympia Dukakis in* Moonstruck *(1987), and Geena Davis in* The Accidental Tourist *(1988). Editing awards go to Thelma Schoonmaker for* Raging Bull *(1980) and Claire Simpson for* Platoon *(1986). Buffy Sainte-Marie shares an Oscar for composing "Up Where We Belong" for* An Officer and a Gentleman *(1982), and Irene Cara shares an Oscar for the lyrics of "Flashdance . . . What a Feeling" (1983), for which she also wins a Grammy as best pop vocalist of the year.*

Murphy, with trombonist Melba Liston leading a big band, play Mary Lou Williams's compositions at a 1981 memorial tribute at New York's Town Hall. Ella Fitzgerald records the Grammy-winning *The Best Is Yet to Come* (1983). Toshiko Akiyoshi forms her own orchestra in 1984. Aretha Franklin records "Sisters Are Doin' It for Themselves" (1985) with British rock star Annie Lennox and wins a Grammy with *Aretha* (1981). Anita Baker's Grammy winners are *Rapture* (1986) and *Giving You the Best That I Got* (1989). Singer and pianist Shirley Horn releases *I Thought about You: Live at Vine Street* (1986). Betty Carter gains her first Grammy with *Look What I Got!* (1988); she also records duets with another legendary jazz diva, Carmen McRae, in 1988.

Other Music: Yoko Ono and John Lennon's *Double Fantasy* wins the Grammy for album of 1981. Lena Horne is Grammy pop vocalist for 1981. Performance artist Laurie Anderson's "O Superman" (1981) is a pop hit. In 1981 Diana Ross releases the album *Why Do Fools Fall in Love?* and leaps to number one on the charts with "My Endless Love," a duet with Lionel Richie. Tina Turner makes her comeback with *Private Dancer* (1984), which includes the hit "What's Love Got to Do with It?" Holly Near and folk singer Ronnie Gilbert release the live album *Lifeline* (1984). Vikki Carr gains a Grammy for *Simplemente Mujer* (1985). Linda Ronstadt's *Canciones de mi padre* wins a 1988 Grammy for best Mexican American performance. With her comeback album *Nick of Time* (1989), Bonnie Raitt garners four Grammys.

Film Industry: Sherry Lansing is the first woman president of a major Hollywood studio, at Twentieth Century Fox, in 1980. She helps produce such films as *Fatal Attraction* (1987) and *The Accused* (1988). Suzanne de Passe, president of Motown Productions in 1981, handles the visual end of the business. Dawn Steel is named president of Columbia Pictures in 1987 but leaves in 1990.

In a 1980 report the Women's Committee of the Directors Guild reveals that in the major studios women directed only 14 films in the last 30 years. On television only 115 of 65,500 hours of prime-time drama were directed by women, and a third of that was by Ida Lupino.

Several women are behind the success of *E.T., the Extra-Terrestrial* in 1982: Kathleen Kennedy is coproducer; Melissa Mathison writes the script; and Carol Littleton edits the film.

Film Performances: Mia Farrow's films with Woody Allen include *Zelig* (1983), *The Purple Rose of Cairo* (1985), and *Hannah and Her Sisters* (1986), also featuring Dianne Wiest, Barbara Hershey, and Carrie Fisher. Barbara Hershey is the first actress to earn back-to-back best actress awards at the Cannes Film Festival, for *Shy People* (1987) and *A World Apart* (1988).

Other films include Jane Fonda, Lily Tomlin, and Dolly Parton in *9 to 5* (1980, with the title song by Dolly Parton); Goldie Hawn in *Private Benjamin* (1980); Eva Le Gallienne and Ellen Burstyn in *Resurrection* (1980); Bette Midler in *The Rose* (1980); Lee Remick, Colleen Dewhurst, and Patty Duke in *The Women's Room* (1980, based on Marilyn French's novel); Meryl Streep in *The French Lieutenant's Woman* (1981), with Cher in *Silkwood* (1984, screenplay by Nora Ephron and Alice Arlen), in *Out of Africa* (1985), and in *A Cry in the Dark* (1989), a Cannes winner; Diane Keaton as Louise Bryant in *Reds* (1981); Sally Field in *Absence of Malice* (1981); Glenn Close with Mary Beth Hurt in *The World According to Garp* (1982) and in *Fatal Attraction* (1987); Sissy Spacek in *Missing* (1982); Mariel Hemingway and Patrice Donnelly in *Personal Best* (1982); Debra Winger in *An Officer and a Gentleman* (1982) and *Terms of Endearment* (1983); Jessica Lange in *Frances* (1983), based on the life of actress Frances Farmer; Jennifer Beals in *Flashdance* (1983); Whoopi Goldberg, Oprah Winfrey, Margaret Avery, and Darcy Glover in *The Color Purple* (1985, based on Alice Walker's novel); Kathleen Turner in *Romancing the Stone* (1984) and *Prizzi's Honor* (1985); Cher in *Mask* (1985), a Cannes winner; Kelly McGillis in *Witness* (1985); Elizabeth Peña in *Crossover Dreams* (1985); Tracy Camila Johns as Nora Darling in *She's Gotta Have It* (1986); Italian-born Isabella Rossellini in *Blue Velvet* (1986); Sigourney Weaver in *Aliens* (1986), as Dian Fossey in *Gorillas in the Mist* (1987), and with Melanie Griffith and Joan Cusack in *Working Girl* (1988); Lillian Gish and Bette Davis in *The Whales of August* (1987); Anjelica Huston in *The Dead* (1987), directed by her father, John Huston, and with Lena Olin in *Enemies, A Love Story* (1989); Lindsay Crouse in *House of Games* (1987), Holly Hunter in *Broadcast News* and *Raising Arizona* (both 1987); Christine Lahti in *Housekeeping* (1987) and *Running on Empty* (1988); Susan Sarandon (Susan Tomaling) in *Bull Durham* (1988); Michelle Pfeiffer in *The Fabulous Baker Boys* (1989); Ellen Barkin in *Sea of Love* (1989); Meg Ryan in *When Harry Met Sally . . .* (1989, screenplay by Nora Ephron); Rosie Perez in *Do the Right Thing* (1989); Andie (Rose Anderson) MacDowell in *sex, lies and videotape* (1989); and Julia Roberts, Sally Field, Shirley MacLaine, Daryl Hannah, and Dolly Parton in *Steel Magnolias* (1989).

Film Directing and Writing: Claudia Weill directs *It's My Turn* (1980), starring Jill Clayburgh. Yvonne Rainer's films include *Journeys from Berlin* (1980) and *The Man Who Envied Women* (1985). Christine Choy films *To Love Honor and Obey* (1980; see also p. 303). Actress Lee Grant directs *Tell Me a Riddle* (1980, based on a Tillie Olsen story), and *Staying Together* (1989), as well as documentaries. Joan Tewkesbury writes and directs such TV dramas as *The Acorn People* (1980). Joan Micklin Silver's new films include *Head over Heels* (1981, a rerelease of an earlier film, based on a book by Ann Beattie) and *Crossing Delancey* (1988), starring Amy Irving. Director Susan Seidelman gains attention with *Smithereens* (1982), the first independent U.S. film in competition at the Cannes Film Festival; her next films include *Desperately Seeking Susan* (1985), with Rosanna Arquette and Madonna; *Making Mr. Right* (1987), with Ann Magnuson; and *She-Devil* (1989). Julie Dash directs the acclaimed short film *Illusions* (1982). Amy Heckerling directs *Fast Times at Ridgemont High* (1982). Kathleen Collins's films include *Losing Ground* (1982) and *Gouldtown: A Mulatto Settlement* (1988),

Dance: 1980s

Lucinda Childs, Simone Forti, Elaine Summers, and other dancers of the 1970s continue to create important new works in the 1980s. Twyla Tharp, for example, choreographs The Catherine Wheel *(1981). Trisha Brown creates* Set and Reset *(1983) and collaborates with artist Nancy Graves and Beverly Emmons on* Lateral Pass *(1985); Laura Dean works with composer Steve Reich on* Impact *and* Force Field *in the mid-1980s. Anna Halprin creates* Circle the Earth *(1987), a planetary dance involving people in 37 countries. "It is necessary for art to express visions that political systems resist," she insists.*

In 1984 the Bessie Awards for dance and performance are established in honor of dance teacher Bessie Schönberg. Choreographers who receive awards include Yoshiko Chuma and her School of Hard Knocks, Stephanie Skura, Susan Marshall, Susan Rethorst, Molissa Fenley, Dana Reitz, and Bebe Miller. Other choreography of note includes Blondell Cummings's Chicken Soup *(1984) and Judith Jamison's* Divining *(1984).*

Among the first dancers singled out for Bessies are Sara Rudner and Valda Setterfield. In ballet one of the new performers is Darci Kistler, who becomes a principal dancer at the New York City Ballet in 1982.

about an African American woman's roots. Lynne Litman directs *Testament* (1983), starring Jane Alexander. Barbra Streisand directs and stars in *Yentl* (1983), which also features Amy Irving. Director Lizzie Borden's films include *Born in Flames* (1983), a feminist fantasy, and *Working Girls* (1986). Donna Deitch films *Desert Hearts* (1985), the first woman-directed lesbian love story with mainstream distribution. Joyce Chopra directs *Smooth Talk* (1985, based on a Joyce Carol Oates story). Penny Marshall, who once played Laverne on TV's *Laverne and Shirley*, directs *Jumpin' Jack Flash* (1986), with Whoopi Goldberg, and *Big* (1988). Randa Haines directs *Children of a Lesser God* (1986), starring Marlee Matlin—a film nominated for best picture Oscar. Martinique filmmaker Euzhan Palcy is the first black woman to direct a Hollywood film: *A Dry White Season* (1989), starring Susan Sarandon.

1990–95

Theater: A few of the many new works by women include Suzan-Lori Parks's *Imperceptible Mutabilities in the Third Kingdom* (1990), directed by Liz Diamond; *The Kathy and Mo Show: Parallel Lives* (1990), by comedians Kathy Najimy and Mo Gaffney; Paula Vogel's *The Baltimore Waltz* (1991), directed by Anne Bogart; Wendy Wasserstein's *The Sisters Rosensweig* (1992), starring Jane Alexander, Madeline Kahn, and Frances McDormand; Deb Margolin's *Lesbians Who Kill* (1992), performed by Lois Weaver and Peggy Shaw; Anna Deveare Smith's *Fires in the Mirror* (1992), in which she performs different characters, drawing on interviews with African Americans and Jews in Brooklyn, and *Twilight: Los Angeles 1992* (1994), which earns an Obie and a special New York Drama Critics' Circle award; Claudia Shear's autobiographical *Blown Sideways Through Life* (1993), which she performs; Cheryl L. West's *Holiday Heart* (1995), and Emily Mann's *Having Our Say* (1995, based on the book by Sarah L. and A. Elizabeth Delany), starring Mary Alice and Gloria Foster. In 1995 the Signature Theater Company begins a year-long production of Adrienne Kennedy's plays. Some of the award-winning performances include Ruth Maleczech playing Lear in a role-reversed *Lear* (1990), Stockard Channing in *Six Degrees of Separation* (1990), Eileen Atkins in *A Room of One's Own* (1990) and *Vita and Virginia* (1994), Mercedes Ruehl and Irene Worth in *Lost in Yonkers* (1991), Sarah Jessica Parker in *The Substance of Fire* (1991), and Glenn Close in *Death and the Maiden* (1992).

Performance: A few of the many new works are Robbie McCauley's Obie-winning *Sally's Rape* (1990), Karen Finley's *We Keep Our Victims Ready* (1990), Sandra Bernhard's film of her one-woman show, *Without You I'm Nothing* (1990), Diamanda Galás's *Vena cava* (1991), Laurie Anderson's *Voices from Beyond* (1991) and *Nerve Bible* (1995), Alyson Pou's *To Us at Twilight* (1993), Laurie Carlos's *White Chocolate* (1993), Rhodessa Jones and Idris Ackamoor's *Big Butt Girls, Hard-Headed Women* (1993), and Theodora Skipitares's *Under the Knife* (1994).

Musicals: Marsha Norman writes the Tony Award–winning book and lyrics and Lucy Simon the music for *The Secret Garden* (1991), starring

Daisy Eagan. Betty Comden coauthors the lyrics for *The Will Rogers Follies* (1991). Susan Birkenhead writes the lyrics for *Jelly's Last Jam* (1992), starring Tonya Pinkins. Jodi Benson stars in *Crazy for You* (1992); Chita Rivera in *The Kiss of the Spider Woman* (1993), winning a Tony; and Glenn Close in *Sunset Boulevard* (1994), earning a Tony.

Opera: Renée Fleming debuts at the Met in 1991. Meredith Monk creates the dance/opera *Atlas* (1991) for the Houston Grand Opera. Thea Musgrave composes *Simon Bolívar* (1992). Libby Brown Larsen's *Mrs. Dalloway* (1993) is performed in Cleveland. Poet June Jordan writes the libretto for John Adams's *I Was Looking at the Ceiling and Then I Saw the Sky* (1995).

Classical and New Music: Christine Berl's *Lord of the Dance* (1991) is commissioned and performed by Peter Serkin. Shulamit Ran receives the 1991 Pulitzer for her Symphony (1989–90), commissioned by the Philadelphia Orchestra. Joelle Wallach's *The Tiger's Tail* (1991) wins a National Orchestral Association award. Ellen Taaffe Zwillich composes her Symphony No. 3 (1992) for the New York Philharmonic's 150th anniversary. Pauline Oliveros creates *Nzinga, the Queen King* (1993), a theater piece.

Academy Awards: Best actress winners include Kathy Bates in *Misery* (1990), Jodie Foster in *The Silence of the Lambs* (1991), Holly Hunter in *The Piano* (1993), and Jessica Lange in *Blue Sky* (1994). Best supporting actresses include Whoopi Goldberg in *Ghost* (1990), Mercedes Ruehl in *The Fisher King* (1991), Marisa Tomei in *My Cousin Vinny* (1992), and Dianne Wiest in *Bullets over Broadway* (1994)

Film Performances: The 1990s bring a number of women's ensemble films, from the buddy film *Thelma & Louise* (1991), with Geena Davis and Susan Sarandon, to *Fried Green Tomatoes* (1992), with Jessica Tandy, Kathy Bates, Mary Stuart Masterson, and Mary-Louise Parker; *The Joy Luck Club* (1993, screenplay cowritten by Amy Tan), with Ming-Na Wen, Kieu Chinh, Tamlyn Tomita, Rosalind Chao, Franie Nuyen, Lisa Lu, and Lauren Tom; Australian director Gillian Armstrong's *Little Women* (1994), with Winona Ryder, Susan Sarandon, Trini Alvarado, Claire Danes, Samantha Mathis, and Kirsten Dunst; Australian director Jocelyn Moorhouse's *How to Make an American Quilt* (1995), with Winona Ryder, Anne Bancroft, Ellen Burstyn, Kate Nelligan, and Alfre Woodard; and several others.

Additional performances include Anjelica Huston and Annette Bening in *The Grifters* (1990); Demi Moore in *Ghost* (1990); Joanne Woodward in *Mr. and Mrs. Bridge* (1990); Julia Roberts in *Pretty Woman* (1990); Michelle Pfeiffer in *Frankie and Johnny* (1991) and with Winona Ryder in *The Age of Innocence* (1993); Mary McDonnell and Alfre Woodard in *Passion Fish* (1992); Susan Sarandon in *Lorenzo's Oil* (1992) and *The Client* (1994); Sharon Stone in *Basic Instinct* (1992); Whoopi Goldberg in *Sister Act* and *Sarafina!* (both 1992); Whitney Houston in *The Bodyguard* (1992) and with Angela Bassett in *Waiting*

Singers: 1990s

At the Grammys: *Mariah Carey is the 1990 best new artist, with her hit "Vision of Love"; she also wins a 1994 award for* Music Box. *Anita Baker's* Composition *and Ella Fitzgerald's* All That Jazz *are both 1990 winners. Natalie Cole's multiple-winning album* Unforgettable *(1991) includes a remixed duet of the title song, with her father, Nat "King" Cole. Vikki Carr earns a Latin pop award for* Cosas del amor *(1991). Linda Ronstadt wins both tropical Latin and Mexican American categories for 1992. Shirley Caesar is a gospel winner in 1992 and 1993. With "Ain't It Heavy," Melissa Etheridge is top 1992 rock vocalist. Cuban-born Gloria Estefan has the best tropical Latin album with* Mi Tierra, *and Selena (1973–95) the best Mexican American album with* Live *(both 1993); Selena's crossover album,* Dreaming of You, *is released after her murder in 1995. The best new artist of 1993 is Toni Braxton and of 1994 Sheryl Crow. The only rappers to receive 1994 awards are Queen Latifah and Salt-N-Pepa.*

Among the new voices are Liz Phair, Tori Amos, and rapper Sister Souljah. Country singer Wynonna Judd releases her first solo album in 1992, after a farewell tour singing with her mother, Naomi. Reba McEntire gains stature with her award-winning album My Kind of Country *(1994).*

Dance: 1990s

Judith Jamison becomes director of the Alvin Ailey American Dance Theater in 1990. In her 1993 autobiography, Dancing Spirit, she writes, "Choreography is a reciprocal moment in the studio . . . an exchange of spirit."

Among the choreographers who receive Bessie awards are Marta Renzi for Vital Signs and Urban Bush Women for their collective work in 1992, as well as Yvonne Meier for The Shining and Sally Silvers for Small Room in 1993. Urban Bush Women are also honored with a Capezio Dance Award in 1994, as are Katherine Dunham and Darci Kistler earlier, in 1991. Susan Marshall presents Spectators at an Event (1994). In 1995 Trisha Brown debuts her large-scale work M.O., choreographed to Bach's music; Jane Comfort presents S/He; Paula Josa-Jones premieres Wonderland; Elisa Monte debuts New York Moonglow, and Twyla Tharp presents Twyla Tharp Red White & Blues.

A dancer to watch is Paloma Herrera, who becomes a principal dancer at the American Ballet Theatre in 1995.

to Exhale (1995, based on Terry McMillan's novel); Basset also as Tina Turner in What's Love Got to Do with It? (1993); Debra Winger in A Dangerous Woman and Shadowlands (both 1993); Isabella Rossellini and Rosie Perez in Fearless (1993); Jodie Foster in Nell (1994), Jamie Lee Curtis in True Lies (1994); Uma Thurman in Pulp Fiction (1994); Jennifer Jason Leigh as Dorothy Parker in Mrs. Parker and the Vicious Circle (1994) and with Mare Winningham in Georgia (1995); Linda (Chlorinda) Fiorentino in The Last Seduction (1994); Sandra Bullock in While You Were Sleeping (1995); Marisa Tomei, Angelica Huston, and Trini Alvarado in Indian-born Mira Nair's The Perez Family (1995); Meryl Streep in The Bridges of Madison County (1995); Patricia Arquette in Beyond Ragoon (1995); plus performances in films by women (below).

Film Directing: The many new films directed by women include Lee Grant's No Place Like Home (1990); Ruby Oliver's Love Your Mama (1990); Jodie Foster's Little Man Tate (1990), in which she stars, as well as her Home for the Holidays (1995), with Holly Hunter and Anne Bancroft; Kathryn Bigelow's Blue Steel (1990), with Jamie Lee Curtis, and Strange Days (1995), with Angela Bassett and Juliette Lewis; Barbra Streisand's Prince of Tides (1991), in which she stars; Martha Coolidge's Rambling Rose (1991), starring Laura Dern and Dern's mother, Diane Ladd, and Three Wishes (1995), with Mary Elizabeth Mastroantonio; Nancy Savoca's Dogfight (1991); Penny Marshall's Awakenings (1991) and A League of Their Own (1992), with Geena Davis, Lori Petty, and Madonna; Julie Dash's Daughters of the Dust (1991), set on Ibo Island off the coast of South Carolina in 1902; Allison Anders's Gas Food Lodging (1992); Camille Billops's Finding Christa (1992), which wins the Grand Jury Prize for best documentary at the Sundance Film Festival; Leslie Harris's Just Another Girl on the IRT (1993); Nora Ephron's This Is My Life (1992, screenplay cowritten by Nora and Delia Ephron), starring Julie Kavner, and Sleepless in Seattle (1993), with Meg Ryan; Maggie Greenwald's The Ballad of Little Jo (1993), with Suzy Amis; Maria Maggenti's The Incredibly True Adventure of Two Girls in Love (1994), with Laure Holloman and Nicole Parker; Rose Troche's Go Fish (1994); Darnell Martin's I Like It Like That (1994), starring Lauren Vélez; Amy Heckerling's Clueless (1995), starring Alicia Silverstone; and Diane Keaton's Unstrung Heroes (1995), with Andy McDowell.

Television: The early 1990s bring Linda Bloodworth-Thomason's Designing Women and Diane English's Love and War. In 1991–92 the two most popular programs after 60 Minutes are Roseanne and Murphy Brown. Women have the top four talkshows in 1994: Oprah Winfrey, Ricki Lake, Jenny Jones, and Sally Jessy Raphael. Standup comic Margaret Cho is the first Asian American to have a sitcom, All-American Girl, on prime-time national television (ABC), in 1994; also in 1994 Claire Danes debuts in My So-Called Life. Judy McGrath becomes MTV president in 1994.

Visual Arts and Design

Nampeyo, a major potter from the Hopi-Tewa pueblo of Hano in the early 1900s (photo by Edward Curtis, Library of Congress)

The First Artists

Baskets woven by Native American women are one of the first art forms, made as early as 9,000 B.C. Before the Spaniards arrive in the Southwest in 1540, women have developed the wicker, plaiting, and coil techniques; they also create geometric and symbolic designs. Pottery by women also dates back thousands of years, with most traditional techniques in place before Columbus. Pueblo women are especially noted for their pots, which incorporate a variety of painted designs. Women also design and build their homes. Ojibwa women not only cut the poles for their wigwams, but also decorate them with colorfully dyed reed mats. Plains women erect the poles for their tipis and create the skin coverings, embroidering them with dyed porcupine and bird quills.

The first known white artist is Henrietta Deering Johnston, who paints pastel portraits in Charleston, South Carolina (1707–20). The Ephrata Sisterhood (p. 199) creates ornate illuminated manuscripts in the 1730s. Other women do needlework painting. A miniature painter in the 1770s is Hetty Sage Benbridge in Philadelphia and then South Carolina. Patience Lovell Wright (1725–86), creates wax portraits in the 1770s, predating Mme. Tussaud. Wright travels to England in 1772 and is believed to have sent information to Revolutionary leaders concealed in her wax figures.

1800–49

Pima, Papago, and western Apache women are expert basketmakers in the 1800s. Navajo women weave their classic blankets from the early 1800s. Plains women add glass beads to their quill embroidery, decorating tipis, clothing, cradleboards, and the like. White women hold quilting bees and do needle paintings. Self-taught watercolorists Eunice Griswold Pinney and Mary Ann Wilson paint around 1810; in the 1820s Ruth Henshaw Bascom creates pastel profile portraits from her sitters' shadows. Top professional artists are sisters Anna Claypoole Peale (1791–1878), Margaretta Angelica Peale (1795–1882), and Sarah Miriam Peale (1800–85). Anna, a miniaturist, exhibits in the first show of the Pennsylvania Academy of Fine Arts in Philadelphia in 1811; she and Sarah are elected members in 1824. Moving to Baltimore in 1831, Sarah is in demand for oil portraits of Lafayette and others. Margaretta specializes in still lifes. In Boston, Sarah Goodridge (1788–1853) paints a miniature of Gilbert Stuart in 1825 and shows regularly. Anne Hall (1792–1863), a miniaturist, is the first woman elected to the year-old National Academy of Design, in 1827, becoming a full member in 1833. In the 1830s Maria Martin (1796–1863) paints plants and insects as backgrounds for John James Audubon's birds. An early cartoonist is Miriam Berry (later Whitcher, 1811–52), who pokes fun at women's "airs" in *Godey's Ladies Book* from 1847 on. Emphasizing industrial arts, Sarah Worthington Peter (1800–77) begins the Philadelphia School of Design (later Moore College of Art and Design) in her home in 1848.

1850–99

Painters/Printmakers: Two popular artists from the 1850s on are Frances ("Fanny") Bond Palmer (1812–76), a lithographer of landscapes for Nathaniel Currier's firm (later Currier & Ives), and Lilly Martin Spencer (1822–1902), whose genre and narrative paintings are engraved for magazines and sold as reproductions. In the 1860s Maria Louisa Wagner (c. 1815–88) is noted for her still lifes. Academic painter Elizabeth Gardner (later Bouguereau, 1837–1922) is the first U.S. woman to exhibit in the Paris Salon, in 1866. In the 1870s Fidelia Bridges shows watercolor closeups of grasses and flowers; Imogene Robinson Morrell does history paintings; Anna Elizabeth Hardy exhibits still lifes; Eliza Pratt Greatorex etches views of old New York; Charlotte Buell Coman and Annie Cornelia Shaw exhibit Barbizon-style landscapes; Cornelia Strong Fassett fits 260 politicians in *The Electoral Commission in Open Session* (1879); and portraitist Susan Macdowell Eakins paints *Two Sisters* (1879). Mary Cassatt (1844–1926) shows with the Impressionists (1879–86), with such works as *Mother about to Wash Her Sleepy Child* (1880). In the 1880s Jennie Brownscombe (1850–1936) is a popular illustrator; Mary Nimmo Moran (1842–99) is the top landscape etcher; Cecilia Beaux (1855–1942) shows her prize-winning *Les Derniers jours d'enfance (The Last Days of Childhood)* at the Pennsylvania Academy in 1885; and Ann Elizabeth Klumpke (1856–1942) wins a medal for *In the Wash House* (1888). In 1891 Mary Cassatt has a solo show in Paris and exhibits innovative color prints, such as *The Coiffure*

(1891). In the 1890s Cecilia Beaux is in demand as a portraitist, with a large 1897 show in Boston; Alice Barber Stephens (1858–1932) is a top illustrator; expatriate Elizabeth Nourse (1859–1938) exhibits realist paintings of peasants in Cincinnati in 1891; Lilla Cabot Perry (1848–1933), a promoter of Claude Monet's work, depicts Japanese scenes; Maria Oakey Dewing (1845–1927) paints realist still lifes; and Claude Raguet Hirst (1885–1942) adopts a trompe l'oeil style in her still lifes.

Design/Craft: Mary Louise McLauglin and Laura Fry help found the Cincinnati Pottery Club in 1879 and develop unusual glazing techniques, as does Maria Longworth Nichols (later Storer, 1849–1932), who opens her Rookwood Pottery in 1880. After working with Louis Comfort Tiffany, Candace Thurber Wheeler (1827–1923) starts an all-woman firm in New York in 1883, which specializes in textile design. Harriet Powers (1837–1911), a former slave, depicts major events in her life in a famous 1880s quilt (later in the Smithsonian); she also stitches *The Creation of Animals* (1898), or Bible quilt. In the early 1890s Nampeyo (see p. 375) adapts ancient Sikyatki forms and designs into her widely collected pots. In 1895 Datsolalee (Louisa Keyser, c. 1835–1925) first sells her innovative Washo baskets to Abram Cohn.

Architecture: Harriet Morrison Irwin patents her hexagonal building in North Carolina in 1869. Louise Blanchard Bethune (1856–1913) is the first woman in the American Institute of Architects, in 1888; she designs schools, banks, and houses in Buffalo. From 1888 in Philadelphia Minerva Parker (later Nichols, 1861–1948) designs houses and women's clubs. Chilean-born Sophia Hayden (1868–1953), paid much less than the male architects, designs the Woman's Building at the 1893 World's Columbian Exposition in Chicago, with murals by Mary Cassatt, Mary MacMonnies, and others. Marion Mahony (later Griffin, 1871–1961) does many of Frank Lloyd Wright's drawings (1895–1905).

Photographers: Portrait photographers of the 1890s include Gertrude Stanton Käsebier (1852–1934, see p. 314), acclaimed for her pictorial shots of mothers and children; Frances Benjamin Johnston (p. 293); Alice Austin; Mathilde Weil; and British-born Zaida Ben-Yusuf.

1900–39

Painting: In 1906 illustrator Angel DeCora (later Dietz, 1871–1919) heads the Carlisle Indian School art department and urges the use of Native designs in painting. In 1910 expatriate Romaine Brooks (1874–1970) has her first solo show in Paris; she does expressive portraits of lesbians, including her companion Natalie Barney. With paintings like *Man among the Redwoods* (1912), Marguerite Thompson Zorach (1887–1968) brings the Fauve style to America. After her abstract drawings are in a 1916 group exhibit, Georgia O'Keeffe (1887–1986) has her first solo show at Alfred Stieglitz's "291" gallery in New York in 1917. Works of the 1920s include O'Keeffe's cityscapes and closeups of flowers, such as *Black Iris* (1926) and *Red Poppy* (1927); Elsie Driggs's precisionist paintings; and Tonita Vigil Peña's watercolors of Pueblo

Early Sculptors

Harriet Goodhue Hosmer (1830–1908) joins expatriate neoclassical sculptors in Rome in the 1850s. She sells 50 copies of Puck *(1856) and carves the marble* Zenobia in Chains *(1859), which critics try to attribute to a man. Emma Stebbins (1815–82) creates a bronze of* Horace Mann *(1865) for the State House in Boston; she later sculpts* The Angel of the Waters *(1873) for the Bethesda Fountain in New York's Central Park. Commissioned by Congress, Vinnie Ream (later Hoxie, 1847–1914) sculpts a full-size marble of Abraham Lincoln for the Capitol rotunda (1866–71). Expatriate Edmonia Lewis, the first known African American–Chippewa sculptor, carves such marbles as* Forever Free *(1867–68),* Hagar *(1868), and* The Death of Cleopatra *(1876), a prize winner at the Philadelphia Centennial Exposition. Anne Whitney (1821–1915) sculpts her beggarwoman* Roma *(1869) and a statue of Samuel Adams for the Capitol (1873), but is denied an 1875 commission once the judges learn of her sex. Prussian-born Elisabet Ney (1833–1907) does marble busts of Sam Houston and other Texans in the 1890s. Helen Farnsworth Mears (1872–1916) sculpts* Genius of Wisconsin *(1892) and later a statue of Frances Willard for the Capitol (1905). Bessie Potter Vonnoh (1872–1955) fashions the widely reproduced bronze* The Young Mother *(1896).*

More Sculptors

Janet Scudder (1869–1940) creates the popular Frog Fountain *(1901). Abastenia St. Leger Eberle (1878–1942) does* Windy Doorstep *(1910), a woman sweeping, and* White Slave *(1913). Meta Vaux Warrick (later Fuller, 1877–1968) sculpts* Spirit of Emancipation *(1913) and* Ethiopia Awakening *(1921). Ann Hyatt (later Huntington, 1876–1973) does an equestrian Joan of Arc for Riverside Drive, New York (1914). Evelyn Longman (1874–1954) sculpts* Genius of Electricity *(1914–16) for the AT&T building; this winged man holding bolts of electricity appears on phonebooks. Gertrude Vanderbilt Whitney (1875–1942) carves her 18-foot* Titanic Memorial *(1914). In 1921 Adelaide Johnson (1859–1955) does the heads of Lucretia Mott, Susan B. Anthony, and Elizabeth Cady Stanton in white marble for the U.S. Capitol. May Howard Jackson (1877–1931) is known for busts of black leaders (1920s). In 1930 Malvina Hoffman (1887–1966) begins two years of travel, studying the world's peoples, to sculpt 100 racial types for Chicago's Field Museum of Natural History. Nancy Elizabeth Prophet (1890–1960) creates* Congolaise *(1930). Four women do sculptures for the 1939 World's Fair: Malvina Hoffman, Brenda Putnam, Gertrude Whitney, and Augusta Savage (1892–1962), whose* Lift Every Voice and Sing *shows a choir of elongated African Americans forming a harp.*

peoples. Florine Stettheimer (p. 350) creates her *Cathedrals of New York* series (1929–42), with its fantastic symbolism. Muralists of the 1930s include Marion Greenwood, Agnes Tait, Rosalind Bengelsdorf (later Browne), Pablita Verlarde (Tse Tsan), and Lucienne Bloch. Two major painters for 50 some years get their start in the 1930s: Isabel Bishop (1902–88), with her urban genre paintings, and Lois Mailou Jones, whose *Les Fétiches* (1938) prefigures later works drawing on her African heritage. In 1939 Anna Mary Robertson ("Grandma") Moses (1860–1961) is "discovered," and three works are displayed in a Museum of Modern Art show. She produces some 2,000 paintings in her lifetime.

Illustrators: Top illustrators include Violet Oakley (1874–1961), Jessie Willcox Smith (1863–1935), and Elizabeth Shippen Green (later Elliott, 1871–1954), who set up a Philadelphia studio together in 1902, and Mary Wilson Preston (1873–1949), the only woman in the Society of Illustrators. In 1909 Rose Cecil O'Neill (1874–1944) creates her cherubic Kewpie figures, which are the rage, used as dolls, salt-and-pepper shakers, and the like. Other cartoonists include Fanny Y. Cory, Grace Gebbie Wiederseim Drayton, and Edwina Dumm. Among 1920s works are Florence Scovel Shinn's humorous sketches, Peggy Bacon's satirical etchings in the *New Masses*, Nell Brinkley's comics with glamourous flappers, Neysa McMein's *McCall's* covers, and Helen Hokinson's *New Yorker* cartoons (1925 on), poking gentle fun at clubwomen. Works of the 1930s include Mabel Dwight's lithographs satirizing city life, Elizabeth Olds's pro-labor lithographs, and Gwendolyn Bennett's covers for the *Crisis* and *Opportunity*. Marjorie Henderson introduces the "Little Lulu" comic strip in 1935, and Jackie (Zelda Jackson) Ormes starts her strip "Torchy Brown in Dixie to Harlem" in the *Pittsburgh Courier* in 1937, and it is soon syndicated to other black papers.

Architecture/Landscape: San Francisco architect Julia Morgan (1872–1957) designs some 800 buildings, including San Simeon (1919–25), William Randoph Hearst's castle. Theodate Pope Riddle (1868–1946) does the Westover School in Middlebury, Connecticut (1908). Beatrix Jones Farrand (1872–1959), a founding member of the American Society of Landscape Architects in 1899, works on her most famous project, Dumbarton Oaks in Washington, D.C. (1920–40).

Design/Craft: Elsie de Wolfe (1865–1950) is the first female interior decorator, designing New York's Colony Club (1905). María Montoya Martínez (1886–1980) with her husband, Julian, develops her influential black-on-black matte-and-polish pottery in the San Ildefonso pueblo, New Mexico (1909–1919). Innovative Washo basketweavers include Sara Jim Mayo (1860–1945) and Lena Frank Dick (1889–1965).

Photography: Gertrude Käsebier helps found the Photo-Secession group in 1906. In the 1920s Imogen Cunningham (1883–1976) does her famous closeups of flowers and other organic forms, and Tina Modotti (1896–1924) portrays workers in Mexico. In addition to 1930s documentary work (see "Journalism"), Laura Gilpin (1891–1979) captures the western landscape; Louise Dahl-Wolfe (1895–1989) photographs fashions for *Harper's Bazaar* (1936 on), Barbara Morgan shoots Martha Graham's dancers, resulting in a 1941 book; and Berenice Abbott (1898–1991) records New York architecture in *Changing New York* (1939).

New Museums: In 1920 painter Katherine Sophie Dreier (1877–1952), with Marcel Duchamp and Man Ray, starts the Société Anonyme, New York's first modern art museum. Abby Aldrich Rockefeller, Lizzie Plummer Bliss, and Mary Quinn Sullivan initiate the Museum of Modern Art (MoMA) in 1929. Gertrude Vanderbilt Whitney establishes the Whitney Museum of American Art in 1931, with Juliana Rieser Force (1876–1948) as director. German-American painter Hilla Rebay (1890–1967) helps Irene and Solomon R. Guggenheim build their collection and directs their new museum in 1939.

1940–69

Sculpture: Selma Burke's 1943 profile relief of Franklin Delano Roosevelt is the source of the image modeled for dimes. Louise Nevelson (1899–1988), Louise Bourgeois, and Elizabeth Catlett all start showing in the 1940s. Nevelson is best known for such sculptural "walls" as *Sky Cathedral* (1958), using milk crates and other scrap wood painted black; she has a retrospective at the Whitney in 1967. Bourgeois's work ranges from her witty *Femme Maison* (1947) print to her 1960s "Lair" series, with organic latex forms. Catlett is noted for such carvings as *Homage to My Young Black Sisters* (1968) and prints such as *Sharecropper* (1968). Marisol (Esobar) shows her satirical wood sculptures of people at Castelli Gallery in 1959. The 1960s bring Anne Truitt's boxes, Dorothy Dehner's abstract wood pieces, neon works by Greek-born Chryssa (Vardea), and eccentric abstractions by Eva Hesse (1936–70). Nancy Graves startles viewers with her life-size *Camels* (1969).

Architecture: With their husbands, Sarah Pillsbury Harkness and Jean Bodman Fletcher form The Architects Collaborative (TAC) in Massachusetts in 1945. Working for Skidmore, Owings, and Merrill, Natalie de Blois helps design such New York landmarks as the Union Carbide Building (1960), but only after 20 years as a senior designer is she even promoted to associate (not partner). Norma Merrick Sklarek is the first black woman in the American Institute of Architects, in 1966.

Cartoons: Dale (Dalia) Messick begins her strip "Brenda Starr, Reporter" in 1940 and inspires other female action heroes. Hilda Terry, creator of the "Teena" strip in the 1940s, is the first woman admitted to the National Cartoonists Society, in 1951, but only after a struggle.

Design/Craft: Aileen Osborn Webb founds what becomes the American Crafts Council in 1943 and New York's Museum of Contemporary Crafts in 1956. Anni Albers has a one-woman show of her weavings at MoMA (1946) and publishes *On Designing* (1959). Lucy Lewis, known for reviving prehistoric Anasazi designs in her pots, wins top prize at the Santa Fe Indian Market in 1950. From the 1950s Lenore Tawney shapes her weavings, increasing their expressive power.

Painters: 1940–69

Georgia O'Keeffe's first retrospectives, including her New Mexico landscapes, are at the Art Institute of Chicago (1943) and MoMA (1946). I. (Irene) Rice Pereira (1907–71) builds abstractions with layers of painted corrugated glass (1940s on) and has a retrospective at the Whitney in 1953. Also from the 1940s are Alice Trumbull Mason's organic abstractions, Kay Sage Tanguy's and Dorothea Tanning's surrealist works, Alice Neel's T.B. Harlem (1940), and Anne Ryan's first delicate collages. Abstract Expressionists of the 1950s include Lee Krasner (1908–84), who waits until 1965 for her first major show, in London; Elaine de Kooning (1920–89); Grace Hartigan; and Joan Mitchell. Helen Frankenthaler paints Mountains and Sea (1952), paving the way for color-field painters by staining unprimed canvas with thinned oils; she wins first prize at the Paris Biennial (1959) but does not receive a New York museum show until 1969, at the Whitney. Other 1950–60s paintings include Nell Blaine's landscapes; Agnes Martin's minimalist abstractions; Pablita Verlarde's narrative images of Native traditions; Lee Bontecou's sculptural paintings, built of canvas and welded steel; Jo Baer's abstractions; and Alice Neel's portraits. For a 1966 Howard University show, Alma W. Thomas (1892–1978) aims for paintings "different from anything I'd ever seen," as if you could see "only streaks of color."

Performance Art

Carolee Schneemann pioneers performance art with her pieces Eye Body (1963) and Meat Joy (1964), as do Yoko Ono and Alison Knowles with their 1960s happenings. The 1970s brings the blossoming of performance art with Adrian Piper's early Catalysis (1970) street performances and other works; Donna Henes's first winter solstice celebration (1974); Theresa Hak Kyung Cha's Aveugle Voix (Blind Voice, 1975); Jerri Allyn and Anne Gauldin's group, "The Waitresses" (1976); Betsy Damon's Seven-Thousand-Year-Old-Woman (1977); Suzanne Lacy and Leslie Labowitz's community pieces such as In Mourning and in Rage (1977, Los Angeles); Eleanor Antin's appearances as a ballerina, nurse, and other characters; as well as works by Tina Girouard, Lynn Hershman, Rachel Rosenthal, Mary Beth Edelson, and others (see also "Entertainment"). A few of the many 1980s pieces are Lorraine O'Grady's Mlle. Bourgeoisie Noire Goes to the New Museum (1981), Martha Wilson's Nancy Reagan impersonations, Linda Montano's Seven Years of Living Art (1984– 91), and Carmelita Tropicana's Memories of the Revolution (1987). In 1992, the quincentennial year, Coco Fusco and Guillermo Gómez-Peña live in a gilded cage as newly discovered people in the Field Museum in Chicago and other sites.

Photography: Works include Helen Levitt's 1940s street shots of children; jarring images of New York night life by Lisette Model (1901–83); Ruth Orkin's famous *American Girl in Italy* (1951); Marie Cosindas's color photos at MoMA (1966); and portraits of drag queens to nudists by Diane Nemerov Arbus (1923–71) at MoMA (1967).

1970–95

Events: After a 1969 protest by Women Artists in Revolution (WAR), Lucy Lippard, Faith Ringgold, and others start the Ad Hoc Women Artists' Group and get the Whitney to more than double the women artists (to 22%) in its 1970 annual. The year 1971 brings New York's "Where We At Black Women Artists" show and Judy Chicago and Miriam Schapiro's Feminist Art Program at the California Institute for the Arts; students in the program create *Womanhouse* (1972), transforming a Los Angeles house into a commentary on womanhood. In 1972 the Women's Caucus for Art forms. Women's galleries include New York's A.I.R. (1972) and Soho 20 (1973), Chicago's ARC and Artemisia (both 1973), Women's Art Registry of Minneapolis (WARM, 1976), and Philadelphia's MUSE (1977). The Los Angeles Woman's Building (1973) has a gallery and community center. Mujeres Artistas del Suroeste (MAS) forms in Austin, Texas, in 1976. Ann Sutherland Harris and Linda Nochlin curate the show *Women Artists 1550–1950* in 1976, and Susanna Torre curates *Women in American Architecture* (1977). Women protest MoMA's 1984 survey of contemporary art with only 14 women of 165 artists. In 1985 the Guerrilla Girls, anonymous agitators wearing gorilla masks, attack art world discrimination with eye-catching posters and zap actions. In 1987 the National Museum of Women in the Arts, founded by Wilhelmina Cole Holladay, opens in Washington, D.C. A 1989 show is *Making Their Mark: Women Artists Move into the Mainstream, 1970–85*. In 1992 the Women's Action Coalition protests discrimination in the opening Soho Guggenheim Museum show. Marcia Tucker organizes *Bad Girls* (1994) at the New Museum in New York, with a sister show curated by Marcia Tanner in Los Angeles.

Painting: The 1970s bring a major show of self-taught artist Clementine Hunter (1886–1988); expressive painterly works by Joan Snyder, Pat Steir, and Susan Rothenberg; Audrey Flack's photorealist paintings; Jennifer Bartlett's *Rhapsody* (1976) with 988 baked enamel steel plates; realist works by Janet Fish and Catherine Murphy; Miriam Schapiro's fan paintings, and Yolanda López's *The Guadelupe Triptych* (1978). A few of the many painters in the 1980–90s are Ida Applebroog, Elizabeth Murray, Melissa Miller, Sherrie Levine, Margo Machida, Helen Oji, Vivian E. Browne, May Stevens, Emma Amos, Kay Walkingstick, Emmi Whitehorse, Jaune Quick-To-See Smith, Santa Barraza, Carmen Lomas Garza, Liliana Porter, and Howardena Pindell. Murals include *Latinoámerica* (1974–76) by Mujeres Muralistas (Patricia Rodríguez, Consuelo Mendez Castillo, Irene Pérez, and Graciella Carrillo de Lopez) in San Francisco; *The Wall of Respect for Women* (1974), directed by Tomie Arai, in New York; *The Great Wall of Los Angeles* (1974–83), a half-mile mural by 500 people, directed by Judy Baca; and *Maestra Peace* (1994) by Juana Alicia and six other women in San Francisco.

Other Forms: Drawings in the 1970s include Michelle Stuart's large graphite scrolls made on site, Vija Celmins's renderings of the ocean, Alexis Smith's collages, Dorothea Rockburne's conceptual wall pieces, and Nancy Spero's *Torture of Women* (1974–76); later Sue Coe does biting social commentaries, such as *Riot* (1981). Works of the 1980s include Linda Nishio's photo text *Kikoemasu Ka (Can You Hear Me?)*; Ilona Granet's offbeat signs, such as "Curb Your Animal Instincts," placed around New York; Barbara Kruger's graphic photosilkscreens, such as *Your Body Is a Battleground* (1982); Joyce Kozloff's decorative ceramic tiles for several subway stations; Sabra Moore's quilted constructions; Faith Ringgold's "story quilts," such as *Who's Afraid of Aunt Jemima?* (1983); and Janet Henry's story dolls. In 1990 Jenny Holzer is the first woman to fill the U.S. pavilion at the Venice Biennale with her work, displaying light-emiting diode (LED) signs with her truisms.

Photography: Diane Arbus is the first U.S. woman photographer in the Venice Biennale, in 1972. Some 1970s works include Abigail Heyman's *Growing Up Female: A Personal Photo-Journal* (1974), Eve Sonneman's side-by-side views of the same scene, Marcia Resnick's *Re-Visions* (1978), Jan Groover's closeups of everyday objects, Cindy Sherman's untitled film stills (using herself as the model), and Lois Greenfield's dancers. The 1980s bring Lynne Cohen's offices, Jolene Rickard's re-interpretations of Native American viewpoints, Nancy Burson's computerized composites, Barbara Kasten's colorful geometric abstractions, Clarissa Sligh's autobiographical works, Laurie Simmons's dolls, Sandy Skoglund's humorous fantasies (such as *Revenge of the Goldfish*, 1981), Lorna Simpson's *Guarded Conditions* (1981), Nan Goldin's *The Ballad of Sexual Dependency* (1986), Tina Barney's large groups, Sophie Rivera's people, Sally Mann's *At Twelve: Portraits of Young Women* (1988), Joyce Tenneson's ethereal figures, and Olivia Parker's enigmatic still lifes. Carrie Mae Weems creates narrative sequences as well as *And 22 Million Very Tired and Very Angry People* (installation, 1990).

Cartoons: Two groups of women cartoonists form in California in the early 1970s: Wimmen's Comix Collective and Tits 'n' Clits. The 1980s brings Lynda Barry's "Ernie Pook's Comeek," Nicole Hollander's "Sylvia," and Barbara Brandon's "Where I'm Coming From," which makes Brandon the first black female cartoonist to be syndicated in the mainstream press, in 1991. *Twisted Sisters*, an anthology of underground comics, edited by Aline Kominsky-Crumb and Diane Noomin, comes out in 1990.

Monuments: In 1982 architect Maya Ying Lin designs the Vietnam Veterans Memorial in Washington, D.C., with 58,000-some names of the Americans killed in the war etched in polished black granite. In 1989 she designs the equally evocative Civil Rights Memorial in Montgomery, Alabama.

Sculptural Works

In 1972 the Guggenheim Museum gives its first major show to a woman, with a posthumous retrospective of Eva Hesse's work. Her playful yet expressive pieces, using such materials as fiberglass, influence many women artists. "It's not the new," she wrote, "it is what is not yet known, thought, seen, touched but really what is not. and that is." Ana Mendieta (1948–85) begins her earth-body sculptures in 1973. The 1970s also offer site works by Mary Miss and Nancy Holt, Mary Frank's Woman (1975), Hannah Wilke's sexual latex pieces, Deborah Butterfield's horses, Jackie Winsor's rope works, Lynda Benglis's gilded knots, Betye Saar's box assemblages, such as The Liberation of Aunt Jemima (1972), Barbara Chase-Riboud's wood and soft fiber pieces, and Sylvia Stone's plexiglas sculpture. A few of the 1980s works are Judy Pfaff's energetic environments, Judith Shea's clothing, Alice Aycock's huge machines, Bessie Harvey's visions, Alison Saar's "modern fetishes," Cecilia Vicuña's fragile assemblages, and Kit-Yin Snyder's wire-mesh pieces. In the 1990s Kiki Smith and Sue Williams create expressive figures. There are also installations, such as Amalia Mesa-Bain's Frida Kahlo altar (1979); Judy Chicago's collaborative The Dinner Party (1979), with 39 place settings for famous women; and Yong Soon Min's Whirl War (1987).

Selected Bibliography

Acker, Ally. *Reel Women.* NY: Continuum, 1993.

Allen, Paula Gunn. *The Sacred Hoop.* Boston: Beacon, 1986.

Ammer, Christine. *Unsung.* Westport, CT Greenwood, 1980.

Auberdene, Patricia, & John Naisbitt. *Megatrends for Women,* Rev. Ed. NY: Fawcett Columbine 1993.

Asian Women United of California, eds. *Making Waves.* Boston: Beacon, 1989.

Bataille, Gretchen M., ed. *Native American Women.* NY: Garland, 1993.

Baxandall, Rosalyn; Linda Gordon; & Susan Reverby, eds. *American Working Women.* NY: Vintage, 1976.

Belford, Barbara. *Brilliant Bylines.* NY: Columbia U. Press, 1986.

Brown, Dorothy M. *Setting a Course: American Women in the 1920s.* Boston: Twayne, 1987.

Broude, Norma, & Mary D. Garrard. *The Power of Feminist Art.* NY: Abrams, 1994.

Buhle, Mari Jo, & Paul Buhle. *The Concise History of Woman Suffrage.* Urbana: U. Illinois Press, 1978.

Carabillo, Toni; Judith Meuli, & June Bundy Csida. *Feminist Chronicles, 1953-1993.* Los Angeles: Women's Graphics, 1993.

Chamberlain, Marian K. *Women in Academe.* NY: Russell Sage Foundation, 1988.

Cotera, Martha P. *The Chicana Feminist.* Austin: Information Systems Development, 1977.

Cott, Nancy F., & Elizabeth H. Pleck. *A Heritage of Her Own.* NY: Simon & Schuster, 1979.

Davidson, Cathy N., & Linda Wagner Martin, eds. *The Oxford Companion to Women's Writing in the United States.* NY: Oxford U. Press, 1995.

Davis, Flora. *Moving the Mountain.* NY: Simon & Schuster, 1991.

DuBois, Ellen Carol, & Vicki L. Ruiz, eds. *Unequal Sisters.* NY: Routledge, 1990.

Edwards, Julia. *Women of the World.* Boston: Houghton Mifflin, 1988.

Ehrenreich, Barbara, & Deirdre English. *For Her Own Good.* NY: Doubleday, 1989.

Evans, Sara M. *Born for Liberty.* NY: Free Press, 1989.

Flexner, Eleanor. *Century of Struggle,* Rev. Ed. Cambridge: Harvard U. Press, 1975.

Foner, Philip S. *Women and the American Labor Movement.* NY: Free Press, 1980.

Garza, Hedda. *Latinas.* NY: Watts, 1994.

Gerber, Ellen W. et al.. *The American Woman in Sport.* Reading, MA: Addison-Wesley, 1974.

Giddings, Paula. *When and Where I Enter.* NY: Bantam Books, 1988.

Goldstein, Leslie Friedman. *The Constitutional Rights of Women,* 2nd Ed. Madison: U. Wisconsin Press, 1988.

Gregorich, Barbara. *Women at Play.* San Diego: Harvest/Harcourt Brace, 1993.

Green, Rayna. *Women in American Indian Society.* NY: Chelsea House, 1992.

Heller, Nancy G. *Women Artists: An Illustrated History.* NY: Abbeville, 1987.

Hine, Darlene Clark; Elsa Barkley Brown; & Rosalyn Terborg-Penn, eds. *Black Women in America,* 2 vols. Bloomington: Indiana U. Press, 1994 .

Holm, Jeanne. *Women in the Military,* Rev. Ed. Novato, CA: Presidio, 1992.

Hymowitz, Carol, & Michaele Weissman. *A History of Women in America.* NY: Bantam, 1978.

James, Edward J., with Janet Wilson James & Paul S. Boyer *Notable American Women 1607-1950,* 3 vols. Cambridge: Harvard U. Press, 1971.

Kaledin, Eugenia. *Mothers and More: American Women in the 1950s.* Boston: Twayne, 1984.

Kass-Simon, G., & Patricia Farnes, eds. *Women of Science.* Bloomington: Indiana U. Press, 1993.

Keller, Rosemary Skinner, & Rosemary Redford Ruether, eds. *In Our Own Voices.* San Francisco: HarperCollins, 1995.

Kerber, Linda K., & Jane Sherron De Hart, eds. *Women's America.* NY: Oxford U. Press, 1991.

Kraditor, Aileen S. *The Ideas of the Woman Suffrage Movement.* NY: Norton, 1981.

———. *Up from the Pedestal.* Chicago: Quadrangle Books, 1968.

Lanker, Brian. *I Dream a World.* NY: Stewart, Tabori, & Chang, 1989.

Lerner, Gerda, *The Female Experience.* Indianapolis: Bobbs-Merrill, 1977.

———. *The Woman in American History.* Reading MA: Addison-Wesley, 1971.

——— ed. *Black Women in White America.* NY: Vintage, 1973.

Levine, Suzanne, & Harriet Lyons, eds. *The Decade of Women.* NY: Paragon, 1980.

Linden-Ward, Blanche, & Carol Hurd Green. *Changing the Future: American Women in the 1960s.* NY: Twayne, 1993.

MacDonald, Anne L. *Feminine Ingenuity.* NY: Ballantine, 1992.

Markel, Robert; Nancy Brooks; & Susan Markel. *For the Record: Women in Sports.* NY: World Almanac, 1985.

McHenry, Robert, ed. *Famous American Women.* NY: Dover, 1980.

Mirandé, Alfredo, & Evangelina Enríquez. *La Chicana.* Chicago: U. Chicago Press, 1979.

Morgan, Robin. *Sisterhood Is Powerful.* NY: Vintage, 1970.

Moynihan, Ruth Barnes; Cynthia Russett; & Laurie Crumpacker. *Second to None,* 2 vols. Lincoln: U. Nebraska Press, 1993.

Nakono, Mei. *Japanese American Women.* San Francisco: Mina Press/National Japanese American Historical Society, 1990.

Niethammer, Carolyn. *Daughters of the Earth.* NY: Macmillan, 1977.

Papachristou, Judith. *Women Together.* NY: Knopf, 1976.

Read, Phyllis J., & Bernard L. Witlieb. *The Book of Women's Firsts.* NY: Random House, 1992.

Robbins, Trina. *A Century of Women Cartoonists.* Northampton, MA: Kitchen Sink, 1993.

Rosenblum, Naomi. *A History of Women Photographers.* NY: Abbeville Press, 1994.

Rossi, Alice S. ed. *The Feminist Papers.* NY: Bantam, 1974.

Rossiter, Margaret W. *Women Scientists in America.* Baltimore: Johns Hopkins U. Press, 1982.

Rubinstein, Charlotte Streifer. *American Women Artists.* Boston: Hall, 1982.

Ruether, Rosemary Radford, & Rosemary Skinner Keller, eds. *Women and Religion in America,* 3 vols. San Francisco: Harper & Row, 1981-86.

Rupp, Leila J., & Verta Taylor. *Survival in the Doldrums.* NY: Oxford U. Press, 1987.

Sadie, Julie Anne, & Rhian Samuel. *The Norton/Grove Dictionary of Women Composers.* NY: Norton, 1995.

Sanders, Marlene, & Maria Rock. *Waiting for Prime Time.* NY: Harper & Row, 1990.

Schlissel, Lillian. *Women's Diaries of the Westward Journey.* NY: Schocken, 1982.

Schoen, June. *Movers and Shakers.* NY: Quadrangle/New York Times, 1973.

Schwarz, Judith. *Radical Feminists of Heterodoxy:,* Rev. Ed. Norwich, VT: New Victoria, 1986.

Sicherman, Barbara, & Carol Hurd Green with Ilene Kantrov & Harriette Walker, eds. *Notable American Women: The Modern Penod.* Cambridge: Harvard U. Press, 1980.

Silver, A. David. *Enterprising Women.* NY: AMACOM, 1994.

Smith, Jessie Carney, ed. *Epic Lives.* Detroit: Visible Ink Press, 1993.

Solomon, Barbara Miller. *In the Company of Educated Women.* New Haven: Yale U. Press, 1985.

Sterling, Dorothy, ed. *We Are Your Sisters.* NY: Norton, 1984.

Stratton, Joanna L. *Pioneer Women.* NY: Simon & Schuster, 1981.

Telgen, Diane, & Jim Kamp, eds. *Notable Hispanic American Women.* Detroit: Gale Research, 1993.

Vare, Ethlie Ann, & Greg Ptacek. *Mothers of Invention.* NY: Morrow, 1987.

Wandersee, Winifred D. *On the Move: American Women in the 1970s.* Boston: Twayne, 1988.

Ware, Susan. *Holding Their Own: American Women in the 1930s.* Boston: Twayne, 1982.

Weatherford, Doris. *American Women's History.* NY: Prentice Hall, 1994.

Weiser, Marjorie P.K., & Jean S. Arbeiter. *Womanlist.* NY: Atheneum, 1981.

Wertheimer, Barbara Meyer. *We Were There.* NY: Pantheon, 1977.

Wheeler, Marjorie, Spruill. *One Woman, One Vote.* Troutdale, OR: NewSage Press, 1995.

Woloch, Nancy. *Women and the American Experience.* NY: Knopf, 1984.

Yung, Judy. *Chinese Women of America.* Seattle: U. Washington Press, 1986.

Index